Romanticism and Consciousness, Revisited

Edinburgh Critical Studies in Romanticism
Series Editors: Ian Duncan and Penny Fielding

Available Titles

A Feminine Enlightenment: British Women Writers and the Philosophy of Progress, 1759–1820
JoEllen DeLucia

Reinventing Liberty: Nation, Commerce and the Historical Novel from Walpole to Scott
Fiona Price

The Politics of Romanticism: The Social Contract and Literature
Zoe Beenstock

Radical Romantics: Prophets, Pirates, and the Space Beyond Nation
Talissa J. Ford

Literature and Medicine in the Nineteenth-Century Periodical Press: Blackwood's Edinburgh Magazine, *1817–1858*
Megan Coyer

Discovering the Footsteps of Time: Geological Travel Writing in Scotland, 1700–1820
Tom Furniss

The Dissolution of Character in Late Romanticism
Jonas Cope

Commemorating Peterloo: Violence, Resilience, and Claim-making during the Romantic Era
Michael Demson and Regina Hewitt

Dialectics of Improvement: Scottish Romanticism, 1786–1831
Gerard Lee McKeever

Literary Manuscript Culture in Romantic Britain
Michelle Levy

Scottish Romanticism and Collective Memory in the British Atlantic
Kenneth McNeil

Romantic Periodicals in the Twenty-First Century: Eleven Case Studies from Blackwood's Edinburgh Magazine
Nicholas Mason and Tom Mole

Godwin and the Book: Imagining Media, 1783–1836
J. Louise McCray

Thomas De Quincey: Romanticism in Translation
Brecht de Groote

Romantic Environmental Sensibility: Nature, Class and Empire
Ve-Yin Tee

Romantic Pasts: History, Fiction and Feeling in Britain, 1790–1850
Porscha Fermanis

British Romanticism and Denmark
Cian Duffy

The Lady's Magazine (1770–1832) and the Making of Literary History
Jennie Batchelor

Mary Wollstonecraft: Cosmopolitan
Laura Kirkley

Romanticism and Consciousness, Revisited
Richard Sha and Joel Faflak

Forthcoming Titles

Romantic Networks in Europe: Transnational Encounters, 1786–1850
Carmen Casaliggi

Death, Blackwood's Edinburgh Magazine *and Authoring Romantic Scotland*
Sarah Sharp

Seeking Justice: Literature, Law and Equity during the Age of Revolutions
Michael Demson and Regina Hewitt

Remediating the 1820s
Jon Mee and Matthew Sangster

Visit our website at: www.edinburghuniversitypress.com/series/ECSR

Romanticism and Consciousness, Revisited

Edited by
Richard C. Sha and Joel Faflak

EDINBURGH
University Press

Edinburgh University Press is one of the leading university presses in the UK. We publish academic books and journals in our selected subject areas across the humanities and social sciences, combining cutting-edge scholarship with high editorial and production values to produce academic works of lasting importance. For more information visit our website: edinburghuniversitypress.com

© editorial matter and organization, Richard Sha and Joel Faflak, 2022, 2024
© the chapters their several authors, 2022, 2024

First published in hardback by Edinburgh University Press 2022

Edinburgh University Press Ltd
The Tun – Holyrood Road
12(2f) Jackson's Entry
Edinburgh EH8 8PJ

Typeset in 10.5/13pt Sabon LT Pro
by Cheshire Typesetting Ltd, Cuddington, Cheshire

A CIP record for this book is available from the British Library

ISBN 978 1 4744 8510 4 (hardback)
ISBN 978 1 4744 8511 1 (paperback)
ISBN 978 1 4744 8512 8 (webready PDF)
ISBN 978 1 4744 8513 5 (epub)

The right of Richard Sha and Joel Faflak to be identified as the editor of this work has been asserted in accordance with the Copyright, Designs and Patents Act 1988, and the Copyright and Related Rights Regulations 2003 (SI No. 2498).

Contents

List of Figures	vii
Acknowledgements	viii
Notes on Contributors	x

1. Introduction: *Romanticism and Consciousness* Redux   1
   Richard C. Sha and Joel Faflak

Part I: New Models of Consciousness

2. Romanticism Against Consciousness   29
   Alan Richardson

3. Romantic Panpsychism   49
   Colin Jager

4. Shelley and the Real of Faith   73
   Joel Faflak

5. Blakean Experience and the Hard Problem of Consciousness Revisited   94
   Richard C. Sha

Part II: States of Consciousness

6. 'Poetry is passion': Lyrical Balladry as Affective Narratology   121
   Mark J. Bruhn

7. After-Affects and Second Thoughts: Wordsworth, Eliot, and the Forms of Emotional Thinking   144
   Nancy Yousef

8. Studio States: Thought Out of Place 167
   Jacques Khalip

9. The Media Ecology of Romantic Consciousness: Knowledge in Charlotte Smith's *Beachy Head* 196
   Ralf Haekel

Part III: Social and Ecological Models of Consciousness

10. Why Reasonable Children Don't Think that Nutcracker is Alive or that the Mouse King is Real 225
    Lisa Zunshine

11. Prone Minds and Extended Selves: *The Cenci* 249
    Yasmin Solomonescu

12. Gothic Ecologies of Mind 268
    John Savarese

13. May Flies and Horseshoe Crabs: Romantic and Post-Romantic Consciousness, Institutions, and Populations 285
    Robert Mitchell

Part IV: Race and Consciousness

14. Shapeshifting Romantic Consciousness 311
    Kate Singer

15. At Peace with Strangers: Feeling Disoriented in the London Panorama of Constantinople, 1801–1802 339
    Humberto Garcia

16. Doubling Down: On White Consciousness, Friends, and *The Friend* 363
    Julie A. Carlson

Index 386

List of Figures

Figure 7.1   Filippino Lippi, *Apparition of the Virgin to Saint Bernard*, 1485–7. 158
Figure 7.2   Pietro Perugino, *Virgin Appearing to Saint Bernard*, c.1490–4. 161
Figure 8.1   William Blake, *Illustrations from the Book of Job*, Plate 20, 'Job and His Daughters,' 1825. Yale Center for British Art, Paul Mellon Collection. 172
Figure 10.1 Albrecht Dürer, *Saint George Slaying the Dragon*. Nuremberg, c.1504. 226
Figure 15.1 Antoine-Ignace Melling, *View of a Part of the City of Constantinople with Seraglio Point taken from the Suburbs of Pera*, 1819. Engraving, 25.6 × 38.2 cm. Getty Research Institute, Los Angeles (93-B15373). 343
Figure 15.2 Henry Aston Barker, *View of Constantinople from the Tower of Galata*, 1801. Engraved key, 15.2 × 12.5 inches. John Johnson Collection Entertainments Folder 6 (4). Bodleian Library, University of Oxford. 345
Figure 15.3 Henry Aston Barker, *View of Constantinople from the Tower of Leander*, 1801. Engraved key, 15.2 × 12.5 inches cut to 9.5 × 8 inches. © Victoria and Albert Museum, London. 346
Figure 15.4 Henry Aston Barker, 'Map of Constantinople,' *A Concise Account of the Views of Constantinople ... at the Panorama, Leicester Square*. London: J. Adlard, 1801. © The British Library Board, shelfmark T.163.(9). 349

For additional online images in colour, please see https://edinburgh universitypress.com/book-romanticism-and-consciousness-revisited.html

Acknowledgements

It seemed daunting as well as foolhardy to revisit Harold Bloom's 1970 epochal volume, *Romanticism and Consciousness: Essays in Criticism*, and imagine that we could match its influence. It was Richard's idea to do so, and as with all his critical instincts, this one has proven to be more than prescient. Since 1970 too much has happened in the fields of Romantic studies and cognitive literary studies, and in the ongoing revolution in brain science and the cognitive neurosciences, to name only a few touchstones, *not* to revisit the topic seemed unthinkable. We hope the results reflect some sense of the excitement of ongoing discovery that these changes reflect. It was Joel's tireless labors and eye for detail that prevented many an error.

Whatever influence this volume has or might have will all be to the credit of our stellar contributors, all of them utterly different in their approaches but all passionate about exploring the always-to-be-discovered, always-undiscovered land that is Romantic consciousness and Romanticism's exploration of consciousness. For their brilliant insights and commitment to this project, our heartfelt thanks.

At Edinburgh University Press we thank Susannah Butler and Michele Houston for their unfailing support for this project and for sharing our sense of its urgency. We also thank the Editors of the Series, Edinburgh Critical Studies in Romanticism, Ian Duncan and Penny Fielding, for their detailed feedback and enthusiasm. For her expert copy-editing, we thank Wendy Lee. We could not have completed this project without the magisterial help of Fiona Conn. For her timely and detailed execution of the index, we thank Dianne Hosmer. Danny O'Quinn provided key advice and also helped to vet some of the chapters.

Richard would like to thank Mary Mintz for bibliographic help and the Mellon Fund at American University for funds to pay for the index. Joel would like to thank the Faculty of Arts and Humanities at Western University for funds to support partial research for this volume.

Finally, we thank our partners and families, whose embodied and extended cognition of life makes consciousness, Romantic and otherwise, worth the pursuit.

Notes on Contributors

Mark J. Bruhn, Professor of English at Regis University (Denver, Colorado), is the author of *Wordsworth Before Coleridge: The Growth of the Poet's Philosophical Mind, 1785–1797* (Routledge, 2018); co-editor (with Donald R. Wehrs) of *Cognition, Literature, and History* (Routledge, 2014); and guest editor of a double issue of *Poetics Today* on 'Exchange Values: Poetics and Cognitive Science' (2011). His work on Wordsworth, style, and cognition appears in *The Oxford Handbook of Cognitive Literary Studies* (2015), *The Oxford Handbook of William Wordsworth* (2015), *The Palgrave Handbook of Affect Studies and Textual Criticism* (2017), and the de Gruyter *Handbook of British Romanticism* (2017).

Julie A. Carlson is Professor of English and Associate Dean of Faculty Equity at the University of California, Santa Barbara. She is author of *In the Theatre of Romanticism: Coleridge, Nationalism, Women* (Cambridge UP, 1994), *England's First Family of Writers: Mary Wollstonecraft, William Godwin, Mary Shelley* (Johns Hopkins UP, 2007), and co-editor, with Elisabeth Weber, of *Speaking About Torture* (Fordham UP, 2012). Her essays focus on cultural politics and poetics, British Romantic-era theater and performance, and mind studies. Her life project, that may someday emerge in a book, concerns the interrelation between friendship and creativity as the means for social change.

Joel Faflak is Professor in the Department of English and Writing Studies and the Centre for the Study of Theory and Criticism, Western University, and Visiting Professor, Victoria College, University of Toronto. He is author of *Romantic Psychoanalysis: The Burden of the Mystery* (SUNY P, 2007), co-author of *Revelation and Knowledge: Romanticism and Religious Faith* (U of Toronto P, 2011), editor of De Quincey's

Confessions of an English Opium-Eater (Broadview P, 2009), and most recently co-editor of *William Blake: Modernity and Disaster* (U of Toronto P, 2020), with Tilottama Rajan, and *Romanticism and the Emotions* (Cambridge UP, 2016), with Richard Sha.

Humberto Garcia is an Associate Professor and Vincent Hillyer Chair of Literature at the University of California, Merced. His research and teaching focus on eighteenth- and nineteenth-century British literature in a global context, with an emphasis on Anglo-Islamic relations in this period. He is the author of *Islam and the English Enlightenment, 1670–1840* (Johns Hopkins UP, 2012) and many articles appearing in academic journals such as *Common Knowledge*, *Studies in Romanticism*, and *Studies in English Literature*. He has completed a second book titled *England Re-Oriented: How Central and South Asian Travelers Imagined the West, 1750–1857* (Cambridge UP, 2020).

Ralf Haekel is Professor and Chair of British Literature at Leipzig University, Germany. His main research interests are Romantic studies, early modern drama and theater, Irish studies, and media studies. From 2008 to 2016 he was Associate Professor (*Juniorprofessor*) of English Literature and Culture at Göttingen University. Furthermore, he was Visiting Professor at the Universities of Mannheim, Frankfurt, Darmstadt, Hannover, and Gießen, as well as Assistant Professor at Humboldt-Universität Berlin and post-doctoral fellow at the graduate school *Klassizismus und Romantik im europäischen Kontext* at Gießen University. In 2003 he received his PhD from the Freie Universität Berlin and in 2013 his *Habilitation* from Göttingen University. His publications include *The Soul in British Romanticism: Negotiating Human Nature in Philosophy, Science and Poetry* (WVT, 2014); together with Caroline Lusin he co-edited *Community, Seriality, and the State of the Nation: British and Irish Television Series in the 21st Century* (Narr, 2019). He is editor of the *Handbook of British Romanticism* (de Gruyter, 2017).

Colin Jager is Professor of English and Director of the Center for Cultural Analysis at Rutgers University. He is the author of two academic monographs, both published by the University of Pennsylvania Press: *The Book of God: Secularization and Design in the Romantic Era* (2007) and *Unquiet Things: Secularism in the Romantic Age* (2015). In 2018 he was Leverhulme Visiting Professor at Lancaster University in the UK. He is at work on two book projects: the first on Romanticism and political possibility, the second on aesthetics and religion.

Jacques Khalip is Professor of English at Brown University. He is the author of *Last Things: Disastrous Form from Kant to Hujar* (Fordham UP, 2018) and *Anonymous Life: Romanticism and Dispossession* (Stanford UP, 2009). He is also the co-editor of *Constellations of a Contemporary Romanticism* (Fordham UP, 2016) and *Releasing the Image: From Literature to New Media* (Stanford UP, 2011).

Robert Mitchell is Professor of English, Chair of the English Department, and Director of the Center for Interdisciplinary Studies in Science and Cultural Theory at Duke University. He is author of *Sympathy and the State in the Romantic Era: Systems, State Finance, and the Shadows of Futurity* (Routledge, 2007), *Tissue Economies: Blood, Organs and Cell Lines in Late Capitalism*, co-authored with Catherine Waldby (Duke UP, 2006), *Bioart and the Vitality of Media* (U Washington P, 2010), *Experimental Life: Vitalism in Romantic Science and Literature* (Johns Hopkins UP, 2013), and *Infectious Liberty: Biopolitics between Romanticism and Liberalism* (Fordham UP, 2021).

Alan Richardson is Professor of English at Boston College. He has published widely on British Romantic literature and culture, especially in relation to issues of gender, childhood and education, race and colonialism, and scientific psychology. His books include *Literature, Education, and Romanticism: Reading as Social Practice, 1780–1832* (Cambridge UP, 1994), *British Romanticism and the Science of the Mind* (Cambridge UP, 2001), and *The Neural Sublime: Cognitive Theories and Romantic Texts* (Johns Hopkins UP, 2011). Honors and awards include a National Endowment for the Humanities Fellowship, a Guggenheim Fellowship, the Keats–Shelley Association Distinguished Scholar Award, the American Conference on Romanticism book prize, and the Alpha Sigma Nu National Jesuit Book Award.

John Savarese is Associate Professor of English Language and Literature at the University of Waterloo, where he teaches British Romanticism, the history and philosophy of science, and gothic studies. He is the author of *Romanticism's Other Minds: Poetry, Cognition, and the Science of Sociability* (Ohio State, 2020).

Richard C. Sha is Professor of Literature and Affiliate Professor of Philosophy at American University in Washington, DC. His most recent book, *Imagination and Science in Romanticism* (Johns Hopkins UP, 2018), won the Jean Pierre Barricelli Prize in that year. In 2020 the National Endowment for the Humanities funded the open publication of this book, one of only twelve titles in the Humanities to be so funded. His most recent articles have been on the Asian American poet, Wing-Tek Lum, and Lacanian Trauma Theory, *Frankenstein* and Embodied Cognition, George Sand, Voltaire, and science and the sublime. With Joel Faflak, he has co-edited *Romanticism and the Emotions* (Cambridge UP, 2016).

Kate Singer is an Associate Professor in the English Department and Critical Social Thought program at Mount Holyoke College. She is the author of *Romantic Vacancy: The Poetics of Gender, Affect, and Radical Speculation* (SUNY Press, 2019) and co-editor, with Ashley Cross and Suzanne L. Barnett, of *Material Transgressions: Beyond Romantic Bodies, Genders, Things* (Liverpool University Press, 2020). She has published essays on Percy Shelley, Mary Shelley, Maria Jane Jewsbury, Letitia Elizabeth Landon, Mary Robinson, Jane Austen, and Mary Wollstonecraft. She is co-editor of the Pedagogies section of the Romantic Circles website, including the journal *Pedagogy Commons*, and is currently working on a project exploring Romanticism, critical theory, tropes of shapeshifting, and notions of ontological change.

Yasmin Solomonescu is Associate Professor of English and Notre Dame du lac Collegiate Chair at the University of Notre Dame. She specializes in British Romanticism with particular interests in persuasion, cognition, epistemology, and literary theory. She is writing a book entitled *Persuasion for the Moment* about how British Romantic writers fundamentally reconceived of the theory and practice of persuasion, including in ways relevant to literary theory and criticism today. She is also the author of *John Thelwall and the Materialist Imagination* (2014), the editor of *John Thelwall: Critical Reassessments* (2011), and the co-editor of *Enlightenment Liberties/Libertés des Lumières* (2018), as well as of John Thelwall's 1801 novel *The Daughter of Adoption* (2013).

Nancy Yousef is Professor of English at Rutgers University. Her work centers on the relationships between literature and philosophy, and on the intersection of aesthetics and ethics. She is the author of *Isolated Cases* (Cornell UP, 2004) and *Romantic Intimacy* (Stanford UP, 2013). Her most recent book, *The Aesthetic Commonplace* (Oxford UP, 2022), explores the valorization of ordinary experience in art and philosophy from Wordsworth to Wittgenstein.

Lisa Zunshine is Bush-Holbrook Professor of English at the University of Kentucky, a former Guggenheim fellow, and the author or editor of twelve books, including *Why We Read Fiction* (Ohio State UP, 2006), *Strange Concepts and the Stories They Make Possible* (Johns Hopkins UP, 2008), *Introduction to Cognitive Cultural Studies* (ed., Johns Hopkins UP, 2010), *Getting Inside Your Head: What Cognitive Science Can Tell Us About Popular Culture* (Johns Hopkins UP, 2012), *The Oxford Handbook of Cognitive Literary Studies* (ed., 2015), and *The Secret Life of Literature* (MIT Press, 2021).

Chapter 1

Introduction: *Romanticism and Consciousness* Redux

Richard C. Sha and Joel Faflak

Romanticism and Consciousness, Then and Now

We begin with a rather sweeping, even reckless claim: perhaps no other essay collection more influenced Romantic studies than *Romanticism and Consciousness: Essays in Criticism* (1970), edited by Harold Bloom. We say this partly in light of the recent passing of Professor Bloom (1930–2019), whose stamp on Romantic studies, not only because of his staggering output, suggests the voice of a kind of undeniable propheticness, however much that voice agitated both for and against critical fashion. Impact is never registered solely by any one critic, however singular and influential, but in the ascendance of Romantic studies as a field unto itself, *Romanticism and Consciousness* appeared at a pivotal moment. British Liberal Humanism and later North American New Criticism had left their marks upon earlier twentieth-century literary studies and embraced Romantic writing and its authors with varying enthusiasm. On the horizon loomed deconstruction, poststructuralism, and their various after-effects in new historicism, feminism, cultural studies, or postcolonialism. As if to mediate this epochal shift in criticism, Bloom's volume emerged to articulate the mind of Romanticism *as* mind, as the consciousness of a single and singular moment in history. Or rather, such a negotiation reified Romantic studies as it had rarely been consolidated before, albeit according to what Jerome McGann would call the critical ideology of what any time imagines Romanticism to be. By this measure, *Romanticism and Consciousness* offered its own sweeping anatomy of the field, one not nearly as multifarious and diverse as we have since found it to be. Yet the volume's claim to apprehend the period as consciousness, which is to say as conscious of itself in a way that earlier periods had not been, marks Romanticism as a watershed moment in the emergence of modernity that makes unthinkable subsequent challenges to criticism's reading of Romanticism as a cognitive synthesis rather than overdetermination of ideas or history. That it is still in print more than five decades later indicates its lasting influence.

This is also to say, then, that since the volume's publication, most of what we thought we knew about consciousness has been challenged. Where Bloom and his contributors privileged a self-consciousness rooted in the singular mind and body, consciousness today is hell-bent on the world and on a version of an embodied subject immersed in the world. For proponents of distributed or enactive cognition, for instance, skin and skull no longer define where consciousness begins and ends.[1] Where, for Bloom, Romantic consciousness maps the internalized quest romance of the individual, self-contained mind, then, today's explorers trace that journey much farther afield. Against advances in the understanding of an embodied consciousness, internalization seems wholly counterintuitive, not just in some earlier abstract notion of mind but as the radical extensions of the Romantic sensorium. If Bloom's muse was Freud, ours is someone like Antonio Damasio, as psychoanalysis has given way to neuroscience – a revolution in the cognitive sciences that is symptomatic of a range of further influences: feminism, queer and trans studies, environmental science, speculative realism, behavioral science, digital and virtual reality, post- and decolonialism, posthumanism. Moreover, whereas *Romanticism and Consciousness* ended with a final section of essays on the 'Great Six' Romantic poets, not to mention that the volume itself was authored almost exclusively by men, our rather more diverse lineup of contributors at once revisits and expands this canon within the context of the complex dialogue of writers, gender, and ideas that now informs our understanding of the period.[2] Their varied contributions are united by a renewed understanding of Romantic notions of consciousness informed by advances in cultural, scientific, and theoretical knowledge over the past fifty years that revisit how Romantic writers understood the term. It is their and our belief that Romanticism's revolution in consciousness continues apace, part of what Richard Holmes calls an Age of Wonder: hence the imperative to revisit Bloom's 1970 volume.

Romanticism and Consciousness appeared on the heels of two earlier field-defining essay collections: *English Romantic Poets: Modern Essays in Criticism* (1960), edited by M. H. Abrams, and *Romanticism Reconsidered* (1963), edited by Northrop Frye. Abrams's volume opens with Arthur O. Lovejoy's 'On the Discrimination of Romanticisms,' which famously called 'any attempt at a *general* appraisal even of a single chronologically determinate Romanticism – still more, of 'Romanticism' as a whole – ... a fatuity' (22).[3] The bulk of the volume divides into essays on each of the Big Six and works against anti-Romantic critical sentiment of the early twentieth century.[4] In his brief Preface Abrams refers to this as the 'great debate about the Romantic achievement which has been the prime index to the shift in sensibility and standards during the generation just past' (v). The Foreword to Frye's volume is rather more pointed, describing the 'anti-Romantic movement in criticism,' dictated by the 'Hulme–Eliot–Pound broadsides of the early twenties' (to which cabal one might add Irving Babbitt), 'now over and done with,' such that 'criticism has got its sense of literary tradition properly in focus again' (v). Such certainty informs Frye's own essay, 'The Drunken Boat: The Revolutionary Element in Romanticism,' which notes Romantic poetry's 'emphasis ... on the constructive power of the mind' (11), a vitally metaphorical capacity that cognitive linguists and philosophers such as George Lakoff and Mark Johnson will later explore in a rather different light.[5] For Frye, the 'vehicular form' of this autonomous creative power signifies a 'heightened state of consciousness in which we feel that we are greater than we know, or an intense feeling of communion' (15). The thrust here is away from a fragmented Romantic legacy toward what William Hazlitt in 1825 called 'The Spirit of the Age' (the subtitle of Abrams's essay) – Romanticism as a unifying force despite the heterogeneous evidence of its ideas and writings, as Lovejoy reminds us.

While both volumes consolidate the emergence of Romantic studies as a distinct field at a time when the New Criticism held sway,[6] they also signal what Jerome McGann would call the Romantic ideology associated with the idealism of the mythopoeic imagination and its ability to overcome political and social disillusionment and thus to redeem the mind from the narrowness of Enlightenment materialism, rationalism, and natural determinism, a transcendental *mythos* explored in Abrams's *Natural Supernaturalism: Tradition and Revolution in Romantic Literature* (1971) or earlier in Frye's groundbreaking study of William Blake, *Fearful Symmetry* (1947). This reparative spirit was in keeping with the social and political idealisms that defined post-World War Two American cultural ascendancy, itself driven by a ceaseless 'vehicular' expansion and innovation reflective of the Romantic achievement itself. On one hand, *Romanticism and Consciousness* marked Romantic forms of psychic response, however heterogeneous, as uniform, even universal guides to a modern understanding of selfhood.[7] How the Romantic mind processed the world offered what Wordsworth in 'Tintern Abbey' called 'abundant recompense' for one's struggle to make sense of things. On the other hand, while the insight that came with the self's internalized quest to find itself was this struggle's payoff, the price was alienation from the world, even from life itself. For Geoffrey Hartman in

'Romanticism and "Anti-Self-Consciousness,"' a touchstone for many of our contributors, the cost was an excess of self-consciousness, the danger of a mind preying upon itself, disconnected from the outside. From the stance of today's embodied and enactive consciousness, such radical disconnection seems nearly impossible, and might be labeled 'autism.' After all, disconnection makes connection the default.[8]

For Bloom or Hartman, reconnection alone would have constituted something like Schiller's naïve poetry. For either critic, the return was made impossible less due to God's flaming sword barring access to knowledge than by the fact that such a retreat to Beulah would be to miss the point of the dialectic of consciousness transpiring between mind and world. How Bloom and company parse this dialectic takes consciousness as the protected encampment of the mind as its own territory, and poetry as its exclusive roadmap, although they sense trouble on the horizon. As Wordsworth writes in his Prospectus to *The Recluse*, the paradigmatic text for Abrams's *Natural Supernaturalism*, 'the individual Mind that keeps her own / Inviolate retirement, subject there / To Conscience only, and the law supreme / Of that Intelligence which governs all' (19–22) is the 'haunt, and the main region of my song' (41), and nothing 'can breed such fear and awe / As fall upon us often when we look / Into our Minds, into the Mind of Man' (38–40). Wordsworth's line break between 'own' and 'inviolate' already violates the individual mind, even as collective fear and awe 'fall upon us' in a kind of introspection that has gravitational force. Yet in spite of his commitment to the 'blended might' of 'How exquisitely the individual Mind … is fitted: – and how exquisitely, too … / The external world is fitted to the Mind' (69, 63–8), that word 'haunt' suggests a more unsettled and uncanny site, like the 'sepulchral recesses' (589) in which Wordsworth means to corral his otherwise miscellaneous poems within the gothic cathedral that is the governing metaphor for his unrealized philosophical poem, *The Recluse*. The false reciprocity of the collective mind and the mind of man ('Into our Minds, into the Mind of Man') is betrayed by the medial caesura's uneven splitting of the iambic pentameter into 4/6, granting the singular mind the larger share, an 'exquisite' fit that seems both labored and belabored, and thus protests too much. It is as if Wordsworth agrees with Blake's annotations to the Preface to *The Excursion*, which includes the Prospectus: 'You shall not bring me down to believe such fitting & fitted I know better & Please your Lordship' (666). Something in the time of Romanticism is, even for Wordsworth, exquisite, and thus always out of joint.

For so many Romantics, the external world – nature, life itself – became the touchstone by which to gauge this disjointure, as if to objectify and authenticate the mind's contemplation of itself. (In Blake's case, what he sees as Wordsworth's natural religion prompts his rhetorical fit denouncing Wordsworth's fitting of the world 'not to Mind but to the Vile Body only & to its Laws of Good & Evil' [667].) Accordingly, Bloom's volume took nature as Romanticism's *modus vivendi* within which the mind's *modus operandi* unfolded how to be and think in the world, organized in three sections that addressed the psychological ('Nature and Consciousness'), the political ('Nature and Revolution'), and the aesthetic ('Nature and Literary Form'). Contributors read the human/nature relation variously in mediatory (Abrams or Frye), agonistic (Bloom or Hartman), or discontinuous (de Man) terms. The volume rarely questioned the centripetal pull of human consciousness towards its own interiority within this dialectic. Today, one arena of debate centers on the degree to which self-consciousness can stand in for all consciousness, and the issue has to do with how much salience to give the first-person account of consciousness and how much to highlight the subpersonal. Antonio Damasio insists on the place of the self in any account of consciousness, and Jesse Prinz counters that 'an adequate theory should allow that consciousness can arise without any experience of the self' (43).[9] Prinz argues that it is perfectly possible to have a stream of sensory information without a sense of self, and indeed Anne McCarthy demonstrates the degree to which Coleridge exploits sublime suspension so that he can make space for multiple subject states that acknowledge the impossibility of subjective mastery (21–49). To sublime suspension, we would add what Mihaly Csikszentmihalyi calls 'flow,' the experience of being so caught up in an activity that nothing else but it matters. It bears noting that though Prinz's and Damasio's models differ on the place of the self within consciousness, they both envision consciousness as porous. For Damasio, consciousness is about the self immersed in the surround through homeostasis; for Prinz, the 'stream' of sensory information, seemingly, is without filter. In this way, even self-consciousness is connected to its surround, and porousness becomes a form of relationality.

So often in Romantic writing, by contrast, is an inner sanctum violated as the human becomes nature's inmate as well as friend, an alienating (and alien) as well as sustaining matrix. Such disconnection defines the troubling character of so many Romantic confrontations with the outside: Charlotte Smith with the indecipherable archaeology of history at Beachy Head; William Wordsworth in the Simplon Pass with the abyss of imagination, in which the hiding places of power perpetually conceal themselves; Mary Robinson's narrativizing of the lyric in *Lyrical Tales* to show repeatedly why empathy *qua* feeling falls flat without the story which shapes the salience of suffering; Percy Shelley with the mute and inaccessible thing-ness of Mont Blanc; James Hogg or Thomas De Quincey with the Spectre of the Brocken. Such encounters remind us, fifty years on from Bloom's volume, that we need to reconsider the treatment of nature itself as what philosopher Peter Sloterdijk calls 'scenery-ontology' or a 'placid background for human operations' (10, 9). Such an approach turned 'the terrestrial sphere' into a 'single great interior' (not unlike the interior space of consciousness itself) for 'human praxis' (15) within which industrial capitalism projected the 'kinetic expressionism' (13) of a freedom not only to advance its interests but even to waste and destroy itself. Now, twenty years into a new century that is witnessing a nature radically altered by monumental shifts in science and technology, not to mention climate change, we need to reassess what new forms or states of consciousness might have been envisioned by a Romanticism whose own restlessness so challenged not only our relationship to and understanding of history as endless progress, but also the current neuroscientific understanding of consciousness in terms of efficiency.

It made sense that Bloom looked to psychoanalysis to map the inroads consciousness made into and onto nature as a debatable land with permeable, shifting boundaries. Psychoanalysis achieved perhaps its greatest influence in a post-World War Two United States haunted by triumph, particularly the 1950s, in the form of ego psychology, which, not unlike the reparative psychic agenda Abrams saw in Wordsworth, championed the ego's ability to surmount threats within and beyond its defenses. But even then, again, there was trouble on the horizon. For post-Freudians such as Jacques Lacan, of course, ego psychology was a betrayal of Freud's more radical insight into consciousness as a divided structure that not only irrevocably split the psychic integrity of the individual subject, but was its constitutive possibility. Paul de Man's essay, 'The Intentional Structure of the Romantic Image,' signaled an emergent displacement of consciousness as determinate and sustaining anchor of any critical universe and works in the more general spirit of the structuralist controversy in which post-Freudian, especially Lacanian, psychoanalysis played such a pivotal role and that found a kindred spirit in Romanticism's own hermeneutic of suspicion.[10]

This psychoanalytical version of Romantic consciousness informs the more recent work of Mary Jacobus, Joel Faflak, or David Sigler, among others.[11] Working in the post-Freudian spirit of Melanie Klein's object relations, Jacobus, for instance, asks the 'question of how things get ... from the outside to the inside – simultaneously establishing the boundary between them and seeming to abolish it': 'What does it mean to call this "interiority"? Where is this place that has neither outside nor inside, and by what process does it come into being?' (18). Such questions speak to porous boundaries of the otherwise sovereign territory mapped by Wordsworth's Prospectus as the imagined community of its own constitution, increasingly unmoored from its goal of self-awareness. So, however much hindsight tells us that psychoanalysis alone cannot account wholesale for Romantic consciousness, it does constellate on behalf of Bloom's volume a central paradox of consciousness, like psychology, as its own self-consuming subject. Put another way, we can understand how we bring the world to consciousness only by virtue of using consciousness itself. To ask a different form of Jacobus's question: How, that is, to observe the very thing that is doing the observing? How does the observer observe herself? Carl Jung, who worked with quantum physicist Wolfgang Pauli to comprehend how 'the Eye altering alters all' (Blake, 'The Mental Traveler' 62) writes: 'I do not imagine for a moment that I can stand above or beyond the psyche, so that it would be possible to judge it, as it were, from some transcendental Archimedean point "outside"' (124). Or as Michel Foucault reminds us, modernity's emergence from the classical episteme as it comes up against the limits of (its own) knowledge confronts us with the unconscious as that which is 'by definition inaccessible to any theoretical knowledge of man, to any continuous apprehension in terms of signification, conflict, or function.' Through this confrontation psychoanalysis reveals the moment 'at which the contents of consciousness articulate themselves, or rather stand gaping, upon man's finitude' (408). It thus constitutes a counter-science that perpetually 'dissolve[s] man' (413) and 'ceaselessly "unmake[s]" that very man who is creating and re-creating his positivity in the human sciences' (414). Thomas Metzinger insists in *Being No One* that the self is no thing but only exists as a process, and if he is right, science must give up thingness if it is to pursue a science of the self.

As our acknowledgement of the porousness of today's consciousness already indicates, many studies of consciousness in our time likewise dissolve the boundary between inside and outside, and yet somehow this dissolution causes no problems. For Chalmers, Clark, Hurley and Noë, for instance, skin and skull are arbitrary boundaries. What they mean here is that the cognitive system includes the brain in direct contact with its environmental surround. Jonathan Kramnick argues that with this notion of direct perception comes the problem of the degree to which our perceptions accurately capture the world, and he shows how literature shapes answers to this question (60). Neuroscientist Stanislas Dehaene argues that functional magnetic resonance imaging (fMRI) technology has rendered skin and skull 'transparent' (116), making consciousness porous at least to observation.[12] Yet rather than overwhelming with an impossible knowledge, this dissolution and transparency of the boundary between inside and outside function to make the environment into forms of contact or 'affordances' that work to support cognition as thinking becomes a form of doing. Andy Clark defines affordances as 'environmental opportunities for organism-salient action and intervention' (*Surfing* 133). Kramnick adds that the affordance is the desire 'to be with the literal thing itself' (9).[13] Paul Cisek introduced an 'Affordance Competition Hypothesis' in 2007, recognizing the possibility of competing affordances and the problem of action selection, but the value of any single affordance diminishes among competition. To the extent that 'cells with different preferences each inhibit each other' (1590), the multiple options in this model cancel each other out, which begs the question when and for whom is an affordance an affordance? In Cisek's model, the affordance ultimately remains an affordance because what used to be considered separate perception, cognition, and action systems, have now become unified into one. Yet when we are watching television or reading a book, is the system necessarily one system?[14] Because for Cisek this work is done by blended populations of neurons that individually and collectively exceed their activation thresholds, how stable and generalizable is this system? Prinz notes that 'components in coupled systems can retain independent entities' (180). And to what extent, then, are specific kinds of embodied responses being generalized into consciousness as a whole? Guy Dove admits that Embodied Cognition researchers have recently acknowledged that 'embodiment might be context dependent and come in degrees' (1). We ask, moreover, with the Romantics, even as they quest for some kind of Absolute, at what price necessary unification? Put more strongly, how is it that 'affordance' manages what to the Romantics often seems an epistemological crisis without borders? With Catherine Malabou we can point our fingers in the direction of versions of brain plasticity that proclaim efficiency. 'Must ... brain plasticity,' she asks, 'constitute the biological justification of a type of economic, political, and social organization in which all that matters is the result of action as such: efficacy, adaptability – unfailing flexibility?' (*What Do We Do* 31). For this reason, she stresses accident and 'negative plasticity' – everything from the death drive through neuroses to Alzheimer's and dementia as the shaping forces of human consciousness (*New Wounded* 210–13), forces that show efficiency to be a Sisyphean boulder.

In one of the most influential models of consciousness today, however, Dehaene builds upon the work of Bernard Baars[15] to propose that what we experience as consciousness is the global availability of information encoded in our 'neuronal workspace,' roughly equivalent to working memory, and roughly localized to the frontal cortex. By emphasizing what scientists call 'access consciousness' – what can be reported – over 'phenomenal consciousness' – what something feels like – Dehaene sought to simplify scientific focus in order to achieve 'objective mechanisms for subjective states' (17). Nonetheless, what begins as a tactical necessity narrows the definition of consciousness itself, and in so doing, produces exactly the kind of efficiency that Malabou warns against, an efficiency condensed into the very terms 'global workspace' and 'mechanism.'[16] Damasio, by contrast, argues for the centrality of the brain stem and thalamus in any account of consciousness because the very brain mapping he considers central to consciousness and to a notion of the self happens there. In Dehaene's 'global neuronal workspace … consciousness is global information broadcasting within the cortex' (13). The brain is not far from a Fordist assembly line of 'pertinent information' (13), an efficiency enhanced by information's ability to stand in for knowledge. Prinz adds that 'we often have conscious experiences that are ephemeral, unclear, peripheral, or irrelevant (31), concluding that Dehaene's correlation between the frontal cortex and consciousness is 'imperfect' (31).[17]

Missing in this picture is the very possibility of normalizing Romantic disjointure, alienation, and disconnection – what Wordsworth named 'fear and awe' and Shelley figures as Rousseau's brain becoming 'as sand' (496) – without which, we hasten to add, relationality has no incentive for improvement.[18] Consider here too not only the published appendix to Mary Prince's history that testifies to the bodily scars of slavery that her own narrative could not sufficiently vouch for (64–5), but also the commonplace, sneering condescension with which her 'owners' named her after the Prince of Wales. They themselves could not live up to the challenge they foisted upon her race. Prince's example further suggests that embodied cognition might bespeak a kind of privilege unavailable or not easily available to the marginalized. Such disjointure is useful even today: Helena de Preester warns that Damasio and others confuse the brain's re-representation of the body with self-awareness (609). Why do we assume the two are or amount to the same thing? She also shows how different brain models stratify different bodily systems differently (606–7). In a larger view, the Romantic awareness of difference and the power of tropes allows greater scrutiny of what really are models of consciousness rather than claims about consciousness itself.

To wit, complicating Dehaene's efficient global workspace model is his claim that it is 'autonomous' (14). He submits 'it is constantly traversed by global patterns of internal activity that originate not from the external world but from within, from the neurons' peculiar capacity to self-activate in a partly random fashion' (14). It is this 'self-activation' that raises deeper epistemological problems, and which reminds us that the internal/external or local/global boundary might be useful from an epistemological perspective. 'Self' here is reduced in scale to the neuronal, as is autonomy, but when does a neuronal affordance scale upwards? We cannot know when we are prompted by random neuronal activity, and when we are acting from input from the external world, especially when we have no introspective insight into which of our neurons are firing. Rather than supporting a world view wherein subject and object become blurred into affordances, would we not be better off heeding Kant's warning that what we take to be the thing itself is really the appearance or form of the thing? What exactly do we think we are in direct contact with? Are our affordances about how the 'world shows up' (Kramnick 76), or about how we want or prime the world to show up? Our point here is that directness can be a liability, as can the loss of skepticism as a stance toward the world and our apprehensions of it. In making the environment actionable, to what extent does 'affordance' permit human appropriation?

Lisa Feldman Barrett illustrates how the idea of direct contact can be a liability in her thesis that affects are about keeping track of our body budgets so that we can be ready to act. 'Affect is like a barometer for how you're doing. Remember, your brain is constantly running a budget for your body' (7½ *Lessons* 106). Affects thus are not necessarily about the world, but rather speak to our energy and other internal needs.[19] She cites a 2011 Israeli study, for example, that shows that judges were significantly more likely to deny parole if the hearing was before lunchtime (*How Emotions* 74–5). The judges experienced their hunger as evidence for their parole decisions. Her sobering warning is that 'brains are not wired for accuracy. They're wired to keep us alive' (7½ *Lessons* 76). In a larger view, the connections between body budgets and affect leads to an affective realism 'because we experience supposed facts about the world that are created in part by our feelings' (*How Emotions* 75). This insight prompts Barrett to reorient the study of emotions away from accuracy and universal models, and towards variability. For her, emotions are generated on the fly, and thus are contextually situated. In this view, context helps us read other minds. Her upshot is that we should see the emotions not in terms of some universal fingerprint, but as about achieving social meaning and consensus (*How Emotions* 40–1). The ability to consider one's affects as being about one's body budget grants skepticism and distance some power to change one's relation to the world, if only in the form of changing one's environment to reduce the impact of our own and other people's body budgets.

As Shelley knew, one person's living is another's 'unprofitable strife' (*Adonais*). Perhaps it is us, the living, who 'decay / Like corpses in a charnel' (422). To wit, today's 'efficiency' was for the Romantics a horror show: *The Prelude* (in fourteen books), the growth of the poet's mind, reduced to a bumper sticker; Coleridge's famous 'Dejection: An Ode' distilled to a headline in *The Morning Post*. Wordsworth's and Coleridge's obsessive revisions suggest less a growth than a series of metastases. Think here also of the Ancient Mariner, compelled to repeat his tale for any wedding guest who happens by, a repetition whose 'strange power' is both efficient and fixated. It is far too easy to lash our minds to its surround, as proponents of embodied cognition arguably do, when both the siren and the odyssey are contained by efficiency. So much for the ten years it took Odysseus to make it home. Likewise, Coleridge's siren was a traumatic Life-in-Death, a point underscored by recent readings of the poem by Debbie Lee and others that suggest his boat is a slave ship, and that the mariner suffers from yellow fever. Another reason why the loss of skin and skull is rarely mourned today is that overcoming the cognitive chauvinism of human beings – the idea that only humans have consciousness – has become far more important than addressing any gap between thinking/consciousness and matter, a shift in values evident in the growing influence of panpsychism today (see Jager's chapter in the present volume (Chapter 5), as well as Chalmers, Goff, and Koch). Indeed, because that very gap between thinking and things has resisted science's incursions into consciousness, Chalmers has argued that positing the universality of consciousness might be the first step necessary to have a science of it. The need for evolution to account for the development of consciousness, furthermore, has made the cost of its reductions less salient. When consciousness is driven by survival, has it become a version of Blake's 'dark, Satanic mill'? By contrast, our contributors chart, to borrow a phrase from Fredric Jameson, a brave new 'aesthetic of cognitive mapping' of Romantic consciousness – Jameson's 'aesthetic' designates the possibility of a theoretical knowing of the world that is beyond accurate representation – in vital and unanticipated ways. Pointedly, Jameson insists this mapping is never mapped.

Since Bloom's volume, such dissolution has been at the center of Romantic studies of consciousness as the product of what Clifford Siskin calls Romanticism's 'self-made mind, full of newly constructed depths' (13), which implicitly reorients Frye's 'constructive power of the mind' as a rather more autonomous and unmoored cognitive apparatus. In *Romantic Identities* (1996) Andrea Henderson explores how the Romantic self 'has no deep truth' and is instead the 'creature of surfaces, of context, and of varying forms' (5); whatever 'core' constitutes the Romantic subject, it is the 'center of movement or circulation,' even 'a place of dangerous fluidity' (9). Subsequent explorations of Romanticism's previously undervalued scientific imagination by Noel Jackson and Richard C. Sha offer a more nuanced Romantic understanding of the interface between minds, bodies, and the world.[20] Research into Romanticism's alternate or paranormal states of being and non-being in work by Anne-Lise François and David Collings or by four of our contributors – Kate Singer, Robert Mitchell, Nancy Yousef, Jacques Khalip – has further demonstrated the period's heterogenous and heterogeneous approach to consciousness.[21] In *British Romanticism and the Science of the Mind* (2001) and *The Neural Sublime* (2010) Alan Richardson, author of this volume's opening chapter, has historicized Romanticism's own contribution to a burgeoning science of consciousness that emerges from what Fernando Vidal calls 'the century of psychology' (90). Richardson's work signals an expanded awareness of Romanticism's achievement beyond what a later methodology such as psychoanalysis might retroactively tell us about that achievement. Or rather, we can now see with the retroactive insight of advances in knowledge beyond those of psychoanalysis the productively uneven and unstable reciprocity between mind and world.

To borrow Sloterdijk's terms again, the Romantics, 'brave enough to consider even the worst as a real possibility,' cultivated the 'prognostic intelligence' of 'experienced apocalypticists' (13) who intuited the fraught 'connection between striving for self-preservation and the will to self-advancement' (19). Accordingly, they sensed how, in the 'interplay between environment and technology,' the 'synergetic rules that evolution is employing and trying to make clear to us' (Buckminster Fuller, cited in Sloterdijk 21) offered nature for a rather different exploitation. We have thus come to see the association between mind, nature, and body in terms of a broader, interactive ecology. Rather than master the world, consciousness orchestrates and is orchestrated by the environment as part of an evolving, systemic interface. Situated between Locke's *tabula rasa* ready for the imprimatur of sense perceptions, somehow to be modified but not negated by reflection; or Hume's theater of the mind that staged identity as merely a bundle of habitual neuronal associations and the self as the vantage point through which one sees; and Coleridge's, Kant's, or Hegel's post-empiricist sense of the labor of abstract cognitive potential, the Romantics came to see consciousness as both a material resource we have only begun to mine, and a trap.²² Such a realization produced narratives of both apocalyptic and utopian intensity that at once liberated, enlightened, and sometimes terrified the subject, in which spirit *Romanticism and Consciousness* took shape.

Romanticism and Consciousness, Now

We are now compelled to reconsider consciousness as a matrix of embedded, intersectional, transactional, dynamic, and 'entangled' associations between consciousness and the world. The popularity of the term 'affordance' alone indexes the seepage of entanglement. Perhaps no other word better captures the changes in what we think we know about consciousness over the past five decades than 'entanglement.' Where perception was once divorced from action, many argue that the sensory–motor system engages in perception for the sake of action. Andy Clark puts it thus: 'whenever a decision is to be reported by (or otherwise invokes) some motor action, there looks to be an entwining of perceptuo-motor processing and decision-making' (*Surfing* 178). Under 'embodied,' 'extended,' or 'distributed' cognition, Clark's dependent clause aside, the gap has become the network, and with the entanglement of our perceptual and motor systems comes the embeddedness of consciousness within its surround, thus making separation of mind from world atypical and even abnormal. Here is Alva Noë: 'it is thus only in the context of an animal's embodied existence, situated in an environment, dynamically interacting with objects and situations, that the function of the brain can be understood' (65). Here is Shaun Gallagher: 'conscious experience is normally ... out ahead of movement, directed at the environment' (64). And yet, we hasten to add, abstraction and skeptical distancing from one's surround also have their uses, and thus question this normativeness. Perhaps our mapping is not yet done.

Our quarrel is not so much with the entangled/ecological or embodied view of cognition, which has at least tamed Cartesian dualism, and taught us that planning and perception are not necessarily separate acts. Indeed, a number of the contributions herein not only espouse that view, but also argue with Lisa Ann Robertson and John Savarese that the Romantics found such a view congenial. Herein, Savarese opens up embodied cognition to historical difference by thinking about how the gothic exploits the idea of 'primitive' meters to shape cognition. Our quarrel is with the compulsiveness of that view and its lack of appreciation for abstraction, idealism – here defined as the ability to see the world from the stance of suspension, as if something were true – and deliberation, which, in our view, Romanticism demands. The world, Wordsworth insists, is sometimes too much with us. Through the mix of sympathy and curiosity, moreover, Joanna Baillie warns that we must attend to and reflect upon our passions, or else, like De Monfort, they become 'strong and fixed ... [not to mention] seemingly unprovoked by outward circumstances' (1:37). Philip Fisher adds that our passions intensify because we never know the radius of our will in advance (160–2).

In what follows, we suggest reasons why the embodied view of consciousness has come to seem compulsory. Chief among the reasons is the rise of entanglement, along with the networks which enable entanglement to thrive. Entanglement is persuasive today partly because it does an end run around linear causality. Since quantum physics, we know that the act of measuring reduces probabilities to a single discrete measure. Entanglement solves this problem by opening up causality to the relation of observed event A to observed event B, thus replacing linear temporal priority with relationality and a web of probable events.[23] In this way, correlation within an ever-expanding web can begin to insinuate causality. With regard to consciousness, the environment has become an affordance for cognition and consciousness, which means that the environment now has a key role to play in the cognitive system that straddles mind and world. Perhaps because so many Romantic writers wanted to change the world, they resisted the necessity of an embodied mind tethered to the world. So too does ecology insinuate networks and entanglement, substituting individual sovereignty for systems of relationality. Recent studies of empathy like Paul Bloom's, which show how the suffering of others easily loses salience, suggest that we are better off not taking relationality as a given, which entanglement can do.

Neuroscientist Antonio Damasio has done much to make persuasive the model of consciousness that entangles mind and world. Against the rational mind, Damasio has underscored how feelings register our homeostasis – think here of Barrett's body budgets – and in this model, feelings are the very stuff of consciousness, without which there would be nothing to be conscious of. Consciousness in this theory is thoroughly embodied, and inextricable from its surround. Hence his somatic marker theory understands feelings as somatic markers that provide the very maps which structure consciousness. His evidence is drawn from patients with damage to the ventromedial sectors of their prefrontal cortices, and as a result they can tell you when something is disturbing, but they themselves are not disturbed by it because, he insists, they lack the somatic marker. They have no Galvanic skin response. Damasio's point is that since they do not feel the danger, even though they cognitively recognize its possibility, they make poor choices.[24] When Damasio insists that 'in reality, emotions and feelings come in multiple flavors, and only a few are disruptive' (*Strange Order* 101), we think Romantic writers would find this view – as Keats puts it in 'La Belle Dame Sans Merci: A Ballad' – a kind of 'kisses four,' partial at best.

Consciousness is now considered hopelessly entangled with what used to be known as the unconscious, and thus access consciousness relies upon the unreportable. And since access consciousness can use the unconscious, the reportable finesses what is unknown. As Katherine Hayles explains, the function of what she calls 'non-conscious cognition' is to keep 'consciousness, with its slow uptake and limited information processing ability from being overwhelmed' (88). In this view, the non-conscious manages the world so that consciousness can imagine its own autonomy. And in this view, the conscious and the non-conscious are bound together into a cognitive assemblage. Because there is nothing but cognition all the way down, there is no epistemological crisis. To wit, head of the Allen Brain Institute Christof Koch offers an Integrated Information Theory, which argues that anything with a 'non-zero maximum of integrated information' can have an experience (158–9).[25] In this view, protozoa have experiences, as do protein molecules. Even a single proton has its own song of experience. However, does this experience help in any way to predict behavior? We are further mindful of Roger Penrose's warning that until computation encompasses understanding – in his view, programming is not understanding – it can offer very limited help in making sense of consciousness.[26]

What was once a Cartesian gap between mind and world is now a span of relationality, entanglement, subject is bound to object, cognition to emotion. If Bloom et al. warned us that re-enchantment to nature was an act of bad faith, never could they have envisioned a version of consciousness so inextricably tethered to the world that mind could never become its own world. It is as if the Alastor poet were never startled by his own thoughts. Tell that to Mary Shelley, who responded with *Frankenstein*. She revises the pastoral 'wedded boughs' and bower Alastor seeks into the novel's wedding night as Alastor's 'bloodless limbs' (l. 513, p. 86) become Elizabeth's 'bloodless arms' (165). Shelley thereby insists that it is Elizabeth who must pay the price for Alastor's and Victor's bloodless ideals. As the gap between mind and world has become an almost unbreakable ecology, to what extent might this unbreakability be a form of special pleading, not to mention a denial of narcissism as an outcome of embodied cognition. Jesse Prinz argues against strong enactivism by insisting that 'motor responses make no constitutive contributions to visual phenomenology' (192).

Put simply, embodied and enactive views of consciousness make strange Romantic resistance and negativity, and threaten once again to make Romanticism unfit. Poststructuralism's nails in the coffin of the subject have shifted our focus to networks. Alan Liu has argued that 'the network is our contemporary intuition of infinity' (42), but how to see or understand anything which is infinitely connected to everything else? Embodied cognition does so by offering the real of particular instances of embodied cognition as standing for cognition and consciousness as a whole, and thereby immerses itself in the problem of how any particular instantiation can capture the totality of the network. Patrick Jagoda puts the problem this way:

> one of the difficulties of even naming, let alone thinking through, networks is that they are inherently emergent – capable of spatiotemporal transformations and scalar shifts. The very notion of a specific and nameable network becomes problematic, thereby signaling the term's instability. (8)[27]

Jagoda argues that network form is more accurately a formation, that is, in process, but the question is to what extent can any particular formation stand in for the network at a whole (29)? At times, instantiation, at other times, metaphor, the network links both. On the one hand, for example, neuroscientist Jean-Pierre Changeux insists 'each component neuron of the assembly possesses its own distinctive patterns of connectivity' (51). On the other hand, 'note that this assumption does not require that an exact topology of anatomical connection be constructed that is reproducible across individual brains in every detail, only that a map of functional relations be established' (54). It is the network's ability to offer metonymy in the form of particular processes that stand in for the whole without looking like metonymy that makes entangled networks so seductive. Within a network, process, system, function, assembly, and emergence conspire to allow particular instantiations to slide into the rule or law, even as any notion of the outside becomes increasingly untenable. Alan Liu insists that the perspective of the production of information must be added to that of its consumption so that the illusion of information as being emancipatory can be tensed against how the information is being managed (42).

To that end, one might say that proponents of embodied cognition elevate embodiment into the law of the cognitive network/consciousness but in reality can offer only many particular instances for the law.[28] That is to say, proponents of embodied cognition overestimate the stability and universality of their embodied networks. They mistake one set of nodes for the totality of consciousness. They thus partake in abstraction even as they turn to embodiment to push abstraction away. When we are reaching for an apple, an embodied cognition model makes total sense, but when we are teasing out this Introduction, embodied cognition is perhaps less useful. We sometimes see without acting. Even Andy Clark, a key proponent of embodied cognition, recognizes that the predictive processing model behind embodied cognition needs to better account for novelty seeking and higher aspirations of art (*Surfing* 265), for in these instances typical embodied behavior can become monotonous. How, then, better to balance action-based forms of embodied cognition that exist to tamp down surprise with the human tendency to become bored and thus seek out novelty. To return to Jameson's aesthetics of cognitive mapping, what the Romantics envisioned was the possibility of a theoretical knowing beyond accuracy – as Blake submits, 'what is now proved, was once only imagined' (36) – that would insist upon the limits of embodied knowing and on network instability. Hence Blake's depiction of Urizen's (reason's) relentless allegorizing and redramatizing of mental and psychological processes and splitting of identities into spectral states of being, which explicitly resist the sovereignty of reason and consciousness.

We have divided this collection into four parts, a kind of Blakean fourfold vision of consciousness. Part I, 'New Models of Consciousness,' concentrates on how the governing models of consciousness have changed. Alan Richardson lays bare the wide array of Romantic models of unconsciousness, and in so doing, highlights their curious phenomenalization of unawareness, suggesting that vacancy may bring its own burdens. Colin Jager then takes on panpsychism as an ontological position, not an epistemological error, and thereby rethinks it as a strategy, both then and now, of dealing with skepticism. Joel Faflak considers how Percy Shelley's desire for the feltness of faith speaks to the pitfalls and possibilities of consciousness itself. Richard C. Sha then situates Blakean experience between Bloom's and today's embodied consciousness, and he shows how and why Blake questions current faith in porousness and relationality.

Part II, 'States of Consciousness,' highlights how affect and trauma theory have reshaped how we understand consciousness to work. Mark Bruhn tackles the affective power of novelty in Wordsworth to show how his balladry sets into motion its production and reception. Challenging current physiological models of affect, Nancy Yousef considers spontaneous forms of Romantic emotion that seem too reflective to count as affective, moments of after-affect that will not partition neatly into thought and feeling. Jacques Khalip then analyzes how Romantic writers constructed consciousness as a state that takes up space without embodying it, enabling a kind of aesthetic thought that he argues is impervious to development and progress. Finally, Ralf Haekel rounds out this section with his turn to media ecology to rethink mental inwardness and Charlotte Smith's *Beachy Head*.

Part III, 'Social and Ecological Models of Consciousness,' foregrounds the field's move away from individual approaches to consciousness and towards embodied and distributed models of social cognition, a growing consensus of the field (some might say a stampede). Lisa Zunshine examines how our social interactions inform our cognitive foundations, and the degree to which E. T. A. Hoffman relies upon a child's unruly imagination to negotiate social reality. Yasmin Solomonescu takes seriously Shelley's metaphor of a prone mind in *The Cenci* to explore the degree to which the self's dissolution into its surround functions as an absorption or as a moral resource. John Savarese considers gothic imitations and experiments with ballad meter to explore cognition's historical variability. Robert Mitchell then argues that Burke, Godwin, and Malthus synthesize individual consciousness and institutions, and in so doing anticipate an alliance between today's extended consciousness and neuronal population approaches to it.

Finally, Part IV takes up 'Race and Consciousness.' Kate Singer charts the swirl of affect within Mary Prince, Mary Robinson, and Percy Shelley to create a field of posthuman consciousness, whereby the circulation of subjects and objects confronts the inequities of race and gender. Humberto Garcia demonstrates how Henry Aston Barker's panorama, *Constantinople from the Tower of Galata*, demands a bodily shift in geographic orientation that inspires viewers to identify with and as strangers, a powerful disorientation that begins to imagine the East getting its due. Last, but not least, Julie Carlson considers Romantic friendship as a white institution, and what it would take to move friendship beyond white supremacy so that it might better promote racial knowledge and caring.

In the spirit of consciousness as process as well as product, then, we offer the volume less as a comprehensive or authoritative summation of the field past or present than as an evolving dialogue among, like the Romantics themselves, productively restless critical explorers. Their tropes for consciousness ideally provoke questioning of ours. Indeed, Malabou hints that the neuron is really a trope, since the network makes it difficult to determine where one begins and ends, and since the cut between the mental and the physical is an interpretative move (*What Do We Do* 62–78). Our growing sense that advances in consciousness will require both first-person and third-person perspectives – both the qualitative feel of consciousness and an 'objective' or scientific view of it – along with contributions from multiple disciplines, perhaps encourages us to learn from how they combined perspectives and sought dialogue.

Through their restless fourfold vision of consciousness, Romanticism continues to matter and helps impel the narrative that makes consciousness possible, and possible to live with.

Notes

1. For a good overview, see Miranda Anderson, George Rousseau, and Michael Wheeler (editors), *Distributed Cognition in Enlightenment and Romantic Culture* (2019), especially the Introduction.
2. Besides Bloom, who edited, wrote the Preface, and contributed an essay on Shelley, the volume included single essays by Samuel H. Monk, Owen Barfield, J. H. Van den Berg, Paul de Man, W. K. Wimsatt Jr, Alfred Cobban, John Hollander, Martin Price, Frederick A. Pottle, Humphry House, and Alvin B. Kernan; and two essays each by Geoffrey H. Hartman, M. H. Abrams, Walter Jackson Bate, and Northrop Frye. Josephine Miles was the sole woman author.
3. Interestingly, Lovejoy treats Romanticism as a 'complex' whose origin we are compelled, through 'an adequate semasiological study of the term,' 'to trace [through] the associative processes through which the word "romantic" has attained its present amazing diversity' in order 'to render it, if possible, psychologically intelligible how such manifold and discrepant phenomena have all come to receive one name' (8). Psychoanalysis thus enters Lovejoy's account through the back door, as if to name the consciousness of Romanticism as a multiple personality resistant to diagnosis.
4. Abrams includes C. S. Lewis's rebuttal of T. S. Eliot's preference for Dryden over Percy Shelley, 'Shelley, Dryden, and Mr. Eliot.'
5. See Lakoff and Johnson, *Metaphors We Live By* (1980) and *Philosophy in the Flesh: The Embodied Mind and Its Challenge to Western Thought* (1990). See also Johnson, *The Body in Mind* (1990).
6. Abrams calls his volume's general methodology 'critical' – which is to say, New Critical – in that, whether or not the essays 'deal with literary history or with the life or ideas of a poet,' they always 'bring these materials to bear on the interpretation and assessment of the poems' (v).
7. Tellingly, Bloom titles his volume 'Essays in Criticism' as opposed to 'Modern Essays in Criticism,' as if to dehistoricize and thus normalize the Romantic ideology of its insights.
8. And from the stance of inactivist theories of consciousness, admittedly less congenial to the humanities today, 'consciousness sidesteps action' (Prinz 169–212). The experiments of Benjamin Libet in the 1980s, which seemed to show that consciousness arrives 300 milliseconds too late to effect action, suggest that consciousness serves a function unrelated to action. Leys (324–7) and Prinz (197–200) detail the limits of Libet's research: most crucially, finger flexing when one feels the urge is hardly a meaningful conscious act, and so it is not clear whether these experiments can be generalized. In *Anti-Externalism*, Joseph Mendola develops a theory of 'qualia empiricism' designed to show both the power of inner resources and that the external has yet to earn its cognitive credits.

9. Damasio (*Self*) divides consciousness into the proto-self, the core self, and the autobiographical self. Proto, of course, implies that everything before is building up to the self. For a sense of the sweep of work on consciousness in addition to Prinz, see Flanagan. We admire Flanagan's ability to see nuance even in approaches to consciousness he disagrees with. So, for example, though he does not agree with epiphenomenalism, he notes that it is useful because we tend to give consciousness too much credit (8), and because information can influence us without our conscious awareness. Prinz believes that consciousness exists to provide menus for action (203–4). Dennett treats arguments about consciousness as 'styles of explanation' even as he seeks to cut it down to size in either an 'intentional stance' or 'multiple drafts' model.
10. One recalls that the landmark symposium 'The Languages of Criticism and the Sciences of Man' at Johns Hopkins University, which included Jacques Derrida's 'Structure, Sign, and Play in the Discourse of the Human Sciences,' was only four years prior to *Romanticism and Consciousness*, and that Bloom would later edit and contribute to the Yale School manifesto, *Deconstruction and Criticism* (1979). De Man did not participate in the Harvard conference but contributed 'Shelley Disfigured' to Bloom's 1979 volume.
11. See Sigler, *Sexual Enjoyment in British Romanticism: Gender and Psychoanalysis, 1753–1835* (2015). See also Daniela Garofalo and Sigler, *Lacan and Romanticism* (2019), and Faflak, *Romantic Psychoanalysis* (2008).
12. Some reasons why fMRI technology is anything but transparent: each brain is unique and must be mapped onto an ideal brain map in order to identify specific voxels; the technology does not work in real time because variations in blood flow have a latency of five seconds or more (Legrenzi and Umiltà 15); what is being measured is oxygenation, not thought; the images capture degrees of oxygenation, but an area that is not lit up is not inactive; and correlation to specific brain areas is not causality.
13. Kramnick's lucid and penetrating *Paper Minds* shows how the forms of literature contribute to the project of embodied cognition. For Kramnick, empiricism requires an image of an object, and is thus object-like, and this prompts him to consider how models of agency and of experience are consequently built. Form, for Kramnick, is 'thinkable only with matter, the substance forms shapes and that makes form apprehensible as, in a word, form' (42), but this is to understand form itself a kind of embodiment and not, say, as a Platonic ideal or Kantian purposiveness. Especially helpful is his sense of the relation of empiricist and computational theories of mind, and his sense that theories of computation, following Jerry Fodor, demand the separation of psychology and epistemology (102–9). By taking on board key terms like 'affordance' and 'ecology,' Kramnick primes us for the embodied view and makes skepticism a heavier lift. One could also see the 'like' in object-like as a marker of difference. Kant's epistemology warned that any noumenon was likely informed by our psychology. He thus turned to the *a priori*, as a way of moving beyond at least individual minds. For a shrewd evaluation of the main evidence for both the enactive and the inactive views of consciousness, see Prinz, 169–212.
14. See Goldinger et al. 'The Poverty of Embodied Cognition.'

15. According to Boly and Baars et al., Global Workspace Theory predicts that conscious perception mobilizes widespread brain resources whereas non-conscious perception should be more localized (10). The authors call for a greater understanding of brain architecture and neuronal computation to make more advances; in particular, they acknowledge that correlational knowledge is not yet causal knowledge.
16. Dehaene's collaborator Changeux insists the 'neuronal workspace hypothesis' is a 'modest' model (87–95). Note that he does not use 'global.' Malabou notes that 'the space and cut that separate the neuronal from the mental … are comparable not to synaptic gaps … but rather to theoretical fissures' (*What Do We Do* 62–3).
17. Prinz details an experiment by Dehaene and his collaborators, whereby, in order to preserve the Global Workspace Theory, they designate a word which was clearly visible but people were told to ignore as 'preconscious' and 'visible but unseen' (31). The fMRI scan showed activity in the visual areas but not in the frontal cortex. Since the people could report it, the word was available to access consciousness, but the frontal cortex, where access consciousness is supposed to take place, did not show activation.
18. See Clark (*Surfing*) on 'efficiency' as a main driver of embodied cognition (271–2).
19. Barrett argues that our feelings begin from 'interoception,' our brain's representation of all sensations from our internal organs and tissues, the hormones in our blood, and our immune systems (*How Emotions* 56). She continues: 'your brain constantly uses past experience to predict which objects and events will impact your body budget, changing your affect. These objects and events are collectively your affective niche' (73).
20. See Sha, *Imagination and Science in Romanticism* (2018), and Jackson, *Science and Sensation in Romantic Poetry* (2008). See also Noah Heringman, *Romantic Science: The Literary Forms of Natural History* (2003), and Andrew Cunningham and Nicholas Jardine (editors), *Romanticism and the Sciences* (1990).
21. See Mitchell, *Experimental Life: Vitalism in Romantic Science and Literature* (2013); Khalip, *Anonymous Life: Romanticism and Dispossession* (2008); Yousef, *Romantic Intimacy* (2013); Collings, *Disastrous Subjectivities: Romanticism, Modernity, and the Real* (2019); François, *Open Secrets: The Literature of Uncounted Experience* (2009); Singer, *Romantic Vacancy: The Poetics of Gender, Affect, and Radical Speculation* (2019). See also Chris Washington and Anne C. McCarthy (editors), *Romanticism and Speculative Realism* (2019).
22. See Alexander M. Schlutz, *Mind's World: Imagination and Subjectivity from Descartes to Romanticism* (2009).
23. To deal with this entanglement and what he calls 'explosive causality,' Dehaene exploits 'Granger causality analysis,' which provides a method 'which asks whether one signal precedes the other and predicts its future values' (139).
24. Our summary of Damasio is indebted to Robinson. For critiques of Damasio's somatic marker theory, see Leys, 377–8, Robinson, 63, and Panksepp. Panksepp argues that Damasio's model strips away 'a life-time accrual of

social meanings and contingencies for affective reward and affective aversion,' thus making human emotion 'thoughtless' (118). See also De Preester.
25. Koch's Integrated Information Theory Model has made important contributions to the care of comatose patients. Integrated Information Theory provides a means of calculating brain activity in these patients; higher integration warrants more treatment and intervention.
26. See BBC4's 'In Our Time,' the podcast episode on consciousness, which features a conversation between the philosopher Ted Honderich and the physicist Roger Penrose (https://www.bbc.co.uk/programmes/p005464j; last accessed December 1, 2021). Penrose argues that we will not know more about conscious materiality until we have a new physics that moves beyond computation, since he believes that computation has nothing to say about understanding.
27. Jagoda adopts a non-sovereign viewpoint from which to examine nodes in the network, and he designates as 'political' any time the network forgets its essential instability. Moreover, he adopts Rancière's concept of 'dissensus' to name the rupture in instability that makes visible the political (23–6).
28. We are mindful here of Dehaene's observation that memory enables 'detachment from pressing environmental contingencies' (101).

References

Abrams, M. H. *Natural Supernaturalism: Tradition and Revolution in Romantic Literature.* New York: W. W. Norton, 1971.
—. 'English Romanticism: The Spirit of the Age.' *Romanticism Reconsidered: Selected Papers from the English Institute.* 26–72.
—, ed. *English Romantic Poets: Modern Essays in Criticism.* New York: Oxford University Press, 1960.
Anderson, Miranda, George Rousseau, and Michael Wheeler, eds. *Distributed Cognition in Enlightenment and Romantic Culture.* Edinburgh: Edinburgh University Press, 2019.
Baillie, Joanna. *A Series of Plays.* 2 vols. London: Cadell and Davies, 1802.
Barrett, Lisa Feldman. *How Emotions Are Made.* Boston: Houghton Mifflin Harcourt, 2017.
—. *7½ Lessons about the Brain.* Boston: Houghton Mifflin Harcourt, 2020.
Boly, Melanie, Anil Seth, Melanie Wilke, Paul Ingmundson, Bernard Baars, Steven Laureys, David Edelman, and Naotsugu Tsuchiya. 'Consciousness in Humans and Non-human Animals: Recent Advances and Future Directions.' *Frontiers in Psychology* 4.625 (October 2013): 1–20.
Blake, William. *The Complete Poetry and Prose of William Blake.* Rev. ed. Ed. David V. Erdman. New York: Anchor Books, 1988.
Bloom, Harold, ed. *Romanticism and Consciousness: Essays in Criticism.* New York: W. W. Norton, 1970.
Bloom, Paul. *Against Empathy.* New York: HarperCollins, 2016.
Chalmers, David. 'How Do You Explain Consciousness?' https://www.youtube.com/watch?v=uhRhtFFhNzQ (last accessed December 2, 2021).

Changeux, Jean-Pierre. *The Physiology of Truth*. Trans. M. B. DeBevoise. Cambridge, MA: Harvard University Press, 2002.
Cisek, Paul. 'Cortical Mechanisms of Action Selection: The Affordance Competition Hypothesis,' *Philosophical Transactions: Biological Sciences* 362.1465 (September 29, 2007): 1585–99.
Clark, Andy. *Supersizing the Mind: Embodiment, Action, and Cognitive Extension*. Oxford: Oxford University Press, 2011.
—. *Surfing Uncertainty: Prediction, Action and the Embodied Mind*. Oxford: Oxford University Press, 2016.
Collings, David. *Disastrous Subjectivities: Romanticism, Modernity, and the Real*. Toronto: University of Toronto Press, 2019.
Csikszentmihalyi, Mihaly. *Flow: The Psychology of Optimal Experience*. New York: Harper Perennial, 2008.
Cunningham, Andrew and Nicholas Jardine, eds. *Romanticism and the Sciences*. Cambridge: Cambridge University Press, 1990.
Damasio, Antonio. *Self Comes to Mind*. New York: Vintage Books, 2012.
—. *The Strange Order of Things*. New York: Pantheon Books, 2018.
Dehaene, Stanislas. *Consciousness and the Brain*. New York: Viking, 2014.
Dennett, Daniel C. *Consciousness Explained*. New York: Little, Brown and Company, 1991.
—. *The Intentional Stance*. Cambridge, MA: MIT Press, 1989.
De Preester, Helena. 'The Deep Bodily Origins of the Subjective Perspective: Models and their Problems.' *Consciousness and Cognition* 16 (2007): 604–18.
Dove, Guy. 'How to Go Beyond the Body: An Introduction.' *Frontiers in Psychology* 6.660 (2105). https://www.frontiersin.org/articles/10.3389/fpsyg.2015.00660/full (last accessed December 2, 2021).
Faflak, Joel. *Romantic Psychoanalysis: The Burden of the Mystery*. Albany, NY: State University of New York Press, 2008.
Fisher, Philip. *The Vehement Passions*. Princeton: Princeton University Press, 2002.
Flanagan, Owen. *Consciousness Reconsidered*. Cambridge, MA: MIT Press, 1992.
Foucault, Michel. *The Order of Things: An Archaeology of the Human Sciences*. New York: Routledge, 1989.
François, Anne-Lise. *Open Secrets: The Literature of Uncounted Experience*. Stanford: Stanford University Press, 2009.
Frye, Northrop. *Fearful Symmetry: A Study of William Blake*. Princeton: Princeton University Press, 1947.
—, ed. *Romanticism Reconsidered: Selected Papers from the English Institute*. New York and London: Columbia University Press, 1963.
—. 'The Drunken Boat: The Revolutionary Element in Romanticism.' *Romanticism Reconsidered*. 1–25.
Garofalo, Daniela and David Sigler, eds. *Lacan and Romanticism*. Albany, NY: State University of New York Press, 2019.
Gallagher, Shaun. *How the Body Shapes the Mind*. Oxford: Clarendon Press, 2009.
Goff, Philip. *Galileo's Error: Foundations for a New Science of Consciousness*. London: Rider, 2019.

Goldinger, Stephen, Megan Papesh, Anthony Barnhart, Whitney Hansen, and Michael Hout. 'The Poverty of Embodied Cognition.' *Psychonomic Bulletin and Review* 23 (2016): 959–78.

Hayles, N. Katherine. *Unthought: The Power of the Cognitive Nonconscious*. Chicago: University of Chicago Press, 2017.

Henderson, Andrea. *Romantic Identities: Varieties of Subjectivity, 1774–1830*. Cambridge: Cambridge University Press, 1996.

Heringman, Noah, ed. *Romantic Science: The Literary Forms of Natural History*. Albany, NY: State University of New York Press, 2003.

Holmes, Richard. *The Age of Wonder*. New York: HarperCollins, 2008.

Hurley, Susan. *Consciousness in Action*. Cambridge, MA: Harvard University Press, 1999.

Jackson, Noel. *Science and Sensation in Romantic Poetry*. Cambridge: Cambridge University Press, 2008.

Jacobus, Mary. *Psychoanalysis and the Scene of Reading*. Oxford: Oxford University Press, 1999.

Jagoda, Patrick. *Network Aesthetics*. Chicago: University of Chicago Press, 2016.

Jameson, Fredric. *Postmodernism: or, The Cultural Logic of Late Capitalism*. Durham, NC: Duke University Press, 1991.

Johnson, Mark. *The Body in the Mind: The Bodily Basis of Meaning, Imagination, and Reason*. Chicago: University of Chicago Press, 1990.

Jung, Carl. *The Practice of Psychotherapy*. 2nd ed. Vol. 16. 1966. *The Collected Works of C. G. Jung*. 20 vols. Ed. Herbert Read, Michael Fordham, Gerhard Adler, and William McGuire. Trans. R. F. C. Hull. Princeton: Princeton University Press, 1954–79.

Khalip, Jacques. *Anonymous Life: Romanticism and Dispossession*. Stanford: Stanford University Press, 2008.

Koch, Christof. *The Feeling of Life Itself*. Cambridge, MA: MIT Press, 2019.

Kramnick, Jonathan. *Paper Minds: Literature and the Ecology of Consciousness*. Chicago: University of Chicago Press, 2018.

Lakoff, George and Mark Johnson. *Metaphors We Live By*. Chicago: University of Chicago Press, 1980.

—. *Philosophy in the Flesh: The Embodied Mind and Its Challenge to Western Thought*. New York: Basic Books, 1990.

Lee, Debbie. 'Yellow Fever and the Slave Trade: Coleridge's "Rime of the Ancient Mariner."' *ELH* 65.3 (Fall 1998): 675–700.

Legrenzi, Paolo and Carlo Umilità. *Neuromania: On the Limits of Brain Science*. Oxford: Oxford University Press, 2011.

Lewis, C. S. 'Shelley, Dryden, and Mr. Eliot.' *English Romantic Poets: Modern Essays in Criticism*. 247–67.

Leys, Ruth. *The Ascent of Affect*. Chicago: University of Chicago Press, 2017.

Liu, Alan. *The Laws of Cool*. Chicago: University of Chicago Press, 2004.

Lovejoy, Arthur O. 'On the Discrimination of Romanticisms.' *English Romantic Poets: Modern Essays in Criticism*. 3–24.

McCarthy, Anne. *Awful Parenthesis: Suspension and the Sublime in Romantic and Victorian Poetry*. Toronto: University of Toronto Press, 2018.

Malabou, Catherine. *The New Wounded: From Neurosis to Brain Damage*. Trans. Steven Miller. New York: Fordham University Press, 2012.

—. *What Do We Do With Our Brains?* Trans. Sebastian Rand. New York: Fordham University Press, 2008.
Mendola, Joseph. *Anti-Externalism.* Oxford: Oxford University Press, 2008.
Metzinger, Thomas. *Being No One.* Cambridge, MA: Bradford Books, 2004.
Mitchell, Robert. *Experimental Life: Vitalism in Romantic Science and Literature.* Baltimore: Johns Hopkins University Press, 2013.
Noë, Alva. *Out of Our Heads.* New York: Hill and Wang, 2009.
Panksepp, Jaak. 'Damasio's Error?' *Consciousness and Emotion* 4.1 (2003): 111–34.
Prince, Mary. *The History of Mary Prince.* Ed. Sarah Salih. London: Penguin Books, 2000.
Prinz, Jesse. *The Conscious Brain.* Oxford: Oxford University Press, 2012.
Richardson, Alan. *British Romanticism and the Science of the Mind.* Cambridge: Cambridge University Press, 2001.
—. *The Neural Sublime: Cognitive Theories and Romantic Texts.* Baltimore: Johns Hopkins University Press, 2010.
Robertson, Lisa Ann. 'Enacting the Absolute: Subject–Object Relations in Samuel Taylor Coleridge's Theory of Knowledge.' *Distributed Cognition in Enlightenment and Romantic Culture.* Ed. Miranda Anderson, George Rousseau, and Michael Wheeler. Edinburgh: Edinburgh University Press, 2019. 118–38.
Robinson, Jenefer. 'Emotion as Process.' *The Ontology of Emotions.* Ed. Hichem Naar and Fabrice Teroni. Cambridge: Cambridge University Press, 2018. 51–70.
Savarese, John. *Romanticism's Other Minds: Poetry, Cognition, and the Science of Sociability.* Athens: Ohio University Press, 2020.
Schlutz, Alexander M. *Mind's World: Imagination and Subjectivity from Descartes to Romanticism.* Seattle and London: University of Washington Press, 2009.
Sha, Richard C. *Imagination and Science in Romanticism.* Baltimore: Johns Hopkins University Press, 2018.
Shelley, Mary. *Frankenstein.* Ed. Marilyn Butler. Oxford: Oxford University Press, 1993.
Shelley, Percy. *Shelley's Poetry and Prose.* 2nd ed. Ed. Donald H. Reiman and Neil Fraistat. New York: W. W. Norton, 2002.
Sigler, David. *Sexual Enjoyment in British Romanticism: Gender and Psychoanalysis, 1753–1835.* Montreal and Kingston: McGill-Queen's University Press, 2015.
Singer, Kate. *Romantic Vacancy: The Poetics of Gender, Affect, and Radical Speculation.* Albany, NY: State University of New York Press, 2019.
Siskin, Clifford. *The Historicity of Romantic Discourse.* Oxford: Oxford University Press, 1988.
Sloterdijk, Peter. *What Happened in the 20th Century?* Trans. Christopher Turner. Medford, MA: Polity Press, 2018.
Washington, Chris and Anne C. McCarthy, eds. *Romanticism and Speculative Realism.* New York: Bloomsbury Academic, 2019.
Wimsatt, W. K. 'The Structure of Romantic Nature Imagery.' *English Romantic Poets: Modern Essays in Criticism.* 25–36.

Wordsworth, William. *Poetical Works*. Ed. Thomas Hutchinson. Rev. ed. Ernest de Selincourt. Oxford: Oxford University Press, 1936.
Vidal, Franceso. 'Psychology in the 18th Century: A View from Encyclopaedias.' *History of the Human Science* 6.1 (1993): 89–119.
Yousef, Nancy. *Romantic Intimacy*. Stanford: Stanford University Press, 2013.

Part I
New Models of Consciousness

Chapter 2

Romanticism Against Consciousness

Alan Richardson

Romanticism and Consciousness, published in 1970, marked a crucial intervention in Romantic studies, one of the most important in the history of the field. At a time when most English departments, at least in the US, remained in thrall to the New Criticism, *Romanticism and Consciousness* presented a number of ways to begin moving, as one of its contributors had put it a few years previously, 'beyond formalism' (Hartman, 'Beyond'). The volume's collective act of provocation began with its very title. For decades, critical surveys of Romanticism had clustered around terms associated with the key notion of the individual: the Romantic self (and its extreme forms in the Wordsworthian solitary and the Byronic hero); Romantic subjectivity; and the 'I' and its attendant genres, including lyric and its 'greater Romantic' variant, the conversation poem (not a conversation at all but an other-directed monologue), the verse autobiography, and the psychologized – or the 'internalized'– quest romance (Abrams, Bloom). This is not to mention the 'Romantic Mind,' transcendent, asocial, autonomous, and, often as not, brooding.

The leading term 'consciousness' offered a way forward. It resonated with a number of the intellectual traditions that – in a loose and inherently uneasy coalition – would underwrite the project of poststructuralism soon to emerge. Hegelian philosophy (which threw the notion of psychic autonomy into crisis) and its various progeny in Marxist theory, structuralist analysis with its turn to language as a sort of collectivized subjectivity, and of course the psychoanalytical theories of Freud and his fractious heirs, from Klein to Lacan, all suggested ways simultaneously to resituate and destabilize the Romantic mind, and all contributed toward a novel critical emphasis on consciousness. Like so many Romanticists of my generation, I returned as a student again and again to *Romanticism and Consciousness* in seeking the terms that would allow my own work to move forward, and my Ph.D. dissertation (later my first book), on 'verse drama and consciousness in the Romantic age,' drew direct inspiration from the post-formalist approaches it represented (Richardson, *Mental*).

And yet the essay that did the most for my own thinking might seem to have taken a contrarian stance in relation to the collection as a whole. Geoffrey Hartman's 'Romanticism and "Anti-Self-Consciousness,"' rather than viewing consciousness primarily as a resource for Romantic-era writers (and their revisionary academic expositors), saw consciousness instead as a 'burden,' even (quoting Wordsworth) as a 'strong disease' (47, 53). 'The Romantic poets do not exalt consciousness *per se*,' Hartman insisted, but rather connected it with self-division, a 'kind of death-in-life' (50). Its representative figures included the Ancient Mariner and the Solitary, Ahasuerus and Faust, Cain and the Wandering Jew – an altogether haunted, tormented, and rather ghoulish crew (51). 'Perilous' and a cause of psychic 'paralysis,' the heightened Romantic consciousness vaunted by other critics emerged instead as a 'wound of self,' a 'problem' in desperate, and dubious, need of solution (51–2, 54–5). This problematic became the key for me to understanding those odd and (still at that time) perennially undervalued works of what Byron called 'mental theatre,' staging in the mind of the reader the process of psychic division and self-alienation afflicting its various protagonists.

For Hartman, however – and for me in *A Mental Theater* – 'consciousness' meant primarily consciousness of self, despite his reference to 'consciousness *per se*' (50). This emphasis on self-consciousness gave Hartman an opening toward resolving or, perhaps better, repeatedly deferring the dilemma of consciousness through consciousness itself, Romantic art becoming a 'means to resist the intelligence intelligently' (50). This 'transition from self-consciousness to imagination' involved less a flight from consciousness than an artistic transformation of it (53). Looking back at the same issues from the distance of several decades on, I would like in this chapter to go further in the direction indicated by Hartman. So, in what follows I will examine some of the ways that writers of the Romantic era turned away from consciousness altogether, to explore those features and processes of the human mind that we now associate with the absence of waking consciousness – with the *un*conscious.

When I first addressed this topic some twenty years ago, it was by no means unprecedented to claim that Romantic-era writers had both explored and helped to popularize notions of the unconscious mind (Richardson, 'Coleridge'). Historians of psychiatry like Henri Ellenberger credited not only proto-hypnotists like Mesmer and Puységur, but literary Romanticism as well with carving out the discursive space from which later accounts of the unconscious would emerge. A few critics and theorists of Romanticism followed suit: Catherine Belsey, for one, claimed that the 'unconscious is *for the first time* produced in discourse' in certain Romantic works (58). These accounts, however, concerned themselves all but exclusively with Romantic formulations and depictions of unconscious mental life that mapped readily onto the later depth psychologies, particularly Freud's psychoanalysis, to come. Such anticipations of the Freudian unconscious were and remain important, revealing (as Joel Faflak has shown) a 'radically disruptive' psychic force haunting such works as *The Prelude*, 'Christabel', and de Quincey's *Confessions* (38).

The wider range of unconscious mental processes addressed within Romantic texts came more fully into view, however, only when scholars of the period began paying serious attention to the cognitive turn in psychology, linguistics, and philosophy of mind. What has been termed both the 'cognitive unconscious' and the 'new unconscious' turned out to characterize by far the greater part of human mental life, vaster and 'far more powerful' than the relatively specialized unconscious theorized by Freud (Kihlstrom, Vermeule 468). For the new cognitive sciences of the late twentieth century, consciousness, by comparison, became a kind of afterthought, recalcitrant to analysis, perhaps epiphenomenal altogether, and scarcely worth investigating (Crick 13).

Research into the cognitive unconscious held special relevance for Romantic studies because, as Jonathan Miller was among the first to point out, the 'new' unconscious strikingly resembled older versions of the unconscious developed in advance of Freud. Miller pointed mainly to a group of mid-nineteenth-century British psychologists like Thomas Laycock and Benjamin Carter, but traced their theories of 'unconscious cerebration' back still further to Mesmer, La Mettrie, the German *Naturphilosophes*, and the early phrenology movement (64). Miller's essay resonated with the earlier efforts of Peretz LaVie and J. Allan Hobson in sketching out a 'rich preFreudian tradition' of thinking about dreams and the unconscious that led from Romantic-era philosophy of mind and physiology to the innovative cognitive and neuroscientific perspectives of the late twentieth century (230). Building on these pioneering studies, in tandem with a great deal of new research into Romantic-era brain-based and embodied or 'corporeal' accounts of mind and mental behavior, Romantic scholarship has by now assembled a robust picture of the 'Romantic unconscious' and its many resonances with (as well as departures from) the cognitive unconscious of the present day (Richardson, *British*; Iseli).

In appreciating the new significance of the unconscious mind and unconscious mental behaviors in the period, one might begin by noting an important shift in the meaning of the term 'unconscious' itself. In earlier writing, to be 'unconscious' of something means not to notice it at all, or to remain entirely ignorant of its existence, or even to be incapable of thought or perception altogether. Thus, in Jane Austen's *Sense and Sensibility*, Marianne is spared any pain caused by the 'puppyism' exhibited by Robert Ferrars through 'remaining unconscious of it at all,' blissfully 'ignorant of what was passing around her' (228–9). In her florid farewell apostrophe to Norland, Marianne notes that the house itself 'will continue the same' without the Dashwoods, 'unconscious of the pleasure or the regret' it occasions (60). Yet in scattered writings by William Wordsworth and related writers, 'unconscious' and such cognate terms as 'subconscious' and 'underconsciousness' began to signify mental contents, acts, and events affecting thinking, feeling, and behavior without registering in conscious awareness. So Wordsworth writes in the early two-part *The Prelude*:

> A child, I held unconscious intercourse
> With the eternal beauty, drinking in
> A pure organic pleasure from the lines
> Of curling mist ... (1.394–7)

'Organic' here refers to sensory and brain organs; this is an embodied 'intercourse' that has no need of, and perhaps remains closed to, conscious awareness, a passive yet saving absorption, a 'drinking in,' that connects the child deeply to his natural environment (Richardson, 'Fungus' 113).

As Marcus Iseli has demonstrated in detail, Wordsworth, S. T. Coleridge, and Thomas de Quincey all contributed to this work of lexical innovation, most likely in tandem with one another (30–5). De Quincey has been widely credited with coining the English word *subconscious* (in 1834), though Coleridge had used the term 'subconsciousness' (in the Notebooks) by 1806. Wordsworth's analogous term, 'underconsciousness' (from a manuscript version of *The Prelude*, c. 1818), seems not to have caught on: the only instance listed in the *Oxford English Dictionary* (*OED*) is from Coleridge (*On the Constitution of Church and State* [1830], a 'sort of under-consciousness blends with our dreams').[1] At least one other Romantic-era writer uses the same term, however: Mary Wordsworth, in a love letter to William ('that underconsciousness that I had my *all in all* about me' [49]). According to the *OED*, Coleridge first uses the term 'the unconscious' as a substantive connoting that part of the human mind influencing behavior and emotion while remaining inaccessible to conscious awareness, once more in the Notebooks (1818).

Writers of the period had, of course, any number of ways to register the decisive shift in the picture of the mind that this shared labor of lexical innovation represented. Other *un*-compounds, in addition to 'unconscious,' sought to convey the mind's activity in the absence of any awareness of that activity. So in 'Tintern Abbey,' ostensibly devoted to the power of memory, Wordsworth resorts twice in four lines to 'unremembered':

>   feelings too
> Of unremembered pleasure; such, perhaps,
> As may have had no trivial influence
> On that best portion of a good man's life;
> His little, nameless, unremembered acts
> Of kindness and of love. (30–5)

Though lost to conscious recall, pleasurable feelings continue to 'influence' not just mental life but ethical behavior, inspiring acts of random kindness that themselves soon drop out of memory, but not necessarily out of one's 'underconsciousness.' Perhaps the most striking example of all concerns 'unaware' in Coleridge's 'Ancient Marinere,' from the same *Lyrical Ballads* volume, marking one of the poem's major hinge moments, the unconscious act that triggers the slow unraveling of the mariner's curse:

> A spring of love gushed from my heart,
> And I bless'd them unaware!
> Sure my kind saint took pity on me,
> And I bless'd them unaware. (*Poems* 276–9)

Where conscious effort ('I look'd to Heaven, and try'd to pray' [236]) has failed, an unconscious movement of heart and brain breaks through, as the albatross drops off the mariner's neck and into the sea.

These constructions are not limited to the Lake Poets and their immediate circle, but can be found in the next generation of Romantic poets as well. A comparable hinge moment occurs in Felicia Hemans's 'A Spirit's Return,' for example, where once more repeated conscious effort ('I taught *one* sound / Unto a thousand echoes') yields to a quiescent, unconscious state:

>   even as the grey church-tower
> Whereon I gazed unconsciously: – there came
> A low sound, like the tremor of a flame –

a sound that at last announces the spirit's much desired, much implored return (*Poetical Words* 371). John Keats, in his 'Ode to Psyche,' gives us not only an embodied psyche (the ode's imagery draws on the brain anatomy Keats studied as a would-be surgeon) but one with unconscious – his term is *un*trodden – depths: 'In some untrodden region of my mind'; 'shadowy thought' also suggests less than fully conscious mental activity (*Poems* 51, 65). In his *Defence of Poetry*, Percy Shelley famously renders poetic composition independent of conscious volition and control: 'Poetry is not like reasoning, a power to be exerted according to the determination of the will ... the conscious portions of our nature are unprophetic either of its approach or its departure' (*Prose* 294). Along with the 'plastic and pictorial arts,' poetry proceeds not from the mind's 'conscious portions' but from 'instinct and intuition,' terms that become increasingly important both to literary writers and to brain scientists during the early nineteenth century (294).

Representations of unconscious mental acts and of the mind's unconscious depths recur throughout the gothic novel of the period as well, as might be expected. M. G. Lewis's *The Monk*, for example, exposes a telling split between conscious and unconscious motivation in recounting Ambrosio's reaction to Matilda's declaration of love: 'such were the sentiments of which he was aware: but there were others also which did not obtain his notice' – a statement that might well have seemed incomprehensible to earlier generations of readers (84). Charlotte Dacre, in *Zofloya*, similarly represents Berenza as unconscious of what truly motivates his desire for Victoria: 'Berenza knew not, so unconscious is the heart of man of the springs of its own movements, that it was the graceful elegant form, and animated countenance of Victoria, that led him to form of her strongly-marked character the best and most flattering estimate' (26). The passage, indeed, even suggests a mechanical, nonconscious character to this heart with 'springs' to guide its movements, like a clock – or an automaton.

In a letter of 1794, at a time when a number of young writers and thinkers were speculating on materialist approaches to mind, Coleridge went so far as to call himself an 'Advocate for the Automatism of Man' (*Letters* 1:147). The automaton had played an outsized role in the gradual rise of materialist and mechanistic accounts of human mental behavior, from Hobbes's 'artificial man' in *Leviathan* through La Mettrie's '*homme machine*' to the animated statue imagined by Condillac in the *Traité des sensations* (Pollin, Mazlish). These famous thought projects (inspired by the technological sophistication of actual automata) suggested that certain cognitive operations might prove not simply *un*conscious but altogether *non*-conscious (a distinction made salient in the recent work of N. Katherine Hayles). Yet for the writers leading up to and traditionally associated with Romanticism, the automaton served more as a metaphor than a precise analogy, given the 'corporeal' or biological bent of the new materialism. Johann Herder, for example, grounds the importance of non-conscious cognition in a proto-evolutionary notion of fitness: 'Our poor thinking organ would certainly not be able to seize every stimulus ... without shuddering with anxiety' – overcome by sheer sensory overload – and 'letting the rudder go from its hands.' And so, 'mother nature took away from it whatever could not be faced by its clear consciousness ... and carefully organized every channel leading into it' (qtd in Whyte 117). For the Romantic writer, even an artificial human assembled from parts – Victor Frankenstein's 'creature' – that might have been made to function altogether non-consciously, shares this biological, organic character in its 'intricacies of fibres' and its 'animal' proclivities. Though apparently jolted into life by electricity, the creature proves far more animal than machine, and indeed is partly constructed from 'slaughter-house' materials, perhaps helping to account for its repertoire of instinctive behaviors (Richardson, 'Wild Minds').

Yet the figure of the automaton, with its clockwork mind, still rises up every so often in Coleridge's poetry of the 1790s. The Ancient Mariner's reanimated crewmates, though they turn out to be operated by angels, work the sails in a voiceless, expressionless, mechanical manner, less like zombies than automata. Christabel, controlled by Geraldine's spell, reacts automatically, like a mechanical doll, to Geraldine's wicked glance:

> The maid, alas! her thoughts are gone,
> She nothing sees – no sight but one!
> The maid, devoid of guile and sin,
> I know not how, in fearful wise
> So deeply had she drunken in
> That look, those shrunken serpent eyes,
> That all her features were resigned
> To this sole image in her mind;
> And passively did imitate
> That look of dull and treacherous hate! (*Poems* 585–94)

Passive and unthinking, reduced to the 'automatism' of imitative behavior, Christabel might also be viewed here in terms of the mesmeric subject, or of the somnambulist. What brings all three figures together is, of course, the spectacle of human action in the absence of conscious volition, seemingly of any conscious awareness whatsoever.

Mesmerism has been widely studied, both for its connections with later depth psychologies and for its presence within Romantic-era writings of many kinds (Tatar, Faflak). Suffice it to say here that mesmerism provided yet another, and for a time quite salient, example of unconscious mental behavior as well as of unconscious influence, surviving to this day in expressions like 'mesmerizing performance' and 'magnetic personality.' To cite the example of just one Romantic writer, Coleridge's interest in mesmerism has been long established (Levere), and both poems mentioned above feature scenes of mesmerizing: the mariner 'holds' the wedding guest with his 'glittering eye,' and Christabel falls into her trance state when Geraldine looks 'askance' at her (*Poems* 17, 575).

Somnambulism has garnered much less critical attention, at least until recently. This may reflect a long-running bias toward studying rapid eye movement (REM) states – a bias shared, whatever their differences, by psychoanalysis and cognitive neuroscience – to the neglect of somnambulism and the other parasomnias. REM dreaming, with its vivid imagery, its narrative structure (however bizarre), and its strong emotionality, holds obvious interest for dream interpretation and literary treatment alike. Yet the parasomnias – sleep walking (somnambulism), talking during sleep (somniloquy), and the like – held comparable if not greater interest for late Enlightenment and Romantic-era writers (Richardson, 'Politics'). Like the hallucinatory dreaming of REM sleep, the parasomnias patently illustrated the continuing activity of the brain during sleep – in the absence of consciousness. Yet, in contrast to the irrationality of the typical dream, the parasomnias struck observers with their appearance of rational behavior, as sleeping subjects dressed, walked about, held conversations, and even composed sermons – and poems – without benefit of conscious volition or awareness. Coleridge's famous introductory note to 'Kubla Khan,' his 'Vision in a Dream,' recounting its composition 'in a profound sleep ... in which all the images rose up before him as things, with a parallel production of the correspondent expressions, without any sensation or consciousness of effort,' makes only the most notorious of many such accounts (*Poems* 249–50).

The year before Coleridge published his dream poem, long retained in manuscript, John Polidori, Byron's sometime doctor and the author of *The Vampyre*, registered his Latin medical thesis on 'Oneirodynia,' a recondite term for sleepwalking and the whole range of parasomnias. Polidori took special interest not only in 'someone who walks while in a dream,' but more pointedly in 'someone who appears to wake up while still asleep, and who performs actions or speaks as if he were awake' (776). His examples include sleepers who carry on coherent conversations, who pour themselves a glass of wine to drink, or who compose (or even edit) essays. All this suggests, as the scholars who have resurrected Polidori's thesis remark, 'how the human body and brain could function mechanically,' without the 'guiding power of the soul' or conscious will, implicitly challenging religious and ideological orthodoxies concerning the integral, self-directed subject (Stiles et al. 790). The soulless yet disturbingly capable vampire might be seen as the fictive embodiment of this very dilemma.

The vampire tale, however, was not the only gothic genre to show an interest in the parasomnias. Ellena, in Ann Radcliffe's *The Italian*, owes her life in part to somniloquy, talking in her sleep and inducing Schedoni to pause in the very act of plunging a dagger into her heart (234). William Godwin's Caleb Williams escapes a similar fate – this one involving a butcher's cleaver – by sensing the murderer's approach in his sleep, hearing her steps and her 'audible breathing,' and translating them into dream imagery, disturbing enough to wake him at the critical moment: 'I shifted my position with a speed that seemed too swift for volition' (231). Caleb, in fact, owes his spectacular dodge to unpremeditated action in the *absence* of conscious volition; had he come more rapidly to full consciousness, the cleaver might instead have split his skull. This gothic parasomnia motif becomes well enough established by 1806 that Victoria, in *Zofloya*, can put it to strategic use. She actually feigns somniloquy in a successful attempt to gain Berenza's unstinting love:

> 'Indeed, Berenza, I love *thee*!' she articulated, starting up, and stretching out her arms, as if under the impression of her dream, attempting to embrace him; when opening her eyes, and affecting surprise and shame at the sight of Berenza, she covered her face with her hands, and turned aside. (79)

Berenza, after a long period of resisting, now falls entirely under Victoria's spell.

Somniloquy in this scene verges on sexsomnia – sleep sex – only recently added to the parasomnias by twenty-first-century sleep science but well known to Denis Diderot, who includes an amusing example in the long somniloquy that dominates *Le Rêve de d'Alembert* (Anderson et al.; Richardson, 'Politics' 11–12). Keats's *The Eve of St. Agnes* walks a fine line between representing rape and sexsomnia when Madeline wakes, while remaining within the aura of her dream – 'Her eyes were open, but she still beheld, / Now wide awake, the vision of her sleep' (*Poems* 298–9) – with Porphyro apparently initiating sex before Madeline awakens altogether: 'Into her dream he melted,' only to tell her, '"This is no dream,"' which seems to surprise Madeline herself: '"No dream, alas! alas! and woe is mine"' (320, 326, 328). Many lines blur here: between sleeping and waking, between violation and willing participation (there is no evidence of struggle or violence), perhaps between dreaming and, like Victoria, feigning to dream. That the scene remains so disturbing – and it should disturb us – speaks to the ways that dreaming and the parasomnias unsettle questions of agency, of volition, and of subjectivity.

Dreaming, once viewed as resulting from divine (or demonic) infiltration or from reflex responses to external stimuli, but now seen as emerging from the brain's ceaseless activity even in the absence of consciousness, struck Romantic-era writers as well on account of its unique cognitive style. In particular, dreaming seemed to loosen habitual patterns of association, the 'bundles of thought,' as William Hazlitt puts it, 'untied, loosened from a common center,' free to 'drift along the stream of fancy as it happens' (12:20). Coleridge also notes the '*streamy* nature' of dream association – 'Fancy and Sleep *stream* on' – as may be seen in his famous account of the dream genesis of 'Kubla Khan' (*Notebooks* 1:1770, 2:2542). Intriguingly, twenty-first-century sleep science has reasserted the 'hyperassociative' character of dreaming, viewing this very feature as a resource for creative thinking and problem solving, activities that P. J. G. Cabanis and Polidori had attributed to the sleeping mind in the early nineteenth century (Cabanis 1:138–9; Polidori 783; Cai et al.).

Yet, in disordering habitual patterns of thought in the absence of conscious control, dreaming could also yield to the insistent voice of bodily urges and desires. Cabanis, a French materialist thinker who found his way into Shelley's notes for *Queen Mab*, found in sexual dreams and nocturnal emissions evidence for the active brain's heightened susceptibility to 'internal impressions' in sleep (1:136). Erasmus Darwin similarly notes how, unchecked by conscious monitoring and external impressions, the 'ceaseless flow of our ideas in dreams' gives expression to the 'internal sensations' of 'hunger, thirst, and lust' (1:199–209). Coleridge seems to rehearse Darwin in his anxious speculation on the 'bad Passions in Dreams' and those 'Impulses from within' that connect dreams with 'motions of the blood and nerves' (*Notebooks* 1:1770, 2:2542). Readers may be forgiven for thinking, at this point, of the notoriously eroticized imagery of 'Kubla Khan' – a poem that, if we can credit Coleridge himself, emerged from the unconscious mind almost verbatim, if cut short thanks to an untimely caller.

Dreams and parasomniac behaviors were not the only channels through which the largely non-conscious internal senses might come to awareness. Internal sensations could also become manifest through 'gut' feelings and other forms of interoception, a term coined only in the early twentieth century, although the phenomena it names were of great interest to Romantic brain scientists and Romantic literary writers alike. Hazlitt includes an especially striking example in 'On Genius and Common Sense,' an essay pervasively concerned with non-rational and non-conscious varieties of cognition ('In art, in taste, in life, in speech, you decide from feeling, and not from reason,' 'unconsciously' basing inductions upon any number of unnoticed perceptions [8:31–2]). The anecdote concerns one of those 'persons who had rendered themselves obnoxious to Government' and been charged with high treason in 1794 – probably the radical writer John Thelwall. Sheltering in the 'romantic valley' of Llangollen some time later and sitting down to breakfast at the local inn, the radical inexplicably loses his appetite, suffering a 'total change' in his 'feelings,' and becomes 'uneasy and spiritless.' A bit later, he sees a figure, barely perceived and disregarded ('flitting, shadowy, half-distinguished') just before breakfast, passing back his way: Taylor, the government spy, linked 'unconsciously and mysteriously' to his travails in London and potential execution. The anecdote exemplifies, for Hazlitt, that 'dim, illegible shorthand of the mind' that, outrunning conscious reason, registers in the viscera (8:34).

Drawing on both the Sensibility tradition, with its commitment to heart, sensation, and feeling, and on what Richard Matlak terms Darwin's 'biomedical' approach to cognition, Wordsworth helps lay the groundwork for a Romantic poetry of interoception in his writings of the 1790s (76–8). 'Tintern Abbey' pays tribute to internal 'sensations sweet / Felt in the blood, and felt along the heart' (*Poems* 27–8). The 1799 *Prelude* celebrates the 'thoughtless hour' of boyhood, times when 'from excess / Of happiness, my blood appeared to flow / With its own pleasure, and I breathed with joy' (2.225–7). In a phrase collapsing heart, brain, and cognition, his was then a 'beating mind' (2.16). In Keats, with his presiding interests in blushing and pallor, in flushing and quickened pulses, in heartache and breathlessness, the Romantic poetry of interoception finds its fullest expression. Drawing on his medical training as well as the Sensibility and earlier Romantic traditions, Keats combines the embodied manifestation of inner sensation with an appreciation for the non-conscious workings of mind, as when a plan fully formed without benefit of consciousness comes flooding into Porphyro's mind, simultaneously flooding his circulatory and somatosensory systems with blood:

> Sudden a thought came like a full-blown rose
> Flushing his brow, and in his pained heart
> Made purple riot. ('The Eve of St. Agnes' 136–8)

The skin, at once our largest external sensory and internal sensory organ, provides another conduit from the viscera to the conscious mind. Reacting to Cynthia's eroticized presence, Endymion's skin rapidly goes from 'pallid' to flushed, striking Endymion himself with the force of his own passion: 'he felt the charm / To breathlessness, and suddenly a warm / Of his heart's blood' (105–7). Conscious volition and the largely non-conscious internal senses stage a kind of battle in *Isabella*, as Lorenzo struggles to give voice to his desire:

>   all day
>   His heart beat awfully against his side;
> And to his heart he inwardly did pray
>   For power to speak; but still the ruddy tide
> Stifled his voice, and pulsed resolve away. (41–5)

Madeline cannot, for reasons of both feminine modesty and ritual convention, express her love for Porphyro, even to herself, so the body speaks it for her: 'But to her heart, her heart was voluble, / Paining with eloquence her balmy side' (204–5). It is as though the physical heart, with its access to the unconscious reaches of desire, needs to inform her metaphorical 'heart' – her conscious emotions – of what her interior monologue itself cannot utter.

Still more obscure messages from the interior of the body were seen to eventuate in instinctive behaviors, themselves the result of non-conscious processes. 'Instinct' remained a controversial term throughout the period as it threatened to undermine the key orthodox distinction between human beings and animals. The older, conservative Coleridge, to cite one prominent example, insisted that inborn animal 'instincts' gave place in humans to gradually developing 'passions' (*Shorter Works* 2:390–1, 1414). Yet any number of prominent medical and scientific writers came to agree with Darwin's recognition, in *Zoonomia*, of the importance of 'natural or connate desires' (1:136). Cabanis held that the internal organs gave rise to instinctive 'tastes, inclinations' and 'desires' already present in newborn infants and no doubt traceable to the 'formation of the fetus' (1:101, 2:580). F. J. Gall gave comparable emphasis to the 'interior ... sensations' and the *'instinctive tendencies'* they promoted, equipping us with rapid, preordained reactions to potential threats in a manner 'involuntary and without consciousness' (1:111, 102). With the growing prominence of Gall and Johann Spurzheim's phrenology movement, a new language of instinct and 'propensity' began seeping into discourses of many kinds. Even a more mainstream figure like the great early neurologist Charles Bell grants a large role in mental life to 'instinctive motions' proceeding from the 'secret operations of the vital organs,' though we remain 'unconscious of the thousand delicate operations which are every instant going on in the body' (*Idea* 14–15).

Literary writers followed suit, particularly as the nineteenth century progressed, and what began as daring avant-garde notions began to find acceptance as home truths. The change in Godwin's writings provides a stark index: beginning his public intellectual life as an associationist, 'blank slate' thinker, by the time he publishes his essays in *Thoughts on Man* (1831) he agrees with Darwin and Gall that human beings are born with 'various dispositions,' evident already in infant behavior, and that even character or 'temper' is in large part innate (29–30, 41). Keats, in his letters, writes easily of the 'instinctiveness' of the 'human animal' – an index, perhaps, of his medical training (*Letters* 2:79–80). Anne, in Austen's *Persuasion*, stands out in a crisis thanks to the 'strength and zeal, and thought, which instinct supplied' – a kind of thinking without thinking (130). And, as noted already, Shelley, in the *Defence*, divorces poetic and artistic creativity from conscious control, making it predominately a matter of 'instinct and intuition' (*Prose* 294).

For Romantic writers, 'intuition' names the immediate apprehension of knowledge or truth, spontaneously and without the mediation of discursive thought or of conscious deliberation. Cabanis gave a theoretical basis for intuition precisely by decentering the conscious subject – the *MOI* – which lacks access to numerous sensations (including most 'internal' sensations). Non-conscious mental processes can 'very sensibly and quickly' affect one's 'entire realm of ideas' as well as emotions, as 'unperceived judgments' make themselves felt (2:547–51, 590). Such intuitive processes were seen to play a significant role in artistic reception as well as production. Bell, for example, in his anatomy lectures aimed at painters and sculptors, expatiates on the 'secret' and 'unconscious' effect of various anatomical forms and facial expressions, signs in a 'universal language' drawn upon by artists throughout time and across cultures (*Essays* 37–8, 49). (Joanna Baillie incorporated these lessons on facial expression into her dramatic theory, most likely reaching her through her brother, the physician and anatomist Matthew Baillie [Richardson, 'Neural Theater'].) De Quincey's great essay 'On the Knocking at the Gate in *Macbeth*' constitutes an extended argument for trusting intuitive judgements in the absence of any conscious chain of reasoning. In aesthetic response, as in our implicit understanding of perspective effects – even when we prove totally unable to explicitly describe or reproduce them – 'feeling' can accurately register what 'consciousness has *not* seen' (10:389–90).

Such is the power of non-conscious cognition, in fact, that, as Darwin states, many of our waking behaviors are nevertheless performed 'as it were inconsciously' – another Romantic neologism that failed to catch on (1:192). Many activities requiring laborious learning eventually become effortless – and largely thoughtless – from learning to walk, to dancing, speaking, writing, negotiating familiar pathways, and musical performance (Darwin 1:41, 50, 192). Godwin, in *Thoughts on Man*, goes so far as to speak of 'human vegetation,' that mental state when reason and conscious volition 'abandon the helm' and we employ our bodies 'mechanically,' with 'no precise consciousness' of the behaviors we routinely perform (152, 159). Godwin includes, in addition to the standard example of walking (a twenty-first-century equivalent might be 'spacing out' while driving to work), such laboring-class activities as farming and factory work, routine housekeeping tasks, and even a good deal of pleasure reading (155, 161). Godwin worries that such 'vegetation,' the habitual state of young children, may monopolize the waking hours of the 'greater part' of humanity (161).

Godwin also uses a less forbidding term for the unthinking life: reverie. A waking yet relaxed and undirected state of mind, dream-like as its name implies, reverie is the term Coleridge initially used to describe the narcotic state in which he composed, or perhaps received, 'Kubla Khan': 'in a sort of Reverie brought on by two grains of Opium' (*Poems* 525). In Wordsworth's 'Reverie of Poor Susan,' reverie functions in hallucinatory fashion to block out conscious perception of Susan's dreary London reality and return her, in a dreamy memory, to her rustic home: 'She looks, and her heart is in heaven' (*Poems* 1:261). As David Perkins has shown, reverie became an expected and even desired condition for the literary reader to enter into. The Scottish Enlightenment figure Lord Kames defines reverie as a condition in which the reader, 'losing the consciousness of self, and of reading,' enters fully and without judgement into a train of poetic images or a fictional world, passively engaging in what would now be termed immersive reading, becoming '"absorbed" in a book' (Perkins 183, 185). Archibald Alison, writing in 1790, describes reading at its most compelling as a 'powerless state of reverie, when we are carried on by our conceptions, not guiding them' (Perkins 184). What Godwin saw as an insufficiently (perhaps even dangerously) uncritical approach to reading could be prized for its very dream-like and escapist qualities.

I will end by noticing one final instance of lexical transformation in the period, this one concerning the word 'vacant.' Ordinarily, 'vacant' implies mere emptiness and, in the context of a human mind, would be pejorative: Austen characterizes the two youngest Bennet sisters in this way in *Pride and Prejudice* ('their minds were more vacant than their sisters" [75]). Yet for certain Romantic writers, regarding consciousness as at once something to be desired, intensified even, and yet alternately to escape, to be freed from, mental vacancy becomes a sign of such freedom. In Wordsworth's 'Guilt and Sorrow,' for example, the mind's emptying out represents a liberation, however temporary, from mental oppression.

> As one whose brain habitual frenzy fires
> Owes to the fit in which his soul has tossed
> Profounder quiet, when the fit retires,
> Even so the dire phantasma which had crossed
> His sense, in sudden vacancy quite lost,
> Left his mind still as a deep evening stream. (*Poems* 1:91–6)

In 'I wandered lonely as a cloud,' mental vacancy – 'when on my couch I lie / In vacant or in pensive mood' – allows for a spontaneous access of feeling and of joyful connection to the natural world that had previously, during the poet's conscious perception of it, kept its distance: 'And then my heart with pleasure fills, / And dances with the daffodils' (*Poems* 1:19–20, 23–4). (Note that 'vacant' here is an alternative to 'pensive': not thoughtful, but unthinking, thought-free.) Dorothy Wordsworth adopts this usage, though in the form of a transferred epithet, in introducing a quite differently transformative moment in 'The Floating Island':

> Perchance when you are wandering forth
> Upon some vacant sunny day
> Without an object, hope, or fear,
> Thither your eyes may turn – the Isle is passed away. (cited in Levin 207–8)

The day's vacancy adheres to the poet's mind, a subject 'Without an object,' as perception becomes passive and the eyes seem to roam of their own accord.

In Shelley's poetry, these states of mental vacancy intensify until they become altogether sublime. In *Alastor*, one finds this occurring twice within the compass of some seventy lines, first when the protagonist-'Poet' haunts the 'ruined temples' of antiquity and

>   ever gazed
> And gazed, till meaning on his vacant mind
> Flashed like strong inspiration, and he saw
> The thrilling secrets of the birth of time. (*Poetry* 125–8)

The lightning 'flash' of realization arrives only when conscious mind has been emptied out, vacant, passive, yawning open like a door into the dark. ('Gazed / And gazed,' of course, echoes Wordsworth's daffodils poem: 'I gazed – and gazed – but little thought' [*Poems* 1:17].) Later, having crossed the Hindu Kush into Kashmir, Shelley's Poet experiences his own vision in a dream – 'A vision on his sleep / There came' (149–50) – that keeps promising to conjoin him with a visionary female counterpart but culminates in a quite unexpected manner:

> She drew back a while,
> Then, yielding to the irresistible joy,
> With frantic gesture and short breathless cry
> Folded his frame in her dissolving arms.
> Now blackness veiled his dizzy eyes, and night
> Involved and swallowed up the vision; sleep,
> Like a dark flood suspended in its course,
> Rolled back its impulse on his vacant brain. (184–91)

Here, the dreaming unconscious mind eclipses consciousness, until unconscious cognition itself gutters out, exposing what Keats, in *Endymion*, calls the 'naked brain' (1.294). The entire passage constitutes a prime example of what has been termed the 'neural sublime,' an anti-transcendent, materialist sublime that first arises in the early nineteenth century (Richardson, *Neural Sublime* 17–37).

Along with their pursuit of heightened states of consciousness, the writers most often associated with Romanticism, however inconsistently, could also seek to evade or extinguish it: Wordsworth's wish to recapture 'self-forgetfulness' (*1805 Prelude* 4.294), Coleridge's Mariner lamenting his sleepless 'agony' (*Poems* 227), Lord Byron's Manfred craving 'oblivion, self-oblivion' (1.1.144), Keats, or his persona, wishing to 'fade away' with the nightingale, 'dissolve, and quite forget' (*Poems* 20, 21). Hartman exposed and brilliantly analyzed this apparent contradiction over half a century ago. From a twenty-first-century perspective, however, we can now add a whole range of psychic phenomena that involve neither an intensification of consciousness nor its extinction. Those overlapping states and processes considered subconscious, unconscious, non-conscious, and 'under'-conscious, along with such mental behaviors as dreaming and the parasomnias, and borderline states like reverie and meditative 'vacancy': all these made part of an avant-garde approach to mind shared by poets and novelists, scientists and medical doctors, critics and philosophers of the era. The full richness, variety, and significance of this revolutionary psychological discourse has only begun to grow apparent with the renewed appreciation for the sheer vastness and hidden complexities of unconscious and non-conscious cognition that characterizes the neuroscience and cognitive psychology of our own era. It may now seem that, in developing the topic of

'Romanticism and Consciousness' some fifty years ago, the eminent scholars and critics gathered together in the collection of that name were telling only half the story.

Notes

1. 'Under-consciousness' in the *Oxford English Dictionary Online*; all references to the *OED* refer to the online version at https://www.oed.com (last accessed October 24, 2020).

References

Abrams, M. H. 'Structure and Style in the Greater Romantic Lyric.' *Romanticism and Consciousness*. Ed. Harold Bloom. New York: Norton, 1970. 201–29.
Andersen, Monica L., Dalva Poyares, Rosana S. C. Alves, Robert Skomro, and Sergio Tufik. 'Sexsomnia: Abnormal Sexual Behavior During Sleep.' *Brain Research Reviews* 56 (2007): 271–82.
Austen, Jane. *Persuasion*. Ed. D. W. Harding. Harmondsworth: Penguin, 1965.
—. *Pride and Prejudice*. Ed. Tony Tanner. Harmondsworth: Penguin, 1985.
—. *Sense and Sensibility*. Ed. Tony Tanner. Harmondsworth: Penguin, 1986.
Bell, Charles. *Essays on the Anatomy of Expression in Painting*. London: Longman, Hurst, Rees, and Orme, 1806.
—. *Idea of a New Anatomy of the Brain: A Fascicle of the Privately Printed Edition of 1811*. London: Dawsons, 1966.
Belsey, Catherine. 'The Romantic Construction of the Unconscious.' *Literature, Politics, and Theory*. Ed. Francis Barker, Peter Hulme, Margaret Iverson, and Diana Loxley. London: Methuen, 1986. 58–76.
Bloom, Harold. 'The Internalization of Quest-Romance.' *Romanticism and Consciousness*. Ed. Harold Bloom. New York: W. W. Norton, 1970. 3–24.
Byron, George Gordon, Lord. *Manfred*. Ed. Joseph Black, Leonard Conolly, Kate Flint, Isobel Grundy, Don LePan, Roy Liuzza, Jerome J. McGann, Anne Lake Prescott, Barry V. Qualls, and Claire Waters. Peterbrough, ON: Broadview, 2017.
Cabanis, Pierre-Jean-Georges. *On the Relations Between the Physical and Moral Aspects of Man*. Trans. Margaret Duggan Saidi. Ed. George Mora. 2 vols. Baltimore: Johns Hopkins University Press, 1981.
Cai, Denise J., Sarnoff A. Mednick, Elizabeth M. Harrison, Jennifer C. Kanaday, and Sara C. Mednick. 'REM, Not Incubation, Improves Creativity by Priming Association Networks.' *PNAS* 106.25 (June 23, 2009): 10130–4.
Coleridge, Samuel Taylor. *Collected Letters of Samuel Taylor Coleridge*. Ed. E. L. Griggs. 6 vols. Oxford: Oxford University Press, 1956–71.
—. *The Complete Poems*. Ed. William Keach. London: Penguin, 1997.
—. *The Notebooks of Samuel Taylor Coleridge*. Ed. Kathleen Coburn. 4 vols. London: Routledge & Kegan Paul, 1957–.

—. *Shorter Works and Fragments*. Ed. H. J. Jackson and J. R. de J. Jackson. 2 vols. Princeton: Princeton University Press, 1995.

Crick, Francis. *The Astonishing Hypothesis: The Scientific Search for the Soul*. New York: Simon and Schuster, 1995.

Dacre, Charlotte. *Zofloya, or The Moor*. Ed. Kim Ian Michasiw. Oxford: Oxford University Press, 1997.

Darwin, Erasmus. *Zoonomia: or, The Laws of Organic Life*. 2 vols. London: J. Johnson, 1794–6.

De Quincey, Thomas. *De Quincey's Works*. Ed. David Masson. 15 vols. Edinburgh: A. and C. Black, 1862–3.

Ellenberger, Henri F. *The Discovery of the Unconscious: An Essay in Cultural History*. New York: Basic Books, 1970.

Faflak, Joel. *Romantic Psychoanalysis: The Burden of the Mystery*. Albany, NY: State University of New York Press, 2008.

Gall, François Joseph. *On the Functions of the Brain and of Each of Its Parts: With Observations on the Possibility of Determining the Instincts, Propensities, and Talents, or the Moral and Intellectual Dispositions of Men and Animals by the Configuration of the Brain and Head*. Trans. Winslow Lewis. 6 vols. Boston: Marsh, Capen, and Lyon, 1835.

Godwin, William. *Caleb Williams*. Ed. David McCracken. New York: W. W. Norton, 1977.

—. *Thoughts on Man, His Nature, Productions, and Discoveries*. London: Effingham Wilson, 1831.

Hartman, Geoffrey. 'Beyond Formalism.' *MLN* 81.5 (December 1966): 542–56.

—. 'Romanticism and "Anti-Self-Consciousness."' *Romanticism and Consciousness*. Ed. Harold Bloom. New York: W. W. Norton, 1970. 46–56.

Hayles, N. Katherine. *Unthought: The Power of the Cognitive Nonconscious*. Chicago: University of Chicago Press, 2017.

Hazlitt, William. *The Complete Works of William Hazlitt*. Ed. P. P. Howe. 21 vols. London: Dent, 1930–4.

Hemans, Felicia. *The Poetical Works of Mrs. Hemans*. London: Frederick Warne, 1884.

Iseli, Markus. *Thomas De Quincey and the Cognitive Unconscious*. New York: Palgrave Macmillan, 2015.

Keats, John. *The Letters of John Keats 1814–1821*. Ed. Hyder Edward Rollins. 2 vols. Cambridge, MA: Harvard University Press, 1958.

—. *The Poems of John Keats*. Ed. Jack Stillinger. Cambridge, MA: Harvard University Press, 1978.

Kihlstrom, John F. 'The Cognitive Unconscious.' *Science* 237 (1987): 1445–52.

Lavie, Peretz and J. Allan Hobson, 'Origin of Dreams: Anticipations of Modern Theories in the Philosophy and Physiology of the Eighteenth and Nineteenth Centuries.' *Psychological Bulletin* 100.2 (1986): 229–40.

Levere, Trevor H. 'S. T. Coleridge and the Human Sciences: Anthropology, Phrenology, and Mesmerism.' *Science, Pseudo-Science, and Society*. Ed. Marsha P. Hanen, Margaret J. Osler, and Robert G. Weyent. Waterloo, ON: Wilfrid Laurier University Press, 1980. 171–92.

Levin, Susan M. *Dorothy Wordsworth and Romanticism*. New Brunswick, NJ: Rutgers University Press, 1987.

Lewis, Matthew G. *The Monk*. Ed. Louis F. Peck. New York: Grove, 1952.

Matlak, Richard. 'Wordsworth's Reading of *Zoonomia* in Early Spring.' *The Wordsworth Circle* 21 (1990): 76–81.
Mazlish, Bruce. 'The Man-Machine and Artificial Intelligence.' *Stanford Humanities Review* 4 (1995): 21–45.
Miller, Jonathan. 'Going Unconscious.' *New York Review of Books* April 20, 1995: 59–66.
Oxford English Dictionary Online. Oxford University Press. https://www.oed.com (last accessed October 24, 2020).
Perkins, David. 'Romantic Reading as Revery.' *European Romantic Review* 4.2 (1994): 183–99.
Polidori, John William. 'An English Translation of John William Polidori's (1815) Medical Dissertation on Oneirodynia (Somnambulism).' Trans. with notes by David Petrain. *European Romantic Review* 21.6 (2010): 775–88.
Pollin, Burton R. 'Philosophical and Literary Sources of *Frankenstein*.' *Comparative Literature* 27 (1965): 97–108.
Radcliffe, Ann. *The Italian*. Ed. Frederick Garber. Oxford: Oxford University Press, 1971.
Richardson, Alan. *British Romanticism and the Science of the Mind*. Cambridge: Cambridge University Press, 2001.
—. 'Coleridge and the Dream of an Embodied Mind.' *Romanticism* 5 (1999): 1–25.
—. 'Erasmus Darwin and the Fungus School.' *The Wordsworth Circle* 33.3 (Summer 2002): 113–16.
—. *A Mental Theater: Poetic Drama and Consciousness in the Romantic Age*. University Park: Pennsylvania State University Press, 1988.
—. *The Neural Sublime: Cognitive Theories and Romantic Texts*. Baltimore: Johns Hopkins University Press, 2010.
—. 'A Neural Theater: Joanna Baillie's *Plays on the Passions*.' *Joanna Baillie, Romantic Dramatist: Critical Essays*. Ed. Thomas Crochunis. New York: Routledge, 2004. 130–45.
—. 'The Politics of Dreaming: From Diderot to Keats and Shelley.' *Romantik* 1 (2012): 9–26.
—. 'Wild Minds: *Frankenstein*, Animality, and Romantic Brain Science.' *Huntington Library Quarterly*, 83.4 (Winter 2020): 771.87.
Shelley, Percy Bysshe. *Shelley's Poetry and Prose*. Ed. Donald H. Reiman and Sharon B. Powers. New York: W. W. Norton, 1977.
—. *Shelley's Prose, or, The Trumpet of a Prophecy*. Ed. David Lee Clark. Albuquerque: University of New Mexico Press, 1954.
Stiles, Anne, Stanley Finger and John Bulevich. 'Somnambulism and Trance States in the Works of John William Polidori, Author of The Vampyre.' *European Romantic Review* 21.6 (2010): 789–807.
Tatar, Maria. *Spellbound: Studies in Mesmerism and Literature*. Princeton: Princeton University Press, 1978.
Vermeule, Blakey. 'The New Unconscious: A Literary Guided Tour.' *The Oxford Handbook of Cognitive Literary Studies*. Ed. Lisa Zunshine. Oxford: Oxford University Press, 2015. 463–82.
Whyte, Lancelot Law. *The Unconscious Before Freud*. New York: Basic Books, 1960.

Wordsworth, Mary and William Wordsworth. *The Love Letters of William and Mary Wordsworth*. Ed. Beth Darlington. Ithaca, NY: Cornell University Press, 2009.

Wordsworth, William. *The Prelude 1799, 1805, 1850*. Ed. Jonathan Wordsworth, M. H. Abrams, and Stephen Gill. New York: W. W. Norton, 1979.

—. *William Wordsworth: The Poems*. Ed. John O. Hayden. 2 vols. Harmondsworth: Penguin, 1977.

Chapter 3

Romantic Panpsychism

Colin Jager

All things are full of gods.

(Thales)

The disenchantment of the world means the extirpation of animism.
(Max Horkheimer and Theodor Adorno, *Dialectic of Enlightenment*)

I am the Lorax. I speak for the trees.

(Dr Seuss, *The Lorax*)

Panpsychism is the belief that *mind* is the fundamental stuff of the universe. According to panpsychism, very simple things – cells and subatomic particles, not to mention rocks and stones and trees – have experiences. Perhaps they are sentient or possess rudimentary consciousness. If panpsychism is right, then the 'mystery of consciousness' is no mystery at all, but a basic fact about the world. This is an idea with a long, though rather marginal, history in the Western tradition.

Before the internet, I owned a four-volume hardbound set of books entitled simply *The Encyclopedia of Philosophy*, published by Macmillan in 1967. The entry for panpsychism reads, in its entirety: 'see animism.' Animism, as described by E. B. Tylor in his pioneering 1871 book *Primitive Culture*, is the conviction that natural objects possess souls or spirits. Tylor ascribed this belief to primitive peoples. That brief entry in the *Encyclopedia of Philosophy* thus reveals a great deal about the philosophical respectability of panpsychism in the middle of the twentieth century.

But things have changed. The invaluable online *Stanford Encyclopedia of Philosophy* has an 11,000-word essay on panpsychism, written in 2017 and filled with learned distinctions and subtle tweakings of the idea: constitutive versus emergent panpsychism, pan-experientialism, panprotopsychism, and so on. Meanwhile, a search for 'animism' in the *Stanford Encyclopedia* yields entries on environmental ethics, childhood, Japanese philosophy, and feminist philosophy of science – but nothing on panpsychism. Clearly, panpsychism's fortunes have risen dramatically in the world of professional philosophy. (If further proof were needed, there is now a *Routledge Handbook of Panpsychism*, published in 2020.) But respectability has come at the price of severing the association with animism, a concept of interest to anthropologists and environmentalists and feminists but apparently not to serious analytic philosophers.

What are we to make of the tangled relationship of these two words? Contemporary panpsychists, now housed in reputable departments of philosophy, might choose to distance themselves from the association with primitivism and religion – to say, in effect, '*that's* not what I mean by panpsychism!' But those with more historical or literary inclinations might choose to dwell on the tendency of the two terms to show up together. Consider, for example, Stanley Cavell's interpretation of Romanticism as a bargain with skepticism.[1] As Cavell explained in his 1988 book *In Quest of the Ordinary*, Immanuel Kant's truce with skepticism preserved knowledge of the world's appearance at the cost of surrendering knowledge of things themselves – a bargain to which Cavell imagined Romanticism responding, 'thanks for nothing!' Cavell's Romanticism named a dissatisfaction with Kant's compromise and a desire to get back in touch with the world itself – but also a recognition that getting back in touch with the world could not happen through the techniques of the human knower, whose sophisticated tools merely pushed the world further away. Recovery and reconnection would come only from the things themselves: seeing into the life of things depended upon the 'life' already in those things. That is the thought Cavell labeled 'animism.'

To declare that every flower enjoys the air it breathes is to make a claim about a flower's capacity for experience, and by extension, about the kind of world in which it exists: a world in which flowers have mental states with qualitative, irreducible properties. Romantic criticism has long viewed such claims with suspicion. Things are 'alive,' we generally think, only in the sense that the poet's language grants them that status; animism is an epiphenomenon of language mistaken for ontological truth. Indeed, panpsychist impulses are built into human language: every anthropomorphic projection, every ascription of sentience or feeling to natural objects, every pathetic fallacy or apostrophe flirts with a latent panpsychism. This can lead to a lot of confusion.

I will have more to say about these anxieties in a moment, but for now I want simply to mark the distance between that attitude toward language (familiar to all of us who read and teach Romanticism) and Cavell's description of Romanticism as 'buying back the thing itself [from Kant] by taking on animism' (65). Cavell's construal of Romanticism as a crisis of knowledge made sense in 1988, during a time when philosophers of mind were largely skeptical about consciousness and literary critics were deeply invested in the linguistic turn. Today, however, we can ask what an animistic Romanticism brings to the renewed discussions of consciousness currently occupying scholars in both philosophy and literature. What would it mean to 'take on' animism – or panpsychism?

It is best to admit at the outset that no Romantic writers were paid-up panpsychists – the word had not yet been invented, for one thing. Nonetheless, the label *panpsychism* gives some shape to the common Romantic-era belief that the universe was responsive and alive, filled with thinking things. We have given this possibility many names over the years – Lucretianism, Spinozism, idealism, vitalism – and each of those names reveals something important about the period and its writers. But framing this impulse as panpsychic helps us to focus specifically on consciousness, which is a more precise matter than the vaguer idea that all things are alive or have agency. 'Consciousness,' here, means awareness: it is the thing I lose when I go under general anesthesia or fall into a dreamless sleep. To have consciousness means that one has a point of view on things: there is something that it is like to feel pain, to smell coffee. And if that property is widely distributed, as panpsychists think, then we are a long way from Bloom's visionary company, for whom consciousness meant separation from nature, an awareness of loss for which the imagination served as recompense.[2]

The first section of this chapter discusses panpsychism's new respectability within analytic philosophy and the complex of commitments and impulses upon which its current revival draws, which I suggest are part of a recognizably Romantic genealogy. The second section dives into some of the disagreements over language – in brief, does it betray or reveal? – that have shaped debates about animism and anthropomorphism in literary studies. In the third section, I identify a fault line in attitudes toward panpsychism that is also present in Romantic thinking about these issues: the question of whether the relevant units of analysis are very small, like subatomic particles, or very large, like the universe. I conclude, in the last section, by trying to specify a version of the latter position, which is sometimes called 'cosmopsychism,' in the writings of Mary Wollstonecraft. I conclude that cosmopsychism avoids some of the conceptual problems that plague other forms of panpsychism and also provides the metaphysical scaffolding for a particularly Romantic kind of political possibility.

Analytic Panpsychism and Romantic Panpsychism

Following decades of relative neglect, consciousness became a hot topic for philosophers and cognitive scientists around the turn of the century. This renewed conversation has been dominated by the so-called 'hard problem,' a variation on an old worry about the relationship of mind and body.[3] Descartes had wondered about the causal interaction between brain and mind and eventually proposed the pineal gland as the place where they came together. Among other things, he was worried about the soul. In 1866 Thomas Huxley, with no such worries, posed the problem in a recognizably modern form: '[H]ow it is that anything so remarkable as a state of consciousness comes about as a result of irritating nervous tissue, is just as unaccountable as the appearance of the Djin when Aladdin rubbed his lamp' (193). Or, as Jerry Fodor put it in 2007, 'How ... could a couple of pounds of grey tissue have experiences?' ('Headaches'). Huxley and Fodor are asking their question from within the domain of philosophical materialism: how do biologically generated physical systems, like human beings, have qualitative experiences – emotions, desires, sensory experiences of color and sound?[4] The general demise of philosophical dualism and the widespread acceptance of some form of physicalism have not made the problem of consciousness any easier; if anything, it has become more intractable.

Of the various possible responses to the hard problem, panpsychism might be the simplest. The panpsychist proposes, quite modestly, that the hard problem is not a problem because matter is conscious. If there is only one kind of stuff in the universe, and that stuff is physical stuff, and we add (what seems self-evidently true) that some of this stuff (like the brain) has conscious experiences, then the most parsimonious conclusion is that physical things must themselves have conscious experience (or, more precisely, that experience must be one of the properties of matter). In this way a panpsychist can be a physicalist and also accept the irreducible nature of the phenomenal experiences of consciousness that we all share. Panpsychism thus offers an elegant answer to the question of how mind and matter interact: simply put, mind was there all along. Unlike dualism, panpsychism's metaphysical demands are modest. And unlike eliminative materialism, panpsychism does not require skepticism regarding common-sense intuitions about the quality of our experiences. It demands only that we generalize from our own introspectively available encounters with the world: if I can be certain that *I* have experiences, then why not everything else?

This may not be as crazy as it sounds. As David Skrbina has laid out in fascinating detail, the history of Western philosophy is a constant encounter with the possibility that all things are conscious.[5] Panpsychist or quasi-panpsychist views were held to varying degrees by the pre-Socratics, by Plato and the Neoplatonic tradition, and by alchemists like Paracelsus. At roughly the same time that Descartes and Newton were distinguishing between primary and secondary qualities (and thereby committing themselves to a form of philosophical dualism), Leibniz spoke of monads that had 'perceptions' and 'appetites,' Spinoza proposed that thought and extension were two aspects of the same basic stuff, and Margaret Cavendish argued that matter could think. Just a bit later, Diderot wrote of 'sensitive matter'; later still, C. S. Peirce and William James deployed panpsychist ideas, and major twentieth-century figures ranging from Bertrand Russell to Alfred North Whitehead to Henri Bergson might also be counted as panpsychists, at least on certain interpretations.

The current analytic interest in panpsychism dates to Galen Strawson's 2006 essay 'Realistic Monism: Why Physicalism Entails Panpsychism,' which appeared in a special issue of the *Journal of Consciousness Studies*. The essay was accompanied by critical appraisals from a number of philosophers and a lengthy response from Strawson. It later appeared as a book. Strawson's subtitle summarizes his proposal: that the now almost-universal commitment to physicalism entails another commitment of the most surprising and apparently radical kind – namely, that 'everything that concretely exists is intrinsically experience-involving' (8). Strawson's announced target was a view he termed 'physicSalism': 'that the nature or essence of all concrete reality can in principle be fully captured in the terms of physics' (4). PhysicSalists, Strawson declared, were a strange intellectual hybrid. They claimed to believe only in one kind of stuff – physical stuff – but they remained in thrall to the dualist intuition that the physical and the experiential were radically different. Thus they backed themselves into the awkward corner of having to claim that conscious experience was an illusion generated by the functioning of physical systems. Yet surely, Strawson wrote, it is more preposterous to claim that experience is illusory than to entertain the possibility that it is a part of the physical world. Most of us, he continued, have too narrow a notion of the physical: '[w]e don't see that the hard problem is not what consciousness is, it's what matter is,' as Strawson put it in the philosophy blog of *The New York Times* ('Consciousness'). Matter is 'experience-involving,' not just inert 'stuff.' And since there cannot be experience without an experiencer, we 'have a rather large number of subjects of experience on our hands' ('Realistic' 26).[6] A very large number, in fact.

Already, there are several implications here worth pausing over:

First, readers trained in the history of Romantic thought will have recognized some of the lineaments of Strawson's story in, for example, Coleridge's complaint in the *Biographia Literaria* that 'all the products of the mere reflective faculty partook of death, and were as the rattling twigs and sprays in winter' (232). The notion is a familiar one: that the commodification, individualism, and environmental devastation that characterize our contemporary world have their roots in a metaphysical crisis that can be traced back to early modernity and the scientific revolution. At the core of the crisis is what Max Weber called disenchantment: draining meaning away from the world and placing it exclusively within the human skull (and in heaven, though that turned out to be optional) and thereby liberating the world, now understood as mere matter, for manipulation by instrumental reason.[7] One finds versions of this narrative in generations of Romantic critics, in the Frankfurt School and the New Left, and in ecological writers from Henry David Thoreau and John Muir to Nan Shepherd and Silvia Federici. It holds that dominating nature, whether conceptually by means of dualism or technologically by means of instrumental reason or politically by means of patriarchy or extractive colonialism, has 'killed' the physical world, emptied it of spirit and animation, and rendered it as mere matter to be manipulated. The only way out of this morass is to reimagine matter itself.

A second implication is that consciousness sometimes seems mysterious because we assume that it is a property restricted to humans and perhaps a few of the higher mammals. If panpsychism is correct, however, consciousness is quite literally everywhere. Consequently, panpsychism may be hard to accept because it destroys the comforting notion that humans are different from the rest of the universe.[8] A common undercurrent in debates about animism, especially, is that resistance to the idea is largely emotional, and thus that we could in principle will ourselves to accept it if we could get over the old-fashioned belief that humans are special.

Finally, there is the question of why one might *want* to be a panpsychist. Strawson describes a scenario in which philosophers are pushed to panpsychism as the best possible option, unlikely as it may at first seem. He portrays himself as someone who long thought that panpsychism was crazy but was eventually convinced that it was the most reasonable option. Once you get over your initial resistance, you see that panpsychism makes things metaphysically easier, since it dissolves some otherwise intractable questions about mind/body relations. With a nod to Occam, I will call this 'Strawson's razor.' Yet as Freya Mathews has noted, the origins of our intellectual identities often go beyond such purely rational explanations. 'One is likely to become a panpsychist,' she writes, 'only as a result of direct experience of a responsive world' (5–6). Lacking that, why would anyone entertain the idea long enough to test its claims analytically? Those without pre-theoretical experiences of a responsive or lively world may remain unmoved by the intellectual pleasures that panpsychism offers.

These three implications (the critique of dualism, the dethroning of the human, and the experience of the responsive world) often come bundled. One does not need to feel the weight of all of them equally, but they nonetheless fit together without too many rough edges. Romantic and post-Romantic writers certainly experimented with all three, in different combinations. For example, consider Ernst Haeckel's observation that '[o]ne highly important principle of my monism seems to me to be, that I regard all matter as ensouled, that is to say as endowed with feeling (pleasure and pain) and with motion' (486). Haeckel is best known for coining the term 'ecology,' thereby giving to Western environmentalist thought its fundamental unit of analysis. And modern ecological thinking is indeed deeply panpsychist, in spirit if not in name or in philosophical rigor. In our age of the Anthropocene, where the consequences of instrumental reason are everywhere apparent, panpsychism might seem a good place to begin constructing a more ecologically centered philosophy. And Romanticism, so often understood as a critique of dualism and disenchantment, might thus receive some credit for glimpsing, even if imperfectly, the implications of philosophical modernity and for beginning to sketch an alternative in which properties typically construed as belonging to subjects, such as agency, intentionality, and communication, belong to objects as well. Here, perhaps, we catch sight of a truly responsive world, not merely attuned to human desires but involved in a complex set of relations with itself.

But before we celebrate this happy turn of events, a stubborn, skeptical question intrudes: are we not just seeing what we want to see? Is panpsychism not simply an anthropomorphic projection of human-like 'minds' onto nonhuman things? One more example of the problem, rather than a solution to it?

Romantic Language

Here is a sharper version of that question: by attributing mindedness to everything, does the panpsychist not take for granted the very thing – mind – that she ought to be demonstrating? Much of what we mean by 'criticism' begins here: we remind our students, and we remind ourselves, that rocks do not mutter and that flowers do not enjoy the air they breathe, whatever poets might say to the contrary. Wordsworth himself, despite saying both of those things, had similar concerns. Under certain conditions, he remarked in 'Note to The Thorn,' words can transform from symbols into '*things*, active and efficient, which are themselves part of the passion' (200). This happens especially with Biblical language, but the impulse seems (in Wordsworth's terms) more primitive still. In 'The Thorn,' for example, the titular spot seems to *know* things merely hinted at in Margaret's repeated refrain of 'Oh misery! oh misery!' Unless they are handled with care, words open a door to the world of those who came to be called animists.

Paul de Man's groundbreaking essay 'Intentional Structure of the Romantic Image,' first published in 1960 and reprinted in *Romanticism and Consciousness*, attempted to shut that door. 'At times,' de Man wrote, 'romantic thought and romantic poetry seem to come so close to giving in completely to the nostalgia for the object that it becomes difficult to distinguish between object and image, between imagination and perception' (7).[9] De Man thought that the desire for unmediated vision, the blurring of object and image, was in fact a determined forgetting of the human (that is, mediated) origin of that very desire. He also thought there was something deeply reassuring – hence primitive, child-like – about the animist impulse. We *want* it to be true, because we want to be at home in the world. The grownup secular critic ought therefore to remind us of the gap between imagination and perception. When we forget this gap, or allow poets to encourage us to forget it, we confuse something that exists in the head with something that exists in the world. And nothing is so good as human language at producing this kind of confusion.

In a well-known 1986 essay entitled 'Apostrophe, Animation, and Abortion,' Barbara Johnson made the political stakes of de Man's argument clear. Apostrophe, she wrote, was 'a form of ventriloquism through which the speaker throws voice, life, and human form into the addressee, turning its silence into mute responsiveness' (30). Writing of 'Ode to the West Wind,' Johnson argued that the poem's 'giving' of animation to the wind presupposed that the speaker had life to give; at the same time, life was what the speaker asked the wind to give to him. Johnson suggested that this paradoxical giving and taking of life also structured disputes about abortion: 'What is the debate over abortion about, indeed, if not the question of when, precisely, a being assumes a human form?' (32). The question of when life begins, who grants it, who dispenses with it – these are rhetorical questions, which is to say that they are questions pertinent to that most distinctive of human capacities, language itself.[10] To forget that the debate is made possible by rhetorical forms of address such as apostrophe is to presume that there is a domain outside the realm of language, and that such a domain is populated by animate things.

This form of deconstructive argument is fundamentally dualist, its professed commitment to materialism notwithstanding. Recall that, according to Strawson, modern-day physicalists remain beholden to a dualist metaphysics; they insist that matter is inert, and then puzzle over where consciousness comes from. In much the same way, Johnson's attention to animacy depends upon a dualist distinction between a thing and its representation. She is agnostic about whether flowers or fetuses actually have consciousness; but she is sure that we only *think* they do because we have projected consciousness there in the first place, by means of language. Moreover, that projection allows us to secure our own identity, and hence to forget that consciousness, ours as much as the flower's, is an effect of language. The role of the theorist is to remind us of these tendencies, even if that means permanent estrangement from what is given to us in experience.

By contrast, panpsychism begins by postulating that consciousness is a property shared by humans and the rest of the world. Compare, for example, Johnson's worry that '[t]o use an anthropomorphism is to treat as *known* what the properties of the human are' ('Anthropomorphism' 551) to Graham Harman's assertion that the possible anthropomorphizing of panpsychism is less worrisome than the 'truly perilous risk of preserving the dominance of the human-world rift' (212).[11] From this perspective, skepticism about consciousness and concerns about the deceptive nature of language simply reify a division between human and world that is a contingent effect of intellectual history whose baneful ethical consequences are becoming more apparent every day. Toward the end of her influential *Vibrant Matter* (2010), Jane Bennett defends anthropomorphism along similar lines:

> Maybe it is worth running the risks associated with anthropomorphizing (superstition, the divinization of nature, romanticism) because it, oddly enough, works against anthropocentrism: a chord is struck between person and thing, and I am no longer above or outside a nonhuman 'environment.' (120)

No reader of Romantic texts would find anything surprising in this sentiment. To put it in Cavell's terms, 'buying back the thing itself by taking on animism' is a bargain worth making, even if animism just turns out to be an anthropomorphic projection.

To be sure, there is still something quite skeptical about this line pursued by Harman, Bennett, and Cavell: even though it might be just a projection, let's behave *as if* animism is true, since the potential ethical gains outweigh the liabilities. Call this skeptical panpsychism. For the non-skeptical panpsychist, meanwhile, anthropomorphism or apostrophe would be not an error of attribution, even an innocent one, but a technique that opens a pathway to the responsive world that really does lie on the far side of language. That one must use language to construct the path to that world (in the case of a poem, anyway) is a complication but not the vicious circle that deconstructive critics thought it to be. To say this is to relativize ethical and epistemological worries about 'speaking for' other entities, and to call into question the premise that there is only one kind of (silent) nature over which human culture spreads its various interpretations. Nature, as Eduardo Viveiros de Castro has argued for some years now, comes in many forms. Jorge Marcone, in his call for an 'Amazonian Environmental Humanities,' has fastened on just this aspect of animist ontologies. '[E]nunciations in any media,' Marcone writes, 'can be thought of as entities originating in the interaction of human and nonhuman actors' (50). A character in a text, for example, is not a mental construct 'supported by language' but has an ontological status more like the 'invisible human and nonhuman beings in Amazonian shamanism' (55). Marcone's invocation of shamanism in this context indicates that animism may not be as entirely comforting and comfortable as de Man, Johnson, and countless other critics assume. Perhaps what is really being protected by the critique of anthropomorphism is a notion of 'text' that secures the special stature of human beings. If all concrete entities are experience-involving, then our received ideas of text as a symbolic depiction of the split between nature and society will not be up to task of attending to the world as it really is. Do we know how to read in such a manner?

John Clare's poem 'The Lament of Swordy Well' at first appears to be written from the perspective of a poor man who cannot speak. Then we read, in the third stanza:

Im swordy well a piece of land
  That's fell upon the town
Who worked me till I couldn't stand
  And crush me now Im down. (21–4)

To the reader's surprise, a 'piece of land' is speaking. Yet this momentary disorientation passes so quickly into the poem's ordinary language as to be scarcely worthy of remark. Such easy travel between human and nonhuman allows the speaker to drive home a claim about the common plight of poor people and decimated land: after enclosure and extraction, neither has anything to offer the other.

Clare's poem reminds us that even if panpsychism is true, it does not follow that the motives and interests of a human and a 'piece of land' will be aligned. The mutuality of shared consciousness, or even shared fate, does not mean that conflict disappears into a love affair with the world. But the fact of shared consciousness *does* place potential conflict on a historical plane rather than on a metaphysical one. 'If I brought harvests twice a year / They'd bring me nothing back,' declares the much-abused Common (47–8), registering the disappearance of a mutual relationship between human and land and thus of a more inclusive sense of the 'common' itself. Clare's poem therefore suggests that panpsychism is, in itself, politically neutral. In this case, it simply means that Swordy Well has experiences – or, more precisely, that a Common is an experience-involving subject. There is *something that it is like* to be a disappearing Common in eighteenth-century England. What we do with that fact is another matter.

Smallism

Earlier, when discussing Strawson's argument for panpsychism, I set aside perhaps the stickiest of its conceptual difficulties. This is known as the 'combination problem.'[12] The combination problem is this: if very basic things like cells or neurons have experiences, then does a collection of such things have different experiences? If a stone has a 'mind,' does a cairn have a different kind of mind? Or is a cairn just a grouping of individual stone-minds? If my individual atoms have experiences, then does the collection of atoms known as my left arm have experiences that are meaningfully different from those of my body as a whole? And why, finally, do some rare things – human brains, for example – support rich and continuous experiences and become aware of themselves doing so? Given that such questions linger even after we have bitten the panpsychist bullet, perhaps we really have not made very much headway at all.

In the second half of this chapter, I would like to use the combination problem as a way to reflect on the political implications of some Romantic texts. Operating in the background here are a set of questions about the relationship between politics and metaphysics. For many readers, I suspect, politics and metaphysics ought to be kept apart. As in the Clare poem just discussed, the question of Swordy Well's ontological standing is analytically distinct from the question of how human beings ought to treat the land. And yet we are also in something of a metaphysical revival, not only in professional philosophy but also in our current Anthropocene moment and its proliferation of ecological criticism and ontological speculation. Undergirding much of that speculation is the supposition that if we got the metaphysics right – if we really grasped what the world was like in all its vibrant, agentive complexity – we would change our behavior. It is, I think, impossible to understand the current revival of interest in both animism and panpsychism apart from this supposition.

The combination problem provides a precise way into these thorny matters. Strawson's version of panpsychism makes consciousness a decidedly ordinary and widely shared property. While this might seem politically promising, it raises difficult questions about how experience 'adds up' in a meaningful way. Taking my cue from the disappearing common in Clare's 'Swordy Well,' I suggest in this section that the combination problem leads to tragic outcomes for literary panpsychism: small units of experience do not add up to something larger, and the advent of panpsychism in a poem thereby points to the loss of meaning, rather than its discovery. Then, in the final section of the chapter, I am going to argue that a passage from Mary Wollstonecraft draws on a different kind of panpsychism that avoids the combination problem. It therefore offers a different way to imagine the political possibilities of Romanticism. But it also confronts the reader with the unavoidability of metaphysics.

I begin with a passage from Dorothy Wordsworth's *Grasmere Journal*, from late January of 1802:

> I found a strawberry blossom in a rock, the little slender flower had more courage than the green leaves, for *they* were but half expanded & half grown, but the blossom was spread full out. I uprooted it rashly, & felt as if I had been committing an outrage, so I planted it again – it will have but a stormy life of it, but let it live if it can. (61)

The panpsychism here is low-key: the flower has 'courage' because it is fully spread out, while its surrounding leaves remain only halfway expanded. Dorothy's uprooting and then replanting of the strawberry, meanwhile, registers as a violation of the small whole to which she attends. It remains unclear whether the 'stormy life' that she anticipates for the plant is the result of its difficult placement in the rock or the fact that she has uprooted it, just as it remains unclear whether the blossom's courage is somehow the product of its placement (courage therefore being the result of a combination of the experiences of these different entities of rock, blossom, and leaves) or whether courage is a property of the blossom on its own. Nonetheless, Dorothy's actions are determined to some extent by that courage, thereby suggesting that the small flower's mental state, modest as it is, has affected a larger entity (that is, Dorothy) dramatically enough to cause her to change her behavior. There are places in the *Journal* where Dorothy exhibits no such compunction – when she describes gathering mosses, for example. But in this case she recognizes in the strawberry a fellow consciousness: experience is a property of this blossom, and it is honored by being returned to its place, though not without some damage.

Initially, panpsychism seems like an extravagant notion: all matter is conscious! But Dorothy's encounter with the strawberry blossom suggests otherwise. The drama is minor, and recognizing the flower as a subject of experience is accompanied by no rhetorical fireworks nor flash of inspiration. Another way to say this is: experience is not special or unique but ordinary – so ordinary that everything is having it, all of the time. It is just something that happens, a process without intentionality or need for representation or even explanation: blossoms exhibit courage, land feels anger, and, as Blake has it, 'every particle of dust breathes forth its joy' (*Europe*, plate 3, line 18). '[B]ringing the world back, as if to life ... may ... present itself as the quest for a return to the ordinary,' writes Cavell (53). This call to Romantic ordinariness (or what used to be called, in a different idiom, natural supernaturalism) has been joined in more recent years by Jane Bennett, Stephen Shaviro, and others.[13] From this angle, panpsychism seems to lend itself to the task of recapturing an ordinary experience that has been distorted or pushed away by enlightened alienation and the hubris of anthropocentrism.

This focus on ordinariness is another way of attending to the most basic levels of reality. In his commentary on Strawson's essay, Sam Coleman calls this attention 'smallism.' This is the view that 'all facts are determined by facts about the smallest things' (40).[14] Smallism is the viewpoint of fundamental physics: that, when we really get down to it, everything is determined by the behavior of subatomic particles. Strawson's panpsychism is likewise smallist: he simply insists that when we finally get down to the very smallest of things ('ultimates,' as he calls them), there we will find experience, and thus subjects of experience. Because, according to this argument, micro-experientiality and macro-experientiality are the same kind of thing, panpsychism need not posit that at some unknown threshold, and experience emerges from the non-experiential. But by avoiding this kind of emergence, Strawson's panpsychism runs smack into the problem of combination – the problem, again, of describing the difference, if any, between a collection of very small subjects of experiences and the whole (a brain, a Common) that they constitute. As Philip Goff puts it in his own response to Strawson, '[s]ubjects of experience are just not the kind of things that could intelligibly join together to form "bigger" subjects of experience' ('Experiences' 59).[15] This is one motivation for the complaint that panpsychism of Strawson's kind does not explain very much.

Poets do not generally write about ultimates (though Blake's 'particles of dust' comes close). Nonetheless, literary versions of the combination problem can be found across the landscape of Romantic panpsychism. The pathos of William Wordsworth's pansies in the 'Intimations' Ode is that they no longer seem connected to the larger whole toward which they gesture:

> – But there's a Tree, of many, one,
> A single Field which I have looked upon,
> Both of them speak of something that is gone:
> The Pansy at my feet
> Doth the same tale repeat:
> Whither is fled the visionary gleam?
> Where is it now, the glory and the dream? (51–7)

Clare's 'piece of land,' too, keeps breaking down into smaller units: 'the muck that clouts the ploughmans shoe / The moss that hides the stone' (37–8); the butterflies and rabbits that leave to seek food elsewhere; the land itself 'turned ... inside out / For sand and grit and stones' (61–2). Is Swordy Well's experience simply the sum of the experiences of the muck, moss, rabbits, sand, and stones? Or does its experience differ qualitatively from that of its constituent parts?

There is a political dimension to this question, for if a piece of land has experiences, it might have rights as well. The Revolutionary-era debate about rights generally treated the question as one limited to humans, with brief forays into the nascent animal rights movement. But conservative critics had no qualm about suggesting what they took to be a *reductio ad absurdum*: if all men, and then women, and then slaves, and then animals were to be granted rights, why stop there? In a satirical 1792 pamphlet entitled *A Vindication of the Rights of Brutes*, Thomas Taylor declared that his aim was 'no other, than to establish the equality of all things, as to their intrinsic dignity and worth' (iii).[16] Taylor took the absurdity of this position to be self-evident, of course, but his strategy is one that a panpsychist needs to take seriously. If panpsychism is true, what kinds of ethical responsibilities follow, and how far down do they go? How radically would society have to be reorganized?

These Romantic-era questions point all the way forward to our present moment and the movement to grant rights to nature. In 2008

Ecuador became the first country to recognize the rights of nature in its constitution, and within the past decade governments from New Zealand to India to Colombia have granted rights to rivers and mountains. In 2017, for example, New Zealand recognized the Whanganui River as a legal person, under the name of 'Te Awa Tupua,' a Maori way of expressing not just the river itself but the entire environment into which it is integrated, stretching from mountains to sea, and including watersheds, river banks, the surrounding area, and the creatures, human and nonhuman, who live there.

From one perspective, the movement to grant rights to nature is part of the history of political liberalism, with its distinction (often contested) between regarding something as property and granting it personhood as a rights-bearing entity. Indeed, contemporary movements for the rights of nature often use liberal notions of personhood as rough approximations for indigenous conceptions that arise from a very different thoughtworld. 'Nature,' accordingly, would be the latest in a line of subjects now legally recognized as bearers of rights. But there is a separate and deeper question here. Is Te Awa Tupua a legal and linguistic fiction, created for the purpose of its own protection – that is, is it a 'person' in name only? Or does Te Awa Tupua have experiences? *Is there something that it is like* to be Te Awa Tupua? If so, why do we think that Te Awa Tupua is something other than the sum of its parts?[17]

Underneath the political and legal matters of rights and persons, in other words, lurks a set of metaphysical questions raised by panpsychism: first, how widely is consciousness distributed, and second, how does consciousness add up? We can see this in the Wordsworth and Clare poems. Both texts point toward social and historical reasons (the course of the French Revolution, enclosure) for the failure of experience to add up meaningfully, and both resort to an anthropomorphic 'voice' to assert the reality of a whole that cannot be demonstrated in fact. But those proximate causes rest on a metaphysical scaffolding. Thus in the final stanza of the Ode, Wordsworth moves to apostrophe: 'And O, ye Fountains, Meadows, Hills, and Groves, / Forebode not any severing of our loves!' (190–1). It is a fully rhetorical plea. Clare, less sanguine but on the same page conceptually, imagines that words without referent will soon be all that remains of the land: 'My name will quickly be the whole / That's left of swordy well,' the piece of land declares (207–8). This grim ending suggests that the combination problem will be 'solved' only when there are no parts left to be accounted for, and the 'whole' becomes a hole, a mere word where there was once a Common. Absent a story about how experience might add up, linguistic fictions are all that remain.[18]

Strawson thinks that panpsychism, as strange as it sounds, makes things easier – and perhaps it does. But these literary examples suggest that panpsychism of this smallist variety cannot resolve the stickiest question of all: how are claims about the nature of matter to be squared with the value to be extracted from it? Confronted with that question, what these literary examples discover is not life but death. I am struck, here, by a casual remark by Cavell: 'If flowers could feel for us what we feel for them, we would not treat them as we treat flowers, for example, arrange them; not even lovingly' (69). I take this to mean that if panpsychism were true, flowers would not be flowers, but something else entirely. Beyond the bare fact of sharing consciousness, would we have a connection to them at all? Would they have any connection to us? Perhaps that is why Dorothy Wordsworth uproots the courageous strawberry – because, like the Ancient Mariner, she wants to be in relationship with it, even if that relationship is marked by death.

Cosmopsychism

I have proposed that smallist versions of panpsychism struggle with the combination problem, and that this manifests itself in Romantic texts as a kind of death or tragedy. For literary studies, this means the separation of metaphysics from politics: it is hard to see how a collection of individual experiences adds up to a 'larger' experience, and thus no normative claim follows from smallist versions of panpsychism. Therefore the messy business of what to do about a piece of land or a strawberry blossom has to be worked out on a case-by-case basis, in the domain of history, and not turned over to metaphysics. This kind of separation might seem a good thing, even a necessary one.

In the final section of this chapter, however, I will turn to a version of panpsychism called 'cosmopsychism' that avoids the combination problem. Rather than beginning with small things like subatomic particles, cosmopsychism begins with the biggest: the universe itself. It belongs to a family of metaphysical views known as 'priority monism' – the view that wholes are prior to parts, and thus that parts are the way they are because the whole (the universe, in this case) is the way that it is.[19] According to cosmopsychism, individual parts of the universe are conscious *because the universe itself is conscious.*[20] Because it does not have the burden of explaining how smaller experiences 'add up' to larger ones, cosmopsychism offers a neat way around the combination problem.

Versions of cosmopsychism were rife in the Romantic period, and they contribute to our sense that the age remained theological despite its widely acknowledged heterodoxy. 'One Mind inhabits, one diffusive Soul / Wields the large limbs, and mingles with the whole,' wrote Erasmus Darwin in the epigraph to *Zoonomia*. Fifteen years later, the young Percy Shelley wrote to his friend, Thomas Jefferson Hogg, that 'the leaf of a tree' and 'the meanest insect on wh. we trample' are evidence that 'some vast intellect animates Infinity –' (December [for January] 3, 181[1]; *Letters* 1:35).[21] Like Darwin, Shelley seemed to think that leaves and insects, along with human beings, were aspects of a single animating force – that is to say, that they were grounded in a larger, fundamental thing, which Darwin called a 'Mind' and Shelley called a 'vast intellect.'[22] Around the same time, Coleridge was adding the lines to 'The Eolian Harp' about the 'one Life within us and abroad / Which meets all motion and becomes its soul' (26–7).[23]

Such cosmopsychist thoughts were associated with free thinking. Controversy turned especially on the question of whether the human soul, conceived as simply a part of some larger whole, survived death.[24] Consider Mary Wollstonecraft's comments about death in the *Letters Written During a Short Residence in Sweden, Norway, and Denmark* (1796). Her arguments seem confused, or ambivalent. Sometimes she is determined to hold on to the individual soul. Humans are more than 'organized dust – ready to fly abroad the moment the spring snaps,' she writes: '[s]urely something resides in this heart that is not perishable' (99). Elsewhere, though, she seems to welcome that very dissolution: 'I cannot tell why – but death, under every form, appears to me like something getting free – to expand in I know not what element; nay, I feel that this conscious being must be as unfettered ... before it can be happy' (134–5). Wollstonecraft's apparently unsystematic thoughts – dualist in the first example, materialist in the second – led some in the conservative press to dismiss her as exemplifying the confused 'cant of modern free-thinkers.'[25] Contemporary critics have reversed the value judgement (now materialism is good and dualism is bad) but have not altered the terms. In other words, we are smallists: we continue to assume that the radical position is the reductive-materialist one, and we privilege the analytic move that shows how a thing like a soul or a poem or an emotion can be dissolved into a host of smaller things that determine it. Humans and pine trees alike are simply organized dust, made of the same stuff; the only debate is whether that stuff is conscious or not. From this smallist perspective, the hope that one is something more than organized dust appears to be a lapse into dualist mystification – a strange lapse for a writer who knew all too well the dangers of simply assuming that nature exhibited an Eolian harp-style responsiveness.[26]

But there is nothing contradictory in Wollstonecraft's claims – if the units of consciousness that make up human beings flee 'upward' rather than downward upon death. Rather than professing belief in an immortal soul, in other words, Wollstonecraft might be proposing a cosmopsychism that rejects emergence (the idea that consciousness arises from the way that non-conscious entities are organized), and indeed any form of smallism. Her panpsychism expands rather than contracts. This is signaled by the grammatical shift from 'I' to 'it' in the passage above ('I feel that this conscious being must be as unfettered … before it can be happy') and in her attention to death 'under every form,' from the human body to an aged pine, its 'fibres whitening as they lose their moisture' (134). In other words, Wollstonecraft's thinking here can be construed as an accurate and consistent depiction of the following metaphysical claims: both the human and the pine are made of the same stuff; that stuff is conscious; its consciousness is grounded in the consciousness of the universe; thus the experience of the parts is explained by the experience of the whole.

It is possible, then, to reconstruct a coherent metaphysical claim out of Wollstonecraft's scattered musings on death in the *Letters* – but only if we reject the smallist premise that truth is always found at lower levels of reality. This becomes clear in another passage in which Wollstonecraft speaks of her melancholy and contemplates suicide:

> I have … considered myself as a particle broken off from the grand mass of mankind; – I was alone, till some involuntary sympathetic emotion, like the attraction of adhesion, made me feel that I was still a part of a mighty whole, from which I could not sever myself … . Futurity, what hast thou not to give to those who know that there is such a thing as happiness! (59)

The first part of the passage asserts unequivocally that wholes precede parts; if that is true, it is incoherent to consider oneself a separate particle, since particles have their being only in relation to a whole (or, otherwise put, conscious particles are aspects of a conscious universe).

The second part of the passage then suggests that acknowledging this fact creates a different possible future. Those who know (in the present) that there is such a thing as happiness create a future (or a futurity) in which happiness exists. We usually think of signs as markers of absence, words substituting elegiacally for things; recall Wordsworth's single tree standing in for the dashed hopes of the Revolution. Wollstonecraft suggests, by contrast, that to know that there is such a thing as happiness is not merely to mark its absence in the present but to actively prepare for its future arrival. Given the priority of whole to part, signs like 'happiness' do not just represent the world; they are grounded in the world. One knows there is such a thing as happiness not because one represents happiness to oneself in its absence, but because the 'mighty whole' is happy, and one is grounded in that whole (whether one likes it or not). This means, finally, that happiness is widely distributed, as suggested again by the grammatical move away from first-person singular and toward a more generalized invocation of 'those who know' – that is, every particle of the whole, given a cosmopsychist picture of the world in which every particle has experiences. As distinct from Blake's particles of dust breathing forth their joy in an ecstatic present, Wollstonecraft's particles are not happy, not yet. But futurity's gift to them is the gift of the whole: that they can experience happiness before, so to speak, they are actually happy.

All this may seem like a cliché about the power of positive thinking – and it would be, if smallism were correct. In that case, happiness would be an example of what Wollstonecraft calls sentiment: a feeling whose parts originate in some lower order of reality and answer to some 'lower' need. In that case, the passage would be Wollstonecraft's Immortality Ode, her effort to make something happen on the page because it was not happening in the world. What the perspective of cosmopsychism strives to bring into view, by contrast, is a 'mighty whole,' which determines experience in the here-and-now. It also offers a metaphysical basis for Wollstonecraft's oft-expressed interest in improvement in the *Letters*, which can otherwise sound like mere bourgeois liberalism.

By using a meditation on death to gesture toward the priority of the whole, Wollstonecraft in effect reverses the smallist forms of panpsychism deployed by Clare and both Wordsworths, who had set out to describe life only to discover death. Wollstonecraft's alternative will be difficult to see, or will seem merely confused, if we have decided beforehand that smallism is true, and thereby committed ourselves to the combination problem, in either its metaphysical or its critical forms. But smallism is not, after all, the only metaphysical option available to us. Wollstonecraft's counter-proposal is that futurity – that is, a meaningful relationship to the whole – requires a grounding in a conscious universe, even if much of the time we do seem to ourselves merely conscious particles, cut off from the whole. If there *is* such a thing as futurity, not just a non-metaphysical future, Wollstonecraft's grammar of a panpsychism oriented toward the whole gives us a glimpse of what it might be like.

Notes

Thank you to Lacey Harvey, Joel Faflak, Richard Sha, Nancy Yousef, and William Galperin, who read earlier versions of this chapter and offered comments and suggestions.

1. See Cavell, *In Quest of the Ordinary: Lines of Skepticism and Romanticism*. On Cavell, Romanticism, and animism, see Fischer. I learned of Fischer's essay only after my own was largely complete, and am pleased to note a certain overlap of interest. Thanks to Lacey Harvey for calling it to my attention.
2. See Sha in this volume. It is important to be clear that, by 'consciousness,' Bloom, Hartman, and the other contributors to *Romanticism and Consciousness* usually meant not mere awareness but something more like self-consciousness. More recently, there has been a persistent tendency among continental theorists like Graham Harman to confuse 'consciousness' with 'self-consciousness' and therefore to dismiss panpsychism as the claim that stones have feelings.
3. The name 'hard problem' comes from David Chalmers. See Chalmers, 'Facing Up to the Problem of Consciousness' and *The Conscious Mind: In Search of a Fundamental Theory*.
4. In the Romantic period, 'idealism' was the popular alternative to philosophical materialism. Although idealism can be compatible with panpsychism, the emphasis is different: panpsychists see consciousness as intrinsic to matter, while idealists see matter as a kind of mental content.
5. I leave aside Asian and African philosophical traditions, which are often more amenable to panpsychist ideas. See Skrbina, *Panpsychism in the West*. See also Skrbina, *Mind that Abides: Panpsychism in the New Millennium*, a collection of essays by a range of contemporary analytic and continental philosophers. See also Harman's comments on panpsychism in *Prince of Networks* (212–14) and Steven Shaviro's two chapters on panpsychism in *The Universe of Things* (65–107).
6. I am following Strawson's usage here in making 'experience' mean 'phenomenal consciousness.' For something to be conscious (or to have an experience) there must be 'something that it is like' to be that thing. Strawson's kind of panpsychism might be accurately termed *panexperientialism*, but I will stick with the more elegant-sounding 'panpsychism.' The claim that experience entails an experiencer is criticized by Carruthers and Schecter. Note that, for Strawson, a 'subject of experience' is not something over and above the experience itself.
7. The bibliography here is enormous. For three representative texts, however, see Horkheimer and Adorno, *Dialectic of Enlightenment*, from the perspective of materialist history; Merchant, *The Death of Nature*, from the perspective of gender and feminism; and Taylor, *A Secular Age*, from the perspective of theological and intellectual history.
8. For this argument, see Koch 132.
9. In de Man's own account of his career this essay belonged to his pre-deconstructive, phenomenological phase, and yet the lineaments of his later obsession with language were already clear.

10. Johnson tends to run together the question of life with the question of consciousness. More recent concerns with biopower, inspired by Foucault, likewise conflate life with consciousness. In any case, biopower is a capacity with which literary language – in the form of elegy, apostrophe, anthropomorphism, and other figures – is deeply familiar.
11. See also de Man, 'Anthropomorphism and Trope in the Lyric': 'Anthropomorphism is … the *taking* of something for something else that can then be assumed to be *given*' (241).
12. The name comes from William Seager. William James is usually credited with identifying this problem. See James 1:160. See also Pinch. Of particular interest is Pinch's claim that, for Victorian panpsychists, the relevant question was not how to explain matter but how to explain spirit; idealism, not materialism, was the default intellectual position.
13. Bennett writes of the ordinary as a site of enchantment in *The Enchantment of Modern Life*. See also Shaviro 82. Along similar lines, Jonathan Kramnick writes: 'For a writer friendly to this bewildering perspective [that is, panpsychism], the work of literature might be to bring it in line with our naïve sense of the real and the ordinary' (140). For a different account of Romanticism and the ordinary, see Galperin.
14. A more celebratory term for smallism might be 'pluralism' (of the metaphysical sort), but I will stick with slightly more pejorative term.
15. This is a good place to note that models of distributed cognition, while not necessarily panpsychist, likewise struggle to account for this summative quality. In eighteenth-century language, both distributed cognition and smallist panpsychism are *mechanical*.
16. The pamphlet appeared anonymously.
17. There is work still to be done to articulate the relationship between Romantic counter-traditions within Western modernity and indigenous ontologies. Aside from Skrbina's essential *Mind That Abides*, see Shaviro and Kohn. Also exemplary are Akeel Bilgrami's essays on enchantment collected in *Secularism, Identity, and Enchantment*.
18. William Galperin has suggested to me that the novel is in fact the literary exemplar of the combination problem, since that is the form sufficient to exploring how a series of discreet experiences and subjects of experience add up (or not) to a larger experience.
19. See Schaffer.
20. Phillip Goff is the most prominent defender of this view. See Goff, *Consciousness and Fundamental Reality*. See also the entry on panpsychism in the *Stanford Encyclopedia of Philosophy* by Goff, Seager, and Sean Allen-Hermanson.
21. Shelley was nothing if not inconsistent on this issue. In 'On a Future State' (1818) he declared that consciousness was merely a particular arrangement of unconscious matter. And by the time of *Adonais* he had swung back toward a kind of monism.
22. Sentiments like these are sometimes labeled idealist. But that is to confuse an epistemological worry about the properties of things (is the red in the apple or in my mind?) for a metaphysical one about the priority of objects (which comes first, the leaf or the vast intellect?).

23. Coleridge, Shelley, and Darwin all took themselves to be saying something about the world, not merely about the power of words. 'I confess,' Shelley concluded, 'that I think Pope's "all are but parts of one tremendous whole" something more than Poetry ...' (*Letters* 1:35).
24. Adela Pinch makes the important point that most Victorian-era panpsychists were often trying to balance a commitment to idealism with a commitment to smallism. Romantic-era writers seem to have felt this tension differently, and were more willing to 'go big.' Romantic writers are not known for their philosophical precision, but here at least they are on firmer ground than their Victorian successors, since idealism is more compatible with metaphysical monism than it is with metaphysical pluralism. See Pinch, 'The Appeal of Panpsychism in Victorian Britain.'
25. *The Monthly Mirror* 1 (1796): 285–9; reprinted in Wollstonecraft 241.
26. In *Letters*, Wollstonecraft calls Eolian-type sentiments 'dangerous,' given the present 'imperfect state of existence' (87) – dangerous, in particular, for a woman in Wollstonecraft's position. Traveling in a foreign country on behalf of a lover of questionable fidelity, she cannot afford to forget that the responsive universe often exists only in the domain of poetry.

References

Bennett, Jane. *The Enchantment of Modern Life: Attachments, Crossings, and Ethics*. Princeton: Princeton University Press, 2001.
—. *Vibrant Matter: A Political Ecology of Things*. Durham, NC: Duke University Press, 2010.
Bilgrami, Akeel. *Secularism, Identity, and Enchantment*. Cambridge, MA: Harvard University Press, 2014.
Blake, William. *The Complete Poetry and Prose of William Blake*. Ed. David V. Erdman. New York: Anchor, 1988.
Carruthers, Peter and Elizabeth Schecter. 'Can Panpsychism Bridge the Explanatory Gap?' Galen Strawson et al. *Consciousness and Its Place in Nature: Does Physicalism Entail Panpsychism?* Ed. Anthony Freeman. Charlottesville, VA: Imprint Academic, 2006. 32–9.
Cavell, Stanley. *In Quest of the Ordinary: Lines of Skepticism and Romanticism*. Chicago: University of Chicago Press, 1988.
Chalmers, David. *The Conscious Mind: in Search of a Fundamental Theory*. Oxford: Oxford University Press, 1996.
—. 'Facing Up to the Problem of Consciousness.' *Journal of Consciousness Studies* 2.3 (1995): 200–19.
Clare, John. *Major Works*. Ed. Eric Robinson and David Powell. Oxford: Oxford University Press, 1984.
Coleman, Sam. 'Being Realistic: Why Physicalism May Entail Panexperientalism.' *Consciousness and Its Place in Nature*. 40–52.
Coleridge, Samuel Taylor. *Biographia Literaria*. *Samuel Taylor Coleridge: The Major Works*. Ed. H. J. Jackson. Oxford: Oxford University Press, 1985. 155–482.

—. *Poetical Works*. Ed. Ernest Hartley Coleridge. Oxford: Oxford University Press, 1980.

Darwin, Erasmus. *Zoonomia*. London: J. Johnson, 1796.

de Man, Paul. 'Anthromorphism and the Trope in Lyric.' *The Rhetoric of Romanticism*. New York: Columbia University Press, 1984. 239–62.

—. 'Intentional Structure of the Romantic Image.' *The Rhetoric of Romanticism*. 1–17.

Dr Seuss. *The Lorax*. New York: Random House, 1971.

Fischer, Michael. 'Accepting the Romantics as Philosophers.' *Philosophy and Literature* 12.2 (1988): 179–89.

Fodor, Jerry. 'Headaches Have Themselves.' *London Review of Books* 29.10 (24 May 2007). https://www.lrb.co.uk/the-paper/v29/n10/jerry-fodor/headaches-have-themselves (last accessed March 3, 2021).

Galperin, William. *The History of Missed Opportunities: British Romanticism and the Emergence of the Everyday*. Stanford: Stanford University Press, 2017.

Goff, Philip. *Consciousness and Fundamental Reality*. Oxford: Oxford University Press, 2017.

—. 'Experiences Don't Sum.' *Consciousness and Its Place in Nature*. 53–61.

Goff, Philip, William Seager, and Sean Allen-Hermanson. 'Panpsychism.' *The Stanford Encyclopedia of Philosophy*. Ed. Edward N. Zalta (Summer 2020). https://plato.stanford.edu/archives/sum2020/entries/panpsychism/ (last accessed December 2, 2021).

Haeckel, Ernst. 'Our Monism: The Principles of Consistent, Unitary World-View.' *The Monist* 2.4 (July 1892): 481–6.

Harman, Graham. *Prince of Networks: Bruno Latour and Metaphysics*. Melbourne: re.press, 2009.

Horkheimer, Max and Theodor W. Adorno. *Dialectic of Enlightenment: Philosophical Fragments*. 1947. Trans. Edmund Jephcott. Stanford: Stanford University Press, 2002.

Huxley, Thomas. *Lessons in Elementary Physiology*. London: Macmillan and Co., 1866.

James, William. *Principles of Psychology*. 2 vols. New York: Henry Holt, 1890.

Johnson, Barbara. 'Anthropomorphism in Lyric and Law.' *Yale Journal of Law and the Humanities* 10.2 (1998): 549–74.

—. 'Apostrophe, Animation, and Abortion.' *Diacritics* 16.1 (Spring 1986): 28–47.

Koch, Christof. *Consciousness: Confessions of a Romantic Reductionist*. Cambridge, MA: MIT Press, 2012.

Kohn, Eduardo. *How Forests Think: Toward an Anthropology Beyond the Human*. Berkeley: University of California Press, 2013.

Kramnick, Jonathan. *Paper Minds: Literature and the Ecology of Consciousness*. Chicago: University of Chicago Press, 2018.

Marcone, Jorge. 'Toward an Amazonian Environmental Humanities.' *Hispanic Ecocriticism*. Ed. José Manuel Marrero Henríquez. Bern: Peter Lang, 2019. 49–67.

Mathews, Freya. *For Love of Matter: A Contemporary Panpsychism*. Albany, NY: State University of New York Press, 2003.

Merchant, Carolyn. *The Death of Nature: Women, Ecology, and the Scientific Revolution*. New York: Harper and Row, 1980.
Pinch, Adela. 'The Appeal of Panpsychism in Victorian Britain.' *RaVoN* 65 (2014–15).
Schaffer, Jonathan. 'Monism: The Priority of the Whole.' *Philosophical Review* 119.1 (2010): 31–76.
Seager, William. 'Consciousness, Information, and Panpsychism.' *Journal of Consciousness Studies* 2.3 (March 1995): 272–88.
Shaviro, Steven. *The Universe of Things: On Speculative Realism*. Minneapolis: University of Minnesota Press, 2014.
Shelley, Percy Bysshe. *The Letters of Percy Bysshe Shelley*. 2 vols. Ed. Frederick L. Jones. Vol. 1: *Shelley in England*. Oxford: Oxford University Press, 2014.
Skrbina, David. *Mind that Abides: Panpsychism in the New Millennium*. Amsterdam: John Benjamins, 2009.
—, ed. *Panpsychism in the West*. 2007. Rev. ed. Cambridge, MA: MIT Press, 2017.
Strawson, Galen. 'Consciousness Isn't a Mystery. It's Matter.' *The New York Times* 16 May 2016. https://www.nytimes.com/2016/05/16/opinion/consciousness-isnt-a-mystery-its-matter.html (last accessed February 19, 2019).
—. 'Realistic Monism: Why Physicalism Entails Panpsychism.' *Consciousness and Its Place in Nature: Does Physicalism Entail Panpsychism?* 3–31.
Taylor, Charles. *A Secular Age*. Cambridge, MA: Harvard University Press, 2007.
Taylor, Thomas. *A Vindication of the Rights of Brutes*. London, 1792. ECCO. https://www.gale.com/primary-sources/eighteenth-century-collections-online (last accessed September 3, 2020).
Viveiros de Castro, Eduardo. 'Cosmological Deixis and Amerindian Perspectivism.' *The Journal of the Royal Anthropological Institute* 4.3 (1998): 469–88.
Wollstonecraft, Mary. *Letters Written During a Short Residence in Sweden, Norway, and Denmark*. Ed. Ingrid Horrocks. Peterborough, ON: Broadview Press, 2013.
Wordsworth, Dorothy. *The Grasmere and Alfoxden Journals*. Ed. Pamela Woof. Oxford: Oxford University Press, 2002.
Wordsworth, William and Samuel Taylor Coleridge. *Lyrical Ballads, 1798 and 1802*. Ed. Fiona Stafford. Oxford: Oxford University Press, 2013.

Chapter 4

Shelley and the Real of Faith
Joel Faflak

Romantic Consciousness and Psychoanalysis

Published in 1970, Harold Bloom's *Romanticism and Consciousness* signals the apotheosis of a surge in Romantic studies that reflected the previous decade's mood swings between optimism and disillusionment. In the struggle between revolution and reaction, if not reform, the volume found its not so uncanny double in the Romantics. The tutelary spirit of this version of Jerome McGann's Romantic ideology, as noted in this volume's Introduction, and despite the diverse critical backgrounds of Bloom's contributors, was psychoanalysis. This orientation made sense, given Bloom's debt to Freud. But it also made sense, given that, especially post-World War Two, American psychoanalysis was dominated by ego psychology, which sought to make the darkness of the unconscious visible and thus champion the subject's ability to conquer inner demons. Yet, at the same time, the Romanticism of Bloom's volume reflects a world at once very and yet never quite sure of itself. This ambivalence heralds a version of psychoanalysis focused more on indeterminacy than resolve, one that took its cue from Continental theory and philosophy, particularly through Jacques Lacan's return to Freud, in which the *cogito* and its consciousness do not add up to the same subject. Lacan was, of course, a key influence on a deconstructive and poststructuralist thought whose impact can already be felt in Bloom's volume in essays by Geoffrey Hartman and especially Paul de Man. So, while *Romanticism and Consciousness* reflects a desire to bring the unconscious to consciousness, particularly by healing the Romantic subject's alienation from the world, it also heralds another psychoanalysis in which this desire for a cure is only one of the plague of fantasies by which we live.[1]

Reassessing Freud's legacy closer to our own time, Adam Phillips argues that 'Freud ... charts the development of the unknowing and largely unknowable modern individual in a culture obsessed by knowledge; of the distracted and disrupted individual whose continuities and traditions are breaking down around him' (10–11). This assessment speaks directly to Romanticism as a process of 'restless self-examination' (Rajan 25) and entails one of the period's central preoccupations with what Coleridge, in *Biographia Literaria*, calls a 'willing suspension of disbelief that constitutes poetic faith' (2:6). Phillips adds that 'Freud moves from wondering who to believe in, to wondering about the origins and the function of the individual's predisposition to believe' (Phillips 111). Put another way, the Romantic subject finds herself less by mapping consciousness as the interiorized space of her own navigation, what Bloom calls the internalization of the quest romance, than constituted by the form taken by the transference between consciousness and the world, consciousness *as* this transference. In this sense, consciousness is what Keats describes as a going out of himself to everyone in a room without any guarantee of return, an alienation that evokes Geoffrey Hartman's sense of a rifted Romantic identity. Yet Keats's sense of 'no Identity ... no self ... no nature' (157) suggests less a nostalgia for return and reparation than the possibility that the subject itself was only a momentary construct required by post-Enlightenment thought to justify its worldly claims. Such a subject was no longer the sole conduit for a Romantic consciousness extending far beyond any notion of subjects as bounded and binding or self-contained and self-containing entities.

I understand this to be Coleridge's sense that we must then take our relation to the world on faith. Here faith is required to assuage the trauma of any disconnect from the world, the inevitable agon that results from the modern notion of what Charles Taylor calls the 'buffered self' or subject 'necessary to have confidence in our own powers of moral ordering' (27).[2] For Taylor, science's capacity to 'disenchant the universe, ... opening the way for exclusive humanism,' superseded a self at once 'open and porous and vulnerable to a world of spirits and powers' (27) associated with religion's earlier hold on individual wills and imaginations and not unlike the persistence of a supernaturalism to which Coleridge's famous statement about poetic faith speaks. The question thus begged here is, what purpose does perception or consciousness serve at all? Rereading Kant in terms of what he calls the principle of sufficient (as opposed to transcendental) reason, Schopenhauer would answer that Kant reverts to perception only

> in order to convince [himself] that [his] abstract thinking has not strayed far from the safe ground of perception, ... much in the same way as, when

walking in the dark, we stretch out our hand every now and then to the wall that guides us. (1:449)

For Schopenhauer, to whom Freud owed a significant debt, perception is precisely what necessarily mires the subject in the sense of its own being as that which it can never possess and so is never at one with itself. However, I read faith in terms of what I would call the preternaturalism of Romantic consciousness, its exploration of what lies beyond the natural or normal. Recent advances in the study of consciousness offer a less buffered, more expansive conception of Romantic subjectivity. I want to address, via the poetry of Percy Shelley, what psychoanalysis might contribute to this revaluation.

Psychoanalysis and the Real of Romanticism

We might say that psychoanalysis informs the political unconscious of Romanticism. Reinflecting Louis Althusser's inflection of the Lacanian unconscious as structured like a language, Fredric Jameson examines the political unconscious as a structure orchestrated around history as an 'absent cause, inaccessible to us except in textual form' (35). Jameson relates this absence to Lacan's account of the Real as 'that which resists symbolization absolutely' (Lacan, *Seminar I* 66). Hence 'our approach to [history] and to the Real itself necessarily passes through its prior textualization, its narrativization in the political unconscious' (35), through symbolic acts, like literature, that respond to a time's social or cultural realities. In this way, psychoanalysis was already in the air by the time of Shelley, for it offered a way of thinking through the various dilemmas of how mind and body situated themselves within and responded to the world, in the same way that Romanticism shaped the political unconscious of psychoanalysis. How Romanticism expresses the mind/body dilemma, which speaks with acute specificity to the dilemma of Romantic consciousness itself, suggests Stanley Cavell's sense of how psychoanalysis had been 'called for in the history of knowledge' (387). Discerning the Real of this dilemma leaves us reconstructing through our readings of Romantic texts how they symbolically form and formulate the 'absent cause' of their articulation.

This problem of representation and reality, of how we represent reality to ourselves and one another, goes back at least to Kant, or Locke or Hume before him. And this goes to the heart of what philosopher and cognitive scientist David Chalmers has called the 'hard problem of consciousness': how to explain the transference between physical processes, like the neuronal structure of the brain, and our experience of the world this structure provides for us – a transference between the cognitive and the phenomenal. Attempting to explain the marriage of mind and nature, Wordsworth's Prospectus to *The Recluse*, for instance, is exemplary of Romanticism's response to this dilemma. Wordsworth is not the only example, of course, however much it seems tailor-made for the version of Romantic consciousness laid out in something like M. H. Abrams's *Natural Supernaturalism,* which appeared the year after Bloom's volume. That is, despite the antagonisms and inconsistencies shaping consciousness, apparent in essays by Hartman or de Man, the volume still took consciousness as a universal, universalizing, and fundamentally human concern. This is also to say, in a different formulation of Phillips's assessment, that Hartman and especially de Man lead us to Jean-Luc Nancy's perception that 'self is what *does not find itself*' (56), even if *Romanticism and Consciousness* as a whole never quite challenges this self's fundamental integrity.

Writing in 1987, Cavell goes on to note that simply 'rediscovering the reality of psychoanalysis' through our reading of texts is 'no longer a sufficient response in our altered environment' (387), when critics like Neil Hertz, Shoshana Felman, or Eve Sedgwick (all named by Cavell) deployed psychoanalysis as a hermeneutic of suspicion troubling our reliance on human experience. However much psychoanalysis offers to us how 'one human being represents to another all that that other has conceived of humanity in his or her life, and moves with that other toward an expression of the conditions which condition that utterly specific life,' it still 'has not surmounted the obscurities of the philosophical problematic of representation and reality it inherits' (393). How psychoanalysis confronts us with our own alien natures makes us strangers to ourselves, as Humberto Garcia's Kristevan epigraph to his chapter in this volume tells us, which in turn suggests how psychoanalysis continues to haunt Romanticism. In their Introduction to *Speculations after Freud* (1994), 'The Censure of the Speculative,' Sonu Shamdasani and Michael Münchow argue that 'psychoanalysis reveals an unmasterable exteriority encrypted within itself' (xv). Jacques Derrida says that the 'greatest speculative power' of psychoanalysis is its 'greatest resistance to psychoanalysis' (86). Moreover, if psychoanalysis locates us at the incompossible punctum between consciousness, thought, and the world, it thus also locates us at the fugitive locus of the human itself. We are unlocatable as human because it is 'virtually' impossible to witness our being at the moment of its becoming, which is always to lead us away from ourselves – although, as Chalmers is more than aware, we most certainly feel this impossibility as the transference between the cognitive and the phenomenal. Cavell himself 'persist[s] in thinking that to lose knowledge of the human possibility of skepticism means to lose knowledge of the human' (390).

Yet for many Romantics, like Shelley, the human was an overhyped concept to begin with, which returns me to my question: what might psychoanalysis still have to tell us about Romantic literature?[3] A recent essay collection, *Lacan and Romanticism* (2019), edited by Daniela Garofalo and David Sigler, argues that the Romantic literary text that 'calls for' psychoanalysis cannot be, or only be, interpolated as part of a broader, autonomous symbolic network of which the text itself is a kind of autonomic expression. They cite, for instance, Franco Moretti's notion of distant reading as an example of a tendency to deprivilege literature's universality, which suggests the bad consciousness of wanting at once to debunk the literary text while at same time enjoying its symptom, to invoke Slavoj Žižek's 'return' to Lacan. I thus take Garofalo and Sigler's principal aim to be how Romantic literature enjoys itself *as* symptom. For Lacan, the symptom's Imaginary mode at once ineluctably and ecstatically structures our realities as necessary fantasies within a Symbolic order that provides their mode of articulation. We might ask what enjoyment – what *jouissance* – we ask from our reading of Romanticism. The Romantic literary text understands itself as always already hoodwinked by linguistic and discursive regimes, what Althusser calls interpellation, which entails a form of misrecognition masquerading as fantasy. Apprehending this misrecognition has long informed Romanticism and the criticism that tracks its ideological unfolding then and since, an evolution whose increasingly thick description – the sheer weight of knowledge that threatens to bury us, as Shelley suggests in *A Defence of Poetry* – tarries with the extinction of Romanticism, Romantic studies, or both. Put another way, is the explosion of materials we continue to gather about Romanticism symptomatic of what Phillips calls an 'obsession with knowledge,' the way in which Romanticism has been 'critiqued into oblivion' (Miles 173), and thus a bulwark guarding against internalizing what this knowledge has to tell us? Yet reading Romanticism *avec* Lacan reminds us of literature's state of Imaginary exception within the Symbolic, precisely because its starting point is an awareness, however implicit or explicit, that the Symbolic itself exists only as an exception to itself.[4] Such exception terrifies, even terrorizes, but also marks our precarious survival, yet not necessarily as humans, or as the humans we thought we were.

This chapter thus tarries with a more general Lacanianism that asks us to think the subject as formed by the Symbolic order as this exception to itself, not at one with itself. This subject, whose out-of-jointness marks her 'fundamental' locus in the world – Hamlet's curse, as Žižek suggests – is less posthuman than nonhuman. For Lacan, to be human and to be a subject are by no means the same thing. Lacanian theory shares an affinity with speculative realism in this regard. In *After Finitude* Quentin Meillassoux queries 'what is truly at stake' in thinking what he calls 'the problem of ancestrality' – a *'past where both humanity and life are absent'* but the effects of which nonetheless demand that we consider their impact as part of what we commonly call our humanity. Or as Meillassoux asks, 'how can a being manifest being's anteriority to manifestation?' (26). How or why does one take responsibility for a world – say, nature or the cosmos – one had no part in making, but in which one nonetheless has and finds one's being, which at the same time makes one's being beside the point, except insofar as one's being shapes and misshapes how the world unfolds, as in climate change?[5] Such questions teased Keats out of thought as he gazed upon the Grecian Urn as an entity without a subject, a visitation from the past that dislocates the poet's place in the world. Urns are not quite what Meillassoux means by 'arche-fossils': 'not just materials indicating traces of a past life ... but materials indicating the existence of an ancestral reality or event,' like a star formed billions of years ago, whose 'luminous emission,' the trace of its reality, 'informs us as to the date of its formation' (10). Yet speculation about the urn's inscrutably alien reality takes us, quite literally, out of thought to a time that had no regard *for* our thought, but which unavoidably arrests our regard.

Preoccupied with the human's traumatic break from nature, *Romanticism and Consciousness* suggested that consciousness can at some level heal this rift. Meillassoux would associate such hope with 'correlationism' – 'the idea according to which we only ever have access to the correlation between thinking and being, and never to either term considered apart from the other' (5). Correlationism entails the Kantian idealism that we can think the *Ding an sich* of being, but only from the perspective of thought. Wrestling thinking from being, however, demands that we think a being beyond our thought *of* being, on its own terms, as it were, which is to say prior to its own 'givenness.' As Meillassoux asks, *'how are we to conceive of the empirical sciences' capacity to yield knowledge of the ancestral realm?'* (25), which begs the answer of what new form consciousness might or need to take in order to circumvent any sense of its exclusive hold on nature and the world. I thus want to pose Meillassoux's question astride Lacan's *The Triumph of Religion*, the text of a 1974 interview Lacan gave at a press conference at the French Cultural Center in Rome. Triumph here has two meanings. One entails a dismissal of how religion triumphs by wresting control from the subject; the other, in a rather Blakean conversion, examines how the idea of religion serves as the *modus operandi* and structuring possibility of consciousness, what we might call, borrowing a phrase from Robert Miles, the 'inner stranger' of consciousness.

Lacan's interview begins by addressing the analyst's 'untenable position' (55)[6] which, like that of one who governs or educates, 'is precisely what everyone rushes toward' in order to avoid dealing with the real:

> The real is the difference between what works and what doesn't work. What works is the world. The real is what doesn't work. The world goes on, it goes round – that's its function as a world. To perceive that there is no such thing as a world – namely, that there are things that only imbeciles believe to be in the world – it suffices to note that there are things that make it such that the world [*monde*] is revolting [*immonde*], so to speak. This is what analysts deal with, such that, despite what one may think, they are confronted with the real far more than even scientists are. Analysts deal with nothing but that. They are forced to submit to it – that is, to brace themselves all the time. (61–2)

Lacan poses the dark irony of this confrontation with 'what doesn't work,' further embedded in the double play on 'revolting [*immonde*],' in terms of science's ability to 'create bacteria that would be resistant to everything, that would be unstoppable' (60). Science's 'true triumph' would be its capacity to 'clear the surface of the globe of all shitty things, human in particular, that inhabit it' (60). Except, as Lacan drops in almost as an aside, the 'animal world is indestructible' (60). The world would go on without us, short of the planet blowing up altogether (and even then, pending the indestructibility of all carbon life), so that science ends up reproducing the same anxiety it allays (the myth of Nietzsche's Socrates as the figure liberated from a fear of death). The same knowledge that makes the world 'work' for us in order to avoid anxiety needs anxiety as its very structuring possibility.[7]

The Real thus marks our virtual inability to take in, except as illusion, our experience of reality. As Žižek argues, the Real stands for 'a certain grimace of reality, a certain imperceptible, unfathomable, ultimately illusory feature that accounts for the absolute difference within identity' (*How to Read Lacan* 80). Leaving the illusion intact allows us to proceed with things as usual. But there is a further twist: the 'Real of the illusion itself' (81), which hides 'the remainder of [our] authenticity whose traces we can discern in an imperfect mechanical reproduction' (45). Žižek summarizes: 'the subject is something that "will have been" in its imperfect representation' (45). The Real is neither where we want to be (which entails the work of desire in the Imaginary) nor where we should be (which is how the Law calls us to being and order in the

Symbolic), neither of which is where we 'truly' are. Put starkly, the illusion *has* to exist as illusion in order to hide the brute reality of who we are, producing instead at once the specter and possibility of a subject who 'will have been.'[8] This is why, Lacan reminds us, religion trumps both science and psychoanalysis:

> We can't even begin to imagine how powerful religion is. [...] If science works at it, the real will expand and religion will thereby have still more reasons to soothe people's hearts. Science is new and it will introduce all kinds of distressing things into each person's life. Religion, above all true religion, is resourceful in ways we cannot even begin to suspect. One need but see for the time being how the place is crawling with it. It's absolutely fabulous. (*Triumph* 64)

Lacan morphs the ab-fab viral expansion of the Real by science into the notion of a 'place crawling with' religion. To this he adds, however, 'for the time being,' which begs the question of what humans will do when the proliferation of knowledge reproduces the terror of a Real that at once generates, justifies, and obliterates the proliferation. One is reminded of the clash between religion and science, faith and knowledge that culminates in Charles Darwin. Shelley's *Queen Mab* (1811) earlier evokes this conflict sensation as a text schizophrenically divided between skepticism and idealism, science and poetry, the symptom of which lack of resolution is a text bogged down by the empiricism of its notes, equal in length to the poem itself, not unlike the hybrid anatomy of Erasmus Darwin's *The Loves of the Plants*, Part Two of his 1791 *The Botanic Garden*.[9]

What differentiates psychoanalysis from science or religion is how it is tasked to deal with the symptom, 'which is not truly the real,' but is nonetheless 'the way the real manifests itself at our level as living beings' (*Triumph* 77). What is an obstacle for 'the scientific pathway' (77) on its road to the real, a sign of its avoidance of the very thing it would attain, is for psychoanalysis its *raison d'être*. For psychoanalysis, the symptom *is* the road to what Lacan calls the 'real real, as it were, the true real' (77). Put another way, we are far from, if ever, done with the symptom for – to reinvoke the 'Real of the illusion itself,' of a 'grimace' or shudder through which the Real announces itself – the symptom is *all we have*. This 'true real' is not Kantian transcendence, nor is it a numinous concept, although the symptom often embodies a numinosity we might, however unconsciously, ascribe to our experience of the true real. Rather, the 'true real' marks how we at once must and cannot ever deal with the Real. However, transcendence *is* what gives 'true religion' (by which Lacan means the 'Roman religion') the upper hand in 'drowning the symptom in meaning, in religious meaning naturally,' which is how 'people will manage to repress [the symptom]' (67). How 'true religion' addresses the Word beyond words, then, bears an uncanny relation to a psychoanalysis tasked to deal with the symptom's impossible access to the 'real.' God gave Adam the power to name things, which 'is altogether within human ken,' but not the Word itself, 'for that would have been too big a deal' (74). The Word structures how we exist in relation to the 'authenticity' of the Real of who we are as subjects but cannot bear to confront, not unlike Dionysus's searing gaze into the light in *The Birth of Tragedy*. Lacan is rather pithy on the matter: 'Human beings ask for nothing more than that the lights be turned down. Light in itself is absolutely unbearable' (74). In another uncanny twist, the Word, as in religion, *does* give life, less as a placeholder for the Real than as the symptom of why subjects, particularly in analysis, put things into words – for, as Lacan says, the Word 'brings *jouissance*' (75). Again, it structures our position as subjects in relation to the unavoidable, but ineluctable Other of our desire, and 'ultimate source' of our *jouissance*. And at the crux of this relation is the symptom that is the knot of our entanglement with, within, and against the Real.

Lacan's 'religion' thus gives us a version of consciousness and the subject that radicalizes Taylor's porous self. The question then becomes: how to enjoy the symptom that is all we have? Getting to this point takes ourselves out of the equation precisely in the way that the Symbolic order, as an exception to itself, interpellates us as subjects that are symptoms *of* this exception – once again, the subject as an exception to the Symbolic and as an exception to herself.[10] This brings me to Shelley's *Adonais*, a poem that confronts rather more than *in utero* the possibility of confronting the Real. *Adonais* rather gothically and ironically turns upon a compulsive return to what is essentially, and quite literally, a rotting corpse in the midst of its unfolding. The blank reality that is the dead Keats himself is the symptom *par excellence*: the absent cause of history read as a subject absent from the scene of their own being. We can locate this exception to the Symbolic order counterintuitively but powerfully in the poem's exquisitely formed Spenserian stanzas, each one an urn for the poet's burial, as if this 'highly-wrought piece of art' (Shelley, *Letters* 2:294) is speaking the Symbolic's exception to itself as the voice of religion's triumph. Gazing upon the oedipal scene of a poet triangulated between his muse/mother, Urania, and his father, Death (the ultimate Law and Name of the Father), Shelley wonders what his place in the poetic order of things among the 'sons of light' (36) might, should, or could be.[11] Accepting death is rather beside the point, which the frankness of the poem's opening line makes apparent: 'I weep for

Adonais – he is dead!' (1). When Urania enters Keats's death chamber, even Death, 'Shamed by the presence of that living Might / Blushed to annihilation' (218–20), so that the corpse's momentary revival becomes part of a larger fantasy structure, the illusion of which the poem will eventually break through. That is to say, the poem tarries with the intensely melancholic enjoyment of its symptoms, as if to work through to some sense of the stakes of the *jouissance* that sustains the poet's being as subject: the repeated outbursts of grief, or the 'quick Dreams, / The passion-winged Ministers of thought' (73–4) – 'All he had loved, and moulded into thought' (118) – which result from Urania's funeral march, 'like an autumnal Night' (199), to Keats's grave that is not yet a grave, 'Even as a ghost abandoning a bier, / Had left the Earth a corpse' (202–3).

Here Shelley witnesses the perverse nature of poetic desire: a mother/muse who, in the presence of death, attempts to revive her son, as if making love to him: '"Stay yet awhile! speak to me once again; / Kiss me, so long but as a kiss may live"' (226–7). Witnessing this primal scene of human thought and creativity – staging the symptom or fantasy structure of its reality – Shelley enters the poem himself as a 'frail Form, / A phantom among men' (271–2) who 'Had gazed on Nature's naked loveliness, / Actaeon-like, and now he fled astray' (275–6), pursued by his own thoughts, 'their father and their prey' (279):

> A pardlike Spirit beautiful and swift–
> A Love in desolation masked; – a Power
> Girt round with weakness; – it can scarce uplift
> The weight of the superincumbent hour;
> It is a dying lamp, a falling shower,
> A breaking billow; – even whilst we speak
> Is it not broken? (280–6)

At this moment we might say that Shelley goes from the illusion of being human to an awareness of the grimace of this illusion's Real, marked so powerfully by the caesura in the middle of line 285 – the awareness of his being a subject ('it') constituted by, and thus subject to, the Symbolic order from which he emerges. He is 'born darkly, fearfully' (492) through the mirror stage of human imagination to a locus where 'the One remains,' even as 'the many change and pass' (460), the place where 'The soul of Adonais, like a star, / Beacons from the abode where the Eternal are' (494–5). Earlier readings, like Earl Wasserman's paradigmatic accounts of the poem,[12] tempt us to see at this moment a Shelley who, torn between skepticism and idealism, the Real and the ideal, politics and poetry, chooses transcendence over mutability, eternal life over death, as if to invoke a Platonic or Neoplatonic possibility. That Shelley turns Keats into Adonais, as he turns himself into the automaton of his own poetry, however, signals a different awareness.

After this, in *The Triumph of Life*, Shelley will instead entertain a world in which 'thoughts which must remain untold' (21) become the structuring possibility of an encounter between a narrator as the uncanny subject of his own dream vision and Rousseau as 'an old root which grew / To strange distortion out of the hill side' (182–3). Such thoughts nonetheless attempt to make sense of the 'multitude' (49) or ineluctable march of life's history whose subjects are 'borne amid the crowd as through the sky / One of the million leaves of summer's bier' (50–1) in search of history's 'absent cause.' Here Shelley enters the strange logic of the dream as the reality we avoid when waking, what Žižek calls the '*hard kernel of the Real*':

> When we awaken into reality after a dream, we usually say to ourselves 'it was just a dream,' thereby blinding ourselves to the fact that in our everyday, wakening reality we are *nothing but a consciousness of this dream*. It was only in the dream that we approached the fantasy-framework which determines our activity, our mode of acting in reality itself. (*Sublime Object* 47)

At the center of this vision, as the blinding drive of desire itself – as if to mark the sheer movement of the drive – we have the 'shape all light' (352) that makes 'All that was seem[ ] as if it had been not' (385).[13] Here enlightenment is not *Aufklärung*, which is 'already a lot [...] already more than we can bear' (Lacan, *Triumph* 74), but rather a gesture toward 'the true real.' It is here, I would argue, that Romanticism pivots us toward a psychoanalysis that Lacan so powerfully gives us as the *pharmakon* of enlightenment. In this way, Shelley's last poem becomes a kind of prelude to *Écrits*, the point of which, Lacan pointedly states, is this: 'I did not write them in order for people to understand them, I wrote them in order for people to read them' (*Triumph* 69). Shelley's final poem exists to be read, not understood, the preparation for which is Shelley shattering 'Life' as a 'dome of many-coloured glass' that 'Stains the white radiance of Eternity, / Until Death tramples it to fragments' (462–4). Shelley implores his reader to 'Die, / If thou wouldst be with that which thou dost seek' (464–5), as 'if' to recognize that his desire has all along been Keats's desire, which was never Keats's to begin with. *Caveat lectorem*, or as neoconceptualist artist Jenny Holzer cautions, as if to blare out the banality of language whose naming shields us from the Word, 'Protect me from what I want.'

If we say that Romanticism 'invents' psychoanalysis, then, and in particular, as I suggest here, the *pharmakon* of analysis that is Lacan's return to Freud, we need to imagine how and when psychoanalysis emerged in Romanticism, not as origin but as primal scene or 'absent cause,' as a phenomenon that makes the thinking of beginnings and ends not only impossible but rather beside the point.[14] In 'From the History of an Infantile Neurosis' (1918), Freud hypothesized behind the Wolfman's dream an *anarche* of sexual trauma, conceding that this scene's empirical reality could be validated as a psychical event only after the fact. Whether the primal scene was repressed reality or phantasy, Freud could 'venture upon no decision' (17:97).[15] Moreover, the distinction was irrelevant. Or as Ned Lukacher, paraphrasing Althusser, adds: '[There] *is no subject to the primal scene; it is the primal scene itself which is a subject insofar as it does not have a subject*' (13–14). Such statements sent and still send hard-nosed empiricists into tailspins. For me, it re-poses Chalmers's point about the hard problem of consciousness. As Freud said, turning to Jung as they sailed into New York harbor en route to Clark University, where Freud would give five lectures, 'They don't realize we are bringing them the plague' (qtd in Jacoby). Psychoanalysis did not bring the plague of fantasies, although it has been debunked ever since for that reason; but it does, as I noted earlier, visit upon us the plague of how to decipher the fantasy structures by which we live. It is to this notion of psychoanalysis in Romanticism as a primal scene without a subject – a subject without a subject – that Shelley turns by turning from *Adonais* to his final poem, opening onto the Real in ways that de Man so powerfully explores in his reading of Shelley's manuscript.[16] In the transformation of poetic vision from Shelley's elegy on the death of Keats to his seemingly interminable analysis with Rousseau as a subject presumed to know[17] we sense the stakes of Lacan's psychoanalysis, which is to say the effect psychoanalysis has on the historical process from which it emerges. This 'entry' into history marks our impossible location within this process as a history always already beyond our grasp.

The Real of Faith

This shift marks a final kind of fulcrum upon which Romanticism pivots: the ineluctable and uncanny divide between belief and faith, encapsulated in Coleridge's famous statement. Coleridge seems haunted by Section X of Hume's *Enquiry Concerning Human Understanding*, 'Of Miracles,' which addresses the fundamental question of how belief sustains perception, especially at the limits of experience, where 'the truth of the *Christian* religion is less than the evidence for the truth of our senses' (73). For Hume, miracles evoke the 'passion of surprise and wonder' and 'give a sensible tendency towards the belief of those events,' but ultimately 'violat[e] [...] the laws of nature' because they work against the 'firm and unalterable experience [that] has established these laws' (78, 76, 76). Susceptible to the forgeries of human testimony, miracles, like prophecy, work by 'Faith, [...] which subverts all the principles of [...] understanding, and gives [...] a determination to believe what is most contrary to custom and experience' (90). Here Hume touches upon the unconscious of eighteenth-century empiricism, if not of perception itself. However reluctantly, he has to entertain the idea that a person's firm persuasion about things, which is what prompts Coleridge's definition in the first place, has to be considered as what Lacan will address as the symptom structure of our lives.

Put simply, belief is a form of knowing – 'I know that something exists' or 'I know that such a thing will happen.' Belief is easy, especially when buttressed by a system that guarantees the attainment of its object, which is where the clash of science and religion comes to a kind of crisis point in the Romantic period. Having faith goes like this: 'I believe such a thing exists or might happen whether I know it will or not, *even if I know it might not.*' In this definition faith seems to correspond to Lacan's imbeciles; yet even they speak to the symptom's fantasy structure as our way to endure reality. Belief depends upon the uncertainty of faith as much as the authority of faith – blindly accepting the apparent irrefutability of fact – sustains belief. Thus belief, which is a fundamental element of human being and knowing, fundamentally depends upon faith, which marks the rub of religion's survival.[18] This uncanny relationship speaks to Žižek's name for the strange logic by which we maintain the illusion of our autonomy and so short-circuit our authenticity: 'interpassivity.' In Western culture, recording television shows does our watching for us, or watching pornography does our fucking for us. Similarly, in some cultures prayer wheels do the work of believing or professional weepers do the work of mourning, a position that defines Shelley's position in relation to the dead Keats or the Narrator and Rousseau in relation to the march of history. In all cases, a Symbolic *manqué* stands in for the 'real' business of living, allowing us to get on with entertaining the perversity of our existence precisely through a prosthetic structure that allows us to avoid the perversity. As Žižek writes, 'We are ashamed of [our] shit because, in it, we expose/externalize our innermost intimacy' (*On Belief* 59). He continues: 'giving way to our innermost self is experienced by the subject as being colonized by some parasitic foreign intruder which takes possession of him against his will' (62). And yet such secreting is fundamentally constitutive of our being, as Julia Kristeva reminds us about the abject. Once we speak this secret – that subjectivity coheres precisely around what is abject within it that we maintain as abject, which is the rotting corpse in the middle of Shelley's elegy – we expose the fundamental rift within an otherwise careful facade. In Shelley's final poem Rousseau emerges from an 'old root,' never a fully formed subject but rather one disfigured by the march of history. This disfiguration intimates the shitty perversity that is our unavoidable, unbearable reality, which confrontation the poem faces (by not being able to face) with such powerfully moving intensity.

In Lacanian analysis the analysand presumes that the analyst 'knows his secret (which only means that the patient is a priori "guilty" of hiding a secret, that there is a secret meaning to be drawn from his acts)' (*How to Read Lacan* 28). Hence the analyst is not an 'empiricist, probing the patient with different hypotheses, searching for proofs' but rather 'embodies the absolute certainty [...] of the patient's unconscious desire' (28). The subject supposed to know, then, gives way to the more fundamental 'subject supposed to believe, which is the constitutive feature of the symbolic order' (29). (We can remind ourselves at this point that the noun form of fundamental, 'fundament,' is a euphemism for shit.) The secret's content is beside the point of how the symbolic order orchestrates our subjectivities around the secret's structuring possibility. The secret becomes the excuse for the subject's being, rather than the other way around. Maintaining the secret as secret means that its impossible knowledge allows us to get on with the business of living our lives. I would argue that if *Adonais* unmasks for us, like Toto pulling aside the curtain to reveal the Wizard's banality, how this secret has, well, secreted itself, *Triumph* hurls us into a locus where we enjoy the symptom *as* symptom. If the point of analysis, Žižek outlines, is to interpret symptoms in order to

> penetrate through them to the fundamental fantasy as the kernel of enjoyment which is blocking the further movement of interpretation; then we must accomplish a crucial step of going through the fantasy, of obtaining distance from it, of experiencing how the fantasy-formation just masks, fills out a certain void, lack, empty place in the Other. (*Sublime Object* 74)

But what if a 'key symptom still persists' (74) for the analysand, having gone through the fantasy? This symptom 'beyond fantasy' is what Lacan explores in Seminar XXIII as *le sinthome*, 'a certain signifying formation penetrated with enjoyment: it is a signifier as a bearer of *jouis-sense*, enjoyment-in-sense' (75).[19] And here we arrive at the 'radical ontological status of the symptom: symptom, conceived as *sinthome*, is literally our only substance, the only positive support of our being, the only point that gives consistency to the subject' (75). Previously conceived as a cryptic message from the unconscious that is potentially decipherable, the symptom as *sinthome* instead marks an impossible position between the need for decryption, a place where one accepts the impossibility of untying the Borromean knot that ties together the Symbolic, the Imaginary, and the Real, and the subject's pure *jouissance* as directed toward no object. I take this directionlessness to evoke the expansion of consciousness at the incompossible space between cognition and phenomenality. *Queen Mab* takes us beyond human perception to the cosmos; *Epipsychidion* or *Adonais* poises and suspends us at the limits of our supposed self-contained being; and the triumph of Shelley's final poem marches relentlessly and simultaneously away from and toward the absent cause of history.

Something of the *sinthome* informs, for instance, what Shelley was for his first readers, starting with Mary Shelley's editing of her husband's writings to render him fit for a future audience. Robert Browning famously said that Shelley, had he lived, would have 'ranged himself with the Christians' (1009). Asking rhetorically, 'should not a poet possess common sense?,' which apparently Shelley did not, Browning instead argues that Shelley's poetry constitutes a 'sublime fragmentary essay towards a presentment of the correspondency of the universe to Deity, of the natural to the spiritual, and of the actual to the ideal' (1012). And the final diagnosis:

> In forming a judgement, I would, however, press on the reader the simple justice of considering tenderly his constitution of body as well as mind, and how unfavourable it was to the steady symmetries of conventional life; the body, in the torture of incurable disease, refusing to give repose to the bewildered soul, tossing in its hot fever of the fancy – and the laudanum-bottle making but a perilous and pitiful truce between these two. He was constantly subject to 'that state of mind' (I quote his own note to 'Hellas') 'in which ideas may be supposed to assume the force of sensation, through the confusion of thought with the objects of thought, and excess of passion animating the creations of the imagination': in other words, he was liable to remarkable delusions and hallucinations. (1011)

Browning's essay, addressing its searing gaze of Victorian common sense against the theoretical speculation of Shelley's writing, has the withering yet ultimately rather banal capacity to drain his verse of its metaphorical vitality. For Shelley in his *Defence*, such vitality signaled how we might 'imagine that which we know' and 'purge[ ] from our inward sight the film of familiarity which obscures from us the wonder of our being'

(533), as if poetry has any 'necessary connexion to consciousness or will' (534). Consciousness, for Shelley, was an altogether different matter which, with the hindsight of fifty years since Bloom's volume, continues to cast a rather different shadow upon our sensate futurity. Recent advances in neuroscience, neurobiology, cognitive science, and cognitive linguistics lead a revolution challenging a Cartesian mind–body binary that continued to haunt our thinking on the matter. Advances in artificial intelligence and neurotechnology have further expanded our understanding of consciousness as the realm of posthuman and nonhuman entities (machines, computers, robots), whose capacity for predictive, anticipatory, even reflective cognition radically alters what it means to 'be conscious.' Rather ironically, Browning's charge of Shelley's drug-induced 'delusions and hallucinations' calls up Michael Pollan's recent account, in *How to Change Your Mind* (2018), of the new science of psychedelics. This science explores 'a universal desire to change consciousness' that not only offers 'tools for healing the mind, for facilitating rites of passage, and for serving as a medium for communicating with supernatural realms, or spirit worlds,' but ultimately 'to enrich the collective imagination– the culture– with the novel ideas and visions that a select few people bring back from wherever it is they go' (13). Here 'psychedelic,' from the Greek meaning 'mind manifesting,' taken in conjunction with the above advances in scientific and philosophical understanding, signals Shelley's sense of consciousness as neither idealistic nor illusory but something altogether different. The opium fantasias of De Quincey's *Suspiria de Profundis* (1845) offer a similarly radical alternative.

So, while we might read Browning's essay as a diagnosis of where the period could have ended up – the Victorians' version of conversion therapy for the Romantics – I am tempted at this moment to enjoy the diagnosis as symptom itself. Explored further in terms of how Lacan wrestles with the 'true religion,' I might wonder if Browning, quite by accident, suggests a different Shelley, one to be read less than understood. The dark Jesuitical interpretation of Pope Francis is telling us something rather different about what the 'Roman religion' might be telling us about the world. This is to contemplate what Shelley might have intuited in our ineluctable capacity to commit to an existence that was never in the first instance of our making, an existence that subtends the ancestrality of our being on its horizon. The Lacanianism of Shelley's *Adonais* and *The Triumph of Life* urges us ever closer toward what we might finally call the *sinthome* of Romanticism. By *this* account, Lacan asks us to consider how the subject, interpellated by the Symbolic order into which they are born, and thus already captured *in utero* and, perhaps most radically, anticipated in the past as a future always yet to come, is at the same time a subject of their own desire, which is not at all, at the same time, their desire. This is, I would argue, as close as Romanticism gets, and perhaps we get, not to desire, but to *jouissance*, which is to say to drive's pure nature. Put another way, in a nod to Lacan's original clinical report in the 1930s on the mirror stage, which is, like Freud's *Interpretation*, the ur-text (un)grounding all of Lacan's subsequent work, Shelley's move from *Adonais* to *Triumph* ushers Romanticism through its own mirror stage to the 'ancestral' place we have always been. It seems to me that Romantic criticism is only beginning to map this alien territory – the point being that it, like Borges's empire, resists all cartographies.

Notes

1. See Faflak, 'What's Love Got to Do with It?'
2. I am indebted here to Robert Miles's use of Taylor's designation in 'Romanticism, Enlightenment, and Mediation: The Case of the Inner Stranger.'
3. I say 'still' to suggest how Romanticism's 'invention' of psychoanalysis remains with us, how psychoanalysis itself – especially Lacan's return to Freud – expresses the psyche's always expectant afterlife. For some, Lacan's baroque theoretical hold on psychoanalysis marks its (arguably) irrefutable stranglehold on theory and modern culture: saying psychoanalysis does not matter, like saying Romanticism does not matter, means we are caught unknowingly – especially unknowingly – by its gaze. See Dufresne, esp. 17, 25, and 182.
4. Merging feminism and poststructuralism, and with a profound sense of bodies and affects, and thus the stakes of human survival, Julia Kristeva, returning to Lacan returning to Freud, speaks of a revolution in poetic language via the semiotic: an energy, at once physiological, libidinal, psychic, and linguistic, that at once generates, sustains, and disrupts the Symbolic. While the Symbolic depends upon the semiotic for its generative articulation, and while the semiotic thus marks a mode of potentiality that registers within the Symbolic as what Nancy calls the restlessness of the negative – once again, a moment of exception to the very rule the Symbolic instantiates – the rule of the Symbolic still prevails, but once again, as an exception to itself. Like hegemony, the Symbolic is an unstable order that insists upon – repeats – itself precisely in order to constitute itself. Paradoxically, its constitution depends upon its instability. And the place where this instability materializes itself is precisely where the subject 'appears.' The subject *is* the Symbolic's exception, as we shall see. See Kristeva, *Revolution in Poetic Language*.
5. See, for instance, Morton, *Hyperobjects: Philosophy and Ecology after the End of the World* and *The Ecological Thought*. My thinking on

speculative realism is indebted to Chris Washington's 'Romanticism and Speculative Realism.' See also Washington and McCarthy's *Romanticism and Speculative Realism.*

6. I thank Allan Pero for bringing this brief but powerful text to my attention.
7. In making the above comments, Lacan refers to his 1962–3 Seminar X on anxiety, the last of his Seminars at St Anne's Hospital.
8. I take this to be Lacan's point that any confrontation with the unconscious is necessarily a missed encounter. Were we able to see reality directly rather than darkly, the unconscious would be a moot point.
9. See Porter.
10. I leave aside the impossible question of whether or not psychoanalysis might end as the end result of this dilemma, for it seems that, for Lacan, posing the question, not answering it, is the issue. Lacan says the analyst will always remain merely a 'symptom,' such that 'humanity will be cured of psychoanalysis' (*Triumph* 67). Psychoanalysis, that is to say, emerges at a specific historical moment, 'as if' (to cite Cavell again) it becomes 'called for in the history of knowledge,' a moment that eventually, Lacan intimates, will pass, after which we will have no further use for psychoanalysis.
11. All references to Shelley's writings are taken from Reiman and Fraistat's *Shelley's Poetry and Prose,* cited hereafter by line number for poetry and page number for prose.
12. See Wasserman, '*Adonais*: Progressive Revelation as a Poetic Mode.' Wasserman reprises readings of the poem in *The Subtler Language: Critical Readings of Neoclassical and Romantic Poems* and most monumentally in *Shelley: A Critical Reading.* It occurs to me that how Wasserman tarries with the poem, despite his implicit insistence on 'critical' distance from it, is not unlike Shelley's or Urania's obsession with the dead Keats.
13. I take up the poem's tension between drive and desire in 'Dancing in the Dark with Shelley.'
14. This is one of my key points in laying out my central argument in *Romantic Psychoanalysis.*
15. Earlier, in 'On the History of the Psycho-Analytic Movement' (1914), Freud writes: 'If hysterical subjects trace back their symptoms to traumas that are fictitious, then the new fact which emerges is precisely that they create such scenes in *phantasy*, and this psychical reality requires to be taken into account alongside practical reality' (14:17). Ned Lukacher defines the primal scene as always already a scene of analysis, an 'ontologically undecidable intertextual event that is situated in the differential space between historical memory and imaginative construction, between archival verification and interpretive free play' (24).
16. See de Man, 'Shelley Disfigured.'
17. I take up the poem as an analytic encounter that at once liberates and entraps its subjects in 'The Difficult Education of Shelley's *The Triumph of Life.*'
18. I take up this issue at greater length in 'Beyond Belief/Having Faith.'
19. On the nature of Romantic *jouissance*, see Sigler and Sha.

References

Browning, Robert. 'Essay on Shelley.' *The Poems*. Vol. I. Ed. John Pettigrew. Supp. and comp. Thomas J. Collins. New York: Penguin, 1981. 1001–11.

Cavell, Stanley. 'Freud and Philosophy: A Fragment.' *Critical Inquiry* 13 (1987): 186–93.

Chalmers, David. *The Conscious Mind: In Search of a Fundamental Theory*. New York: Oxford University Press, 1996.

Coleridge, Samuel Taylor. *Biographia Literaria*. Ed. James Engell and W. Jackson Bate. Princeton: Princeton University Press, 1983.

De Man, Paul. 'Shelley Disfigured.' *The Rhetoric of Romanticism*. New York: Columbia University Press, 1984. 93–123.

Derrida, Jacques. *Resistances of Psychoanalysis*. Trans. Peggy Kamuf, Pascale-Anne Brault and Michael Nass. Stanford, CA: Stanford University Press, 1998.

Dufresne, Todd. *Tales from the Freudian Crypt: The Death Drive in Text and Context*. Stanford: Stanford University Press, 2002.

Faflak, Joel. 'Beyond Belief/Having Faith.' *Revelation and Knowledge: Romanticism and Religious Faith*. By Ross Woodman, with Joel Faflak. Toronto: University of Toronto Press, 2011. xiii–xlix.

—. 'Dancing in the Dark with Shelley.' *Constellations of a Contemporary Romanticism*. Ed. Jacques Khalip and Forest Pyle. New York: Fordham University Press, 2016. 166–85.

—. 'The Difficult Education of Shelley's *The Triumph of Life*.' *Keats–Shelley Journal* 58 (2009): 53–78.

—. *Romantic Psychoanalysis: The Burden of the Mystery*. Albany, NY: State University of New York Press, 2007.

—. 'What's Love Got to Do with It? *Frankenstein* and Monstrous Psychoanalysis.' *Frankenstein in Theory: A Critical Anatomy*. Ed. Orrin C. Wang. New York: Bloomsbury, 2021. 85–100.

Freud, Sigmund. 'From the History of an Infantile Neurosis' (1918). Vol. 17. *The Standard Edition of the Complete Psychological Works of Sigmund Freud*. 3–122.

—. 'On the History of the Psycho-Analytic Movement.' 1914. Vol. 14. *The Standard Edition of the Complete Psychological Works of Sigmund Freud*. 24 vols. Trans. and ed. James Strachey. New York: Vintage, 2001. 3–66.

Garofalo, Daniela and David Sigler, eds. *Lacan and Romanticism*. Albany, NY: State University of New York Press, 2019.

Hume, David. *An Enquiry Concerning Human Understanding*. Ed. Eric Steinberg. 2nd ed. Indianapolis: Hackett, 1993.

Jacoby, Russell. 'When Freud Came to America.' *The Journal of Higher Education* 21 (September 2009). http://www.chronicle.com/article/Freuds-Visit-to-Clark-U/48424 (last accessed December 2, 2021).

Jameson, Fredric. *The Political Unconscious: Narrative as a Socially Symbolic Act*. Ithaca, NY: Cornell UP, 1981.

Keats, John. *Letters of John Keats*. Ed. Robert Gittings. Oxford: Oxford University Press, 1977.

Kristeva, Julia. *Revolution in Poetic Language*. Trans. Margaret Waller. New York: Columbia University Press, 1984.

Lacan, Jacques. *The Triumph of Religion*. The Triumph of Religion *Preceded by Discourse to Catholics*. Trans. Bruce Fink. Cambridge: Polity, 2013. 55–85.

Lukacher, Ned. *Primal Scenes: Literature, Philosophy, Psychoanalysis*. Ithaca, NY: Cornell University Press, 1986.

Meillassoux, Quentin. *After Finitude: An Essay on the Necessity of Contingency*. Trans. Ray Brassier. London: Continuum, 2008.

Miles, Robert. 'Romanticism, Enlightenment, and Mediation: The Case of the Inner Stranger.' *This is Enlightenment*. Ed. Clifford Siskin and William Warner. Chicago: University of Chicago Press, 2010. 173–88.

Morton, Timothy. *The Ecological Thought*. Cambridge, MA: Harvard University Press, 2012.

—. *Hyperobjects: Philosophy and Ecology after the End of the World*. Minneapolis: University of Minnesota Press, 2013.

Nancy, Jean-Luc. *Hegel: The Restlessness of the Negative*, trans. Jason Smith and Steven Miller, Minneapolis: University of Minnesota Press, 2002.

Phillips, Adam. *Becoming Freud: The Making of a Psychoanalyst*. New Haven, CT: Yale University Press, 2014.

Pollan, Michael. *How to Change Your Mind: What the New Science of Psychedelics Teaches Us About Consciousness, Dying, Addiction, Depression, and Transcendence*. Harmondsworth: Penguin Press, 2009.

Porter, Dahlia. 'Scientific Analogy and Literary Taxonomy in Darwin's Loves of the Plants.' *European Romantic Review* 18.2 (April 2007): 213–21.

Rajan, Tilottama. *Dark Interpreter: The Discourse of Romanticism*. Ithaca, NY: Cornell University Press, 1980.

Schopenhauer, Arthur. *The World as Will and Representation*. 2 vols. Trans. E. F. J. Payne. LaSalle, IL: Open Court, 1974.

Sha, Richard C. *Perverse Romanticism: Aesthetics and Sexuality in Britain, 1750–1832*. Baltimore: Johns Hopkins University Press, 2009.

Shamdasani, Sonu and Michael Münchow, eds. *Speculations After Freud: Psychoanalysis, Psychology, and Culture*. London: Routledge, 1994.

Shelley, Percy Bysshe. *The Letters of Percy Bysshe Shelley*. 2 vols. Ed. Frederick L. Jones. Oxford: Clarendon Press, 1964.

—. *Shelley's Poetry and Prose*. 2nd ed. Ed. Donald H. Reiman and Neil Fraistat. New York: W. W. Norton, 2002.

Sigler, David. *Sexual Enjoyment in British Romanticism: Gender and Psychoanalysis, 1753–1835*. Montreal and Kingston: McGill-Queen's University Press, 2015.

Taylor, Charles. *A Secular Age*. Cambridge, MA: The Belknap Press of Harvard University Press, 2007.

Washington, Chris. 'Romanticism and Speculative Realism.' *Literature Compass* 12.9 (September 2015): 448–60.

Washington, Chris and Anne C. McCarthy, eds. *Romanticism and Speculative Realism*. New York: Bloomsbury Academic, 2019.

Wasserman, Earl. '*Adonais*: Progressive Revelation as a Poetic Mode.' *ELH* 21.4 (1954): 274–326.

—. *Shelley: A Critical Reading*. Baltimore: Johns Hopkins University Press, 1971.

—. *The Subtler Language: Critical Readings of Neoclassical and Romantic Poems*. Baltimore: Johns Hopkins University Press, 1959.
Žižek, Slavoj. *How to Read Lacan*. London: Granta Books, 2006.
—. *On Belief*. London: Routledge, 2001.
—. *The Sublime Object of Ideology*. New York: Verso, 1989.

Chapter 5

Blakean Experience and the Hard Problem of Consciousness Revisited

Richard C. Sha

What does Blake mean by 'experience?' Since a prevailing definitive feature of consciousness is experience, I posit an answer by situating his *Songs of Innocence and of Experience* between Bloom and company's version of Romantic consciousness, and current approaches to consciousness.[1] Together, the models span the gamut of possible relations between mind and world, and thus offer useful frames for thinking about Blakean experience. Briefly, whereas Bloom et al. took for granted human consciousness's divorce from nature and likely alienation from the world, today, ecological approaches to consciousness situate it within a necessary relationality to that world that amounts to a cognitive partnership with the environment and others. What was an abyss between nature and consciousness, is now an ecology, and what is striking beyond the conceptual whiplash is the fact that what was absence is now the constitutive presence that is our cognitive system.[2] The declining fortunes of the subject and of individuality have increased our faith in relationality and ecology, but has the pendulum swung too far? In the *Songs*, Blake explores through innatism and panpsychism the shifting boundary between mind and world that is entailed in experience, and in the process teaches us about the limits of porousness and relationality. Since both consciousness and ideology – what Blake refers to as 'mind-forged manacles' – have a stream-like immersive feel, Blake warns that the porousness of consciousness cannot be a necessary good. He thus turns to a range of prepositions to question the givenness of one's relationality towards the world.

For Bloom and company, Romantic consciousness became a hard problem insofar as it entails an estrangement from nature, mandating a new, iconoclastic map of the mind (Bloom 3, 147). In this view, the imagination can 'sustain its own integrity' or yield to 'the illusive beauty of nature' (5). Any autonomy purchased by this version of consciousness was at the cost of the social self (6), and underscored both the precarity and the achievement of Romantic art. For de Man, 'nostalgia' was the only bridge between Romantic nature and consciousness, a pathological fusion of matter and imagination that cedes consciousness 'to the realities of the object' (70). The object 'marks instead a possibility for consciousness to exist entirely by and for itself, independently of all relationship with the outside world, without being moved by an intent aimed at a part of this world' (76–7). Hartman depicted the Romantic vision of a 'mind that knows itself almost without exterior cause or else as no less real, here, no less indestructible than the object of its perceptions' (290). For our purposes here, one idealism – the mental foundation of reality within an individual – is replaced by another, human consciousness as alienated language.

Today, consciousness is literally shaped by theories of embodied or enactive cognition.[3] Embodied and enactive theories cleave to the idea that states of the body shape states of mind, that cognition is connectionist. Buttressed by growing recognition of the crosstalk between our visual and motor brain pathways, and the idea that perception might be for the purpose of action, these new theories of consciousness situate it firmly within the world, insisting that the relationality between mind and world fosters perception–action couplings that not only are themselves the very site of consciousness, but also bring mind and world into simultaneous being. Enactive theories recognize that perception and action are not necessarily separate acts. They further admirably question the degree to which previous theories glorified the human at the expense of animal, plant, and even cellular or atomic consciousness, and the degree to which cognitive systems are spread into the world.

But perhaps they go too far. In the embodied view, the body circumvents the need for complex internal mental representation – Francisco Varela, Evan Thompson, and Eleanor Rosch bid adieu to complex mental symbols (98–100) – and we are in necessary touch with the world. The current simultaneous enactive reduction of consciousness to autopoiesis and spread of the scale of consciousness – its necessary embeddedness within its surround – has made consciousness no longer the prerogative of the human (a good thing), and to the extent that consciousness is a kind of autopoiesis, which locates the identity of the living system in the very processes of survival (Levinson 83), then it is widespread. But note that while autopoiesis simplifies consciousness, it has become the activity of a system and not so much an individual experience; left behind is much of what it feels like to have this activity.[4] And note how, in this view embodiment, has shifted from an epistemological problem – the Kantian idea that our perceptual systems condition how we know – to the very engine of consciousness insofar as thinking has become doing and our immersion in our surround is what generates consciousness.[5]

While older models of consciousness certainly underestimated the mind's relation to the world, to what degree is our consciousness necessarily tied to the world, and what price is paid for this embeddedness? Alva Noë, a prominent enactivist, stipulates the 'environmentally imbedded unity' of organisms, and makes the problem of consciousness, the problem of life (41), thereby spreading the hard problem.[6] The spread potentially includes 'non-evolved physical systems previously assumed to be mindless' (Koch 155). In the rush to lower the stakes of consciousness, and to de-emphasize the feel of what it is like to perform actions or the first-person account of them because what this feels like is very difficult for science to account for, some enactive thinkers make consciousness inclusive and necessarily of the world.[7] Shaun Gallagher, for instance, submits that, under enaction, intentionality has become 'operative intentionality,' which he defines as being 'intrinsic to movement; it is in one's action, in one's environmentally attuned responses' (80). 'Operative intentionality' shifts an otherwise distant mental state into a visible action in the form of movement, granting the human subject environmental attunement. This move towards enaction diminishes phenomenality insofar as consciousness is thus impoverished by a behavioralist frame, orienting it towards movement, even as it replaces the need for narration with cognitive assemblies, and subjectivity itself with attunement. The egological (Butler 10) has become the ecological. Jonathan Kramnick concludes: 'experience becomes something one does [an action], as opposed to something one has [a collection of objects, or representations of objects]' (131).

By converting consciousness into an action, theories of embodied and enactive consciousness wish away the possibility of abstraction and idealism under cover of ecology, and with them, the dark sides of autonomy: solipsism and narcissism.[8] This attunement to environment is rarely optional. Missing here is a kind of sustained engagement over time, like Wordsworth's returns to Tintern Abbey, not to mention the very possibility of nostalgia or the complexities of moral reflection.[9] The view is behavioralist, a kind of phenomenality lite, because the rich terrain of the subjective has been replaced with behaviors and affordances. Indeed, Varela, Thompson, and Rosch welcome a return to a 'behavioralist orientation' (92). However embedded within the environment consciousness is, I question both the necessary openness of 'mind' to world, and the assumption that this porousness must be a good thing.[10] Moreover, necessary openness to the world puts too much faith in porousness, and perhaps mistakes porousness to information as porousness to meaning. It disallows the possibility that sympathy works through the bracketing of one's own feelings, a kind of disembodiment – as well as embodiment (Chandler 272); yet without disembodiment the other is never truly other, and sympathy risks projection. Martin Jay submits that the very tension between subject and object endemic to accounts of experience can be harnessed to enable an encounter with otherness, along with moments of passivity within experience (221). And since embodied cognition in this view removes the very particularity of bodies – marks of gender, race, class, sexuality – it does not consider how some bodies might have more access to these interactions over others. Finally, although dualism may be a fiction, it is a useful fiction. Body versus mind stipulates two levels of thought, and emplots cognitive development by providing stages for it. Without dualism, can we even emplot cognitive development?

Hence if enactivism heals the Cartesian separation of mind and body and mind and world insofar as both object and subject are replaced by a verb, this healing comes, at least in theory, at the considerable costs of denying the value of abstraction (and distance), and irony along with the value of the subjective feel of experience: in short, idealism and narration. In the process, one idealism – the Bloomian human possession of an albeit alienated consciousness that is eventually subsumed by (human) language, the *wording* of consciousness – has been replaced by another idealism – the *worlding* of consciousness, even as idealism has come to seem bankrupt. Under Bloom et al. idealism was already nostalgia. One advantage of making consciousness a verb instead of an object is that it seems less possessable, and action replaces both the representational work of language along with the constitutive power of ideas over our conceptions of reality. I harp upon the idealism entailed in both sides because enaction makes idealism pathological or impossible – the immediacy of the interaction between mind and world replaces a reflexive model of mind – because the ecology it advocates has become its central activity. Such immediacy and enaction is guaranteed, moreover, by an ideal grammar that has transformed objects into verbs, thereby moving us closer to the posthuman while preserving the kind of autonomy that perseveres through action. As we shall see, for Blake, passionate action is most often a cry for help, and a denial of vulnerability.

Blake and the Hard Problem of Experience

According to David Chalmers, the hard problem of consciousness is the problem of experience:[11] how to explain how physical brain processes get us to experience, which has a qualitative dimension. Functionalism in this view offers no help, as the function of consciousness in the form of first-person awareness would seem to be beside the point. The standard retort here is why should anything have a consciousness at all? Chalmers himself insists upon a separation of phenomenal experience from causality: 'why the causal role [of experience] is played and why the phenomenal quality is present are two entirely different questions' (15), but is there no possible shared ground? The solutions to the hard problem include panpsychism, reductionism, and dualism, and more recently, enactivism. According to panpsychism, which the Romantics flirted with, if everything is in some time-scale conscious, then consciousness has become a universal. According to reductionism, consciousness is the product of nervous mechanisms of some kind, and some go so far as to claim consciousness to be an epiphenomenon. And according to dualism, there are mental things and physical things. Spinoza's retort would be that the mental and physical are simply two ways of looking at the conatus or striving of the thing. The idea encapsulated in enactive theories is that because consciousness exploits the body, it thus entails a necessary relationality to the world, an enactive ecology. In this view, 'sensory–motor contingencies and environmental affordances take over the work that had been attributed to neural computations and mental representations' (Gallagher 7). Just how necessary that relationality is, is open to debate. Chalmers himself argues for panpsychism, on the grounds that a universal consciousness will enable science to have purchase on it. In Romanticism, the fact that scientific experiment and experience were not so far apart as they are now perhaps provides resources to consider, especially since so much of the current debate about consciousness has to do with how science can study it.

Unsurprisingly, Blake takes different routes through the hard problem of consciousness and he does so by tackling the meaning of 'experience,' along with the subjective feel of it. In *Songs of Innocence and of Experience*, Blake asks not only why we have experiences at all, but also under what circumstances can experience ground knowledge. What, if anything, does experience empower us to do? Writing at a time when, according to Martin Jay, experience narrowed from the full body to the five senses (42), Blake resists such confinement.[12] Contrary to the empiricism of Locke and Hume, Blake insists that conventional experience cannot be the driver of epistemology, writing in *The Marriage of Heaven and Hell* 'what is now proved was once, only imagined' (8; E36).[13] Blake highlights the belatedness of proof because it merely confirms what the imagination made possible to begin with. By framing the proof of experience retroactively, Blake makes revelation the cause of epistemology and minimizes the role of proof. Blake thus wrests experience from the deadly grip of empiricism, making the conventional empiricist account a posthumous version of experience, a fallenness ('Introduction' to *Songs of Experience*), and the effect of society and culture instead of its origin.[14] Hence his frontispiece to *Songs of Experience* frames experience as a kind of mourning, and indeed this loss may entail a poetic loss figured in the stereotyped letters that announce EXPERIENCE. That Los is his figure for the poet hints that the loss that comes with experience is not without recompense. And hence in the 'Introduction' to *Songs of Innocence*, Blake insists that the water must be stained in order to achieve clarity, implying of course that even the origin is already stained, and that the stain itself is not necessarily evil, especially since without it there would be only translucence and no image. Blake, then, is with Kant, when Kant argues that although our cognition starts with experience, it does not arise from it (45), and that cognitions arise through the intuitions made possible by imagination.

There is more. Eighteenth-century moral psychology boiled human feeling down to pleasure or pain, and motivation thereby acquires the possibility of an on-and-off switch and of being translated into a simple binary. Blake's agitation resists pain or pleasure, signaling an unease that is in between (Goldsmith). To that end, innocence is unexpectedly littered with anxiety: beguiling, bearing, despair, weeping, lostness, loneliness and envy. Even in innocence, Blake's palette of emotional and anxious states is rich and burdened with negativity, suggesting that first-person accounts of motivation and unease cannot be dispensed with, and that eighteenth-century moral psychology is really an ideology when these states of agitation do not count.[15]

Aesthetically, Blake further complicates experience by unbinding *pictura* from *poiesis*. What W. J. T. Mitchell referred to as Blake's composite art, becomes in this view a peeling back of the layers of consciousness to show how the sausage is made, how experience acquires the illusion of being a unified field. (We refer to this today as binding.) Where Locke understood perception to be awareness (Yolton 55), Blake highlights the gaps between perception and awareness that make the potential costs of experience as unity visible. Here I disagree with Nicholas Williams, who helpfully links ideology and utopia in Blake, but then insists that ideology entails contradiction while utopia delivers unity. For Williams, the unity of utopia is the backdrop against which one sees the fissures of ideology, but Blake understands ideology sometimes to present as unity. When Blake's images and words refuse alignment, the very nature of perception is at issue, and the degree of activeness within perception also becomes part of the debate. Only active perception reveals contraries: the kind of split screen Blake delineates in many of his title pages demands such activeness.

In this way, perception and awareness move from being the given to show the mediatedness of the given, and consequently lived experience must earn its authenticity instead of presuming it. This presumption of mediatedness of the given is what enables distancing from ideology, along with the possibility of empiricism as an ideology. It is also what enables any relationality to mobilize transference. In psychoanalysis, transference refers to the unconscious projection of feelings onto one's analyst, which leads to counter-transference. The issue becomes how to treat any new relation within terms of its own particularity. In 'On Another's Sorrow,' Blake questions the necessary good behind relationality by showing sympathy to be a form of transference. I feel what I think you feel, but how do I know my feelings are not just transference? Blake sums up by insisting 'Till our grief is fled & gone / He doth sit by us and moan' (17:35–6; E17). On the one hand, Blake wrote in his annotations to Berkeley, 'Jesus considerd Imagination to be the Real Man & says I will not leave you Orphanned and I will manifest myself to you' (E663), and thus Jesus's presence counts for something. On the other hand, that Jesus moans with us changes or accomplishes what, exactly? Tellingly, the fact that Jesus sits *by* us prevents the 'our' pronoun from bridging the gap between our and He, transforming physical proximity into distance. In the process, sympathy has become an undecidable transference and a kind of mimicry, hardly the kind of relationality to warrant any kind of ethical gold star.

We see Blake's distrust of coherence and unity most clearly in 'The Chimney Sweeper' of Innocence. Tom Dacre is told that if he does his duty, 'He'd have God for his father & never want joy' (12:20; E10). Tom, whose own father sold him, is manipulated into this view, and returns to his dangerous work, 'happy & warm' (12:23; E10). The work of religious ideology here is to make coherent Tom and the world that oppresses him, even as his very name marks his status as commodity. According to the *OED*, 'Dacre' is related to dicker, a unit of ten hides. By making unity a problem, Blake demands the ability to distance oneself from unity, so that its mediations and reasons for mediation become visible. Visually, Blake makes this unity a problem, by depicting the chimney sweeps being crushed by the poem. Tom may feel happy and warm, but he has no real reason to do so, since doing the duty of the sweeper absolutely places him in harm's way. Formally, Blake advances his argument in the 'Holy Thursday' of Innocence by changing the equipoise of the couplet from a Popean defense of rationality into the mere appearance of order: as the children march two by two, so do

Blake's couplets, but as the lines describe the thousands of raised hands and 'harmonious thunderings' (19:10; E13) the couplet form and human sensation have been overwhelmed by a mathematical sublime. Crucially, Blake slowly introduces eye rhymes that demand what initially counts as awareness to become an appearance. 'O what a multitude they seemd these flowers of London town / Seated in companies they sit with radiance all their own,' Blake writes (19:5–6; E13). Town looks like but does not rhyme with own, introducing the possibility that the given is an appearance. Of course, 'seemd' is in the past tense, implying that they no longer seem so. It is also hard to reconcile the children's ownership with the radiance, given the poem's insistence on multitudes and group think. That radiance is perhaps the only thing that these orphans could own reminds us again that cognitive embeddedness may be a privilege.

Blakean experience, I argue, lies somewhere in between Bloom's and today's models of consciousness: between word/representation and world, object and action, and pleasure and pain.[16] To the extent that both sides rely upon idealism, the separability of mind and world and representation do not have to be the enemy, and the task at hand is to remind us that this separation can be a cognitive resource. In making ecology the law of consciousness, current approaches rely upon distance, but this distance is not seen as a form of distancing, and that is because consciousness now ecologizes itself into necessary mind and world couplings. That enactive consciousness transpires under cover of what is really a theory of embodiment in which embodiment is always both a verb and a relationality that preserves the status quo heightens the irony. Enaction seizes upon particular examples of, say, sensory–motor interactions or subcortical affects as illustrative of consciousness writ large.[17] But what about cognitions and consciousness that have nothing to do with movement, and what about what used to be known as higher cognition?

Blake's *Songs* trouble both approaches to consciousness by asking: how far does experience leach into the surround?[18] When Blake claims in *The Marriage of Heaven and Hell* that 'Man has no Body distinct from his Soul' (4; E34) he seems like a proto-enactivist, or at very least a proponent of embodied cognition, but he also claims à la Bloom that 'where Man is not, nature is barren' (10; E38). Because Blake equated nature with a vegetative state, he was wary of any synthesis between people and environment. Blake's concepts of self and self-annihilation, which require conscious effort, moreover, support the self as a moving boundary but reject the allure of total porousness, since even in self-annihilation, there must be a self to annihilate. Because 'mind-forg'd manacles' show Blake understanding how ideology provides what seems like a natural stream of consciousness, but one whose unity is suspect, he highlights what is lost when intentionality becomes intentionality light, a Urizenic behavioralism that amounts to a drive. Blake's boundary between consciousness and the world is not totally porous, and thus serves as a prompt for thinking about the dangers of this porousness. As Gallagher's 'operationalized intentionality' suggests, enactivism substantially cedes the ability to control the traffic between mind and world to an embodiment that is bereft of higher cognition and what Locke considered reflection.[19]

Judith Butler helps us tabulate these costs by reminding us that the ecological papers over a destructive relationality: since systematic racism (then and now) structures relationality,

> relationality is not by itself a good thing, a sign of connectedness, an ethical norm to be posited over and against destruction: rather relationality is a vexed and ambivalent field in which the question of ethical obligation has to be worked out in light of a persistent and constitutive destructive potential. (10)[20]

Nor is an ecology devoid of built-in hierarchies. Insofar as one of its goals is to widen the tent of consciousness to include all living things, enactive theories share a posthuman agenda, one that Ruha Benjamin warns 'assumes that we have all had a chance to be human' (32) and that foundational societal structures are neutral rather than racist (Chapter 2). Simply put, when relationality and ecology are ethical norms, one loses the incentive to evaluate the quality and conditions of that relationality. Orc, thus, can only promise revolution to the extent that his version of relationality marks an improvement over Urizen's, and Blake's insistent doubling of Urizen/Orc asks the degree to which the promise has yet to be imagined.

Blake also wonders about the extent to which action has the power to shed light on consciousness, and the degree to which relationality must be a necessary good. What Northrop Frye labelled as Blake's plotlessness (121) puts a useful spin on this question, for if there is action in the poet's works, it often does not propel the narrative forward but rather signifies a kind of rut. Furious action in Blake is often denial, suppression, obsession, violent domination. Frye suggests instead a 'unity of energy and consciousness' in Blake (132), but where today's enactive theorists orient energy into action, because action alleges survival, Blake promises only agitation and action that resist any forward plot momentum.

Steve Goldsmith highlights Blake's Kantian non-participatory but vital enthusiasm as a way of reflecting upon the degree of critical agency within emotion. Insofar as agitation resists action in Blake, it offers an important corrective to enactive theories of consciousness. In insisting upon agitation, Goldsmith's Blake only guarantees the capacity for movement. Couple this insight with Chandler's observation that Blake mines lyric compression for syntactic turns and transformations, whereby objects become verbs, and we see how consciousness, for Blake, transforms images into a capacious grammar for manipulation, but it can do so only by not abandoning objects and representational images, not to mention the feel of experience, and the fact that it can mislead. I here build upon Butler, to argue that Blake insists that relationality is not a necessary good, but rather involves a field of relations that can work for good or ill. Blake's agitation thus neither presupposes any single ethical trajectory, nor assumes any single course of action. Against autopoiesis, Blake's agitation thereby becomes a form of activity under which homeostasis is the start of something, not its end, and action entails the possibility of objectification.

In 'Little Black Boy,' we witness the boy's mother educating him in the meaning of blackness. When 'blackness' begins as a kind of bereftness – 'bereav'd of light' (9:4; E9) – it cannot signify on its own terms, and the best the mother can do is to shift its meaning to an ability to bear. Though the shift merely exchanges one justification for racism and slavery for another – bereftness signifies irredeemability, where blackness as an ability to bear God's light and heat invites even more burden – blackness at least acquires a shade of positivity, and this positivity is what enables the boy to embrace this definition. In the final stanza, the boy comments:

> Ill shade him from the heat until he can bear,
> To lean in joy upon our fathers knee.
> And then I'll stand and stroke his silver hair,
> And be like him and he will then love me. (10:25–8; E9)

The boy adopts his mother's definition of blackness as an ability to bear, which enables him to embrace his shade-providing role. After all, he contentedly stands and strokes the white boy's hair, even taking on the 'our' pronoun, notwithstanding his own submission and the fact that the white boy's burden, to learn how to lean, requires significantly less subservience. Here, unity is the outcome of ideology – his subordination – and there is no evidence that the boy sees the irony of the final line's stipulation of Christ's conditional love. Although the boy is determined to 'be like' Christ, race is still an obstacle to united being, as unity and societal relationality are themselves predicated upon a racialized hierarchy. Blake's infinitive verbs, moreover, remind us of the perpetuity of that hierarchy.

In Blake's illustrations, the little black boy sometimes appears black, other times white, still other times shadow – and in this way blackness becomes part of the language of chiaroscuro, the very light and shade which is the ground of an engraving's meaning. In this way, Blake unleashes a plot against a plot, as blackness as line and intellect counters blackness as bereftness.[21] Blake's unbinding of experience through the multiplicity of meanings for blackness thus returns us to the problem of the given, and the ways in which on the one hand ideology makes it possible to inhabit a world that oppresses by managing contradiction. On the other hand, since blackness means no one thing, it has become, as Fred Moten sees it, a blur, and the poet's exploitation of its competing meanings reminds us that the given must include the cultural work of mediation and the ways in which racialized bodies mean. Experience thus can be seen as a form that shapes content instead of being shaped by it. Such a distinction between consciousness and immediate awareness does not limit consciousness to what is before it. Experience here is necessarily metonymic of a larger awareness, a frame, and that larger scale thereby makes a space for the revised salience and meaning of the current experience.[22] Embodiedness therefore does not heal the Cartesian gap between mind and body because any particular experience of it is metonymic and cannot stand in for the whole.[23] To wit, racial and class embodiment alienates, as opposed to immerses, the subject within her surround.

Being poor does not bode well for an embedded consciousness either. The little vagabond of Experience, for example, in his opening stanza, recognizes two pictures of his reality, and he juxtaposes one to the other:

> Dear Mother, dear Mother, the church is cold.
> But the Ale-house is healthy & pleasant & warm:
> Besides I can tell where I am use'd well.
> Such usage in heaven will never do well. (45:1–4; E26)

The preposition 'besides' indicates the child's parallel views of the cold church and warm ale-house, and the fact that he is 'use'd well' in the church does not sit well with him, even as the contrast between heaven and the church, rendered as it is through the *rime riche* of 'use'd well/ do well,' indicates wellness as appearance only. This parallel leads to a further parallel, between the church and heaven, and all these parallels suggest embeddedness in one's surround as a problem, not a solution. The ear hears unmistakable correlation in the rhyme, but any actual correlation between church and heaven is a hollow echo. Blake's rhyme clarifies that what appears to the outside as doing well is, in fact, a using up. In calling attention to the speaker's ability to distance himself from his surround and presumably from his mother's preference for church over the ale-house, Blake challenges enactive theories which insist upon a perception–action loop that immerses subject in his surround. Blake's repeated end-stopped lines resist anything like stream of consciousness, and the goal here is to say, cognizer beware. Indeed, Blake's pun on 'ne'er do well' foists the charge that the poor are poor because they are lazy right back upon the accuser, who will receive a proper comeuppance in heaven for his usury of poor souls. Blake's mobile parallels shift the context for the meaning of his lines, demanding different kinds of abstraction through which to funnel experience. Insofar as unity requires abstraction of particularity, abstraction is neither good nor bad, but must be evaluated. Only in this way can adjacency not be mistaken for intimacy. And only in this way can prepositions shift the meaning of and relationality to one's embodiment.

Innatism and Idealism

Blake's approach to the hard problem of experience begins precisely with what Locke resolutely rejected: innatism. Locke had insisted that 'truths imprinted on the soul which it perceives or understands not' was unintelligible, and that universal consent was hardly evidence of the innateness of any idea (*Essay* 2: 1–5). Because Locke insisted that metaphysics is beyond human empirical knowledge, the claim of innate ideas itself presumes what could only be divine knowledge. Innate ideas would, accordingly, amount to an impression without an impression, a logical inconsistency. The assumption of a *tabula rasa* grants experience generative force, and with experience, the loss of the possibility of certainty.[24] When Blake ties experience to loss, experience shifts from being the cause of our learning to its effect.

Innatism furthermore enhances Blake's emphasis on idealism and imagination. Without these, the mind cannot bring itself into being, but must passively rely on sensations to reflect upon (Quinney 72). If consciousness starts with ideas, it has contents before experience, and in this way, consciousness starts off with something to combine. Because Blake frames innocence and experience as 'contrary states of the human soul,' he suggests that the meaning of consciousness must derive from the dialectical energy of their opposition, and indeed value only comes into view in the gamut of the binary.[25] Consciousness thus is partly combinatorial, partly idealist. Only after experience can we perceive fully the value of innocence. Dialectic is a crucial resource because, within it, experience is necessarily both cause and effect, and hence, consciousness takes form which shapes and reshapes the contents of consciousness. In this way, the particular contents of awareness at any given moment do not subsume consciousness, and the self that can be more than a hostage to experience. Through dialectic, experience is never essentialized into its own evidence. And through dialectic the salience of an experience shifts, which means learning is possible. Finally, in the temporal delay within dialectic, what was a first-person experience becomes an as-if third person experience, as the self looks back on itself and wonders the degree to which then and now overlap. Some consciousness researchers now believe that the study of consciousness should focus on combining the objective third-person perspective with the first-person subjective one, which allows narrative to help construct consciousness by forging connections between viewpoints. In this view, the binding that enables consciousness to seem like a unified field is itself a construction.

Innatism has recently found a defender in the neuroscientist Stanislas Dehaene, although Dehaene's name for it in *How We Learn* is evolution. Dehaene refutes Locke and argues that 'despite its immaturity, the nascent [infant] brain already possesses considerable knowledge inherited from its long evolutionary history' (53). What he means by this is that babies come into the world both with concepts of objects, numeracy, and probability, and with an ability to exploit abstraction and thereby create a grammar for language and learning. For evidence he cites neuroscientific studies of infant surprise. When objects defy laws of physics, two-month-old infants show surprise. When infants are repeatedly shown slides with two objects, they grow bored, but stare longer when three objects are introduced, which suggests an innate idea of numeracy.[26] Dehaene concludes that infants possess 'deep intuitions of the physical world, and ... are stunned when their expectations turn out to be false' (54). Circling back to Locke for a moment, let me point out that when Locke refutes hunger, thirst, and warmth as innate ideas (*Essay* Vol. 1, Ch. 4, section 2), he raises the stakes from idea to 'settled idea' and goes on to imply an idea is not an idea until it is clearly settled. When he argues 'nature, I confess, has put into man a desire of happiness and an aversion to misery' (*Essay* 1:3.3), the blank slate is no longer empty, and we are forced to ask what the difference is between innate desire/aversion and innate ideas.

Like Dehaene's infants, Blake's infants, of course, are not innocent of concepts and intuitions. James Chandler has shown how Blake disrupts sentimentalism within innocence by claiming the ewes' 'tender reply' to the shepherd, and the fact that 'the shepherd follows the sheep rather than the other way around' (277). Rather than modifying reply, 'tender' here functions as a verb that commodifies sentimentalism, rather than framing it as a given. In 'Infant Sorrow' the infant already has a concept of freedom, as he or she objects to being swaddled, and decides 'to sulk upon [his or her] mother's breast.' Crucially, the concept of freedom has been imagined well before any experience of it, and one recalls here Kant's argument that human freedom is a regulatory ideal that may well be beyond experience. In this view, embodied cognition would offer no way of encountering freedom. All this restriction entails sorrow and disappointment, and disappointment suggests that expectations are perhaps innate, are already being frustrated, but this frustration perhaps incentivizes us to learn how to make better predictions or at least to see the limits of our predictive powers.

Blake therefore considers the etymology of innocence, which means 'no poison,' and the linkage between experience and poison incentivizes both the consideration of other engines for consciousness besides experience, and the opening up of a category for experiences that are not poison. In what ways, then, might experience mitigate its necessary poison? To ask the question is already to see why Blake refuses the notion of the mind's embeddedness in its surround as a necessary good. Yet since Blake assumes the possibility of poison, he needs a strategy so that one can distinguish 'mind-forg'd manacles' from reality, a strategy which entails an epistemological idealism. To return briefly to 'Little Black Boy,' the poem demonstrates that the experience of blackness solely in the contexts of racism and slavery makes it difficult indeed to associate it with something positive.

To the extent that ideas are the contents of consciousness, abstraction is not necessarily the enemy, and indeed, as Dehaene argues, abstraction may be a key to understanding why human learning is at least presently so much more powerful than machine learning. In seeking to account for the differences between the two, Dehaene alights on both abstraction and grammar, a system of rules that allows information to build upon itself. Because code limits machines to rules, abstraction is especially tricky for machines to learn. Hence the use of CAPTCHA on websites to prove that one is human: unlike machines, human beings easily apply abstract rules to identify different examples of traffic lights or buses. Dehaene writes that 'to recognize an object, for instance, [machines] often rely on the presence of a few shallow features in the image, such as a particular color or shape' (28). He adds that although humans initially make the same kinds of mistakes as machines, in time they learn how to correct errors, to modify the rules. For Dehaene, then, innatism and abstraction give human learning a measure of superiority over machines. For Blake, innatism reminds us of the divinity of imagination, but any hierarchy implied in a divine gift is collapsed within his concept of the human form divine.

From Blake's perspective, because coherence or the feel of unity with the world can be the product either of ideology or of consciousness, Blake requires the ability to probe the unity, especially since innocence may falsely credit the unified point of view. The sense of embodiedness is not itself to be trusted since both ideology and reality can deliver the feel of unity. Kant had warned that if it feels good, it must be bad. Hence in 'Holy Thursday' of *Innocence*, Blake highlights the verb 'seemd' when referring to the appearance of the poor children, and he puts appearance in the past, thus signaling the potential to move beyond appearances, and the need to create rules so that the given can be evaluated as an appearance. His repetition of the word 'multitude,' moreover, thrice signals that the orchestration of differences is taking place, which logically leads one to ask: what have the beadles to gain by this organization of innocence? To probe the unity, one must be able to evaluate the abstractions that made a unified view possible to begin with. For unity to overcome difference and particularity, these must be abstracted so that commonality is possible. To this end, Blake insists on a division between the way things appear to a speaker or character in his poems, and any corresponding reality.

Embodiedness can feel like unity in part because it makes consciousness feel like a continuous stream.[27] Owen Flanagan asks the degree to which this stream is necessary to consciousness itself, and he suggests that since most patients with mental disorders do not experience a dried-up stream (155), this sense of a stream may be essential to consciousness. If Blake is right that something like ideology is also capable of delivering this stream-like immersive feel, then how to distinguish between the stream of ideology and of consciousness? For instance, when we are told the innocent children of 'Holy Thursday' like Thames water flow, we have to reconcile their 'clean and innocent' faces with the sewage of the Thames; the fluid movement of water with the flow of Blake's artificial couplets. Here the natural imagery does not seem natural, and the given shades into appearance.[28]

Blake's 'A Divine Image' offers incentives for thinking through when abstractions are helpful and when they are a liability. Abstractions can help provide universal ethical rules and can facilitate learning. By highlighting how 'all must love the human form' but by juxtaposing this rule with examples that test its resolve – 'heathen, turk or jew' – Blake shows the work of prejudice, and how easily good intentions are derailed (18:17, 18; E13). In this view, the abstract ethic needs to be tested by the particulars. And by underscoring the degree to which human beings resort to prayer only in a time of need, Blake encourages humanity to find the self-reliance that comes with the idea that the human imagination is itself divine. But abstractions and rules are not necessarily to be relied upon because they may be influenced by prior misleading abstractions. Here, because the divine has been abstracted into an externalized image, an idol, humanity has lost sight the divinity within.

Panpsychism

Blake couples innatism with a version of panpsychism, perhaps because panpsychism helps level innatism's hierarchies, thus preventing kinds of priesthood. Once again, Blake does not presume relationality to be a given, nor is it a necessary good. Since Blake in *The Marriage* writes 'Where Man is not nature is barren,' his panpsychism may be a thought experiment against hierarchy. Blake may have in mind that when the idea of man as master of nature is abandoned, then so is the idea of nature as mere object subject to man's creativity.[29] In 'The Clod and the Pebble,' for instance, Blake deliberately associates stones and clay with animacy, thereby flirting with panpsychism. Consciousness here becomes recursive, and such recursiveness, the arena for development. The clod that is downtrodden with the cattle's feet surprisingly has the optimistic outlook: no mere clod, he believes that 'Love seeketh not Itself to please' (32:1; E19). Blake's choice of the preposition 'with' (and not by) suggests that the clod and the cattle's feet engage in a kind of collaboration. There is no necessary opposition here, just as there is no necessary victim. Crucially, the preposition shapes the form of the relationality instead of assuming it. Meanwhile, the one who keeps its shape, the pebble, believes in the selfishness of love. Blake denies experience the power to adjudicate between these orientations to the world, and thus it cannot be the ground zero of consciousness. That both points of view are given equal measure – six lines apiece – further takes measure (and with it, empiricism) off the table as a necessarily reliable way of sorting things out. The poem pivots around a central stanza that grants clod and pebble two lines each, and the combination hints that in time the pebble will erode into a clod. Essence thereby moves from materiality to point of view, or consciousness, even as prepositions help shift the relationality one has to the world from the given to an orientation. That mobility in point of view offers the potential for learning, even as relationality becomes a form to be evaluated, and as narrative builds consciousness.

Surprisingly, today panpsychism is experiencing a revival of sorts, and this revival is underwritten by the embeddedness of mind within world and its allegedly flat ontology.[30] Hence, Clark submits 'mind itself leaches into body and world' (29), and underscores 'relations between movement or change and resulting patterns of sensory stimulation' (22). Noë argues 'it is thus only in the context of an animal's embodied existence, situated in an environment dynamically interacting with objects and situations, that the functions of the brain can be understood' (65). He concludes, 'the world itself can be described as belonging to the very machinery of our consciousness' (65). However, Clark cautions that Noë takes enaction too far because 'strong sensorimotor models of perceptual experience do us a service by foregrounding embodied skills ... but they fail to do justice to the many firewalls, fragmentations, and divisions of cognitive labor that characterize our engagements with the world our senses reveal' (195). These firewalls take the names of abstraction, idealism, and irony, and thus are the unacknowledged legislators of embodied cognition.

Head of the Allen Brain Institute, Christof Koch, is sympathetic to panpsychism, and submits not only that 'some level of experience can be found in all organisms' (155), but also that 'experience is in unexpected places, including in all animals, large and small, and perhaps even in brute matter itself' (167). He turns to integrated information theory, however, to develop a scientific theory of consciousness over panpsychism, because it has nothing to say about machine consciousness and because Koch credits anything with a non-zero maximum of integrated information with consciousness, including machines and atoms. Koch insists, despite his geometrical method of postulates for experience, that 'experience is the only way you know about the world' (xi). In so doing, Koch builds upon Giulio Tononi's integrated information theory, which sees experience as a fundamental quality of the universe in much the same way as mass, charge, and energy are (Kramnick 139). Koch transforms five phenomenological properties of experience into methodological axioms that form the basis of his information theory (75). For Koch, every experience exists for itself, is structured and informative, does not contradict another experience, and is independent and complete (75). The making of phenomenal properties into axioms belies Koch's empirical claim that experience is the only route to epistemology. Integrated information theory requires geometrical postulates to become axioms. In a larger view, then, since ecological views fear abstraction because abstraction means that enaction may not be the law of consciousness, enactive and panpsychist theories need to consider both their indebtedness to abstraction, and whether enaction is axiomatic or applies only to a subset of consciousness.

I have argued that embodied or enactive cognition has swung the pendulum too far towards ecology and relationality, and away from abstraction and idealism, and that neither ecology nor relationality is a necessary good. Enactivists recognize this when they promote embodied cognition to a cognitive law. Hartman's take on Romantic consciousness highlights a cost to it largely ignored by today's enactivists. For Hartman, Romantic consciousness is in part a burden, a divorce from the immediacy of being. Hartman submits that 'the mind that acknowledges the existence or past existence of immediate life knows that its present strength is based on a separation from that life' (50). Today's consciousness, by contrast, largely casts this burden to the wind, especially because present versions of consciousness are underwritten by efficiency. Catherine Malabou has denounced neuroscientific accounts of neural plasticity for touting efficiency and flexibility at the expense of apoptosis, cell death. She reminds us that plasticity requires the death of nervous connections, and thus efficiency always has costs. We now cannot forget that the average human brain consumes 20 percent of the total oxygen available to the body while tipping in at 2.2 percent of its average weight, and we leverage this awareness to shape our fantasies of cognitive efficiency. Perhaps the last thing our ethical choices should be is efficient.[31]

Blake's poetry and designs everywhere frustrate efficiency. Even the repeated line 'Little Lamb God bless thee' in 'The Lamb' warns that despite the fact that the lamb symbolizes both divine and the human, any blessing has yet to be performed. It is, moreover, not clear that ritual has any performative powers, since the bland repetition seems more like a phatic utterance. In so doing, Blake reminds us of costs and rewards of consciousness, and also the potentially high costs for an enactive consciousness: cognitive efficiency, a relationality blind to structured hierarchy, and a consciousness that cannot separate itself from ideology. In short, a consciousness whose embeddedness is not only shorn of prepositions, but also deaf to the nuances of repetition.

Notes

1. Marshall Brown argues with Kant's help that the Romantics dissociated consciousness from experience. I think it is more correct to say that, for Kant, the experience of the object, such as it is, amounts to the knowledge we can have of it. That is to say we can experience objects only through our senses, and thus our accounts of objects are really accounts of the form of objects as we experience them. Add to this the fact that Kantian beauty is inescapably subjective, but that such subjectivity must be accounted for as if it were universal to be aesthetic.
2. Many would object to any equivalence between cognition and consciousness, on the grounds that cognition often is predicated on information, and information specifically excludes meaning, whereas consciousness often

assumes meaning. Since Robert Zajonc, we have known our brains to be porous to information: we are influenced by information without awareness. Shaun Gallagher notes that proponents of weak embodied cognition consider bodily anatomy and movement trivial for cognition (37–8). In this chapter, my focus is on 'stronger' versions of embodied cognition or enactive cognition. For helpful readings of drafts of this chapter, I would thank Colin Jager, Joel Faflak, and Marjorie Levinson. I thank Scott Phelps for wonderful conversations about consciousness.

3. See, however, the important History of Distributed Cognition Series published by Edinburgh University Press, especially the work of John Savarese and Lisa Ann Robertson.
4. J. Kevin O'Regan submits that our feels are the 'quality of interaction with the world' (116). He claims this definition helps solve the hard problem in that our feelings gauge our interaction. One advantage of this view is that when consciousness is an interaction between brain and world, the problem of the homunculus needed to correct sensory distortions drops away. Yet Rodolfo Llinás argues that our 'brain functions as a closed system most of the time' (81). Lisa Feldman Barrett, moreover, argues that our emotions help us gauge our body budgets (*How Emotions* 67–72), meaning that our brains are constantly predicting our energy needs. My point is that raw feels are not just about qualities of interaction but include interoception, not to mention selfishness. So, the hard problem of consciousness is solved by creating another. Interoception challenges the ecological view of consciousness insofar as something like an internal state must differentiate itself. An example: one should never come before a judge around noon because s/he might mistake hunger for evidence to deny parole.
5. Owen Flanagan's incisive critique of Colin McGinn's insistence that consciousness is cognitively closed to us frames McGinn's position not in terms of closure but rather in terms of the problem of embodiment (122). This helped me to see how enaction has shifted embodiment from a problem to the solution of consciousness. Flanagan persuades us that McGinn's standard of perfect intelligibility is much too high.
6. Manzotti argues in *The Spread Mind* that 'my experience of the object is the object I experience' (15), implying that consciousness is experience, and moreover that 'we are our experience. We are not our bodies' (21). While this has the virtue of getting rid of any inside and of replacing the identity of brain with experience with object and experience (92), it comes at the cost of the loss of the ability to think about which bodies – able ones and white ones get to immerse themselves in a surround – and the inability to distance objects from experience. He further submits that illusions are misbeliefs, not misperceptions (Chapter 4), but in this view how can empiricism recognize its false beliefs?
7. Gallagher argues 'I see the other's actions as an affordance for my own possible responsive action' (80). How does one know this affordance is not a projection? Flanagan imagines why human beings evolved towards experience: 'the special vivacity of perceptual experience might enable quicker, more reliable, and more functional responses than a less robustly phenomenological system, and these might have resulted in small selection

pressures in favor of becoming a subject of experience' (42). Here he grants consciousness as experience a function.
8. Andy Clark, philosopher of enaction, surprisingly admits that enaction in the form of the sensory–motor model can foster narcissism. '[B]y linking the contents and character of experience rather directly to acquired expectations concerning patterns of sensorimotor dependence, the interpretative framework is able to do justice both to the notion of an objective, mind independent reality and to the sense in which the world as perceived is the world of a specific type of embodied agent' (176). David Chalmers rightly notes that the older rational model falsely idealizes the amount of complexity human cognition is capable of dealing with, and also idealizes thought by making any thought universally possessable (62–5). In this sense, enactive cognition is right to go after this version of idealism. Enactivism rejects cognitive idealism, but is nonetheless invested in other kinds of it, insofar as certain cognitive acts are generalized as actions.
9. Amanda Anderson laments psychology's reductive approaches to the complexity of moral reflection and of human experience within time.
10. Barrett (*Seven*) complicates embeddedness in several ways: she insists that the brain is about making predictions, suggesting a kind of temporal gap within that embeddedness (63–82). Moreover, she highlights how the brain compresses information, and this compression entails both sensory integration and abstraction simultaneously (114–18). She uses 'abstraction' psychologically to mean the ability to find meaning in patterns. Roitblat argues that algorithms will never get to generalized intelligence because they are tethered to their narrow objectives and cannot create their own paths through a problem (81–108).
11. On the various responses to the hard problem, see Jager, paragraph 6. Jager worries about what literary studies stands to gain by tackling the problem of consciousness, and he argues consciousness talk can help us refine our understanding of how novel properties emerge from material determinants. Phillip Goff argues all options have a hard problem: materialists need to show how subjective qualities can be accounted for by objective quantities; dualists need to explain why empirical brain investigation shows no trace of mind–brain interaction (171).
12. With Agamben, Jay questions the reduction of experience from a kind of totality in Montaigne to mere cognition in Descartes. To resist this reduction, along with the loss of appreciation for ambiguity and uncertainty, his chapters focus on religious and aesthetic experience.
13. All references to Blake are from David V. Erdman's *The Complete Poetry and Prose of William Blake*, cited by plate and/or line number, followed by page number in Erdman's edition (E).
14. Laura Quinney submits Wordsworth's empiricism 'dissolves the confidence and integrity of consciousness' (69). Elsewhere, she suggests that the empirical subject in Blake can only despair because the very longing for transcendence that marks subjectivity must be abandoned (34). She defines subjectivity in terms of the experience that resists the concept of the self. Yet since empiricism itself cannot justify its primary postulate – all knowledge comes through experience – it too longs for transcendence.

15. Michael Clune faults the majority of literature and science studies of experience because they fail to show why experience might make a scientific difference. See Chapter 2 of *Writing Against Time*.
16. Recall here Saree Makdisi's attention to Blake's recycled images, which transform relationality into a play of sameness and difference, which I argue has the power to improve relationality (18–28).
17. Joseph LeDoux and Richard Brown argue that the scientific study of emotion has overemphasized subcortical circuits while scientific studies of consciousness have not paid enough attention either to general networks of cognition or to subjectivity. They propose 'a higher order theory of emotional consciousness.'
18. To what extent has the rise of contextualism bolstered our faith in permeability?
19. Clark offers three grades of embodiment that add ethical nuance: 'mere, basic, and profound' (42). The danger is always that the mere will be made into the profound, especially when the enemy is Cartesian dualism, and the mere can be dragooned to support an anti-dualism. These grades of embodiment are also helpful in that they do not simply hand cognition over to embodiment. Clune reminds us that even small-scale automatic behaviors may be part of some larger plan (85).
20. Though even Butler considers porousness to be a necessary good: 'without that overarching sense of the interrelational, we take the bodily boundary to be the end rather than the threshold of the person, the site of passage and porosity, the evidence of openness to alterity that is definitional of the body itself' (16). Body in this view shifts from boundary to openness to alterity, but how open is body to alterity, and is that unconditioned openness a necessary virtue? Imagine, for example, a white supremacist as the example of alterity, and porousness no longer cashes out ethically. Butler's concept of grievability – who or what is grievable and who or what is not – offers an important way to assess relationality.
21. I adapt 'plot against plot' from Moten (68). Morris Eaves argues that line in Blake represents the human being (40).
22. O'Regan argues that our feeling of wholeness is generated by our exploratory actions (25). In this view, experience is a kind of sampling, and the act of sampling generates the feel. If experience is a kind of sampling, then the point must be to ever widen the sampling. I find intriguing the idea that experience is metonymic, but does the act generate the feel, or do the act and feel mutually combine? The theory of enaction requires the action to generate the feel. Kant, of course, would credit the imagination's synthesis of presentations for the feel, and then bracket the feel as our perception of the object.
23. In this view, the spread mind returns us to the Hume problem, the endless bundles of perception that do not empirically cohere into identity or self.
24. Jay argues that reading Locke is about the experience of the value of probability, and probability in his view makes experience less of a possessable object, which, for Jay, is a loss (49).
25. Frye, of course, famously argued against any notion of a private mythology in Blake and maintained that innocence and experience were keys to Blake's mythology. He defined Blakean innocence in terms of 'the assumptions that

the world was made for the benefit of human beings, [and] has a human shape and a human meaning, and a world in which ... "mercy, pity, peace and love" have a genuine function' (237). In the poem, these characteristics are skeletal and do not even rise to the status of personifications.
26. Dehaene argues that babies perceive numbers within a few hours of life (57).
27. Dennett notes that although consciousness feels continuous, it is essentially gappy, and he cites as evidence saccades, blindsight, and the fact that there is no Cartesian theater in the brain where experience all comes together (8–9, 54, 356). Flanagan retorts that the stream does not require a Cartesian theater (174), and that Dennett's argument here exists to protect his multiple drafts theory of consciousness. Embodiedness supports physicalism while seemingly making experience physicalist, but the problem is that physicalism cannot speak to what it is like to feel an experience. See Flanagan 101.
28. Is the current fascination with embodied cognition within the humanities a symptom of our exhaustion with ideological critique?
29. Thanks to Marjorie Levinson for this suggestion.
30. Panpsychist Goff argues that 'basic forms of consciousness ... are postulated to exist as basic properties of matter' (174).
31. Clune highlights how addicts become fascinated by their addictive objects as a way of making subjective experience matter to science (82–6). See also Anderson on how models of emotion versus cognition gerrymander both and oversimplify moral reflection. My own view is that the emotions are about the perception of value, and thus both direct our attention and compel us to act.

References

Anderson, Amanda. *Psyche and Ethos*. Oxford: Oxford University Press, 2018.
Barrett, Lisa Feldman. *How Emotions Are Made*. Boston: Houghton Mifflin Harcourt, 2017.
—. *Seven and a Half Lessons About the Brain*. Boston: Houghton Mifflin Harcourt, 2020.
Benjamin, Ruha. *Race After Technology*. Cambridge: Polity Press, 2019.
Blake, William. *The Complete Poetry and Prose*. Rev. ed. Ed. David Erdman. New York: Anchor Books, 1988.
Bloom, Harold, ed. *Romanticism and Consciousness: Essays in Criticism*. New York: W. W. Norton, 1970.
Brown, Marshall. *The Gothic Text*. Stanford: Stanford University Press, 2004.
Butler, Judith. *The Force of Non-Violence*. London: Verso, 2020.
Chalmers, David. *The Conscious Mind: In Search of a Fundamental Theory*. New York: Oxford University Press, 1996.
Chandler, James. *An Archeology of Sympathy*. Chicago: University of Chicago Press, 2013.
Clark, Andy. *Supersizing the Mind: Embodiment, Action, and Cognitive Extension*. Oxford: Oxford University Press, 2011.

Clune, Michael. *Writing Against Time*. Stanford: Stanford University Press, 2013.
de Man, Paul. 'Intentional Structure of the Romantic Image.' *Romanticism and Consciousness*. 65–76.
Dehaene, Stanislas. *How We Learn*. New York: Viking, 2020.
Dennett, Daniel. *Consciousness Explained*. New York: Little, Brown, 2017.
Eaves, Morris. *William Blake's Theory of Art*. Princeton: Princeton University Press, 1982.
Flanagan, Owen. *Consciousness Reconsidered*. Cambridge, MA: MIT Press, 1992.
Frye, Northrop. 'The Keys to the Gates.' *Romanticism and Consciousness*. 233–54.
Gallagher, Shaun. *Enactivist Interventions: Rethinking the Mind*. Oxford: Oxford University Press, 2017.
Goff, Philip. *Galileo's Error: Foundations for a New Science of Consciousness*. London: Rider, 2019.
Goldsmith, Steven. *Blake's Agitation: Criticism and the Emotions*. Baltimore: Johns Hopkins University Press, 2013.
Hartman, Geoffrey. 'Romanticism and "Anti Self Consciousness."' *Romanticism and Consciousness*. 46–56.
Jager, Colin. 'Can We Talk about Consciousness Again? (Emergence, Natural Piety, Wordsworth).' *Romantic Praxis*, 'Romantic Frictions' (September 2011). https://romantic-circles.org/praxis/frictions/HTML/praxis.2011.jager.html (last accessed December 2, 2021).
Jay, Martin. *Songs of Experience*. Berkeley: University of California Press, 2005.
Kant, Immanuel. *The Critique of Pure Reason*. Ed. Werner Pluhar. Indianapolis: Hackett Books, 1996.
Koch, Christof. *The Feeling of Life Itself*. Cambridge, MA: MIT Press, 2019.
Kramnick, Jonathan. *Paper Minds: Literature and the Ecology of Consciousness*. Chicago: University of Chicago Press, 2018.
LeDoux, Joseph and Richard Brown. 'A Higher-Order Theory of Emotional Consciousness.' *Proceedings of the National Academy of Sciences of the United States of America*. 114.10 (March 7, 2017): E2016–E2025.
Levinson, Marjorie. *Thinking Through Poetry: Field Reports on Romantic Lyric*. Oxford: Oxford University Press, 2018.
Llinás, Rodolfo. *I of the Vortex: From Neurons to Self*. Cambridge, MA: MIT Press, 2001.
Locke, John. *An Essay Concerning Human Understanding*. 2 vols. Freeport: Books for Libraries Press, 1969.
Makdisi, Saree. *Reading William Blake*. Cambridge: Cambridge University Press, 2015.
Malabou, Catherine. *What Should We Do with Our Brain?* Trans. Sebastian Rand. New York: Fordham University Press, 2008.
Manzotti, Riccardo. *The Spread Mind*. New York: OR Books, 2017.
Mitchell, W. J. T. *Blake's Composite Art*. Princeton: Princeton University Press, 1978.
Moten, Fred. *Black and Blur*. Durham, NC: Duke Univeristy Press, 2007.
Noë, Alva. *Out of Our Heads*. New York: Hill and Wang, 2009.
O'Regan, J. Kevin. *Why Red Doesn't Sound Like a Bell*. Oxford: Oxford

University Press, 2011.
Oxford English Dictionary. 2nd ed. 1989. *OED Online*. Oxford University Press. http://dictionary.oed.com/. January 19, 2021.
Quinney, Laura. *William Blake on Self and Soul*. Cambridge, MA: Harvard University Press, 2009.
Roitblat, Herbert. *Algorithms Are Not Enough: Creating General Artificial Intelligence*. Cambridge, MA: MIT Press, 2020.
Varela, Francisco, Evan Thompson, and Eleanor Rosch, eds. *The Embodied Mind*. Cambridge, MA: MIT Press, 1993.
Williams, Nicholas. *Ideology and Utopia in the Poetry of William Blake*. Cambridge: Cambridge University Press, 2008.
Yolton, John. 'The Concept of Experience in Locke and Hume.' *Journal of the History of Philosophy* 1.1 (October 1963): 53–71.

Part II
States of Consciousness

Chapter 6

'Poetry is passion': Lyrical Balladry as Affective Narratology

Mark J. Bruhn

From a cognitive literary studies perspective, verbal art is informative about consciousness and other aspects of human cognition insofar as it indexes the designing mind of the author, represents the diverse minds of characters, speakers, and narrators, and affects the variously disposed minds of readers. All three dimensions – the expressive, the mimetic, and the rhetorical – merit study, yet critical attention in the original *Romanticism and Consciousness* was devoted almost exclusively to the mimetic dimension: that is, to consciousness treated as an explicit theme in Romantic literature rather than as its underlying cause or ultimate effect. Published in 1970, the volume reprised essays mostly from the two previous decades, a period dominated, especially on the American front, by the behaviorist prohibitions of the intentional and affective fallacies, which forbade any attempt to read the literary artifact in terms of the black-box subjectivities of its author or reader on the grounds that neither the expressive intentions of the one nor the affective experiences of the other are publicly available and reproducible for critical investigation. What *is* publicly available and reproducible is the literary artifact itself or, more exactly, the relation(s) between its mimetic 'content' and its verbal 'technique'; claims about such 'objective' relations are 'testable' in the sense that they are 'susceptible of discussion' and informed debate (Wimsatt xviii, 32, 34). William K. Wimsatt, Jr, one of the co-legislators (with Monroe Beardsley) of the fallacies, was also among the many brilliant contributors to *Romanticism and Consciousness*, but his status as first among equals registers in the volume's nearly total silence concerning the actual minds that create and construe the after-all-debatable literary object.

Ironically, even as the intentional and affective fallacies were gaining traction across the literary critical landscape, psychology itself and related fields such as computational science, neurobiology, and psycholinguistics were being rapidly transformed by what is now termed 'the cognitive revolution.' Where behaviorism had confined psychological attention to observable and measurable behaviors, cognitivists across the human sciences began formulating ingenious models, complex algorithms, and ever more sophisticated experimental technologies and procedures in a collective effort to open the black box of the mind–brain to empirical investigation. By 1970, the revolution was in full force, but few literary critics were at that time paying much attention; the allied fields of cognitive literary studies and empirical literary studies began effectively consolidating only in the 1990s. In the interim, pioneering studies in the expressive and rhetorical dimensions of literary art made their necessary case insufficiently, and indeed wound up retreating to the mimetic ground they were supposed to be getting beyond.

Let one major instance stand for many. At the outset of *The Art of the Lyrical Ballads*, published just three years after *Romanticism and Consciousness*, Stephen Maxfield Parrish urges a rhetorical approach to the poems based on Wordsworth's theoretical statements about his poetic purposes and practices, which chiefly 'concern [...] the reader's response, and the artful means by which the poet plays upon it' (8). When applied, such a rhetorical criticism would evidently require some explicit and significant correlation of the poem's 'artful means' with actual readers' 'responses,' yet in his subsequent readings of individual poems, Parrish himself nowhere meets this demand, for he has no principled method to collect and analyze a data set of actual responses to the poem. Short of these, he has no option but to treat the poems' represented responses as proxies for the ones his argument really requires, thereby substituting the mimetic dimension for the affective dimension he is really after. For example, in his discussion of 'The Thorn' as an experimental dramatic monologue, Parrish famously argues that it is not Martha Ray but the narrator who is the 'subject of the poem,' for Wordsworth explicitly 'intended [it] to be a psychological study, a poem about the way the mind works' (98). Yet 'the mind whose workings are revealed is that of the narrator' – a verbally represented mind, in other words, rather than one or more actually affected ones (98). Shifting narrative interest from the story told to the story's teller still leaves one squarely in the realm of the mimetic, as Parrish himself clearly understands: 'Wordsworth – to put the matter in another way – sought to imitate nature [...] by simulating dramatically the passions of real men' (141). By the close of his book, however, the critical rhetorical question of how such dramatic simulations affect actual readers remains unposed, for Parrish lacked any means – apart from the impressionistic self-reporting proscribed under the affective fallacy – to answer it if he had.[1]

It falls precisely within the remit of cognitive and empirical literary studies to hypothesize and test possible answers to such questions concerning the actual rhetorical effects of verbal art. The case I will pursue here will be the one Parrish aptly theorized but insufficiently demonstrated, that of Wordsworth's affective narratology in *Lyrical Ballads* and 'The Thorn' in particular. My aim is twofold: to side-step the affective fallacy by concentrating on possible empirical approaches that make readers' actual responses meaningfully objective, and to suggest at the same time how such approaches might be used to test key tenets of Wordsworth's poetic theory, from the primary role of emotion in (literary) cognition to the reformative power of his experiments in lyrical balladry.

A note on terminology before I proceed. Under the heading 'affective,' Wimsatt and Beardsley broadly designated any psychological and physiological effects of a work of literature upon its audience, from 'vivid images, intense feelings, or heightened consciousness' to shivers, quickened pulse, horripilation, and other 'motor discharges attendant upon reading' (30–2). For contemporary theorists of emotion and affect such as Antonio Damasio and Brian Massumi, such physiological and psychological effects are more or less conscious results of activity in homeostatic feedback circuits that stimulate and regulate emotional response. While these theorists contract for distinct definitions of such blanket folk-psychological terms as 'affect,' 'emotion,' 'feeling,' and 'passion,' all agree in distinguishing pre-reflective and reflective forms. Insofar as 'we are always already actively engaged in an emotionally charged situation by the time we become aware of it,' the reflectively aware state (which Damasio calls 'feeling' and Massumi 'emotion') never fully comprehends or represents the pre-reflectively 'charged situation' (Damasio's 'emotion' and Massumi's 'affect') (Stanley 107). More a homespun folk psychologist than a hardboiled affect theorist, Wordsworth uses 'affections,' 'feelings,' 'passions,' and 'emotions' interchangeably, but he nevertheless consistently distinguishes original excitement from subsequent reflection, most famously in his definition of poetry as 'spontaneous overflow of powerful feelings [...] recollected in tranquillity' (*Lyrical Ballads* 756).[2] Though I follow Wordsworth's practice and treat 'affect' and 'emotion' in particular as synonyms (as do the cognitive and empirical researchers most closely engaged below), in this chapter I am chiefly interested in pre-reflective affectivity, especially where it proves 'irreducible to static and limiting cognitive and conceptual structure' that reflective awareness can hardly do without (Stanley 98).

Permanent Impressions in 'The Thorn'

As arguably the earliest of the 'lyrical ballads' to be conceived as such, 'The Thorn' effectively set Wordsworth's poetic agenda for the joint enterprise with Coleridge. According to Coleridge's later account, 'Mr. Wordsworth [...] propose[d] to himself as his object, to give the charm of novelty to things of every day, and ... excite a feeling analogous to the supernatural, by awakening the mind's attention from the lethargy of custom' (qtd in *Lyrical Ballads* 5). Notice that Coleridge identifies Wordsworth's poetic 'object' less with the represented 'things of every day' than with readers' excited feelings and awakened attention when 'novelty' surprises expectation. With specific regard to 'The Thorn,' Wordsworth recollected that 'a stormy day' awakened his attention

> to a thorn which I had often past [*sic*] in calm and bright weather without noticing it. I said to myself, 'Cannot I by some invention do as much to make this thorn permanently[3] an impressive object as the storm has made it to my eyes at this moment.['] (*Lyrical Ballads* 350)

This individual hawthorn tree had always been an unremarkable 'thing of every day' until the storm awakened Wordsworth's attention to it, exciting feelings that made it from that moment on a 'permanently [...] impressive object' in Wordsworth's mind. In the poem inspired by this revisionary encounter, Wordsworth challenged himself to make a verbally represented 'thorn' similarly impressive – that is, attention-awakening and passion-exciting – for his readers. Readers' poetic experience would thus mirror by affective analogy the perceptual experience of the poet.

Wordsworth's emphasis on 'permanent impressions' here in the Fenwick note recollects a touchstone passage from the two-part *Prelude* of 1799 that Wordsworth excised when he repurposed the spots of time for later books of the 1805 *Prelude*. Appearing just after The Drowned Man of Esthwaite sequence and just before the Visionary Dreariness and Waiting for the Horses sequences, the passage explains that all three episodes are meant to illustrate how 'accidents,' 'distresses,' 'disasters,' and 'tragic facts of rural history'

> ... impressed my mind
> With images to which in following years
> Far other feelings were attached – with forms
> That yet exist with independent life,
> And, like their archetypes, know no decay. (*1799* 1.280–7)

'Images' that were originally 'impressed' with one feeling tone (such as curiosity, fear, anticipation) are subsequently complicated and enriched with 'far other feelings' (for example, of beauty, ardor, or guilt). The resulting 'form' or 'image-feeling' complex persists in consciousness, 'independent' of the original impressive occasion and without 'decay,' which is to say permanently.

Wordsworth took such an impression from a stunted thorn on a stormy March day in 1798, and the conclusion of the spots of time sequence suggests why: in 'storm and rain,' even 'in this later time,' Wordsworth writes, 'unknown to me / The workings of my spirit thence are brought' – that is, brought from the image-feeling complex that registered its first impression when the schoolboy Wordsworth ascended 'a crag, / An eminence' to wait for the horses that would bring him home for Christmas – and his father's death (*1799* 1.335–6, 371, 373–4). Though Wordsworth had not yet penned *this* sequence when he encountered the storm-tossed hawthorn on Quantock Hill, he had already attempted a decade before to versify the enduring impression of that stormy December evening,

> ... when the wintry blast
> Through the sharp Hawthorne whistling pass'd
>
> * * * *
>
> Long Long upon yon steepy rock
> Alone I bore the bitter shock
> Long Long my swimming eyes did roam
> For little Horse to bear me home
> To bear me what avails my tear
> To sorrow o'er a Father's bier. (*Early Poems* 446)

The rudimentary image-feeling complex described here resurfaces in sublimated form in the brief 'Description of a Thorn' that Wordsworth sketched out on March 19, 1798 to capture the visual and emotional tenor of the permanently impressive experience he had that day. Indeed, through a figurative allusion to the final line, just before 'The Epitaph,' of Thomas Gray's 'Elegy Written in a Country Churchyard' – which reads, 'Grav'd on the stone beneath yon aged thorn' (116) – Wordsworth subtly reinters his father even here:

> A summit where the stormy gale
> Sweeps through the clouds from vale to vale –
> A thorn there is which like a stone
> With jagged lychens is o'ergrown[.] (*Lyrical Ballads* 283)

Richard Gravil similarly correlates the 'image cluster' of the full-blown poem with the 'equally well-known' cluster of the Waiting for the

Horses sequence, observing that, through such affective ramification, even 'simple objects become valued indices of feeling and memorials of a state of being: they acquire, also, a power – or become the hiding place of power' (109). David Collings extends this view, arguing that, for Wordsworth, 'a given scene's ability to exceed his interpretive capacity is a sign of its privilege, its proximity to an affect too early and dense for him to decipher' (177). In 'The Thorn,' Wordsworth evidently drew directly upon such excessively and indecipherably affective scenes in his own psychological experience to render a virtual scene that might potentiate an analogous experience in his readers. As Collings implies, such experience may be permanently impressive, as it was for the poet, to the extent that it encodes a 'dense' or complex affect that cannot be comprehensively decoded upon reflection.

'Impressive effects out of simple elements'

In a long 'Note' appended to 'The Thorn' in 1800, Wordsworth defines imagination as 'the faculty which produces impressive effects out of simple elements,' so we might reframe the preceding discussion as an empirical question: which 'simple elements' of 'The Thorn' produce the most permanently 'impressive effects' in actual readers, and how would we know? An obvious candidate element is meter, for Wordsworth himself singles it out as instrumental to his affective as opposed to mimetic purposes in the poem:

> I had two objects to attain; first, to *represent* a picture which should not be unimpressive yet consistent with the character that should describe it, secondly, while I adhered to the style in which such persons describe, to take care that the words, which in their minds are impregnated with passion, should likewise *convey* passion to Readers who are not accustomed to sympathize with men feeling in that manner or using such language. It seemed to me that this might be done by calling in the assistance of Lyrical and rapid Metre [...]. (*Lyrical Ballads* 351; emphases added)

Wordsworth's reference to meter here provides a helpful gloss on his related claim in the 'Preface' that he purposely cast his *lyrical* ballads in 'a more impressive metre than is usual in Ballads' (757). As the note to 'The Thorn' confirms, 'more impressive' means not worthier of admiration but more affecting, that is, more effective in 'convey[ing] passion to Readers,' even ones not prone to be moved by ballad narrators ('men feeling in that manner') or ballad style ('such language'). While the meter or, more properly, the stanzaic form of 'The Thorn' is certainly admirable – at eleven lines rhyming ABCBDEFFEGG, it is the longest and most complex 'ballad' stanza that Wordsworth invented for *Lyrical Ballads* (Sheats 95) – at issue here is where and how precisely its constituent 'elements' affect actual readers.

Paul Sheats broached this issue some time ago, arguing that Wordsworth 'shifts the burden of rhetorical effect from diction to formal arrangement' in a way that 'manipulates the reader's attention with great power and subtlety' (93). Sheats's declaration is in truth just a hypothesis – formal arrangement manipulates readers' attention (whether they know it or not) – and it can be further specified by recourse to related theoretical and critical arguments. For instance, though Wordsworth departed from conventional ballad forms to the extent that he invented a variety of his own, he nevertheless intended that his innovations should evoke more traditional 'works of rhyme or metre of the same or similar construction,' thereby producing a 'blind association of pleasure' contributing 'imperceptibly' to the 'complex feeling of delight' that he aimed to arouse (*Lyrical Ballads* 757). In 'The Thorn,' Wordsworth evokes the traditional ballad metrically in the opening quatrain of his stanza, in which three tetrameter lines are rounded off with an end-stopped trimeter line and a completed B rhyme, 'marking an emphatic close to the structural unit' (O'Donnell 131). Brennan O'Donnell groups the remaining seven lines as 'a modified tail-rhyme stanza,' and a note makes clear that Wordsworth's chief modification is to leave the first of these seven lines, which is to say the fifth in the stanza, unrhymed (62; see 258n16). This unrhymed fifth line is thus potentially doubly impressive: it arrives on the heels of a 'most basic and familiar' stanza form that has come to its customary close (O'Donnell 133), thereby incompleting (if I may revive a word) what should feel like a completion, and it introduces a potential new rhyme word that, in the ensuing seven-line unit, will not find its conventional mate. The double disturbance thus effected registers in the following comment from Corinna Russell, who, though she follows O'Donnell's analysis, nevertheless tellingly mischaracterizes his 'tail-rhyme' unit: 'The rhymed second and fourth lines of the initial quatrains enact [...] the return on the reader's memory of the profoundly familiar four-line ballad stanza, which is subsequently modulated by the "tail rhyme" of the final six lines' (108). As 'final' confirms, the line missing from her count is line five, which gets its distinct due just two paragraphs on: 'the unrhymed line 5 [of the first stanza] offers a negative comparison for the tree: it stands "Not higher than a two-years' child"' (108).

With this much in mind, Sheats's working hypothesis can be considerably refined. Wordsworth claims that his meter is 'more impressive than is usual in Ballads' and then begins his 'Thorn' stanza with a traditional ballad rhythm, 'rhetorically valuable by virtue of its pleasing familiarity' (O'Donnell 133). But that same familiarity or expectedness should make these lines comparatively unimpressive. So, as a first refinement, we might hypothesize that this formal arrangement will manipulate readers to pay more attention to, and thus potentially be more affected by, the more impressive tail-rhyme unit than the less impressive ballad unit. Further, within the more impressive tail-rhyme unit (fifth to eleventh lines), we might predict that its unrhymed opening line is likely most impressive of all.

As a preliminary test of these hypotheses, we can use an empirical method called 'citation analysis,' whereby one examines which lines of a given poem (or passages of a prose text) are most frequently and least frequently cited in a random but sizable sample of professional interpretations of that poem (or text). The relative citation frequency of a given line serves as a proxy for that line's attention-getting power on the assumption that, in their reading experience as in their interpretive follow-up, critics paid more attention to the lines they ultimately cite than to the lines they do not.[4] I accordingly collected thirty-three professional interpretations of 'The Thorn' published between 1881 and 2020, identified which lines of the poem were cited in each interpretation, and then tallied the results to determine relative frequency of citation. For example, in this particular data set, the first line of the poem was cited by ten of the thirty-three critics, yielding a relative frequency of 0.3030; line 127, in the exact middle of the poem, was cited by thirteen of thirty-three, yielding a higher relative frequency of 0.3939; the last line of the poem was cited by sixteen of thirty-three, yielding a still higher relative frequency of 0.4848. Put more simply, fewer than one in three critics cite the first line, two out of five cite the middle line, and nearly one in two cite the final line. The high relative frequency of citation for the final line is unsurprising, given that the final position in a segment of discourse is considered most emphatic, but this suggests an alternative hypothesis with regard to the stanza sequence, in which line eleven occupies the final position and might therefore command even more attention than unrhymed line five. O'Donnell lends weight to this alternative hypothesis when he somewhat incongruously recharacterizes 'The Thorn' as consisting of a ballad stanza plus the five-line stanza of 'The Idiot Boy' plus a two-line couplet. In this three-part structure with 'a rhythmically familiar beginning, an elaborated middle, and a summarizing end' (O'Donnell 134), the gravitas of summative finality could well outweigh the impressive elaboration of lines five through nine.

There are many ways to parse and interpret the results of a citation analysis, but with our hypotheses, frequency of citation by line position within the stanza is of greatest interest. Across the poem, are first, second, third, and fourth lines of stanzas cited less frequently than fifth through eleventh lines? And within this latter group, are fifth lines more frequently cited than sixth through tenth and especially eleventh lines? The following table divides the citation results into three roughly equal frequency groups: most frequently cited lines, meaning lines cited by eight or more of the thirty-three critics (relative frequency ≥ 0.2424); somewhat frequently cited lines, meaning lines cited by five to seven of the thirty-three critics (relative frequency between 0.1515 and 0.2121); and least frequently cited lines, meaning lines cited by four or fewer of the thirty-three critics (relative frequency ≤ 0.1212). Numbers in each column indicate how many lines occupying that stanzaic position (out of a total of twenty-three in the poem) appear in each frequency group.

Stanza Position	Most Frequently Cited (n = 83)	Somewhat Frequently Cited (n = 83)	Least Frequently Cited (n = 87)
First Line	7	7	9
Second Line	6	9	8
Third Line	4	9	10
Fourth Line	6	6	11
Fifth Line	12	6	5
Sixth Line	10	5	8
Seventh Line	9	8	6
Eighth Line	9	7	7
Ninth Line	5	9	9
Tenth Line	6	10	7
Eleventh Line	9	7	7

Were lines cited purely by chance, we would expect (on average) a fairly even distribution across the table and down, roughly seven to eight instances of each kind of line (first, second, and so on) in each frequency group. In this respect, the eighth and eleventh lines of the twenty-three stanzas fall very close to a chance (or null hypothesis) distribution. By significant contrast, the distribution of fifth lines strongly skews to the most frequently cited group, at a rate 50 percent greater than chance would predict. Even within this most frequently cited group, fifth lines are especially high-ranking. For example, six of the thirty-four lines cited by one in three critics or more are fifth lines, which is twice as many as chance would predict. Citation analysis thus preliminarily confirms the hypothesis that fifth lines are more likely to impress actual readers of 'The Thorn' than lines in any other position.

The table likewise shows that groups of lines are more or less impressive pretty much as predicted. Among most frequently cited lines, the ballad unit of lines one through four is clearly outranked by the tail-rhyme unit of lines five through eleven, while the reverse holds among the least frequently cited lines. Stunningly, no first or second lines and only one each of third or fourth lines appear within the subset of thirty-four lines cited by one in three critics or more, where chance would predict three of each. Correlatively, in the subset of thirty-two lines cited by two or fewer critics, the balladic unit is heavily overrepresented with two first lines, five second lines, six third lines, and five fourth lines – that is, eighteen of the thirty-two lines, where chance would predict fewer than twelve. Thus, the preliminary test confirms the hypothesis that the ballad unit is significantly less impressive than the tail-rhyme unit.

Within the tail-rhyme unit, the final couplet, despite its emphatic position, is clearly less attention-getting than the five-line unit that precedes it, which appears to be most impressive at its outset, in the stanzas' fifth lines and, as the next most frequently cited position, sixth lines. Interestingly, the high relative frequencies of sixth lines can be partially explained with reference to the fifth lines that precede them. In nine of the ten instances of a most-frequently-cited sixth line, the syntax of the foregoing fifth line is left-shifted or otherwise prospectively enjambed, so that main clause structure is delayed or incomplete until the sixth line, for example:

> Not higher than a two-years' child,
> It stands erect this aged thorn; (5–6)

> And with this other maid to church
> Unthinking Stephen went – (126–7)

> For many a time and oft were heard
> Cries coming from the mountain-head[.] (170–1)

A previous citation analysis study of Wordsworth's 'The Last of the Flock,' 'To My Sister,' 'To Joanna,' and 'Stepping Westward' likewise showed that prospective enjambment predicts frequency of citation (Bruhn, 'Citation').

Citation analysis can be used preliminarily in this way to winnow more viable from less viable hypotheses in the criticism on record. According to these data,[5] Sheats is right to claim that Wordsworth's 'stanza-form permits effects unique to this poem' but wrong to assert that 'the five-line middle sequence, in particular, postpones and then concentrates the gratification of meter and rhyme' (95). If the five-line subdivision within the seven-line tail-rhyme unit 'postpone[d]' then 'concentrate[d]' the gratifications of meter and rhyme, we would expect its final two lines (that is, the eighth and ninth of the stanza) to be more frequently cited than its first two (the fifth and sixth of the stanza). Likewise, Sheats's claim that trimeter 'short lines add emphasis at the close of the first and second parts' (95) seems wholly mistaken; according to citation analysis, neither the fourth nor the ninth line position is especially impressive. More locally, Sheats suggests that in the ninth stanza of the poem, because 'the concrete nouns and adjectives [...] have all appeared before' (with only one exception), 'they have no power to arrest the accelerated syntax [...] or the darting, circling movements of attention, and the reader's eye (and mind) is denied any resting place' (96). Sheats's hypothesis that repeated diction loses its novelty and thus its power to arrest attention appears to be confirmed by the fact that eight of stanza nine's eleven lines appear in the least frequently cited group in the table above, including the stanza's fifth and sixth lines, which collocate diction, imagery, and figuration that has recurred from the start of the poem:

> The heap that's like an infant's grave,
> The pond – and thorn, so old and grey ... (93–4)

Citation analysis reveals that the words, images, and simile repeated in these infrequently cited fifth and sixth lines are, in their first appearances (that is, lines 4, 30, 36, 52), very frequently cited indeed, by more than one in three critics in every case.

Measuring Primary Affect

If Wordsworth's rhetorical 'object' was to 'awaken' (Coleridge) and 'manipulate' (Sheats) readers' attention, particularly through the employment of 'a more impressive metre than is usual in Ballads,' citation analysis suggests that he achieved his end in some significant measure. Importantly, aroused attention is not just a precondition for affective response but is itself a product of such response: we attend to what we are affected by, just as we are affected by what we attend to. Attention is already a form of 'excited feeling,' indexing what contemporary cognitive science calls 'the primacy of emotion,' the view, well grounded 'on neurophysiological evidence in particular[,] that emotion is at the basis of, and shapes the purposes of, all cognitive activity,' including the processing of literary narratives (Miall 324). As Terrence Deacon explains, emotion 'is the prioritizing marker attached to every cognitive object that enables an independent sorting of it with respect to other competing cognitive objects'; emotion thus plays a 'precognitive role' in that it 'organiz[es] interpretations and activities according to a largely hidden and sometimes orthogonal matrix of emotional associations' (37). In other words, emotion not only commands attention to a cognitive object (such as a particular line of verse) but also then governs, usually in unconscious ways, how that object is interpreted and used; it is thus a 'hiding place' of considerable cognitive 'power.'

The lines to which Wordsworth most frequently manipulates readers' attention, by that very token, presumably involve such primary affective power. But what specific affect(s) do they bear, and with what consequence for interpretive understanding? Citation analysis is uninformative about the specific kind or quality of affect that commands critical attention to a particular position or feature of a text, or about how such affect plays out in subsequent reading experience and/or the process of interpretation. Citation analysis indicates only where and (to a certain extent) to what a critic has paid attention, yet these where and what data, coupled with critical commentary, can help to formulate and rank possible hypotheses concerning the affective whys and wherefores, hypotheses that can then be submitted to more sophisticated forms of experimental verification. For example, in 'The Thorn' stanza, fifth lines are more likely to be attention-getting than any other. Converging evidence for this where hypothesis can be found in criticism of Wordsworth's poems that have the same or very similar structure, such as 'The Idle Shepherd-Boys' or 'The Danish Boy.' Analyzing the latter, Roy Sellars likewise finds that

> line 5 stands out with an end rhyme [...] that does not in fact rhyme, lying as an open spot between the [rhyming] rills of lines 1–4 and 6–9. These [...] spots, while isolated from their fellows, also form a kind of series over the course of the poem, and together give the following pastoral sentence as a contribution to knowledge: 'dell ... home ... wears ... near ... grave ... blest'. The chain of monosyllabic fragments, each one patiently awaiting a [rhyme] that would complete it, makes as much or as little sense as a prose summary of the [poem's] six stanzas would. (307–8)

Sellars turns from the where question to the what question, suggesting that attention-getting fifth lines offer a sort of précis of the poem that contains them. His very good point holds even more truly for 'The Thorn': the poem's fifth lines alone, lifted from the poem and read in sequence, offer what might oxymoronically be called a 'complete epitome' of the poem.

Space forbids printing this twenty-three-line epitome, but I urge readers to pause here and read through just the fifth lines of 'The Thorn' in the order they occur. We know from citation analysis that these fifth lines are especially attention-worthy but also that they are less likely to be cited when they contain repeated diction, imagery, and figures. Reading them through in order confirms just how much repetition these fifth lines, like the poem they completely epitomize, involve. Notably, almost all of this repeated diction, imagery, and figuration appears, in its first iteration, in the subset of most frequently cited lines that are cited by one in three critics or more, listed out here by line number:

4	It looks so old and grey.
5	Not higher than a two-years' child,
6	It stands erect this aged thorn;
8	It is a mass of knotted joints,
9	A wretched thing forlorn.
10	It stands erect, and like a stone
17	And this poor thorn they clasp it round
20	To drag it to the ground;
27	Not five yards from the mountain-path
29	And to the left, three yards beyond,
30	You see a little muddy pond
31	Of water, never dry;
32	I've measured it from side to side:
33	'Tis three feet long, and two feet wide.
36	A beauteous heap, a hill of moss,
52	Is like an infant's grave in size
63	A woman in a scarlet cloak,
65	'Oh misery! oh misery!
66	Oh woe is me! oh misery!'
77	'Oh woe is me! oh misery!'
126	And with this other maid to church
127	Unthinking Stephen went –
197	Instead of jutting crag, I found
214	I cannot tell; but some will say
215	She hanged her baby on the tree,
216	Some say she drowned it in the pond,
219	The little babe was buried there,
225	Some say, if to the pond you go,
227	The shadow of a babe you trace,
228	A baby and a baby's face,
247	And this I know, full many a time,
251	That I have heard her cry,
252	'Oh misery! oh misery!
253	Oh woe is me! oh misery!'

These thirty-four most-frequently-cited lines chiefly involve descriptive imagery and figuration, supplemented by only one narrated action (ll. 126–7) and seven lines of interpretive speculation (ll. 214–16, 219, 225, 227–8). For most readers, in other words, the perceptual dimensions of 'The Thorn,' its haunting and possibly haunted sights and sounds, are more salient than its narrative or heuristic dimensions, a point which could equally be made of the permanently impressed poet in relation to the storm-tossed thorn on Quantock Hill. Jerome Christensen accordingly 'suggest[s] that the reader courts futility if he seeks an explanation of the thorn's curious power in this sublime scene' divested of any 'cause or consequence' (281–2), and Christian La Cassagnère likewise emphasizes the inexplicable power of the poem's stubborn perceptual remainder:

> to the hermeneutic questions of the narratee ('Now wherefore thus … ?,' 'And why … ?') and to the causal perspective they establish, the displacements of the narrator respond […], ceaselessly deflecting the questioning toward the hypnotic adventure of a vision and its experience. (33; my translation)

James Averill similarly characterizes the 'doleful cry' of lines 65–6, 77, and 252–3 as a nearly pre-semantic 'hard core of language to which the narrator's mind returns and from which he recoils as from an impenetrable mystery' (176), and Peter McDonald adds that,

> whatever the speaker's (or the poem's) narrative satisfactions, the primacy of the repetition of Martha Ray's cry remains the poem's most secure fact, and is something in advance of the attempted explanations right to the end. Repetition, in other words, does not present a problem that can be solved, but remains at some level beyond interpretation … . (63)

McDonald's comments return us to the notion of the 'primacy' of emotion that is always prior to and 'at some level beyond interpretation,' what Collings variously calls 'emotion without content,' 'primary affect,' and 'pure potentiality' (171) and in terms of which he rightly explains the enduring power of Wordsworth's permanent impressions.

As I have argued elsewhere from different evidence,[6] such critical characterizations of Wordsworth's narrative methods and their affective results dovetail, unintentionally but point-by-point nonetheless, with the premises of Patrick Colm Hogan's 'affective narratology,' in particular its fundamental distinction between 'emotional incidents' and 'emotional events.' In Hogan's model, these core elements of narrative structure correspond to distinct emotion-processing systems in the human brain, one of which is 'largely subcortical and responds to perceptual information and emotional memories,' while the other is 'neocortical and involves appraisal-like elaboration of the full perceptual situation' in terms of explanatory 'causes' and calculated 'outcomes' (87). According to Hogan (29–67), tellable happenings begin as emotional incidents, which are typically unexpected departures from a homeostatic norm due to a perceived, remembered, or imagined elicitor that activates the subcortical emotion system and initiates automatic and not necessarily conscious physiological responses (such as repulsion or attraction, a grimace or gasp, increased heartrate or blushing, and so on). Beyond a certain threshold and duration, this felt, preconceptual experience of disturbance feeds forward to the neocortical system, initiating a much more conscious appraisal process concerning the causes of the disturbance, its probable consequences, possible responses, and so forth. In this way, the originating incident scales up to an 'emotional event,' which is the basic structural unit of any narrative episode; prototypically, the goal of emotional event elaboration is the reduction of the original, 'incidental' emotional excitement and a return to (unconscious) homeostasis. In Hogan's terms, Wordsworth in 'The Thorn' communicates an emotional incident that exceeds any corresponding event structure on offer in the poem (for example, the background tale of Martha Ray's abandonment by Stephen Hill) or available elsewhere (in balladic analogues, in Wordsworth's other poems or critical commentary, and so on) and thereby repeatedly foils the drive to restore homeostatic balance through appraisal and understanding.

Given such close parallels between critical commentary on 'The Thorn' and Hogan's theory of affective narratology, we might expect that the poem's affective impression would register primarily in the subcortical emotion system rather than the neocortical one, but the neuroprocessing situation is considerably more complex than that, especially in literary cognition, where any 'bottom-up' effect from emotion systems is mediated in the first place by 'top-down' processing from the language system. According to the more recent 'quartet theory of human emotion,' humans in fact have four interrelated emotion systems, two at the subcortical level (in the brain stem and diencephalon) and two higher up in the allocortex (the hippocampus) and prefrontal cortex (the orbitofrontal cortex or OFC) (Koelsch et al. 1). Not only do these four 'affect systems' influence one another, but they also interact with other 'effector systems' of the mind–brain, including

> motor systems (which produce actions, action tendencies, and motoric expression of emotion), peripheral physiological arousal [for example, horripilation], as well as attentional and memory systems. Activity of affect systems and effector systems is synthesized into an *emotion percept* (preverbal subjective feeling), which can be transformed (or *reconfigured*) into a symbolic code

such as language. Moreover, conscious cognitive appraisal (involving rational thought, logic, and usually language) can regulate, modulate, and partly initiate, activity of affect systems and effector systems. (Koelsch et al. 1)

On this account, Hogan's 'incident structure,' which is here termed an 'emotion percept,' may integrate activity from four distinct affect systems, while his 'event structure,' at least to the extent that it involves 'conscious cognitive appraisal,' appears to be more of a conceptual and interpretive process than an affective or emotional one.[7] The conceptual–interpretive process can serve to 'regulate, modulate, and partly initiate' emotion percepts, but this process is to some degree frustrated for most readers of 'The Thorn,' such that affects initiated during the top-down linguistic process of reading cannot be easily identified, regulated, or otherwise reflectively contained.

Such uncontained or excessive affect would likely register at the very top of the emotion-systems complex, in the OFC, which (among a host of other functions) is directly involved in 'automatic' or unconscious cognitive appraisal, including ongoing 'normative significance evaluation' through 'stimulus evaluation checks' that 'are performed with reference to internalized knowledge of social norms' (Koelsch et al. 10–11). In this way, the OFC generates unconscious 'expectancies, and is sensitive to breaches of expectancy (which give rise to feelings of surprise)' (Koelsch et al. 12). Breaches of expectancy – also known as 'defamiliarization' or 'estrangement' – generate specifically 'moral affects,' where 'moral' is understood in the widest sense as having to do with any and all internalized 'representations of relatively complex social norms, roles, and conventions,' including literary ones (Koelsch et al. 12; see also 16). In 'The Thorn,' Wordsworth courts then flouts his readers' unconscious expectations with regard to genre conventions, beginning with his stanza form itself, which evokes the 'native rhythm' and 'pleasing familiarity' of ballad measure, only to breach that satisfied expectancy with the onset of the fifth line. The felt disturbance, initiated in the OFC, should 'awaken [...] the mind's attention,' in Coleridge's phrase, 'from the lethargy of custom,' thereby 'exciting a feeling analogous to the supernatural' that may not become conscious but that nevertheless orients and colors the reader's unfolding response. In the terms of Koelsch et al., 'according to the outcome of such evaluation and appraisal of [for example, prosodic] information, the OFC also performs immediate, automatic, and non-conscious imbuement of [that] information with emotional valence' (11). Such non-conscious valence, I submit, then attaches to the diction, imagery, and figuration that the fifth lines repetitively hammer home, making them unforgettably yet also inexplicably impressive.

An experimental paradigm for testing these predictions has yielded promising results for a team of researchers based at Freie Universität in Berlin. The stimuli in this elegant fMRI study consisted of familiar proverbs ('Rome was not built in a day'), unfamiliar proverbs ('Not every cloud rains'), proverb substitutions that retain the sense of a familiar proverb but not its form ('Rome was not constructed in a day'), proverb variants that reverse the sense of a familiar proverb ('Rome was not destroyed in a day'), and baseline sentences not in proverbial form ('Salt makes some foods taste better') (Bohrn et al. 2–3). Of these five conditions, only two were hypothesized to be defamiliarizing: the proverb substitutions (which preserve the conventional sense but deviate in form) and the proverb variants (which are deviant in both sense and form). The key finding for our purposes is that only the latter 'activated areas related to affective evaluation' including the OFC (Bohrn et al. 8). Noting that these 'affect-related areas [...] have often been attributed to moral emotions,' Bohrn et al. explain this differential finding in terms of participants' conventional expectations:

> While proverbs express traditionally valued and accepted cultural norms and beliefs, proverb-variants often oppose, or at least question traditional value. Proverb-substitutions, which do not question the content of the corresponding familiar proverbs, did not recruit this moral emotion network. (10)

Following this model and Wordsworth's formal directives, a range of simplified stimuli could be created involving systematic manipulations of familiar ballad refrains or rhythms, some of which involve an unexpected fifth line, and some of these involving an unexpected word, image, or figure. Wordsworth's first stanza models both kinds of deviance, insofar as the simile of the fifth line, 'like a two-years' child,' represents a conceptual reversal of the semantic import of the preceding ballad quatrain, which insists through repetition that the thorn 'looks so old and grey.' By contrast, Wordsworth's fourth stanza models only the first kind of deviance, insofar as its fifth-line reference to 'All lovely colours [that] there you see' sustains the sense of the foregoing quatrain ('There is a fresh and lovely sight') rather than subverting it. By adding a sixth line to such stimuli, one could test whether left-shifted or prospectively enjambed syntax in the fifth line amplifies the predicted effect of greater OFC activation in the doubly deviant condition (fifth line + conceptual reversal) than in the singly deviant condition (fifth line + conceptual consistency).

Primary Affect as an Agent of Moral Change

Increasingly heightened activity in the 'moral affect' region of the OFC in response to Wordsworth's deviant (in rhythm only), doubly deviant (in rhythm and concept), and/or triply deviant forms (in rhythm, concept, and syntax) would offer empirical support for the success of Wordsworth's rhetorical experiment in 'The Thorn' and for the validity rather than fallaciousness of critical arguments based on readers' affective responses to the poem. More generally, such a finding would begin to clarify what Wordsworth meant when he proposed to give his readers 'new compositions of feeling' that would 'render their feelings more sane, pure, and permanent, in short, more consonant to nature, that is, to eternal nature' (*Letters* 355).[8] By 'eternal nature,' Wordsworth means 'human nature' in its speciated as opposed to its socialized character, human nature 'as it has been [and eve]r will be' notwithstanding the 'false refinements, wayward and artificial desires, false criti[ci]sms, [and] effeminate habits of thinking and feeling' that distort and conceal it, especially among the literate (355). John Wilson's cultivated 'aversion' for the representation of 'idiots' is the case in point. His 'pre-established code of decision' ('Advertisement' to *Lyrical Ballads* 739) concerning the subject matter pre-empts his authentic response to 'The Idiot Boy' and thus defeats in advance the poem's reformative purpose of stimulating a 'new composition of feeling' grounded in a 'sane[r], pure[r], and [more] permanent' affectivity. 'So with respect to many moral feelings, either of [lo]ve or dislike,' Wordsworth goes on to say: conventional 'modes of sentiment' usurp the place and reduce the force of natural human responses (*Letters* 356). The rhetorical task of Wordsworth's balladry is to reverse this moral calculus, artfully short-circuiting 'false notions' of habit and convention and thereby creating an opening and outlet for pre-reflective affectivity in which natural moral feelings may revive and recombine (356).

Given the contemporaneity of its ostensible theme, 'The Thorn' presented the same problem as 'The Idiot Boy' to a greater degree, and Wordsworth responded accordingly with the most radically experimental strategy on display in the volume. As scholars have long noted, many ballads and poetic tales of abandoned mothers and infanticide were circulating in books and periodicals when 'The Thorn' first appeared in 1798.[9] Had Wordsworth told his tale in the traditional way, with the narrator largely backgrounded and the story of Martha Ray foregrounded and delivered in chronological order in conventional ballad stanzas (*à la* 'The Lass of Fair Wone,' translated from Bürger by William

Taylor and reprinted in the *Monthly*, *Edinburgh*, and *Scots Magazines* in 1796), readers' expectations would have been well ahead of their line-by-line experience, reducing it wherever possible to the conventional script and anticipated response (for example, 'love or dislike' of sensational incidents, suffering characters, moral justice, popular verse forms and style, and so on). To forestall this knowing-in-advance that too effectively impedes feeling-in-process, Wordsworth displaces the traditional story from the narrative present, defers its introduction for many stanzas, fragments and disorders its sequence, and, by focusing instead on the 'superstitious' and 'credulous' narrator of such a tale, calls into irresolvable question the facticity of its rumored events (*Lyrical Ballads* 351). In lieu of the expected tale of passionate crime and punishment, Wordsworth represents a mind 'of slow faculties and deep feelings,' 'not loose but adhesive' (351), in a stanza tailor-made to produce a similarly adhesive cast of mind in the reader, in which the operations of integrative understanding are retarded and the play of feelings thereby deepened. Wordsworth thus 'take[s] care' that the very words and images which in the narrator's mind 'are impregnated with passion, should likewise convey passion to Readers,' especially those 'not accustomed to sympathize with men feeling in that manner, or using such language' (351). The words of the poem should thus function not merely as mimetic 'symbols of [...] passion, but as things, active and efficient, which are themselves part of the passion' and in the reader's experience wholly productive of it (351).

Because the issue of Martha Ray's displaced maternity cannot be decided, the poem's two other passionate impregnations, the virtual one that is mimetically represented and the actual one that is rhetorically evoked, can never come to full conceptual term. As Wordsworth suggests through the embedded figure of a 'listener', readers should expect to be, not satisfied with the narrator's tale, but perplexed and superstitiously haunted by its affect-laden imagery. James Averill accordingly finds that '[t]he redundancy that reflects "a craving in the mind" [...] is equally present in the reader [...] In the course of the telling, the thorn, the pond, and the heap of moss become as important to the listener as they have been to the narrator' (174–5). Citation analysis bears Averill out: of the thirty-four most-cited lines printed above, sixteen concern the thorn, pond, and heap of moss; add to that tally the lines that represent Martha's cry and fully two-thirds of the most cited lines turn out to be devoted to the same perceptual counters that haunt the narrator's adhesive imagination. Critically, none of these twenty-three lines carries narrative or actional content, and of the remaining eleven, only two (126–7) provide narrative information that is beyond question.

In other words, the majority of the most attention-getting lines do not bear determinate interpretative significance and have not been cited for that reason. Rather, because 'we cannot "know" the cause, the "why" and "wherefore" so insistently demanded by the questioner and denied by the speaker,' our narrative 'hunger for motive and incident is satisfied by the sheer presence of images, or in the language of sceptical empiricism, of impressions' (Sheats 98). 'Satisfied' is too strong a term, for the 'sheer presence' of perceptual 'impressions' must persistently stoke interpretative reflection rather than answer its conceptual need. This is why, for Swinburne, for example, even 'on a sixth or seventh reading the effect remains identical – an effect of unmodified and haunting horror' (781). 'Unmodified' indicates that his affective response to 'The Thorn' is not (yet) narratively contextualized or otherwise conceptually contained; consequently, it is 'haunting,' which is to say, permanently impressive. An eighth reading was unlikely to alter the affective situation.

Wordsworth may not have intended to excite the specific affect of 'horror' but he would be gratified to know that his lyrical ballad persistently caused such a strong 'moral disturbance' in a reader as sensitive as Swinburne (Gravil 108). For Wordsworth, the significant issue is whether unmitigated 'horror' had ever previously colored Swinburne's response to 'cruel mother' ballads and tales: if not, in reading 'The Thorn' he was experiencing a salutary 'new combination of feeling' that swamped his habituated expectations for the genre and opened the way (perhaps never again to be foreclosed) to a recalibration of his 'moral feelings of love or dislike' concerning it. Wordsworth would beg much the same question of Wilson's response to 'The Idiot Boy': if Wilson brought predetermined feelings of 'loathing and disgust' to the poem, then the question is the extent to which Wordsworth's design (including the five-line metrical unit that plays a key role in the affective dynamics of 'The Thorn' stanza) may have tempered such feelings by bringing them into combination with unanticipated feelings of 'exquisite delight' (*Letters* 356, 358). In Wordsworth's view, the resulting spot-of-time-like complex, in which one kind of feeling to a 'far other' kind of feeling is 'attached,' could be morally consequential, regardless of whether that consequence is consciously appraised or articulated as such. Even local effects of attention recruitment and affective valence imbuement orchestrated by meter and rhyme are, on this account, potential agents of moral change.

Empirical literary research is now poised to confirm this truly radical affective hypothesis, which can be restated in contemporary terms as follows:

The registering of such [attentional and affective] movements in the neural system, just below the level of habitual mental categorization[, and] the excited sense of cognitive matter happening speedily and almost physically *before* cognition can take place: these seem to point to deep pre-articulate sources of excited feeling not exhausted by any subsequent ratiocination and worthy of being an acknowledged part of our experience. (Davis 23)

The echoes here of Coleridge's characterization of Wordsworth's prime directive in *Lyrical Ballads* – to 'excite [...] feeling [...] by awakening the mind's attention from the lethargy of custom' – are likely deliberate, for Philip Davis begins his brilliant polemic on behalf of affective poetics with none other than Wordsworth himself, who 'spoke of remembering *how* he felt at a particular time, but *what* exactly he felt he could not recall' (1). Davis quotes the relevant passage from *The Prelude* and then paraphrases Wordsworth's 'how' in terms of 'the obscure, possible, growing feeling of inchoate thoughts' (1). The cultivation of such 'deep pre-articulate sources of excited feeling' was the express goal of Wordsworth's affective narratology in *Lyrical Ballads*, one he appears to have achieved more frequently than not but which his readers over two centuries have struggled to articulate, for reasons that are only now becoming clear. Wordsworth's dictum that 'Poetry is passion,' pointedly offered with reference to 'The Thorn' (351), provides a long-standing warrant for the kinds of affective research, from citation analysis to neuroimaging, that this chapter illustrates and advocates.

Notes

1. The problem bedevils subsequent scholarship that likewise argues that 'the real concern of these poems is tale-telling and tale-listening' (Griffin 393), involving an 'insistently tentative exploration of the relations between the poetic object and its audience' (Averill 149) that leads to an 'affective engagement with the reader [...] defined through [poem's] affective potentialities' (Regier and Uhlig 8). This is all well and good for just the reason Parrish specified – Wordsworth himself said so – but, unsubstantiated by verifiable evidence, such claims play more or less directly into Wimsatt and Beardsley's hands.
2. See Bruhn, 'History' 675–9.
3. Reprinting this Fenwick note in the Cornell edition of *Lyrical Ballads* (350), Butler and Green show that 'prominently' has been deleted from the fair copy DCMS 153 but not that 'permanently' has been written in above in pencil. The same penciled handwriting supplies other corrections in the MS, including missing and misspelled words, which suggests that 'permanently' is most likely what the poet wanted and/or what Isabella Fenwick's autograph MS, now lost but from which DCMS 153 was copied, originally read.

Thanks to Jeff Cowton, curator of the Wordsworth Trust, for assistance in sorting this out.
4. See Bruhn, 'Citation' for details.
5. Postscript: a subsequent citation analysis of thirty-five additional interpretations of 'The Thorn' published between 1914 and 2019 replicates these findings and further supports the conclusions drawn here.
6. See Bruhn, 'History.'
7. In addition to Hogan, see Cupchik 39ff, for extensive overviews of two broad classes of emotion theory known as 'natural kinds' and 'conceptual-act' theories. Koelsch et al.'s quartet model is an example of a 'natural kinds' theory.
8. For further discussion of this point, see Bruhn, 'Ambiguity,' 31–4.
9. See Mayo 496n14; Parrish 91–2; Jacobus 241–2.

References

Averill, James. *Wordsworth and the Poetry of Human Suffering*. Ithaca, NY: Cornell University Press, 1980.
Bohrn, Isabel C., Ulrike Altmann, Oliver Lubrich, Winfried Menninghaus, and Arthur M. Jacobs. 'Old Proverbs in New Skins – An fMRI Study on Defamiliarization.' *Frontiers in Psychology* (4 July 2012): 1–18.
Bruhn, Mark J. 'Ambiguity in Affect: The Modernity of Wordsworth's *Lyrical Ballads*.' *Romantic Ambiguities: Abodes of the Modern*. Ed. Sebastian Domsch, Christoph Reinfandt, and Katharine Rennhak. Trier: Wissenschaftlicher Verlag Trier, 2017. 21–36.
—. 'Citation Analysis: An Empirical Approach to Professional Literary Interpretation.' *Scientific Study of Literature* 8 (2018): 77–113.
—. '"The History and Science of Feeling": Wordsworth's Affective Poetics, Then and Now.' *The Palgrave Handbook of Affect Studies and Textual Criticism*. Ed. Donald R. Wehrs and Thomas Blake. Cham: Springer Nature, 2017. 671–93.
Christensen, Jerome. 'Wordsworth's Misery, Coleridge's Woe: Reading "The Thorn."' *Papers on Language and Literature* 16 (1980): 268–86.
Collings, David. 'Emotion Without Content: Primary Affect and Pure Potentiality in Wordsworth.' *Romanticism and the Emotions*. Ed. Joel Faflak and Richard C. Sha. Cambridge: Cambridge University Press, 2014. 171–91.
Cupchik, Gerald C. *The Aesthetics of Emotion: Up the Down Staircase of the Mind-Body*. Cambridge: Cambridge University Press, 2016.
Davis, Philip. *Reading and the Reader*. Oxford: Oxford University Press, 2013.
Deacon, Terrence. 'The Aesthetic Faculty.' *The Artful Mind: Cognitive Science and the Riddle of Human Creativity*. Ed. Mark Turner. New York: Oxford University Press, 2006. 21–53.
Gravil, Richard. *Wordsworth's Bardic Vocation, 1787–1842*. New York: Palgrave Macmillan, 2003.
Gray, Thomas. 'Elegy Written in a Country Churchyard.' *The Poems of Gray and Collins*. Ed. Austin Lane Poole. London: Oxford University Press, 1961.

Griffin, Andrew L. 'Wordsworth and the Problem of Imaginative Story: The Case of "Simon Lee."' *PMLA* 92 (1977): 392–409.
Hogan, Patrick Colm. *Affective Narratology: The Emotional Structure of Stories*. Lincoln: University of Nebraska Press, 2011.
Jacobus, Mary. *Tradition and Experiment in Wordsworth's Lyrical Ballads (1798)*. Oxford: Oxford University Press, 1976.
Koelsch, Stefan, Arthur M. Jacobs, Winfried Menninghaus, Katja Liebal, Gisela Klann-Delius, Christian von Scheve, and Gunther Gebauer. 'The Quartet Theory of Human Emotions: An Integrative and Neurofunctional Model.' *Physics of Life Reviews* 13 (2015): 1–27.
La Cassagnère, Christian. 'Histoire d'un regard: Une lecture de "The Thorn" de Wordsworth.' *Études Anglaises* 37 (1984): 28–40.
McDonald, Peter. *Sound Intentions: The Working of Rhyme in Nineteenth-Century Poetry*. New York: Oxford University Press, 2013.
Mayo, Robert. 'The Contemporaneity of the *Lyrical Ballads*.' *PMLA* 69 (1954): 486–522.
Miall, David S. 'Emotions and the Structuring of Narrative Responses.' *Poetics Today* 32 (2011): 323–48.
O'Donnell, Brennan. *The Passion of Meter: A Study of Wordsworth's Metrical Art*. Kent, OH: Kent State University Press, 1995.
Parrish, Stephen Maxfield. *The Art of the Lyrical Ballads*. Cambridge, MA: Harvard University Press, 1973.
Regier, Alexander and Stefan H. Uhlig, eds. *Wordsworth's Poetic Theory: Knowledge, Language, Experience*. New York: Palgrave Macmillan, 2010.
Russell, Corinna. 'A Defense of Tautology: Repetition and Difference in Wordsworth's "Note" to "The Thorn."' *Paragraph* 28 (2005): 104–18.
Sellars, Roy. '"Wallowing in the rubbish of departed ignorance": Poetic Knowledge in Peacock, Wordsworth and Adorno.' *European Journal of English Studies* 11 (2007): 301–13.
Sheats, Paul D. '"Tis Three Feet Long, and Two Feet Wide': Wordsworth's "Thorn" and the Politics of Bathos.' *The Wordsworth Circle* 22 (1991): 92–100.
Stanley, Kate. 'Affect and Emotion: James, Dewey, Tomkins, Damasio, Massumi, Spinoza.' *The Palgrave Handbook of Affect Studies and Textual Criticism*. Ed. Donald R. Wehrs and Thomas Blake. Cham: Springer Nature, 2017. 97–112.
Swinburne, Algernon Charles. 'Wordsworth and Byron.' *The Nineteenth Century: A Monthly Review* 15 (1884): 764–90.
Wimsatt, Jr, W. K. and Monroe C. Beardsley. *The Verbal Icon: Studies in the Meaning of Poetry*. Lexington: University of Kentucky Press, 1954.
Wordsworth, William. *Early Poems and Fragments, 1785–1797*. Ed. Carol Landon and Jared Curtis. Ithaca, NY: Cornell University Press, 1997.
—. *Lyrical Ballads, and Other Poems, 1797–1800*. Ed. James Butler and Karen Green. Ithaca, NY: Cornell University Press, 1992.
—. *The Prelude: 1799, 1805, 1850*. Ed. Jonathan Wordsworth, M. H. Abrams, and Stephen Gill. New York: W. W. Norton, 1979.
Wordsworth, William and Dorothy Wordsworth. *Letters of William and Dorothy Wordsworth: The Early Years*. Ed. Chester Shaver. Oxford: Oxford University Press, 1967.

Chapter 7

After-Affects and Second Thoughts: Wordsworth, Eliot, and the Forms of Emotional Thinking

Nancy Yousef

Sudden excitations and strange fits of passion are not unusual in Romantic poetry; indeed, we might credit Romanticism for instructing us to notice how bursts of spontaneous reaction disrupt the ongoing flow of experience – so frequently as to destabilize the distinction between the momentous and the mundane. Dilation of spontaneity is made possible by the temporal distentions and cumulative parataxes of lyric description. Typically, a single, and singular, instance of heightened response extends through successive figurations, deepened with memory or regret, amplified by expectation or anxiety. It is as if lyric time suspends the difference between reaction and reflection. Recent years have seen an intense and often selective interest in the reactive immediacy of feeling, in what Wordsworth termed the 'pressure of the passions' and characterized as the 'animal sensations, and the causes which excite' them (598). Memorably articulated by the Romantic poet, the task of capturing the 'spontaneous overflow' of visceral affects is evidently also an undertaking of the literary and cultural theory of our time.[1] That said, it takes only the most glancing of second readings to recall that by 'animal sensations' Wordsworth does not mean purely physical or unthinking modes of being, and to be reminded that the 'powerful feelings' he associates with poetry are, at once and without contradiction, spur-of-the-moment and reflective: 'All good poetry is the spontaneous overflow of powerful feelings: but,' Wordsworth qualifies, 'Poems to which any value can be attached, were never produced' except by one who 'had also thought long and deeply' (598). With the 'but' that introduces a crucial additional specification to the definition of 'good poetry,' Wordsworth links affective spontaneity to the practice of long and deep thought, joining terms that would ordinarily be set in opposition. Such generative complications are so ubiquitous in the 'Preface' as to count as a deliberate procedure or mode of argument, whereby every evocation of the passions as primal, immediate, and bodily also involves a transfiguring qualification of those terms. The interdependence of formal aspirations, rhetorical complexity and affective expression in the 'Preface' will be addressed more fully near the end of this chapter; here it will suffice to note that even as certain familiar features of Romanticism, especially the incitements and provocations of Romantic lyric, seem to cohere with contemporary interest in the visceral energies of affect, first impressions are misleading.

The appeal to feelings, or more precisely, the appeal *of* feelings is always also an articulated appeal. The reader, the analyst, the critic can attend to the occasion only when emotion – paralyzing fear, or burning shame, or sharp aversion – is named, narrated, or described. The self-evident is often underemphasized: the cultural theorist or literary historian whose work must be constructed from textual evidence must of necessity fix upon moments when feelings are made explicit. Language is always, after all, what makes affect legible. But the interpretive tendency to compare instances, find patterns, and identify synonymous usages is also liable to simplify and stabilize a partial or static taxonomy of 'basic emotions' or 'core affects.'[2] Emotional range, the complexities of mixed or compounded emotions, and the flux and reflux of emotions, cognitions, and sensations that are themselves rarely discernibly separate are bound to fall out of view when the theoretical aim – deliberately pursued or unintentionally presupposed – is to 'class the cabinet of sensations' and account for each 'as of a single independent thing' (to borrow Wordsworth's caution against the scientizing philosophies of mind of his own day) (*The Prelude* 2.228–9, 231). One way to attend to indistinct, unclassifiable forms of emotional experience is to consider the aftermath of affectively charged spontaneous reaction, to become curious about what comes next, after the moment of explicit emotional intensity subsides into relatively unremarkable, relatively subdued, but nevertheless still moving goings-on of thought and feeling.

My title, 'After-Affects and Second Thoughts,' is intended to signal a turn away from theoretical emphases on affective immediacy and embodiment, a movement past the exciting moment, or moment of excitation, that most obviously presents itself as a significant affective event in order to notice what follows – and to notice also how often what follows is not necessarily a consequence or result of the emotional upsurge, nor simply a resumption or relapse back into whatever state of being prevailed before the extraordinary excitation. Attending to what comes after spontaneous response means noticing forms of emotional experience that seem too composed or too reflective or perhaps simply too thoughtful to fall under the definition of affect – an exclusion that might itself provoke second thoughts about the tendency, or temptation, to construct affect as a discrete category. At stake are the conceptual and aesthetic implications of assuming that feeling can be isolated, even if only for analytic purposes, from a flow of experience that includes thinking – that we can separate affects from after-affects.[3] What happens, then, when a pressing urgency eases, when excitement subsides, and yet feelings remain pooled as in a full basin of water that has been tipped but not altogether spilled?

Post-Romantic Affect: Picturing the Morning After

The textual scene that initially provoked these second thoughts about affect is lodged in George Eliot's *Middlemarch* (1871–2), a novel that I want to designate as post-Romantic, by which I mean belonging to a much longer account of Romanticism that would include its precursors and its successors. Eliot's novels fully assimilate the Romantic negation of the distinction between the momentous and the commonplace; indeed, that negation is explicitly espoused in the memorable metafictional reflections on artistic practice embedded in her work. The realist's reclamation of Wordsworth's aspiration to cherish the everyday ought to be important for the student of Romanticism not only as a reminder of the still under-appreciated afterlife of the period, but also for the proleptically edifying implications of a radically different formal approach to the poet's aesthetic imperative.[4]

The temporal distentions of lyric often obfuscate sequence in ways that narrative does not, and precisely because the events of a novel either unfold in a linear series or can be retrospectively reconstructed as a succession of events, it is perhaps easier to see that what counts as affectively consequential is not exhausted by the force of immediate reactivity – that what follows the spontaneous fit of passion is in itself emotionally eventful. The scene from *Middlemarch* that prompted these reflections occurs in the wake of climactic plot developments near the end of the novel, when the heroine's consciously deliberated charitable resolutions are brought into startling collision with romantic and erotic longings that have only barely, and only through the negations of abstention and renunciation, been admitted to her awareness. When, with characteristic good will, Dorothea undertakes to help the young Dr Lydgate withstand scandal and financial ruin by calling on his wife, Rosamond, she glimpses Will Ladislaw, the man she loves (though she has not quite admitted that to herself), clasping Rosamond's hands and speaking to her in urgent tones as she gazes at him with a flushed and tearful face. The melodramatic staging is unusual in Eliot – Dorothea is on the threshold of the

Lydgate drawing room, peering through a crack in the door left ajar. The scene provokes an overwrought eruption of feelings in a heroine who, up to this point, has not been given to the vehemence of contempt, jealousy, and rage; her reactions under the pressure of these passions are initially and emphatically defined and described as physical, even physiological events. Dorothea 'was never animated by a more self-possessed energy,' we are told, 'as if she had drunk a great draught of scorn' and, thus fortified, 'felt the power to walk and work for a day, without meat or drink' (738–9). This initial surge of affect makes the ensuing surrender to grief more poignant for having been deferred. It also intensifies our sense of the power of the emotions to take hold of the subject, to excite and transport or, as happens later, to overcome and exhaust. Such energies rapidly exceed the bounds of 'self-possession.' Once alone in her home, Dorothea finds herself held in the 'clutch of inescapable anguish,' at the mercy, and in the throes, of sensations and physical reactions over which she has no control (749). 'Her heart was palpitating violently,' leaving her 'helpless,' incapable of 'recovery' and 'resistance,' engulfed by 'waves of suffering [that] shook her too thoroughly to leave any power of thought' (749). The emotional upheavals described thus far correspond to familiar and still current accounts of affective energy as a visceral, physical response, constitutive of experience, and independent of conscious cognition – too powerful to leave any power for thought.[5] While giving this reaction its due, the novel also compels us to attend to what happens next, specifically the morning after this dark night, when Dorothea herself asks 'What should I do – how should I act now, this very day, if I could clutch my own pain, and compel it to silence?' (751)

The narrator tells us that:

> It had taken long for her to come to that question, and there was light piercing into the room. She opened her curtains, and looked out towards the bit of road that lay in view, with fields beyond ... On the road there was a man with a bundle on his back and a woman carrying her baby; in the field she could see figures moving – perhaps the shepherd with his dog. Far off in the bending sky was the pearly light; and she felt the largeness of the world, and the manifold workings of men to labor and endurance. She was part of that involuntary, palpitating life, and could neither look out on it from her luxurious shelter as a mere spectator, nor hide her eyes in selfish complaining.
>
> What she would resolve to do that day did not yet seem quite clear, but something that she could achieve stirred her as with an approaching murmur which would soon gather distinctness. (751)

This justly famous passage seems to deliver a Dorothea recovering herself, resuming the shape of the character with whom readers of the novel have grown familiar, someone again striving to be something other than selfish. But what, if anything, comes to be settled or resolved here? Does Dorothea succeed in mastering her pain and stoically compelling it to silence, or does that remain a wistful articulation of an impossible desire? ('*If only* I could clutch my own pain' and thereby escape the 'clutch of inescapable anguish.') The scene outside her window moves her – even if only with the indeterminate, undetermined resolve to do something that 'did not yet seem quite clear.' 'She felt' – not knew, or considered, or even glimpsed, but *felt* – 'the largeness of the world' under a pearly light, more opalescent than transparent. Beyond this evocative vagueness, we do not know what Dorothea is thinking, or what it might mean to feel that feeling and to experience it as an impetus to action that is literally, and in the ordinary idiom of the emotions, *moving*. The narrator informs us that 'she was part of that involuntary, palpitating life,' but it is by no means clear that this is Dorothea's revelatory thought rather than the narrator's observation, nor even, were we to attribute it to Dorothea, how such an insight could amount to a motive, or inspire the idea of 'something that she could achieve,' however indistinct.

I would not be the first to notice that the scene upon which Dorothea gazes is framed, as a painting, by her window, and that she necessarily stands removed from it, taking in the view from the 'luxurious shelter' of her position as the proprietor of all that she beholds. To rehearse a familiar kind of critical argument: if Dorothea is looking at road and field and figures of man, woman, shepherd, and dog as if at a painting of them, a rustic landscape, then she is not after all really seeing them, but only seeing-them-as, and even making them into, consoling means toward the desired goal of self-mastery – fulfilling the wish of 'clutch[ing] ... pain, and compel[ling] it to silence' by seizing on an image that overlooks the pain of others. Are we content to think that the aestheticization of the scene exposes the facticity or bad faith of the ideas and sentiments it conveys? The novel itself contains this very critique in an earlier episode, when Mr Brooke deigns to visit the poor homestead on the edge of his property called Freeman's End. There, the narrator initially and deliberately indulges in painterly description that explicitly approaches the tenant farm as a piece of picturesque. We are told that a 'mouldering garden wall with hollyhocks peeping over it was a perfect study of highly-mingled subdued color,' adjacent to which are seen 'an aged goat lying against the open back-kitchen door,' 'the mossy thatch of the cowshed,' 'pauper labourers in ragged breeches ... unloading a wagon of corn,' 'cows being tethered for milking' (376). All these elements appear arrayed on the same plane, all equally 'objects under the quiet light of a sky marbled with high clouds,' precisely, the narrator notes, as they would be in the 'sort of picture we have all paused over as a "charming bit"' (376). The description knowingly points to the distraction from material conditions that this 'sort of picture' beautifies – an aesthetic remove admonished in the immediately subsequent scene when Mr Brooke is affronted by the crudely indignant hostility of his tenant. Let us take the painterly view of 'Freeman's End' together with the ensuing rebuke of that image as a reminder that *Middlemarch* is a novel fully aware that moral blindness can take the form of aestheticizing distance, that persons and things can be made into undifferentiated objects under a beautifully colored sky. To credit Eliot with deliberation in configuring the later scene of Dorothea's looking out her window as a moment of aesthetic receptivity is to suggest that we are meant to distinguish her becalming act of seeing from a mindless 'pause over a charming bit' of picturesque, and that the novel in effect asks us to apprehend the difference between being charmed by the appearance of hollyhocks, old goats, and poor laborers together as so many 'objects under the light of a quiet sky' and being impressed, as Dorothea is, by figures that are, after all, so abstract as to be impossible to picture.

'Far off in the bending sky was the pearly light,' under which no thing is actually seen, but something indistinct and only vaguely articulated comes to be 'felt.' Dorothea 'feels,' not sees, 'the largeness of the world and the manifold workings of men to labour and endurance,' an aspect of the real that itself entails a manifold of sensing, conceiving, and imagining. The connection between 'feeling the largeness of the world' and resolving to move, or moving with resolve – though not with clarity of aim – is made precisely when and because Dorothea attends to the world before her as if to a work of art, subject to its effects but also actively implicated in conjuring those effects – able to feel what cannot be seen: the 'largeness of the world' and the 'manifold workings of men.' Far from being repressed, or even attenuated in the morning light, affect reshapes itself into an animating resolution when given a form around which to compose itself. Surely this too counts as being moved by a feeling – not of a kind so powerful as to leave no power for thought, but precisely powerful enough to lend its power to thought.[6]

If, in the end, 'what she would resolve to do that day did not seem quite clear,' then there has been no clarifying transcendence of pain or palliative relief, only an impulse toward an indeterminate 'something that she could achieve.' This movement occurs not just by virtue of time, but of time passed in a state of attention and responsiveness that Eliot presents as akin to aesthetic experience – a 'looking out' on the world behind a glass and beyond a frame. If nothing more definitive happens here than an intermingling of feeling, thinking, and intending, then perhaps it is precisely just this occurrence – the co-presence of feeling, thinking, intending with no one being the cause of the other, no one being separable from the others as a distinct faculty – that the novel invites us to apprehend.

Conjunctions of Art and Affect: 'Form itself becomes the object and material of emotion'

I proposed earlier that Eliot's fiction instantiates the persistence of Romantic aspirations later in the nineteenth century, in particular the effort to define aesthetic practice in terms of attention to the commonplace and the related but not contradictory insistence that attending to the commonplace is not a matter of representing the already-given but rather entails a making-of-interest in the heretofore unnoticed. The ordinary in Wordsworth and Eliot is often evoked in conjunction with an ethically inflected imperative to recall or remember what the poet repeatedly terms – without elaboration or definition – 'important.'[7] The novelist gives that vague importance some precision when she argues that, in the regions of the everyday, 'emotion links itself with particulars' ('The Poet Young,' *Essays* 199). Elsewhere I have argued that the emotional investment in particulars is both a formal element and a conceptual commitment to counteract the theoretical force of generalization and abstraction.[8] At issue here is the effort to register forms of emotional experience at once so common and so sedate as to pass unremarked and without account among the sensational and passional intensities typical of the representation of emotions at the end, and in the aftermath, of the 'age of sensibility.' In both Wordsworth and Eliot, the imbrication of affective receptivity and aesthetic attention occurs *en passant*, as it were – as a momentous but barely discernible pause, a looking-about before going on, rather than an emphatic reaction to an extraordinary provocation.

It will be useful, in this context, to recall that the anxieties driving Wordsworth's critique of artificial poetic diction in the 'Preface' to *Lyrical Ballads* and the wider Romantic critique of the facile moral psychology associated with 'sensibility' in which it participates retain a recognizable urgency in Eliot's writing on the unstable relationship between poetic language and the emotions. In a series of remarks from her journals, collected under the title 'Notes on Form in Art' (written in 1868, proximate to the composition and publication of *Middlemarch* in 1871), Eliot begins by urging us to withhold definition of the key term: 'to any but those who ... cannot afford to wait for a meaning,' she writes, 'it must be more fruitful to ask what relations can be properly included under the word "Form" as applied to artistic composition' than to use the word and take its meaning for granted (231). She proposes that 'Poetic form was not begotten by thinking it out or framing it as a shell which should hold emotional expression, any more than the shell of an animal arises before the living creature' (235). A speculative history is sketched: the 'spontaneous' passions captured in 'the earliest poetic forms' include the 'rhythmic shouts' of zealous hunters and warriors, the 'funeral or marriage sing-song,' and even the 'monotonous burthen chanted by an Arab boatman on the Nile' because monotony too may be understood as an 'emotional state' in need of utterance (234–5). But this harmonious conjunction of spontaneity and formal expression is only an originating moment: 'A form once started must by and by cease to be purely spontaneous: the form itself becomes the object and material of emotion' until at last 'it preoccupies the room of emotional thinking' (235).

Eliot's incomplete remarks end abruptly with what seems a story of degeneration, in which 'tricks with vocables' take the place of 'living words filled with the blood of relevant meaning' (235). The 'Notes on Form' are unfinished, and if we were to imagine an essay concluding where Eliot leaves off, then we would have to count her among those who find that art has fallen away from an ideal of animated, spontaneous expression. Nevertheless, these remarks about the inevitable disappearance of spontaneously generated forms, and the resulting importance of form as that which holds 'emotional thinking,' may be more cautionary than elegiac. If form 'preoccupies the room of emotional thinking,' then it is also at risk of dislocation and evacuation. The danger may not lie in the fact that form has become the 'object and material of emotion,' but in the carelessness of its handling or the abuse of its power. The 'want of genuine emotion' Eliot elsewhere associates with rhetorical artifice and conceptual abstraction (*Essays*, 198–9) needs to be understood as reclaiming and acknowledging the continued relevance, or modernity, of the alarm sounded in the 'Preface' to *Lyrical Ballads*, in which Wordsworth offers a conjectural history of poetic diction similar to that found in Eliot's 'Notes.' The 1802 appendix to the 'Preface' traces a devolution in the correspondence between emotion and utterance from a time when poets wrote 'naturally,' 'from the passion excited by real events' to the current period in which the 'corruption' of poetic diction is mistaken for refinement, and the 'plain humanities of nature' are hopelessly obscured by the modern 'masquerade of tricks ... hieroglyphics and enigmas' that passes as poetry (617).

The condemnation of the language of sensibility – the 'extravagant and absurd' excesses Wordsworth denounces in the 'Preface' (606) and the pretensions Eliot excoriates in essays on the poetry of Edward Young and what she calls the 'silliness' of lady novelists (*Essays*, 199, 155) – betrays an anxiety about how stylized rhetorical artifice obscures, disfigures, and corrodes the distinctive forms of truth lodged in ordinary language and which the poet and the novelist are uniquely – that is to say, especially, as specialists – committed to render legible. The commitment to write in the 'language really used by men' in order to make 'ordinary things ... [and] incidents and situations interesting' is a culturally urgent project for Wordsworth and for Eliot because it is linked to a recognition of the dangers of factitious forms and facile expressions – like 'thoughts and prayers' – that leave us with no index of truth other than 'matter of fact or science' in the public life we construct and conduct through language.[9]

Rendered powerless, vacuous, and insubstantial by its sadly predictable utterance on maddeningly avoidable occasions of violence, 'thoughts and prayers' reminds us also of abuses of the language of feeling in the political sphere. If, as I have been suggesting, Wordsworth and Eliot both imagine a revitalized conjunction of aesthetics and affect as a recovery of 'relevant meaning' and 'importance,' then it perhaps bears emphasizing that the need for such a recovery is first articulated in response to crises of moral and political language brought on by the pressing conflicts of the era (abolition and the French Revolution principal among them). Wordsworth writes in the immediate aftermath – hardly even the aftermath – of these crises in and for the language and politics of 'sensibility' and by turning briefly to the sharp diagnosis of these crises in the work of Mary Wollstonecraft, my aim is to thicken the cultural context for the far-reaching claims both Wordsworth and Eliot later make for literature as a generative and vital form of 'emotional thinking.'

'Emotions that reason deepens': Wollstonecraft Rethinks Affect, and Eliot Follows

A Vindication of the Rights of Men (1790), Wollstonecraft's sharp, hastily written reaction to Edmund Burke's *Reflections on the Revolution in France* (1790), styles itself as a spontaneous response animated by indignation and scorn. The denunciation of what Wollstonecraft terms the cultural 'mania' (6) for sensibility and of the corrupting usages of false sentiment in political discourse is evidently an important precedent for Wordsworth's censure of affected and artificial poetic diction. But this short polemical work also mounts an incisive critique of moral sentimentalism with implications beyond its immediate political occasion. In taking aim at the value accorded to thoughtless automaticity, or spontaneity, in the theories of emotion prevalent in her day, Wollstonecraft's arguments also have a bearing on related emphases in currently influential theories of affect.

'We ought to beware of confounding mechanical instinctive sensations with emotions that reason deepens and justly terms the feelings of humanity,' Wollstonecraft writes, warning in particular against the loss of the aspirational sense of the latter: 'this word [humanity] discriminates the active exertions of virtue from the vague declamation of sensibility' (54). What are 'emotions that reason deepens'? Are emotions intensified by reason, or attenuated by it, or does Wollstonecraft's phrase instead undermine the very opposition it invokes? These questions pertain to current theories of affect shaped by a fascination with the physiology of the emotions as much as they compel reflection on Wollstonecraft's doubts about what – her own writing helps us see – were related philosophical emphases on sensuous and affective immediacy in her own time. While Burke's sentimental rhetoric is her immediate target, in denying the ethical value of 'instinctive sensations' and what she elsewhere terms 'quick emotions,' Wollstonecraft rejects the basis of influential eighteenth-century theories of a natural moral sense. David Hume, for example, had famously invoked the 'force of sympathy thro' the whole animal creation and the easy communication of sentiments from one being to another' as the origin of moral judgements in his *Treatise of Human Nature* (234). Wollstonecraft is troubled by this apparent reduction of sympathy to automatic impulse. Hume had observed that sympathy causes the 'blood [to] flow with a new tide' and the 'heart [to be] elevated' (228).[10] For Wollstonecraft, not only does this attention to physical response risk turning sympathetic insight into mere sensation, it also risks expending itself entirely in complacent absorption with the feeling. 'The being who is not spurred on to any virtuous act still … boasts of its feelings,' Wollstonecraft observes. 'Why? Because the sight of distress, or an affecting narrative, made its blood flow with more velocity, and the heart, literally speaking, beat with sympathetic feeling. We ought to beware of confounding mechanical instinctive sensations with emotions that reason deepens' (54). To be moved by a scene or story is not necessarily to be stirred into exertion – and here it is worth recalling the difference between this affective current of sympathy that flows through Wollstonecraft's idle subject and the 'resolve to do … something,' however indeterminate, that arises when Eliot's heroine 'feels the largeness of the world' – feels *that*, let us say, instead of the pulse of her own heart beating.[11]

Wollstonecraft's 'emotions that reason deepens'; the 'powerful feelings' of Wordsworth's poet that depend on his having 'thought long and deeply': these formulations deliberately conjoin categories that are typically separated in theories of the emotions. The practical purposes or analytic usefulness of distinguishing affect from cognition should not obscure the importance of the ordinary, lived experience of feeling mingled with thinking, and of thinking entangled with feeling. Indeed, perhaps precisely because the mingled entanglement of thought with feeling and of feeling with thought is so unremarkably humdrum, so ordinary, it lacks theoretical interest.

The momentous and the uneventful may nevertheless be imagined as occasionally coinciding, as when George Eliot's heroine 'feels the largeness of the world' in the scene from *Middlemarch* with which I began. The mood, or mode, I am calling 'after-affect' succeeds an emotional excitation 'too powerful to leave any power for thought.' Composure appears to arise through a lingering mode of attention modeled on aesthetic receptivity. Earlier, I suggested that Eliot would have us distinguish Dorothea's 'look[ing] out' and 'feel[ing]' (not seeing) the 'largeness of the world' from a distancing, aestheticizing view of the landscape as a 'charming bit' of picturesque. The later scene and the after-affect it composes are nevertheless evocative of engaged attention to a work of art, which is to say that Dorothea does indeed look at the scene outside her window *as if* at a painting, but not with the impassive appropriation frequently associated with an instrumentalizing gaze, and not with the idle surrender often given the name absorption either.

'Feeling' what can be neither seen nor represented – the 'largeness of the world' and the 'manifold workings of men' – involves a creative responsiveness, a generative and expansive confusion of perception, affect, and abstract thought that are (it turns out) easily enough comprehended as occurring together if we allow Eliot's choice of the verb 'to feel' its full range of ordinary significations. (Consider how the word is used in the following phrases: 'I feel cold'; 'I feel so alone'; 'I feel the time has come'; 'I feel the earth move under my feet.' I am suggesting that the scope of our ordinary usage of the word includes phenomena that cannot be reduced to or isolated as 'affect,' and that Eliot's use of the word in this passage should serve as a reminder of this fact about the role 'feeling' plays in language.) Finally, it is consequential that Dorothea does not lose herself in the scene, and that this feeling, which is also an imagining, allows an opening for the resolution to 'do ... something,' however undefined and uncertain. The 'resolve to act' engendered by the feeling composed in and by the mode of attention described here is presented as explicitly ethical (a decision not to hide one's eyes in 'selfish complaining') but it is also left deliberately indeterminate. This after-affect that seems to amount to no more than a passive openness to being moved nevertheless matters when (precisely at the moment when) all illusion of agency, or even hope in modest efficacy, is lost. Feeling an incitement to go on, in the aftermath of despair, with no clear sense of an end in view: how momentous and yet how uneventful.

Wordsworth's Not So 'Simple Affections'

Dorothea's dark night ends as morning light breaks into her room; the straightforward temporal and narrative sequence makes plain the distinction between immediate pained reaction and the complex after-affect of a responsive attention in which feeling is not separable from thinking, observing, intending. Such a movement does not terminate in an identifiable emotional state – fear, say, or anger, or some other 'core affect.' Bearing this in mind, I hope it is now possible to return to Wordsworth's poetics with a renewed interest in its deliberate qualifications of affective excitement: 'good poetry is the spontaneous overflow of powerful feelings' but also the work of one who has 'thought long and deeply' (598). More famously, 'the spontaneous overflow of powerful feelings' originates in 'emotion recollected in tranquillity'; consequently, and consequentially for this discussion, there is no 'spontaneous overflow of feeling' in the composition of poetry after all, but an 'emotion kindred to that which was before,' fostered in contemplation, and coalescing into what Wordsworth calls the 'mood' in which poetry is written (611).

The inclination to temper or qualify emotional excitement occurs repeatedly in the 'Preface,' and is most memorably connected to the poet's discussion of the harmonizing power of meter. 'If the images or feelings [of a poem] have an undue proportion of pain connected with them, there is some danger that the excitement may be carried beyond its proper bounds,' Wordsworth notes (609). Meter, then, is the 'something regular' in a poem that averts the danger of over-excitement, balancing out 'an undue proportion of pain' (609). Without questioning the special importance of metrical form in the argument, it is nevertheless also worth noticing how an attenuation of affect-as-excitement informs Wordsworth's understanding of all feelings, however painful, however powerful.

Consider, for example, the unexpected source of the 'agitation' shaping the poems. The 'excitement' of the poetry arises from 'follow[ing] the fluxes and refluxes of the mind when agitated by the great and simple affections' (598): the feelings are no less moving for being the source of an agitation that sets '*the mind*' in motion, rather than being themselves the sole cause of the poet's (and of poetry's) excitement.

The poet's pursuit is not a passive registration of the impact of the affections, but a formal practice involving attention and composition. Here are Wordsworth's examples of what is entailed in 'following' the 'simple affections': 'tracing the maternal passion through many of its more subtle windings'; 'accompanying the last struggles of a human being at the approach of death'; 'showing the perplexity and obscurity which in childhood attend our notion of death'; 'displaying the strength of the fraternal, or to speak more philosophically, of moral attachment when early associated with the great and beautiful objects of nature' (598). A paratactic series of parallel but non-synonymous verbs ('tracing,' 'accompanying,' 'showing,' 'displaying') correspond to the elaborate specification of affections that can hardly be termed 'simple.' Even the 'maternal passion' is rendered complex, unfolding in 'subtle windings.' (And this is to say nothing of the poems Wordsworth adduces as examples – 'The Mad Mother,' 'We are Seven,' 'Simon Lee,' 'The Forsaken Indian Woman' – each of which wends a complicated way around the ostensibly 'simple affection' they aim to follow, and all of which are also highly self-conscious in rendering the acts of tracing, accompanying, and displaying involved in poetic composition.)

Second thoughts about the composition of Wordsworthian affects are called for as well in reflections on the subjects of the poems later in the 'Preface.' The poet's 'passions and thoughts and feelings are the general passions and thoughts and feelings of men. And with what are they connected?' Wordsworth asks: 'with our moral sentiments and animal sensations' (607). The conjoining of sentiment and sensation, moral and animal is itself notable, as is the ensuing specification of the 'causes which excite' them. 'Passions and thoughts and feelings' are connected 'with the operations of the elements and the appearances of the visible universe; with storm and sunshine, with the revolutions of the seasons, *with cold and heat, with loss of friends and kindred*, with injuries and resentments, gratitude and hope, with fear and sorrow' (607–8; emphasis added). There is a stutter here; it is difficult to follow the unmarked transition from the turbulences of nature to human attachments and their severance, from our exposure to cold and heat to our vulnerability to loss and injury. The affective distance between 'cold and heat' and 'loss of friends and kindred' is closed by a mere comma, a forcefully abbreviated and condensed expression of the work Wordsworth is doing throughout the 'Preface' to attenuate oppositions, not so as to dissolve distinctions altogether but to compel a reflective pause over the tendency, and the desire, to draw sharp distinctions between the moral and animal, the thoughtful and emotional, the spiritual and the passionate, the poetic and the philosophical.

* * *

The attention Wordsworth and Eliot devote to complex modes of feeling compels acknowledgement of the ways in which sensation, will, memory, emotion, and cognition are almost always conjoined. This is obvious, but its conceptual importance is easy to overlook. The refusal to mark out a clear distinction between feeling and thinking, reacting and reflecting is representative of a rich and persistent line of intellectual culture that strains against the analytic partitioning of psychological life into discrete categories. Affects and after-affects are inseparable in Wordsworth and Eliot and that insistence on the dynamic interrelationship between emotion, thought, and attention is a vital aspect of their shared aspiration to interest us in the ordinary and unremarkable features of experience.

Coda: *Romola*, Reading, and the Art of Calm Resolve

The scene, the after-affect, and the subtle impact of Dorothea opening the curtains and gazing out at road and fields and human figures gathered under the bending sky in *Middlemarch* has an important antecedent in *Romola* (1862–3) when, at a moment of acute crisis, the titular heroine takes refuge in a church, parting the curtains at the door and 'sinking down on the step of the altar in front of Filippino Lippi's serene 'Virgin appearing to Saint Bernard' (443) (Figure 7.1; for full-colour image, see https://edinburghuniversitypress.com/book-romanticism-and-consciousness-revisited.html). Beneath this painting, we are told that Romola 'waited in hope that the inward tumult which agitated her would by and by subside' (443).

Filippino Lippi's canvas, painted in the 1480s, remains *in situ* at the Church of the Badia in central Florence, as it was during Eliot's travels to the city in 1860 and 1861. Like all of her art historical references in *Romola*, the novelist's choice of this painting is contextually precise, for the legend that is its subject and the sweetness of Lippi's style offer a beautiful and soothing version of heavenly revelation following fast upon the fanatical threats from Savonarola's followers to which the heroine has just been exposed. Lippi's painting conjures the remarkable moment

Figure 7.1   Filippino Lippi, *Apparition of the Virgin to Saint Bernard*, 1485–7.

when divine compassion for dreadful weariness and painful misgiving bodies itself forth in the form of angelic messengers delivering inspiration to the saint. In her *Legends of the Monastic Orders, as Represented in the Fine Arts* (1850), a book Eliot certainly studied and likely had with her in Florence, the art historian Anna Jameson reminds us that the 'Vision of St Bernard' typically represents the moment when, 'employed writing his famous homilies on the "Song of Songs," [Bernard] was so ill that he could scarcely hold the pen, [and the Virgin] graciously appeared to him, and comforted and restored him by her divine presence' (166). Offering this painting by Lippi and another by Giotto as examples of the legend in painting, Jameson adds (superfluously one imagines) that the subject must be considered 'mystical and devotional, not historical' (166). Presumably, it is in anticipation of some comforting illumination that Romola turns to the altarpiece, 'waiting in hope' while gazing at its image of spiritual vision.

But – and this is where it is important to remain alert to the difference between the heroine and Eliot's narrator – neither church nor work of art is a portal for mystical or secular transcendence. The novel as a whole abides no such expectations (nor does Eliot, translator of David Strauss and Ludwig Feuerbach). Indeed, at an earlier moment of crisis in the novel, a dark night of the soul during which Romola wavers wearily between resolve and despair, the narrator breaks in to deny her heroine the prospect of otherworldly enlightenment: 'no radiant angel came across the gloom with a clear message for her,' we are told in an emphatic negation (324). Nevertheless, the miracle that is not-to-be may be taken as a blessing in disguise insofar as it makes way, in the narrator's account, for the possibility of support nearer to hand, and poignant in its very imperfection.

> In those times, as now, there were human beings who never saw angels or heard perfectly clear messages. Such truth as came to them was brought confusedly in the voices and deeds of men not at all like the seraphs of unfailing wing and piercing vision ... The helping hands stretched out to them were the hands of men who stumbled and often saw dimly, so that these beings unvisited by angels had no other choice than to grasp that stumbling guidance along the path of reliance and action which is the path of life, or else to pause in loneliness and disbelief, which is no path, but the arrest of inaction and death. (324–5)

No angel lights a path on this earlier night of distress, nor will the miraculous guidance pictured in Lippi's 'Apparition' exert extraordinary influence on the later occasion of crisis and despair in the Badia – but the novel does not quite forsake the possibility of something that might be done by earthly dim-sighted beings like Romola herself.

Though the heroine is described as 'wait[ing] in hope' for composure before the altarpiece, the novel does not sanction her anticipation of a calming illumination. It is no wonder that 'calmness would not come' to Romola from 'looking at the serene picture, where the saint, writing in the rocky solitude, was being visited by faces with celestial peace in them' – a picture which beautifully imagines the kind of claim to spiritual authority from which Romola (newly disillusioned by Savonarola) now 'shrink[s] with newly-startled repulsion' (445). And yet, if 'calmness [does] not come' to Romola on the altar step, it is not because the serenity of Lippi's vision of Saint Bernard fails to impress her. She evidently discerns the distance and incommensurability between the genial, wish-fulfilling world of the painting and her own. But in spite of that dispiriting awareness, the moments passed before the painting remain poised between a forsaken expectation for clarifying revelation and the prospect of utter disillusionment that is glimpsed – and ultimately averted. From this suspension there arises a prompting, a resolve to move that coincides with no resolution beyond that of ceasing to wait for the 'calmness that would not come.' 'She rose from her knees that she might hasten to her sick people in the courtyard, and by that immediate beneficent action, revive that sense of worth in life which at this moment was unfed by any wider faith' (445): nothing in the painting restores a 'sense of worth' in life and activity, and yet time with the painting somehow unfolds into this possibility of going on in the absence of any conviction about 'what makes life worthy.' This indeterminate resolution, which recovers nothing and resolves nothing and yet stirs the subject to movement composes itself in relation to the artwork.

Although Eliot allows Romola no miraculous intervention, no angelic guidance or spiritual transcendence, the overdetermined choice of the painting before which she places her heroine offers her readers other prospects. Bernard is, after all, the reader's saint. His 'Sermons on the *Song of Songs*' (1135–53) remain a touchstone for the text-based form of spiritual practice they develop. *Lectio divina* ('divine reading') – a sustained meditation on the scripture – is meant to cultivate personal response to the written word by involving the reader's mind and body in contemplative exercise, leading to the incorporation of textual meaning through affective experience and quasi-corporeal memory. Jean Leclercq, the French Benedictine and scholar whose work has illuminated the relationship between medieval monastic culture, exegesis, and mysticism, offers this description:

> *Lectio divina* is what inscribes the sacred text in the body and the soul. This repeated mastication of the divine words is sometimes described by use of the theme of spiritual nutrition ... the vocabulary is borrowed from eating, from digestion ... sometimes described by the very expressive word *rumination*. (73)[12]

Hence Bernard opens the first of his sermons with this invitation: 'Solomon has bread to give that is splendid and delicious, the bread of the book called "The Song of Songs." Let us bring it forth then and break it' (342). It signifies, in this context, that Eliot describes Romola turning away from the image of Bernard composing that very text to resume a life 'unfed' by any wider faith. I do not mean to suggest that Eliot deliberately weighted this scene in *Romola* with the burden of such historical and philosophical signification, but nor do I think it wholly fortuitous that the image of a figure associated with the spiritually transformative practice of close reading and meditation appears at this moment in the work of an author whose knowledge of the visual arts was extensive, who kept detailed accounts of works she saw on her travels and in museums, and who often employed allusion and ekphrasis in metafictional reflections on her own artistic methods.[13]

It also matters that Eliot chose Lippi's 'Apparition' in the Badia for this important scene of resolve-without-enlightenment in *Romola*. Compared to a nearly contemporaneous version by Perugino, for example (Figure 7.2; for full-colour image, see https://edinburghuniversitypress.com/book-romanticism-and-consciousness-revisited.html), Lippi's version is busy with earthly doings. Instead of being isolated in a sanctuary to receive the heavenly messengers who seem hardly to pause from the *sacra conversazione* from which we are excluded, Lippi's Bernard is pictured as a member of the monastic community, seated

Figure 7.2 Pietro Perugino, *Virgin Appearing to Saint Bernard*, c.1490–4.

out of doors, visited by angels whose feet touch the earth, directed to a specific place by a hand that touches the same page as his own. Realistic as many of the details are, especially the plant life in the foreground, and the misty hillside in the far background, the painting is nevertheless also unabashed in its display of artistic invention, particularly the ingenious fashioning of the rocks into bookshelves, bench, and writing desk. Finally, in the far upper right, three figures are depicted in midmotion, heads down, moving away from and presumably oblivious to the miraculous scene unfolding beneath them. There is an entirely superfluous detail: two young men carrying a third older man on their shoulders. He still grips the cane he had used for support until these two came along to bear him up. Do these figures amount to an image of what Eliot's narrator has identified as 'beings unvisited by angels' who grasp the 'helping hands ... of men who stumble and often see dimly'?

Nothing is resolved during Romola's time with this painting, waiting in vain for a calm that does not come; nothing more happens than a resolution to act. Nevertheless, some settlement takes place before the artwork: not enlightenment, to be sure, certainly not inspiration, but perhaps forbearance of those very desires. The experience Eliot recounts does not follow the ascendant trajectory of *lectio divina*, but neither is her heroine's movement one of unreflective spontaneity. With the 'vision' before her, but 'attention turned inwards' as Bernard himself advises readers to do, somehow the possibility of acting arises – without clarity of thought, and without passionate intensity either. As in *Middlemarch*, feeling is composed after intense and painful excitation by means of a lingering and subdued attentiveness, and this after-affect seems to be the condition for the possibility of doing something in the absence of any revelatory answer to the question 'What should I do now?' No definitive end is in sight for either of Eliot's heroines, or at least no end beyond the bare possibility of moving on toward some action that might 'revive a sense of worth' (in *Romola*), toward a vague 'something that she could achieve' (in *Middlemarch*). Neither a lucid enunciation, then, nor an unintelligible roar, perhaps it is just this kind of approaching murmur to which we attend in reading.

I have linked the sight of Lippi's painting in *Romola*, visible when the curtains at the door of the church are parted, to the scene in *Middlemarch* visible when Dorothea opens the curtains of her room to see a bit of road and fields, a man with a bundle and a woman with a baby, all moving under the bending sky. What does it mean, then, that in one case we have a 'real' work of art and in the other a word picture of the real world? I would suggest that, in *Middlemarch*, Eliot has no need for the densely allegorized mediation of the painting in order to represent a form of attention to the world that she associates with the aesthetic. In the later scene, the importance and interest of what Wordsworth terms 'incidents and situations of common life' are *made*, not given, by the workings of 'feeling' that – like the poet's 'powerful feelings' – involve deep thought as well as an affective sensitivity. And it is precisely in this generative fusion of perception, emotion, and ideation in the imagination of responsiveness to ordinary things that I would locate Eliot's inheritance of Wordsworth's specifically Romantic aesthetics of the everyday.

Notes

1. For its pertinence to affect theory and its concision in linking powerful feelings to animal sensations, see Deleuze. To recognize 'a deep identity, a zone of indiscernibility more profound than any sentimental identification' between 'man and beast,' he argues, is to see that 'every man who suffers is a piece of meat' (23–5).
2. Ruth Leys was first to notice that theories of affect as purely physiological and non- or pre-linguistic tend also to draw on scientific research aimed at isolating, naming, and classing the 'basic emotions' (434–72). In a different context, Fiona Somerset has argued that a methodological preference for explicitly named feelings among historians entails an over-reliance on the kinds of affect hypothesized, and perhaps also hypostasized, as 'basic' or 'universal' by psychologists and evolutionary biologists. Consequently, she argues, the 'emotional alterity' of different historical periods remains illegible even to critics committed to a constructivist account of the emotions (301–3).
3. On the need for a 'theory of affect that at least gives it the possibility of recognizing the value of further cognitive processing,' and the conceptual and ethical losses entailed when the 'personal history that comes with emotion is subsumed into affects,' see Sha (259).
4. Eliot's iteration of Wordsworth's project in the remarkable metafictional digression of her first full-length novel – in which she entrusts art with the task of 'giving the loving pains of a life to the faithful representing of commonplace things' – ought to be as familiar to the Romanticist as it is to the Victorianist.
5. See, for example, Brian Massumi's emphasis on the affective 'dimension of viscerality' that registers as 'intensity' (61). On the conceptualization of affect as corporeal, non-conscious, and non-intentional, see Greg and Seigworth.
6. Though I cannot develop the comparison here, the aesthetic response I understand Eliot to be rendering is not unrelated to the 'non-discursive' awareness that Hegel understands as the special affordance of art. See especially Raymond Geuss on Hegel's aesthetics in the context of nineteenth-century efforts to account for the cognitive value of art (80–7).
7. Wordsworth terms his subject 'important' or 'interesting' repeatedly in the 'Preface' (595, 597, 598, 599, 600, 603, 607, 608, 613, 615). On Romanticism and the ordinary, see especially Cavell 6 and Galperin 27–48.

8. 'The General, the Particular, and the Art of Everyday,' in *The Aesthetic Commonplace*, 37–73.
9. On the different but equally valuable forms of 'knowledge' proffered by the poet and the 'man of science,' see 'Preface' (606–7). See also Eliot's remarks on the incommensurability of the 'universal language' of the sciences with the 'fitful shimmer of many-hued significance' in ordinary language in 'The Natural History of German Life' (*Essays* 128). Contemporary versions of these positions are to be found in recent academic arguments against the possibility and desirability of consilience between scientific and humanistic research programs and methodologies. See, for example, Kramnick (18–23) and De Caro and Macarthur (1–17).
10. Hume's physicalism, his emphasis on embodiment and on the instability of identity, account for his appropriation by scientistically inclined philosophers of mind such as Jerry Fodor (*Hume Variations*) and poststructuralists like Gilles Deleuze.
11. Eliot approvingly addresses Wollstonecraft's skepticism toward the moral valence of 'instantaneous emotions' in her review essay on 'Margaret Fuller and Mary Wollstonecraft' (1855) (338). Reservations about the ethical force of quick emotional response and reaction belong to a long history of thinking about the cognitive value of feelings that extends to present-day critique of 'affect theory' by Ruth Leys, Robert Solomon and others. It bears emphasizing that neither Wollstonecraft nor Eliot is a moral rationalist. They urge an understanding of 'emotions that reason deepens,' such that intellect might be said to 'cooperate' with feeling, as Eliot puts it (*Essays* 45), rather than to overrule, or guide, or displace feeling. For fuller discussion of Wollstonecraft and moral sensibility, see Yousef (167–8).
12. See also E. Ann Matter on Bernard's commentary on the 'Song of Songs' as an important 'Christian mystical text' in its own right (151). On *lectio divina* and modern theories of reading in the academy, from the New Criticism to reader response and poststructuralism, see Robertson.
13. Eliot certainly knew Bernard's work – he is a frequent point of reference for Feuerbach in the *Essence of Christianity*, especially in his treatment of the mystery of the incarnation. The saint also occupied a privileged place in Florentine culture of the late Middle Ages and early Renaissance, which Eliot tirelessly researched. It is Bernard who guides Dante toward his vision of the Virgin Mary in *Paradiso*, and pictorial representation of Bernard's vision is fairly specific to Florence and Tuscany in this period.

References

Bernard of Clairvaux, Saint. 'Sermons on the *Song of Songs*.' *Readings in Medieval History: The Later Middle Ages*. Ed. Patrick J. Geary. Toronto: University of Toronto Press, 2010. 342–50.

Cavell, Stanley. *In Quest of the Ordinary: Lines of Skepticism and Romanticism*. Chicago: University of Chicago Press, 1994.

De Caro, Maria and David Macarthur. 'The Nature of Naturalism.' *Naturalism in Question*. Ed. Mario de Caro and David Macarthur. Cambridge, MA: Harvard University Press, 2004. 1–20.

Deleuze, Gilles. *Francis Bacon: The Logic of Sensation*. Trans. Daniel Smith. New York: Continuum, 2003.
Eliot, George. *Middlemarch*. Introd. A. S. Byatt. Notes by Deborah Lutz. New York: Modern Library/Random House, 2000.
—. *Romola*. Ed. Dorothea Barrett. New York: Penguin, 1996.
—. *Selected Essays, Poems and Other Writings*. Ed. A. S. Byatt and Nicholas Warren. New York: Penguin, 1990.
Galperin, William. *The History of Missed Opportunities: British Romanticism and the Emergence of the Everyday*. Stanford: Stanford University Press, 2017.
Geuss, Raymond. 'Art as Theodicy.' *Morality, Culture, History: Essays on German Philosophy*. Cambridge: Cambridge University Press, 1999. 78–115.
Greg, Melissa and Gregory Seigworth. 'An Inventory of Shimmers.' *Affect Theory Reader*. Ed. Melissa Greg and Gregory Seigworth. Durham, NC: Duke University Press, 2010. 1–27.
Hume, David. *A Treatise of Human Nature*. Ed. David Fate Norton and Mary Norton. Oxford: Oxford University Press, 2000.
Jameson, Anna. *Legends of the Monastic Orders, as Represented in the Fine Arts*. New York: Houghton Mifflin, 1901.
Kramnick, Jonathan. *Paper Minds: Literature and the Ecology of Consciousness*. Chicago: University of Chicago Press, 2018.
Leclercq, Jean. *The Love of Learning and the Desire for God: A Study of Monastic Culture*. Trans. Catherine Misrahi. New York: Fordham University Press, 1961.
Leys, Ruth. 'The Turn to Affect: A Critique.' *Critical Inquiry* 37.3 (2011): 434–72.
Lippi, Filippino. 'Appartition of the Virgin to Saint Bernard.' 1485–7. Badia, Florence. https://commons.wikimedia.org/wiki/Category:Apparition_of_the_ Virgin_to_Saint_Bernard_(Filippino_Lippi)#/media/File:Bernardo_claraval_ filippino_lippi.jpg (last accessed December 2, 2021).
Massumi, Brian. *Parables for the Virtual: Movement, Affect, Sensation*. Durham, NC: Duke University Press, 2002.
Matter, E. Ann. 'Lectio Divina.' *The Cambridge Companion to Christian Mysticism*. Ed. Amy Hollywood and Patricia Z. Beckman. Cambridge: Cambridge University Press, 2012. 147–56.
Perugino, Pietro. 'Virgin Appearing to Saint Bernard.' c.1490–4. Alte Pinakothek, Munich. (Originally, Santa Maria Maddelena dei Pazzi, Florence.) https:// commons.wikimedia.org/wiki/Category:Apparition_of_the_Virgin_to_Saint_ Bernard_(Perugino)#/media/File:Perugino,_apparizione_della_vergine_a_ san_bernardo,_monaco.jpg (last accessed December 2, 2021).
Robertson, Duncan. '*Lectio Divina* and Literary Criticism.' *Cistercian Studies Quarterly* 46.1 (2011): 83–93.
Sha, Richard. 'The Turn to Affect: Emotions without Subjects, Causality without Demonstrable Cause.' *The Palgrave Handbook of Affect Studies*. Ed. Donald Wehrs and Thomas Blake. London: Palgrave Macmillan, 2017. 259–82.
Solomon, Robert, ed. *Thinking about Feeling: Contemporary Philosophers on Emotion*. Oxford: Oxford University Press, 2004.

Somerset, Fiona. 'Emotion.' *The Cambridge Companion to Christian Mysticism*. Ed. Amy Hollywood and Patricia Z. Beckman. Cambridge: Cambridge University Press, 2012. 294–304.

Wollstonecraft, Mary. *A Vindication of the Rights of Men*. Ed. Janet Todd. Oxford: Oxford University Press, 1993.

Wordsworth, William. 'Preface to *Lyrical Ballads*.' *William Wordsworth. The Oxford Authors*. Ed. Stephen Gill. Oxford: Oxford University Press, 1984. 595–615.

—. *The Prelude, 1799, 1805, 1850*, ed. Jonathan Wordsworth, M. H. Abrams, and Stephen Gill. New York: Norton, 1979.

Yousef, Nancy. *Romantic Intimacy*. Stanford: Stanford University Press, 2013.

Yousef, Nancy. *The Aesthetic Commonplace: Wordsworth, Eliot, Wittgenstein and the Language of Every Day*. Oxford: Oxford University Press, 2022.

Chapter 8

Studio States: Thought Out of Place

Jacques Khalip

I have often said that man's unhappiness springs from one thing alone, his incapacity to stay quietly in one room.
(Blaise Pascal, *Pensées and Other Writings*, 44)

… this inability to think through anything but the materials right now in my room, wherever or whatever my room might be, whether bubble or cell or gallery or mausoleum or website.
(Wayne Koestenbaum, 'Fag Limbo' 197)

Like Coleridge's Mariner or Keats's 'living hand,' Romanticism has often been read with and through figures of beholding, holding onto, or letting go of concepts: mind and world, subject and object, idealism and materialism, inside and outside, lyric and narrative, persons and things. 'Insofar as Romanticism holds together, then as now,' writes Jerome Christensen, 'it coalesces as a writing about how things or persons (or things *and* persons) hold together' (xxi). The wager that Romanticism holds 'then as now' suggests that whatever it was and is, Romanticism continues to exert its adhesiveness by thinking about how persons and things coalesce, how they fall apart, and how thinking itself is a thing. And even more, it is about how thought orients us around things that may be obstacles. Take the following well-known orientation lesson:

> In the darkness, I can orientate myself in a familiar room so long as I can touch any one object whose position I remember. But it is obvious that the only thing which assists me here is an ability to define the position of the objects by means of a *subjective* distinction: for I cannot see the objects whose position I am supposed to find; and if, for a joke, someone had shifted all the objects round in such a way that their relative position remained the same but what was previously on the right was now on the left, I would be quite unable to find my way about a room whose walls were in other respects identical.
> ('Orientation' 239)

Immanuel Kant here navigates a dark room via a familiar feeling of difference, but whenever I read the paragraph, I am oddly taken with the line 'and if, for a joke, someone had shifted all the objects round ...,' not because I want to imagine who that 'someone' is, but because of the way Kant's well-kept room is infiltrated by a joker who disorients him and, in so doing, turns the room into a space for something and someone else – room, in other words, for both a joke and a joker. According to Scott J. Juengel, Kant follows the subject as 'a plot point in thought and feeling,' and as a point of formalization, subjectivity is inevitably vulnerable to the vagaries of thoughts and feelings that put it at odds with itself (272). 'When the illusion [of the joke] disappears into nothing,' writes Kant in the *Critique of Judgment*, 'the mind looks back again in order to try it once more, and thus is hurried this way and that by rapidly succeeding increases and decreases of tension and set into oscillation' (210). The joke triggers an embodied sense of disorientation: whoever steals into the dark room trips up the mind and sends it oscillating, and by permitting the joke, Kant unintentionally sets up philosophy for a pratfall. Who would so childishly tease the philosopher? 'Enlightenment is the human being's emancipation from its self-incurred immaturity. Immaturity is the inability to make use of one's own intellect without the direction of another.' Only the immature tell jokes in the dark, 'but only he who, himself enlightened, is not afraid of shadows ... can say what a free state may not dare say' ('Answer' 17, 23).

Kant's vignette reveals the distinctly anachronistic and anatopic features of thinking-as-orientation: one *must* think beyond the room's darkness precisely because we are already out of place and out of time. And even if thinking, for Kant, is premised on an *a priori* feeling of spatio-temporal grounding, its scenography is haunted by a far more disorienting set of possibilities – that we do not think we know what room we are in, that someone or something else might trash our room, that the room was never ours to begin with. Indeed, it is as if Kant, unbeknownst to himself, approaches a border of ecstasy in the darkness: affectively standing out of place (*ekstasis*), exposed without transport in the delimited confines of the room. Thinking in and out of the dark is perilous because neither confirms that we and our thoughts will ever find their place.[1]

Ian Baucom has glossed the historicist's task as that of placing 'that thing ['event, text, or phenomenon'] within its determinate moment, to "situate" it,' which means establishing the pre-conditionality of the situation, as it were, in order to corroborate persons and things *as* interpretably spatio-temporal phenomena: 'a fundamental preliminary to the act of placing an object within its situation ... is the invention of the categories of the situation and the period themselves. Absent those categories historicist method could not exist' (Baucom 43).[2] In the historicist's dream, thought is pluralized as an orienting principle for the 'historical,' imagining multiple places and times for its extensive, virtualizing force. But as Thomas Pfau has remarked, the 'deep-structural situatedness [or mood] of individuals within history [is] something never actually intelligible to them in fully coherent, timely, and definitive form' (7). How would we begin to write and make room for the history of a curiously placeless Romantic thought? How would we 'place' it, and where are its place(s)?

In the following pages, I want to approach these questions slowly, closely reading three conceptual 'places' of study or studios (*stadium*) where a certain aesthetic thinking occurs but remains unfinished and placeless. These studios are versions of what Maurice Blanchot calls the 'space of literature' – space that is alien to itself, a 'void' (10), and is irreducible to the logic of socio-material spatiality.[3] Studios are both within and outside of the historical and psychosocial dimensions of space, unthoughts, or negativities that shade modernity's projects. Foucault's bravura reading of Kant's idea of enlightenment (*Aufklärung*) famously interprets it

> as an *Ausgang*, an 'exit,' a 'way out' … He is not seeking to understand the present on the basis of a totality or of a future achievement. He is looking for a difference: What difference does today introduce with respect to yesterday. (305)

Kant's pedagogy of the exit steers us out of the space of immaturity; even the concept of *today* figures difference as spatialized separation, a cleaving away from yesterday. I must confess that as I write this chapter, hunkered down in my apartment in Providence and observing social distancing guidelines (and, I might add, in the temporary darkness of a winter power outage), it is not hard to want to refract all of this through the bleak poetics of quarantine and inertia. But what I am after here is to the side of isolation, retreat, or solitude, all of which are partly marked by internalization and privation. A studio, after all, is not 'private space' in a bourgeois sense but rather *minor*: it reconfigures (after Deleuze and Guattari) the dualistic norms or standards through which something like privacy might be sought in a majoritarian culture.[4] The studio is close to what Giorgio Agamben describes as a 'topology of the unreal,' *stanzas* (rooms) that figure for 'something more original than space' and which demand 'an *analysis situs* (analysis of site) in opposition to *analysis magnitudinis* (analysis of magnitude),' the former being 'adequate to the *topos outopos,* the placeless place' (*Stanzas* x–xix). This topology is less alternate reality or Morean *utopia* than a thought of space that space cannot accommodate, an elliptical non-place for thinking the inappropriable. A studio (like a queer backroom) is a monadic topology that tarries with, but does not house or shelter, the ungovernable thoughts that (un)make it – in other words, the thoughts that take place there but do not *take up place*. In a brilliant reading of how Leibniz's theory of monads anticipates Romantic poetic theories of obscurity and enclosed perception, Daniel Tiffany remarks that poems, like monads, have their own dark internal codes of conduct and thinking.[5] The paradox of the monad – that its perspective is partial and self-enclosed, and yet communicates with other monads *in the medium of its partiality* – describes just this kind of undefinable 'studio state,' an evocative turn of phrase I borrow from David L. Clark's work on Goya, where he uses it to describe an interstitial world 'where worlds have not formed and may never form.' Clark underlines that this is a 'state' and not a 'life' because the studio is a figure for the unlived or what within life cannot be lived, 'emphasizing the phenomenon – from acts to objects to concepts – for which productivity, potentiality, or vitality don't easily apply' (91, 111, 116).[6]

The studio states that interest me are life-less, enclosed, and (more on this) *sealed*; they are not formally bound by anything like closure or terminus, both of which imply a completion of processes.[7] They are inconclusive but only insofar as the kind of thinking that transpires there does not reason with doubt, dispute, or contradiction: to stay and think in the room and not experience it as a situating principle for orienting our life through thinking; to not imagine orienting thought *out of it* or beyond it, but to tarry in a room and not be *en route*. Aesthetic thought insists but does not create a space, a world, or a life; it 'does not appear as a form of space – not haven or enclave or utopia – but precisely as an *insistence*, as something that was *never not there*, however obscured, overlooked, or repressed it might have been' (Pyle). It insists because it goes nowhere in its non-claustrophobic impasse; and even more, it can be ecstatic even without leaving space. To be sure, compensatory tropes for intellectual sequestration appear throughout Romantic texts as spaces that set the stage for the freedom of either leaving or adjusting to them: in Wordsworth's 'Nuns fret not,' for example, the sonnet's 'scanty plot of ground' becomes a philosophical refuge for those 'who have felt the weight of too much liberty' (401–2).[8] It goes without saying, however, that feeling 'too much liberty' is a rare experience for the world populations of the eighteenth century, where *too little* liberty is a far more devastating weight: the 'earless den' of the sonnet on Toussaint Louverture is the violent trace of sentimentalized capture that enacts the very violence it otherwise tries to sublime over (407). Catherine Malabou has remarked that philosophy often affirms 'captivity ... [as] the very form of being in the world,' which is to say that philosophy guards life, and in so doing, preserves it as a central object of study, 'as if life itself was the privileged victim of philosophical concepts' ('Life and Prison'). The studio, by contrast, is a paraform that focalizes how disorienting and disoriented thinking can be (an insurgency that is itself insurgent), and how it takes place to the side of the belief that thinking constitutes a form of living only when thought actively externalizes itself – what Coleridge describes as the phenomenon of how 'Ideas passing forth into action reinstate themselves again in the world of Life' (cited in Litchfield 133). Ideas performatively 'reinstate' themselves because, tending towards life, they must continually restore and institutionalize themselves in order to take part *in* life. But how ideas become intentional, how they 'pass forth into action,' is murky; it is as if Coleridge cannot withhold an idea, cannot prevent it from socialization. The studio state, however, is closer to the work of his notebooks, or poems like 'Kubla Khan,' 'Christabel,' or 'Frost at Midnight,' where the restriction on reinstating ideas is put aside.[9] 'Passing forth' in the studio state is less a transitioning towards (*passer à l'acte*) and more like an act of relief or voiding – passively passing a thing along into inconsequential disappearance.

To think in the studio state, this chapter argues, is to treat thought elliptically: it brooks no forward or backward movement but, like the dots of the ellipsis, occurs by way of omission – presentation without representation.[10] 'Something invisible is missing in the grammar of this repetition,' writes Jacques Derrida on the ellipsis, which does not invite revelation but rather figures for a redundancy that both enables *and* disables thinking: 'once more passing through each point along its circuit, nothing has budged ('Ellipsis' 296). Returning to the ellipsis in *Rogues*, Derrida refers to it as 'not only lack but a curved figure with more than one focus. We are thus already between the "minus one" and the "more than one"' (*Rogues* 1). The elliptical betweenness of the 'minus one' and the 'more than one' neutralizes the idea that thought is additive or subtractive. But how does one think such a dead spot?

Let's begin with Blake.

Staring at Cracks

In Plate 20 of William Blake's *Illustrations from the Book of Job* (1825), we encounter the following scene: the titular character takes up the

Figure 8.1 William Blake, *Illustrations from the Book of Job*, Plate 20, 'Job and His Daughters', 1825. Yale Center for British Art, Paul Mellon Collection.

focus of the image, forming a quasi-pyramid with his daughters seated beneath him as he seemingly relates his trials, illustrated on the curved, tripartite wall behind him, his arms fully outstretched and fingers cued to the roundels. Job gesturally illustrates the illustrations just as *he* is illustrated by them, graphically rhyming with their forms as foreground and background meld: Job's beard and lower half combine with his daughters' bodies, which are, in turn, sculpturally draped in clothing that collects on the ground like objects. The composition of the print reflects Blake's idea of treating illustration as (1) something that is ongoing and underway, and (2) something undergone *in* his images and *by them*, as if images were also subject to a kind of aesthetic tutelage. Images need to learn to read each other and us, Blake intimates, but in a language that is something other than merely rhetorical.

This kind of learning, moreover, cannot happen through conventional guidance or stewardship; if illustration exemplifies a thing by illuminating or giving light (*illustrare*), it is also complicit in dimming that candle. Samson-like, Job points to and holds the illustrations in the dark world of this print, holding them together in imitation of an architecture that supports the outer frame or the other 'room' of the illustration itself, a room within a room. T. J. Clark has glossed the print as Blake's fantasy of a 'life he thought images might lead in a better world,' which is to say that Blake is picturing how to bring his own images into the topology of the print in order to situate them, to enroll them into the life that they should have elsewhere. Blake, however, is not one to take solace in prospective claims: In his annotations to Swedenborg's *Divine Providence* he writes: 'What is Enrolling but Predestination?' (609).[11] Blake is responding here to Swedenborg's rulemaking statement that the 'Man who doth not suffer himself to be led to, and enrolled in Heaven, is prepared for his place in Hell' (609). For Swedenborg, not to submit to enrollment in one place means being punitively guaranteed a spot in another; in this sense, enrollment is underwritten by a corrective logic of placement regardless of where one wants to be, as if it were impossible to imagine a mode of being that is allergic to habitation, or a history within which one does not desire to dwell.

If enrolling evokes pre-inscription or pre-registration (scripting something in anticipation of its materialization), Blake imprints his images otherwise – in a 'topology of the unreal' where images think in the absence of any afterlife or what Jean-Luc Nancy calls their ground (*fond*): 'it disappears in its essence as ground, which consists in its not appearing' (*Ground* 7). And we, as Blake's readers and spectators, are also not to be enrolled in the groundless images, tempted neither to predestinate nor to place *our* thinking in them as if images were museal placeholders. Perhaps it is for this reason that Job's daughters look away from him in the print, neither listening to, nor seeing, nor reading what their father apparently says or shows. Furthermore, it is not clear if Job himself listens, teaches, or looks at them or us, if *look* is even the appropriate word here to describe what his eyes do or show: looking 'out' frontally and not toward his daughters, Job does not appear to be directed at some kind of beyond; nor does he solicit an implied future spectator. *Staring* might be the better word, an empty ocular fixity that is materially inscriptive and 'nonrelational' in Leo Bersani's sense, a visual structure of being 'in a world in which we no longer *are*' (*Receptive* 107). Staring is visually immobile and uncomprehending, a looking that does not absorb things as relational conditions of our being. Bersani remarks that one of the few places it is safe to stare is in museums, and there is a way in which Blake appears to confront the privilege of the knowing spectator who seemingly arrives before his images and encounters a stare fixed on her as if she was a work of art, but does not recognize her *as* a spectator. The room here, to be sure, is something other than a gallery or a museum: in other painted versions of the scene, Blake sets things outside *en plein air*, although what this outside might be is still circumscribed by him.[12] Like Coleridge with his 'unclos'd lids' or an 'eye / Fix'd with mock study on my swimming book' in 'Frost at Midnight' (*Poetry and Prose* 121), Job's studying is inhibited and fixed, unmoved by a world it does not know or, put differently, a worldlessness that cannot be made manifest. Here there is only planarity, a negativity of surface which, like Blake's acid-resistant etching techniques, concentrates on the 'underworld' or non-place of the image. This is not a form of studying that observes a thing as subject to knowledge; rather, it is an impersonal studying and staring *of* the studio. Hence the compression of Job's studio state, the prephotographic intensity that condenses and fixates upon it but does not place it. Blake spaces it away, nearby but far from the rhetorical 'world' of the caption above it: 'How precious are thy thoughts / unto me O God / how great is the sum of them.' The scaled magnitude here between God's thoughts and Job's tribute to them – his veneration of them but inability to address or absorb them – hovers like a hashtag outside the frame, as if what the caption says can be pictured but cannot be made available to the image. To ask 'how precious are thy thoughts … how great is the sum of them' also can be read in the form of a question: what *is* the quality and weight (*pensée, pensare*) of thoughts?[13] The open-endedness of the question crowns but does not convert the image below it into a response. Rather, the uncoordinated relation here between word and image – their non-relation – evokes speech that has yet to find its image, and an image that has not found speech.

Blake's singular 'enlightenment' thus does not so much illustratively bring to light various things, persons, and events as it breaks away *from them*. On the subject of method, Alan Liu has written that 'the only thing that registers is a break in the tight, clenched little history of our selves; and the most accurate statement of that break is a method … that enacts a certain alienation or remove from ourselves' (22–3).¹⁴ If the first step of such a break involves self-othering, I want to adjust Liu's phrase to allow for an implosion *within* that 'little history': with his back turned to his images like Klee's angel, Job breaks with his own 'tight, clenched little history' by staying with it in his studio state. He does not turn from a historical past since such a turn *from* would be like a turn *to* – a confirmation of a relation with that history; rather, Job remains with a groundless thought that is outside of that history and has a history of its own, or a thought within history that remains to be thought through.¹⁵ In this way, Job's studio thinking cannot be seen or possessed; it resembles what Blake calls in *Milton* 'a Moment in each Day' that cannot be found, but 'when it once is found / It renovates every Moment of the Day if rightly placed' (136). Perhaps the studio is the place from where Job stares inconclusively at something that is not given to view – not a better world, certainly, and not another world, but *a* world just as it is.

'All is to [historians] a dull round of probabilities and possibilities; but the history of all times and places, is nothing else but improbabilities and impossibilities; what we should say, was impossible if we did not see it always before our own eyes' (543). By staring indefinitely, Job and his daughters might be Blakean anti-historians who attend the impossibility of a thought whose history cannot be absorbed, a thought *within* history that is not yet to come or yet to be conceived, but is non-transferable and unyielding to 'that saving transformation of the real' (Makdisi 10). It would be a species of (non-)history that has not been situated (and thus rendered thinkable). When Blake, in *The Marriage of Heaven and Hell*, says to the Angel 'Here said I! is your lot, in this space, if space it may be calld' (42), he reminds us of the illusion of deixis, of the unrealness of a kind of *a priori* philosophical spacing that makes a claim upon an idea by trying to situate it, but in so doing, it places itself *in* the idea's situation, only to be disoriented by a perspective that it cannot abide with. The studio state of the print evokes an *Umwelt* that is not open for enrollment; it is an experiment with insulated perception under conditions where images and the spectators who look at and read them find no mutual way through which to redeem their incommensurability to each other. The three obscure roundels in the print, as if conjured from the tips of Job's fingers in varying degrees of shadow and illumination from left to right, solicit a kind of reading scansion, but the image does something else with them: Blake arranges and stacks them like things in a junkshop, their 'value' only barely hinted at by their adjacency to each other. And as junk, their seemingly auratic history is spread on their etched surfaces, unyielding to a visual economy of commodity exchange. Unperturbed, they show nothing at all.

In Job's studio state, 'history' does not have his back; the impossible topology of the print insists like an (im)material plane without support. Vincent de Luca long ago described Blake's texts as a 'kind of wall, against which [Corporeal Understanding] presses itself, groping along, trying to peer through chinks in the hard, opaque surface' (32). The present tense of de Luca's formulation hints that whatever understanding presses up against, it happens in the now-time of intimately enclosed conditions. Blake's print values enclosure as a way of imagining what thinking looks like in the absence of an outside or a transformative real that tries to claim and legitimize it, of staying in one room and staring with and alongside the image. It is thinking undertaken for the sake of *a* now, not policed by either a past or a future: 'this inability to think through,' writes Wayne Koestenbaum, 'anything but the materials right now in my room, wherever and whatever my room might be, whether bubble or cell or gallery or mausoleum or website' (197). To think only with what is 'right now in my room' might be a sign of frugality, satisfaction, carelessness, or exhaustion, but Koestenbaum's observation turns on how to dwell with modes of writing and reflection that are unfinished, undeveloped, immature.[16] This is a curtailed volition, thought that does not pass into action because it never goes too far. In a certain sense, 'Job and his Daughters' echoes what Rei Terada has described (after Deleuze) as the 'trapped thought' that characterized post-Waterloo Romantic culture, where revolutionary and restorative politics came to be perceived as at a standstill, and any way out of the situation was neutralized by despair: 'the whole point is that what's required to find "the way out" is missing ... "trapped thought" finds not a chink in the wall but the wholeness of the false' ('Looking' 295). Those chinks might be dents, scratches, or dry paint. But the impetus for Blake is to work with the materials of his room just as they are. And for an instant, perhaps, the image will lower its eyes.[17]

Freedom and Ruin

In an interview with the critic David Sylvester, Cy Twombly states the following:

> Painting a picture is a very short thing if it goes well, but the sitting and thinking ... I usually go off on stories that have nothing to do with the painting, and sometimes I sit in the opposite room to where I work. If I can get a good hot story going I can paint better, but sometimes I'm not thinking about the painting, I'm thinking about the subject. Lots of times I'll sit in another room and then I might just go in. It takes a lot of freedom. (180)

Sitting and thinking, not sitting and not thinking, leaving and not painting, and then, perhaps, painting: in order to do the work, Twombly confesses to thinking about something else ('a good hot story'), to leaving the studio and entering 'the opposite room.' There is no pretense made about skilled coordination. Everything happens by way of detachment or putting off – a deferral *of* deferral – as if to further loosen Twombly's experiences of thinking and painting from one another. In order for painting to begin, it needs to be estranged from thinking but still in the same space with it – *in* the studio but also *of* the studio. Brian O'Doherty has observed that 'it is not so much a question of the pictures that can be made in [the] studio as of the thoughts that can be thought there' (9), and for Twombly, to leave or return to a painting implies turning away from an obligation to relate to whatever may or may not be picturable in that non-place since the kind of thinking that can only be thought *there* is decidedly unpicturable or, at the very least, anterior to picture-making.

When Twombly says that 'it takes a lot of freedom,' the 'it' is enigmatic. On the one hand, he is referring to the entire process he has just described, but on the other hand, 'it' might be less about *his* freedom and more about the worldless freedom of his studio state. 'Might just go in': the tentativeness of the verb 'might' is less about a voluntary act or decision than a sense that preference here tends to one option while keeping the other in view, holding apart disparate work spaces (where one thinks and paints) and states of mind (thinking/painting). Like Bartleby's 'I prefer not,' Twombly's 'I might just go in' is feebly declarative, as if he were saying: *I might go into a studio I already inhabit, but I will inhabit it as a stranger, not in order to be doing something but in order to allow myself the possibility of not doing.* Imagine a painter painting for the freedom of the studio to be with or without him, the studio as the situation that does not need any things or persons in it.

In *Visconti: Insights into Flesh and Blood*, Alexander García Düttmann writes that

> the artist makes things in ignorance of what they are; he does not know how these things are made and why he makes them, irrespective of how great his technical skill may be ... Does the artist make things? This question indicates the point at which the artist brushes up against the border of making or intentionality: the border of aesthetic seriousness. (10–11)

To make things in ignorance of what they are (a phrase Düttmann borrows from Adorno, who in turn takes it from Kierkegaard) invokes an unusual theory of intentionality. Aesthetic intention is insistently preoccupied with a making from within the enclosure of artistic work, and by 'making' Düttmann does not mean manufacturing, handicraft, or skill; rather, the poiesis of a work – *how* it happens – is inscribed in its non-meaning, and the artist cannot help but remain ignorant of that kind of thinking if he or she wants to seriously make something that is not subordinate to the prosaic, or what he calls the 'possible.'

> Between the artist's making and every conceivable observation which cancels it as a making, as an intentional action, a gulf opens up, precisely because the making requires no additional observation, because no gulf may open up between it and the world if it is to validate itself as a making. (8)

An artist's making does not need to be observable because this would imply that its meaning depends on an external verification. Observing would only assimilate the making to prior recognitions, rendering it too easily interpretable and possible.

What Twombly and Düttmann are suggesting about art is that it happens but is not made because the studio state evokes something inassimilable to the life of the artist *and* the 'life' he or she works over in art. But what is this species of studio 'life'? Take another example:

> The different accidents of life are not so changeable as the feelings of human nature. I had worked hard for nearly two years, for the sole purpose of infusing life into an inanimate body. For this I had deprived myself of rest and health. I had desired it with an ardor that far exceeded moderation; but now that I had finished, the beauty of the dream vanished, and breathless horror and disgust filled my heart. Unable to endure the aspect of the being I had created, I rushed out of the room and continued a long time traversing my bedchamber, unable to compose my mind to sleep. At length lassitude succeeded to the tumult I had before endured; and I threw myself on the bed in my clothes, endeavoring to seek a few moments of forgetfulness. But it was in vain: I slept, indeed, but I was disturbed by the wildest dreams. I thought I saw Elizabeth, in the bloom of health, walking in the streets of Ingolstadt. Delighted and surprised, I embraced her; but as I imprinted the first kiss on her lips, they became livid with the hue of death; her features appeared to change, and I thought that I held the corpse of my dead mother in my arms; a shroud enveloped her form, and I saw the graveworms crawling in the folds of the flannel. I started from my sleep with horror; a cold dew covered my forehead, my teeth chattered, and every limb became convulsed; when, by the dim and yellow light of the moon, as it forced its way through the window shutters, I beheld the wretch – the miserable monster whom I had created. He held up the curtain of the bed; and his eyes, if eyes they may be called, were fixed on me. His jaws opened, and he muttered some inarticulate sounds, while a grin wrinkled his cheeks. He might have spoken, but I did not hear; one hand was stretched out, seemingly to detain me, but I escaped and rushed down stairs. I took refuge in the courtyard belonging to the house which I inhabited; where I remained during the rest of the night, walking up and down in the greatest agitation, listening attentively, catching and fearing

each sound as if it were to announce the approach of the demoniacal corpse to which I had so miserably given life. (Shelley 57–8)[18]

What if we were to read Victor Frankenstein's behavior (after Twombly), however high-strung, as expressing a studio-freedom *from* life? What if, by leaving the creature behind, turning away with revulsion from it, Victor in fact wants to think *with-out* it, away from the creature in order to maintain his studio state for the sake of a non-negotiable thinking that (*contra* Coleridge) does not want 'ideas [to pass] forth into action [in order to] re-instate themselves again in the world of Life'? Might dreaming in the studio – or the dream state of the studio – be a way to stop thinking from acting and reinstating itself in life?

'The beauty of the dream vanished': what *was* that particular beauty? If Kantian beauty is to have a purposive purposelessness – if beauty is to be contemplated but not had – the beautiful must contain a purpose for judgement, but one that is of another cognitive order. Its vanishing from the dream of work suggests a disappearance of that purposelessness, but it also compels us to read the project of making the creature as a dreamwork, unconscious and latent. By turning from the coercive encounter with the newly risen creature, it is as if Victor stays with the impotentiality of the dreamwork he initiated prior to its reification – in other words, a work that is still dreamt of, but cannot be actualized and turned into action ('A sight to dream of, not to tell!' as Coleridge exclaims in 'Christabel' [*Poetry and Prose* 169]). He might just want to make a creature in ignorance of what it is and allow it to live as it wishes, but to undertake its living *to the side* of biopolitical life.[19] And perhaps this is the kind of unlivable life that Victor stays with inside his own studio state: 'In a solitary chamber, or rather cell, at the top of the house, and separated from all the other apartments by a gallery and staircase, I kept my workshop of filthy creation' (Shelley 55). The sentence calls to mind a dark version of Keats's reflections on the 'Chamber of Maiden Thought' which we move into after temporarily living in the 'infant or thoughtless Chamber in which we remain as long as we do not think.' But even as we move out of thoughtlessness, the new chamber 'becomes gradually darken'd and at the same time on all sides of it many doors are set open – but all dark – all leading to dark passages' (*Letters* 1:281). Like Keats, Victor describes a 'chamber of Maiden-Thought' within a larger structure that is part of it but also necessarily excluded from it. Keats conveys that life is like a 'Mansion of Many Apartments' because it is a fragment of 'dwelling' that we can never fully own or inhabit.[20] Victor's 'home,' however, is not an architectural simulation of human life striving for acculturation, however much it falls into 'dark passages'; rather, his 'workshop' or studio state arranges and rearranges life as something unthinkable and brought in from elsewhere – from the 'vaults and charnel-houses' (Shelley 52) that figurally underwrite his space ('Darkness had no effect on my fancy' [51]). And whatever the space is, it is not a home; multipurpose in some respects, it is non-identifiable and changeable – a 'solitary chamber,' 'cell,' 'top of the house,' and 'workshop.'[21]

Tiffany helpfully reminds us (after Walter Benjamin) that whereas *topography* maps out physical space as a social phenomenon, *topology* refers to the imperceptible, monadic qualities within space – '"the void," the "nothingness" across the frontier' (163). Victor's workshop is this 'nothingness' found in and *of* the house, rearranged through its negating topology – an uncanny space, to be sure, but also a more perverse kind of homelessness that, *pace* Heidegger, refuses to be given thought to.[22] Victor does not think to dwell because, in the studio state, thought does not dwell to live – something that even Shelley alludes to in her prefatory remarks about the composition of the work as an 'abortion,' a messy thing that is part novel, part epistolary correspondence, part testimonial, part confession. Formless as much as it is formed, *Frankenstein* is, like the creature, 'of component parts animated' but stillborn (9). Warren Montag has noted that the novel's elliptical withholding of the details of work and production covers over science with the rhetoric of theology, of 'creation' over 'workshop,' in the same way as the shift from 'chamber' to 'cell' evokes prison labor but also the insulated 'closed world' of a monk's cell (309). To be sure, omission is key, but not because of contextual suppression; rather, the 'workshop' figures its 'filthy' creativity as obscene (outside or off scene). And instead of imagining that we need to 'restore to the work that peculiar form of dependence that its very structure is designed to mask or deny' (300), the novel, like the workshop, marks itself out in a topology that is impossible to pin down or arrange.[23] Might the 'catastrophe' (Shelley 57) of the novel signal its own exhaustion with itself *as a novel*, an exhaustion with the genre's commitment to covering over the void within relationality, the disconnection that is compensated by the desire to relate in novels as a function of overprotecting characters and plots? Perhaps Victor's hatred and disgust towards the creature convey a refusal to allow it to exit the studio state and join the world as a biopolitical figure. But do the creature and Victor ever truly *leave* the novel? Their leavings, after all, are tellingly different: Victor dies by the time we read Robert Walton's narrative, the residual corpse haunting the peripheries of the text; but the creature, as a figure of *envoi*, just leaves, departing without the novel troubling itself to let us know if he has killed himself or not. In fact, the creature forces the novel, as it were, to take leave of itself.

What *Frankenstein* insistently reflects upon are the reversals through which life, like dreaming, rehearses visions that are closed off or inaccessible to the intervention of others. When Victor does dream again after settling down in bed after his disastrous creation, it is as if in the horror of his nightmare he is able to think and perceive (but not be consoled by) the latency of thoughts and their technics, 'the globalized mobility of significance in an era of mechanical reproduction' (Redfield, '*Frankenstein's* Cinematic Dream') which gothically morphs Elizabeth into the mother to enact the production of sexual difference as a symptom of a hallucinatory machinery. But *this* dream, like another of vanishing beauty, if it functions along the lines of Freudian dreamwork, resembles Twombly's account of deferred thinking and painting: walking off and dreaming after the animation of the creature, Victor dreams another deferred dream, another animation or restitching of a creature – his adopted sister/lover/wife to his mother – and thus returns and repeats the earlier dream but without being forced to actualize it (to let an idea pass into action and life), as if the dream here were the studio state where one could keep thinking and creation away from each other in order to facilitate something else to be dreamt. Thus Victor's fear of replicating a 'companion' for the creature (who gazes on him in his useless work as if to verify it) evokes a parallel desire to vouchsafe the studio's apartness, to refuse a 'race of devils ... propagated upon the earth,' and to disavow the reproductive futurism invading the studio space [Shelley 165]). Dreaming manages to hold Victor, the one who dreams, apart from himself, as if the dream were repeating from within itself that initial separation. After all, we experience and speak about dreams in the past tense of recollection: *I dreamt that dream* rather than *I am dreaming it*, in all of its unrecoverable disarray. The 'creator' of the dream is not the dreamer; the dreamer is only the placeless place where the dream, in turn, takes place, but where the creator is not.

To dream about failing in creation would be a dream-failure that paradoxically does not express lack or non-fulfillment; as Bersani notes, the dream is a state that is 'blind to the temporal anomaly ... of fearing or desiring failure *after* success' (*Thoughts* 60). Sharon Sliwinski writes that 'reporting a dream is a rather unusual method of inserting oneself into the public realm, not least because these strange speech acts operate without mastery of their content' (xiv). But Victor's report to Walton (and insertion into the framework of the novel) strangely (dis)engages with the notion of 'the public': like *Frankenstein* itself, Victor tries to impart to his interlocutor that everything 'reported' is discarded, non-transferrable content, the detritus or 'ruin' (Shelley 41) of dreams that cannot be redeemed or given over to others. 'Now, once again,' Shelley declares in her Preface,

> I bid my hideous progeny go forth and prosper. I have an affection for it, for it was the offspring of happier days ... Its several pages speak of many a walk, many a drive, and many a conversation, when I was not alone; and my companion was one who, in this world, I shall never see more ... But this is for myself; my readers have nothing to do with these associations. (10)

Having dreamt 'unbidden' her novel in its preliminary shape, Shelley 'wished to exchange the ghastly image of my fancy for the realities around,' but her wishing, like Victor's reporting, holds to the ruin of a thought within that dream, a ruin that cannot be economized: 'I see them still; the very room, the dark *parquet*, the closed shutters, with the moonlight struggling through' (9–10). When Shelley states that her readers do not need to know everything about her life and should read the novel as it is, even as she proceeds to tell her life, she is reporting on how the unthought of the dream is both inside but also separate from the different life of the novel. While *Frankenstein* can be nominally for others to read, Shelley suggests there is something built into it that cannot be handed over, a 'terrible destruction' (42) that has 'nothing to do with these associations' because the abjection of *her* life, a life she aligns with the (de)composition of her novel, lies outside the revelatory dynamics of the literary public sphere.

When Victor wakes up from his dream and sees the creature staring at him in the bedroom, he experiences, I think, something close to what he (and Shelley) might be after – a tacit observance of an ignorant reader who reads without knowing what things are:

> He held up the curtain of the bed; and his eyes, if eyes they may be called, were fixed on me. His jaws opened, and he muttered some inarticulate sounds, while a grin wrinkled his cheeks. He might have spoken, but I did not hear; one hand was stretched out, seemingly to detain me, but I escaped and rushed downstairs.

The held curtain, the disembodied eyes, jaws, the grin, the cheeks – all of these detached gothic figures hold and hail Victor, but they do so without recognitional force. The scene becomes a studio state *cum* queer zone of therapy where the creature takes on the role of the analyst, who cedes interpretation to Victor in order to keep the space from quick monopolization – to estrange it by reordering it in terms of what André Green calls the 'ventilated space' of therapy, 'which is neither that of "this is meaningless" nor that of "this means that but one of "this may mean that"' (42). Disarticulated into figures of holding, muttering, grinning, and stretching, the creature is a non-communicable, inhuman presentation, something movingly captured at the end of the novel as it extends its hand over Victor's corpse in the cabin of Walton's ship, 'in color and apparent texture like that of a mummy' (Shelley 218). Though recriminatory, what if we were to read the creature not as a reminder of Victor's failure, but of the *creature-as-failure,* as a presence that is neither awake nor dreaming but something quite other than life? A ruin, perhaps? Both outside the dream but still staring down Victor back into his studio state, the unspeaking creature figures for the hermeneut of the unthought of the dream, the placeless place that it occupies but can never coincide with. When the creature stares at Victor, he models what it would be like to stare *at* the novel and see it in a defamiliarized light as a mass of sketches and deletions.

> Thus strangely are our souls constructed, and by such slight ligaments are we bound to prosperity or ruin. When I look back, it seems to me as if this almost miraculous change of inclination and will was the immediate suggestion of the guardian angel of my life. (41–2)

If Victor requires Walton to hear his ruin, it is because, like Shelley to her readers, Victor reports his 'associations' so as to make them available to be contemplated but not appropriated, as if to present conflict by showing but not resolving it. This kind of reporting is queerly cruisy, allowing for desired thoughts (thoughtful desires) to be both repressed and intensified; by offering this to Walton, he might be cruising him, saying: perhaps you, too, are already ruined, and I love you. And perhaps, Victor also leaves the creature as a way of lovingly (and ruinously) staying with it by not wanting to properly have it.

Unsought Thoughts

In *An Essay Concerning Human Understanding,* John Locke asks whether it is possible to imagine (and he does) that '*the soul thinks not always*': 'I confess myself, to have one of those dull souls, that doth not perceive itself always to contemplate ideas, nor can conceive it any more necessary for the *soul always to think,* than for the body always to move' (112). If the body can be at times inactive or unwilling to act, then the soul likewise does not need to always think. Infinite thinking and acting are, Locke observes, 'the privilege of the infinite Author and Preserver of things, "who never slumbers nor sleeps"; but is not competent to any finite being, at last not to the soul of man' (113). Perhaps Locke's soul is not always thinking, but his phrasing leaves open the possibility that thinking still occurs, just not by his soul. Indeed, Locke does not say that thinking does not happen all the time; just that the soul is not always thinking. Can thoughts occur in the absence of soul thinking? Elsewhere in a letter, Locke calls these 'unsought' thoughts: 'The thoughts that come often unsought, and, as it were, drop into the mind, are commonly the most valuable of any we have, and therefore should be secured, because they seldom return again' (*Works* 10:317).[24] Where do unsought thoughts come from? From what placeless place do they originate? Presumably an 'outside' that cannot be located or pinned down. The quote 'who never slumbers nor sleeps' cites Psalm 121: 'He will not suffer thy foot to be moved: he that keepeth thee will not slumber. / Behold, he that keepeth Israel shall neither slumber nor sleep.' God's thinking is cast as an overprotective watchfulness (the repetition of 'slumber' and 'sleep' spells out this defensiveness) in contrast to a far sleepier and undefended being who does not always think and act, and as a result is less capable of ascertaining what or when he thinks or when he does not. In a reading of this passage, Kevis Goodman has suggested that the 'gaps or syncopes of thought' introduced (though left unexplored) by Locke become places where poetry is left 'open to context, so that the affective consciousness represented is not a recess or retreat but a mediating aperture through which the world's strangeness enters' (90). For Goodman, these syncopes give way to opening and unsealing, letting glimpses of the world in; at the same time, however, it would not be inconceivable to think of a soul's non-thinking as a medium without mediation, neither transferring over nor interfacing with worlds. Unsought thoughts would fail to register in their abstention. 'But supposing that all watches, whilst the balance beats, think, and it is sufficiently proved, and past doubt, that my watch thought all last night' (113). While Locke's point is that conjecture or opinion is not hard evidence, the other side of his example makes the point that things indifferent to our thinking, like watches, *are* thinking, sleeping, or not thinking, too.

Within every philosophical problem, many things are lost and remain unsought. The world does not always enter; it disappears. And quite often, it does not even know poetry has been written, nor what to do with it.

>A slumber did my spirit seal;
>I had no human fears:
>She seemed a thing that could not feel
>The touch of earthly years.
>
>No motion has she now, no force;
>She neither hears nor sees;

Rolled round in earth's diurnal course,
With rocks, and stones, and trees. (Wordsworth 115)

Simon Jarvis has stated that Wordsworth's singular contribution was to show how poetry is 'fitted to stand for what makes us see our *thinking* ... not as "thinking that," "judging that," "knowing that," but as the irreducibly affective fact of experience' (179). In a poem which notably begins with slumbering and sealing, how do we 'see our thinking' under and *with* these conditions? And is it *ours*? Whichever way we read the first line, 'a sealing (seal: from *signum*, sign) is at work,' writes Marc Redfield. 'It inscribes, stamps, closes up, and – if slumber is taken to seal spirit (*spiritus*: breath, wind) – it stifles. Slumber stamps itself onto breath and seals it up; breath, acting as an inscriptive force, stamps and seals slumber' (*Theory* 73). As a 'parable of reading' (73), sealing, closing up, and stifling all reify the poem as an object that reflects back the hermeneutical task of unsealing it. At the same time, the poem is more experimental with its stanzas, thinking how to make room for us to think about what we cannot have access to beyond its contours – what is unsought, lost, subtracted, or slept through. This is not knowledge we missed and would have wanted to have; rather, it is close to the fallible non-knowing that Locke reflects upon, a 'thinking not always' that raises questions about what thinks or does not think when we do not, and how our own privilege not to think is an alibi for other things that think and do not think.

Something illegibly available, neither present nor withheld, occurs in these eight lines, which read like a 'studio of words' (Britzman 52). Perhaps this is what accounts for the powerful hold the poem has continually exerted on readers and scholars in its cramped textual space. Its uncanniness derives from the fact that it is so declaratively simple in its complexities just as it is, as if it were presenting a thought that is so freely obtainable – and always has been so – and not up for purchase or loan that we have no way (nor have ever had a way) of knowing it because the poem's 'sense' was given away long before it could ever have become claimed. And we do not feel at all diminished by this dispensation. To put it in these terms, I believe, reverses the traumatic language that often enfolds it as a text of what Cathy Caruth calls 'unclaimed experience.' 'A slumber' is weirdly diffident, enclosed, an antechamber of evaporative thought; it does not reckon with the inaccessibility of past experiences, histories, and lives, but rather unemphatically insists that its thinking is not precious or rare, that it is *there* in its mereness. It can be read, spoken, stared at, and seen, but the thinking it shows is not the kind we can properly possess. In spite of the poem's minimal plot, whenever I read it I intensely feel that each line is strangely non-sequential, detached and detaching like the movement of thinking and not-painting Twombly describes in his studio. Not a single line bears a triumphalist confidence; each one stands at a distance from the other, doing nothing.

In the 'Preface' to the *Lyrical Ballads*, Wordsworth defends himself from 'the most dishonourable accusation which can be brought against an Author, namely, that of an indolence which prevents him from endeavouring to ascertain what is his duty, or, when his duty is ascertained, prevents him from performing it' (78). Indolence brings about two things: it cancels out the will to 'ascertain' or find out a poet's 'duty' and why, namely, it is thought to be his (and only his) to define; and, in the event the task is found out, it stops him from performing it. Indolence scrambles poetic duty as both concept and performance, something the poet should prove by way of showing and doing it. 'A slumber,' I wager, continues this line of reflection but in an odder direction: it ascertains that a thought occurs because we cannot think or act, and that this thinking is a making that is specific to the poem's studio state. Sealing the spirit (or the slumber) is, like signing, stifling, or closing, a form of inscription, to be sure, but it is also a gesture of incompletion: to seal or to close is also to cut, to change and remake the substance of what is being closed – to imagine that the poem will always be unreadable and unthinkable because *its* making is not something we can wakefully observe or follow. Wordsworth thus seems to suggest that while the poem's 'duty' to make might be *there* or *somewhere*, it is at a distance from the poet's own capacity to ascertain it – to think it. In its indifference, the poem does not require another's watchfulness in order to be a poem.

Wordsworth's 'turn towards poetry ... must embrace the risk,' states Peter de Bolla, 'that some things are known to things' (58), which is to say that knowing transpires with or beside things, but is not a transaction between them as in commodity exchange. Not only do things know and think about each other relationally, but they make and unmake each other in their knowing. What I am describing here is not craft. It is a making of things in ignorance of what they are, a sealing (which is to say a signing or inscribing) of ignorant, ignoring, unsought things. It is as if we are invited to peer over into the studio state of a lyric like anthropologists, looking at things that are making other things we either can or cannot bring to reason with eyes wide shut.

'She seemed a thing that could not feel / The touch of earthly years.' At this point in the chapter, I cannot help but read Wordsworth's poem as a massively condensed revision of Victor's dream: an ungendered 'I' dreams of a 'she' who may or may not have been, and like the dream, the poem materializes gender difference as the precipitate of an error of reading that takes simultaneous events / words / things and translates them into a temporally unfurling narrative, separating 'I' from 'she,' masculine from feminine, dreamer from dream. Difference is bestowed by the fantasy of temporal succession – a consequence, in other words, of the allegory of temporality that Paul de Man long ago detected in the poem's rhetorical desire to 'to give duration to what is, in fact, simultaneous within the subject' (225). To push the *Frankenstein* comparison even further, shifting from 'I' to 'she' is like gothic substitutability, each thing no less meaningful than the other as words grasp for an ineluctable empiricism. But substitutability here suggests a chain of replacements and appropriations; in Wordsworth's two 'sealed' rooms or stanzas, change, putatively indicated in the simple shift from 'I' to 'she,' is less transition or alteration than a non-dualistic setting down or letting be of two things beside each other in what Eve Kosofsky Sedgwick has called a 'spacious agnosticism' – letting ideas be just as they are and as they are not, 'though not an infinity of them' (8). Pronouns here have nothing to do with discursive participants; they are alibis in the poem (and used *by* the poem) to singularly materialize its inhibited making and thinking. To say, for example, that 'she seemed a thing that could not feel' is not only to qualify the 'she' as an unfeeling substance, but also to hint that 'seeming' is touched *by* that unfeeling, too, deriving its sense of thingliness by coming up against the 'she' as a thing that cannot feel. Similarly, 'the touch of earthly years' in the fourth line emphasizes how seeming / sensing is gleaned from that touching, a calendrical tactility, as it were, that is not so much geological but aesthetic ('earthly'). How do we begin to think the touch of that? And how do years, after all, touch?

'No motion has she now, no force; / She neither hears nor sees; / Rolled round in earth's diurnal course, / With rocks, and stones, and trees': 'no, now, no' acoustically redistributes the *n* and *o*, but the phrase also lets the words resonate beside each other, each calmly insisting on its own specificity. The durability of the 'now' does not denote the present as a point in time; rather, this 'now' is thingly, weighty and yet light, material and immaterial, pushing up against the 'she' as if to stop the motion of the line and render it indifferent to the expectation that the poem seems driven to meet but finally does not quite push toward or pull back from. This indifference is, I suggest, Wordsworth's unsought *un*force: something imperceptible has been achieved but not quite finished, impossible to point to and know but still tenaciously, laterally *there*, 'with rocks, and stones, and trees' but also, movingly, with *with*ness itself, like a prior mark of relation or being-there. It cannot be sought, but it is made and unmade in the enclosure of the poem.

De Bolla has remarked that the poem stages how knowing can be stolen from us in its reading: he argues that even the word 'seal' – the charismatic totem of the poem – verges on being replaced by the word 'steal,' an aural simulacrum that names the theft it enacts.[25] What is stolen away, however, can often appear to be unsought, as I think Locke knew: on the one hand, to feel that a thought has been stolen from me means that, at some point, I believed it was uniquely mine, and feared it could be taken away – a presumption that 'it' was something I had at some prior moment acquired and sought to make my own. Unsought thinking, however, intimates that something can be felt to pass through me, but without any fear of loss because that thing was never mine to begin with ('I had no human fears'). Such experiences, not necessarily lived or undergone, give evidence to what it means to be stolen away *from* oneself, to be disoriented or displaced by a poem.

This brand of unsought disorientation in 'A slumber' partly evokes, I believe, one species of the Romantic studio state's aesthetic thinking. To bring it into fuller view, I want to close with a famous example, Friedrich Schiller's ekphrastic reflection on the Juno Ludovisi, as a way to create a juxtaposition that appreciates the 'unsought-ness' that the poem is noiselessly after:

> It is neither charm, nor is it dignity, that speaks to us from the superb countenance of a Juno Ludovisi; it is neither of them, because it is both at once ... The whole form reposes and dwells within itself, a completely closed creation, and – as though it were beyond space – without yielding, without resistance; there is no force to contend with force, no unprotected part where temporality might break in. Irresistibly seized and attracted by the one quality, and held at a distance by the other, we find ourselves at the same time in the condition of utter rest and extreme movement, and the result is that wonderful emotion for which reason has no conception and language no name. (81)

Admiring the massive head in its serene 'repose,' we are 'seized and attracted ... we find ourselves at the same time' empathetically absorbing and identifying with it. We submit to and realize this unnamed, emotional equilibrium of 'utter rest and extreme movement' which remains nameless because that equilibrium can be instituted or prescribed only by an experience that is the somatic correlative of the aesthetic state. We submit to harmony, to the suspension instantiated by the Schillerian aesthetic. Jarvis has stated, however, that Wordsworth's own relation to the aesthetic does not easily submit to Schiller's insofar as the 'separation of pleasures into sensual pleasures, on the one hand, and disinterested (or, alternatively, 'ideological') pleasures on the other, is governed by the progressive perfection of the distinction between production and consumption in modern economic reason' (126). On this reading, the Juno Ludovisi, in Schiller's prose, harmonizes that necessary 'separation.' But like 'A slumber,' its figuring of rest and non-resistance is not lived; rather, the Juno insists on something archaically *unlived*, something anterior to economistic thinking – less the accomplishment of a state than a trace of unfinished materiality found in its 'closed creation.'

Schiller encounters the Juno as a thing floating on the page, a sheer expression of an efficiently conserving power, motivated but without volition. It is as if he imagines the way space admits 'her.' He remakes the head in language by imagining how *not* to retroactively produce her, or perhaps how to unmake the Juno from a *her* into an *it*. Detached from context, the head appears as a ruin that is out of place, an aestheticized decapitation. It exists artifactually in museums and institutions but it is also a phenomenon that is irreducible to them. Jacques Rancière has remarked that Schiller's version of the Juno articulates a singular leveling idea: 'The statue thus comes paradoxly to figure what has not been made' (135). As a model of apparent aesthetic autonomy, the head bestows that sense of autonomy on any prosaic thing which now can partake of the aesthetic while also being unassimilated to the 'high' category of art (144). To be sure, the Juno, as the figure *of* a figure, is a phenomenalized surface topology, serving as the groundless ground (*le fond*) of the aesthetic. And as a colossal gendered fragment, its charisma, 'without yielding, resistance,' sublimes over the directive to its imputed masculine viewers to submit, to 'find ourselves' in a seized relation with it, as if here and now we have finally found our heteronormative place in a groundless world. But, *pace* Rancière, I want to dwell a bit more with the head as a 'closed creation ... as if beyond space.' Note that he calls it a 'statue,' as if hallucinating a body into spectral sight in order to organize 'her,' render 'her' legibly sensible according to the humanistic standards of a conforming liberal visibility, ultimately redeeming 'her' as an object of recognition and spectatorship. I do not believe, however, that the Juno figures authorless autonomy: the head neither sees, hears, nor feels; it captures no memory of its making and, like the 'she' in 'A slumber,' it is not a kind of 'material anamnesis' that records its unique time and history in stone for us to archaeologically reclaim.[26] Similarly, Wordsworth's 'she' is outside of memory, just as the poem's monadic studio state does not remember but remakes, putting 'her' beside or alongside 'rocks, and stones, and trees,' not in order to give 'her' a pantheistic burial, or return 'her' to 'nature,' but to push her out of place, to displace and disorient 'her' – to make it possible to see, ultimately, from within the studio's sealed partiality, that a thing can think next to other things and *apart from us*, in another part (or *partage*) of the poem's space. In this very moment, Wordsworth shows us something quite extraordinary and profoundly queer: an indifferent ecstasy. 'She' is put out of place, out of memory, out of life, but all of this happens *in* the placelessness of the poem. Such *ekstasis*, moreover, is not something the poem or anyone else undergoes; rather, it is an ecstatically formal relation to the unsought – the thought without anyone or anything to think it, but which nevertheless is an outside within the studio of the poem, as ordinary as the commas that discretely separate rocks from stones from trees, and shes, pushing words away from each other.

This muted ecstatic thinking is anything but empathetic – in other words, it is contrary to the belief that when we see a thing like the Juno Ludovisi, that experience already transcends the brute matter of the head and solicits our submission to the 'humanity' that is missing from it like its invisible body. In an 'aesthetics of empathy,' writes Claire Colebrook, 'the hand of the artist is led by the idea of a world that is not materially presented but that can be indicated or thought through matter ... [a] positing of an immateriality that transcends matter' (156, 155). There is no 'interiority' to the Juno: it neither is a head without a body nor is it journeying to find one. The 'Juno' is just a head and nothing more. From what point of view does a ruinous head think? Might it be another version of Kant in the dark room, a head but without a body in the darkness? Before it enters into the patterns of connoisseurship in the 'show-rooms of Romanticism,'[27] the head thinks within its own 'closed creation,' its occulted point of view which is beyond reach or touch. In Wordsworth's studio of words, other inhuman modalities think and make, as well as unthink and unmake: years can touch, and things cease to feel. Romanticism's aesthetic seriousness consists in allowing for the unsought, for the making *of* and *in* studios where images and texts can happen but are not immediately owned, rendered relevant or publishable, or made to luminously appear outside a miraculously inhibiting and placeless dark.

Notes

1. Compare this with Giorgio Agamben's argument that the 'contemporary' is the thinker who trains perception on the obscurity or illegibility of 'the darkness of his time' over and against a hegemonic enlightenment. In this sense, darkness evokes 'an activity and a singular ability ... a neutralization of the lights that come from the epoch' ('What is the Contemporary?' 45). Forest Pyle and I discuss this passage in our introduction, 'On the Present Darkness of Romanticism,' in *Constellations of a Contemporary Romanticism* 1–15.

2. Baucom here is responding to James Chandler's notion of a dislocated historicism in *England in 1819: The Politics of Literary Culture and the Case of Romantic Historicism* 37ff.
3. See also Rajan.
4. I refer, of course, to the concept of the 'minor' in Gilles Deleuze and Félix Guattari's *Kafka: Towards a Minor Literature*.
5. See Tiffany, *Infidel Poetics*.
6. Clark here reflects on Goya's studio as the material 'space' where he worked on *The Disasters of War* (c.1810–20; published 1863), prints he endlessly labored over but withheld from public view during his lifetime. Clark explores the impotentiality or non-productivity of Goya's images, held back as if in refusal of their recognition.
7. See Catherine Malabou's comments on how the concept of 'plasticity' imagines psychic transformation in the absence of an outside, a 'fleeing without going anywhere' or how to 'think of the formation of a way out in the absence of a way out' (*Plasticity* 67). Also see her book *The Ontology of the Accident: An Essay on Destructive Plasticity*.
8. All citations from Wordsworth's writing are from *Wordsworth's Poetry and Prose*.
9. See Rei Terada, 'Coleridge Among the Spectra.'
10. I allude here to John Paul Ricco's remark that the ellipsis is 'neither a matter of absence of presence nor even of the not presentable, but in a sense is the lexicographic presentation of presentation. It is the stage/scene that summons neither a word ... nor a concept' (82).
11. All citations from Blake are from *The Complete Poetry & Prose of William Blake*.
12. Blake returned to the story of Job multiple times in various media, producing watercolors for Thomas Butts and John Linell between 1805 and 1827. There is one important difference in some of those versions: the angels surpass the frame in some and not in others, as if Blake were experimenting with what the room of the engraving is, and what it must make room for.
13. I refer to Jean-Luc Nancy's 'The Weight of a Thought.'
14. Stephen Best adopts Liu's perspective in a chapter entitled 'My Beautiful Elimination,' from *None Like Us*, where he imagines how to think of a negative orientation to history once one begins to 'think like artworks' (37).
15. I am reformulating here Joel Faflak's remarkable phrase on the alterity or 'matter of history' as 'a being within being that cannot be thought, but also a thought within being that has a being of its own that cannot be thought.'
16. In an article on Camille Pissarro, T. J. Clark calls his painting 'not a journey to a horizon: it is *here where we are*, an immense proximity, a total intuition of "place" and "extent." And Time is not becoming, not endless contingency: it is a Now that goes on being Now as we live it, a unique kind of permanence' ('Strange Apprentice').
17. I am citing Georges Didi-Huberman's marvelous phrase, 'For the film itself to lower its eyelids for an instant' ('Out of the Dark' 149).
18. See my other reading of this passage in 'Is That All There Is? No Regrets (After 1818).'
19. I take this term from Bersani and Ulysse Dutoit, 'this side of – *en-deça de*': 'that which has not yet happened, a before-stories' that manifests *before*

'more officially sanctioned connections,' social or aesthetic, become symbolically legible (6–8).
20. Thomas Ford has read the passage from the letter as evocative of 'an atmospheric state of not knowing' or 'breathing chamber' of modernity, as stifling as it is seemingly enlivening (154).
21. Beyond the workshop, one could think of other multiple 'topologies of the unreal' in the novel: the hovel in which the creature lives and from which he surveys the De Laceys; the two-room 'hut' Victor sets up in the Orkneys (a retreat from retreat, as it were); the house in which Victor is imprisoned awaiting the arrival of the magistrate, and even the cabin on Walton's ship, where his corpse lies.
22. 'What if man's homelessness consisted in this, that man still does not even think of the *real* plight of dwelling as *the* plight? Yet as soon as man *gives thought* to his homelessness, it is a misery no longer' (Heidegger 161).
23. Anne K. Mellor (54–5) has pointed to the historical non-specificity of events in the novel.
24. John Locke to Samuel Bold, May 16, 1699. I thank David L. Clark for pointing me to this passage and a reading of it.
25. De Bolla writes: 'Something might be, even has been, stolen from me. Something has been lifted from me which causes a certain lightness – it is as if I have been divested of a part of what I had thought to be inalienably mine, what I think of as my being human' (57).
26. 'Material anamnesis' is from Georges Didi-Huberman's *Being a Skull: Place, Contact, Thought, Sculpture*.
27. Rancière, 'The Aesthetic Revolution and its Outcomes,' 144.

References

Agamben, Giorgio. *Stanzas: Word and Phantasm in Western Culture*. Trans. Ronald L. Martinez. Minneapolis: University of Minnesota Press, 1993.
—. 'What Is the Contemporary?' *What Is An Apparatus? and Other Essays*. Trans. David Kishik and Stefan Pedatella. Stanford: Stanford University Press, 2009. 39–54.
Baucom, Ian. *Specters of the Atlantic: Finance Capital, Slavery, and the Philosophy of History*. Durham, NC: Duke University Press, 2005.
Bersani, Leo. *Receptive Bodies*. Chicago: University of Chicago Press, 2018.
—. *Thoughts and Things*. Chicago: University of Chicago Press, 2015.
— and Ulysse Dutoit. *Forms of Being: Cinema, Aesthetics, Subjectivity*. London: BFI Publishing, 2004.
Best, Stephen. 'My Beautiful Elimination.' *None Like Us: Blackness, Belonging, Aesthetic Life*. Durham, NC: Duke University Press, 2018. 29–62.
Blake, William. *The Complete Poetry & Prose of William Blake*. Rev. ed. David V. Erdman. New York: Anchor Books, 1988.
Blanchot, Maurice. *The Space of Literature*. Trans. Ann Smock. Lincoln: University of Nebraska Press, 1989.
Britzman, Deborah P. *A Psychoanalyst in the Classroom: On the Human Condition in Education*. Buffalo: State University of New York Press, 2015.

Caruth, Cathy. *Unclaimed Experience: Trauma, Narrative, History.* Baltimore: Johns Hopkins University Press, 1996.
Chandler, James. *England in 1819: The Politics of Literary Culture and the Case of Romantic Historicism.* Chicago: University of Chicago Press, 1998.
Christensen, Jerome. *Lord Byron's Strength: Romantic Writing and Commercial Society.* Baltimore: Johns Hopkins University Press, 1993.
Clark, David L. 'Goya's Scarcity.' *Constellations of a Contemporary Romanticism.* 86–121.
Clark, T. J. 'A Snake, A Flame: Blake at the Ashmolean.' *London Review of Books* 5 February 2015. https://www.lrb.co.uk/the-paper/v37/n03/t.j.-clark/a-snake-a-flame (last accessed October 20, 2020).
—. 'Strange Apprentice.' *London Review of Books* 8 October 2020. https://www.lrb.co.uk/the-paper/v42/n19/t.j.-clark/strange-apprentice (last accessed October 15, 2020).
Colebrook, Claire. *Death of the PostHuman: Essays on Extinction, Vol. 1.* Ann Arbor, MI: Open Humanities Press, 2014.
Coleridge, Samuel Taylor. *Coleridge's Poetry and Prose.* Ed. Nicholas Halmi, Paul Magnuson, and Raimonda Modiano. New York: W. W. Norton, 2004.
De Bolla, Peter. 'What is a Lyrical Ballad? Wordsworth's Experimental Epistemologies.' *Wordsworth's Poetic Theory: Knowledge, Language, Experience.* Ed. Alexander Regier and Stefan H. Uhlig. London: Palgrave, 2010. 43–60.
Deleuze, Gilles and Félix Guattari. *Kafka: Towards a Minor Literature.* Trans. Dana Polan. Minneapolis: University of Minnesota Press, 1986.
De Luca, Vincent. *Words of Eternity: Blake and the Poetics of the Sublime.* Princeton: Princeton University Press, 1991.
de Man, Paul. 'The Rhetoric of Temporality.' *Blindness and Insight: Essays in the Rhetoric of Contemporary Criticism.* Minneapolis: University of Minnesota Press, 1983. 187–228.
Derrida, Jacques. 'Ellipsis.' *Writing and Difference.* Trans. Alan Bass. Chicago: University of Chicago Press, 1978. 295–300.
—. *Rogues: Essays on Reason.* Trans. Pascale-Anne Brault and Michael Naas. Stanford: Stanford University Press, 2005.
Didi-Huberman, George. *Being a Skull: Place, Contact, Thought, Sculpture.* Trans. Drew S. Burk. Minneapolis: University of Minnesota Press, 2016.
—. 'Out of the Dark.' Trans. Gila Walker. *Critical Inquiry* (Autumn 2020): 149–71.
Düttmann, Alexander García. *Visconti: Insights into Flesh and Blood.* Trans. Robert Savage. Stanford: Stanford University Press, 2009.
Faflak, Joel. 'Still Here.' *The Future of Shelley's Triumph. Romantic Circles Critical Praxis.* Ed. Joel Faflak. https://romantic-circles.org/praxis/triumph/praxis.2019.triumph.faflak.html (last accessed December 1, 2020).
Ford, Thomas. *Wordsworth and the Poetics of Air.* Cambridge: Cambridge University Press, 2018.
Foucault, Michel. 'What Is Enlightenment?' *Ethics: Subjectivity and Truth.* Ed. Paul Rabinow. Vol. 1 of *Essential Works of Foucault, 1954–1984.* New York: New Press, 1997. 303–19.
Goodman, Kevis. *Georgic Modernity and British Romanticism: Poetry and the Mediation of History.* Cambridge: Cambridge University Press, 2004.

Green, André. *On Private Madness*. Trans. Kim Lewison and Dinora Pines. New York: Karnac Books, 1997.

Heidegger, Martin. 'Building, Dwelling, Thinking.' *Poetry, Language, Thought*. Trans. Albert Hofstader. New York: HarperCollins, 1971. 143–61.

Jarvis, Simon. *Wordsworth's Philosophic Song*. Cambridge: Cambridge University Press, 2007.

Juengel, Scott J. 'What is Orientation in Sinking?' *European Romantic Review* 30.3 (2019): 265–74.

Kant, Immanuel. 'An Answer to the Question: What is Enlightenment?' *Toward Perpetual Peace and Other Writings on Politics, Peace, and History*. Ed. Pauline Kleingeld. Trans David L. Colclasure. New Haven, CT: Yale University Press, 2006. 17–23.

—. *Critique of Judgment*. Ed. and trans. Paul Guyer. Cambridge: Cambridge University Press, 2000.

—. 'What is Orientation in Thinking?' *Kant: Political Writings*. Ed. H. S. Reiss. London: Cambridge University Press, 2003. 239–47.

Keats, John. *The Letters of John Keats, 1814–1821*. 2 vols in 1 vol. Ed. Hyder Edward Rollings. Cambridge, MA: Harvard University Press, 2001.

Khalip, Jacques. 'Is That All There Is? No Regrets (After 1818).' *Frankenstein In Theory: A Critical Anatomy*. Ed. Orrin N. C. Wang. New York: Bloomsbury, 2021. 221–39.

— and Forest Pyle. 'On the Present Darkness of Romanticism.' *Constellations of a Contemporary Romanticism*. Ed. Jacques Khalip and Forest Pyle. New York: Fordham University Press, 2016. 1–15.

Koestenbaum, Wayne. 'Fag Limbo.' *My 1980s & Other Essays*. New York: Farrar, Straus and Giroux, 2013. 192–200.

Litchfield, Richard Buckley. *Tom Wedgwood, The First Photographer*. London: Duckworth and Co., 1903.

Liu, Alan. *Local Transcendence: Essays on Postmodern Historicism and the Database*. Chicago: University of Chicago Press, 2008.

Locke, John. *An Essay Concerning Human Understanding*. Ed. Roger Woolhouse. New York: Penguin, 1997.

—. *The Works of John Locke, in Ten Volumes*. London: Otridge and Son, etc., 1812.

Makdisi, Saree. *William Blake and the Impossible History of the 1790s*. Chicago: University of Chicago Press, 2002.

Malabou, Catherine. 'Life and Prison.' *Alienocene/Dis-Junction* (October 2018). https://alienocene.com/2018/10/23/life-and-prison (last accessed September 5, 2020).

—. *The Ontology of the Accident: An Essay on Destructive Plasticity*. London: Polity, 2012.

—. *Plasticity at the Dusk of Writing: Dialectic, Destruction, Deconstruction*. Trans. Carolyn Shread. New York: Columbia University Press, 2010.

Mellor, Anne. *Mary Shelley: Her Life, Her Fiction, Her Monsters*. New York: Routledge, 1989.

Montag, Warren. '"The Workshop of Filthy Creation": A Marxist Reading of *Frankenstein*.' *Case Studies in Contemporary Criticism: Mary Shelley, Frankenstein*. Ed. Johanna M. Smith. Boston: Bedford Books, 1991. 300–11.

Nancy, Jean-Luc. *The Ground of the Image.* Trans. Jeff Fort. New York: Fordham University Press, 2005.
—. 'The Weight of a Thought.' *The Gravity of Thought.* Trans. François Raffoul and Gregory Recco. Atlantic Highlands, NJ: Humanities Press, 1997. 75–84.
O'Doherty, Brian. *Studio and Cube: On the Relationship Between Where Art is Made and Where Art is Displayed.* New York: Princeton Architectual Press, 2008.
Pascal, Blaise. *Pensées and Other Writings.* Trans. Honor Levi. Oxford: Oxford University Press, 2008.
Pfau, Thomas. *Romantic Moods: Paranoia, Trauma, and Melancholy, 1790–1840.* Baltimore: Johns Hopkins University Press, 2005.
Pyle, Forest. 'Introduction: "The Power is There": Romanticism as Aesthetic Insistence.' *Romanticism and the Insistence of the Aesthetic.* Ed. Forest Pyle. *Romantic Circle Praxis Series* (February 2005). https://romantic-circles.org/praxis/aesthetic/pyle/intro.html (last accessed November 21, 2020).
Rajan, Tilottama. 'Unspacing: The Architecture of Poetry in Shelley's *Alastor* and Keats's *The Fall of Hyperion.' Studies in English Literature 1500–1900* 55.4 (Autumn 2015): 787–815.
Rancière, Jacques. 'The Aesthetic Revolution and its Outcomes: Emplotments of Autonomy and Heteronomy.' *New Left Review* 14 (March/April 2002). https://newleftreview.org/issues/ii14/articles/jacques-ranciere-the-aesthetic-revolution-and-its-outcomes (last accessed February 15, 2021).
Redfield, Marc. '*Frankenstein*'s Cinematic Dream.' *Frankenstein's Dream.* Ed. Jerrold Hogle, *Romantic Circles Praxis Series* (June 2003). https://romantic-circles.org/praxis/ frankenstein/ redfield/redfield.html (last accessed 1 November 2020).
—. *Theory at Yale: The Strange Case of Deconstruction in America.* New York: Fordham University Press, 2016.
Ricco, John Paul. *The Decision Between Us: Art and Ethics in the Time of Scenes.* Chicago: University of Chicago Press, 2014.
Schiller, Friedrich. *On the Aesthetic Education of Man.* Trans. Reginald Snell. Mineola, NY: Dover, 2004.
Sedgwick, Eve Kosofsky. *Touching Feeling: Affect, Pedagogy, Performativity.* Durham, NC: Duke University Press, 2003.
Shelley, Mary. *Frankenstein.* Ed. M. K. Joseph. Oxford: Oxford University Press, 1998.
Sliwinski, Sharon. *Dreaming in Dark Times: Six Exercises in Political Thought.* Minneapolis: University of Minnesota Press, 2017.
Sylvester, David. *Interviews with American Artists.* New Haven, CT: Yale University Press, 2001.
Terada, Rei. 'Coleridge Among the Spectra.' *Looking Away: Phenomenality and Dissatisfaction, Kant to Adorno.* Cambridge, MA: Harvard University Press, 2009. 35–72.
—. 'Looking at the Stars Forever.' *Studies in Romanticism* 50 (Summer 2011): 275–309.
Tiffany, Daniel. *Infidel Poetics: Riddles, Nightlife, Substance.* Chicago: University of Chicago Press, 2009.
Wordsworth, William. *Wordsworth's Poetry and Prose.* Ed. Nicholas Halmi. New York: W. W. Norton, 2014.

Chapter 9

The Media Ecology of Romantic Consciousness: Knowledge in Charlotte Smith's *Beachy Head*

Ralf Haekel

Charlotte Smith's late masterpiece, *Beachy Head*, published posthumously one year after the author's death, begins in a manner that is still widely considered to be typically Romantic:

> On thy stupendous summit, rock sublime!
> That o'er the channel reared, half way at sea
> The mariner at early morning hails,
> I would recline; while Fancy should go forth,
> And represent the strange and awful hour
> Of vast concussion ... (1–6)

Nature, the sublime, subjectivity, imagination – these topics seem to pave the way for a poem based on a thoroughly dualistic concept of the human. According to this dualistic concept, consciousness is interior, based on the subjective mind which, in turn, is clearly opposed to the material world. Smith's speaker is situated in a recognizable setting within nature, reclining on top of Beachy Head, the cliffs in East Sussex looking down on the English Channel. The rich history of the spot, as well as its proximity to France, triggers the complex meditations that characterize the bulk of the poem. In this sense it is, in Smith's own words, a 'local poem' (Smith, *Collected Letters* 705) or, as Jacqueline Labbe states, a 'contemplative blank-verse poem' that 'participates in the Romantic revival of the prospect poem' (Labbe 142–3).

The first part covers the time span of an entire day, from early morning to night. In other traditional Romantic poems, like Wordsworth's 'Tintern Abbey' or Coleridge's 'Frost at Midnight,' such an opening sequence would then – according to M. H. Abrams's influential description of the 'greater Romantic lyric' – turn into an extended inward meditation. In *Beachy Head*, however, these expectations are thwarted as the poem takes an entirely different course:

> Contemplation here,
> High on her throne of rock, aloof may sit,
> And bid recording Memory unfold
> Her scroll voluminous ... (117–20)

The mediation of the stream of consciousness, to apply the term for the most famous modernist narrative technique, is not rendered invisible, mimicking the ongoing associations of ideas; rather, it is made discernible through Smith's fragmentation of the mind. Readings of Smith's poem tend to characterize this fragmented narration either as caused by different speakers[1] or as different forms of a gendered self-fashioning persona.[2] Yet, this passage suggests that Smith's poem presents the speaker's consciousness as different faculties of the mind, which appear as personifications, in these lines as Contemplation and Memory. These allegorical figures, reminiscent of the traditional faculties of the soul well established since the early modern period, do not represent an inner self but rather remain outward and use media: 'recording Memory' unfolds her 'scroll voluminous.' The faculty of memory relies on written documents, which in their totality establish the discipline of history and later natural history: that is, science. This outward consciousness is inextricably linked with forms of writing: it quotes, makes references, discusses contradictory opinions.

Seen from this perspective, the opening lines already pave the way for the fragmentation of the mind. While the speaking 'I' reclines, her 'Fancy' takes over to imagine the scene. Here the I is immediately separated and set in opposition to Fancy. The speaker's position is crucial in this context. She reclines, and her body almost merges with the ground, the eponymous rock, while all she can see is (presumably) the sky. All of the following discourses are therefore the creations of the conscious mind, which are, however, not rendered as subjective but rather in and through media. In other words, *Beachy Head* constructs a non-dualistic conception of the human mind in which consciousness not only intertextually relies on media – through reading, writing, communication – but also is synonymous with a complex media ecology thus established.

This is particularly evident with regard to the poem's treatment of science. The speaker displays a vast knowledge of natural history, focusing on the expertise gathered and systematized in the just emerging scientific disciplines of geology, ornithology, and botany. Smith's extensive use of endnotes, in which she discusses and sometimes also destabilizes the arguments made in the main text, further emphasizes this knowledge. Yet this knowledge relies not only on the developing sciences but also on the rapidly changing mediascape: its storage, procession, and proliferation through the modern media system. During the Romantic age, science became dispersed in popular culture through a variety of media that had originated in the Enlightenment: encyclopedias, popular periodicals, or museums made scientific knowledge publicly accessible. This popular discourse, in turn, influenced how science was developed and presented, for instance, in public lectures or in the self-fashioning of the scientific genius.

Smith's *Beachy Head* bears witness to this change of the modern media system and its effects not only on society but also on the development of the concept of consciousness around 1800. The poem's complex treatment of narrative voice in particular reflects this evolution: just as the poem is itself a fragment, the speaker presents herself as fragmented. Christoph Reinfandt explains the difficult narrative arrangement of *Beachy Head* by identifying the different narrative voices of 'the Poet,' 'the Narrator,' and 'the Historian' ('Textures' 107), further subdividing the poet into four different speakers. As Reinfandt argues, 'the poem is concerned with pitting authoritative voices against each other in print' (107). This interpretation, which argues against the notion that there is one identifiable speaker or narrator representing a unified self, is itself based on Labbe's influential reading of *Beachy Head*:

> The idea that Smith may be playing with the idea of subjectivity – that she may be less concerned with establishing a speaking 'I' or exploring personal memories than with experimenting with poetic form and identity – is suggested not only by the multiple speakers she creates but also by the parallels she embeds in the poem. (150–1)

My approach proposes an alternative to Reinfandt's and Labbe's assumption that the poem features many speakers or identities. I argue instead that the poem's voices demonstrate how different conceptions of knowledge engender distinct ways of reading the world. The poem displays a mind that is itself fragmentary and multifaceted, depending on which scientific discipline shapes and constructs consciousness. *Beachy Head* thematizes how the point of view changes depending on the perspective: the significance of the same cliffs in the eyes of a historian differs from that of the geologist or poet. And all of these perspectives depend on discourses and their medial manifestations. Thus, *Beachy Head* is a sophisticated reflection on the change of consciousness as an 'event in the history of mediation' (Siskin and Warner 1). To make my point clear, I will touch upon the different ways Smith's use of media constructs consciousness. I first discuss the concept of knowledge in literature and its connection to consciousness before turning to media theory. Here I emphasize the theory of media ecology, which differs from other media-theoretical approaches in its rejection of techno-centrist arguments.

Finally, I will read *Beachy Head* as a poem that self-reflexively refers to and highlights the media change around 1800 and, more importantly, absorbs this change by turning what I call the media ecology of consciousness into its very own formal and aesthetic principle. Rather than 'explain' Smith's poem or her approach to consciousness in *Beachy Head*, media theory provides a vocabulary that enables us to understand her own reflexive and theoretical take on the problem of knowledge and epistemology.

Harold Bloom begins his influential volume *Romanticism and Consciousness* (1970) with a quote taken from Sigmund Freud's *New Introductory Lecture on Psychoanalysis* (1933). This reference suggests the psychoanalytical definition of the psyche as subdivided into the Id, the Ego, and the Superego. The Romantic concept of consciousness, however, rather than foreshadowing Freud's twentieth-century theory of the human mind, is more indebted to Kant's critical philosophy, as Bloom goes on to state: 'Subjectivity or self-consciousness is the salient problem of Romanticism, at least for modern readers, who tend to station themselves in regard to the Romantics depending on how relevant or adequate they judge the dialectic of consciousness and imagination to be' (Bloom 1). Further on, he states that 'the central spiritual problem of Romanticism is the difficult relation between nature and consciousness' (Bloom 147), which evokes the philosophical problem of epistemology. The main argument of my chapter will thus be that *Beachy Head* runs counter to this typically Romantic conception of consciousness, so heavily indebted to German philosophy. Instead, Smith's poem proposes a non-Kantian, non-dualistic approach to consciousness, drawing on fundamental changes in the emerging field of science. *Beachy Head* makes use of scientific theories and discourses, but also shows how this knowledge is to be understood as material rather than subjective or immaterial – how consciousness relies on and is made up of media such as books, journals, or scientific periodicals. In other words, the poem proposes a concept of consciousness that takes the form of a media network or media ecology.

Literature, Media Theory, Remediation, and Media Ecology

Knowledge in literature is closely linked to the debate about the relationship between science and literature. In distinction to the British discussion that dominated much of the nineteenth and twentieth centuries,[3] a controversial German debate evolved in the 1990s in the wake of an edited collection by Joseph Vogl, *Poetologien des Wissens um 1800* [*Poetologies of Knowledge around 1800*].[4] Conducted by Tilmann Köppe, Gideon Stiening, Roland Borgards, and others, this debate is noteworthy because it shows the extent to which the concept of knowledge is still based on traditionally dualistic assumptions. In his attack against Vogl's concept of a poetology of knowledge, Köppe focuses not on the historical influence of science on literature but solely on the conception of knowledge by distinguishing two different theories: personal and impersonal knowledge – that is, the knowledge of people and the knowledge of books. The argument is simple. 'Personal knowledge,' Köppe argues, 'is, according to its logical structure, a *bipartite* predicate: it describes a relationship between a person and something this person knows. Somebody who knows something enters a specific relationship – that of knowledge – with a specific content or subject matter' (400).[5] Köppe claims that it is nonsense that a text or a book can *know* something: 'Texts are not people; therefore, they cannot know anything' (402).[6] One may dismiss this 'analytic' literary theory as a nit-picky witticism, but it helps to see the premises on which the concept of knowledge within the debate is based. Köppe's definition of knowledge presupposes a thoroughly dualistic conception of human nature grounded on the firm conviction that knowledge is interior and subjective, something to be separated from the thing that is known. This knowledge can be stored or communicated in media – that is, in texts or books – but these media do not 'have' any knowledge themselves.

Köppe's strict dichotomy has a long tradition of which the mind-and-body problem is perhaps the most important strain. There have been several attempts to transcend this dualism in recent years, most notably in the field of cognitive literary studies (Zunshine), the theory of embodied mind (Varela et al.), and studies on embodied cognition (Shapiro). I contend, however, that the necessarily mediated quality of knowledge runs counter to any form of dualism. Scientific knowledge depends on discourse, language, and thus on media. In a word, knowledge is always already mediated and cannot be separated or abstracted from its medial conditions. Taking its cue from recent developments in media studies, particularly actor-network theory and media ecology, my approach thus focuses on the historical conditions of knowledge as a complex, dynamic, and non-hierarchical social network formed by the interplay of people, media, and practices. Accordingly, the human mind – that is, the concept of consciousness and its 'content,' knowledge – cannot be separated from these processes. The mind not only participates in this 'circulation of social energies' (Greenblatt 1), but is established in and through this participation. Indeed, the mind can be understood and analyzed only through its material manifestations – signs, speech, texts, and so on. Furthermore, these material manifestations are what constitutes the mind: this media ecology is necessary to construct consciousness and knowledge in the first place.

While it is clear that literature is mediated through manuscripts, printed books, or other forms, media studies within literary theory has been less clear about what constitutes a medium in the first place. As opposed to poetics or theories of literature, a theory of mediation was seemingly non-existent prior to the invention of new media technologies in the middle of the nineteenth century.[7] Just as modern media technology was missing, there was also apparently no theoretical or conceptual reflection on media and mediation. Recent investigations by Clifford Siskin, Celeste Langan, Andrew Burkett, James Brooke-Smith, and Christoph Reinfandt ('Popular and Media Culture'), however, have argued to the contrary and shown that media theory is indeed central to Romanticism.[8] Jay David Bolter and Richard Grusin's theory of remediation is especially helpful in approaching the media ecology of *Beachy Head*. According to Bolter and Grusin, remediation is characterized by a 'double logic,' a productive tension between immediacy and hypermediacy. Media tend to render themselves transparent in order to simulate a direct – immediate – access to mediated objects, especially in our present age: virtual reality or the desktop metaphor on our personal computers but also realism in photographs or, indeed, television. As Bolter and Grusin state: 'The transparent interface is one more manifestation of the need to deny the mediated character of digital technology altogether' (24). But they also show that this is neither a new nor a surprising aspect of mediation. For instance, the technique of linear perspective in Renaissance painting or eighteenth- and nineteenth-century realist novels also tends to efface their mediality. The aim is to render a depiction most realistic and natural, foregrounding the illusion whilst denying the technique. The double logic of remediation, however, can work only with immediacy's counterpart, hypermediacy:

> Where immediacy suggests a unified visual space, contemporary hypermediacy offers a heterogeneous space, in which representation is conceived of not as a window on to the world, but rather as 'windowed' itself – with windows that open on to other representations or other media. (Bolter and Grusin 34)

Hypermediacy breaks the naturalist illusion and foregrounds the medium or media technology.

This paradigm shift leads to a wholly new concept of literature, according to which content is increasingly distinguished from medium and form:

'"content" is not a substance, but rather the production through reading of an interior, of (literate) subjectivity as a virtual space modelled on the page' (Langan 58). According to the logic of remediation, media tend to render themselves either invisible or, by means of a self-reflexive hypermediacy, highly conscious of their own medial constitution. Around the turn of the nineteenth century, the dominant mode is the remediation of earlier, predominantly oral, media into print.[9] The apparently dualistic state of consciousness in Romantic literature has its origin here, as consciousness is largely perceived as wholly inward, which is ultimately the result of the silent 'invisible, inaudible medium of print' (Langan 54). The immediacy of the poetic medium, particularly the blank-verse meditative poem and its focus on subjectivity and imagination, may be the prevailing form in the Romantic period, but it is by no means the only one. *Beachy Head*, for instance, is highly self-reflexive and hypermedial in Bolter and Grusin's sense. The poem's extensive use of notes, scientific discourses, and intertextual references which include a poem that does the exact opposite – Wordsworth's 'Tintern Abbey' – thus renders the purported immediacy of Romantic consciousness *visible* and shows it to be a medial construct. This highly conscious sense of its medial status hinges on the fact that the poem is not a remediation of an oral song but rather of earlier media of knowledge – scientific knowledge in particular and its impact on the gendered speaking subject. But the poem also highlights the fact that any form of consciousness is necessarily the result of mediation, a point made by more dynamic media theories such as cultural technique technography, and particularly media ecology.

The materialist focus on the impact of new media technology in media-theoretically informed literary studies has made way for a more open approach. This approach sees media not as mere objects used for storing, processing, and proliferating information, but rather as part of a dynamic interplay between technological inventions, *techné*, cultural techniques, dynamics, and agency encompassing literacy, writing, education, and knowledge acquisition. This more recent focus on mediation rather than media technology, be that remediation, actor-network-theory, or cultural techniques, offers a possible alternative to the common problem of dualism and the difficulty of correlating two diametrically opposed factors: mind/body, consciousness/nature or reality, technology/human, and so on.[10] The theory of media ecology perhaps best captures this non-essentialist and non-techno-centrist approach to media and mediation. The traditional approach to media ecology, first used by the Toronto School, in particular Marshall McLuhan and Neil Postman, has been criticized for its strictly hierarchical structure by a number of scholars after 2000. As Matthew Fuller argues, Postman's approach to a technological medium and its immediate environment – the people who use it and to which purpose and in what way it is put to use – 'describes a kind of environmentalism: using a study of media to sustain a relatively stable notion of human culture' (3).[11]

Fuller's less static and hierarchical and more dynamic theory is influenced by the poststructuralist writings of Gilles Deleuze and Félix Guattari, particularly Guattari's *The Three Ecologies*. As Michael Goddard and Jussi Parikka maintain,

> Media ecologies are quite often understood by Fuller through artistic/activist practices rather than pre-formed theories, which precisely work through the complex media layers in which on the one hand subjectivation and agency are articulated and, on the other hand, the materiality of informational objects gets distributed, dispersed and takes effect. (2)

In essence, the theory of media ecology encompasses the whole of culture, as Ursula Heise argues:

> Based on the assumption that media are not mere tools that humans use, but rather constitute environments within which they move and that shape the structure of their perceptions, their forms of discourse, and their social behavior patterns, media ecology typically focuses on how these structures change with the introduction of new communications technologies. (151)

Although Heise here refers mainly to digital technology, the introduction of new communication technologies, if applied to the Romantic period, also calls up the new media associated with the storage, processing, and proliferation of science and knowledge around 1800: scientific transactions, popular periodicals, encyclopedias, and museums, but also lectures, and poems such as Erasmus Darwin's *The Botanic Garden* (1791). Although none of these medial forms was absolutely new at the time, the upsurge of the capitalist print market created an entirely new medial landscape[12] that in turn left its mark on literature, and these repercussions are reflected, and reflected upon, in Smith's poem. The following media-theoretical reading of *Beachy Head* will therefore focus on the self-reflexive nature of the medial artifacts, since, as Jussi Parikka states, 'a media-ecological perspective relies on notions of self-referentiality and autopoiesis' ('Universal Viral Machine').

The Media Ecology of Consciousness in *Beachy Head*

Most critical readings of *Beachy Head* focus on one of the following four aspects: first, the poem's complex narrative construction; second, its use of natural history, particularly in scientifically informed endnotes; and third, on the most famous passage which starts with a reference to sea-shells and becomes a reflection on the nature of science. The fourth and final aspect regularly concerns the poem's fragmentary form and whether the epitaph mentioned at its close is actually missing or not. My own approach will touch upon these questions while at the same time retaining a focus on the mediality of consciousness. Consciousness in *Beachy Head* is made up of observations, ideas read or heard, scientific findings, and historical writings, but also popular opinions and folklore. These mediations of knowledge combine to establish a form of consciousness that is starkly opposed to the mind–body dualism in the wake of the Cartesian *cogito*. As such, this form of consciousness is not only influenced by various texts and media but also relies on or is created by them in the first place. *Beachy Head* is both a reflection on and an enactment of human consciousness as dependent on different forms of media.

The concept of media ecology captures this dynamic best, which becomes clear when considering how the poem treats scientific knowledge and literature. There is one theme that connects all the disciplines, perceptions, allusions: the poem is a prolonged, sophisticated, and multifaceted meditation on epistemology, particularly on how a given perspective or discursive approach changes the way nature is perceived and understood. The new sciences that take the place of natural history and natural philosophy fundamentally challenge the individual's consciousness of the world. Not only does science take the place of religious world views, it also questions any form of immediate perception and understanding of the world. Geology plays a key role here, as it theorizes the history of the world in unforeseen ways. Thus, the new sciences not only create modernity as a differentiated concept but also bring about a rupture between the individual's immediate perception and the new knowledge of the world that the same individual encounters through, and stores in, other media. Kevis Goodman describes this as a fundamental shock to human self-understanding:

> The charged tableau of that coastal stare captures the emergent recognition, which is not unique to Smith but rendered with particular intensity in her poetry, of a complex historical present, one that exists beyond sense perception, even beyond complete conceptualization, yet paradoxically seeps into everyday experience. (984)

With reference to Theodor W. Adorno and Fredric Jameson, Goodman concludes that the differentiation of modern society creates a 'rift between the lived experience of the individual and the historical forces that shape such experience in ways not usually apparent, or even conceivable, to it'

(984). The radically changing mediascape in the wake of the Industrial Revolution, new forms of readership, and new medial forms of the distribution of knowledge contribute to this crisis of the traditional dualistic concept of consciousness. An understanding of the world is increasingly shaped by new medial forms, and any scientific world-making is accessible only through them. *Beachy Head* thus offers a stark and brilliant contrast between how the world had been conceived and understood previously, and the fragmentation of consciousness graspable only as a display of a media network of different perspectives on the world, time, and history in the wake of this paradigm shift.

As indicated above, the poem's contemplative opening section 'follow[s] the course of one day from sunrise to sunset during which the speaker is reclined on the cliffs, watching the view and meditating, in which Fancy watches the scenery throughout one entire day' (Radu 441). Labbe attributes these opening 117 lines to a 'masculinized "I"' (147), but more importantly a clearly identifiable 'I' assisted by the faculty of Fancy (4). Accordingly, the passage is decidedly poetic, and it is little wonder that it ends with a reference to *Hamlet*: 'Yet more remote, / Where the rough cliff hangs beetling o'er its base, / All breathes repose' (110–12). Nevertheless, the passage marks an unsettling disruption between what is accessible to sense perception and a world beyond immediate approach. This gap widens when the speaker refers to a faraway ship that calls up associations of commerce, which in turn trigger, with the help of the imagination or fancy, images of the orient as literary creation:

> While more remote, and like a dubious spot
> Just hanging in the horizon, laden deep,
> The ship of commerce richly freighted, makes
> Her slower progress, on her distant voyage,
> Bound to the orient climates, where the sun
> Matures the spice within its odorous shell,
> And, rivalling the gray worm's filmy toil,
> Bursts from its pod the vegetable down;
> Which in long turban'd wreaths, from torrid heat
> Defends the brows of Asia's countless casts. (40–9)

Even in this orientalist construction of the world of commerce, however, the characteristic opposition between surface and depth, which the poem later explores with regard to the rock of Beachy Head, illuminates the abuse on which this world is built:

> There the Earth hides within her glowing breast
> The beamy adamant, and the round pearl

> Enchased in rugged covering; which the slave,
> With perilous and breathless toil, tears off
> From the rough sea-rock, deep beneath the waves.
> These are the toys of Nature; and her sport
> Of little estimate in Reason's eye:
> And they who reason, with abhorrence see
> Man, for such gaudes and baubles, violate
> The sacred freedom of his fellow man –
> Erroneous estimate! (50–60)

Two aspects are remarkable here. First, the poem's theme of antagonism and exploitation that is the result of ambition and the loss of innocence discloses Smith's sympathies for the ideals of the French Revolution: reason and equality. Second, the speaker introduces in passing the central theme of mediation as something that is hidden and needs to be disclosed. The diamond that is hidden under 'rugged covering' foreshadows the secret history of the earth that the poem will turn to next.

With Memory taking over, the subject matter turns from the poetic to historiography and its 'scroll voluminous.' The poem makes clear that the whole of history and of learning is not an end in itself but only valuable if it is relevant for the present day. All these influxes – perception, meditation, imagination, and knowledge – culminate in the speaker's consciousness, the 'reflecting mind' that shapes a complex, often contradictory, media ecology. The speaker's mind occupies a middle ground between the simple peasants and the world of knowledge that is always already mediated. As readers we are keenly aware that the poem is not only informed by books and texts about history, science, and commerce, but that these texts constitute the knowledge of the speaker's mind in the first place. One important aspect of this media ecology is, of course, Smith's use of notes. Reinfandt has stressed that it is important for the texture and the reading process of the poem that these are printed at the end of the poem, not the bottom of the page; the verses in the original edition do not contain marks, so that readers need to check at the back of the book to find out whether a line is annotated or not. This turns the arrangement of the poem within the medium of the book into a metaphor of mind and consciousness: while the poem's main body, the ongoing flow of blank verses, resembles the speaker's seemingly immaterial mind, the hidden endnotes lay bare the texts – and thus the material and medial dimensions – that are its foundation.

The passage concerned with history and historiography works towards establishing a media-ecological network of the mind and of consciousness. Here the faculty of Contemplation asks the faculty of Memory to tell the history of the place:

                                – Bid her retrace
The period, when from Neustria's hostile shore
The Norman launch'd his galleys, and the bay
O'er which that mass of ruin frowns even now
In vain and sullen menace, then received
The new invaders; a proud martial race,
Of Scandinavia the undaunted sons,
Whom Dogon, Fier-a-bras, and Humfroi led
To conquest ... (120–8)

Here is the corresponding note on the Vikings and their raids:

> The Scandinavians, and other inhabitants of the north, began towards the end of the 8th century, to leave their inhospitable climate in search of the produce of more fortunate countries.
>   The North-men made inroads on the coasts of France; and carrying back immense booty, excited their compatriots to engage in the same piratical voyages: and they were afterwards joined by numbers of necessitous and daring adventurers from the coasts of Provence and Sicily.
>   In 844, these wandering innovators had a great number of vessels at sea; and again visiting the coasts of France, Spain, and England, the following year they penetrated even to Paris; and the unfortunate Charles the Bald, king of France, purchased at a price, the retreat of the banditti he had no other means of repelling.
>   These successful expeditions continued for some time; till Rollo, otherwise Raoul, assembled a number of followers, and after a descent on England, crossed the channel, and made himself master of Rouen, which he fortified. Charles the Simple, unable to contend with Rollo, offered to resign to him some of the northern provinces, and to give him his daughter in marriage. Neustria, since called Normandy, was granted to him, and afterwards Brittany. (Smith, *Beachy Head* 146–8)

Rather than being merely explanatory, the note offers an independent historiographical narrative, a mini-treatise that, linked to Memory, stresses the non-dualistic and medial quality of consciousness. Moreover, Smith wrote *Beachy Head* while writing a comprehensive *History of England*, which contains this corresponding passage:

> A new danger, however, threatened in the year 876. Rollo, the Dane, a general of such reputation as made him particularly dreaded, attempted to settle another colony in the island: but finding so much of it in possession of his own countrymen that there was not room for his ambition on one side, while Alfred was prepared for him on the other, he changed his intention of committing hostilities on England, and directed his course to France. (29)

Both the notes to the poem and Smith's history book, along with the poem's main text, serve a broader pedagogical purpose (according to their full title, the three volumes of Smith's history book – the third volume was witten by Mary Hays – take the form of 'a series of letters to a young lady at school'). Together, these media convey a deepened understanding that is not an end in itself but a form of education whose poetic purpose is to enhance originality and novelty, a point to which I will return.

The historical overview itself in *Beachy Head* is quite extravagant. It begins with a reference to the Vikings who started their raids in the ninth century, setting sail, according to the speaker, from Normandy, establishing the antagonism between France and England symbolized by Beachy Head. This scope quickly widens spatially and temporally to include the fact that the Vikings also raided 'Trinacria' (128), or Sicily, and 'Parthenope' (130), or Naples, thus offering a pan-European perspective: 'But let not modern Gallia form from hence / Presumptuous hopes, that ever thou again, / Queen of isles! shalt crouch to foreign arms' (143–5). The reference to Anglo-French war immediately links past and present: just as the Vikings were present across Europe in the Middle Ages, Napoleon set out to conquer Europe in Smith's day. Such ambition is at odds with the humility of English peasants, establishing the poem's dichotomy between the simple here and now and a bewildering, confusing, and complex world beyond immediate observation and experience:

> From even the proudest roll by glory fill'd,
> How gladly the reflecting mind returns
> To simple scenes of peace and industry,
> Where, bosom'd in some valley of the hills
> Stands the lone farm ... (167–71)

Smith further stresses this opposition of innocence and experience in her description of a country boy:

> Ah! who *is* happy? Happiness! a word
> That like false fire, from marsh effluvia born,
> Misleads the wanderer, destin'd to contend
> In the world's wilderness, with want or woe –
> Yet *they* are happy, who have never ask'd
> What good or evil means. The boy
> That on the river's margin gaily plays,
> Has heard that Death is there – He knows not Death,
> And therefore fears it not; and venturing in
> He gains a bullrush, or a minnow – then,
> At certain peril, for a worthless prize,
> A crow's, or raven's nest, he climbs the boll,
> Of some tall pine; and of his prowess proud,
> Is for a moment happy. (255–68)

Here Smith plays with her public persona of the suffering, melancholy woman she half-created in her *Elegiac Sonnets*. But she also sketches an image of England modeled on the Garden of Eden and the innocence of prelapsarian humans, a reference to original sin informed by *Paradise Lost* and its concept of freedom. The boy may be happy, but without access to a knowledge of good and evil, he is not free. The one voice capable of choosing between right and wrong, the one voice that mediates between immediate perception and scientifically and historically informed knowledge, is the poet-speaker's consciousness.

Beachy Head refers not only to the emerging scientific discourse but also to poetry as an alternative medial approach to understanding the objective world. For instance, line 221 quotes Thomas Gray's *Deserted Village* and includes the reference in a note. Furthermore, towards the end of the poem, Smith includes and thus remediates the oral poetry of the stranger's song (531–55) and the written fragment of the hermit's rhapsody (577–654) in full. More importantly, she references and mimics the style of Wordsworth's 'Tintern Abbey' and its approach to the world through an all-encompassing subjective consciousness: 'An early worshipper at Nature's shrine; / I loved her rudest scenes' (436–47). However, the poem immediately subverts this form of understanding nature:

> warrens, and heaths,
> And yellow commons, and birch-shaded hollows,
> And hedge rows, bordering unfrequented lanes
> Bowered with wild roses, and the clasping woodbine
> Where purple tassels of the tangling vetch
> With bittersweet, and bryony inweave,
> And the dew fills the silver bindweed's cups –
> I loved to trace the brooks whose humid banks
> Nourish the harebell, and the freckled pagil;
> And stroll among o'ershadowing woods of beech,
> Lending in Summer, from the heats of noon
> A whispering shade; while haply there reclines
> Some pensive lover of uncultur'd flowers,
> Who, from the tumps with bright green mosses clad,
> Plucks the wood sorrel, with its light thin leaves,
> Heart-shaped, and triply folded; and its root
> Creeping like beaded coral; or who there
> Gathers, the copse's pride, anémones,
> With rays like golden studs on ivory laid
> Most delicate: but touch'd with purple clouds,
> Fit crown for April's fair but changeful brow. (347–67)

Smith's detailed description of flowers and plants is informed by the speaker's expert botanical knowledge, supplemented by numerous notes with references to their Latin names. These details at once undermine and parody the Wordsworthian poetic principle, typical of male Romantics, according to which nature serves merely to enhance the poet's mind, and thus offer an equally legitimate approach to nature. Moreover, the remediation of 'Tintern Abbey' makes the poetic medium *visible*[13] as it demonstrates that Wordsworth's 'immediate' rendering of subjective consciousness is just one medial construct among others.

Perhaps most importantly with regard to Smith's self-fashioning as a poet and author, the passage demonstrates a non-dualistic conception of consciousness, one that challenges early feminist readings of *Beachy Head* as a powerful argument for female agency and the inclusion of women in scientific discourses.[14] I contend that Smith's much bolder point transcends the gender argument. Being one of the most successful poets of her day, Smith does not need to defend the rights of women to participate in discussions of science. She does not argue for equality but rather for the superiority of a poetic principle and epistemology that rely on science, education, reading, and thus on medially available scientific discourses. The speaker's approach to knowledge is fundamentally shaped by science mediated through books and journals. This is particularly obvious in the poem's most famous passage:

> Ah! hills so early loved! in fancy still
> I breathe your pure keen air; and still behold
> Those widely spreading views, mocking alike
> The Poet and the Painter's utmost art.
> And still, observing objects more minute,
> Wondering remark the strange and foreign forms
> Of sea-shells; with the pale calcareous soil
> Mingled, and seeming of resembling substance.
> Tho' surely the blue Ocean (from the heights
> Where the downs westward trend, but dimly seen)
> Here never roll'd its surge. Does Nature then
> Mimic, in wanton mood, fantastic shapes
> Of bivalves, and inwreathed volutes, that cling
> To the dark sea-rock of the wat'ry world?
> Or did this range of chalky mountains, once
> Form a vast bason, where the Ocean waves
> Swell'd fathomless? What time these fossil shells,
> Buoy'd on their native element, were thrown
> Among the imbedding calx: when the huge hill
> Its giant bulk heaved, and in strange ferment
> Grew up a guardian barrier, 'twixt the sea
> And the green level of the sylvan weald. (368–89)

While later passages informed by ornithology and botany are much more precise and scientifically educated, the above passage's approach to geology, while it may be inaccurate, dismisses scientific theories as mere conjectures.[15] Here the speaker focuses more on the disruption caused by these very findings.

Read through the lens of media ecology, the passage's scientific references to geology pose an interesting challenge to Kantian epistemology. The quintessentially Romantic philosophical question – how the subjective mind can access the world – is still a key problem, recently tackled by French philosopher Quentin Meillassoux in *After Finitude*, the most important publication in the field of speculative realism. Here, Meillassoux addresses the Kantian principle that the thing-in-itself (*Ding an sich*) can never be grasped by the human mind. According to Meillassoux, philosophy since Kant remains unable to move beyond this basic insight of Kant's *Critique of Pure Reason*, that one cannot comment on reality outside of its relation to consciousness. He terms this problem 'correlationism':

> By 'correlation' we mean the idea according to which we only ever have access to the correlation between thinking and being, and never to either term considered apart from the other ... . Correlationism consists in disqualifying the claim that it is possible to consider the realms of subjectivity and objectivity independently of one another. Not only does it become necessary to insist that we never grasp an object 'in itself', in isolation from its relation to the subject, but it also becomes necessary to maintain that we can never grasp a subject that would not always-already be related to an object. (5)

There is a telling coincidence between Meillassoux's 'arche-fossil' (10 and passim), his image of an ancestral time before consciousness came into being, and Smith's image of the fossilized sea-shell, which calls up the deep time of history. Meillassoux's ancestrality leads to the conclusion that reasonable scientific statements can be made about aspects of reality that clearly predate the existence of consciousness. In other words, 'it is possible to think beyond human knowledge, to move further into a world without cognition' (Colebrook 67). Positive knowledge of the world is contingent but nevertheless possible as it first and foremost depends on science:

> When I maintain that this or that entity or event is contingent, I know something positive about them – I know that this house can be destroyed, I know that it would have been physically possible for this person to act differently, etc. *Contingency* expresses the fact that physical laws remain indifferent as to whether an event occurs or not – they allow an entity to emerge, to subsist, or to perish. (Meillassoux 39)

Meillassoux's proposition that a positive, scientific statement about the ontological world no longer depends on the correlation of mind and world but on scientific insight echoes Smith's use of science in *Beachy Head*, which may therefore also be read as a criticism of Kant's transcendental idealism with regard to the concept of consciousness. According to Kant's transcendental idealism, the intuition of objects is not identical with the object world, which remains unobtainable:

> The transcendental concept of appearances in space, on the contrary, is a critical reminder that absolutely nothing that is intuited in space is a thing in itself, and that space is not a form that is proper to anything in itself, but rather that objects in themselves are not known to us at all, and that what we call outer objects are nothing other than mere representations of our sensibility, whose form is space, but whose true correlate, i.e., the thing in itself, is not and cannot be cognized through them, but is also never asked after in experience. (Kant 161–2)

While Kant's critical philosophy influenced male Romantic poets such as Coleridge or Wordsworth, Smith's critique of its particular dualism differs in the sense that she does not problematize the correlation of subjective consciousness and objective world, but rather establishes consciousness as medially conditioned and realized.

This aspect of Smith's poem corresponds with contemporary media-theoretical approaches to epistemology. Mark B. N. Hansen made the claim that media theory may overcome the epistemological dualism in Kantian philosophy: 'media institute a theoretical oscillation that promises to displace the empirical–transcendental divide that has structured western meditation on thinking' (297). By focusing on the oscillation between phenomenology and materiality, he aims to show how media are not passive instruments which humans use to communicate, but rather that they define humanity in the first place. Quoting German media theorist Bernhard Stiegler, Hansen describes 'the human as an originarily prosthetic being' (299). It is thus possible to read *Beachy Head* as a poem that proposes a concept of human consciousness that differs fundamentally from Kant's correlationism as well as from the dominant male approach to poetry, as it concentrates on science, knowledge, and media.

Smith's reference to fossilized sea-shells expands the poem into a reflection on the media ecology of knowledge that includes not only geology but also other new scientific approaches to nature. Yet a few lines on, the speaker appears to object to any kind of science:

> Ah! very vain is Science' proudest boast,
> And but a little light its flame yet lends

> To its most ardent votaries; since from whence
> These fossil forms are seen, is but conjecture,
> Food for vague theories, or vain dispute,
> While to his daily task the peasant goes,
> Unheeding such inquiry; with no care
> But that the kindly change of sun and shower,
> Fit for his toil the earth he cultivates. (390–8)

This rejection of science is puzzling, given the poem's preoccupation with botany and ornithology, yet it makes sense in the face of Smith's emphasis on the function and purpose of knowledge in poetry and thus on the *poetic* purpose of science and scientific education. A further note briefly refers to *Essay on the Application of Natural History to Poetry* by John Aikin, Anna Laetitia Barbauld's brother, which stresses the importance of scientific knowledge not for its own sake but as a new and expanding source of original poetic imagery. Aikin dismisses contemporary poetry as fraught 'with a perpetual repetition of the same images, clad in almost the same language' (2), a lack of novelty based not on a lack of genius but on a lack of knowledge:

> Hitherto it has been chiefly attempted to shew that the accurate and scientific study of nature would obviate many of the defects usually discoverable in poetical compositions. The more pleasing talk succeeds, of exhibiting to view the beauties which the poet may derive from this source. (32–3)

This approach is akin to Wordsworth's claim that he visited the lectures held by Humphry Davy to 'renew [his] stock of metaphors' (Hartley 45). Smith's reference to Aikin makes it clear that the poem is less a showcase for her proficiency in botany and ornithology, or lack thereof in geology; rather, historiography and natural history serve to make her a more original poet. What is more, the poem regards this knowledge as not merely something a human being 'has,' for it does not even represent her inner or subjective self or consciousness. This consciousness is rather expressed as a new form of knowledge that is made available to a new readership established through a massive expansion of the Romantic mediascape. What is remarkable about *Beachy Head*, unlike Wordsworth's 'Tintern Abbey' or Coleridge's 'Dejection: An Ode,' which largely place the medium of poetry in the service of expressing consciousness, is that Smith's poem exposes how knowledge is available only in and through the new mediations of a growing print market, and thus how knowledge, human consciousness, and media are interdependent.

Conclusion

The meandering consciousness of the speaker, its paradoxical plurality of voices, time and again refers to cultural techniques of inscription that read nature itself as forms of mediation:

> But near one ancient tree, whose wreathed roots
> Form'd a rude couch, love-songs and scatter'd rhymes,
> Unfinish'd sentences, or half erased,
> And rhapsodies like this, were sometimes found ... (573–6)

Christoph Bode argues:

> Thus the mediality of poetry is highlighted exactly when – with symptomatic fuzziness and obscurity – it is suggested that the visionary has somehow literally inscribed himself into the scene, into nature: 'rhapsodies like this, were sometimes found' – either on 'leaves', one supposes, or literally scratched into the bark of a tree atop Beachy Head or even into the rock that is Beachy Head. Add to this that the auto-referentiality of this inscription into nature is ambiguously hinted at ('rhapsodies *like this*' refers to the following poem to Amanda as well as to the frame text that rhapsodizes about Beachy Head) and it becomes apparent that *Beachy Head*, in its attempt to inscribe itself into a natural medium, is more than just superficially about itself. More than this, it is not only *about* the way the natural landscape is overwritten, quite naturally it also *enacts* such an overwriting. It is itself an instance of what it is about; it is its own example, at once a signification and the very thing itself. (64)

Bode calls attention to the fact that any form of subjectivity or selfhood is fractured through its mediation: the poem leaves no doubt that there is no immediate access to anything like a subjective, authentic, or true self. Instead, consciousness is an auto-reflection of its own mediation and remediation. Bode again:

> We seem to be slightly uneasy with the inescapable alternative that a subject can only be made visible *in a medium* but that the medium can, of course, never comprehend the subject, since any medium can only register and represent traces of the absenting movement of the subject. (65)

The one thing that holds these multiple reflections together is the massive rock of Beachy Head, which in itself is a giant medium and metaphorically represents the principle of mediation. The ending with its reference to the hermit's epitaph is most significant in this context:

> Those who read
> Chisel'd within the rock, these mournful lines,

> Memorials of his sufferings, did not grieve,
> That dying in the cause of charity
> His spirit, from its earthly bondage freed,
> Had to some better region fled for ever. (726–31)

I follow Bode's reading that these lines do not refer to a missing poem but rather self-reflexively refer to *this* poem – 'these mournful lines' – that we are asked to read as this epitaph. This way, *Beachy Head* is inscribed into Beachy Head.

If one combines these different strands, one can see how Charlotte Smith's *Beachy Head* unfolds its media ecology so that literally everything in the poem can become a medium, and the poem itself is a powerful reflection on mediation. However, it takes Smith's experienced speaker to decipher these different media or texts. The way a given medium is read depends on genre and scientific discipline. Beachy Head, the rock that looks out over the sea, can be a sign for the antagonism between Britain and France during the time of war; it can be seen as the place at which centuries of invasions have taken place; it can be read as a medium in which fossilized sea-shells tell a natural history of the deep time of the earth; or it can be read as the place in which this poem has been inscribed which tells the story of all these histories leading up to the present. The reclining speaker figuratively merges with the ground and the rock becomes an external medial extension of her consciousness. The opposition between this knowledge and the innocence of the peasants is of key importance here. These simple people, if we believe the speaker, may be happy, but they in no way have the kind of access to the scientific knowledge available to the speaker, who is free to choose between different readings of the world. The different voices are not different speakers but rather different approaches to this knowledge. At the dawning of modernity, this knowledge creates a fundamental disruption within the human, a disruption between immediate perception and a scientifically informed view of the world. And these different readings combined establish the speaker's consciousness.

To come back to my initial observation, the depiction of consciousness in literary texts is traditionally associated with inwardness and hence subjectivity, selfhood, and the psyche. This dualistic conception of consciousness has its origin in the writings of the Romantics themselves but it is ultimately centered around a reductive canon focusing on Coleridge, Wordsworth, and a few other male poets. Consciousness in *Beachy Head* is a far cry from the 'egotistical sublime' characteristic of *The Prelude* and may be described as non-individual, all-encompassing, materialist, and non-dualistic. *Beachy Head* is therefore a powerful theoretical reflection on the insight that consciousness around 1800 – of the world and of the self – is necessarily part of an increasingly complex media ecology. In this sense, we can read the poem, as it constructs consciousness based on cultural practices of mediation, as a self-reflexive theory about the effects of media change on human consciousness.

Beachy Head opposes innocence – the world of simple, true, yet ignorant workers, of flowers and birds, botany and ornithology – to experience, a world beyond perception and consciousness but nonetheless inscribed into the very rock on which the speaker reclines. This hidden world registers the deep time of history explored by geology, but also the deeply historical and political time fraught with the antagonisms of numerous invasions from the Romans and the Vikings to William the Conqueror to war between France and Britain. The speaker, the melancholy persona 'Charlotte Smith' of the massively successful *Elegiac Sonnets*, sympathizes with the innocent, even (figuratively speaking) prelapsarian people dwelling there. But she belongs to the side of experience and the knowledge of good and evil signified through the poem's various forms of mediation. Self-reflexive and multifaceted, *Beachy Head* is pieced together like a consciousness that bears the scars of its fragmented, and always contingent, textual nature. It perceives the world as a puzzling multiplicity of medial discourses, and it envisions epistemology, the knowledge of this world, and consciousness as a complex media ecology at the dawn of modernity.

Notes

1. See Reinfandt, 'Textures of Romanticism' 107.
2. See Labbe 142–51.
3. See Pethes, esp. 188–91. The most prominent contribution to the debate is arguably C. P. Snow's lecture on the by now proverbial two cultures. In his systematic and comprehensive overview of the history of science and literature, the German scholar Nicolas Pethes summarizes the main trends of this debate from Thomas H. Huxley onwards. Up until the end of the twentieth century, the field had been dominated by British contributions. This changed in the 1990s, when a sometimes fiercely fought-out debate about its legitimacy and systematic validity arose in Germany. This is relevant for the present context because it helps to highlight the preconditions that shaped the historical conceptions of consciousness and knowledge, in particular its rootedness in a mind-and-body dichotomy.
4. Vogl's works are influenced by Michel Foucault's discourse theory and based on earlier studies by Gaston Bachelard and Ludwik Fleck. In these studies, he aims to show that scientific knowledge is shaped by pre-existing

questions that are the outcome of historically determined discourse formations: 'The constitution of the fact does not lead from the object to the concept, rather it proceeds in the opposite direction; observation and experiment are only possible under the compulsion of previous trails' (Vogl 114).

5. '"personales Wissen" ist, seiner logischen Struktur nach, ein zweistelliges Prädikat: Es bezeichnet eine Beziehung zwischen einer Person und etwas, das die Person weiß. Wer etwas weiß, tritt, wie man auch sagen kann, in eine bestimmte Beziehung – eben die des Wissens – zu einem bestimmten Inhalt oder Gehalt' (my translation).

6. 'Texte sind keine Personen, sie können daher nichts wissen' (my translation).

7. Media-theoretical approaches to literature have changed fundamentally during the past decades. Friedrich Kittler's ground-breaking *Gramophone, Film, Typewriter* still mainly focused on the impact of technological inventions, arguing that new technology invented in the nineteenth century, which had no immediate connection to literary works themselves like photography or sound recording devices, nonetheless changed the very nature of literature. The innovation of recording technologies, according to Kittler, displaced literature as the prime medium to record human emotions, thoughts, and activities. Before this invention, literature had been the paradigmatic medium to store what is quintessentially human, while after the technological paradigm shift, this task was passed on to other media such as film. Kittler distinguishes traditional print media (paper, letters, books) from technological media invented in the nineteenth century: photography, phonograph, telephone, film. To these one might add today's technology: radio, television, computers, cellphones, and even the internet – Kittler writes about 'fibre networks' (1) at a very early stage. Kittler relies on the following distinction: literature relies on language as an arbitrary sign system that bears no resemblance to its subject matter and thus has to rely on the power of the imagination. Since newer technologies were able to record and store human activity, literature became more self-reflexive and experimental. This is a powerful and convincing argument, yet it focuses solely on the technological means of artistic communication, which is why Kittler's approach is often dismissed as techno-determinist.

8. In 'Genesis of the Media Concept,' John Guillory states: 'The very fact of remediation ... suggests that premodern arts are also, in the fully modern sense, media but that for some reason they did not need to be so called, at least not until the later nineteenth century' (322). Guillory thus argues 'that the concept of a medium of communication was absent but *wanted* for the several centuries prior to its appearance, a lacuna in the philosophical tradition that exerted a distinctive pressure, as if from the future, on early efforts to theorize communication' (321). In other words, although new technological media had not yet been invented, a theory of communication, media, and mediation existed from the sixteenth century onwards. Thus, new media technologies in the nineteenth century do not suddenly change the discourse, as suggested by key aspects of Romantic poetry such as the concept of modern authorship, imagination, and subjectivity.

9. Medial self-reflexivity can be traced to the eighteenth century. Christina Lupton (5) defines mediation in contradistinction to both form and discourse on the one hand, and materiality on the other. Quoting Lisa Gitelman's insight that media are 'socially realized structures of communication' (7), Lupton focuses not so much on the technological dimension but rather on the question of how self-conscious – that is, 'knowing' – books have an impact on the consciousness of the readers by addressing 'the phenomenological question of what happens when mediation registers in discourse' (10). Gitelman shows how media work only in a social network 'where structures include both technological forms and their associated protocols, and where communication is a cultural practice, a ritualized collocation of different people on the same mental map, sharing or engaged with popular ontologies of representation' (Gitelman 7). By distancing herself from the tradition of technological determinism, Lupton likewise highlights the performative and processual dimension of mediation within a cultural network. With reference to Hegel's dialectic of mediation, Lupton asks

> how it is that self-conscious books contribute to the perceived autonomy of print mediation. The recognition of the reader, which shows up in the consciousness modelled by the book of its own mediation, and of the reader's categories of understanding, qualifies the book to perform as a partner in what is by rights a human process. (Lupton 16)

10. James Purdon (2018) aims to move media theory beyond its purported techno-centrism. Building on studies published in media archaeology (see Parikka, *What Is Media Archaeology?*) and cultural techniques (see Siegert; Bayerlipp et al.), Purdon elaborates on the meaning and scope of the more recent methodology of 'technography' (see also Pryor and Trotter). Referring to Heidegger's take on the term, he stresses technology's performative dimension. In order to highlight technology as dynamic as well as mechanical, Purdon states that technology in Greek 'meant not a domain of objects but a genre of discourse' (5). Hence literature, through technology and technography, has always been linked to mediation: literature as well as 'writing is technological, through and through' (8). One may venture further to claim that the technology of writing creates interiority in the first place, a point already made by Canadian scholar Eric Havelock in *Preface to Plato* (1963). Havelock claims that subjective selfhood is not a naturally existing entity but the immediate outcome of the invention of the technology of writing (cf. Haekel, *The Soul* 199). Writing as the 'separation of the knower from the known' (Havelock 197) enabled people to store knowledge which led to self-reflection and the discovery of the soul. Consequently, it also enabled them to forget, which made writing a technology and medium that creates consciousness in the first place.
11. Fuller's game-changing book on media ecology begins with a reference to Kurt Schwitters's description of a Dadaist collage as an illustration of Fuller's approach to media ecology. Dada is the juxtaposition and confrontation of fragments, cut-outs, appropriated elements that, in this new arrangement, reject the notion of an organic work and highlight the dynamics and transience of culture.

12. See St Clair.
13. See Gillory 324.
14. See Pascoe.
15. In the note, the speaker claims that she is ignorant of the latest findings in the field of geology: 'The appearance of sea-shells so far from the sea excited my surprise, though I then knew nothing of natural history. I have never read any of the late theories of the earth, nor was I ever satisfied with the attempts to explain many of the phenomena which call forth conjecture in those books I happened to have had access to on this subject' (Smith, *Beachy Head* 159). In a further note, she claims that the theory that even the highest mountains were once at the bottom of the sea was triggered by Gilbert White's *Natural History of Selbourne*, first published in 1789. In the third letter of this book, White mentions fossil shells, but the scientific theory mentioned by Smith rather stems from Hutton's *Theory of the Earth*, published in 1788 as part of the *Transactions of the Royal Society of Edinburgh*: 'There are few beds of marble or limestone, in which may not be found some of those objects which indicate the marine origin of the mass. If, for example, in a mass of marble, taken from a quarry upon the top of the Alps or Andes, there may be found one cockle-shell, or piece of coral, it must be concluded, that this bed of stone had been originally formed at the bottom of the sea, as much as another bed which is evidently composed almost altogether of cockle-shells and coral. If one bed of limestone is thus found to have been of a marine origin, every concomitant bed of the same kind must be also concluded to have been formed in the same manner' (220).

References

Aikin, John. *An Essay on the Application of Natural History to Poetry.* Warrington: W. Eyres, 1777.

Bayerlipp, Susanne, Ralf Haekel, and Johannes Schlegel. 'Cultural Techniques of Literature.' *Zeitschrift für Anglistik und Amerikanistik: A Quarterly of Language, Literature and Culture* 66.2 (2018).

Bloom, Harold. *Romanticism and Consciousness: Essays in Criticism.* 1st ed. New York: W. W. Norton, 1970.

Bode, Christoph. 'The Subject of Beachy Head.' *Charlotte Smith in British Romanticism*. Enlightenment World: Political and Intellectual History of the Long Eighteenth Century. London: Pickering & Chatto, 2008. 57–69.

Bolter, J. David and Richard A. Grusin. *Remediation: Understanding New Media.* Cambridge, MA: MIT Press, 1999.

Borgards, Roland. 'Wissen und Literatur: Eine Replik auf Tilmann Köppe.' *Zeitschrift für Germanistik* 17.2 (2007): 425–8.

Brooke-Smith, James. 'Remediating Romanticism.' *Literature Compass* 10.4 (2013): 343–52. https://onlinelibrary.wiley.com/doi/epdf/10.1111/lic3.12052 (last accessed March 4, 2021).

Burkett, Andrew. *Romantic Mediations: Media Theory and British Romanticism.* Albany, NY: State University of New York Press, 2016.

Colebrook, Claire. 'Extinct Theory.' *Theory after 'Theory.'* Ed. Jane Elliott and Derek Attridge. New York: Routledge, 2011. 62–71.
Fuller, Matthew. *Media Ecologies: Materialist Energies in Art and Technoculture.* Leonardo. Cambridge, MA: MIT Press, 2005.
Gitelman, Lisa. *Always Already New: Media, History and the Data of Culture.* Cambridge, MA: MIT Press, 2006.
Goddard, Michael, and Jussi Parikka. 'Editorial: Unnatural Ecologies.' *The Fibreculture Journal* 17 (2011): 1–5.
Goodman, Kevis. 'Conjectures on Beachy Head: Charlotte Smith's Geological Poetics and the Ground of the Present.' *ELH* 81.3 (2014): 983–1006.
Greenblatt, Stephen. *Shakespearean Negotiations: The Circulation of Social Energy in Renaissance England.* Berkeley: University of California Press, 1988.
Guillory, John. 'Genesis of the Media Concept.' *Critical Inquiry* 36.2 (2010): 321–62.
Haekel, Ralf. *Handbook of British Romanticism.* Berlin: De Gruyter, 2017.
—. *The Soul in British Romanticism: Negotiating Human Nature in Philosophy, Science and Poetry.* Trier: WVT, 2014.
Hansen, Mark B. N. 'Media Theory.' *Theory, Culture & Society* 23.2–3 (2006): 297–306.
Hartley, Harold. *Humphry Davy.* London: Nelson, 1966.
Havelock, Eric A. *Preface to Plato.* History of the Greek Mind. Cambridge, MA: Belknap Press, Harvard University Press, 1963.
Heise, Ursula. 'Unnatural Ecologies: The Metaphor of the Environment in Media Theory.' *Configurations* 10.1 (2002): 149–68.
Hutton, James. 'Theory of the Earth: Or an Investigation of the Laws Observable in the Composition, Dissolution, and Reparation of the Land upon the Globe.' *Transactions of the Royal Society of Edinburgh* 1 (1788):209–304.
Kant, Immanuel. *Critique of Pure Reason.* Trans. and ed. Paul Guyer and Allen W. Wood. Cambridge: Cambridge University Press, 1998.
Kittler, Friedrich. *Gramophone, Film, Typewriter.* Stanford: Stanford University Press, 1999.
Köppe, Tilmann. 'Vom Wissen in Literatur.' *Zeitschrift für Germanistik* 17.2 (2007): 398–410.
Labbe, Jacqueline M. *Charlotte Smith: Romanticism, Poetry and the Culture of Gender.* Manchester: Manchester University Press, 2003.
Langan, Celeste. 'Understanding Media in 1805: Audiovisual Hallucination in the Lay of the Last Minstrel.' *Studies in Romanticism* 40.1 (2001): 49–70.
Lupton, Christina. *Knowing Books: The Consciousness of Mediation in Eighteenth-Century Britain.* 1st ed. Philadelphia: University of Pennsylvania Press, 2012.
Meillassoux, Quentin. *After Finitude: An Essay on the Necessity of Contingency.* London: Continuum, 2008.
Parikka, Jussi. 'The Universal Viral Machine: Bits, Parasites and the Media Ecology of Network Culture.' *CTheory* 12.15 (2005). https://journals.uvic.ca/index.php/ctheory/article/view/14467/5309 (last accessed March 4, 2021).
—. *What Is Media Archaeology?* Cambridge: Polity Press, 2012.
Pascoe, Judith. 'Female Botanists and the Poetry of Charlotte Smith.' *Re-Visioning Romanticism: British Women Writers, 1776–1837.* Ed. Carol

S. Wilson and Joel Haefner. Philadelphia: University of Pennsylvania Press, 1994. 193–209.
Pethes, Nicolas. 'Literatur- und Wissenschaftsgeschichte. Ein Forschungsbericht.' *Internationales Archiv für Sozialgeschichte der deutschen Literatur* 28.1 (2003): 181–231.
Pryor, Sean and David Trotter, eds. *Writing, Medium, Machine: Modern Technographies*. London: Open Humanities Press, 2016.
Purdon, James. 'Literature – Technology – Media: Towards a New Technography.' *Literature Compass* 15.1 (2018).
Radu, Anca-Raluca. 'Charlotte Smith, Beachy Head (1807).' *Handbook of British Romanticism*. Ed. Ralf Haekel. Berlin: Walter de Gruyter, 2017. 439–58.
Reinfandt, Christoph. 'Popular and Media Culture.' *Handbook of British Romanticism*. Ed. Ralf Haekel. Handbooks of English and American Studies: 6. Berlin: De Gruyter, 2017. 116–34.
—. 'The Textures of Romanticism: Exploring Charlotte Smith's Beachy Head (1807).' *Proceedings of the Conference of the German Association of University Teachers of English* 43 (2013): 99–114.
Shapiro, Lawrence A. *Embodied Cognition*. New Problems of Philosophy. New York: Routledge, 2011.
Siegert, Bernhard. *Cultural Techniques: Grids, Filters, Doors, and Other Articulations of the Real*. Meaning Systems. New York: Fordham University Press, 2015.
Siskin, Clifford. 'More Is Different: Literary Change in the Mid and Late Eighteenth Century.' *The Cambridge History of English Literature, 1660–1780*. Ed. John Richetti. Cambridge: Cambridge University Press, 2005. 797–823.
— and William Warner. *This Is Enlightenment*. Chicago: University of Chicago Press, 2010.
Smith, Charlotte. *Beachy Head: With Other Poems*. London: J. Johnson, 1807.
—. *The Collected Letters of Charlotte Smith*. Bloomington: Indiana University Press, 2003.
—. *The History of England, from the Earliest Records to the Peace of Amiens: In a Series of Letters to a Young Lady at School*. 3 vols. London: Richard Phillips, 1806.
St Clair, William. *The Reading Nation in the Romantic Period*. Cambridge: Cambridge University Press, 2004.
Stiening, Gideon. 'Am "Ungrund" oder: Was Sind und zu welchem Ende studiert Man "Poetologien des Wissens"?' *KulturPoetik: Zeitschrift für Kulturgeschichtliche Literaturwissenschaft / Journal of Cultural Poetics* 7.2 (2007): 234–48.
Varela, Francisco J., Evan Thompson, and Eleanor Rosch. *The Embodied Mind: Cognitive Science and Human Experience*. Cambridge, MA: MIT Press, 1991.
Vogl, Joseph. *Poetologien des Wissens um 1800*. Munich: Fink, 1999.
White, Gilbert. *The Natural History and Antiquities of Selborne*. London: T. Bensley, 1789.
Zunshine, Lisa. *The Oxford Handbook of Cognitive Literary Studies*. New York: Oxford University Press, 2015.

Part III

Social and Ecological Models of Consciousness

Chapter 10

Why Reasonable Children Don't Think that Nutcracker is Alive or that the Mouse King is Real

Lisa Zunshine

E. T. A. Hoffmann's tale *The Nutcracker and the Mouse King* (1816) contains several wonderful, one may even say magical, events. First, it celebrates the birthday of a man who died in his early thirties, then came back from the dead for a couple of days, and then disappeared from view completely, while still managing to stay alive, somewhere (possibly, behind the clouds), for almost 2,000 years. To commemorate him, the grownup characters of Hoffmann's story buy toys for their children and tell them that these gifts come from that man, who brings goodies to hundreds of thousands of well-behaved youngsters of Europe, and who, incidentally, has now become an infant again.[1] So, what we have here is a gift-bearing, omnipresent, 2,000-year-old infant.

Another wonderful event involves a nutcracker, perhaps delivered by that energetic infant. Shaped like a little man with a large mouth, the nutcracker comes alive at night and commandeers a regiment of toy soldiers to fight an army of mice led by their king: a large seven-headed mouse. The battle is witnessed by a seven-year-old girl, who then reports what she has seen to her parents and to her younger brother, Fritz.

One would expect that this event should not strike the parents as very strange because they may already be familiar with its broad outlines, again, through stories involving the two-thousand-year-old infant. When that infant was still a man, he was reported to have successfully fought basilisks, dragons, and many-headed serpents.[2] Somewhere in his 800s, however, he lost interest, so by the eleventh century, the job of dragon-trampling was assumed by St George. St George's exploits were commemorated by many famous artists. One of these artists was Albrecht Dürer (see Figure 10.1), a particular favorite of Hoffmann's,[3] who used to live in the same city of Nuremberg as do several characters in *The Nutcracker*. This is to say that an appearance of a seven-headed monster, right around the birthday of the infant, and its subsequent defeat by the very Nutcracker whom the infant may have

Figure 10.1   Albrecht Dürer, *Saint George Slaying the Dragon*. Nuremberg, c.1504.

providently insinuated into the household, should not raise the parents' eyebrows.

Yet eyebrows are raised. Far from being honored to learn that this year's installation of the sacred battle against evil is unfolding in their living room,[4] Dr Stahlbaum and his wife vehemently deny their little girl, Marie's, eyewitness report. First, together with the family physician, they attribute it to her 'wound fever,' for, in the process of assisting Nutcracker in his fight against the Mouse King, Marie has broken 'the glass of the toy cabinet' and 'cut her arm very badly' (35). When, after several days of staying in bed and, presumably, having gotten over her delirium, Marie still persists in her account, her mother is 'horrified' and her father moved to ask, 'Where on earth does the child get such crazy ideas?' (62) When Marie tells her parents about her subsequent journey to the 'Land of Dolls,' on which the victorious Nutcracker has taken her, her mother calls it 'a long, beautiful dream' and insists that Marie now 'must really forget all that nonsense' (95).

No amount of evidence can make the parents change their mind. When they see signs of a large, inexplicable mice infestation, all that the mother can say is, 'I can't understand how all those mice could get into our living room' (64). When Marie produces tangible proof of her adventure – the seven tiny crowns that used to belong to the Mouse King – the parents keep urging her to tell them where they have *really* come from. When Marie desperately turns to the one man who could confirm her story – her Godfather Drosselmeier – and begs him to tell her parents that her Nutcracker is, in fact, his nephew, 'young Mr. Drosselmeier from Nuremberg, and that he gave [her] the little crowns,' the father responds by bringing out the big guns:

> Dr. Stahlbaum looked severely at his daughter and said: 'Look here, Marie. You're to forget about this foolishness once and for all. And if I ever again hear you saying this ugly simpleminded Nutcracker is Judge Drosselmeier's nephew, I'll throw Nutcracker out of the window and all your other dolls as well, including Mistress Clara.' (97)

'Of course,' Hoffmann observes dryly, faced with such an irrefutable argument, Marie has no choice but to fall silent.

Here is the question that I want you to consider. Why is Marie's story treated as utterly unreasonable (that is, 'crazy' and 'foolish') while the story of the man who has come back from the dead is not? Or, at the very least, why can Marie's family not afford her narrative some of the same easygoing and pragmatic attitude that they afford to the narrative of a 2,000-year-old gift-bearing infant, which they treat as true or ignore, depending on their current pedagogical needs?

The answer to this question may seem obvious. One can say, for instance that it is much more unreasonable for a child to believe in the story of Nutcracker battling the Mouse King than it is for her to believe in the story of Christ battling dragons, turning back into a baby, and distributing gifts 2,000 years after his death, if only because the story of Christ is a familiar cultural narrative, deeply embedded within a broad variety of communal practices. What I hope to show, however, is that, while cultural familiarity certainly matters, yet another factor is at play in deciding which story will be treated as contingently plausible and which will not, hence marking the child who believes in the latter as unreasonable (or else, unusually imaginative).

Emerging from studies by cognitive psychologists and anthropologists, this factor has to do with social functions of reason, and it sheds new light not just on the strong emotional response of the older Stahlbaums to Marie's story, but also on the long critical tradition of thinking of Marie as a quintessential Romantic child, whose lively imagination outstrips that of her philistine parents. The proponents of the social view of reason emphasize its dialogic and interactionist nature, which, I believe, makes this approach of particular interest to literary theorists who seek to integrate literary criticism with cognitive science.

I have divided my chapter into five parts. The first part, 'Coexistence Thinking,' draws on work of cognitive psychologists to show that, in principle, the adult protagonists of Hoffmann's tale could engage with Marie's story in ways other than pronouncing it foolish and crazy. Part two, 'Naïve Skepticism and Metacognitive Limitations,' suggests that Marie's stubborn insistence on the reality of Nutcracker and the Mouse King is well in keeping with what developmental psychologists today would expect from children of her age group. In part three, 'Social Functions of Reason,' I turn to the recent work of cognitive evolutionary anthropologists and psychologists Hugo Mercier and Dan Sperber, who consider reasons 'constructs' intended 'primarily for social consumption' (127), and I show that Marie's parents are subjected to a very particular kind of social pressure when they are called to respond to their daughter's account of her adventures. Part four, 'Metacognitive Instability and Critical Imagination,' shows how literary scholars have attempted to come to terms with the two seemingly incommensurable realities depicted in the story (that is, that of Marie and that of her parents), first, by idealizing Marie's 'Romantic' imagination, and, more recently, by treating *Nutcracker* as the foundational text of the children's fantasy genre. Both of these approaches, I suggest, are deepened and complemented by the cognitive perspective. Finally, the fifth and concluding part, 'But They Didn't Have that Word!,' discusses the legitimacy of using recent research by cognitive scientists for examining the psychology and interpersonal dynamics of early nineteenth-century fictional characters.

Coexistence Thinking

Let us start by taking a closer look at how members of the Stahlbaums' household integrate certain types of magical thinking into their daily routine. *The Nutcracker and the Mouse King* begins with Marie and Fritz, locked out of the parlor, which their parents are decorating for Christmas, trying 'to guess what their parents' and Godfather Drosselmeier 'would give them this time.' Fritz asserts that he likes 'the things Mama and Papa give ... a lot better' because the children 'can keep them and do what [they] like with them, while the elaborate mechanical toys that their Godfather makes for them are so special that their parents take them away and lock them up (2). As Marie and Fritz assure each other that their parents are well aware of what specific items they want this year, their 'big sister Louise' feels it is incumbent on her to remind them that,

> [It] was always the Christ Child who, by the hands of their dear parents, brought children things that would give them true enjoyment, since he knew what those would be better than the children themselves. So … instead of hoping and wishing for all sorts of things, they should wait quietly like well-behaved children for whatever the Christ Child would bring. (2)

Although Fritz grumbles, in response, that he would still like 'a chestnut horse and some hussars,' neither he nor Marie has any problem combining natural and supernatural explanations for the origins of their gifts, or, to be more precise, for the origins of the *joy* that they would experience from their gifts. Although, only a moment ago, they were saying that they like what their parents give them more than the gifts from their Godfather, and were proudly recalling with what skill and tact they had conveyed to the adults what they really wanted ('Marie also remembered how Mama had smiled at her being so delighted with her doll Gretchen's little parasol'), now they are perfectly willing to attribute their impending pleasure in their parents' gifts to the blessings of the Christ Child:

> So the children knew that their parents had bought them all sorts of lovely presents, and were busy imagining them, but they were just as certain that the Christ Child was looking on with tender loving eyes, and that Christmas gifts, because he had blessed them, gave them more pleasure than any others. (3)

Developmental psychologists have a particular term to describe this kind of thinking: they call it 'coexistence.' As Christine Legare and her colleagues put it, 'both natural and supernatural explanations frequently operate within the same mind to explain the very same event or phenomenon.' In this view,

> supernatural explanations do not always appear early in development; nor are they primitive or immature ways of thinking that are suppressed over the course of development. Instead, like natural explanations, they are constructed and elaborated through socialization and cultural learning and may be founded on earlier intuitive explanations. (781)

Marie, Fritz, and Louise have certainly been socialized by their parents to integrate magic and realism in their thinking about Christmas. We see a bit of that socialization at work when the parents, who had toiled the whole day on decorating the tree and preparing the gifts (the children could hear 'murmuring and shuffling and muffled hammer blows in the locked rooms'), now throw open the doors, take 'their children by the hand,' and say: 'Come in, come in, dear children, and see what the Christ Child has brought you' (3). Nobody, including readers, seems to find it strange that the same phenomena – that is, gift-giving and the particular pleasure derived from some gifts but not others – are given two very different ontological explanations, which function parallel to each other or are flexibly combined when an occasion calls for it.

For our present purposes, what is most interesting about coexistence thinking is that it is more prevalent in adults than in children. Traditionally, it has been thought that 'young children gradually abandon a belief in supernatural causation and instead acquire a more objective, rational, or scientific appreciation of cause and effect.' Recent studies, however, have shown that coexistence thinking grows stronger with age and that adults exhibit it more consistently than children.[5] 'The endorsement of allegedly competing epistemologies is commonplace in both Western and Non-Western contexts,' and not just in such 'emotionally charged domains' as the origin of species, illness, and death, but also in 'accounts of procreation, wrongdoing and marriage.' Converging 'developmental data from diverse cultural contexts,' both within 'highly educated, industrialized communities' and 'highly traditional, non-industrialized communities,' demonstrates that 'natural explanations involving natural or scientific causes and supernatural explanations involving divine or religious causes are used by the same individuals to interpret the same to-be-explained phenomena.' When 'faced with different explanatory frameworks – including those that are potentially in conflict with one another – adults and children might endorse both, either by recruiting them in different contexts, by ignoring potential contradictions, or by finding ways to combine and coordinate them' (Legare et al. 780, 781, 789).[6]

What forms does coexistence thinking take in the elder Stahlbaums? On the one hand, they know exactly where the Christmas gifts come from, so it is reasonable to assume that, when they are telling their children that 'the Christ Child has brought' them, they are taking part in an elaborate cultural ritual rather than accurately reporting what they know about the origins of the gifts. On the other hand, were someone to ask them about what Marie, Fritz, and Louise think about where the gifts come from, the parents would be likely to attribute to their children some form of coexistence thinking, perhaps acknowledging, for instance, that while they believe that the Christ Child has brought them, they also know that the parents did the actual choosing, buying, and arranging of the presents. Though seemingly incompatible, these beliefs would not be considered so. Instead, the Stahlbaums would come up with some explanation that would reconcile them – not unlike the explanation that their children came up with (above) about the Christ Child conferring a special blessing on the gifts brought by the parents (as opposed to those, for instance, made by Drosselmeier).

Moreover, it probably would not take very long to get the parents to display more coexistence thinking, were one to ask them a couple of follow-up questions about the exact ontological status of the 2,000-year old infant. Unless they would pronounce themselves staunch atheists and materialists – which is, clearly, not a viable alternative for characters in a Hoffmann storyworld – the older Stahlbaums would have to come up with explanations that would draw on both natural and supernatural elements, 'by ignoring potential contradictions, or by finding ways to combine and coordinate them.'

Here is where it all leaves us in respect to my initial question, which is why Marie's story about the Mouse King is treated as unreasonable while the story of the 2,000-year-old infant is not. While I am not yet in a position to answer that question (I hope to do so in part three), what we have established so far is that the older Stahlbaums do *not* lack a broad explanatory frame that would allow them to domesticate a supernatural event. Coexistence thinking is always an option, so if Marie's parents refuse to engage in it (for instance, by naturalizing some parts of her story while treating other parts as a Christmas miracle), they must have good reason for it.

Naïve Skepticism and Metacognitive Limitations

What enables Marie to persist in her belief in the reality of her adventures in the face of her parents' strong disapproval and their insistence that it was either a delirious vision or a dream? Putting aside, for a moment, traditional literary-critical explanations (that is, that Marie is a uniquely imaginative child, a fitting icon for the Romantic age, and an embodiment of Hoffmann's own contempt for philistinism), we can ask what other children of her age would have done in her place. To see if Marie's behavior is unusual, especially for a seven-year-old, we turn to research from developmental psychology which focuses on the development of metacognitive abilities in young children.[7]

To begin with, coexistence thinking explains only so much when it comes to children's reality judgement. Although they can and do engage in such thinking, it does not mean that they are ready to treat any fantastic event as real, as long as they can come up with a combination of natural and supernatural explanations to account for it. In fact, as developmental psychologists Jacqueline D. Woolley and Maliki E. Ghossainy point out, young children, be they from New Jersey or Madagascar, tend to display 'a strikingly large amount' of skepticism and 'assign reality status much more sparingly than one might expect' (1497), although as they grow older, their skepticism becomes somewhat weaker. This is to say that a typical seven-year old is not likely to rush to adapt what we may call a 'Romantic' outlook – which privileges her imagination over the grownups' realism – unless she has good reasons to do so.

Considerations that are likely to influence her perspective include her own first-hand evidence; verbal testimony of trusted others; context (for instance, 'instruction in church or Sunday school has the potential to confer reality status on events that might otherwise seem fantastical'); and the quality of her emotional arousal (when stirred by an 'angry or frightening event,' children's 'reasoning about reality status errs on the side of dismissing real events as fictional,' while happy or neutral events may be judged as 'real regardless of their fantastic content') (1502).

How are these considerations weighted in relation to each other? Individual differences certainly play a role. Some children tend more 'toward initial credulity and others toward initial skepticism' (1503). These initial differences can then be reinforced by paying selectively more or less attention to, for instance, contexts and the testimony of others, as opposed to personal experience and emotional charge.

But here is another factor that may underlie the strong skeptical stance generally espoused by children between three and nine. Children of that age are less able to reflect on the limitations of their knowledge. (This is not to say adults never overestimate their knowledge – of course they do! – merely that the gradual maturation of metacognitive abilities is an important developmental phenomenon.[8]) What it means is that when children are asked to estimate the reality status of improbable and impossible events, they are likely to judge it as low or high depending on whether or not they have experienced such events themselves. For instance, when they are told about a radically novel entity – such as a real or made-up animal which they have never encountered before – they tend to remain highly skeptical and disregard the testimony of adults who claim that it exists.

It may be 'perplexing' to an adult that 'a young child could believe that his or her knowledge of the world is complete enough to deny the existence of anything new,' for it 'would seem that young children would understand that there are many things that exist in the real world that they have yet to experience.' Yet, as 'intuitive as this seems, it appears not to be the case.' The ability to rely less on one's own knowledge and experience and use, instead, 'a wider range of strategies for assessing reality status, including, for example, seeking more information, assessing contextual cues, and evaluating the quality of the new information,' is something that does not come online until later in development (1505).[9]

What we have in Hoffmann's tale is the same dynamic of skepticism, only reversed to accommodate Marie's particular expertise. As a naïve skeptic, the seven-year-old Marie is less likely to be swayed by the testimony of her parents if it contradicts her own first-hand experience, especially given the sensory richness and narrative coherence of that experience. So many factors corroborate her account, from her memory of the active participation in the battle with the mice army (and the arm wound she incurred in the process), and the gift of the seven little crowns, to Drosselmeier's 'Story of the Hard Nut' (which provides a compelling account of the motivations of both Nutcracker and the Mouse King[10]), that she would have to be an unusually metacognitively precocious child to disregard all that evidence in favor of the testimony of her parents. This is to say that she would have to exhibit a truly remarkable insight into how fallible her judgement of reality can be. That we, as readers, apparently expect her to possess that kind of insight – and thus pronounce her a particularly imaginative, 'Romantic' child when she does not – demonstrates, primarily, that we may not be aware of the important differences between metacognitive abilities of children and grownups.

Somewhat ironically, it may also be the case that her family's frequent references to the magic Christ Child have provided Marie with a broader context for believing in the reality of some supernatural occurrences. You may recall that, when Louise reminds Marie and Fritz that it is the magical Christ Child who brings them their gifts (for he knows what gifts 'would give them true enjoyment ... better than the children themselves'), Marie sits 'deep in thought' – apparently more impressed than her brother, who keeps muttering that, 'all the same,' he knows what he wants for Christmas (3). That the elder Stahlbaums then expect that Marie would attend *selectively* to the cultural contexts of various improbable and/or impossible events[11] – that is, that she would believe the story about the miraculous infant (for which she has only circumstantial evidence), yet would disbelieve the story of Nutcracker (for which she has overwhelming personal evidence) – shows them to be rather typical parents. They assume, as we would (and as I myself do as a parent), that a child should be properly humble about the status of her knowledge about the world and trust her parents' judgements implicitly, a humbleness that would certainly feel gratifying to adults but would hardly be developmentally realistic.

To sum up, Marie's resistance to her parents' argument is not different from what any other child of her age would do, faced with the same kind of evidence. Her skeptical view of their opinion reflects metacognitive limitations typical for this developmental stage, for she yet has to learn to question various aspects of her memory, knowledge, and experience. Note that I do not mean to say by this that Marie's parents are correct and that she has dreamt up Nutcracker's battle with the Mouse King – merely that we should not overly romanticize Marie's imagination. Given the immediate evidence of her senses, the background tale of the Hard Nut provided by her Godfather Drosselmeier, and the overall magical context of Christmas, her insistence on the truth of her story may be perfectly reasonable.

What is reasonable for Marie, however, is not so for the older Stahlbaums. What is at stake for them is not the actual ontological status of the nutcracker toy: they could have easily sidestepped around that issue the same way they sidestep around other potentially thorny issues involving magic/religion: that is, through coexistence thinking. But it so happens that the older Stahlbaums are typically called on to respond to Marie's story in the presence of other people, and that puts a different kind of pressure on their own metacognitive capacities. To see how their reactions are shaped by that pressure, we turn to the work of cognitive psychologists and anthropologists who study social functions of reason.

Social Functions of Reason

To make sense of Dr and Mrs Stahlbaum's predicament, I rely on the framework developed by Hugo Mercier and Dan Sperber in their book *The Enigma of Reason* (2017), which considers reason in the context of mindreading (that is, attribution of mental states to oneself and others) and metacognition (capacity to evaluate one's mental states). Specifically, Mercier and Sperber argue that our production and evaluation of reasons is shaped by our need to (1) convince others of the truth of our opinion, (2) decide if others' opinion is worth adopting, and (3) manage reputational costs involved in these processes. According to this 'interactionist approach, the normal conditions for the use of reason are social, and more specifically dialogic,' while outside 'of this environment, there is no guarantee that reasoning acts for the benefit of the reasoner' (247). Reasons, then, are 'constructs' intended 'primarily for social consumption':

> [Reasons] are constructed by distorting and simplifying our understanding of mental states and their causal role and by injecting into it a strong dose

of normativity. Invocations and evaluations of reasons are contributions to a negotiated record of individuals' ideas, actions, responsibilities, and commitments. This partly consensual and partly contested social record of who thinks what and who did what for which reasons plays a central role in guiding cooperative or antagonistic interactions, in influencing reputations, and in stabilizing social norms. (127)

Here is what is at stake in thinking of reasons as social – that is, relational, dialogic, and interactional – rather than as internal, immanent, and abstract. First, it alerts us to the appealing but ultimately false story that we tell ourselves about our reasoning, for we tend to assume that we reason and *then* act, whereas, in reality, this process may be reversed: we act and *then* look for reasons to justify our actions in the eyes of others. In general, we are not able 'to bring to consciousness reasons that have guided us unconsciously' (114).[12] Worse than that, we are 'systematically mistaken in assuming that we have direct introspective knowledge of our mental states and of the processes through which they are produced.' Even in the case 'of seemingly conscious choices, our true motives may be unconscious and not even open to introspection; the reasons we give in good faith may, in many cases, be little more than rationalizations after the fact' (115).[13]

Second, this perspective on reason emphasizes the importance of debates, arguments, and other contexts in which one has to submit one's reasons for external scrutiny and is, in turn, asked to critically evaluate other people's reasons. The 'backward procedure' through which we infer our reasons from our actions 'is not designed for objective thinking, let alone intellectual discovery,' because it has an inbuilt confirmation bias or 'myside bias' (219). While this bias works well for us when we think of how to persuade others (which involves, to begin with, persuading *ourselves*), it works against us when we attempt to objectively evaluate our own opinion. But this bias is *not* at play when we scrutinize reasons given by others who hope to convince us. On the contrary, we approach those with a critical eye, which means that there is a greater chance for objective critique and, hence, genuine advance in thinking.

Finally, let us not lose track of how these two functions of reason – 'to justify oneself in the eyes of others, and to evaluate the justifications of others (often critically)' – are implicated in managing one's reputation:

> Thinking about good reasons for their actions is something that people often do proactively, anticipating that they may be called upon to explain or justify themselves. The minute you have engaged in a course of action that may

have reputational costs – and sometimes even before, when you are merely considering it – a different mental mechanism may start working. Its function is to manage your reputation and for this, to provide an explanation that will justify your behavior. (124)

In light of the imperative to manage reputational costs, it is important that Marie's parents are always forced to respond to her stories about Nutcracker and the Mouse King in the presence of other people. When Marie first informs her mother that there 'had just been a big battle between the dolls and the mice,' the family physician, Dr Wendelstern, is in the room, and, following his cue ('a meaning look'), her mother attempts to humor her, by saying that 'the mice are all gone, and Nutcracker is safe in the toy cabinet.' Then her father comes in, feels Marie's pulse, hears of her story, and talks to the doctor about her 'wound fever' (35). Similarly, when Marie first explains to her assembled family that Nutcracker is Drosselmeier's nephew and 'a prince, or rather a king,' her mother and Louise laugh, but Drosselmeier, who is also present, remains 'unsmiling.' While we (and Marie) interpret his gravity as a sign that he takes her story seriously, it appears that Marie's father experiences it differently, for it is then that he first becomes cross with her and asks, 'Where on earth does the child get such crazy ideas?' (62). Finally, when Marie asks Drosselmeier to confirm that his nephew, also known as Nutcracker, gave her 'the little crowns,' and Drosselmeier betrays her, muttering 'Stuff and nonsense!,' Dr Stahlbaum gets really angry and threatens that unless she forgets 'about this foolishness once and for all,' he will throw Nutcracker and all her other dolls 'out of the window' (97).

While we have no way of knowing for sure what Marie's parents, and especially her father, might have said, had there been no strangers in the room on any of those occasions, I do not think that the presence of these strangers is a coincidence. It changes the social dynamics of those scenes and creates a very particular kind of pressure on the father. Because Dr Wendelstern and Judge Drosselmeier are there, Dr Stahlbaum's priorities shift from engaging with his daughter to managing his and his family's reputation in their community. Any attempt to take Marie's story seriously or even to pretend to take it seriously (for example, by deploying coexistence thinking) would open the possibility that he and his wife would be reported as believing 'stuff and nonsense,' or else, encouraging their children to believe it, or, at the very least, allowing their children to treat other members of their community disrespectfully (as Marie allegedly does when she seems to be claiming, according to her father, that Judge Drosselmeier's nephew is as 'ugly' and 'simpleminded' as a nutcracker). In other words, it is in anticipation 'that they may be called to explain or justify themselves' (Mercier and Sperber 124), and that their reputations would suffer because no good justification appears to be immediately forthcoming, that Dr Stahlbaum describes his daughter's behavior as delirious, crazy, and foolish.

Keep in mind, too, that a reaction that may have started as a response to anticipated reputational cost can then take on a life of its own. This is the dynamic that Mercier and Sperber describe when they say that we do not have direct introspective knowledge of our motives and that 'the reasons we give in good faith may be … little more than rationalizations after the fact.' If it is indeed the case that the real reason that Dr Stahlbaum, in his initial conversation with Dr Wendelstern, pronounced Marie's story a product of her 'wound fever' was that he was concerned about his reputation in the community, he is not likely to be aware of that reason. What this means is that he may now *sincerely believe* that he has always considered his daughter's story nonsensical and that *this* is why he is now becoming increasingly angry about her recalcitrant repetitions of that story. Thinking that his daughter is willfully defying him (as opposed to being aware that he is scared of incurring a reputational cost) leaves smaller and smaller space for engaging in any kind of coexistence thinking (which, after all, calls for a certain kind of creativity and mental flexibility), and no amount of physical evidence (the mice infestation, the seven little crowns) can make him change his mind.

Hence the reason that reasonable (that is, not delirious, crazy, or foolish) children think that the 2,000-year-old infant is real while the Mouse King is not, is that believing in the first would (in the eyes of their parents) maintain the parents' reputation in the community, while believing in the second would (again, in the eyes of those parents) damage it. That the parents are mistaken – at least in the case of Judge Drosselmeier, who actually shares their daughter's belief in the world of Nutcracker and the Mouse King – is, of course, deeply ironic, but hardly surprising. After all, evolution had never bestowed upon us the capacity to read each other's minds *correctly*, only the capacity to think that others have mental states and to act on our fallible inferences of what those mental states may be.

A central conflict of *The Nutcracker and the Mouse King* thus could be said to arise from a clash between two different aspects of metacognition. On the one hand, we are presented with the compelling sensibility of a child whose developmentally appropriate metacognitive limitations make her privilege her memories, sensory impressions, and logical deductions over the verbal testimonies of her parents. On the other hand, we have the compelling-in-its-own-right perspective of the parent, whose (not necessarily conscious) anticipation of incurring reputational costs leads him to question – quite sincerely, too, as far as he is concerned – his daughter's sanity. And then, of course, there is also Drosselmeier, who maintains a precarious foothold in both worlds, now confirming the truth of Marie's story, now throwing her to the wolves. For he, too, has reputational costs to manage, as Dr Stahlbaum indirectly reminds him when, upon hearing Drosselmeier agree with Marie, he feels his pulse, suggests that the Judge is 'suffering from cerebral congestion,' and offers to write him out 'a prescription' (62).

Metacognitive Instability and Critical Imagination

Where does all this leave the reader, or to be more precise, literary critic reading the story? I see two main payoffs of adding the cognitive–psychological perspective on Hoffmann's tale to other literary-critical readings. First, it enriches our understanding of the characters' motivation, because it shows that they act in response to very different metacognitive challenges. Marie sticks to the truth of her lived experience, as a typical seven-year-old would, while her father attempts to manage his reputation by pronouncing Marie unreasonable and refusing to listen to her story. Both try to make the best of the hard spots that their creator put them in, and neither can appreciate the problem faced by the other. In fact, they cannot appreciate their own problems either, for the father is not likely to realize that he says what he says because of the presence of strangers, and Marie is not likely to realize that she lacks the fully developed cognitive machinery for questioning the reality of her lived experience.

In addition to highlighting the particular psychological predicaments of the characters, talking about metacognition in relation to *The Nutcracker and the Mouse King* also allows us to understand better the trajectory of its critical reception. Briefly, this trajectory can be described as moving away from the romanticized view of Marie and recategorizing the genre of the tale. Let us consider each of them in turn, first on its own, and then from the 'cognitive' perspective.

Hoffmann's tale used to be read in the context of the Romantic 'idealization of imagination and childhood,' informed by the Rousseauian 'cult of sensibility,' and representing a backlash against what was seen as the preceding century's emphasis on moral didacticism in education. In this reading, Marie's philistine parents are not capable of sharing her marvelous visions because they are blinkered by their rationalism and/or fatally deficient imagination.

A critique of this view, voiced by such scholars as Alan Richardson and Jeanette Sky, emphasizes that the notion that children 'have an elevated imagination [was] a cultural construct,' serving specific ideological needs of the Romantics:

> Alan Richardson has argued that those who urged the importance of fairyland in forming the minds of children were in fact tending towards conservative views on social and political affairs. They had turned away from their youthful radicalism towards the conservatism that would mark their later careers. The Romantics' idealization of imagination and childhood was therefore perhaps less an act of liberation, and more a conservative reaction to the radical ferment of the 1790s with its unprecedented upsurge in literacy and a hunger for ideas demonstrated by the popularity of political pamphlet literature. What the so-called moralists were urging was educational literature that would help children become rational individuals. What the Romantics proposed in return was a literature that turned its back on reality and engaged in a religious and quasi-mythological sacralisation of child and imagination. (Sky 366)[14]

Perhaps particularly important for our present purposes is the critical insight that 'the idea of the child was more important for the Romantics than the real child itself.' Imagination made this ideal child impervious to political manipulation, and, as such, 'naturally resistant to both radical and conservative indoctrination alike.' Hence,

> the efforts by Romantics like Wordsworth and Coleridge to reinforce the fairy tale in opposition to the more educational literature that flourished in the late eighteenth and early nineteenth century can actually be seen as a reaction against an informed and politically engaged lower-class readership. (Sky 371)

From the cognitive perspective, this view of the child as naturally shielded from ideological indoctrination is extremely fascinating, for, on the one hand, it is not altogether wrong. As we have just seen, according to developmental psychologists, metacognitive limitations can make the child between the ages of three and nine privilege her experience and knowledge over the testimony of adults. In this respect, the child may, indeed, be somewhat insulated from their manipulation. On the other hand, to idealize this stage in the child's cognitive development and to sacralize the special quality of imagination that presumably underlies it does mean to ignore the 'real child.'[15] Worse yet, treating this 'liberating' imagination as something to aspire to can, in practice, translate into locking politically vulnerable (due to race, gender, class, and age factors) populations into 'assumptions of infantilism and even primitivism' (Sky 368). As a political move, it can thus be particularly insidious because it taps, intuitively, into a real cognitive phenomenon (that is, children's metacognitive immaturity), which it misinterprets to serve specific ideological agendas.

You can see, based on just this example, how insights from cognitive science (here, research into children's metacognitive development) can complement and deepen the existing literary-historical perspective (in this case, the critique of some aspects of Romantics' view of childhood and imagination). Still, excited as I am about this case of interdisciplinary synergy, I do not want it to be taken to mean that it is up to cognitive science to validate or invalidate this or that critical interpretation. Instead, I want you to note that when a work of fiction foregrounds metacognitive instability – which is to say, challenges its characters' and readers' capacity to evaluate their own mental states – readers will continue seeking ways of resolving this instability.[16] Different cultural and historical contexts could make some resolutions more immediately appealing than others, but it is not clear that any one of them would ever decisively settle the question and dissipate the metacognitive tension.

Emphasizing the protagonist's unusual – childish and/or romantic – imagination is one way of dealing with this tension. Changing the generic optics through which we view the story is another. Moreover, the two can peacefully coexist. In the case of *Nutcracker and Mouse King*, even though the tendency to read it as a Romantic fairy tale for adults never completely went out of fashion, another reading has become possible with the increasing cultural prominence of the fantasy genre.

Thus, speaking of the origins of fantasy, 'which has become one of the key genres of children's literature,' Emer O' Sullivan points out that it 'was founded in Germany with E. T. A. Hoffmann's *Nußknacker und Mausekönig*,' even if 'its subsequent development took place in other countries' (that is, Denmark, Britain, and Sweden). In fact, it was not until 1949, with the German translation of Astrid Lindgren's Pippi Långstrump, that, 'for the first time since the Romantic era,' there was 'a favorable climate for the reception and creation of fantasy for children in Germany,' which led to 'a boom in this genre by German authors such as Michael Ende and Cornelia Funke' ('Comparative' 194).[17]

Note that readers well versed in the fantasy genre are not likely to consider Harry Potter's or Percy Jackson's sojourns in various magical worlds as evidence of their vibrant imaginations. By the same token, when J. K. Rowling's and Rick Riordan's ordinary adults are shown to lack access to the alternative universes of the young protagonists and sometimes literally cannot see amazing events taking place before their eyes, we do not explain it by their philistinism and imaginative deficiency.[18] There is simply no need for us to question the characters' powers of perception in order to vindicate our own.

And so we remain comfortably anchored in the reality that allows the respective worlds of muggles and wizards, and of humans and (demi) gods to exist parallel to each other, without roughing up our 'metacognitive self-confidence' (Mercier and Sperber 66).[19] This is to say that while Hoffmann may have been 'a founding father of children's fantasy' (O'Sullivan, *Comparative* 26), not many latter-day practitioners of the genre remained committed to the metacognitive instability animating his tale.[20]

But They Didn't Have that Word!

Throughout this chapter, I have been unabashedly psychologizing little Marie and her parents. In fact, I seemed to all but imply that, had Mrs Stahlbaum brought her daughter into a university laboratory for an experiment conducted by a developmental psychologist today, she would fit right in with other seven-year-old 'subjects,' answering questions about the reality status of this or that novel animal and, inadvertently, revealing her metacognitive limitations.

Now, how anachronistic is that? Not only do I conveniently forget that Marie is not a real child but a fictitious construct, who cannot have any cognitive limitations, much less reveal them, but I also talk about her metacognitive ability, even though the word metacognition did not even exist in 1816. Its first recorded use, according to the *Oxford English Dictionary*, was in 1972.[21] Ought I not, at least, to limit my discussion of Marie's so-called psychology to terms and concepts that Hoffmann and his contemporaries were conversant with?

These two objections to cognitive-literary approaches are still sometimes voiced by literary critics, which is why I will conclude my chapter by addressing them. To start with the first objection, cognitive-literary scholars have no quarrel with the notion that fictional characters are narrative constructs whose 'reality' is a mere illusion. Still, one cannot help noticing that this illusion is what makes both literary-critical and classroom conversations possible. As Andrew Elfenbein observes,

> Literary scholars assume that characters are not real people and that the questions appropriate to ask about them are not the same ones that we might ask about real people. Yet no matter how often we stress such a point, both students in literature classes and many critics find that it never fully takes hold. For all our efforts, readers persist in treating literary characters as if they were people they had met. (59)

The reason that we persist in treating literary characters as if they were people we had met is that we cannot help using the same cognitive mechanisms (that is, mindreading adaptations) to make sense of the actions of fictional characters that we use when we make sense of the actions of flesh-and-blood people. On some level, these adaptations do not distinguish between the two: as soon as they register behavior, they start churning up representations of mental states (thoughts, feelings, and intentions) that may have plausibly caused that behavior.

To keep constantly reminding oneself that it is all an illusion (as in: 'Marie stops talking about Nutcracker because she is *afraid* that her father would throw her dolls out the window; but, wait: not really! Marie can't be "afraid" because she doesn't really exist, she is a fictitious construct! So the reason this construct stopped "talking" about Nutcracker is because, had she been a real girl and had her father been a real man, and had he threatened her that way, that's what that real girl would have felt, but as this Marie is not a real girl, she clearly cannot be afraid') would make the process of reading about as much fun as I have just made it sound.

Attributing mental states to fictional characters is thus what makes reading fiction, and talking about it possible. One key difference between doing that on your own, as opposed to in a classroom or in a literary-critical essay, is that the latter contexts encourage us to go *beyond* mental states of fictional characters. That is, as scholars and teachers we are expected (and expect our students) to attribute mental states not just to characters, but also to narrators, to actual and implied authors, to variously historically situated readers, as well as to living and dead literary critics and philosophers. We may ask, for instance, what would this or that luminary think about this or that aspect of Hoffmann's tale? What would Viktor Shklovsky say/think about it? What would Freud? What would Wittgenstein? What would Eve Kosofsky Sedgwick?

As I have argued elsewhere, when we ask our students to consider such questions, it may seem that we encourage them to move away from treating fictional characters 'as if they were people they had met' and train them instead to see a work of fiction as a historically situated artifact that uses a variety of narrative techniques to engage with ideological, aesthetic, and psychological agendas – techniques that may come into sharper focus if we consider them via conceptual frameworks developed by various classical and modern thinkers. And train them we do. Make no mistake, however: the only way we can achieve this is by expanding the circle of entities whose minds we read *as if they were real people.*[22]

Let us now turn to the second potential objection, which is that we cannot have a meaningful conversation about the limitations of Marie's metacognitive capacity or about her parents' coexistence thinking because, back in 1816, those concepts did not exist, which implies – so this objection would go – that the phenomena that these terms describe did not exist either. To quote Elfenbein again,

> [Cognitive-literary] investigations open themselves to an easy charge of anachronism: since most psychological findings derive from participants who postdate [the past centuries], we cannot know if those findings apply to earlier periods. Yet literary scholars routinely apply approaches and insights honed in the twentieth- and twenty-first century academy to works written in earlier periods. Nervousness about the use of cognitive science is an arbitrary invocation of rigor that misrecognizes the field's enabling anachronisms. Also, there is no reason to decide a priori that contemporary psychological findings are irrelevant to the past. If it is wrong to assume that there is no difference between now and then, it is equally wrong to assume that there are no continuities either; assertions of historical difference do not guarantee truth any more than do ones of continuity. (168)

In fact, as Patrick Colm Hogan has argued, to increase 'ecological validity' of cognitive literary criticism, we should make a point of reaching out to literary texts from 'other historical periods and cultures.' Although there may be 'great enthusiasm' in literary studies today to read 'literary works in relation to theories that were or are contemporary with those works,' such texts are 'usually just the sort of project that lacks independent value for cognitive research.' For instance, if a scholar interested in memory takes up a late twentieth-century novel that explicitly draws on a particular neuroscientific account of memory, this novel 'probably does not tell us anything new about memory, beyond the account given in its source.' It cannot even be said to '"converge" with cognitive research, since it actually derives from that research' (25).

In deciding whether a work of literature is theoretically significant for a cognitivist investigation one should thus consider 'at least two factors':

> First, that significance is contingent on the work's independence from the theoretical and empirical studies with which one seeks to synthesize it. Second, its significance is in many ways proportionate to the degree to which it affects readers or viewers. The durability of a work suggests that it has represented a human condition in a way that is emotionally and cognitively affective for readers or viewers in different contexts and with different backgrounds. [This] does not mean that it is necessarily accurate. But its inaccuracies themselves may suggest something about human emotional and cognitive response. (25)

In contrast, Hogan observes, we would be 'hardly justified in concluding anything from an ineffective work or work whose effectiveness may be a function of ephemeral factors,' which can range from the work's topical references to contemporary scientific research to its particularly deft handling of current political preoccupations.

This is why we are better off, as researchers, focusing on 'emotionally and cognitively affecting' texts that are epistemologically independent – that is, removed in space or time – from contemporary psychological findings. The processes that are at work in such texts 'are largely unselfconscious, a matter of implicitly understanding patterns in human relations and conveying that implicit understanding representationally, which is to say, through the depiction of situations that manifest the patterns – usually in a heightened or more salient form than we would encounter in everyday life' (26).

In other words, Hoffmann did not need twenty-first-century cognitive-evolutionary insights into metacognition and reputation management to intuit that a respectable paterfamilias may become defensive and angry when faced with (what he experiences as) social pressure, and that he would rather pronounce his daughter's ideas 'crazy' and threaten to throw away her toys than reach out for a type of coexistence explanation that he and his family might have happily adapted in more relaxing circumstances. Both Marie's insistence on the truth of her lived experience and her father's insistence on her 'foolishness' ring true to us – and we explain those respective behaviors by enlisting research in cognitive psychology. But, then, those behaviors also rang true to early nineteenth-century audiences, and they explained them through conceptual frameworks available to them, which is to say, by evoking the unfettered imagination of the child and the hopeless philistinism of the parent. Literature, as Blakey Vermeule puts it, 'is so powerful because it eats theories for breakfast,'[23] and that includes theories originating in Rousseauian/Romantic outlook *and* in cognitive-psychological research. We can hope to gain a better understanding of cognitive foundations underlying our social interactions, but keep in mind that writers had gotten there first.

To return, then, to this chapter's title, children may very well be put in circumstances in which it feels reasonable to them to think that Nutcracker is alive and Mouse King is real. But then, their parents, too, can be put in circumstances in which it feels reasonable to them to pronounce their children's stories crazy and foolish and forbid repeating them. Taking our cue from Mercier and Sperber, who emphasize the interactionist, dialogic approach to reason, we begin to see the predicament of Hoffmann's characters, particularly that of the older Stahlbaums, in social rather than ontological terms. Is the Mouse King real? Who knows? But one's peers and neighbors surely are.

Notes

1. E. T. A. Hoffmann refers to Christ now as 'der liebe Heilige Christ mit gar freundlichen frommen Kindesaugen' ['the dear Holy Christ with kind and pious eyes of a child'] (77) and 'das Christkind' ['Chist Child'] (78). Various translations render that differently, ranging from 'holy Christ' to 'infant Christ.' Ralph Manheim's acclaimed version has it as 'Christ Child' (3) throughout.
2. Stephenson 179–82.
3. In fact, at the time of his death, Hoffmann was working on a story about Dürer, called 'Der Feind,' which was never finished and published posthumously in 1823.
4. For a discussion of the Mouse King's resemblance to 'the dragon representing evil incarnate in the Book of Revelations (12:3),' see Blamires, position 21.
5. In general, adults tend to be more supernatural in their thinking than children. For a discussion, see Woolley and Ghossainy, 1498, as well as Astuti and Harris, 'Understanding Mortality,' and Astuti et al., *Constraints*.
6. As Woolley and Ghossainy observe, 'different aspects of people's situations will favor or elicit different ways of thinking' (1497). See also Subbotsky, *Magic*, and Harris, *Trusting*. For a related analysis of 'epistemic switching' practiced by 'educated adults' (109), see Gottlieb and Wineburg. What they have demonstrated is that people can use a variety of 'strategies of coordination' to 'navigate multiple' – and conflicting – epistemologies (99), and that they can sometimes 'display self-awareness' (103) about doing so. Compare, also, Luhrmann's argument about 'flexible ontologies' (5).
7. For a broader review of metacognition – that is, 'the ability to represent, monitor and control ongoing cognitive processes,' which 'helps us perform many tasks, both when acting alone and when working with others' (349) – see Heyes et al.
8. For a study of the neural bases of the development of metacognitive abilities in early childhood, see Elisa Filevich et al. See also Yana Fandakova et al. for a study of the neural changes underlying the development of 'metamemory monitoring' in seven- to fifteen-year-old children, which 'showed continued longitudinal improvements in introspection on memory accuracy into adolescence' (7582).
9. See also Harris's 'Early Constraints' for a discussion of children's 'empirical bias.' As he points out, young children's imagination is 'ordinarily guided by what they know of reality' (477).
10. For a discussion of the connections between the main tale and the story within the story, see Blamires, positions 18–20.
11. But see Skolnick and Bloom's 'What Does Batman Think?,' as well as their 'The Intuitive Cosmology of Fictional Worlds,' for a discussion of children's capacity to keep different fictional worlds apart.
12. In fact, as Richardson demonstrates in his contribution to this volume (Chapter 1), early insights into a wide 'range of unconscious mental processes' were already articulated by Romantics.
13. See also Hogan, *Sexual Identities* 232.

14. See Richardson, 'Wordsworth, Fairy Tales' 40. See also Richardson, *Literature, Education, and Romanticism*.
15. Compare to Harris's observation that, although findings of developmental psychologists 'do not show that young children are unreceptive to the departures from everyday reality that they encounter in children's fiction, especially in fairy tales, ... they do show that it may be misleading to draw conclusions about children's own imaginative dispositions and capacities from the fictional materials that adults create for them' ('Early Constraints,' forthcoming).
16. See Spolsky's discussion of 'the interface of cultural change and cognitive possibilities' (43), particularly in the context of generic adjustment.
17. For an account of a somewhat different generic genealogy, see Zipes's *Relentless Progress*. As Zipes argues, Hoffmann wrote 'disturbing fairy tales that we might today designate as tales of magic realism that celebrated the utopian potential of art and the artist. His unique style and approach to fairy tales has been carried on well into the twenty-first century as can be seen in Aimee Bender's two collections of startling short stories, "The Girl in the Flammable Skirt" and "Willful Creatures"' (130).
18. And if they *are* imaginatively deficient philistines, as are, for instance, the Dursleys, it is a reflection on them and not on their status as muggles.
19. For a discussion of anchoring, see Scullion and Treby, 46.
20. For an important analysis of Hoffmann's aesthetics in the context of the 'Schlegelian concept of elevation' see Scullion and Treby. As they point out, Friedrich Schlegel urged writers and artists to '"hover in the middle (in der Mitten schweben) on the wings of poetic reflection" in order to maintain a state of creative balance between spirit and matter .... Hoffmann was ever receptive to and well informed about contemporary aesthetic debate. In *The Serapion Brothers* (1819–21), for example, Brother Theodor, one of the main contributors to aesthetic dialogue, describes poetic inspiration as follows: "I think that the bottom of the ladder to heaven on which one wants to climb up into higher regions must be grounded in life ... If, having climbed higher and higher, he [the writer or artist] then finds himself within a fantastic magical realm, he will come to believe that this realm too is part of his life, and that this realm is actually the most wonderful part of it"' (vol. 4, p. 721) (43).
21. See https://www.oed.com (last accessed December 15, 2021).
22. See Zunshine, 'Cognitive Alternatives.' See also Zunshine, 'Who Is He?' and *The Secret Life*.
23. Blakey Vermeule, personal communication, November 20, 2002.

References

Astuti, Rita, and Paul L. Harris. 'Understanding Mortality and the Life of the Ancestors in Madagascar.' *Cognitive Science* 32 (2008): 713–40.
—, Gregg E. A. Solomon, and Susan Carey. 'Constraints on Conceptual Development: A Case Study of the Acquisition of Folkbiological and Folksociological Knowledge in Madagascar,' with commentary by Tim

Ingold and Patricia H. Miller. *Monographs of the Society for Research in Child Development* 69.3 (2004): vii–135.

Blamires, David. '13. E. T. A. Hoffmann's *Nutcracker and Mouse King.*' *The Impact of Germany on English Children's Books, 1780–1918.* Cambridge: Open Book Publishers, 2009. 223–44. https://books.openedition.org/obp/612 (last accessed December 3, 2021).

Elfenbein, Andrew. *The Gist of Reading.* Stanford: Stanford University Press, 2018.

Fandakova, Yana, Diana Selmeczya, Sarah Leckey, Kevin J. Grimm, Carter Wendelken, Silvia A. Bunge, and Simona Ghetti. 'Changes in Ventromedial Prefrontal and Insular CortexSupport the Development of Metamemory from Childhood into Adolescence.' *PNAS (Proceedings of the National Academy of the Sciences of the United States of America)* 114.29 (July 2017): 7582–7. https://doi.org/10.1073/pnas.1703079114 (last accessed December 3, 2021).

Filevich, Elisa, Caroline Garcia Forlim, Carmen Fehrman, Carina Forster, Markus Paulus, Yee Lee Shing, and Simone Kühn. 'I Know that I Know Nothing: Cortical Thickness and Functional Connectivity Underlying Meta-Ignorance Ability in Pre-schoolers.' *Developmental Cognitive Neuroscience* 41 (February 2020): 100738. https://doi.org/10.1016/j.dcn.2019.100738 (last accessed December 3, 2021).

Gottlieb, Eli and Sam Wineburg. 'Between Veritas and Communitas: Epistemic Switching in the Reading of Academic and Sacred History.' *Journal of the Learning Sciences* 21.1 (2012): 84–129.

Harris, Paul L. 'Early Constraints on the Imagination: The Realism of Young Children.' *Child Development,* 92.2 (2021): 466–83.

—. *Trusting What You're Told: How Children Learn from Others.* Cambridge, MA: Harvard University Press, 2012.

Heyes, Cecilia, Dan Bang, Nicholas Shea, Christopher D. Frith, and Stephen M. Fleming. 'Knowing Ourselves Together: The Cultural Origins of Metacognition.' *Trends in Cognitive Sciences* 24.5 (2020): 349–62. https://doi.org/10.1016/j.tics.2020.02.007 (last accessed December 3, 2021).

Hoffmann, E. T. A. 'Nussknacker und Mausekönig.' *Werke in Fünf Bänden, Band 4: Die Serapionsbrüder (Ausgewählte Erzählungen).* Based on the edition by Prof. Dr. Georg Ellinger, newly edited by Dr. Gisela Spiekerkötter. Frankfurt: Stauffacher Verlag Ag. Zurich, 1965. 76–126.

Hoffmann, E. T. A. *Nutcracker.* Translated by Ralph Manheim, illustrations by Maurice Sendak. New York: Crown Publishers, 1984.

Hogan, Patrick Colm. *Sexual Identities.* New York: Oxford University Press, 2019.

Legare, Cristine H., Margaret E. Evans, Karl S. Rosengren, and Paul L. Harris. 'The Coexistence of Natural and Supernatural Explanations Across Cultures and Development.' *Child Development* 83.3 (2012): 779–93.

Luhrmann, Tanya M. *How God Becomes Real: Kindling the Presence of Invisible Others.* Princeton: Princeton University Press, 2020.

Mercier, Hugo and Dan Sperber. *The Enigma of Reason.* Cambridge, MA: Harvard University Press, 2017.

O'Sullivan, Emer. *Comparative Children's Literature.* New York: Routledge, 2005.

—. 'Comparative Children's Literature.' *PMLA* 126.1 (2011): 189–96.

Richardson, Alan. *Literature, Education, and Romanticism: Reading as Social Practice, 1780–1832.* Cambridge: Cambridge University Press, 1995.

—. 'Wordsworth, Fairy Tales, and the Politics of Children's Reading.' *Romanticism and Children's Literature in Nineteenth-Century England.* Ed. James Holt McGavran, Jr. Athens and London: Georgia University Press, 1991. 34–53.

Scullion, Val and Marion Treby. 'The Romantic Context of E. T. A. Hoffmann's Fairy Tales, *The Golden Pot, The Strange Child* and *The Nutcracker and the Mouse King.*' *English Language and Literature Studies* 10.2 (2020): 40–52.

Skolnick, Deena and Paul Bloom. 'The Intuitive Cosmology of Fictional Worlds.' *The Architecture of the Imagination: New Essays on Pretence, Possibility, and Fiction.* Ed. Shaun Nichols. Oxford: Clarendon Press, 2006. 73–86.

—. 'What Does Batman Think About Sponge Bob? Children's Understanding of the Fantasy/Fantasy Distinction.' *Cognition* 101 (2006): B9–B18.

Sky, Jeanette. 'Myths of Innocence and Imagination: The Case of the Fairy Tale.' *Literature and Theology* 16.4 (2002): 363–76.

Spolsky, Ellen. *Gaps in Nature: Literary Interpretation and the Modular Mind.* Albany, NY: State University of New York Press, 1993.

Stephenson, Paul. *The Serpent Column: A Cultural Biography.* New York: Oxford University Press, 2016.

Subbotsky, Eugene V. *Magic and the Mind: Mechanisms, Functions, and Development of Magical Thinking and Behavior.* New York: Oxford University Press, 2010.

Woolley, Jacqueline D. and Maliki E. Ghossainy. 'Revisiting the Fantasy-Reality Distinction: Children as Naïve Skeptics.' *Child Development* 84.5 (2013): 1496–1510.

Zipes, Jack. *Relentless Progress: The Reconfiguration of Children's Literature, Fairy Tales, and Storytelling.* New York: Routledge, 2008.

Zunshine, Lisa. 'Cognitive Alternatives to Interiority.' *Cambridge History of the English Novel.* Ed. Robert L. Caserio and Clement C. Hawes. Cambridge: Cambridge University Press, 2011. 147–62.

—. *The Secret Life of Literature.* Cambridge, MA: MIT Press, 2022.

—. 'Who Is He to Speak of My Sorrow?' *Poetics Today* 41.2 (2020): 223–41.

Chapter 11

Prone Minds and Extended Selves: *The Cenci*

Yasmin Solomonescu

In the 1970 collection *Romanticism and Consciousness*, in an essay that aimed to make Percy Shelley more palatable to contemporary readers, Harold Bloom insisted on the acuity of the poet's portrayals of the mind. A case in point was Shelley's 1819 drama *The Cenci*, about a sixteenth-century Roman family of that name, and specifically about the tyrannical Count Cenci's rape of his daughter, Beatrice. Departing from historical accounts of the actual Cenci family (particularly those accounts' indeterminacy about a rape), and departing also from the ethos of forbearance articulated in the Preface to the drama, Shelley has the fictional Beatrice succumb to bloodlust in turn as she arranges for her father's murder and is then arrested and sentenced to death.[1] By Bloom's account, behind this tragic outcome lies the Cenci family's skill of introspection, or what the prelate Orsino describes as their capacity for 'self-anatomy,' whereby the mind peels back the layers on '[d]angerous secrets' and thus 'tempts' itself '[i]nto the depth of darkest purposes' (2.2.110–13). Alluding to this passage, Bloom presents *The Cenci* as a classic instance of 'Romantic, experimental tragedy, in which a crime against nature both emancipates consciousness and painfully turns consciousness in upon itself' (391).

While there can be no doubt about the perils of mental inwardness in the drama, as a copious amount of criticism since Bloom makes clear, equally remarkable is Shelley's treatment of the mind's capacity to turn painfully outward.[2] This concern emerges suggestively in Act I as Beatrice pleads with the guests at a banquet for protection from her father's sadism:

> Oh, think what deep wrongs must have blotted out
> First love, then reverence in a child's prone mind
> Till it thus vanquish shame and fear! O, think! (1.3.108–10)[3]

In the Longman *Poems of Shelley*, the term *prone* in that striking phrase 'a child's prone mind' is glossed as 'ready' or 'eager,' as in *Cymbeline*

('I never saw one so prone') and *Measure for Measure* ('in her youth / There is a prone and speechless dialect / Such as move men').⁴ However, not only was this usage already archaic in Shelley's day (although admittedly not in the Cencis'), but the ensuing lines draw out a different sense altogether. Beatrice speaks of having 'borne much, and kissed the sacred hand / Which crushed us to the earth, and thought its stroke / Was perhaps some paternal chastisement!' (I, iii, 111–13). In this context, the 'prone mind' evokes a state of susceptibility and even vulnerability to external harm ('prone, *adj.*,' def. 1.b). Given the later mentions of Count Cenci's tendency to drag his daughter around the palace by her hair, we might also connect this sense of *prone* with the face-down, horizontal posture from which it derives etymologically (def. 5.b).⁵ But just as 'stroke,' in Beatrice's account of her father's touch, can mean both 'vicious blow or loving caress' (Cheeke 148), so too is a further polysemy at work in *prone*, which commonly denotes intrinsic disposition (def. 1). In *St. Irvyne* (1811), for instance, Shelley writes of 'a nature prone to the attacks of *appetite*' (158). Beatrice's use of *prone* thus carries the same ambiguity that *inclined* does in the exchange between the hired assassins Marzio and Olimpio when, in answer to Marzio's question about whether he is 'inclined' to the murder of Cenci, Olimpio speaks of both extrinsic and intrinsic motivations: 'If one should bribe me with a thousand crowns / To kill a serpent which had stung my child, / I could not be more willing' (IV, iii, 24–7). The image of the prone mind, then, raises a question implicit throughout the drama of the relative efficacy of external and internal influences on the mind, and also, by its very ambiguity, the corollary question of whether the internal and external can be so tidily distinguished. Another major question concerns the proneness of the adult mind: what causes Beatrice to turn no less criminal than her father?⁶ These fundamental problems raise the further question of the extent to which moral and mental forms of proneness are implicated in each other.

Recent criticism has stressed the extent to which Romantic writers' interest in 'internal' proneness – more typically referred to as the innate or the hereditary – represented an important turn away from Lockean constructivism. Alan Richardson, most notably, links the concern with what is bred in the bone (or body) with the period's new brain science, which challenged the idea that the self was dependent on or identical with an immaterial soul to regard it instead as contingent on a material brain and its relation to the environment.⁷ That such science deeply influenced Shelley is now well established. Paul Hamilton has argued that Shelley's poetry is often concerned with the 'shock of our subordination to natural processes' (144); Sharon Ruston has explored Shelley's poetic debts and allusions to medical practitioners, practices, and debates; and Mark J. Bruhn has shown how Shelley's treatment of cognition in his prose and poetry overlaps in key areas with present-day theories of mind.[8] Certainly, *The Cenci* bears out such alignments as well, notably by its numerous references to the brain and nerves as the material substrata of thoughts and truths.[9] Yet as the metaphor of the prone mind suggests – and, indeed, as the whole drama makes clear – Shelley was interested in the mind's environment not merely as an independent, clearly demarcated source of influence (as in the *tabula rasa* model) but as potentially bound up with the mind in a mutually dependent system. Beatrice's brother Bernardo may be speaking only metaphorically when he remarks, of Beatrice's refusal to desert their stepmother, 'I am of my sister's mind' (II, i, 98), but the drama entertains the possibility of a literal meaning. Can one be *of* another's mind more than metaphorically, not just sharing its opinions but actually bound up in its processes? Shelley dramatizes the consequences of an affirmative answer, notably in Beatrice and her father.

In so doing, Shelley offers a serious and sustained exploration of the phenomenon that contemporary cognitive theorists call mental extension: the process whereby the mind extends beyond the boundaries of skin or skull and into the world, including into other minds. However, whereas scientists and philosophers debate whether and to what extent the mind is thus extended, Shelley directs attention to a separate but related problem. Through Beatrice and her father Shelley suggests that, whatever the mind's actual boundaries, it is at least capable of thinking itself extended, and this self-understanding can pose a real threat to its integrity and that of the self.[10] Contrary to much contemporary theory, that is, Shelley treats the possibility of mental extension as entailing not functional efficacy but existential threat. He also exceeds current cognitive discourse in his exploration of the role of language, especially figurative language, in creating a sense of mental extension, as well as in potentially mitigating its dangers. To put the point more broadly: while Shelley would seem to anticipate, or at least have affinities with, arguments in cognitive theory for the mind's extension, something more than anticipation or affinity is at stake. Establishing this requires a fuller engagement with the theory in question.

Extended Minds, Extended Selves

The idea that the mind might be not just embedded in (or causally dependent on) a material brain and body but extended beyond them was first advanced in Andy Clark and David Chalmers's controversial 1998 paper, 'The Extended Mind.' The basic premise is that the body and its environment do not merely facilitate cognitive processes (as with maps, diagrams, pens and paper, and sundry digital devices) but intrinsically drive those processes, as integral parts of them. Clark and Chalmers give the often-cited hypothetical case of Otto, who suffers from memory loss and relies on a notebook for information about his environment, such as the location of the Museum of Modern Art. They compare Otto's mode of navigation with that of Inga, who relies on no such notebook, getting herself to the same museum based on her beliefs about its location. Clark and Chalmers contend that there is no essential difference between the modes of cognition employed by each agent. Rather, we must extend our definition of 'belief' – and of mind and cognition more generally – to account for the functional parity: the fact that Otto's notebook entries have the same impact on behavior as Inga's mentally stored information. As Clark has more recently elaborated in *Supersizing the Mind* (2008), 'thinking and cognizing may (at times) depend directly and noninstrumentally upon the ongoing work of the body and/or the extraorganismic environment' (xxix).

A notebook, however, is by no means the most significant mode of cognitive extension. Rather, as Clark and Chalmers note, it is above all language that spreads cognitive processes into the world, and may even have evolved to support such extension (11–12). It follows that extended cognition often has a profoundly social character. Clark and Chalmers address this point briefly but suggestively:

> Could my mental states be partly constituted by the states of other thinkers? We see no reason why not, in principle. In an unusually interdependent couple, it is entirely possible that one partner's beliefs will play the same sort of role for the other as the notebook plays for Otto. What is central is a high degree of trust, reliance, and accessibility. In other social relationships these criteria may not be so clearly fulfilled, but they may nevertheless be fulfilled in specific domains. For example, the waiter at my favourite restaurant might act as a repository of my beliefs about my favourite meals (this might even be construed as a case of extended desire). In other cases, one's beliefs might be embodied in one's secretary, one's accountant, or one's collaborator. (17–18)

Taking the argument one step further, Clark and Chalmers suggest that where cognition extends, so too extends the self. Since the information in Otto's notebook is 'a central part of his identity as a cognitive agent,' then 'Otto *himself* is best regarded as an extended system, a coupling of biological organism and external resources.' The alternative would be 'to shrink the self into a mere bundle of occurrent states' (18) – a prospect that returns us to David Hume's skeptical view of the self as a mere bundle of perceptions. 'Far better,' Clark and Chalmers insist, 'to take the broader view, and see agents themselves as spread into the world,' with all that might entail for our understanding of what it means to think and act, individually or socially (18).

While many theorists of cognition have heeded Clark and Chalmers's call to overthrow 'the hegemony of skin and skull' (18) – and have likewise echoed their enthusiasm for the explanatory gains thus achieved – others have questioned the arguments, evidence, and assumptions involved in that position. To take one prominent instance, Robert Rupert has contested the notion that the forms of memory employed by Otto and Inga are equivalent and argues instead that cognitive phenomena rely on 'integrated ... architectures' contained within the bounds of the human organism (*Cognitive Systems* 8). The mind and the self, though embodied, are 'nonextended' (8), however much they may 'utilize environmental resources on an ad hoc basis' (12).[11] Rupert has also taken issue with the hypothesis of socially extended cognition entertained by Clark and Chalmers and elaborated elsewhere. Advocates of both group-mind theory and collective epistemology contend that two or more minds can sometimes be treated as a single mind: under certain circumstances (notably of shared purpose and reasoning, or at least of shared commitment to a given proposition), they can form cohesive, intelligent systems, as in the case of courts, labor unions, or political parties, or less formal groupings like collaborative research teams, poetry reading groups, or friends arranging a vacation together.[12] Rupert, by contrast, sees no explanatory gain, and many logical problems, with the position, particularly as it comes into conflict with the theory (a contested one, though Rupert treats it as widely accepted) that cognitive systems possess capacities of mental representation – of matching particular mental states with particular referents in the world.[13]

Theories of extended mind are, of course, more various and fraught than this overview can suggest.[14] My aim, however, is not to survey or lay deep stakes in this terrain but to draw out lines of inquiry that can be put into productive dialogue with Shelley. While transformations in concepts of the mind and self across the eighteenth century and Romantic period have received careful attention in recent years, Shelley's contributions, particularly in *The Cenci*, remain relatively overlooked.[15] This is a significant oversight, given both the weight of those contributions and their expression across several of his works. The question of 'the existence of distinct individual minds,' for instance, receives explicit attention in the essay 'On Life' (1819). Shelley contends there that the personal pronouns '*I, you, they* are not signs of any actual difference subsisting between the assemblage of thoughts thus individuated, but merely marks employed to denote the different modifications of the one mind.' He adds, however, that this does not make any one 'I' equivalent to the one mind, but only 'a portion of it.' Shelley also writes rhapsodically of the state of reverie in which individuals, particularly children, 'feel as if their nature were dissolved into the surrounding universe, or as if the surrounding universe were absorbed into their being' and are 'conscious of no distinction' (*Prose* 174). In children and adults, the driver of such experiences of communion is ideally love, which Shelley defines in the essay 'On Love' (1818) and elsewhere as the self's 'thirst[ing] after its likeness' (*Prose* 170). Yet Shelley's attitude toward the prospect of such self-dissolution is also ambivalent. In his unfinished treatise on morals (c.1812–15) he insists, on the one hand, that '[t]he use of the words *external* and *internal*, as applied to the ... distinction' between thought and the objects of thought, is mere verbiage – 'an affair of words' (*Prose* 186). On the other hand, however, Shelley also affirms a fundamental awareness of individuality when he remarks that 'We are intuitively conscious of our own existence and of that connection in the train of our successive ideas which we term our identity. We are conscious also of the existence of other minds; but not intuitively' (*Prose* 183). As Earl R. Wasserman remarked, although Shelley recognized the illusoriness of distinctions between self and other, internal and external, thoughts and their objects, he also regarded such illusions as necessary to the existence and transformation of individual adult minds (147–9).

This ambivalence is even more apparent in Shelley's verse. Whereas in *Prometheus Unbound* (1820) he represents the relation of parts to whole positively, notably in the scene of Panthea's 'absor[ption]' into Prometheus (II, i, 82), in *Laon and Cythna* (1817) he has Cythna pointedly reject her brother's fantasy of a revolutionary brotherhood that dissolves all differences of identity and opinion. This is the case notably when she adopts her brother's name with a crucial difference, the addition of an 'e' (Laone), and more explicitly when she insists on the dangers that will result 'If our own will as others' law we bind; / ... / If as ourselves we cease to love our kind!' (5.2153–5). *Laon and Cythna* more generally insists on a clear distinction between loving our kind as versions or extensions of ourselves and loving them in the same spirit with which we love ourselves, with respect for their individuality.[16]

The Cenci is often read as the dark twin of *Prometheus Unbound*, as representing not the triumph but the tragic failure of the mind and self to transcend injuries committed against them. It nonetheless also pursues Shelley's critique in *Laon and Cythna* of a vision of reform predicated on the total melding of individual consciousnesses. Whereas Clark and

Chalmers are keen for the 'hegemony of skin and skull' to be 'usurped' by the notion of selves, minds, and cognitive processes that are 'spread into the world' (18), including into other selves and minds, Shelley shows that hegemony can work both ways, as extended minds also threaten unjust domination.

'This particle of my divided being'

Cenci's rape of Beatrice is often interpreted as symbolizing the corruption of the late sixteenth-century patriarchal, Roman Catholic society that refuses to check his predations. But Shelley is also interested in the deeper logic of that system of injustice, specifically, in the tendency of its participants to rely, in justification of their crimes, on what we might call a logic of extension. This is not quite the same as the metonymic logic, so prominent in the drama and its criticism, that connects Cenci-as-father with the papal Father and the divine Father such that a challenge to one represents a challenge to all. (As Cenci puts it, 'The world's Father / Must grant a parent's prayer against his child / Be he who asks even what men call me' [IV, i, 106–8].)[17] More central to Cenci's machination is the idea that another might not just stand in symbolically for the self but actually extend it. Cenci cannot pretend that the wine he drinks at his banquet is truly the 'mingled blood' of his dead sons – the perversion of the Eucharist he wishes it were ('Then I would taste thee like a sacrament' [I, iii, 82]). Nevertheless, he seems earnestly to understand himself and his daughter as joined by blood more than metaphorically. When Beatrice refuses to enter his apartment at the castle of Petrella, he excoriates her as

> this my blood,
> This particle of my divided being;
> Or rather, this my bane and my disease,
> Whose sight infects and poisons me; this devil
> Which sprung from me as from a hell[.] (IV, i, 116–20)

While there is certainly an apt Miltonic resonance here, in the allusion to the birth of Sin from the cleft brain of her father Satan (Richardson, *Mental Theater* 109), also noteworthy is the idea that Beatrice is in some sense a part of Cenci, connected to him by 'blood' and 'being.' The blurring of boundaries is also enacted by Cenci's shifting figures of speech as metaphor, an association of dissimilar terms or objects (here, Beatrice and blood), is refigured as synecdoche, an association of part and whole (or 'particle' and whole: Beatrice and Cenci).

The suppression of difference finds extreme expression in Cenci's rape of Beatrice, a deed meant to 'confound both day and night' for them both (II, i, 183), and to confound many other distinctions besides. Cenci's chief concern after he has committed the rape is to subdue Beatrice's mind:

> 'tis her stubborn will
> Which by its own consent shall stoop as low
> As that which drags it down.
> ...
> She shall become (for what she most abhors
> Shall have a fascination to entrap
> Her loathing will), to her own conscious self
> All she appears to others[.] (IV, i, 10–12, 85–8)

Cenci's utmost desire is to make his daughter's will exactly replicate his own – to make her will further violations and the social stigma they entail. As Alan Richardson observes, Cenci more generally wishes to impose his whole self-consciousness on Beatrice, including his mixed feelings of horror and desire, his desire for social supremacy, and his awareness of a dependence on others that thwarts his autonomy (*Mental Theater* 107). Incest thus becomes a motif for the conquest and assimilation of one mind by another.[18] Still more tragically, however, it also becomes a figure for one mind's *extension* into another, as Beatrice's subsequent remarks reveal.

Having often interposed, with 'firm mind' (II, i, 48), between her father and the rest of the family before the violation, Beatrice tries in the immediate wake of that act to continue resisting the logic of extension. On being ordered to Cenci's apartment, she refuses on grounds that she sees 'a torrent / Of his own blood raging' between them (IV, i, 113–14). His blood is emphatically not hers, but a channel that divides them. Yet her grasp on this sense of distinction after the violation is only fitful, as indexed by her remark, 'Am I not innocent?' (III, i, 70), readable as both a rhetorical question (I am) and an unrhetorical one (I doubt whether I am). The more her stepmother urges her to explain herself, moreover, the more the horror of the event erodes her sense of self:

> Oh, blood, which art my father's blood,
> Circling through these contaminated veins,
> If thou, poured forth on the polluted earth,
> Could wash away the crime, and punishment
> By which I suffer. ... no, that cannot be! (III, i, 95–9)

If Beatrice were conflating her blood and her father's only figuratively (as Cenci did of the wine he wished were his sons' blood), there would be no need for her to contemplate self-decontamination by suicide, the act represented by the ellipsis, which 'cannot be' because it is divinely prohibited. Rather, Beatrice, too, takes the shared-blood metaphor literally, seeing herself as physically and psychically polluted by the crime.[19] The assault leaves her feeling engulfed in a 'clinging, black, contaminating mist' that 'dissolves / [... Her] flesh to a pollution' and poisons the 'inmost spirit of life' (III, i, 17, 21–3). Cenci has similarly imagined the rape as shrouding Beatrice in such a 'bewildering mist / Of horror' (II, i, 184–5), and Beatrice now directly associates the phenomenon with her father when she wonders whether after death she will discover 'all things' to be pervaded by his 'spirit / [...] / The atmosphere and breath of [... her] dead life!' [V, iv, 60, 62]).[20]

Such doublings of thought and language become even more salient as Beatrice has recourse to another key element of Cenci's ideology, revenge. Renouncing 'Forbearance and respect, remorse and fear, / And all the fit restraints of daily life' (III, i, 209–10), she presents herself as an instrument of divine retribution, 'A sword in the right hand of justest God' (IV, iv, 127), echoing Cenci's self-description as 'a scourge' wielded by God on humankind (IV, i, 63).[21] Subsequently denying involvement in his murder, Beatrice also displays a Cenci-esque pride in the family name: 'stain not a noble house' (IV, iv, 151), she asks of her eventual prosecutor, sublating her identity to that of her father. Numerous critics have noted that the tragedy turns less on Beatrice's decision to have Cenci killed than on her endorsement of some of the most pernicious aspects of his ideology.[22] Yet Shelley also goes to the length of suggesting that Beatrice has come to be of her father's mind in more than just a colloquial sense. This is not just the effect of external influence, as if Cenci had actively persuaded Beatrice to see things his way (he fails notably to make her will her own violation).[23] Nor is it a clear case of group think, the unilateral imposition of opinion.[24] Rather, in significant ways Beatrice participates in a shared process of cognition, her beliefs being 'partly constituted' (as Clark and Chalmers put it) by her father's. Her remarks on the 'child's prone mind' are worth revisiting in this regard. The mind that was once prone in the sense of being susceptible to external influence – reliant on the parent's mind as a repository of un- or under-developed cognitive abilities – has become prone in the sense of internal disposition, continuing in adulthood to sustain parental ways of thinking by its own means and accord. In the parlance of cognitive theory, Cenci forms part of Beatrice's mental 'scaffolding'; in key respects their two minds form one system, in a dynamic that such theory often describes positively as 'coupling,' and that Shelley epitomizes darkly as incestuous rape.[25]

In short, Beatrice is ultimately 'lost' in much more than the moral sense lamented by her brother Giacomo (III, i, 381) and insinuated by Orsino (III, i, 176). Reeling from the violation, she remarks, 'I thought I was that wretched Beatrice / Men speak of, whom her father sometimes hales / From hall to hall by the entangled hair' (III, i, 43–5). Not the least horrific aspect of Cenci's crime is that it reduces Beatrice to the status of an entangled *heir*, a perpetuator of his mentality and sinful reputation.[26] To pursue the wordplay (as Shelley himself does): the 'hair undone' by the violence of the assault (III, i, 6) stands in for the heir undone by it, as Beatrice loses both a distinct self and a distinct mind, and this mental proneness precipitates a moral proneness.[27] The stage direction that describes her as 'absorbed in thought' (III, i, 179) as she ponders parricide is therefore remarkably apposite: the way that she and her father insist on regarding his actions effectively absorbs her individuality, much like the noxious mist they imagine enveloping her.

That, at least, is how Beatrice and Cenci jointly see it. Shelley's clever stage-management of the language of the drama urges audiences to see it otherwise.

Splitting Hairs/Heirs

Over against the large body of criticism about the ethics, psychology, and political symbolism of Beatrice's revenge, Stephen Cheeke reminds us that Beatrice also functions as a 'textual site' wherein Shelley expresses complex ideas about language, notably the 'familiar language of men' that he employs in the drama (Cheeke 155; *Shelley's Poetry and Prose* 144). Much like Beatrice, that is, Shelley, in his refusal to name so *un*familiar an act as incestuous rape, becomes embroiled in a 'radical language economy' in which words lose their connection to shared systems of meaning and ethical values, whether through willful abuse (as when Beatrice makes *parricide* synonymous with *piety*) or equally willful omission (as when Cenci tells his wife that Beatrice will become the target 'Of public scorn, for acts blazoned abroad, / One among which shall be ... What? Canst thou guess?') (Cheeke 155; *Cenci* IV, i, 83–4). Certainly, there is no shortage of sly verbal indirection in the drama, as we see likewise in Orsino, the prelate and suitor in whom Beatrice detects a 'sly, equivocating vein' (I, ii, 28). In fact, Orsino's very name is shot through with equivocation: Or-si-no or, indeed, Or-sin-o – the conjunction 'or' that serves to link alternatives being itself linked, in the first syllabication, with the Italian words for *yes* and *no*, and in the second with a sort of false alternative between 'sin' and nothing ('o'), and the name as a whole constituting an anagram (or disordering) of a synonym for prayer, *orison*. Yet not all equivocation in *The Cenci* is linked to sin, disorder, or false alternatives.[28] From the Latin *aequivocāre* for 'to call by the same name' ('equivocation, *n*.'), equivocation is also the basis for various forms of semantic doubling – especially of name and sound – that turn out to be the drama's chief countermeasures against pernicious indirection.

Figuration might seem a paltry defense against cognitive conquest. What makes the two acts meaningfully interdependent is not just Shelley's characteristic recourse to analogy – yoking the macrocosmic and the microcosmic, the revolutionary and the aesthetic – but also the particular nature of Beatrice and Cenci's cognitive bond. That bond, after all, depends on figuration, specifically the metaphor of familial flesh and blood that Cenci treats as synecdoche in regarding Beatrice as a 'particle' of his 'divided being.'[29] In regarding disparate objects as intrinsically united in a part–whole relationship, Cenci, and Beatrice after him, commits the error that Shelley in the treatise on morals and elsewhere denounces as the 'abuse of a metaphorical expression to literal purpose' (*Prose* 288). Shelley not only dramatizes such error, however, but also urges audiences to avoid it by cultivating the kind of critical distance his protagonists lack. The effect is akin to the one Richard C. Sha discerns in William Blake's 'London': an invitation to recognize the mobility of the boundary between mind and world – its susceptibility to being drawn in different places by different subjects at different moments – and thus to recognize its status as representation, this recognition in turn freeing one up to 'evaluate the kinds of [cognitive] distribution that are possible' and to avoid those in league with pernicious ideologies (247).

This kind of re-cognition evokes what Shelley, in the Preface to *The Cenci*, calls the 'restless and anatomizing casuistry with which men seek the justification of [the historical] Beatrice, yet feel that she has done what needs justification' (142), but it also stands apart from such casuistry in that it applies primarily not to moral cases but to minute elements of language and thought.[30] Aptly enough, since a kind of hair-splitting is at issue, the hair/heir homophone is representative of Shelley's strategy. References to Cenci's dragging of Beatrice by the 'entangled hair' are repeated in several places and associated there with filial abuse and revenge, as in the reference to Beatrice's 'hair undone' by the violence of the assault or her mention of the 'tangled hair' of the trees that lead to the castle of Petrella, forming a cover for an attempt on Cenci's life (III, i, 622).[31] More explicit associations with Cenci's actual heirs also occur, including in Cardinal Camillo's early remarks to Cenci:

> How hideously look deeds of lust and blood
> Through those snow white and venerable hairs! —
> Your children should be sitting round you now,
> But that you fear to read upon their looks
> The shame and misery you have written there. (I, i, 38–42)

Juxtaposing the patriarch's white hairs with his familial heirs ('your children'), the passage at once tempts us to follow Cenci and Beatrice in conflating the referents and urges us to discern their difference – one emphasized by both the line break and the fact that the heirs are *not* in fact sitting reverentially around their father. Sonic and semantic doublings thus underscore differences that the logic of extension would deny.[32] This is likewise the case when, within hearing of her father's banquet guests, Beatrice orders him to hide himself '[w]here never eye can look upon thee more' (I, iii, 147), a rebuke all the more severe if the company hear 'I' in place of 'eye' and understand Beatrice to be elevating herself above her father, effectively banishing him from her sight. Similarly subversive is the pun Shelley works into Camillo's description of Pope Clement VIII as 'grave, / Pious, and just' (V, ii, 192–3), the adjective alluding to Pius VII, the pope in power during Shelley's time in Italy and notorious for overseeing a virtual police state.[33]

As a means of counteracting the logic of extension, however, Shelley's most effective and meaningful verbal doubling may be the one involving that polysemous phrase, 'prone mind.' At once evoking and calling into question the standard distinction between internal and external cognitive influences, the phrase also suggestively encompasses, in its spelling, the 'one mind' – the essential reality to which, as Shelley affirmed in 'On Life,' all things, including individual minds and selves, belonged. As a kind of *reductio ad absurdum* of Shelley's own ideals, what *The Cenci* makes arrestingly clear is that such extension has limits. The 'prone mind' should no more be conflated with the cosmic 'one mind' – or indeed with any terrestrial one mind – than any '*I, you,* [or] *they*' should be, whatever their degree of relation or mutual reliance. The phrase, then, is an index of the play's overall attitude toward cognitive extension. As Beatrice puts it, albeit in a morally problematic attempt at self-exoneration, it would be far better for the world not to 'lose all discrimination' (V, ii, 153) between closely related cases – far better, in the case of cognition, to keep the 'prone mind' an *own* mind.

The tragedy of *The Cenci*, then, pivots on the capacity of the mind to turn painfully not just inward but also outward. It explores the dark side of Shelley's interest in, and frequent idealization of, concepts of interpersonal absorption, self-dissolution into the environment, and the one mind. This is not to say that Shelley takes a decided stance on the question of mental extension.[34] What we see in *The Cenci* is not that the mind is definitely extended but that it is capable of thinking itself so, and that this self-understanding, proceeding through the logic of extension inherent to figuration when it is literalized, can pose a real threat to the integrity of both mind and self. Incest may be Shelley's foremost motif for this dangerous dissolution of boundaries – physical, mental, and moral – but it is, above all, his subtle verbal doublings that mount a challenge to forms of extension that obliterate individuality. Shelley thus dramatically (in both senses) widens out what, in Clark and Chalmers, was only a small tear in the hypothesis of socially extended cognition. 'Could my mental states be partly constituted by the states of other thinkers? We see no reason why not, in principle' (17). 'In principle,' but perhaps not in practice, lest we find ourselves on the slippery slope to endorsing the kind of cognitive 'coupling' that *The Cenci* so carefully and horrifically explores.

Notes

For their helpful comments on earlier iterations of this article I thank the collection editors as well as Joseph Rosenberg, Stefan H. Uhlig, and the members of the 18th- and 19th-Century Subfield in English at the University of Minnesota, especially Moinak Choudhury, Andrew Elfenbein, Brian Goldberg, and Amit Yahav.

1. On Shelley's departures from the historical record see Rossington 874–5.
2. On *The Cenci* as 'the period's most complex dramatization of the romantic protagonist's turn to the interior' see, for instance, Cox 139–68, 141.
3. Unless otherwise noted, all Shelley citations are from *Shelley's Poetry and Prose*, cited parenthetically by act, scene, and line number for drama, by canto and/or line number for poetry, and by page number for prose.
4. Rossington 755, quoting *Cymbeline* V, iv,197 and *Measure for Measure* I, ii, 175–7, and citing the *OED*'s entry for 'prone, adj.,' which at def. 2 quotes the lines from *The Cenci*. Shelley references the *Cymbeline* passage in a footnote to *Oedipus Tyrannus* I, i, 227.
5. Shelley uses *prone* in this sense in *Prometheus Unbound* (III, ii, 17), 'Ode to Naples' (166), and 'The Witch of Atlas' (638).
6. Jerrold Hogle aptly describes this moral tendency as 'proneness' when he remarks of Beatrice that 'the [patriarchal] logic she assaults ... [leads] her by her own consent to be as prone to scapegoating and self-concealment as the mimetic power-plays directed so brutally against her' (160). Collocated with 'by her own consent,' Hogle's use of *prone*, much like Shelley's, expresses both necessity and intent, attesting to the enduring

problem of the relationship between internal and external influences in *The Cenci.*

7. See, notably, Richardson, *Science of the Mind* 93–113. Although Richardson does not discuss Shelley's works, he notes that Shelley 'uses the term "brain" more extensively than any other canonical Romantic poet, and in ways that reflect his interest in materialist or quasi-materialist thinkers like [Joseph] Priestley, [Erasmus] Darwin, and [Pierre-Jean-Georges] Cabanis'; 212n77.
8. On Shelley's adaptation, in his prose, of eighteenth-century theories of association to explain human morality while eschewing the apparent problem of contingency and the argument for transcendental oversight, see Bruhn, 'Shelley's Theory of Mind'; on Shelley's complex treatment of metaphor, especially in 'To a Sky-Lark,' as it stands to enhance cognitive theories of metaphor, see Bruhn, 'Harmonious Madness.'
9. Beatrice, for instance, is said to 'anatomize' others' minds 'nerve by nerve' (I, ii, 85); see also II, ii, 82; III, i, 1; IV, i, 7; and V, ii, 88.
10. This is not to say that Shelley in *The Cenci* denies the existence of a self. Romantic writers' explorations of the impersonal and the dispossessed have recently been lauded for constituting 'an ethics of engaged withdrawal or strategic reticence' whereby subjectivity 'remains open to change and redescription' by virtue of its refusal to inhabit static social categories (Khalip 3). In his study of such Romantic 'anonymity,' Khalip singles Shelley out for defining sympathy not as an interpersonal bond of mutual recognition but as a sensitivity to the elusiveness or inapprehensibility of the other and the self (see especially 98–9). While Khalip's account is finely attuned to the notes of skepticism about the self audible in 'On Life' and amplified in *A Defence of Poetry* and *Prometheus Unbound*, Shelley's frequent poetic and rhetorical recourse to the concept of selfhood, as well as his sense of the necessity of such a concept, remain to be reckoned with, especially as they pertain not just to ontological questions but also to political, linguistic, and cognitive ones.
11. For another major rebuttal of Clark and Chalmers's position, see Adams and Aizawa, who coin the phrase 'coupling-constitution fallacy' (11) for the slippage from the claim that a given environmental feature Y interacts with a cognitive process to the claim that Y is itself (part of) that process. Adams and Aizawa argue for the need to elaborate a 'mark of the cognitive' (10) – criteria for a process to count as cognitive – and emphasize the difference between extended cognitive systems (in which diverse elements outside the body and brain contribute causally to brain-bound cognitive processes) and a wholesale extension of cognition beyond the body and brain.
12. On the criteria of collective purpose and collective reasoning see Pettit; on the criterion of commitment to believing a given proposition see Gilbert.
13. See, for instance, Rupert, 'Minding' and 'Empirical Arguments.'
14. For a fuller account of positions and debates in the field of extended cognition, see Anderson et al., 'Distributed Cognition and the Humanities.'
15. See, notably, the essays collected in Anderson et al., *Distributed Cognition in Enlightenment and Romantic Culture*, on notions of brain–body–world interaction in European literature of the long eighteenth century; Taylor on Romanticism's 'expressivist' conception of the self as defined by inwardness

and emotion (368–90); Martin and Barresi on eighteenth-century associations of the self with the mind rather than the soul; and Keymer on the sense of an unstable, elusive, and profoundly imaginative self in both eighteenth-century fiction and Romantic autobiography. Wahrman, in his study of the late eighteenth-century transition from a sense of the self as fluid and performative to a sense of it as interiorized and stable, positions William Godwin as the representative of a vestigial and newly politicized insistence on mutability, but that 'counter trend' (310) could evidently be extended to encompass Shelley (making it questionable to what extent it constituted merely a vestige of older perspectives).

16. For fuller discussion of this distinction see Solomonescu 1123–4.
17. On this metonymic system see Peterfreund 249–66.
18. For a reading of *The Cenci* that emphasizes such conquest see, for instance, Hogle 147–62. On incest as an element of Shelley's attack on Christian theology in the drama, see Potkay.
19. The literalism is all the more emphatic if, as Curran suggests, blood is understood here as a 'euphemism for [...] semen' (116).
20. Henderson is therefore surely right that in the Cencis' world, 'one can easily make the mistake of overestimating the body's role in identity-formation' (112). Yet her argument that the tragedy turns on Beatrice's failure to bridge, by means of imagination, the divide between an inner, authentic self and its outer, theatrical embodiment stands in tension with Shelley's resistance to such dualism in *The Cenci* and elsewhere.
21. On Beatrice's mimicry of her father's speech, see also Bruhn, 'Prodigious mixtures' 750–3.
22. See, for instance, Hogle 155; Peterfreund 248–66; and Dempsey.
23. The unlikelihood of attempts at overt persuasion is implied by the relative lack of dialogue between Beatrice and her father, a lack paradoxically underscored by Shelley's choice of the dialogic genre of drama for his tragedy.
24. On group-think as the achievement of concurrence without regard to individual, potentially dissenting voices, see Theiner 307–8.
25. On cognitive 'coupling' see, for instance, Clark and Chalmers 8, 18. I borrow the concept of cognitive 'scaffolding' from Clark, who uses it in a wholly positive sense, as when he writes of linguistic scaffolding that it 'opens up' new 'opportunities' for thought, 'supports the development' of new expertise, and 'contribute[s]' to self-reflection (*Supersizing* 45). It is worth elaborating here on how Beatrice fulfills the criteria for cognitive extension. According to Clark and Chalmers, extension occurs when an environmental feature serves as a consistent, accessible, and trusted part of cognitive processing – conditions that may be fully met only in an 'unusually interdependent couple,' but that can be partially fulfilled in 'other social relationships' (17). Beatrice evidently does not trust her father (she is immediately suspicious of the motives for the banquet at which he announces the deaths of two sons [1.3.36–8]), but she can nevertheless be said to put trust in certain aspects of his ideology (such as the sanctity of a family's good name), and she certainly has direct access to his way of thinking, as well as a potentially long-standing reliance on it, as discussed above.

26. While one of Cenci's motivations for the rape is the transcendence of all moral codes and forms of authority (Dempsey 887–8), another is surely a transcendence of the death he knows is approaching, whether from old age or conspiracy. Not only does he hope to beget a child by Beatrice, but he also plans to incinerate his possessions and thus make the crime his sole legacy, 'an inheritance to strip / Its wearer bare as infamy' (IV, i, 61–2).
27. Lest the substitution of *heir* for *hair* seem too fanciful, it is worth nothing that the drama provides a bridge between the homonyms in Beatrice's reference to her 'entangled will' (III, i, 220) concerning the murder.
28. Orsino notably lays out the false alternatives on parricide or inaction when he remarks of Cenci's crime that it leaves Beatrice 'only one duty, how she may avenge,' her stepmother Lucretia 'but one refuge from ills ill endured,' and himself 'but one counsel' (III, i, 200–2). Beatrice similarly asks Marzio, 'Am I, or am I not / A parricide?' (V, ii, 156–7), as if the question admitted of a straightforward yes/no answer and not a 'restless and anatomizing casuistry.'
29. *The Cenci* thus explores the dark side of what Lakoff and Johnson have theorized as the bodily origins of the metaphors we use to conceptualize and navigate the world.
30. In this respect, the response is also distinct from the 'pernicious casuistry' of a Satan (or a Count Cenci), as well as from the 'sublime casuistry' that Shelley describes in a review of Godwin's *Mandeville* (but with reference to *Caleb Williams*) as 'persuad[ing] us personally to love' the criminal Falkland (*Prose* 309). For thoughtful disambiguation among these diverse forms of casuistry see Wasserman 115–28 (with emphasis on morality); and Chandler 498–515 (with emphasis on historicity).
31. On hair as a metaphor for social entanglement in the drama see Walker 240–5.
32. This is not to deny that in other works Shelley uses figuration to encourage cognitive and affective linkage. Carlson argues that simile is Shelley's preferred trope for achieving such effects because, by its use of a comparative *as* or *like*, it encourages awareness of the disparate objects thus linked (92–3).
33. The pun is noted by Reiman and Fraistat 195n9.
34. We might think of him on that issue, as Kenneth Neill Cameron describes him on numerous others, as 'noncommittal and agnostic ... because intellectual honesty demanded that he [... be] so' (158).

References

Adams, Frederick and Kenneth Aizawa. *The Bounds of Cognition*. Malden, MA: Blackwell, 2008.

Anderson, Miranda, George Rousseau, and Michael Wheeler, eds. *Distributed Cognition in Enlightenment and Romantic Culture*. Edinburgh: Edinburgh University Press, 2019.

Anderson, Miranda, Michael Wheeler, and Mark Sprevak. 'Distributed Cognition and the Humanities.' *Distributed Cognition in Enlightenment and Romantic Culture*. 1–17.

Bloom, Harold. 'The Unpastured Sea: An Introduction to Shelley.' *Romanticism and Consciousness*. Ed. Harold Bloom. New York: W. W. Norton, 1970. 374–401.
Bruhn, Mark J. 'Harmonious Madness: The Poetics of Analogy at the Limits of Blending Theory.' *Poetics Today* 32.4 (Winter 2011): 619–62.
—. '"Prodigious mixtures and confusions strange": The Self-Subverting Mixed Style of *The Cenci*.' *Poetics Today* 22.4 (Winter 2001): 713–63.
—. 'Shelley's Theory of Mind: From Radical Empiricism to Cognitive Romanticism.' *Poetics Today* 30.3 (Fall 2009): 373–422.
Cameron, Kenneth Neill. *Shelley: The Golden Years*. Cambridge, MA: Harvard University Press, 1974.
Carlson, Julie. 'Like Love: The Feel of Shelley's Similes.' *Romanticism and the Emotions*. Ed. Joel Faflak and Richard C. Sha. Cambridge: Cambridge University Press, 2014. 76–97.
Chandler, James. *England in 1819: The Politics of Literary Culture and the Case of Romantic Historicism*. Chicago: University of Chicago Press, 1998.
Cheeke, Stephen. 'Shelley's *The Cenci*: Economies of a "Familiar" Language.' *Keats–Shelley Journal* 47 (1998): 142–60.
Clark, Andy. *Supersizing the Mind: Embodiment, Action, and Cognitive Extension*. Oxford: Oxford University Press, 2008.
— and David Chalmers. 'The Extended Mind.' *Analysis* 58.1 (January 1998): 7–19.
Cox, Jeffrey N. *In the Shadows of Romance: Romantic Tragic Drama in Germany, England, and France*. Athens: Ohio State University Press, 1987.
Curran, Stuart. *Shelley's* Cenci: *Scorpions Ringed with Fire*. Princeton: Princeton University Press, 1970.
Dempsey, Sean. '*The Cenci*: Tragedy in a Secular Age.' *English Literary History* 79.4 (Winter 2012): 879–903.
'Equivocation, *n*.' *OED Online*. Oxford University Press, June 2020. 5 September 2020.
Gilbert, Margaret. 'Collective Epistemology.' *Episteme* 1.2 (October 2004): 95–107.
Hamilton, Paul. *Metaromanticism: Aesthetics, Literature, Theory*. Chicago: University of Chicago Press, 2003.
Henderson, Andrea K. *Romantic Identities: Varieties of Subjectivity, 1774–1830*. Cambridge: Cambridge University Press, 1996.
Hogle, Jerrold E. *Shelley's Process: Radical Transference and the Development of His Major Works*. New York: Oxford University Press, 1988.
Keymer, Thomas. 'The Subjective Turn.' *The Oxford Handbook of British Romanticism*. Ed. David Duff. Oxford: Oxford University Press, 2018. 311–26.
Khalip, Jacques. *Anonymous Life: Romanticism and Dispossession*. Stanford: Stanford University Press, 2009.
Lakoff, George and Mark Johnson. *Metaphors We Live By*. Chicago: University of Chicago Press, 1980.
Martin, Raymond and John Barresi. *Naturalization of the Soul: Self and Personal Identity in the Eighteenth Century*. London: Routledge, 2000.
Peterfreund, Stuart. *Shelley among Others: The Play of the Intertext and the Idea of Language*. Baltimore: Johns Hopkins University Press, 2002.

Pettit, Philip. 'Groups with Minds of Their Own.' *Socializing Metaphysics: The Nature of Social Reality.* Ed. Frederick F. Schmitt. Lanham, MD: Rowman and Littlefield, 2003. 167–93.

Potkay, Monica Brzezinski. 'Incest as Theology in Shelley's *The Cenci.*' *Wordsworth Circle* 35.2 (Spring 2004): 57–65.

'Prone, *adj.*' OED Online. Oxford University Press, June 2020. 5 September 2020.

Reiman, Donald H. and Neil Fraistat, eds. *Shelley's Poetry and Prose.* 2nd ed. New York: W. W. Norton, 2002.

Richardson, Alan. *British Romanticism and the Science of the Mind.* Cambridge: Cambridge University Press, 2001.

—. *A Mental Theater: Poetic Drama and Consciousness in the Romantic Age.* University Park: Pennsylvania State University Press, 1988.

Rossington, Michael, ed. *The Cenci: A Tragedy in Five Acts.* By Percy Bysshe Shelley. *The Poems of Shelley.* Vol. 2: *1817–1819.* Ed. Kelvin Everest and Geoffrey Matthews. Harlow: Longman, 2000. 713–875.

Rupert, Robert. *Cognitive Systems and the Extended Mind.* Oxford: Oxford University Press, 2009.

—. 'Empirical Arguments for Group Minds: A Critical Appraisal.' *Philosophy Compass* 6/9 (2011): 630–9.

—. 'Minding One's Cognitive Systems: When Does a Group of Minds Constitute a Single Cognitive Unit?' *Episteme* 1.3 (February 2005): 177–88.

Ruston, Sharon. *Shelley and Vitality.* 2005. Houndmills: Palgrave Macmillan, 2012.

Sha, Richard C. 'Blake and the Mark of the Cognitive: Notes Towards the Appearance of the Sceptical Subject.' *Distributed Cognition in Enlightenment and Romantic Culture.* 204–18.

Shelley, Percy. *Laon and Cythna.* Ed. Jack Donovan. *Poems of Shelley.* Vol. 2: *1817–1819.* Ed. Kelvin Everest and Geoffrey Matthews. Harlow: Longman, 2000. 10–250.

—. *Oedipus Tyrannus; or, Swellfoot the Tyrant. The Poems of Shelley.* Vol. 3: *1819–1820.* Ed. Jack Donovan, Cian Duffy, Kelvin Everest, and Michael Rossington. Harlow: Longman, 2011. 654–710.

—. *Shelley's Poetry and Prose.* Ed. Donald H. Reiman and Neil Fraistat. 2nd ed. New York: W. W. Norton, 2002.

—. *Shelley's Prose: The Trumpet of a Prophecy.* Ed. David Lee Clark. New York: New Amsterdam, 1988.

—. *St. Irvyne; or, The Rosicrucian: A Romance.* London: J. J. Stockdale, 1811. *Nineteenth Century Collections Online.* link.gale.com/apps/doc/UGTJMR745439889/NCCO?u=nd_ref&sid=gale_marc&xid=4e45b8ab&pg=162 (last accessed September 5, 2020).

Solomonescu, Yasmin. 'Percy Shelley's Revolutionary Periods.' *English Literary History* 83.4 (Winter 2016): 1105–33.

Taylor, Charles. *Sources of the Self: The Making of the Modern Identity.* Cambridge, MA: Harvard UP, 1989, repr. 2001.

Theiner, Georg. 'A Beginner's Guide to Group Minds.' *New Waves in Philosophy of Mind.* Ed. Mark Sprevak and Jesper Kallestrup. Houndmills: Palgrave Macmillan, 2014. 301–22.

Wahrman, Dror. *The Making of the Modern Self: Identity and Culture in Eighteenth-Century England*. New Haven, CT: Yale University Press, 2004.

Walker, Leila. 'Percy Bysshe Shelley and the Ekphrasis of Hair.' *European Romantic Review* 24.2 (2013): 231–50.

Wasserman, Earl R. *Shelley: A Critical Reading*. Baltimore: Johns Hopkins University Press, 1971.

Chapter 12

Gothic Ecologies of Mind

John Savarese

This chapter proposes that the gothic ballad revival, and the formal experimentation it engendered, also became an opportunity for Romantic-era writers to experiment with different models of mind. From the poems Matthew Lewis included in his novel *The Monk* to the 'new principle' of meter Samuel Taylor Coleridge claimed to have invented for 'Christabel,' metrical inventiveness was one way that poets gave shape to a gothic interest in alterity and idiosyncrasy.[1] In his reading of gothic metrical experiments, Daniel Robinson has described this neogothic love of nonce meters – poetic forms that invent their own idiosyncratic lines and stanzas – as 'weird form,' aligned with a broader interest in historical difference and gothic excess (155). On my argument, that interest in 'weird form' also had implications for longer-standing conversations about the history of cognition. In particular, this chapter reads gothic imitations as a response to an earlier moment in the eighteenth-century ballad revival, which had framed ballads as the products of an early phase in cultural development – and which, consequently, read them as artifacts shaped by common, pre-cultural features of the human mind. Joseph Addison's emphasis on ballads' formal simplicity and universalizable sentiment, for example, implied a uniformitarian account of mental development, where simplicity of form and feeling pointed back to a common origin point. Another way to put this is that eighteenth-century writings on the ballad revival often double as claims about the history of cognition. Those claims frequently emphasize continuity over time: literary artifacts were made to uncover and naturalize aspects of mental functioning that came to appear universal, timeless, and embodied. Neogothic experiments, in contrast, show that ballad studies also afforded a different approach to the history of cognition.

The idea that poetic meter reflected the rhythmic, embodied movements of thought itself had a long history in eighteenth-century aesthetics. Recently, that attention to rhythmic thinking has helped recover

Romantic writers' commitment to the mind's embodiment: to the idea that thinking happens in and through the body's rhythms.[2] Yet even as gothic nonce meters and irregularities suggest that kind of embodied movement – in Robinson's words, marking 'the pulses and beats of English meters and, at the same time, in the human psyche' – they can still seem strangely decorporealizing, especially when the 'weird' seems to pull in the direction of 'other-worldly or subconscious sources' or an 'evocation of the uncanny' (164). While the eighteenth-century gothic is invested in both of those things, this chapter argues that 'gothic' also became a keyword attached to a different picture of the mind's foundations and history: it often designated a medieval moment aligned not with cognitive origins, or with persistent features of psychology across time; but with a middle stage of cultural growth, or even overgrowth, characterized by pervasive social institutions and a maximalist or baroque aesthetics. Accordingly, gothic revivalism also pointed toward a different model of mind: one that was thoroughly embodied, but that also saw bodies and minds as entangled with their local environments.

In keeping with the gothic interest in surfaces, material institutions, and aesthetic excess, the gothic ballad revival became a place where the logic of an embodied mind could be pushed even further, beyond the boundaries of the body altogether. To invoke the terminology of philosophers Andy Clark and David Chalmers, neogothicism asks readers to 'extend' the mind out into the built environment and its artifacts. As they drew on earlier theories of the literary mind, gothic revivalists could have it both ways: poetic rhythm could be an embodied activity that spoke to the mind's underlying structures; and at the same time, it could offer evidence about cognition's dependency upon external, scaffolding artifacts, and about the ways minds changed with changing cultural and technological environments. The gothic, in other words, offers an alternative way to frame Romanticism's connection of the inner mind and the outer world, one that differs substantially from the dialectic of mind and nature emphasized by many of the essays in *Romanticism and Consciousness* (1970). Instead, gothic imitations and experiments can highlight another impulse at work in Romantic poetics, one that pictured thought itself as a less centralized, more distributed or 'ecological' process. In their emphasis on historical variation and idiosyncrasy, gothic metrical experiments imply that the mind has a diverse history.

The first part of this chapter surveys a long-running eighteenth-century conversation that made historical poetry evidence about the human mind's foundations and its historical stages of development. Joseph Addison's early eighteenth-century essays on ballad aesthetics made popular poetry a window into basic, universal elements of human nature, and pointedly opposed that 'natural' aesthetic to gothic poetry's 'wrong, artificial taste.' However, for other writers, gothic artificiality and excess spoke to the way that the apparatus of culture – including ballads themselves – structured and scaffolded the individual mind's development. That approach to artifact-mediated cognition became particularly pronounced later in the century, as I will show in reference to Anna Letitia Barbauld's remarks on gothic forms and institutions. The second part of the chapter turns from those histories of artifact-mediated cognition to the experimental verse of one of Barbauld's own students, William Taylor. In his influential translation of the German ballad 'Lenora,' Taylor negotiates between standard English common meter and a reconstructed accentual meter, in ways that draw on Barbauld's theories of poetic form and mental development. Like Coleridge in his Preface to 'Christabel,' Taylor correlates looser, accentual rhythms with an earlier moment in the mind's progress from 'barbarous' liberty to developed civilization. Ultimately, I argue, gothic experiments like Taylor's say less about Romanticism's drama of subjectivity than about an overlapping interest in cognition's historical variability, environmental embeddedness, and material contingency.

Poetic Histories and the Scaffolded Mind

Against the background of ballad antiquarianism, gothic revivalists could have it both ways: poetry could be an embodied activity that spoke to the mind's underlying, pre-cultural foundations; and, at the same time, it could offer evidence of the ways that cognition was itself culturally dependent or historically contingent. If ballad simplicity was aligned with common humanity (those ways antiquarians asserted we are all alike because of presumed universal properties of the human mind), then its opposite – gothic excess and idiosyncrasy – afforded a different model of mind, with as much emphasis on historical variation as transhistorical consistency, and with as much of a stake in externalist accounts of cognition as internalist accounts.

I begin with the first of those propositions: that ballads seemed to be a window into pre-cultural, universal features of the human mind. By the later eighteenth century, ballads had been made into a type of empirical evidence about human nature.[3] For Addison, ballads track general, universal principles of taste that have been features of the human mind from the beginning and have not changed over time. One common way to put this was that ballads were not just cultural artifacts, but could also be considered as natural specimens that revealed human nature.

So, to explain ballads' universal appeal, Addison asserts that nothing artificial could please people of different times and different social positions: 'it is only nature that can have that effect' (383). Thomas Percy, who differs from Addison in some important ways, still says that his poetic relics 'are presented ... not as labours of art, but as effusions of nature, showing the first efforts of ancient genius' (vi). On these arguments, the ballad is a window into early phases of development, at once rudimentary and – for that very reason – frameable in terms of underlying or universal properties of natural taste or genius.

This brand of poetic universalism is a central part of the story of the ballad revival, but it is a part of the story for which the gothic ballad, in particular, is an uncomfortable fit. In fact, in his first 'Chevy Chase' paper, Addison takes great pains to distinguish those universally human ballads from a later strain of gothic artifice. If ballads display the 'essential and inherent perfection of simplicity of thought,' then, in contrast, Addison writes, 'that which I call the Gothic manner in writing' is unnatural, acculturated, and artificial. Where ballad aesthetics are universally pleasing, gothic mannerisms please 'only such as have formed to themselves a wrong artificial taste' (378). Addison is referring to affected, ornamental, or overly complex writing, at the level of style or sentiment: anything, that is, that departs from the 'simplicity of thought' that pleases the universal taste (378). 'Gothic' in this sense designates a state of cultural growth or development that was – at least for the aesthetics of simplicity or nature – problematically aligned with the unnatural and artificial. In that sense, ballad studies' characterization of gothic style links up to a broader eighteenth-century gothic imaginary with its emphasis on material ritual, architectural enclosures, and aesthetic excess. That focus on the built environment pushes in the direction of external institutions and influences, the cultural trappings that an account like Addison's frames as categorically distinct from human nature and from the mind's native dispositions.

Addison's claims about natural taste focus on matters of diction and sentiment, with a preference for simplicity on both counts. Eighteenth-century poetic theory extended that link between poetic form and original cognition to include questions of rhythm, or of the movement of thought. For Johann Gottfried Herder, the ancient ode reflected the original form of the faculty of sensibility, with its irregular, spasmodic structure echoing the rhythmic movements of consciousness itself ('Fragment' 36). For Adam Ferguson, early poetry is 'occasioned, probably, by the physical connections ... between the emotions of a heated imagination, and the impressions received from musical and pathetic sounds' (312). For John Aikin, brother of the poet Anna Letitia Barbauld, the historical origins of poetic language are to be found in 'the effects which the passions produce upon the body ... the fluttering pulse, the changing colour, the feverish glow, the failing heart and the confused senses,' and as a result the history of poetics makes possible a 'general deduction of the progress of the mind through the different stages of poetical composition' (6, 21). In other words, there is something about the early, immature, uncultivated, unrestrained mind that generates the stylistic features of poetic language, and so poetic language in turn tells us about what the mind is like, at base. These arguments can sound quite essentializing, insofar as their turns to embodied cognition imply a cognitive architecture and a developmental schema that all people are presumed to have in common.

Yet studies of poetry and cognition have also recovered the way that such theories can frame thinking as a set of discrete, individuated processes that happen in language and unfold in real time. This is the basis, for example, for Simon Jarvis's argument for 'prosody as cognition' and for the studies of historical meters that follow from that argument.[4] More recently, Jonathan Kramnick has offered a reminder that an embodied approach to poetic cognition does not just stop at the boundaries of the body itself, but can extend beyond the body's limits to include environmental objects. In James Thomson's poetic apprehensions of the landscape, for example, Kramnick identifies the marks of 'an antirepresentational model of perceptual experience' that emerged in response to eighteenth-century empiricist philosophy. Against the model of perception as an internal representation of the outside world, eighteenth-century locodescriptive poetry helped develop an account of perception as situated or enactive – for example, in the way that visual perception of a distant object can be calibrated or altered by changing one's position relative to that object. 'With its emphasis on skilled action and its embrace of naïveté,' Kramnick argues, that poetic approach 'has some bearing on the way we now talk about ecologically situated or embodied cognition' (57). Kramnick's study of locodescriptive verse points to features of eighteenth-century poetry that capture cognition's enactive dimensions – that is, the aspects for which an enactivist approach like Alva Noë's offers a good explanation, and where cognitive acts are best seen not as internal or computational processes but as bodily interactions with the surrounding environment.

Moving from locodescriptive poetry to the ballad revival, I would suggest, highlights a related but distinct set of approaches to distributed cognition. Put simply, eighteenth-century ballad studies developed approaches to cognition that highlighted ways of thinking with and through traditional forms. Thinking with ballad form, or with the building blocks of traditional balladic materials, was also an environmentally or ecologically situated kind of thinking, but one that relied more directly on the built environment of artifacts. As an artifact-focused field, ballad antiquarians' theories of cognition are better captured by 'embedded' or 'extended' approaches to distributed cognition. In their introduction to the eighteenth-century background of distributed cognition, Miranda Anderson, Michael Wheeler, and Mark Sprevak suggest that there is 'a natural route from embodied cognition to ... *embedded* cognition,' a view which holds that 'intelligent thought and action is regularly, and perhaps sometimes necessarily, causally dependent on the bodily exploitation of certain environmental props and scaffolds' (3). Those props might include tools, memory aids, or indeed language, insofar as these things support and structure cognition or (more radically, for proponents of 'extended' cognition) directly bear some of the process's cognitive load.

Embedded or extended approaches to cognition are particularly relevant to eighteenth-century ballad antiquarianism because of that field's investment in cultural artifacts, and because of its claims about how the history of literature tracks the history of intellectual development. These approaches are also particularly relevant for ballad studies because of a long-standing recognition of the ways that the ballad revival set collective or traditional models of creativity against models of individual genius.[5] To students of the ballad revival, the idea that thinking recruits and relies on the scaffolding of received tradition might seem like second nature. Read this way, ballads would not only need to speak to the history of cognition because (as they did for Addison) they pointed the way back to the mind's underlying, unchanging foundations. They would also speak to the history of cognition because they were artifacts of a cultural environment that was part of the medium in which thinking happened, and were continuous with its embodied components. In this sense, if gothic style speaks to an artificial taste or the trappings of culture, those exteriors and that artificiality were not clearly outside or separate from the historical shape of cognition itself.

This focus on exteriors came into sharper focus – and was frequently recuperated – in the decades of the gothic revival. For example, in her 1773 essay 'On Monastic Institutions,' Anna Letitia Barbauld reframes gothic artifacts as a technology of mental functioning and growth. The essay appears in *Miscellaneous Pieces in Prose*, a collaborative volume with her brother, John Aikin, to which Barbauld also contributed an imitation of ancient poetry in the style of Macpherson's Ossian; a gothic tale; and celebrations of technological improvements, for a volume that blends glimpses of human origins together with meditations on culturally scaffolded development.[6] The essay itself performs a heavily situated kind of thinking, a meditation made possible, and directly prompted, by the environment in which it takes place. It begins: 'I happened the other day to take a solitary walk amongst the venerable ruins of an old Abbey. The stillness and solemnity of the place were favourable to thought, and naturally led me to a train of ideas relative to the scene' (88). Barbauld explicitly describes her meditation as a 'train of thought' that is prompted and carried along by the external scene, as it acts upon learned and taught predispositions such as her religious upbringing. The ruins initially prompt a feeling of Protestant superiority over these relics of the Catholic past, as 'like a good protestant, I began to indulge a secret triumph in the ruin of so many structures which I had always considered as the haunts of ignorance and superstition' (88–9). The train of thought then changes rails, as the particular contemplative mood those ruins encourage leads Barbauld to soften her tone and to think about her relation to history: the way the monastery played a role, however distantly or externally, in her own mental development.

As the scene-prompted meditation took a different turn, she 'gradually fell into a different train of thought' that led her to reconsider the ruins (90). Rather than merely offering 'to remind us from what we have escaped, and make posterity for ever thankful for this fairer age of liberty and light,' the monastery ultimately serves as a relic of an earlier age's distributed cognitive apparatus (90). In this second phase of the essay, the monastery comes to feature as a repository or safeguard of memory, and an important link in the chain that would eventually lead to enlightened modernity. Specifically, Barbauld writes:

> [T]o this it is owing, to the books and learning preserved in these repositories, that we were not obliged to begin anew, and trace every art by slow and uncertain steps from its first origin. Science, already full grown and vigorous, awaked as from a trance, shook her pinions, and soon soared to the heights of knowledge. Nor was she entirely idle during her recess. (93)

In the 'trance' of that medieval moment – a period during which the progress of collective intellect seemed to be paused, or asleep – the monastery functioned as a sort of unconscious machinery, an apparatus that was not 'idle' but that kept working in the background. In short, Barbauld's essay shows that there was a desire to reclaim gothic forms of external or alienated knowledge and to see them as being part of the story of individual intellect, rather than being at odds with it.

A similar impulse is behind many of the gothic ballad revival's discussions of metrical form: in the conversation about imitating or translating gothic ballads, the key points of reference were common meter, the specific accentual-syllabic form most often associated with popular poetry of a distinctively British stamp; and accentual meter, a more general category aligned with earlier moments in the history of British literature. In the next section of this chapter, I want to point to an example of how experimenting with accentual meter drew on a few different, overlapping approaches to what John Aikin called those 'stages of poetical composition' (21).

Gothic Exteriors, Gothic Ballads

The English ballad revival received a major infusion from the German gothic tradition in 1796, due to a translation of Gottfried August Bürger's 'Lenora.' Appropriately, the translation was the work of one of Barbauld's students, William Taylor, who had studied with her at the Palgrave Dissenting academy. As her niece, Lucy Aikin, recounts in the memoir that prefaces the 1825 *Works of Anna Letitia Barbauld*, two of Barbauld's students at the Palgrave Academy became well-known poets:

> It fortunately happened, that two of the eight pupils with which Palgrave school commenced, were endowed with abilities worthy of the culture which such an instructress could alone bestow. One of these, William Taylor, Esq. of Norwich, known by his English Synonyms, his exquisite Iphigenia in Tauris from the German, his Leonora from Bürger, and many other fruits of genius and extensive learning, has constantly acknowledged her, with pride and affection, for the 'mother of his mind.' (xxiv–v)

The other, Frank Sayers, took his medical degree and subsequently became a well-known writer of mythological poetry, especially with his *Dramatic Sketches of the Ancient Northern Mythology* (1790). Lucy Aikin tells us that he, too, attributed his abilities to 'the lessons in English composition superintended by Mrs. Barbauld' (xxv).

The story continues further, as a chain or a network of influence remediated by many hands. First, Taylor named Barbauld as the 'mother of [his] mind.' Subsequently, Barbauld claimed to propagate that influence further when, visiting Edinburgh and finding herself in the house of philosopher Dugald Stewart, she recited Taylor's 'Lenora' translation. Stewart subsequently recited it to Walter Scott, who some years later claimed that as a result of this second- or third-hand delivery of the ballad, Barbauld (or, rather, Taylor via Barbauld) 'made me a poet.' Word of this claim reached Barbauld, who closed the loop by passing the news back to Taylor in 1815, writing: 'are you aware that *you* made Walter Scott a poet?'[7] The questions around Barbauld's approach to neogothic literature, then, are also part of a fairly canonical account of the lineage of Romantic-era gothic imitations. It is also appropriate that this important development in the gothic ballad tradition should form a node connecting Stewart (the coiner of the term 'conjectural history') with Barbauld, Taylor, and Scott.

Taylor thought a lot about prosody. He wrote about Bürger's own stylistic irregularity in the original German text, and argued that Bürger's 'extraordinary powers of language are founded on a rejection of the conventional phraseology of regular poetry, in favour of popular forms of expression, caught by the listening artist from the voice of agitated nature.'[8] As for Addison, 'popular' form for Taylor offers a conduit back to nature and away from convention. For his part, in his translation of the poem, Taylor approximated those popular forms by using English common meter, though he also introduced a good deal of extrametrical substitution to create an impression of irregularity, motion, or variation. As an example, here is the poem's description of the ghostly William, as his spectral body melts away to reveal his material remains beneath:

> And when hee from his steede alytte,
> His armour, black as cinder,
> Did moulder, moulder all awaye,
> As were it made of tinder.
>
> His head became a naked skull;
> Nor haire nor eyne had hee:
> His body grew a skeleton,
> Whilome so blithe of blee. (237–44)

Based on the sound of these lines, it is surprising to hear this poem described, in an early review by Edward Whyte, as possessing 'the genuine unaffected simplicity of our old English Ballad.'[9] It is hardly as irregular or idiosyncratic as the poems Matthew Lewis would become known for. Yet 'unaffected' seems a stretch, too, partly because of the archaisms and inverted syntax, and partly because there is something about the common meter that is not quite right. As Daniel Robinson suggests, Taylor 'rejects foot verse in favor of syncopated effects that resist conventional scansion and that imitate the archaic style' of Percy's *Reliques of Ancient English Poetry*, largely by creating lines with an 'anapestic feel' (160). The ghost of triple meter is present in these lines not just due to their extrametrical or 'feminine' endings, but also because the stress in these iambic lines often falls on short vowels and weak syllables, as in the line 'his body grew a skeleton' (243). The effect is of an older, accentual verse straining against the common meter that seeks to contain it.

The readiest way to interpret that conflict might be as a struggle between an individual poet's movements of mind and the communal or received forms into which the poem needs to be fitted. That is the struggle that John Hollander, writing in the *Romanticism and Consciousness* volume this current book revisits, called the tension between a poet's specific linguistic choices and the higher-order 'metrical contract' that establishes a poem's 'basic schematic fabric' (183). To be sure, Taylor's metrical substitutions may owe a lot to the notion that early verse form had a looser relationship to that metrical contract. Yet there is also a sense that Taylor is not just varying the schematic of common meter, but is gesturing toward a different schematic altogether, or at least a different moment in its historical development. The poem's meter seems meant to suggest something eccentric or idiosyncratic, but at the same time it is presented as a gothic form that should be typical or representative of a particular era. In that sense, the poem's stylistic eccentricity would match the eccentricity of its content—in the quoted passage, for instance, the play with superstition, or with historical differences in concepts of matter and spirit. To that end, it is worth noting that Taylor's translation choices actually emphasize the materiality of the ghost beyond Bürger's original: where the German text frames William's apparition as an allegorical figure of death in general – a skeleton that appears with the stock symbols of hourglass and scythe – Taylor emphasizes that it is William himself. Taylor's English version introduces more room for ambiguity: 'And inn his witherde hand you might / The scythe and hour-glasse see' (247–8). It is as if William seems, to the beholder, as if he could be the very image of death. It seems relevant that rather than a mere apparition or allegorical figure, Taylor toyed with the idea of an embodied, material revenant that melts away before the reader's eyes.

In its gothic content as well as its style, Taylor's version of 'Lenora' leans heavily on the idea of an early, rudimentary phase of literary production, marked by primitive superstition as well as an only loosely or incipiently regular meter. In both of those senses, the poem suggests an early, undeveloped style in the process of development or cultivation. It also suggests a text that is undecided about some of its historically specific features: whether they should be understood as early and universal – a common belief in returning spirits; a simple, early-intuited common meter – or whether they were being singled out as the characteristics of a strange and singular moment. If Taylor's metrical substitutions create an effect of straining against common meter, it is tempting to read that push-and-pull, too, in terms of eighteenth-century arguments about early poetry's looseness of form. For example, it is easy to imagine Taylor's prosody as reaching back to a primordial liberty or irregularity – with Herder, a poetics of the spirit and not of the 'dead letter' ('Extract' 156); or with Adam Ferguson, 'the language of early ages' which is 'varied and free,' and 'allows liberties, which to the poet of after-times, are denied' (314).

One major context that encourages that reading – perhaps the best-known association between accentualism and primordial 'liberty' – is Coleridge's Preface to 'Christabel,' in which he claims to have invented a 'new principle' of meter for the poem (435).[10] A brief turn to that Preface will help clarify the context of Taylor's 'Lenora' translation and, more broadly, the tension between ideas about historically specific forms and the lure of early liberty *as* form. Coleridge's supposedly new metrical principle – 'namely, of counting in each line the accents, not the syllables' – has been variously described as an assertion of the poet's autonomous, form-giving imagination; and as a nod to an older, traditional type of accentualism (435). Paul Fussell, for example, suggests that Coleridge's remarks on 'Christabel' capture 'the essence of the accentual aesthetic, the malleability of the prosody to the "Passion and Meaning" of the poetry' (151). Insofar as this flexibility grants Coleridge license to shape the poem as he deems necessary, it reinforces what Kevis Goodman has called a Coleridgean poetics of the 'free spirit;' and what Margaret Russett has described – in reference to this specific passage from the Preface to 'Christabel' – as a defense of the individual will in the face of received or determined poetic forms. In Russett's words, Coleridge's faith here is in the way that 'a truly original spirit would imbue an iterable pattern with unaccountable variation' (75). Moreover, on Russett's reading, Coleridge's motivation here has to do specifically with overcoming the externally determined or distributed nature of ballad composition: he 'sophisticates the rude accentualism of balladry' and introduces a 'law of license or self-abrogation, by which the irregularities of passion are reinscribed as the transcendence of automatism' (83). As in his remarks on the 'gothic mind,' Coleridge's tactic seems to be to reframe things that seem to be deterministic or automatic in terms of a free spirit.[11]

Recruiting accentual aesthetics in this way is characteristic of what John Hollander, in that *Romanticism and Consciousness* essay on 'Romantic Verse Form and the Metrical Contract,' calls a particularly Romantic temptation. For Hollander, a poet's variation of stress and a (perhaps impassioned) strain against the metrical grid are not, properly speaking, metrical features at all, but are among the 'mysterious choices which must occur in actual composition' as a poet writes within the constraints of a chosen meter (183). Hollander takes pains to separate Romantic metrical inventiveness from the claim to free spirit that he thinks Romantic writers frequently mistake it for – when William Blake, for example, announces a metrical liberty-taking 'in the guise of a declaration of rhythmic independence,' but '[w]hat emerges from this experimentation' really turns out, like Coleridge's experiment in 'Christabel,' to be more of 'a commitment to a traditional-sounding accentualism' (198, 196).

Hollander is right that there is a tendency in Romantic poetics – as this chapter shows in Taylor and Coleridge – to reduce metrical experimentation to accentualism, and to do so in the interest of an ideology of the free spirit. That tendency was conditioned by eighteenth-century antiquarian poetics, which framed ancient or early poetic forms as irregular and rudimentary because they were closer to the mind's underlying, original conditions. But that impulse was not the only one in play. What is more interesting, for my purposes, is the other principle at work in gothic metrical experiments: the idea that there is a multiplicity of alternate metrical patterns that could be mined or simulated from the past, and which could be aligned with discrete moments in the history of cognition.

Eric Weiskott suggests what that alternative might look like in his study 'Early English Meter as a Way of Thinking.' Though that essay examines historical medieval poetics rather than its Romantic imitations and reimaginings, I would suggest that Weiskott's approach to early English meter – as a kind of a thinking made possible by a historically specific use of an available form – matches a different, more diversitarian impulse in neogothic poetics.[12] Weiskott's basic premise is that poetic form is a part of the thought it enables. Medieval 'alliterative meter,' for example, 'does not think the same way pentameter thinks' (43). From this historicizing perspective, using an accentual meter would represent an individual, phenomenologically distinct type of thinking, but one that should also be considered 'a historically mediated event that occurs in the minds of poets, scribes, and readers' through that deployment of linguistic, textual, and artifactual form (Weiskott 43).

By way of conclusion, I would suggest that Taylor's (if not Coleridge's) imitation of archaic meter is built on a similar premise about the work of poetic form and its historical variations. That desire for a historically specific, scaffolding medium is there, in Taylor's 'Lenora' translation, though it may also come under the sway of an ideology of primitive poetic liberty. Romantic-era gestures toward accentualism may often be committed, at least at some level, to the idea of a universally shared condition of human freedom. But just as important was an orientation toward a past made up of a proliferation of differences: differences which were not just the singular acts of free spirits, but that represented a plurality of external forms that gave the history of literature, and the history of cognition, its changing and contextually specific shape. In this sense, the question for Romantic-era gothic imitations is the one that Noel Jackson has asked in *Science and Sensation in Romantic Poetry*: 'Is the principal function of meter, then, to reinforce existing norms and [what Wordsworth calls] "known habits of association"? Or is meter rather intended, through formal innovation and experiment, to loosen our unconscious attachment to those conventions?' (127). In the context of gothic imitation and experimentation, a different way to put this would be that meter was not, in all of these cases, just the 'basic schematic fabric' against which the individual poet always strains (Hollander 183). Rather, it was also a marker of historical difference that let readers imagine the mind, itself, as having a history in the first place.

Finally, then, I am not convinced that what is going on in Taylor's metrical scheme – or in Matthew Lewis's nonce meters or other instances of gothic 'weird form' – works exclusively according to that principle of ancient liberty we tend to associate with Coleridge's Preface to 'Christabel.' It may have more to do with the 'set of critics' Coleridge is pushing back against in that Preface. He is proactively defending himself against any charge of having plagiarized that metrical plan, and notes that critics these days tend to balk at the very idea of an 'original' poetic idea:

> For there is amongst us a set of critics, who seem to hold, that every possible thought and image is traditional; who have no notion that there are such things as fountains in the world, small as well as great; and who would therefore charitably derive every rill they behold flowing, from a perforation made in some other man's tank. (434)

Coleridge may just be taking aim at a straw target here: at his own caricature of the antiquarian or communalist, who denies that any mind is autonomous unto itself, and who thinks any thought in one mind – and, crucially, the rhythmic shaping of that thinking, too – must have come from some other, external location. But what I hope this chapter has started to do is to recover more about this discussion Coleridge was pushing back against, where experimental meters might have been just as easily recruited to histories of an external or traditional mind. Taylor's varied, irregular take on common meter might not be best read as a Coleridgean assertion of the individual will, or the particular cadences, fits, and starts the poet deems appropriate to the passion expressed. It is also possible that the idiosyncrasy is doing the work of extravagant and traditional form, of something collectively mediated. Specifically, in keeping with developmentalist accounts of language and of verse form, it might be a reconstruction of a certain stage in the development of common meter, and a reminder that the external, traditional, or collective component of individual thinking is not fixed, stable, or singular. The proliferation of neogothic 'nonce meters' would not be, in that case, a throwback to the poetic freedom of a barbarous age, but could also be a gesture toward a wider taxonomy of traditional forms, considered as forms of cultural growth. Like Barbauld's monastery, they would still tell us about the history of mind; but rather than sketching the big picture – what John Aikin calls a 'general deduction of the progress of the mind through the different stages of poetical composition' – it would focus in on its local histories, microhistories, or alternate histories (21).

Another way to put this would be that the gothic ballad revival discovers the cognitive to have a historical, materially embedded component in the first place. In tandem with the earlier, Addisonian focus on the timeless and unchanging, the gothic emphasis of historical difference gives rise to a method closer to what Alan Richardson has termed 'cognitive historicism.'[13] Like the cognitive historicist, gothic revivalists set a synchronic concept of human nature in dialogue with the mind's diachronic and changing features, and show, as Richardson puts it, that 'even aspects of mind and mental activity that seem to occur with minimal variance over time and across cultures have histories.' To some degree this is a question of setting cognition in context: of recognizing that any stable or unchanging feature of the mind is still 'interpreted, represented, and valued in relation to specific historical and cultural milieus' (Richardson 16). But even beyond that, the gothic ballad further suggests that cognition itself changes with those milieus. Collectors and imitators of gothic ballads still point to a developmental history of human intellect, but their version of that history is not marked as clearly by a categorical distinction between foundational or 'primitive' features of mind on the one hand, and later cultural growth on the other. In keeping with theories of an embedded or extended mind, the context or milieu is *part of* the cognition. This shift in recent cognitive theory – the turn to distributed cognition – is also a shift that can be seen in some facets of eighteenth-century literary antiquarianism. Gothic ballads, in particular, map out the common territory that some of these approaches share. Gothic prosody, for example, points in a few possible directions at once. By invoking ideas about primitive liberty, their rhythms point in the direction of enactive, situated cognition: of cognitive acts that depend on their shape, on their unfolding in sound and embodied utterance. At the same time, by invoking a background of traditional, gradually shifting received forms and meters, these poems also acknowledge the facets of poetic cognition that might more properly be referred to as embedded or extended: the way that, in its rhythmic movements and utterances, the mind leans on an existing set of received scaffolding structures. As a result, gothic experiments with meter were also experiments with models of cognition. They show how the conceptual vocabulary of an earlier era might help map out the points of connection or convergence between more recent theories, and how those theories might in turn speak to the history of literary forms.

Notes

1. On Lewis's 'Alonzo metre,' as typified in his poem 'Alonzo the Brave and Fair Imogine,' see Robinson 158–60. For Coleridge's claim to a new metrical principle, see 'Christabel' 435.
2. See Richardson, *British Romanticism* 66–92. On later nineteenth-century movements that use meter in similar ways see Rudy.
3. On the relation between ballad antiquarianism and 'conjectural histories' of human nature see McLane, *Romanticism* 43–83; Regan; and Savarese. On Addison and Percy in this regard see Savarese 25–36.
4. See, for example, Weiskott, discussed below.
5. See especially McLane, *Balladeering* and Newman.
6. On the relation between 'On Monastic Institutions' and Barbauld's broader approach to cultural scaffolding, see Savarese 89–90.
7. On this anecdote (which appears in slightly different versions in Scott's 1820 *Miscellaneous Poems* and his 1830 'Essay on Imitations of the Ancient Ballad') see McCarthy 353n51.
8. *Monthly Magazine* (March, 1796) 117.
9. For a discussion of Whyte's remarks see Jacobus 222.
10. For a more material connection between Coleridge's poetic theory and Taylor's 'Lenora,' see John Livingston Lowes on Coleridge's response to the translation (*The Road to Xanadu* 308n111).
11. See *Literary Remains* 1.68.
12. I should note that I am thinking here of Romantic diversitarianism as discussed by Manu Chander in a recent essay on A. O. Lovejoy: as a historiographical impulse that might not be as distinct from 'nationalistic narcissism' as one might assume (299).
13. See Richardson, *Neural Sublime* 1–16.

References

Addison, Joseph. *Selections from Addison's Papers*. Ed. Thomas Arnold. Oxford: Clarendon Press, 1907.

Aikin, John. *Essays on Song-Writing*. London: Joseph Johnson, 1772.

Anderson, Miranda, Michael Wheeler, and Mark Sprevak. 'Distributed Cognition and the Humanities,' *Distributed Cognition in Enlightenment and*

Romantic Culture. Ed. Miranda Anderson, George Rousseau, and Michael Wheeler. Edinburgh: Edinburgh University Press, 2019.

Barbauld, Anna Letitia. 'On Monastic Institutions,' *Miscellaneous Pieces in Prose. Ed.* John Aikin and Anna Letitia Aikin. London: Joseph Johnson, 1773. 88–118.

—. *Works of Anna Letitia Barbauld*. Ed. Lucy Aikin. London: Longman, 1825.

Chander, Manu Samriti. 'Romantic Diversitarianism: Problems and Promises.' *European Romantic Review* 31.3 (2020): 295–300.

Clark, Andy and David Chalmers. 'The Extended Mind.' *Analysis* 58.1 (January 1998): 7–19.

Coleridge, Samuel Taylor. 'Christabel.' *Lyrical Ballads 1798 and 1800*. 434–52.

—. *The Literary Remains of Samuel Taylor Coleridge*. Ed. Henry Nelson Coleridge. London: Pickering, 1836.

Ferguson, Adam. *An Essay on the History of Civil Society*. 2nd ed. London: Miller and Cadell, 1768.

Fussell, Paul. *Theory of Prosody in Eighteenth-Century England*. Hamden: Archon, 1966.

Goodman, Kevis. 'Reading Motion: Coleridge's "Free Spirit" and its Medical Background.' *European Romantic Review* 26.3 (May 2015): 349–56.

Herder, Johann Gottfried. 'Extract from a Correspondence on Ossian and the Songs of Ancient Peoples.' *German Aesthetic and Literary Criticism: Winckelmann, Lessing, Hamann, Herder, Schiller and Goethe*. Ed. H. B. Nisbet. Cambridge: Cambridge University Press, 1985. 154–61.

—. 'Fragment of a Treatise on the Ode.' *Selected Early Works, 1764–1767: Addresses, Essays, and Drafts; Fragments on Recent German Literature*. Ed. Ernest A. Menze and Karl Menges. Trans. Ernest A. Menze and Michael Palma. University Park: Pennsylvania State University Press, 1992. 35–51.

Hollander, 'Romantic Verse Form and the Metrical Contract.' *Romanticism and Consciousness*. Ed. Harold Bloom. New York: W. W. Norton, 1970. 181–200.

Jackson, Noel. *Science and Sensation in Romantic Poetry*. Cambridge: Cambridge University Press, 2008.

Jacobus, Mary. *Tradition and Experiment in Wordsworth's Lyrical Ballads*. Oxford: Clarendon Press, 1976.

Jarvis, Simon. 'Prosody as Cognition.' *Critical Quarterly* 40.3 (Autumn 1998): 1–14.

Kramnick, Jonathan. *Paper Minds: Literature and the Ecology of Consciousness*. Chicago: University of Chicago Press, 2018.

Lowes, John Livingston. *The Road to Xanadu: A Study in the Ways of the Imagination*. 1927. Princeton: Princeton University Press, 2014.

McCarthy, William. *Anna Letitia Barbauld: Voice of the Enlightenment*. Baltimore: Johns Hopkins University Press, 2008.

McLane, Maureen N. *Balladeering, Minstrelsy, and the Making of British Romantic Poetry*. Cambridge: Cambridge University Press, 2008.

—. *Romanticism and the Human Sciences: Poetry, Population, and the Discourse of the Species*. Cambridge: Cambridge University Press, 2000.

Newman, Steve. *Ballad Collection, Lyric, and the Canon*. Philadelphia: University of Pennsylvania Press, 2007.

Noë, Alva. *Action in Perception*. Cambridge, MA: MIT Press, 2004.

Percy, Thomas. *Reliques of Ancient English Poetry.* London: Dodsley, 1765.
Regan, John. 'Ambiguous Progress and its Poetic Correlatives: Percy's *Reliques* and Stadial History.' *ELH* 81.2 (Summer 2014): 615–34.
Richardson, Alan. *British Romanticism and the Science of the Mind.* Cambridge: Cambridge University Press, 2001.
—. *The Neural Sublime: Cognitive Theories and Romantic Texts.* Baltimore: Johns Hopkins University Press, 2010.
Robinson, Daniel. 'Gothic Prosody: Monkish Perversity and the Poetics of Weird Form.' *Transnational Gothic: Literary and Social Exchanges in the Long Nineteenth Century.* Ed. Monika Elbert and Bridget M. Marshall. Farnham: Ashgate, 2013. 155–71.
Rudy, Jason. *Electric Meters: Victorian Physiological Poetics.* Athens: Ohio University Press, 2009.
Russett, Margaret. *Fictions and Fakes: Forging Romantic Authenticity.* Cambridge: Cambridge University Press, 2006.
Savarese, John. *Romanticism's Other Minds: Poetry, Cognition, and the Science of Sociability.* Columbus: Ohio State University Press, 2020.
Sayers, Frank. *Dramatic Sketches of the Ancient Northern Mythology.* London: Joseph Johnson, 1790.
Stewart, Dugald. 'Account of the Life and Writings of Adam Smith, LLD.' *Glasgow Edition of the Works and Correspondence of Adam Smith.* Vol. 3. Ed. W. P. D. Wightman, J. C.Bryce, and I. S. Ross. Oxford: Clarendon Press, 1980. 263–351.
Taylor, William. 'Lenora.' *Lyrical Ballads 1798 and 1800.* 517–25.
Weiskott, Eric. 'Early English Meter as a Way of Thinking.' *Studia Metrica et Poetica* 4.1 (2017): 41–65.
Wordsworth, William and Samuel Taylor Coleridge. *Lyrical Ballads 1798 and 1800.* Ed. Michael Gamer and Dahlia Porter. Peterborough, ON: Broadview Press, 2008.

Chapter 13

May Flies and Horseshoe Crabs: Romantic and Post-Romantic Consciousness, Institutions, and Populations

Robert Mitchell

The extraordinary power of *Romanticism and Consciousness: Essays in Criticism* (1970) was, in the first instance, a consequence of the collective interpretative insight of the contributors, such as Harold Bloom, Geoffrey Hartman, M. H. Abrams, and Paul de Man. Yet the critical acumen of these critics was itself enabled by elective affinities between many of their theoretical orientations, especially psychoanalysis and deconstruction, and Romantic literature itself. Some of these affinities had genealogical origins: as Henri Ellenberger documented in *The Discovery of the Unconscious: The History and Evolution of Dynamic Psychiatry* (1970), Freud's concept of the unconscious was heavily indebted to Romantic-era authors such as F. W. J. Schelling, while deconstruction and poststructuralism relied on an assimilation of Martin Heidegger's philosophy with an anthropological version of G. W. F. Hegel's Romantic-era idealism (Descombes; Borch-Jacobsen 1–20). Bloom's, Hartman's, and de Man's scintillating illuminations of Romantic structures of intergenerational antagonism, ambivalence toward nature, and approaches to poetic language (among other topics) were thus in part a consequence of these critics' uncanny reinventions and reoccupations of Romantic-era approaches.

If there is a lesson here for the project of revisiting relationships between Romanticism and consciousness in light of early twentieth-first-century neuro-approaches, it is that these latter are most likely to have a real interpretative grasp on the literature of the period when they themselves resonate with, or even have their distant origins within, Romantic theories, practices, and approaches. This is, at any rate, my approach here, and I suggest that a basic conceptual matrix first established in the Romantic period persists in many contemporary neurological accounts of consciousness. This conceptual matrix connects three kinds of agents or entities – institutions, individuals, and populations – by means of two kinds of process: automatic processes that occur below the level of consciousness and self-conscious acts of cognition. While we can discern this conceptual matrix in the work of many Romantic-era authors and discourses, I focus here on the debate among Edmund Burke, William Godwin, and Thomas Malthus over the foundations of social order. Burke argued that social order required that traditional institutions do some of our thinking for us (a claim echoed in Germany by Hegel). Godwin opposed that claim in the name of the individual exercise of reason, while Malthus opposed both Godwin and (to a lesser extent) Burke by arguing that the problem of social order depended on the institutions of liberal political economy, which alone were capable of addressing the primary biological struggle of populations over food.

Drawing on the evolutionary rereading of Malthus initiated by Charles Darwin, twentieth-century cognitive science theories have often silently (and likely without the awareness of their theorists) reconfigured relationships among the elements of this conceptual matrix. I focus here on two examples: the neuronal population model, which proposes that the explicit content of consciousness is the result of Malthusian-like struggles of populations of neurons; and the 'extended mind' approach to consciousness, which suggests that mind and cognition are limited neither to the brain nor even to the body, but occur among the brain, the body, and the environment (with the latter including, in the case of humans, institutions such as private property and law).

In the first three sections of this chapter, I suggest that we can best understand the commitments (and aporiae) of these contemporary neurotheories of consciousness by recognizing them as reconfigurations of the conceptual matrix originally developed in the Romantic period. In the chapter's fourth and fifth sections, I employ these contemporary theories to help us recognize anew aspects of Romanticism that were less apparent to theorists who sought to understand the relationship of Romanticism and consciousness through psychoanalytical and deconstructive methodologies. Focusing on several of Immanuel Kant's suggestions in the *Critique of Judgment* (1790) about the relationship of cognition to populations, and William Wordsworth's engagement with the logic of populations in *Lyrical Ballads* (1798), I argue that these new neuro-approaches help us to see that both Kant and Wordsworth linked consciousness and populations in ways decidedly more pacific than either Malthus or Darwin.

Romantic Institutions and Populations

While I begin by providing a schematic summary of the well-known Romantic-era political debate among Edmund Burke, William Godwin, and Thomas Malthus, I do so in a way that stresses aspects of this debate not always brought to the fore. I suggest we understand this as a debate about the relationship among three terms: institutions, learning, and collective progress.[1] For all three authors, the rapid and deep transformation of political, legal, and economic institutions in France in the 1790s established the obvious horizon of significance for this debate, in the sense that the French Revolution underscored both the urgency of answers to these questions, and the fact that these questions concerned the basic sources of social stability.

Burke articulated his position in his open letter, *Reflections on the Revolution in France* (1790). Concerned about what the book's subtitle described as 'the proceedings in certain societies in London' that explicitly supported the revolution in France, Burke criticized the French revolutionaries by contrasting a bad with a virtuous mode of political experimentation. Burke castigated the leaders of the French Revolution as political experimentalists who desired that 'the whole fabric [of the French government] should be at once pulled down, and the area cleared for the erection of a theoretic experimental edifice in its place' (188). Such ground clearing was dangerous, Burke asserted, because though the 'science of constructing a commonwealth, or renovating it, or reforming it' *was* an 'experimental science,' it required a mode of experimentation dependent upon 'even more experience than any person can gain in his whole life, however sagacious and observing he may be' (90). The knowledge sufficient for constructing, renovating, or reforming government was to be found neither in the mass of those who were governed (whom Burke described dismissively as the 'swinish multitude' [117]) nor exclusively in legislators, but rather in the traditions and long-standing institutions that mediated between the people and their legislators. Burke contended that traditions and institutions were the results of successful experiments, and it was through – and only through – traditions and institutions that the experience of the past was stored and made available for the present.

Burke acknowledged that traditions and institutions changed over time, but stressed that they did so at a pace generally and necessarily imperceptible to members of any given generation. Imperceptible and slow change was the necessary cost of social progress; the alternative, exemplified for Burke by the French revolutionaries, was a state of constant change that destroyed the very possibility of progress itself:

> By this unprincipled facility of changing the state as often, and as much, and in as many ways as there are floating fancies or fashions, the whole chain and continuity of the commonwealth would be broken. No one generation could link with the other. Men would become little better than the flies of a summer. (141)

For Burke, it was only by means of traditions and institutions that generations could be linked to one another and, hence, collective experience extended and progress enabled.

For William Godwin, by contrast, institutions were precisely what prevented both the attainment of knowledge about social relations and the implementation of that knowledge in social life. The political philosophy Godwin developed in *Enquiry Concerning Political Justice* (1793, 1796, 1798) pursued to its logical conclusion the Enlightenment project of identifying and criticizing social structures that created shadows of illusion and error. Earlier eighteenth-century Enlightenment authors focused their critique on specific institutions, usually those of 'kings and priests' (that is, bad government and false religion). Godwin went further, arguing that the real impediments to enlightenment were not just specific institutions, but institution itself. Godwin argued that institutions, by their nature, forced individuals to adopt the opinions of others, rather than allowing one to employ one's own reason. For Godwin, taking on the opinion of another was the real obstacle to enlightenment and social perfectibility, and so he opposed all institutions, including those of politics, religion, economy (such as private property), and private life (such as marriage). Because he understood himself to be living in an era in which institutions did most of the individual's thinking for him or her, Godwin did not support the immediate overthrow of institutions, but rather advocated for the gradual elimination of institutions. He argued that this process would slowly and safely increase occasions for perfecting the exercise of individual reason, and – because reason was the same for everyone – would eventually enable the perfection of social relations.

Malthus's *Essay on the Principle of Population* (1798) explicitly attacked Godwin's philosophy, and represented a narrowing and refinement of Burke's defense of institutions. Malthus's 'principle of population' was intended to trump Godwin's principle of perfectibility by locating a non-institutional register of darkness – namely, the dynamics of living populations – that was inaccessible to the enlightening exercise of reason. Malthus claimed that populations tend to expand infinitely, but that otherwise exponential growth was naturally regulated by the death of the portion of the population for which no food was available (21). He argued that this first form of natural regulation could itself be regulated – that is, made more regular and less acute in its effects – through rigorous commitment to a second form of self-regulation, namely, economic self-regulation of supply and demand of the sort described by the new science of political economy. Malthus suggested that the knowledge of population dynamics described in his book could not be employed to change those dynamics themselves, since these depended upon blind urges of sexuality that could be neither enlightened nor changed.[2] Yet knowledge of population dynamics was nevertheless politically useful, for it made it possible to identify *which* traditional social institutions were necessary for social order: namely, those of private property, commercial exchange, and law. Malthus thus ended up with a modified Burkeanism: where social stability for Burke depended on the maintenance of all traditional social institutions and the generational wisdom they contained, for Malthus one needed only those traditional institutions associated with the maintenance of liberal commerce.

In order to understand the relationship between learning and progress, Burke, Godwin, and Malthus drew on a matrix of terms – institutions, individuals, and populations – that was both productive for, and helps us to understand better, many Romantic-era developments in political theory. The fact, for example, that Burke's abstract defense of traditional institutions was, in his context, also implicitly a defense of the particular liberal economic and political structures of his day helps us to account for subsequent difficulty in determining how best to categorize his political theory; Malthus, by contrast, was very clearly an advocate of what we now call 'classical liberalism.' Other Romantic-era authors opened up new possibilities for political theory by recombining the elements of this matrix. In Germany, for example, Hegel followed Burke's lead in seeing institutions as repositories of collective knowledge. However, rather than gesturing vaguely at progress over time, Hegel instead posited that institutions were expressions of a super-subject – *Geist* – that came to know its own nature over time. For Hegel, the *telos* of institutional form was not, *pace* Burke and Malthus, mere survival, but rather self-development and self-knowledge. Hegel agreed with Godwin that reason spoke to all individuals in one voice, but contended in his *Philosophy of Right* (1820) that – *pace* Godwin – the political, legal, economic, and social institutions of early nineteenth-century Germany were the necessary structures by means of which *Geist*'s process of self-knowledge was completed.

This same matrix also facilitated many Romantic-era literary projects. James Chandler argues compellingly, for example, that Burke's conservatism served as the muse of Wordsworth's poetry, even in the poet's supposedly 'radical' period in the 1790s. Percy Bysshe Shelley's admiration for Godwin's philosophy led both to his courtship of Godwin's daughter Mary and to the poet's accounts of social progress within his poetry.[3] And Malthus and Malthusian figures of population surplus made their way into a variety of Romantic-era texts, including Wordsworth's 'Preface' to the 1800 *Lyrical Ballads* and Mary Shelley's *Frankenstein* (1818).[4]

Late eighteenth- and nineteenth-century authors also opened up new possibilities by redefining terms within this matrix, or reconfiguring relationships among its elements. The term *population* was an important site of reconfiguration. Malthus's attempt to counter Godwin's attack on institutions depended upon a very specific understanding of the term population: namely, the process of filling up an empty geographic space with living human bodies (Foucault, *Security* 67). However, Malthus reversed the valence of this process from positive to negative: where earlier authors saw increasing population as intrinsically good, Malthus presented it as a threat (Hazlitt 44; Ferguson 106–11). Yet by the mid to late eighteenth century, the term population denoted not just a homogenous mass of individuals that increased or decreased in size, but also heterogeneous collections of individuals who differed in key respects from one another. This latter understanding of population was not precisely a competitor of Malthus's understanding of the term, for it emerged in discourses focused on other concerns. Understanding populations as made up of individuals who differed from one another allowed eighteenth-century advocates of smallpox inoculation, for example, to determine whether age differences among individuals within a population had an effect on the efficacy of inoculation (Foucault, *Security* 57–63), and it assisted eighteenth-century and nineteenth-century life insurers such as Richard Price in establishing economically viable policy pricing models that varied premium cost by age and health of the insured.

Order from Pandemonium: Neuronal Populations

In the late nineteenth century, Charles Darwin combined these two approaches to populations, thereby establishing a powerful new paradigm for biological evolution that persists into our own moment, and which is foundational for both neuro-approaches I consider here. Darwin was explicit about the importance of Malthus for his project, noting in *The Origin of Species* (1859) that readers should understand his book as 'the doctrine of Malthus, applied to the whole animal and vegetable kingdoms' (5).[5] More precisely, Darwin drew from Malthus the image of individuals competing with one another for resources. Yet equally central to Darwin's approach was an emphasis on *variations* among individuals, for these differences, in combination with forces of selection, enabled new species to emerge from older species. The contemporary 'neuronal populations' approach takes its direction from Darwin's replotting of the consequences of Malthusian competition. Drawing on an understanding of populations as the unit within which differences among individuals enable adaptive change to the environment, the neuronal population reinterprets this struggle as a mode of learning, and then proposes that individual brains learn by means of their own populations of neurons.

This 'internalization' of competition among individuals into competition among neurons within an individual has its origins, like much of cognitive science, in the mid-twentieth-century cybernetics movement, which aimed to understand technology in terms of cognition, and cognition in terms of technology. Computer engineer Oliver G. Selfridge, who studied under the arch-cybernetician Norbert Wiener, set out the rudiments of the neuronal population approach. However, he did so in the context of attempts to determine how computers could replicate cognitive processes normally associated with humans, such as learning to recognize letters and words. As Selfridge stressed in his seminal paper 'Pandemonium: A Paradigm for Learning' (1959), computerized pattern recognition did not seem to work when the programmer attempted to stipulate in advance the formula or rule for recognizing a letter. As Selfridge noted, for 'a large class of pattern recognition ensembles there has never existed any adequate written or statable description of the distinctions between the patterns' (514). Pandemonium is thus a model for 'recogniz[ing] patterns which have not been specified' (513); that is, it is a computer model that *learns* to recognize something. It learns, moreover, in the way that humans (or, arguably, institutions) learn – namely, by being taught:

> we present to the model examples of patterns taken from some set of them, each time informing the model which pattern we had just presented. Then, after some time the model guesses correctly which pattern has just been presented before we inform it. (513–14)

Pandemonium's learning ability depends upon a hierarchy of levels, each of which contains a population of 'demons,' which each performs a simple task. In a simplified version of this model, each demon in the population of demons at the lowest level would be 'assigned one letter of the alphabet, so that the task of the A-demon is to shout as loud of the amount of 'A-ness' that he sees in the image' (516). The 'decision demon' at the next higher level has to determine only which demon shrieked the loudest, and then 'makes a choice of that pattern belonging to the demon whose output was the largest' (514). However, since recognizing something like 'A-ness' is in fact what Pandemonium has to learn, the actual implementation of the program requires more than two levels, with the lowest-level demons devoted to recognizing elements of letters, such as corners, lines, and curves, while those on the next level make guesses as to which letters those elements instantiate.[6]

The key to Pandemonium's learning ability is that in its learning phases – that is, the phase when the experimenter corrects wrong guesses – the program contains a quasi-Darwinian method for eliminating from within the population of a level those demons who guess incorrectly, and also for combining those demons within a level who are more successful in their guesses. Or, as Selfridge put it, the program 'eliminate[s] those subdemons with low worths,' but also 'generate[s] new subdemons by mutating the survivors and reweighting the assembly'; this 'mutation' either can be random, or can involve taking 'two "useful" subdemons' and 'generat[ing] a new subdemon' from parts of both of the 'parent' subdemons (522). Selfridge noted the origins of this approach in biological evolutionary considerations:

> One of the things a species learns is not only how to survive but to have exactly the right variants in its members. The reason horseshoe crabs have not changed much is not because they don't adapt; they can adapt, but there is no variation, so they can only adapt very little, and they are about as good as they can be; whereas there are all kinds of people. (530)

Pandemonium was a method for translating the importance of differences among members of biological populations such as humans into a method that would allow a computer to learn to recognize patterns such as letters.

Selfridge transformed his model into working hardware and software for recognizing Morse code, and so-called 'Selfridge' or 'Pandemonium architecture' – computer programs that learn by employing levels of demon populations – is central to many forms of contemporary pattern recognition and computer learning. However, as has often been the case in cognitive science, a model for computer emulation of a human mental process quickly became a model for that human mental process itself. This reverse translation happened immediately after Selfridge delivered his initial paper: in the seminar participant comments in the original article, computer and cognitive scientist John McCarthy noted that '[i]f one conceives of the brain as a pandemonium – a collection of demons – perhaps what is going on within the demons can be regarded as the unconscious part of thought, and what the demons are publicly shouting for each other to hear, as the conscious part of thought' (527).

This model has been used by contemporary neuroscientists to explain a variety of human perceptual and cognitive processes, most focusing on pattern recognition of some kind. In *Reading in the Brain: The New Science of How We Read* (2009), cognitive neuroscientist and Collège de France lecturer Stanislas Dehaene uses this model to explain how humans learn to read. Dehaene suggests that cognitive neuroscientists should approach reading as an 'enigma' and 'paradox' (4). The first half of the reading paradox is that 'the literate brain contains specialized cortical mechanisms that are exquisitely attuned to the recognition of written words,' and 'the same mechanisms, in all humans, are systematically housed in identical brain regions, as though there were a cerebral organ for reading' (4). Yet the second half of the paradox is that 'writing was born only fifty-four hundred years ago in the Fertile Crescent, and the alphabet itself is only thirty-eight hundred years old,' 'time spans [that] are a mere trifle in evolutionary terms,' which means that evolution did not 'have the time to build specialized reading circuits in *Homo sapiens*' (4).

Dehaene employs the concept of neuronal populations to resolve this paradox. Citing Selfridge, Dehaene suggests that the human ability to read depends on a Pandemonium architecture; that is, our

> mental lexicon can be pictured as an immense semicircle where tens of thousands of daemons compete with one another. Each daemon responds to only one word, and makes this known by yelling whenever the word is called and must be defended. When a letter string appears on the retina, all the daemons examine it simultaneously. Those that think that their word is likely to be present yell loudly. Thus when the word 'scream' appears, the daemon in charge of the response to it begins to shout, but so does its neighbor who codes for the word 'cream.' 'Scream' or 'cream'? After a brief competition, the champion of 'cream' has to yield – it is clear that his adversary has had stronger support from the stimulus string 's-c-r-e-a-m.' At this point the word is recognized and its identity can be passed on to the rest of the system. (42–3)

According to Dehaene, this capacity to read letters 'recycles' a more primary capacity of the human brain to recognize objects: '[t]hose shapes constitute useful invariants for recognizing objects... . [W]hen we learn to read, part of this neuronal hierarchy converts to the new task of recognizing letters and words' (121). Dehaene cites the plasticity of the human brain, especially in developing children, as the foundation of its capacity to recycle evolved structures in this way (142–50).[7]

Dehaene draws specific and general implications from his resolution of the reading paradox. Specific implications bear upon how reading can be most effectively taught in schools (Dehaene favors the Montessori method) and how dyslexic readers can be best helped. His more general implications concern the plasticity of the human brain. Dehaene stresses that his approach differs from 'the "no constraints" approach so common in the social sciences, according to which the brain is capable of absorbing any form of culture' (146). He argues, by contrast, that '[o]ur genome ... specifies a constrained, if partially modifiable, cerebral architecture that imposes severe limits on what we can learn' (146). In the realm of reading, these limits determine which kinds of shapes can be used in alphabets or in morphosyllabic writing systems such as Chinese; in other realms of culture, they determine the contours of, for example, classification systems, mathematics, art, and religion (308–12).

Dehaene's interest in clarifying the concept of mental plasticity brings his project back, in uncanny ways, to Romantic-era efforts to determine the limits of mental flexibility, and the relationship of those limits to questions of reading and writing. Dehaene notes that contemporary efforts – misguided, in his view – to protect student freedom and creativity by eliminating rote memorization of letters repeat criticisms first advanced in the late eighteenth century in Nicolas Adam's *Pedagogical Dictionary* (1787).[8] Even more significant, the seemingly ultra-contemporary concept of neural plasticity turns out to be, as Catherine Malabou documents, an uncanny repetition of Hegel's discussions of plasticity (Malabou, *Future*), though with the twist that many neuro-accounts align this purportedly innate capacity with the needs of contemporary capitalism (Malabou, *What Should We Do*). Given this, it is perhaps not surprising that Dehaene models the 'recycling' component of his theory of 'neuronal recycling' on the French sense of *se recycler* as 'students or employees who take a refresher course or train for a new job better adapted to the job market' (147). In this sense, the recycling of neurons that enabled reading and human culture more generally turns out, in Dehaene's account, to prefigure the contemporary imperative that we remain flexible and entrepreneurial within an ever-changing employment environment.

Institutions and the Extended Mind

Where the neuronal population approach takes its direction from Malthus and Darwin, the contemporary 'extended mind' approach finds itself tending toward Burkean and Hegelian conclusions about the role of institutions in enabling individual and collective cognition and consciousness. Robert A. Wilson and Lucia Foglia helpfully distinguish between contemporary accounts of cognition as *embodied*, on the one hand, and as *embedded or extended*, on the other. Both approaches dispute the more dominant cognitive science model of cognition as solely a property of the brain. However, where embodied cognitive approaches assert that 'cognition deeply depends on aspects of the agent's body other than the brain,' embedded or extended approaches claim that 'cognition deeply depends on the natural and social environment.' That is, for advocates of embodied cognition, the nature and contents of cognition cannot be divorced from the kinds of bodies cognizers have, but extended and embedded cognitive approaches go further in arguing that cognition also depends on the specific ways in which those bodies are embedded within environments. The latter approach was inspired in part by successful robotics projects that enabled complicated tasks such as walking, and did so not by first generating complex mental maps of the robot's environment, but rather via simple routines that allowed the robot to engage its environment physically (Clark).

Advocates of the extended mind approach stress the role of external tools used by individual human agents to extend cognitive capacities such as memory, belief, and judgement. In 'The Extended Mind' (1998), for example, Andy Clark and David Chalmers ask readers to consider the hypothetical case of 'Otto':

> Otto suffers from Alzheimer's disease, and like many Alzheimer's patients, he relies on information in the environment to help structure his life. Otto carries a notebook around with him everywhere he goes. When he learns new information, he writes it down. When he needs some old information, he looks it up. For Otto, his notebook plays the role usually played by a biological memory. Today, Otto hears about the exhibition at the Museum of Modern Art, and decides to go see it. He consults the notebook, which says that the museum is on 53rd Street, so he walks to 53rd Street and goes into the museum. (12–13)

For Otto, '[t]he information in the notebook functions just like the information constituting an ordinary non-occurrent belief; it just happens that this information lies beyond the skin' (13). Clark and Chalmers suggest that though the extended nature of cognition is especially evident in the case of Otto, in fact such cognitive extensions are found everywhere, for every individual, and include tools such as pen and paper, and 'the general paraphernalia of language, books, diagrams, and culture' (8).

Shaun Gallagher and Anthony Crisafi extend significantly the range of examples of cognitive extensions by recognizing an important affinity between this approach and earlier Romantic accounts of the relationship between thinking and institutions. As Gallagher and Crisafi put it in their (non-ironically entitled) essay 'Mental Institutions' (2009), '[t]here is no good reason, once we start along the path of the extended mind, to stop short of considering the larger processes, such as the processes involved in social, educational, and legal institutions, as cases of extended cognition' (51). Gallagher and Crisafi seek 'to extend the Clark–Chalmers version of the extended mind, usually exemplified in terms of notebooks and such' by considering the role of *institutions* as extensions of mind, and they find Hegel helpful in this connection (Crisafi and Gallagher 128). This is because, for Hegel,

> social institutions, like cultural practices and legal systems, are pieces of the mind, externalized in their specific time and place, and activated in ways that extend our cognitive processes when we engage with them. We create these institutions via our own (shared) mental processes, or we inherit them as products constituted in mental processes already accomplished by others. We then use these institutions instrumentally to do further cognitive work – to solve problems and to control behavior – and we do so, not simply by using them as tools, as neutral bits of technology, that might be considered external to cognitive processes, but by engaging with them in ways that extend our cognitive reach. (124–5)

They note Hegel's accounts of private property, legal contracts (and the legal system more generally), and educational institutions as examples of such embodiments of mind (Gallagher and Crisafi 50–1; Crisafi and Gallagher 125–6), and they read Hegel's philosophy as 'an enactive concept of the mind' *avant la lettre* (Gallagher and Crisafi 50).

Gallagher and Crisafi are not, however, willing to endorse Hegel's absolute idealism, which leaves their account of mental institutions closer to a half-committed Burkeanism than to a Hegelian position. The importance of Hegel's philosophy, they argue, is that it allows us to 'see that human cognition relies not simply on localized brain processes in any particular individual, or on short-term uses of notebooks, tools, and technologies, but often on social processes that extend over long periods of time' (Crisafi and Gallagher 127). Gallagher and Crisafi also contend that Hegel's account allows advocates of the extended mind approach to consider how social institutions can place *limits* on thinking:

> we want to argue ... that it is important to take a closer look at how social and cultural practices either extend or, in some cases, curtail mental processes... . Institutional structures, especially, can shape the way that we use

certain technologies and can allow us to see certain possibilities even as they blind us to others. (Crisafi and Gallagher 128)

Though Gallagher and Crisafi's emphasis on institutions as both extending and limiting mental processes is ecumenical, it begs what Romantic authors such as Burke, Malthus, Godwin, and Hegel saw as the essential questions. Is the curtailment of mental processes induced by institutions the necessary cost of social stability (Burke and Malthus)? If so, is there, as Malthus claimed, a set of absolutely necessary social institutions that cannot change (for example, private property, commercial exchange, and law), while other institutions can be made less limiting? Or, channeling Hegel, is what Gallagher and Crisafi see as arbitrary institutional 'curtailing' of mental processes in fact better described as *necessary* limits on individual thought and action: a distinction which would be more apparent to Gallagher and Crisafi if they took seriously Hegel's key point that the mental processes extended through institutions are not those of individuals, but rather of a collective subject, *Geist*?

In pointing out the questions begged by Gallagher and Crisafi's account, I aim neither to criticize their extended mind approach, nor to knuckle-rap these authors for abstracting an element of Hegel's philosophy without determining whether that then entails acceptance of the whole. It is a reminder, though, that however much the extended mind approach may be indebted to new technological developments in robotics and cognitive science, it ends up propelling us back into Romantic-era questions about the relationship of cognition to institutions and progress.

Kant on Populations, Standard Ideas, and Common Human Understanding

The preceding two sections aimed to illuminate the premises and commitments of contemporary cognitive science approaches by reading these as extensions of Romantic-era authors and debates. The remainder of my chapter draws on these contemporary cognitive science approaches to help us reinterpret the aims and methods of Romantic authors. I focus first on the neuronal populations approach, noting that while contemporary neurotheorists draw upon a Darwinian reinterpretation of Malthus that understands populations in terms of competition and survival, a Romantic-era author such as Immanuel Kant understood the relationship between populations and consciousness in terms of more pacific and synthetic processes.

An implicit concept of mental populations underwrites Immanuel Kant's reflections in the *Critique of Judgment* (1790) on the origins of the mental 'standards' that individuals employ to make judgements of beauty (as well as other kinds of judgements). Kant suggested that an individual comes to have a 'standard idea' (*Normalidee*) of various entities by abstracting from a population of actual perceptions of those entities. He exemplified this process through the example of a population of perceptions of individual human beings:

> when the mind wants to make comparisons, [it] can actually proceed as follows, though this process does not reach consciousness: the imagination projects, as it were, one image onto another, and from the congruence of most images of the same kind it arrives at an average that serves as the common standard for all of them. For instance: Someone has seen a thousand adult men. If now he wishes to make a judgment about their standard size, to be estimated by way of a comparison, then (in my opinion) the imagination projects a large number of the images (perhaps the entire thousand) onto one another … . Now if in a similar way we try to find for this average man the average head, for it the average nose, etc., then it is this shape which underlies the standard idea of a beautiful man in the country where this comparison is made. That is why, given these empirical conditions, a Negro's standard idea of the beauty of the [human] figure necessarily differs from that of a white man, that of a Chinese from that of a European. (*CJ* 82 [Ak. 234])[9]

For Kant, a particular individual's standard of beauty for a human being depends upon his or her actual experience, which in turn implies that this standard can – and should – be revised by means of additional experience. Though Kant distinguished among the standards of beauty of different – and, in fact, heterogenous kinds of – groups (Negro, white man, Chinese person, European), his point is that each human individual has a unique standard of beauty for a human being generated from, and hence limited to, his or her individual experience with that subpopulation of the human species with whom he or she has come into contact.[10] This account of the genesis of the standard idea of beauty of a human suggests that an individual ought to understand judgements of beauty as provisional and always open to revision upon the basis of a wider experience of the globe and its inhabitants.

Where standard ideas are based on unconscious processes, what Kant called 'common human understanding' involves a conscious process of seeking to 'think from the standpoint of everyone else' (*CJ* 160 [Ak. 294]), which means 'transferring himself to the standpoint of others' (*CJ* 161 [Ak. 295]). Hannah Arendt and Linda Zerilli have developed useful accounts of this dimension of Kant's philosophy. Zerilli notes, for example, that what Kant calls 'think[ing] from the standpoint of everyone else' does *not* mean thinking from an abstract, 'universal' position, but rather denotes attempts to think from the position of concrete human beings, and especially those who differ most significantly from me (28–40). This process of thinking from the position of other people is, in effect, the conscious, deliberative version of the unconscious, automatic process by means of which each individual's standard idea of the human form emerges. Where the latter process automatically creates a standard idea by running through the specific corporeal particularities of that population of individuals that I have encountered, the former names my conscious effort to think from the standpoints of many other unique individuals.

Neither Kant's account of the unconscious generation of standard ideas nor his description of the conscious activity of common human understanding contests the neuronal population model. One could imagine explaining, for example, both the generation of standard ideas and the activity of common human understanding as enabled by competition among neuronal populations, as perhaps it is a 'decision demon' that selects the standard idea of an object at time T, or concludes with a final decision at time Y the process by which I seek to occupy the standpoint of others. Yet Kant's accounts stress that the competition among neurons that is central to the neuronal population approach, and which has its ultimate origins in Malthus's image of individuals fighting over scarce food, is not the only way of understanding the relationship among members of a population. Moreover, even if such competition among neurons exists – and this is, it is worth stressing, a model that cannot really be 'proven' – then such competition does not necessarily have to be replicated at the level of social relations, but can instead lead to the more pacific activity of engaging the standpoints of others.

Wordsworthian Populations and Institutions

Though, for Kant, 'think[ing] from the standpoint of everyone else' seemed to be a relatively straightforward matter, it is less clear to us now that one can easily understand how the world is experienced by others, especially those who occupy different racial, sexual, and class positions. That is, one may need to *learn how* to think from the standpoint of those many others who make up the globe's populations. As it turns out, other Romantic authors, such as Wordsworth, also believed that one needed to learn how to think from the positions of others (both human and nonhuman) and developed poetic techniques for enabling this.

Though Wordsworth drew on Malthusian logic in his concern, in the 1800 'Preface' to *Lyrical Ballads*, that the rapid growth of the population of print publications would overwhelm and eventually wash away valuable instances of poetic genius (Newlyn 42–8; Fulford 361–3), the poems within *Lyrical Ballads* take a different, non-Malthusian approach to populations. Many of the poems in the collection present a 'type' of individual: the naïve young child of 'We are Seven'; the superstitious narrator of 'The Thorn'; the superstitious (or cursed) drover in 'Goody Blake and Harry Gill'; and the 'Female Vagrant,' 'The Mad Mother,' and 'The Idiot Boy,' to mention just a few examples. The self-reflexive nature of these poems encourages readers to encounter these individuals first as types distinct from the reader. However, in a second, more reflexive moment, these types turn out to speak within and through the reader herself. The reader of 'We are Seven,' for example, is not supposed to conclude, as does the narrator, that "[t]was throwing words away' (114) to try to understand why the child with whom he speaks counts her two dead siblings among those who exist in the present ('we are seven'). Rather, the reader is encouraged to consider the strange affinities between this child's sense of an eternal present and the poem's own commitment to allowing the reader to occupy a 'now' that re-emerges whenever the poem is read, and which seems to encompass the girl, the narrator, and the reader.[11] Or, to take another example, 'The Thorn,' according to Wordsworth, seeks 'to exhibit some of the general laws by which superstition acts upon the mind' by presenting a type of person who has 'become credulous and talkative from indolence' (*Lyrical Ballads* 211). Yet the ultimate aspiration of the poem is to 'convey passion to Readers who are not accustomed to sympathize with men feeling in that manner or using such language' (212).

Lyrical Ballads does not aim, from this perspective, to create a prose human zoo by means of which the reader can observe strange 'others' within the human population. Rather, it seeks to produce within a reader an awareness of the extent to which his or her seemingly individual consciousness is, in fact, a meeting point of, and constituted in part by, differences that characterize populations. Though *Lyrical Ballads* is not itself an example of individuals speaking in their own voices – it is two poets' channelings of what they imagine to be the viewpoints of others – it nevertheless aims to abate the struggle of populations, so that individuals can learn how to allow populations to speak within and through themselves. Repurposing Jonathan Culler's brilliant deconstructive reading of apostrophe as a means by which lyrical poems establish a non-narrative temporality (135–54), we might say that the poems in *Lyrical Ballads* address their readers by means of a population of types precisely in order to sidestep Malthusian (and subsequent Malthusian–Darwinian) narratives of struggles for existence, in which one element of the population must eventually triumph over another.

Where the neuronal population approach encourages us to consider alternative approaches to population within Romantic texts, the extended mind approach provides another way of reading Romantic authors' engagements with both human institutions and the 'institutions' of the natural world. Chandler's brilliant documentation of Wordsworth's Burkean commitment to institutions and traditions undermined claims that the poet was ever a political radical. Yet more recent work, such as Katey Castellano's *The Ecology of British Romantic Conservatism, 1790–1837* (2013), underscores resonances between Burke's commitment to tradition and the emphasis of environmental and ecological thinkers on the need for patterns of collective living that enable continuity over many generations, and which oppose the liberal drive for economic growth at all costs. From this perspective, we could read Wordsworth's famous assertion that he 'was often unable to think of external things as having external existence, and I communed with all that I saw as something not apart from, but inherent in, my own immaterial nature' (*Poetical Works* 4:463) less as an indication of what Keats called (in his 27 October 1818 letter to Richard Woodhouse) the 'Wordsworthian or egotistical sublime' (226) than as evidence of Wordsworth's awareness of the *dependence* of thought on the external world. From the individual's point of view, this may feel like an incorporation of the external world into the ego, as Wordsworth notes. Yet this relationship between individual consciousness and the external world cannot be a one-way street, and one can just as correctly say that the thoughts of Wordsworth's individual 'I' could not persist apart from, but were rather maintained by means of, those external things. As Geoffrey H. Hartman showed in compelling fashion in *Wordsworth's Poetry, 1787–1814* (1964), Wordsworth always feared being extinguished by too close an embrace of nature. Yet his thought nevertheless proceeded through – that is, by means of the necessary support of – natural (that is, external) objects.

The dependency of Wordsworth's thinking on the assistance – and, in many cases, persistence – of the concrete natural objects and processes that made up his natural environment, as well as many of those institutions and traditions which made up his 'second nature,' seems to be the lesson of a poem such as 'Tintern Abbey.' The poem's full title stresses the narrator's return to a specific place that he had visited five years earlier: 'Lines written a few miles above Tintern Abbey, on revisiting the banks of the Wye during a tour, July 13, 1798.' The poem's narrator perceives the same landscape and objects that he had observed on his earlier trip: again he hears '[t]hese waters, rolling from their mountain-springs / With a sweet inland murmur,' and again he reposes 'under this dark sycamore, and view[s] / These plots of cottage-ground, these orchard-tufts' (Coleridge and Wordsworth 201–2). The narrator is certain that memories of these external things have enabled important thoughts and experiences in the meantime, even if he is not able to trace precisely the dependencies of his thoughts and experiences on memories of this landscape. As the poem's title stresses, though, the particular expression of consciousness that is this poem emerges not just from the *memories* of the past experience of this landscape, but by the *persistence* of these external objects through time, which enables the narrator to encounter these natural objects again, and to bring to consciousness and expression their meaning for him. And as the rather surprising quasi-apostrophic address to the narrator's sister near the end of 'Tintern Abbey' underscores, this is also a poem about the transmission of consciousness and experience from one person to another (and, implicitly, across generations). This transmission of experience through poetic language – a transmission from the narrator to his sister, and to everyone who reads the poem – is also thus dependent upon the persistence of this natural landscape, without which this poem could not exist.

This perspective gives us another way of understanding Marjorie Levinson's important reading of what is puzzlingly absent from the poem: namely, Tintern Abbey itself and the homeless people who were living in and around this religious ruin when Wordsworth visited it; the industrial processes staining the river around the town of Tintern; and the political context indirectly referenced in the date in the poem's title (which includes both the French Revolution and more general processes of enclosure and industrialism responsible for the changes to the area around the abbey). To account for the peculiar way in which the poem references but does not represent these places, processes, and events, Levinson argues that the 'primary poetic action' of 'Tintern Abbey' is 'suppression of the social,' in the sense that the poem

> achieves its fiercely private vision by directing a continuous energy toward the nonrepresentation of objects and points of view expressive of a public – we would say, ideological – dimension: that knowledge which is neither nature nor individual but which defines and hides within the former and constructs a certain kind of consciousness as the latter ... . Wordsworth cancels the social less by explicit denial and/or misrepresentation than by allowing no scope for its operation. (37–8)

From this perspective, Tintern Abbey was not represented within Wordsworth's poem precisely because the real site that Wordsworth visited was overrun with reminders of the losers in capitalist class conflict. 'Despite his genuine commitment to the Revolution,' Levinson contends,

> Wordsworth cannot abide the desecration of hallowed ground. The reaction – sometimes disproportionate and always conflictual – suggests an immediate existential issue: fear of losing the housed associations that make thought possible and that permit the poet to know himself to be a continuous, integrated personality ... . We might consider the fact that a land stripped of its sacred spots offers the individual no escape from the social body and the historical moment. (33)

Levinson's point is that though the poem does not erase 'historical consciousness,' it actively suppresses the latter – albeit in such a way that a literary critic such as Levinson can locate and describe the mechanism of suppression and what was suppressed.

The extended mind approach allows us to think further about the 'immediate existential issue' that Levinson attributes to Wordsworth: namely, the 'fear of losing the housed associations that make thought possible and that permit the poet to know himself to be a continuous, integrated personality.' Levinson reads that fear as derived from Wordsworth's sense that 'a land stripped of its sacred spots offers the individual no escape from the social body and the historical moment.' Wordsworth, Levinson suggests, believed that he had to make a choice: either he could shelter his 'continuous, integrated personality' within a geographically specific sacred spot *or* he could remain open to the social body and his historical moment, but he could not do both. Since to have chosen for the social body and historical moment – by, for example, representing the homeless people residing within the ruins of the abbey – would have threatened his continuous, integrated personality, Wordsworth chose to leave the sacred spot referenced but unrepresented. The extended mind approach suggests, though, that both of these choices – openness to the social body, on the one hand; individuality protected by a sacred spot, on the other – would require sustaining institutions. Openness to the social body and history is not the 'other' of a continuous, integrated personality, but is itself a way of instantiating such a personality. Wordsworth's poem thus suggests that one cannot be 'for or against' the link between institutions and integrated personalities; what is rather at stake are choices about the specific *kinds* of institutions and the specific continuous, integrated personality those enable.

This in turn suggests that Wordsworth's poem was less a desire to escape from the social body and history than an analysis of the importance of what Raymond Williams called 'residual' institutions (121–7) for enabling modes of consciousness that can resist the dominant institutions of the moment.[12] The poem's merely titular reference to Tintern Abbey underscores that the modes of religious life and consciousness that that institution made possible had already disappeared by the time Wordsworth wrote his verse, and this point is not necessarily strengthened by depicting either the abbey itself or the homeless people who now occupied its ruin. The poem merely references Tintern Abbey, in other words, to underscore the point that valued, or sacred, modes of thought and life indeed cease to be when their sustaining institutions fall to ruin. By staging the narrator's efforts to establish institutions that will enable forms of 'housed associations' that both draw on, but also necessarily depart from, the now-disappeared sacred modes of life of Tintern Abbey, Wordsworth's poem encourages readers to reflect on the kinds of thought and individuality that they themselves value, to consider which institutions and natural objects make that thought possible, and hence, to reflect on which institutions, natural objects, and thoughts they wish to pass on to the future.

This point is perhaps even more pressing in our own moment than when Wordsworth wrote his poem, not least because poetry itself has now arguably become one of Williams's residual institutions. We are also now quite a bit further down the road than was Wordsworth – or even Levinson in 1986 – toward an elimination of all institutions except those of private property, contract, and law (and the necessary corollary of the latter, the police). The latter processes have made clear that there is no necessary conflict between housed associations which produce integrated personalities, on the one hand, and market-oriented institutions, the social body, and the crises of the historical moment, on the other, since what Michel Foucault has identified as the 'entrepreneurial' individuality of neoliberalism appears to be able to combine all of these seamlessly. We are also better able to see the extent to which these same market forces produce ecological catastrophes that make many modes of human habitation on earth – including those which enabled Wordsworth's verse and Levinson's analysis of these poems – increasingly precarious. All of this suggests that we are approaching Burke's 'may flies' scenario from another direction, as the transmission of knowledge from generation to generation is narrowed down to nothing but Malthusian-cum-Hobbesian economic competition. Against this backdrop, Wordsworth's poem gives us, just as Tintern Abbey gave him, resources to reflect on how we can best seek to reform relationships among institutions, consciousness, and nature.

Notes

My thanks to Joel Faflak and Richard Sha for their extremely helpful comments on an early draft of this chapter, and to the Hanse-Wissenschaftskolleg Institute for Advanced Study, Delmenhorst, Germany for a Fellowship that supported this chapter.

1. This section draws some prose from *Infectious Liberty*, in which I argue that classical liberalism emerged from this same matrix, and also from my essay 'Population Aesthetics.'
2. Beginning in the 1803 edition of his text, Malthus suggested that 'moral restraint' (43–4, 71–2) might have some effect on these dynamics, but never saw this as a force that would have widespread appeal or efficacy.
3. Shelley cites and references Godwin admiringly in the Notes to *Queen Mab* (1813); see, for example, 130, 143, 210.
4. For the role of Malthus in Wordsworth's 'Preface,' see Newlyn 42–8 and Fulford 361–3; on the role of Malthus in *Frankenstein*, see McLane 13–23, 84–108, Mitchell, *Experimental Life* 74–180, and Mitchell *Infectious Liberty*.
5. Hale provides a helpful reading of the role of Malthus in Darwin's theory and the reception of the latter by late nineteenth- and early twentieth-century biological and social theorists.
6. Though I do not have space here to expand on the more general resonance of Selfridge's concepts of 'demons' and 'pandemonium' with Romantic-era literature, Hookway stresses the Miltonic origins of these terms, and expands on the widespread importance of Selfridge's approach to learning, populations, and computation for our current high-tech moment.
7. Dehaene notes that Selfridge's Pandemonium architecture is compatible with the notion of 'cell assemblies' developed in the 1940s by the neurophysiologist Donald O. Hebb. Hebb proposed that learning was equivalent to groups of cells – for example, neurons – developing via experience an increased tendency to 'fire together' (a process summarized as 'Hebb's Law', and often captured through the phrase 'cells [or neurons] that fire together wire together'). Selfridge's model provides one architecture for such wiring, which, for Dehaene, explains why Selfridge's Pandemonium structure 'has been a source of inspiration for many theoretical models of the nervous system' (44).
8. For analogous debates in Romantic-era Britain about how reading and writing should be taught, see Richardson; for Germany, see Kittler 27–53.
9. 'Ak.' refers to the standard *Akademie Edition* of Kant's works. The *Critique of Judgment* (*Kritik der Urteilskraft*) is in section 1, volume 5 of this edition.
10. For useful discussions of Kant's racialized claims about standards of beauty, see Kleingeld, 'Kant's Second Thoughts on Race' (2007), and Hoffmann, 'Kant's Aesthetic Categories' (2016). Hoffmann provides an especially nuanced reading, acknowledging that Kant is, in fact, divided on the question of race: precisely because Kant 'believes that nature intends diversity, he longs to keep races apart' (73). Following Zerilli's lead, I stress Kant's

commitment to diversity, rather than Kant's attempt to keep diversity channeled within purported racial groups.
11. I expand on this reading in Mitchell, 'Experience of Experiment.'
12. Williams described the oppositional potential of residual institutions with the example of organized religion, which, though it operates primarily in service of dominant values, also valorizes virtues such as 'absolute brotherhood' and 'service to others without reward' that can be reference points for struggle against dominant values and institutions (122).

References

Arendt, Hannah. *Lectures on Kant's Political Philosophy*. Chicago: University of Chicago Press, 1982.
Bloom, Harold, ed. *Romanticism and Consciousness: Essays in Criticism*. New York: W. W. Norton, 1970.
Borch-Jacobsen, Mikkel. *Lacan: The Absolute Master*. Trans. Douglas Brick. Stanford: Stanford University Press, 1991.
Burke, Edmund. *Reflections on the Revolution in France, and on the Proceedings in Certain Societies in London Relative to That Event. In a Letter Intended to Have Been Sent to a Gentleman in Paris*. London: ed for J. Dodsley, in Pall-Mall, 1790.
Castellano, Katey. *The Ecology of British Romantic Conservatism, 1790–1837*. New York: Palgrave Macmillan, 2013.
Chandler, James K. *Wordsworth's Second Nature: A Study of the Poetry and Politics*. Chicago: University of Chicago Press, 1984.
Clark, Andy. *Being There: Putting Brain, Body, and World Together Again*. Cambridge, MA: The MIT Press, 1997.
— and David Chalmers. 'The Extended Mind.' *Analysis* 58.1 (1998): 7–19.
Coleridge, Samuel Taylor and William Wordsworth. *Lyrical Ballads, with a Few Other Poems*. London: Printed for J. & A. Arch, 1798.
Crisafi, Anthony and Shaun Gallagher. 'Hegel and the Extended Mind.' *AI and Society* 25.1 (2010): 123–9.
Culler, Jonathan. *The Pursuit of Signs: Semiotics, Literature, Deconstruction*. Ithaca, NY: Cornell University Press, 1981.
Darwin, Charles. *The Origin of Species by Means of Natural Selection; Or the Preservation of Favoured Races in the Struggle for Life*. London: John Murray, 1859.
Dehaene, Stanislas. *Reading in the Brain: The New Science of How We Read*. New York: Viking, 2009.
Descombes, Vincent. *Modern French Philosophy*. Trans. L. Scott-Fox and J. M. Harding. Cambridge: Cambridge University Press, 1980.
Ellenberger, Henri F. *The Discovery of the Unconscious: The History and Evolution of Dynamic Psychiatry*. New York: Basic Books, 1970.
Ferguson, Frances. 'Malthus, Godwin, Wordsworth, and the Spirit of Solitude.' *Literature and the Body: Essays on Populations and Persons*. Ed. Elaine Scarry. Baltimore: Johns Hopkins University Press, 1988. 106–24.

Foucault, Michel. *The Birth of Biopolitics: Lectures at the Collège de France, 1978–79.* Trans. Graham Burchell. New York: Palgrave Macmillan, 2008.
—. *Security, Territory, Population: Lectures at the Collège de France, 1977–78.* Trans. Graham Burchell. New York: Palgrave Macmillan, 2007.
Fulford, Tim. 'Apocalyptic Economics and Prophetic Politics: Radical and Romantic Responses to Malthus and Burke.' *Studies in Romanticism* 40.3 (2001): 345–68.
Gallagher, Shaun and Anthony Crisafi. 'Mental Institutions.' *Topoi* 28.1 (2009): 45–51.
Godwin, William. *Enquiry Concerning Political Justice, and its Influence on Morals and Happiness.* 3rd ed. 2 vols. London: printed for G. G. and J. Robinson, 1798.
Hale, Piers J. *Political Descent: Malthus, Mutualism, and the Politics of Evolution in Victorian England.* Chicago: University of Chicago Press, 2014.
Hartman, Geoffrey H. *Wordsworth's Poetry, 1787–1814.* New Haven, CT: Yale University Press, 1964.
Hazlitt, William. *A Reply to the Essay on Population, by the Rev. T. R. Malthus. In a Series of Letters. To Which are Added, Extracts from the Essay; with Notes.* London: printed for Longman, Hurst, Rees, and Orme, 1807.
Hegel, G. W. F. *Hegel's Philosophy of Right.* Trans. T. M. Knox. Oxford: Oxford University Press, 1967.
Hoffmann, John. 'Kant's Aesthetic Categories: Race in the *Critique of Judgment*.' *Diacritics* 44.2 (2016): 54–81.
Hookway, Brendan. *Pandemonium: The Rise of Predatory Locales in the Postwar World.* Princeton: Princeton Architectural Press, 1999.
Kant, Immanuel. *Critique of Judgment.* Ed. and trans. Werner S. Pluhar. Indianapolis: Hackett, 1987.
—. *Gesammelte Schriften.* 23 vols. Berlin: Koeniglich-Preussischen Akademie der Wissenschaften zu Berlin, 1902– .
Keats, John. *The Letters of John Keats.* 4th ed. Ed. Maurice Buxton Forman. London: Oxford University Press, 1952.
Kittler, Friedrich A. *Discourse Networks 1800/1900.* Trans. Michael Metteer, with Chris Cullens. Stanford: Stanford University Press, 1990.
Kleingeld, Pauline. 'Kant's Second Thoughts on Race.' *The Philosophical Quarterly* 57.229 (2007): 573–92.
Levinson, Marjorie. *Wordsworth's Great Period Poems: Four Essays.* Cambridge: Cambridge University Press, 1986.
McLane, Maureen N. *Romanticism and the Human Sciences: Poetry, Population, and the Discourse of the Species.* Cambridge: Cambridge University Press, 2000.
Malabou, Catherine. *The Future of Hegel: Plasticity, Temporality, and Dialectic.* Trans. Lisabeth During. New York: Routledge, 2005.
—. *What Should We Do With Our Brain?* Trans. Sebastian Rand. New York: Fordham University Press, 2008.
Malthus, Thomas R. *An Essay on the Principle of Population.* Ed. Donald Winch and Patricia James. Cambridge: Cambridge University Press, 1992.
Mitchell, Robert. *Experimental Life: Vitalism in Romantic Science and Literature.* Baltimore: Johns Hopkins University Press, 2013.

—. *Infectious Liberty: Biopolitics between Romanticism and Liberalism*. New York: Fordham University Press, 2021.

—. 'Population Aesthetics in Romantic and Post-Romantic Literature.' *Constellations of a Contemporary Romanticism*. Ed. Jacques Khalip and Forest Pyle. New York: Fordham University Press, 2018. 267–89.

—. 'Romanticism and the Experience of Experiment.' *The Wordsworth Circle* 46.3 (2015): 132–42.

Newlyn, Lucy. *Reading, Writing, and Romanticism: The Anxiety of Reception*. Oxford: Oxford University Press, 2003.

Price, Richard. *Observations on Reversionary Payments; On Schemes for Providing Annuities for Widows, and for Persons in Old Age; On the Method of Calculating the Values of Assurances on Lives; and on the National Debt*. London: Printed for T. Cadell, 1772.

Richardson, Alan. *Literature, Education, and Romanticism: Reading as Social Practice, 1780–1832*. Cambridge: Cambridge University Press, 1994.

Selfridge, Oliver G. 'Pandemonium: A Paradigm for Learning.' *Proceedings of the Symposium on Mechanisation of Thought Processes*. Ed. D. V. Blake and A. M. Uttley. London: Her Majesty's Stationery Office, 1959. 511–29.

Shelley, Mary Wollstonecraft. *Frankenstein, or, The Modern Prometheus*. Ed. David Lorne Macdonald and Kathleen Dorothy Scherf. Peterborough, ON: Broadview Press, 2012.

Shelley, P. B. *Queen Mab: A Philosophical Poem*. Ed. Jonathan Wordsworth. New York: Woodstock Books, 1990.

Williams, Raymond. *Marxism and Literature*. Oxford: Oxford University Press, 1977.

Wilson, Robert A. and Lucia Foglia. 'Embodied Cognition.' *The Stanford Encyclopedia of Philosophy* (Spring 2017 Edition). Ed. Edward N. Zalta. https://plato.stanford.edu/archives/spr2017/entries/embodied-cognition/ (last accessed August 20, 2020).

Wordsworth, William. *Lyrical Ballads, with Other Poems. In Two Volumes*. London: Printed for T. N. Longman and O. Rees, Paternoster-Row, 1800.

—. *The Poetical Works of William Wordsworth: Edited from the Manuscripts with Textual and Critical Notes*. 5 vols. Ed. Ernest De Selincourt. Oxford: Clarendon Press, 1952–63.

—. 'The Thorn.' In Wordsworth, *Lyrical Ballads*, 38–53.

—. 'Tintern Abbey.' In Coleridge and Wordsworth, *Lyrical Ballads*, 201–10.

—. 'We Are Seven.' In Coleridge and Wordsworth, *Lyrical Ballads*, 110–14.

Zerilli, Linda M. G. *A Democratic Theory of Judgment*. Chicago: University of Chicago Press, 2016.

Part IV
Race and Consciousness

Chapter 14

Shapeshifting Romantic Consciousness

Kate Singer

In 'Romanticism and "Anti-Self-Consciousness,"' Geoffrey H. Hartman articulates this classic formulation of the relation between the natural world and human consciousness: 'It is the destiny of consciousness, or as the English Romantics would have said, of Imagination, to separate from nature, so that it can finally transcend not only nature but also its lesser forms' (49). Hartman inveighs against both the naïve 'return to nature' that had become signal and sound of Romanticism and also the degraded, overly mediated self-consciousness of young William Wordsworth and Matthew Arnold. The uncomfortableness with a naïve return to nature has persisted in Romantic studies, particularly when investigating the relation between an embodied imagination and the world it inhabits.[1] Proto-cognitive science and a robust array of scientific discourses have unveiled a materialist brain at the center of Romanticism processing a world of dynamic materiality. This scientific materialist turn has been sung in polyphonic dissonance with posthuman approaches to materiality, especially new feminist materialisms, speculative realism, and object-oriented ontology, which each posit a retro-futuristic version of the 'return to nature.' Their ontological project assumes the human and nonhuman as always already entangled, whether by a monist substance or as a series of separate but interacting objects.

Perhaps not unsurprisingly, these approaches to Romantic matter parallel the debate in consciousness studies surrounding the provenance of the consciousness itself. Materialists such David Chalmers postulate a materialist brain not split from a Cartesian mind but amassing enough complexity to allow consciousness to emerge – even while still searching for a means to explain how emergence occurs. Meanwhile, vigor has returned to those, such as Thomas Nagel, who espouse panpsychism as a more elegant solution to the brain–mind–consciousness debates, suggesting that all matter already has within it experiences of mentality, whether or not we have human access to those nonhuman antics.[2] Panpsychism has particular affinity with the ontological turn since both espouse the entanglement of mind and matter of one kind or another – whether Stacy Alaimo's trans-corporeality, Karen Barad's intra-active entanglements, Jane Bennett's vibrant matter, or Graham Harman's objects. Steven Shaviro presupposes that all things have both interior lives and exterior qualities, however different they might be (107).

I draw these parallels not to engage in a further binaristic debate about whether new materialism and panpsychism flatten ontologies and destroy the thinking, conscious subject, however it arises from matter. Rather, I want to highlight two questions about the relation of materiality to consciousness, which Romantic-period writers were especially keen to ponder. The first question revolves around whether consciousness arises via the individual (brain or brain–body), or whether it might sometimes or already be a corporate phenomenon. If, as Hume famously argued, stable consciousness was merely custom and narrative drawn through bundles of perceptions, might these bundles arise from and even be processed by trans-corporeal bodies and beings, wrapped up with corporate selves, mentality, or experiences? If so, would that pave the way for a consciousness that is already posthuman? This issue, I will argue, is more complex than a naïve Blakean all things come from 'corporeal energy.' It leads to the second, tricksy epistemological question. How could consciousness be assembled from mutual experiences of different beings, and perhaps even different substances? In a reversal of Hume's driving dictum to find resemblance, contiguity, and constancy that assure a stable conscious identity, Romantic writers perversely ask how moments that refuse to coalesce into a self-same identity enact a continual change paramount to less individualistic, humanistic iterations of consciousness. While much discussion of consciousness has revolved around mentality, experience, awareness, perception, sentience, or animacy, what happens to our understanding of 'what it is to be like' when we consider change as not only the sign of consciousness (its ontology) but also its epistemology (how we know it to exist)?

Asking these questions of consciousness and materiality as a sometimes-prior posthuman experience also leads us, I hope, to reconsider how consciousness has been composed as humanistic, individualized, and universal. Black studies in particular has challenged such an ideological frame for conscious experience, exhorting us to rework our ideas of mentality when we consider histories of commodity (objects seemingly denuded of their self-directed ability to change or bear sentience) and of dehumanization (via animality or commodity). Although it is not the only way to approach these issues, thinking of consciousness as posthuman – thinking from outside the Enlightenment individualized Western masculine subject – might give us a way to redraw the relation between the human and the nonhuman that new materialist feminists exhort as a means of outwitting the logic of subjects and (oppressed) objects. While new materialists have given lip service to undoing the commodification of objects (especially female bodies as objects in traffic), they have likewise been critiqued for their inability to account for the historical erasure of Black being. In this inquiry I follow Zakiyyah Iman Jackson, who writes, 'the antiblack formulations of gender and sexuality are actually essential rather than subsidiary to the metaphysical figuration of matter, objects, and animals that recent critical theory hopes to dislodge' (9). Yet, rather than attempting to recognize personhood, humanity, or the liberal human subject, Jackson looks to African diasporic culture for 'nonbinaristic models of human–animal relations, advancing theories of trans-species interdependency, observing trans-species precarity, and hypothesizing cross-species relationality in a manner than preserves alterity while undermining the nonhuman and animality's abjection' (18). Jackson's work might encourage Romanticism to 'return to nature' differently, to outrun the necropower of white consciousness by finding other forms of differences in relation that avoid becoming either universalizing or post-racial, the twinned liberal and neoliberal white ideologies.

Romantic writers similarly look to the posthuman – concatenations of humans, animals, plants, things, and incorporeals – to reconfigure both the posthuman and conscious sentience together. They repeatedly ask whether the ability to think unlike a human – to change the nature of thought itself – might create a new genre of human and of consciousness. Using figures such as prosopopoeia as a trope of metamorphosis rather than human animation, they formulate corporate or mutual consciousness among bodies, or within entities that entail multiple forms of materiality. This kind of posthuman consciousness occurs not through empirical observation and not entirely through our imaginations of it, nor through panpsychic assumptions of universal consciousness. Rather, bodies and things come into relation through affect – a 'posthuman affect' – a responsivity and movement that put bodies in intimate relation without flattening their respective ontologies. Consciousness, in these cases, arises through transformations and movements that bespeak sentience, what Shaviro calls 'an active self-transformation or becoming-other' (89). Because affect is both material and figural movement (all the moves a body might make, real and abstract, as Brian Massumi defines it), we know such consciousness through those movements most often signaled by shapeshifting, by changes in shape and body, such as prosopopoetic changes of face. This posthuman consciousness figured and enacted through change not only discovers forms of mutuality in the period other than empirical sensibility or universalizing spirit. It also, and perhaps importantly for our own times, offers a possible way to think about racial subjectivity in the age of necropolitics, by thinking through a shape of consciousness that routes both dehumanized objectification and the guilt-ridden self-reflections of the individual shut inside his white, Western consciousness.[3] What follows is a survey of five Romantic-era texts that wander through different shapes of these questions as they manifest in lyric poetry, epistolary travelogue, closet drama, and slave narrative – examples that are in no way meant to be exhaustive but rather exploratory, differential, and moving along with the forms of mindful encounter they open.

Conspiring with Mutual Consciousness

What would it mean to move, feel, and be sentient along with the nonhuman? What would it be to exist amid them, to have a 'what it is like' with them, beyond or aside from projection, fancy, or fantasy? Would such an experience be merely imaginative, even as much of new materialism is 'speculative' realism, or is there some other real possibility of 'the practice of thinking from within and as part of the material world' (Alaimo, 'Thinking' 20)? If we already exist as trans-corporeal subjects, are we already processing and speaking from within entangled ontologies of corporate selves or shared sentience? Mary Robinson's poem 'January, 1795' spins us a line of urban flight that offers London as a corporate entity created by the mutual, entangled movements of its groups, buildings, and goods. However sado-masochistic that mutuality, the experience of London entails group awareness, city sentience, and incorporeal figures that jointly embrace them all.

The poem's trochaic mechanism operates by pounding out a series of impressions that swerve into, or already hum along to, the city's pulsing, corporate, confederate being. The bulk of the first four stanzas is driven by a motor of participles, as people, places, entities, and things of London move both paratactically and mutually, at similar rates and frequencies.

> Pavement slipp'ry, people sneezing,
> Lords in ermine, beggars freezing;
> Titled gluttons dainties carving,
> Genius in a garret starving.

Lofty mansions, warm and spacious;
Courtiers cringing and voracious;
Misers scarce the wretched heeding;
Gallant soldiers fighting, bleeding.

Wives who laugh at passive spouses;
Theatres, and meeting-houses;
Balls, where simp'ring misses languish;
Hospitals, and groans of anguish.

Arts and sciences bewailing;
Commerce drooping, credit failing;
Placemen mocking subjects loyal;
Separations, weddings royal. (1–16)

The trochaic rhythm, along with the repeated 'ing' rhyme of the entire first quatrain and couplets in the second and fourth quatrains, create a pushy, urgent movement that seems as energetic (and potentially dynamic) as it is tyrannical and all-encompassing. All London denizens seem dancers in sway to this tune of modernity, whether gluttonous lords or starving geniuses. The paratactic listing of people and places that often begins the lines ('Lords,' 'Titled gluttons,' 'Courtiers,' 'Misers,' 'Gallant soldiers,' 'Wives,' 'Placemen,' 'mansions,' 'Theatres,' 'Balls,' Hospitals') levels social groups and their establishments as mutual agents even as it exposes the differential power structures that place the 'Lords in ermine' and 'Titled gluttons' at the top of the poem, weighing down the 'wretched' and soldiers bleeding below.

The poem is at great pains to point out that parallel arrangement does not guarantee equality or freedom, even when organization through asyndeton emancipates actors from clear lines of empirical succession and causation. Stuart Curran has remarked on Robinson's propensity for postmodernism's slick surfaces of non-signifying sound,[4] yet the poem is not without its Marxist depth. Robinson's categorical attention to groups arranged by rank, occupation, and labor offers a proto-Marxian analysis of class struggle that identifies the aristocratic lords, courtiers, ladies, and dames, as well as the bourgeois 'Gallant soldiers,' 'Gen'rals,' 'lawyers, doctors, politicians,' and the 'poets, painters, and musicians' (2, 6, 25, 27, 8, 38, 34, 33). In lieu of a proletariat class, however, she offers a sort of bare life of impoverishment by naming the 'wretched,' beggars, rogues, misers, fugitives, and knaves (7, 2, 18, 20, 19, 42).

While it is the groups of human actants that end their lines with participles acting in motion, the places for that motion most often evince adjectival affects: 'spacious,' 'voracious,' 'languish,' and 'anguish.' The poem's energy summons the city's motion that upends even the reinstantiation of monied groups. Rather than an analysis of work (or classes of people that do certain forms of labor), the poem performs the 'logistics' of modernity, what Stefano Harney and Fred Moten describe as 'to do without thinking, to feel without emotion, to move without friction, to adapt without question, to translate without pause, to desire without purpose, to connect without interruption' (87). Despite the poem's near continual motion that convenes the force of commerce, there is no mobility, only repetition that leads to depletion, if not cliché. Everyone and everything are caught in the fluidity of lines that 'dispense with the subject altogether' in favor of this movement without friction (Harney and Moten 87). The poem does not merely display and satire such urbane logistics, where all people and their groups become abstractions of capital's all too easy movements. Rather, at the very moments where class consciousness almost emerges, the poem acknowledges socio-economic difference but does not solidify its humanistic, Hobbesian tendencies (for example, struggle between groups of people). Instead, it rides the flow of logistics into another form of motion, a posthuman consciousness that redirects the fluidity of exchange and commodity movement.

Embodying both perpetual flux and customary motion, the ways and means of the city echo what David Hume famously writes in *A Treatise of Human Nature*: 'I may venture to affirm of the rest of mankind, that they are nothing but a bundle or collection of different perceptions, which succeed each other with an inconceivable rapidity, and are in a perpetual flux and movement' (300). These patterns of urban life give London a character. As Hume explains, the identity of person or thing is therefore a 'fictitious one' and 'nothing really belonging to these different perceptions, and uniting them together; but is merely a quality, which we attribute to them, because of the union of their ideas in the imagination when we reflect upon them' (306, 307). These qualities entail the relations of resemblance, contiguity, and causation; the greater the change in matter, the less able we are to ascribe identity to it, or ourselves. Akin to Hume's bundles of perceptions, Daniel Dennett similarly posits multiple threads of perceptions engaged in the brain at once. As some processes are selected, the self becomes the 'center of narrative gravity,' so that what manifests is not so much 'identity' *per se* but unity via customary selection or the narration of various impressions grouped together. What is so provocative about Robinson's poem, however, and perhaps nightmarish to Hume's desire to unite perceptual flux into customs and identities, is that even as it maps bundles in London's impersonal groups, there is no real narrative center of gravity. The poem's lyricism suggests that the only constant is continuous movement and metropolitan thrum. The experience of the city – having a mind of the city – means moving to its beat of modernity, whatever one's place in the cycles of consumption. The poem's jubilance intimates that the city's movements entrap individual actants even as they exhilaratingly propel them into urban mentality.

All things abruptly come to a head in fourth stanza, where the abstractions 'Art,' 'Science,' 'Commerce,' and 'Credit' take on affect and motion, 'bewailing' and 'failing.' Although it would be easy to assess this turn in the poem, as early scholars of Romantic women's poetry did,[5] as the crutch of eighteenth-century abstract personification, Robinson's careful architecture asks that we read this moment as an involution where abstract forces appear to run 1790s London, in a mutual, paratactic motion parallel to and encompassing that of human agents. The abstractions couple with the concatenation of movements, of affects, and together they veer in the direction of what Alaimo calls 'environmental posthumanism, insisting that what we are as bodies and minds is inextricably interlinked with the circulating substances, materials, and forces' (*Exposed* 158). Alaimo's concept of 'trans-corporeality' sketches the blurry intermixing of bodies, domestic spaces, objects, chemical pollution, and the media that record and reproduce them. The fourth stanza's abstractions ask us to consider their seeming contingent provenance: how human movements and the places that house their affects together co-create or are co-created by a mutual motion – the (unstoppable) forces of vitiating commercial Credit and of contingent, enthralling Genius.[6]

Both of these forces posit a relationality and a putting-into-motion that resemble new materialist ideas about material affect, though Robinson, unlike those theorists, uses figuration to turn affect throughout the city. Bennett, questioning our understanding of human agency in *Vibrant Matter*, proposes a 'congregational agency' similar to *shi*, as 'the style, energy, propensity, trajectory, or élan inherent to a specific arrangement of things' (35). While Bennett cannot really account for what enters into or leaves any specific 'vibratory' assemblage, she does sketchily intimate its motor:

> in the case of a complex body or mode, conatus refers to the effort required to maintain the specific relation that defines the mode as what it is … . What it means to be a 'mode,' then, is to form alliances and enter assemblages: it is to mod(e)ify and be modified by others. (22)

Bennett's 'impersonal affect' is not simply the responsive, empirical tendency to affect and be affected by others but rather a transformative moving together, in the same rhythmic time. All vibrate on a certain frequency that might change as the assemblage alters. Brennan would specify such an environment as a chemical and hormonal one, passed from individual to individual, but also available in groups through combination or mimesis, or often pre-existing in the environment already (as in a maternal womb), and certainly Michael Marder and Donna Haraway would agree that such an environment would include plants and animals, if not Jeffrey Cohen's stone.

Robinson's London might be an assemblage of lords, their dainties, their mansions, the misers, and the wives, but whatever they are, they are all sharing their *shi* – their 'ing' – as they move throughout the city. Not unlike the sneezing contagion that begins the poem, the force of Credit has them all vibrating to both Commerce and Genius. Such quasi-personifications register more than either an abstract 'mode' (e.g., one of the imagination's Kantian quasi-concepts[7]) or a dynamic materiality that is limited to the perceptual, phenomenal world enclosed within the human sensorium. Such entities, created by the mutual yet differential movements of human and nonhuman agents, offer an awareness, a posthuman being, an 'as,' an along-with. Corporate consciousness manifests not through an amount or dearth of sentience (vivacity or deanimation) but an assemblage with a shared affect, or series of affects, with similar movements, or potentiality of movements as Massumi would say.

Prosopopoeia can help us understand this metamorphosis into the city, not as a figure of address or apostrophe but as a trope of posthuman transformation, not only into and out of person-like things but as groups of things that act together as entities with consciousness. The long line of Romantic criticism attending to the poetics of address, including Barbara Johnson, Paul de Man, and Sara Guyer, has understood this giving-face-to as an attempt to revivify the dead or the nonhuman. More recently, Mel Y. Chen has considered similar forms of animacy as a means of disfiguring personhood. Although I have argued elsewhere that Romantic forms of address often give nonhuman life vibrancy to interact in non-teleological ways with the human, Robinson's prosopopoeia tracks a different sort of movement aside from animacy or disfiguration. It shapes a tropic turning, the making of a person or a 'doing' of a face – a metamorphosis, a change that becomes the deixis of consciousness itself, and a posthuman one at that. Robinson is at pains to reproduce all the cheap, human and nonhuman 'ing' of urbane logistics. Yet, Art – with its contradictory forms of value in artifice and creation, skill and genius, with its dually human and nonhuman ontology – puts into motion allegorical figurings with their own propulsions. Art speaks back to – moves against – Commerce and Credit with punning, aporetic motions that cannot easily be contained by value, labor, or capital. Art is rewarded not by monetary gain, since the Genius marks a Keatsian figure frozen in eternal starvation. Rather, its creative activity incorporates all into the city's artifice through a speculative, prosopopoetic volta that transforms the non-subject of humanistic logistics into the bounty of a posthuman consciousness, an assemblage of 'ing' potentially not subject to erasure, automation, or a universalizing abstraction.

Before looking more closely at the way consciousness entails change amid multiplicities that form and reform it, I want to look at the example of John Keats's 'Ode to Autumn,' which reconfigures and offers what Barad would say are different 'cuts' or 'intra-actions' of cross-species consciousness, or what I would say are three different posthuman faces, three alternative tropic turns of prosopopoeia, which each manifests how consciousness might bundle together. The tripartite odic structure of strophe–antistrophe–epode formalizes the movements from object-oriented but evanishing materiality to the personified Ceres asleep on the furrows to, finally, a nonhuman network of creatures twittering in latent protest. The poem moves through a series of figurations that, separately and together, index different movements of posthuman consciousness. As Evan Gottlieb notes in his object-oriented reading of the poem, 'it is quite literally subjectless …, and therefore perfectly machinic' (217). The first stanza aligns with an object-oriented realism as it lists the scene's fruit vines, thatch-eves, apples, moss'd cottage trees, ripe fruit, swelled gourds, plump hazel shells, flowers, and bees. What Graham Harman would call the external appearances of ripeness, however palpable, allude to but resist our desires to penetrate their withdrawn, interior cores, kernels, and clammy cells. So many species grow together, into both organic teleologies (swelled gourds) and non-purposive forms (moss'd cottage trees).

Yet, the poem, as it describes the season's 'conspiring' with the 'maturing sun,' adumbrates this tension between external appearance and internal privacy that Shaviro has argued is evidence of panpsychism. He writes,

> I might just as well say that I am inwardly isolated and imprisoned while outwardly able to make affiliations and pursue enlivening relations. Panpsychism is the recognition that this doubleness of privacy and relationality is not just a human predicament but the condition of all entities in the universe. (107)

The poem offers a double sense of conspiring – the internal plotting of the sun and season that humans have no access to except in the imagination and the breathing together of two entities through the measure of the lines. As ripe as these objects are, they reveal a double consciousness of external relation and an open secret that is their growing together in different ways.

In the second stanza, this poem turns from an array of nonhuman consciousness to what would seem to be an explanatory personification. Echoing the pulses of Commerce and Credit but in more muted tones, we find 'Thee' idling in the granary, perhaps as Ceres, a worker, or Autumn more generally. The stanza alludes to harvest labor, yet 'Thee' does not inaugurate a working-class consciousness so much as the anticipatory movements and rests around furrows, brooks, and presses, themselves in various stages of slowing seasonality. The figural 'Thee' sleeps off opiate intoxication on a 'half reap'd furrow,' 'drows'd with the fume of poppies,' then like a gleaner, surveys the fields and watches the cider press: 'thou doest keep steady / Thy laden head,' 'with patient look / Thou watchest' (14, 16, 17, 18–19, 20–1). The intoxicated sitting and patient watching certainly appear humanistic. If we read 'Thee' as Ceres, though, we end up with a paradoxical figure of the Harvest goddess acting more like a weary laborer. A similar category confusion occurs with 'laden head,' which reaches back to the first stanza's over-ripe fruit, the furrows (of the brow, of the field), and Ceres too, her melancholy at the anticipated loss of her daughter, Spring. This Keatsian mix of mythology, labor, and the georgic/biological imbricates harvest, gleaner, and the elemental through those doings that are variably or simultaneously human, nonhuman, and godly. They are connected through the 'laden head' of consciousness created by a stanza's worth of prosopopoeia that addresses a deeply ambiguous 'Thee,' recognizable by its cross-category, if sluggish, metamorphoses. This stanzaic turn refracts labor as that Autumnal work done together by human and nonhuman actors, through physical activity that changes bodies, landscapes, climates – and consciousness.

The poem ends with songs not sung by human workers or gods but by the animals and insects that may die at the season's end (by human hands or not). The communal congregations that voice this music offer a third but perhaps parallel turn to corporate consciousness in multiple species each singing their song but also intoning a song together: lambs, crickets, red-breast, and swallows in differential chorus alongside the light wind and blooming clouds. In odic fashion, the animal world redounds upon the botanic sentience of the first stanza but seems shot through with the working-class consciousness of the second, as a choir of communal protests facing death (Peterloo, agricultural, biological). This epode harmonizes or synchronizes the object consciousness of stanza one with the prosopopoetic consciousness of stanza two into a climactic animal sentience, now aware of its own metamorphic change through the act of singing, of vibration's repetition, growth, and variation. Keats manages the prosopopoetic turns in the stanzaic interstices to intimate a shifting 'poetic center of gravity,' to adjust Dennett's phrase, which perhaps fictionalizes but nonetheless creates a mutual, seasonal consciousness among developing entities. The economy of the poem furnishes a triptych of 'what it is like to be' in different groups of things, perhaps even unifying them all, however temporarily, in the metamorphic turns of about-face. This multiplicity locates local, affective movement, in all its varieties, as the shape of consciousness, a responsive, posthuman being-with. In the various turnings of prosopopoeia, the shifting shapes of autumn epitomize change so that it becomes an epistemology for consciousness itself, in its changing multiplicity and turning mutuality. Autumn's most hidden workers differentially give voice to their laboring bodies' sundry tunes, which can be heard together, but not in bourgeois unison.

Knowing Skeins / Shapely Sciens

If there is something to mutually created sentience, more needs to be said about how exactly such an experience is co-created. The transformations that produce posthuman consciousness – interruption, growth, intensification, entanglement – evolve through figures of shapeshifting.[8] Not entirely empirical or embodied, figures change shapes due to the collision, coincidence, or conversation between affects, or what I have been calling posthuman affect – movements that occur across materialities and mediums, including the figural. These affects include all the moves a body might make, actual or potential, and they likewise include the dispersed materiality that makes up an environment – including Brennan's hormones and pheromones, Massumi's fields of intensity, Bennett's impersonal affect, and the incorporeal animacies of inorganic matter. Romantic writers perhaps most importantly insist that figuration's own movements do not just mediate matter but compose and inhabit it.[9] These shiftings produce new skeins of beings *and* new shapes of consciousness. Richard Sha has detailed the analogy of 'forces of attraction' that are 'proximate to an intentional state or emotion like love' as 'motion is what allows us to encounter matter in the sense of perceiving it,' such that it is not clear whether motion (as force) belongs to the universe or to individual (as love) (76, 77). Romantic writers are also interested in less analogical representations of co-constituted affect, especially because those affects posit new forms of posthuman consciousness even as they offer an epistemology for it. That means that we come to know posthuman consciousness through the very motions – sometimes material and sometimes abstract – that produce it.

Although Mary Wollstonecraft may seem to be a staunch associationist in *A Vindication of the Rights of Woman* (1792), her *Letters Written in Sweden, Norway, and Denmark* (1796), aided by their more gauzy epistolary movement, offers moments of affective entanglement between the speaker and her ever-changing environment, not between Wollstonecraft and her erstwhile addressee. The speaker veers from her first sociological encounter with Norwegians to the bay of Tønsberg, itself a border town of Norway that had been battered by the Swedes, including it one of the volume's many naturalistic interludes. 'Here,' she announces, 'I have frequently strayed, sovereign of the waste,' napping on the 'mossy down,' in repose with the 'soft gales' and 'the tinkling bells on the necks of the cows' (49, 50). In this liminal state of awakening – coming back into consciousness, surrounded as she is by the materialities of nature in flux through the moving winds, waves, mossy earth, lolling cows – the speaker of the *Letters* pointedly sketches an ecology where human and nonhuman bodies, as well as more diffuse matter, share and exchange affects, and then change their shapes. This technique reveals Wollstonecraft moving past her earlier critique of eighteenth-century sensibility's bodily sensations and toward a descriptive habitus of being in, and within, the world by moving along within it.

Not unlike Heidegger's *Mitsein*, though in a pointedly less humanistic mode, Wollstonecraft's corporate consciousness might be well described by Jonathan Kramnick's insight, via Maurice Merleau-Ponty, that 'physical action brings objects into view through attention and movement and so smears or spreads the locus of experience from interior states of the brain to entire bodies located in specific ecologies' (2). Kramnick's methodology has the benefit of 'coupling these [internal] states with external objects and environments' (6). In his study, such mutually constituted experience – even of panpsychism – often entails 'points of view that are plural and vary in scale' (140), whether at the behest of multiple beings articulating their experience serially or through a perspective wrought by a sentence that 'instantiates a set of nerves that belong to no one in particular' (153). If both of these models depend on a material monism, in Wollstonecraft, the uniting factor is their mutual movement; whatever the materialities (or immateriality) they are, they move together.

As the speaker repeatedly gazes at the scenery, in that prototypical act of Romantic-era perception, she 'gazed again, losing my breath through my eyes – my very soul diffused itself in the scene – and, seeing to become all senses, glided in the scarcely agitated waves, melted in the freshening breeze, or taking its flight with fairy wing, to the misty mountains,' and she becomes 'entranced' (50). The speaker's subjective collapse into the scene, her 'seeing to become all senses,' occurs through the repeated movements of the waves, the breeze, or 'fairy wing.' The enchantment the speaker experiences, the awareness of mutual movement that occurs in this assemblage, may be partially a result of perceptual understanding, but it is more fully rendered through a mutual conatus, a 'seeking to become,' enacted through the 'tion' and 'ing' of agitation, melting, freshening, and taking flight. Even these motions augur different shapes to movement, which might arrive in upset, liquidity, renewal, or alternative spaces. Janina Wellmann's work on embryology and rhythm tells us that formation and growth in the mid-eighteenth century was characterized by repetition, regularity, and variation (95). Wollstonecraft achieves her own 'rhythm of repetition and variation,' composed not through one body's force and teleology but through a variety of differential movements across human and nonhuman bodies.

It is in this vein that William Godwin's figuration of Wollstonecraft's literary and affective practices in Memoirs of the Author of A Vindication of the Rights of Woman (1798) becomes seminal: 'she was like a serpent upon a rock, that casts its slough, and appears again with the brilliancy, the sleekness, and the elastic activity of its happiest age' (88). This comment appears just after Godwin's revelation of Mary's lovesickness for Henry Fuseli and for Gilbert Imlay, the apex of which is his declaration that she was 'endowed with the most exquisite and delicious sensibility ... Mary was in this respect a female Werther' (87–8). Godwin may have quite missed his mark in characterizing Mary as a woman of arch sensibility, praising her for not loving unavailable men by halves. His subsequent figuration of her as a serpent, however, tropes something more than sensibility. Her ability to shed her skin – her complicated arrangements, her habitus, the shape of her livelihood – transpires through simultaneous growth and movement.

Her radiant sentience materializes through an 'elastic activity' of self-transformation, formalized by her tackling of all manner of literary forms, including the pedagogical primer, children's literature, literary reviewing and criticism, political and social philosophy, the epistolary travel narrative, and finally fiction. That Godwin uses the snake metaphor wryly insinuates Wollstonecraft's devilish pursuit of knowledge (she is the serpent, not Eve) saves rather than condemns her by moving into new skins of biographical and literary life. Her nonhuman figuration arguably routes the sexual implications (which Godwin miserably misestimates in the work's reception) by associating her brilliance with a great ability for bodily movement – not merely for sexual pursuit but, more grandly, for shapeshifting.[10] If posthuman consciousness was figured through a corporate prosopopoeia, the epistemology of change that signals new turns to such consciousness becomes enacted through shapeshifting – shifts that move through, and blur, the animacy hierarchy of human/animal/plant/inorganic matter/incorporeals. Such transmogrifications, and the capacities to enact them, undermine the anthro- and androcentric category hierarchies that constitute the Enlightenment human. They entertain the possibility of resistance to and the inhabiting of alternative consciousnesses unstuck in gendered, raced, binaristic bodies and minds.

Racial Ness-Ness

Plasticity of shape and of consciousness is not without its detriment. The celebratory, gender-bending aspects of human–nonhuman equality that Wollstonecraft pursues are tempered by the class consciousness of Robinson and Keats, as non-aristocratic bodies become sick, disabled, slow, and vulnerable to harm in ways that imbricate them quite differently within their environments. Perhaps the most trenchant critique of this damage comes from those writers alert to the histories of racial consciousness. As Jackson argues in *Becoming Human*,

> [p]lasticity ... describes what Stephanie Smallwood, in her study of the Middle Passage and slavery, identifies as 'an enduring project of the modern Western world': the use of black(ened) flesh for 'probing the limits up to which it is possible to discipline the body without extinguishing the life within (36). (10)

Although plasticity may seemingly spell freedom during the age of revolution, it has a subterranean end: 'a praxis that seeks to define the essence of a black(ened) thing as infinitely mutable, in antiblack, often paradoxical, sexuating terms as a means of hierarchically delineating sex/gender, reproduction, and states of being more generally' (Jackson 11). Jackson's skepticism about new materialism's theoretical equalities reminds us that mutability has a use and abuse value all its own, particularly in creating the fungible slave body that is by turns sexed for white pleasure and reproduction, ungendered for labor, made flesh for commodification, turned animal for the aggrandizement of civilization, and infantilized for sentimental coercion.[11]

Looking more closely at Romantic fluidity and dynamic materiality within Romantic writers, if not various strands of new materialism, gives a more nuanced and subtle ontological account of both shapeshifting's metaphysical violence and its possible swerves from subsequent double consciousness or objectification that denudes racialized consciousness.

Posthuman consciousness has the potentiality to subtend the racialized erasure of sentience and the manipulation of affects by offering a mentality that sidesteps either white Western individual humanistic consciousness that slaves were denied or the nonhuman status that racialized bodies are most often given. Moving along with other bodies and affects finds other shapes and rhythms not bound to racist necro-capitalist consciousness.

Percy Shelley's closet drama *Prometheus Unbound* contemplates such a 'mental theater,' to use Alan Richardson's phrase, during Asia's transformation into light, the lamp of love, and an enchanted boat. For Asia, after she vapes Delphi's oracular vapors and comes to consciousness of Jupiter's colonial, patriarchal tyrannies, does not simply dispute his reign but turns into a boat of light that then doses the globe with her intoxicating affects – which literally change the world in Act IV. With this material and figural shapeshifting, Asia seems to attain a new medial form of light that inverts both Jupiter's lightning (with all its phallic, Rochesterean libidinal weight) and the starlight of universal love we see in 'The Triumph of Life.'[12] Her stream of light, unlike a singular ray of white supremacy, bestows on the world a rainbow of materialities, which in their dynamisms and multiplicities reach toward posthuman forms of gender, sex, and race. Asia, as she turns into light, shirks the gender that produces her critique of Jupiter's reign and becomes something beyond the humanistic dimorphic binary of sexed bodies or heteronormative genders. Yet, neither does she transform into a post-racial being. She – perhaps now they – also does something more to the categories of light and dark. Something happens beyond simply subsuming into the knighted whiteness the dark fathoms of the increasingly colonial seas that long ago birthed Asia, an Oceanid. Similarly, Asia's Enlightenment does not simply evanish the South Asian vale of the Hindu Kush, the scene of *agon*, for an unrealistic utopia of spirits and panpsychic mentalities bound through a universalizing, monadic substance.

Rather, Asia seems much more a figure for what Alexis Pauline Gumbs in *M Archive: After the End of the World* calls the 'black feminist metaphysicians,' who articulate an ontology where the origin of light becomes the blackness at the bottom of the oceans, a blackness which is as much oceanic as it is illuminating (6).[13] Heroes of this archive built after an apocalypse,

> they were the first ones who learned to light themselves and find each other. The critical black marine biologists, scientists of the dark matter under fathoms, suggest that there may be a causal relation between the bioluminescence in

> the ocean and the bones of the millions of transatlantic dead … . [S]o any light you find in the ocean right now cannot be separated from the stolen light of those we long for every morning. (11)

Light comes from blackness; light is shared with blackness. The light of the nonhuman is 'recut,' as Barad would say, with the bioluminescence from the lasting bones, now turned into (al)chemical elements.[14] This kind of light is not merely the pervasive climate of whiteness but also the light of persistent and changing matter that inhabits the oceanic sways and organic and inorganic matter in its fathoms, as well as the life that survives titanic apocalypses of modernity, especially racialized injustice.

With this reading, I do not mean to appropriate Black feminist theory to valorize Shelley, or to suggest that he anticipates or pre-empts Jackson, Gumbs, or others I mention below. Rather, placing Shelley within the theoretical reworlding created by Black feminist theory may provoke us to reread the racial tensions within the closet drama as a racially aware posthumanism, with its attendant problems. Such a reading is meant to open up a line of inquiry that then, as this chapter will do, ardently moves us to read other Black Romantic-era authors, to hear further versions of such theoretical, figural crisis.

Gumbs offers another form of shapeshifting that allows us to read Asia's alchemical transformations as what Sylvia Wynter would call Asia's 'Third Event,' a retelling of her own origin story as something other than either a becoming human or nonhuman. As Panthea and Ione first see her light, they repeat and retool Asia's origin story as an Oceanid who, like Aphrodite, arrives on a vein'd shell. This Western provenance might seem to whitewash Asia by giving her a Greco-Roman backstory as Venus/Aphrodite and by installing her in a white supremacist tale of Westernized universality:

> love, like the atmosphere
> Of the sun's fire filling the living world,
> Burst from thee, and illumined earth and heaven
> And the deep ocean and the sunless caves
> And all that dwells within them, till grief cast
> Eclipse upon the soul from which it came. (II, iv, 26–31)

With Asia's birth, the clear translucence of the ocean is split upon her arrival on the half-shell, and love emoted from Asia herself fills the world, penetrating the depths of the ocean and caves at once. Grief redoubles on its source, as if to stop negative affects through their very reflection. Where does 'grief' come from? Who casts an eclipse onto the deep ocean and its sunless caves? Both Love and Grief intertwine a force of affect and affinity but, even more, a prosopopoetic, posthuman figure: the corporate consciousness of oceanic matter, replete with photosynthetic light and with buried, osseous calcium.[15] This prosopopoetic turning of love into grief and grief into love registers the loss of Asia within her birth of light, even as her light commemorates and brings to light the shadows of the dead buried within the deep ocean and its caves. While 'all that dwells within them' is dredged up, so not forgotten, the signifier for blackness or for the enslaved dead remains somewhat figurative and abstract, and thus subterranean, perhaps hiding or engaging in the realities of blackness's fungibility. Nevertheless, these movement may be materially fluid, as Tiffany Lethabo King suggests, in order to find movement outside the economies of Black flesh:

> To be rendered Black and fungible under conquest is to be rendered porous, undulating, fluttering, sensuous, and in a space and state at-the-edge and outside of normative configurations of sex, gender, sexuality, space, and time to stabilize and fix the human category. (23)

Whether or not Shelley fails to move outside the whiteness of his own subject position, Asia's allegorical play and flickering figurality attempt to reimagine blackness's fungibility as moving outside normative configurations of Romantic-era racialization and gender tied to a static or easily read biological, human body. Asia's eclipse, the momentary darkness, which ends her Grecian birth and turns us to her rebirth as global light, remixes darkness and light, such that endemic to her enlightenment is the brilliant and repeated movement from dark to light and back again. She figures and enacts a movement through Enlightenment and its darkness so that she might, finally, move into other materialities outside the continuum of racial, sexualized visuality.

Asia herself does not remain the light of love but transmogrifies, twice again, into other shapes and vessels of posthuman consciousness. Her light redoubles on its source, and, nearly faster than the speed of light, her metaphorical vehicle becomes a vehicle, as she manifests as an 'enchanted boat,' able 'to float ever, forever' in multiple times and places at once '[u]pon that many-winding river,' until she emerges back into the sea of 'ever-spreading sound.' Such a profound description of consciousness seems to spread concentrically from boat to waves to phonic vibrations, back through the wilderness that leads to the sea of profundity and redounding sound. These materialities occur and then mix within Shelley's pulsing echolalia. They move into and out of one another not by way of perception and reflection but through a movement that enables the reciprocal touching of their rippling motions, which are both common and differential.

By the end of the passage, Asia is back in a wilderness 'peopled by shapes too bright to see,' where raced flesh or even sexual dimorphism gives way to 'shapes' that are 'bright.' Such abstraction does not totalize a universal humanity but rather offers a materiality that refuses the politics of either invisibility or visibility. This shape blocks the specularity and empirical observation that would recreate embodied, racial categories. Not necessarily amorphous or plastic shapes, these are futuristic 'pod people' who can, without already being erased or violated by descriptive practices, self-determine their bodily information.[16] Their posthuman shapes reroute humanistic, racial biopolitics even as they allow for a repeopling of the earth that is not so much indeterminate as Afrofuturistic, with newly mythologized beings. Shelley's metaphysicians, Asia and her sisters, lean their oceanic sways away from the contingencies of racialized plasticity and the abuse of power and violence – though, of course, such figural aversion to harm may itself avert direct abolitionary action, even as abolitionary rhetoric turned from the shapes of anti-racism. The sisters' metamorphic consciousness nonetheless accretes shapes of posthuman relation without erasing the history of their violent and improvisatory ontologies.[17] Their brightness is shared by all who come from and return to the bottom of the ocean, the unfathomed shapes that are not denuded of their blacknesses but are bright with them. Shelley's poetics at least strives to create a model of difference without othering. It attempts to translate racial difference into a different key that both defamiliarizes growing discourses of biological or species-based race and recreates material differences as complementary – as those which do not hierarchize or erase othered pasts even as they move harmonically alongside each state, condition, or quality, a togethering fulminating ness-ness.

Ever-spreading sound working through an alliance of touching, shifting shapes reverberates in even more pointed and brilliant ways through texts that deal most palpably with violence and its effects on (racial) consciousness. Rather than recording a subjectivity erased by equivalence with nonhuman animal-commodity, Mary Prince's seminal account of shapeshifting violence allows her to articulate a consciousness that slips the knot of human/nonhuman altogether. As she experiences intellectual and physical violence, what she describes might be categorized as a special kind of shapeshifting wrought through laceration, trauma, survival, and persistence. The vocalizations of the affects that change her shape – and that of the earth, her tools, and other people – disrupt any white rhetoric of sympathy affixed by her amanuensis, Susanna Strickland, or her editor, Thomas Pringle.[18] Rather, they respond to the erasure of black being with aural repetition, a 'weep, weep, weep' whose rippling affects intone a shapeshifting that moves through and beyond racial violence.

No simple pandering to the abolitionary uses of sentimentality to humanize the former slave (now evangelicalized), Prince's breathy vocalization insists that not only do black people have sensibility that demands white sympathy, but they have affect – they can be moved and move others in turn. As she writes in *The History of Mary Prince* (1831), 'Oh the Buckra people who keep slaves think that black people are like cattle, without natural affection. But my heart tells me it is otherwise' (18). The classic dehumanization of slaves by comparison to animals, especially those commodified for profit like chattel, allows for the erasure of black subjectivity and being as part and parcel of the necropolitical right to kill. As Jackson writes, 'the categories of 'race' and 'species' have coevolved and are actually *mutually reinforcing* terms' (12). Calvin L. Warren explains this complication of mutuality (being 'black people' and 'cattle' at once) as a double problem – one of excess and negation of being that further entails a shifting between them. He argues: 'the paradox of black being ... is the excess of form in an anti-black world, but also the interruption of form, the formless' (33). The formless Being of (white) metaphysics is plagued by the anthropological differences of racialized form. Thus, not only is, as Jackson writes, the black body a form of plasticity that can be used and shaped in all sorts of (excessive, violent) ways, but it is also the form of difference that disrupts formlessness, and therefore both violently visible as difference yet also invisible as constantly fungible. While, as Ruha Benjamin, for one, has noted, '*posthumanist visions assume that we have all had a chance to be human*,' black feminists, including Wynter, King, and Jackson, suggest that to recover humanity one must paradoxically move aslant to the category of the human rather than simply recover it for those excluded (32). For Prince, this means finding or creating a posthuman consciousness that entails humanity without the inhumane, materiality without flesh, a difference that is neither visible nor invisible.

In Prince's narrative we see a different linking of human and non-human things over and against this Fanonian double consciousness, another shape that parlays the desire for white subjectivity and the loss of the ego through the 'lick lick' lashings of humanistic black subjection (15). Michele Speitz has argued that Prince's narrative literalizes the entanglement of laboring body and environment through slave labor in the salt ponds, akin to Monique Allewaert's 'swamp sublime.' Likewise, Prince's experience adumbrates the violence exacted on both ponds and body through her swollen limbs and later rheumatism, which figuratively echo the aqueous expansions of bodies of water. Prince's narrative clearly issues a critique of slavery that treats the ponds (and enslaved flesh) as an endless resource of salty capital. It also serves as an invective against those labor practices that permanently disable the enslaved body. If her body's shape becomes repeatedly distended through labor and its contact with the environment, the apex of her disability becomes fully realized only later, in England, when she refuses to immerse her limbs once again in the polluted water of the washbasin. This petit marronage, what Neil Jordan terms a 'desire for the brief avoidance of forced labour' and of the enslaved environment, signals a sort of workers' consciousness, one that resists the white warping of the Black body and its means of movement (98).

The connection between environment, body, and consciousness, however, occurs even earlier than Prince's experience in the salt mines, when she tells a comparatively long anecdote about an episode with a broken jar that causes a severe lashing followed by an earthquake. The length of the story, its triple fracturing of jar, body, and earth, and the apocalyptical feel of the natural disaster together give the episode an allegorical weight. These bodies become connected through their breaking and through Prince's repetitive lyrical descriptions, her own 'ever-spreading sound,' which amasses an unchatteled posthuman consciousness. She begins the episode with the death of Hetty, a beloved companion severely beaten to death, by remarking,

> It was then, however, my heavy lot to weep, weep, weep, and that for years; to pass from one misery to another, and from one cruel master to a worse. But I must go on with the thread of my story. (16)

The ululation of 'weep, weep, weep' sounds out an iterative and percussive repetition that vocalizes a mode of conscious experience of moving from one misery-inducing master to the next – an uncanny return of violence and weeping, the invasion, distortion, and, ultimately, shedding of the harmed body through the plasticity of tears.

Prince then picks up the story with an account of being sent to fetch a large earthen jar. 'The jar was already cracked with an old deep crack that divided it in the middle, and in turning it upside down to empty it, it parted in my hand' (16). When she tells her mistress the jar has 'come in two,' she is duly blamed for it and, later that night, roundly beaten by her master 'with several heavy blows' and 'with every ill name he could think of, (too, too bad to speak in England)' (16). She proceeds to recount the lashing she next receives, interrupted only by her master needing to catch his breath and take a drink, but more permanently by 'a dreadful earthquake' (17). The empty jar itself seems a potent allegory for the slave body broken in two by overuse and impoverishment, into the double consciousness of nonhuman flesh and disabled-but-human enslaved body. As she brings a jar already ruptured, and now breaking on its own, so the allegedly affect-less slave body is an insuperable resource of labor and repetitive movement – already disabled and always already coming apart. This vessel, too, might allegorize a reproductive fecundity that has become defunct with the death of pregnant Hetty, or the double bind of Black women as reproductive vessels already broken by their overuse in miscegenation. In the published version of the narrative, Prince avoids being subject to the psycho-social biopolitics of colonial reproductive futurity,[19] and in this way, she has broken the bell jar of maternal slave labor. Yet, the jar, in its shapeshifting, seems to double as an allegory for the double consciousness that renders slave affect both excessive (in labor, in weeping, in subjection to beating) and also erased and made invisible (the slave as chattel whose body is unfeeling enough to avoid injury). The jar moves from filled to broken, as black being is overdetermined and non-existent, excessive, and voided, formed and formless.

Yet, Prince's adumbration of the imputation of violence as a kind of tyrannically enforced shapeshifting is answered, in turns, by the pervasive and repetitive lyric lilt of her phrases, such as 'weep, weep, weep.' The earthquake brings more of these echoes: 'Part of the roof fell down, and everything in the house went – clatter, clatter, clatter. Oh I thought the end of things near at hand' (17). When other slaves see her lying on the steps of the house's piazza, they exclaim, "Poor child! Poor child!'; 'too, too bad'; 'clatter, clatter, clatter'; and 'Poor child! Poor child!' (17). These repetitive, spondaic phrases move in relation to the cracked jar, with its old, deep crack divided in the middle, the several heavy blows, the hundred-lashed flogging, and the earthquake, as if in fugitive movement from the very violent motions that occasion them. Her lyricism resounds in the text as what Fred Moten calls 'the antiphonal accompaniment to gratuitous violence,' the hapticality of sound that is 'a way of feeling through others, a feel for feeling others feeling you' (95, 98). This mutual sentience entangles jar/earth/slave/body/child. Born in pain, these aural–material affects shift into a moving antagonism, one that resides not in one place or body but within the repetitive chanting that breaks and then continues, breaks and continues. This is the racial consciousness, a posthuman 'ness, ness': the quality of knowing, along with other things, their breaking and continuing. Their sentience enacts and figures a constant self-transformation in the shape of what is lacerated and held by antiphonal waves of differential materiality. These harmonic voices emit their own movements and tambors, calling back and forth to the forcible movements of logistical slavery. The voice is always a materiality in/of/as marronage, the friction of one body moving amid, alongside the world's body.

Prince's moving reiterations likewise speak an earthly vocality, a tectonic shifting that allegorically chants, as if in protest against colonial extraction: 'The earth was groaning and shaking; everything tumbling about; and my mistress and the slaves were shrieking and crying out, "The earthquake! the earthquake!"' (17). The earth moves as if in response to or harmony with Prince's own, earlier utterances that groan and shake and tumble about the most violent sections of the narrative. The chthonic protest resists the anthropocentric mining of salt ponds and enslaved flesh, fracturing the totality of the landscape and the entire scene of labor. Prince's alliances with jar and earth are not simply born from three objectified bodies bridged by a sentimental imagination. Their mutual, responsive motions, wrought by labor and misuse, create an alternative to human subjectivity. These Romantically ruined bodies route the desire for wholeness or white being with their polyphonic utterances that do not attest to a 'being-with' that would demand a supplementary other but that assert a layering of ever-spreading sounds, a motion that harmonizes posthuman allies in ever-changing sentience.

This is not to say that these texts never voice a desire for human subjectivity or never assert a more individualized consciousness through classic Romantic self-reflexivity. It is to suggest that Romantic-era writers, as much as they worried over the Wordsworthian 'half-perceived, half-created' self and its separateness from nature, were likewise moved to create models of experience and transformation that depended upon collaborative mutual affects, movements, and changes of shape among multiple entities with different kinds of materiality. The art of these differences calls out to be understood in harmonic together*ness*, in a key other-than-white universality. Not all corporate, posthuman consciousness was beneficial to all parties, but cross-species alliances – created through shared material affects that transgress bodily and mental boundaries – discover another way to route the denigrating effects of Western, individualized, white consciousness. Such affects subtend the twinned Enlightenment gods of 'thought' and 'feeling' with a sentience confabulated through movements and rests of multiple materialities, including whimsical and violent posthuman figurality. This figurality is something writers live and breathe with, which conspires to make us, too, as we share our 'ing' with it, moving in more ways than the human.

Notes

1. Two recent and nuanced examples of complex arguments about the relation between nature and the poetic imagination include Orrin N. C. Wang's *Techno-Magism: Media, Mediation, and the Cut of Romanticism* and Richard Sha's recent *Imagination and Science in Romanticism*. Wang resists the 'return to nature' approach of new materialisms to avert a philosophy seemingly blind to the object as commodity, as well as 'calls to erase the subject object divide not to rescue the subject but to insist upon the primordial notion of a divide, break, or split – *différance*, if you will – that inflects the radical notion of figure bequeathed to us by deconstructive thought' (10). For Wang, the deconstructive figure (*qua* poetry but also other forms of visual mediation) rescues what Graham Harman has called the primordial goo of new materialism's smoorging of subject and object into a seemingly undifferentiated materiality (Harman, 'Agential'). I take the term 'smoorg' from Walt Kelly's *Pogo*, vol. 1 (New York: Fantagraphics Books, 2011). Bruno Latour refers to a 'flat ontology' that allegedly engulfs both Enlightenment subject and the commodified, differential object – not to mention, as others have argued, the commodified object of slavery's non-being. Sha, in a very different register, investigates 'the new materialism's Romantic past,' but with one insuperable caveat: 'From Shelley's perspective, the new materialists have lost the skepticism that comes with the need to think about matter as necessarily imagined. If materiality is entwined with imagination, then it can neither rescue the imagination from the charge of fecklessness nor serve as a counterweight to imagination. Instead, the force of Romantic materiality lies within the worlds it makes epistemologically available and open to question' (33).
2. In literary scholarship, see Jonathan Kramnick's chapter on panpsychism (*Paper Minds*) and Adela Pinch's recent article on Victorian panpsychism, along with scholarship on Blake such as Joseph Fletcher's analysis of Leibnitzian echoes in early writings.
3. I use Achille Mbembe's term 'necropolitics' to denote the 'right to kill' that colonial regimes and empires used to transplant and control their slave labor.
4. See Stuart Curran's 'The I Altered.'
5. See Marlon B. Ross, *The Contours of Masculine Desire*.
6. See Richard Sha's essay on force in *Romanticism and the Emotions*.
7. See Robert Kaufman's 'Red Kant, or The Persistence of the Third *Critique* in Adorno and Jameson.'
8. There were, of course, other scientific accounts of change – chemical affinity, geological sedimentation, neurological transmission, Galvanism, to name a few. I have resorted to a post-Humean version of affect that certainly takes some of its energy from contemporaneous accounts of force and electricity, as well as the passions, but conceptualizes change through figuration and more posthuman ideas about affect.
9. Shaviro likewise intimates a form of posthuman affect in his discussions of panpsychism, although he might not acknowledge it as such: 'the value activity of an entity that persists through time is not just a matter of

self-perpetuation or of the continually renewed achievement of homeostatic equilibrium. It may well also involve growth or shrinkage and assimilation or expulsion, or an active self-transformation and becoming-other. Such processes are more akin to … "the will to change" … the active self-valuation of all entities is in fact the best warrant for their sentience, for "value activity" is a matter of feeling and sometimes responding' (89).

10. For another version of Godwin's account of Wollstonecraft's intellectual endeavors, see Anne C. McCarthy's 'Falling in Love with the Author in Godwin's *Memoirs* of Wollstonecraft.'
11. Saidiya V. Hartman makes the seminal claim in *Scenes of Subjection* that the slave cannot be defined simply as/by labor but rather as a fungibility that becomes figurative and abstract, as a vessel for all sorts of demands and desires.
12. See Lussier and Sha (*Imagination*) on dynamic materiality tied to contemporaneous science, Washington on the figuration of light in 'Triumph of Life,' and Linda Brigham for a French feminist reading of the after-effects of Asia's transformation.
13. I want to be very clear that I do not mean to elide South Asian liberationist struggles against the British empire, with which Shelley was quite familiar, and Black theorists (then or now). The use of Gumbs's 'black feminist metaphysicians' is meant to position Asia as a theorist of race who attempts to find a way out of the humanist white/objectified non-white bind. The constellation of Gumbs's archive with Shelley's drama is meant to be a provocation for us to think about how Shelley may be struggling with race in his own attempt to reconstruct consciousness without universalizing it.
14. Barad's quantum analysis has its echoes in Shelley's understanding of early quantum physics, as both Mark Lussier and Arkady Plotnitsky have argued. For a Baradian reading of the late Shelleyan poetics of light, see Chris Washington's essay, 'The Dark Side of the Light: The Triumph of Love in Shelley's *The Triumph of Life*.'
15. For another, recent reading of Shelley's liberationist similes and affect see Julie Carlson's chapter in *Romanticism and the Emotions*.
16. Karen Swann offers another reading of 'other-worldly or unworldly figure' in Shelley's 'The Witch of Atlas' in her essay 'Shelley's Pod People.'
17. I use shape rather than form here to suggest that shape is a more improvisatory way to acknowledge, rather than mark, appearance, body, or figure. Form, even despite the Kantian purpose without purposiveness and its alleged sidestepping of teleology, was often used in scientific and literary discourses as a specific structure, particularly inflected by anatomy. For more on form see Dahlia Porter, Richard Sha (*Imagination*), and David Fairer's accounts of mixed forms, among others.
18. Much of the criticism on Mary Prince has been devoted to discussing the mediation of her narrative by both her amanuensis and her editor. While it is true that Prince's 'voice' was appropriated by the white abolitionary movement, and while we cannot know how much of the narration uses her words and how much has been erased and rewritten by white writers, as Gillian Whitlock recounts, my argument here is that the repetitive intonations of the text resemble an aurality Prince would have heard in spirituals

and other songs. If there were a place that we might hear Prince's voice, or an intimation of it, it might very well be these repetitions. For a deconstructive reading of the silence of Mary Prince, see Kerry Sinanan, 'The "Slave" as Cultural Artifact: The Case of Mary Prince.'
19. Prince does not have children or nor does she intimate the possibility of her own pregnancy (either by her masters or her later husband). The libel trial that followed the publication of her *History* does allege sexual lasciviousness in her relations with Captain Abbot as a means of discrediting her character. While such accusations of lying and promiscuity are part and parcel of undermining women's writing in the Romantic period, Prince's sexuality is nevertheless separated from a biopolitical agenda – in ways damning for her within the Christian abolitionary circuit but perhaps revealing to us as a means by which she was in marronage from the demands of reproductive labor and the bodily disability that resulted from such work.

References

Alaimo, Stacy. *Exposed: Environmental Politics and Pleasures in Posthuman Times*. Minneapolis: University of Minnesota Press, 2016.
—. 'Thinking as the Stuff of the World.' *O-Zone: A Journal of Object-Oriented Studies* 1 (2014): 13–21.
Allewaert, Monique. 'Swamp Sublime: Ecological Resistance in the American Plantation Zone.' *PMLA* 123 (2008): 340–57.
Barad, Karen. *Meeting the Universe Halfway: Quantum Physics and the Entanglement of Matter and Meaning*. Durham, NC: Duke University Press, 2007.
Benjamin, Ruha. *Race After Technology: Abolitionist Tools for the New Jim Code*. Cambridge: Polity Press, 2019.
Bennett, Jane. *Vibrant Matter: A Political Ecology of Things*. Durham, NC: Duke University Press, 2010.
Brennan, Teresa. *The Transmission of Affect*. Ithaca, NY: Cornell University Press, 2004.
Brigham, Linda. 'The Postmodern Semiotics of *Prometheus Unbound*.' *Studies in Romanticism* 33.1 (1994): 31–56.
Chalmers, David. 'The Hard Problem of Consciousness.' *The Blackwell Companion to Consciousness*. Ed. Max Velmans and Susan Schneider. Malden, MA: Blackwell, 2007. 225–35.
Cohen, Jeffrey Jerome. *Stone: An Ecology of the Inhuman*. Minneapolis: Minnesota Press, 2015.
Curran, Stuart. 'The I Altered.' *Romanticism and Feminism*. Ed. Anne K. Mellor. Bloomington: Indiana University Press, 1988. 185–207.
Dennett, Daniel C. *Consciousness Explained*. Boston: Little, Brown and Company, 1991.
Fairer, David. *Organising Poetry: The Coleridge Circle, 1790–1798*. Oxford: Oxford University Press, 2009.
Fletcher, Joseph. 'Leibnitz, the Infinite, and Blake's Early Metaphysics.' *Studies in Romanticism* 56.2 (Summer 2017): 129–55.

Godwin, William. *Memoirs of the Author of* A Vindication of the Rights of Woman. Ed. Pamela Clemit and Genia Luria Walker. Peterborough, ON: Broadview Press, 2001.
Gottlieb, Evan. *Romantic Realities: Speculative Realism and British Romanticism.* Edinburgh: Edinburgh University Press, 2016.
Gumbs, Alexis Pauline. *M Archive: After the End of the World.* Durham, NC: Duke University Press, 2018.
Haraway, Donna. *Tentacular Thinking: Anthropocene, Capitalocene, Chthulucene.* Durham, NC: Duke University Press, 2016.
Harman, Graham. 'Agential and Speculative Realism: Some Remarks on Barad's Ontology.' *rhizomes* 30 (2016). http://www.rhizomes.net/issue30/harman.html (last accessed December 15, 2021).
—. *The Quadruple Object.* New York: Zone Books, 2011.
Harney, Stefano and Fred Moten. *The Undercommons: Fugitive Planning & Black Study.* Minor Compositions, 2013.
Hartman, Geoffrey. 'Romanticism and "Anti-Self-Consciousness."' *Romanticism and Consciousness: Essays in Criticism.* Ed. Harold Bloom. New York: W. W. Norton, 1970.
Hartman, Saidiya V. *Scenes of Subjection: Terror, Slavery, and Self-Making in Nineteenth-Century America.* Oxford: Oxford University Press, 1997.
Hume, David. *A Treatise of Human Nature.* Ed. Ernest O. Mossner. New York: Penguin, 1969.
Jackson, Zakiyyah Iman. *Becoming Human: Matter and Meaning in an Antiblack World.* New York: New York University Press, 2020.
Jordan, Neil. *Freedom as Marronage.* Chicago: University of Chicago Press, 2015.
Kaufman, Robert. 'Red Kant, or The Persistence of the Third *Critique* in Adorno and Jameson.' *Critical Inquiry* 26.4 (Summer 2000): 682–724.
Keats, John. *Keats's Poetry and Prose.* Ed. Jeffrey N. Cox. New York: W. W. Norton, 2008.
King, Tiffany Lethabo. *The Black Shoals: Offshore Formations of Black and Native Studies.* Durham, NC: Duke University Press, 2019.
Kramnick, Jonathan. *Paper Minds: Literature and the Ecology of Consciousness.* Chicago: University of Chicago Press, 2018.
Latour, Bruno. *Reassembling the Social: An Introduction to Actor-Network-Theory.* Oxford: Oxford University Press, 2005.
Lussier, Mark. *Romantic Dynamics: The Physicality of Matter.* New York: Palgrave Macmillan, 1999.
McCarthy, Anne C. 'Falling in Love with the Author in Godwin's *Memoirs* of Wollstonecraft.' *Essays in Romanticism* 25.2 (2018): 123–39.
Marder, Michael. *Plant-Thinking: A Philosophy of Vegetal Life.* New York: Columbia University Press, 2013.
Massumi, Brian. *Parables for the Virtual: Movement, Affect, Sensation.* Durham, NC: Duke University Press, 2002.
Mbembe, Achille. *Necropolitics.* Trans. Steven Corcoran. Durham, NC: Duke University Press, 2019.
Moten, Fred and Stefano Harney. *The Undercommons: Fugitive Planning & Black Study.* Brooklyn, NY: Autonomedia, 2013.

Nagel, Thomas. *Mind and Cosmos: Why the Materialist Neo-Darwinian Conception of Nature is Almost Certainly False.* Oxford: Oxford University Press, 2012.

Pinch, Adela. 'The Appeal of Panpsychism in Victorian Britain.' *Romanticism and Victorianism on the Net* 65 (2014). https://doi.org/10.7202/1069867ar (last accessed December 7, 2021).

Plotnitsky, Arkady. 'All Shapes of Light: Quantum Mechanical Shelley.' *Shelley: Poet and Legislator of the World*, ed. Betty T. Bennett and Stuart Curran. Baltimore: Johns Hopkins University Press, 1995. 263–174.

Porter, Dahlia. *Science, Form, and the Problem of Induction in British Romanticism.* Cambridge: Cambridge University Press, 2018.

Prince, Mary. *The History of Mary Prince.* Ed. Sara Salih. New York: Penguin. 2000.

Robinson, Mary. *The Selected Poems of Mary Robinson.* Ed. Judith Pascoe. Peterborough, ON: Broadview Press, 2000.

Ross, Marlon B. *The Contours of Masculine Desire: Romanticism and the Rise of Women's Poetry.* Oxford: Oxford University Press, 1990.

Sha, Richard. *Imagination and Science in Romanticism.* Baltimore: Johns Hopkins University Press, 2018.

—. 'The Motion behind Romantic Emotion.' *Romanticism and the Emotions.* Ed. Joel Faflak and Richard Sha. Cambridge: Cambridge University Press, 2016. 19–47.

Shaviro, Steven. *The Universe of Things: On Speculative Realism.* Minneapolis: University of Minnesota Press, 2014.

Sinanan, Kerry. 'The "Slave" as Cultural Artifact: The Case of Mary Prince.' *Studies in Eighteenth-Century Culture* 49 (2020): 69–87.

Singer, Kate. 'Surfing the Crimson Wave: Romantic New Materialisms and Speculative Feminisms.' *Romanticism and Speculative Realism.* Ed. Chris Washington and Anne C. McCarthy. New York: Bloomsbury Press, 2019. 111–32.

Speitz, Michele. 'Blood Sugar and Salt Licks: Corroding Bodies and Preserving Nations in *The History of Mary Prince, a West Indian Slave, Related by Herself.*' *Circulations: Romanticism and the Black Atlantic.* Ed. Paul Youngquist and Fran Botkin. *Romantic Circles Praxis* (2011). https://romantic-circles.org/praxis/circulations/HTML/praxis.2011.speitz.html (last accessed December 7, 2021).

Swann, Karen. 'Shelley's Pod People.' *Romanticism and the Insistence of the Aesthetic.* Ed. Forest Pyle. *Romantic Circles* (February 2015). http://romantic-circles.org/praxis/aesthetic/swann/swann.html (last accessed December 7, 2021).

Wang, Orrin N. C. *Techno-Magism: Media, Mediation, and the Cut of Romanticism.* New York: Fordham University Press, forthcoming.

Warren, Calvin L. *Ontological Terror: Blackness, Nihilism, and Emancipation.* Durham, NC: Duke University Press, 2018.

Washington, Chris. 'The Dark Side of the Light: Triumph of Love in Shelley's *The Triumph of Life.*' *The Futures of Shelley's* Triumph. Ed. Joel Faflak. *Romantic Circles* (2019). http://romantic-circles.org/praxis/triumph/praxis.2019.triumph.washington.html (last accessed December 7, 2021).

Wellmann, Janina. *The Form of Becoming: Embryology and the Epistemology of Rhythm, 1760–1830*. Trans. Kate Sturge. New York: Zone Books, 2017.

Whitlock, Gillian. *Postcolonial Life Narratives: Testimonial Transactions*. Oxford: Oxford University Press, 2015.

Wollstonecraft, Mary. *Letters Written in Sweden, Norway, and Denmark*. Ed. Tone Brekke and Jon Mee. Oxford: Oxford University Press, 2009.

Wynter, Sylvia. 'Unsettling the Coloniality of Being/Power/Truth/Freedom: Towards the Human, after Man, Its Overrepresentation – An Argument.' *The New Centennial Review* 3.3 (2003): 257–337.

Chapter 15

At Peace with Strangers: Feeling Disoriented in the London Panorama of Constantinople, 1801–1802

Humberto Garcia

Strangely, the foreigner lives within us: he is the hidden face of our identity, the space that wrecks our abode, the time in which understanding and affinity founder.

(Kristeva 1)

Most relevant for the study of social cognition and affect is how the imagination estranges the self, as elucidated in *Romanticism and Consciousness*. In Romantic literature, the introspective subject overcomes solipsism by identifying with the stranger within, a psychic alienation that helped forge a common national culture.[1] Hospitality is put to the test in terms of what Julia Kristeva conceives as global modernity's socio-psychological imperative: to live with others is to live as others. To illustrate this self-othering, my chapter examines the panorama of Constantinople painted by Henry Aston Barker (1774–1856) on site in 1800. His *Constantinople from the Tower of Galata* and *Constantinople from the Tower of Leander* compliment one other as Europe and Asia, respectively. The first view was reproduced in 1813 as colored aquatints in eight plates (Barker, *A Series*; see https://edinburghuniversitypress.com/book-romanticism-and-consciousness-revisited.html). The original paintings (now lost) appeared on a 10,000-square-foot cylindrical canvas hung inside a rotunda in London's Leicester Square, immersing the Muslim nobleman Mirza Abu Talib Khan Isfahani (1752–1806) in a 360-degree simulacrum. He left Calcutta for London in 1799 and returned to his hometown, Lucknow, via Constantinople during the Peace of Amiens in 1802, as commemorated in his exuberant Persian poetry about Barker's life-like artwork. In the poet's eyes, panoramic Constantinople epitomizes the divine mandate to welcome strangers. This vision of peace, I argue, is intrinsic to a metropolitan self-consciousness oriented toward Islamic–Ottoman understandings of social relationality.

Reorienting England through this visual modality brings home the exotic Orient as imagined by Europeans. The knowledge–power nexus that Edward Said dates to the Napoleonic occupation of Ottoman Egypt and Syria in 1798–1801 was to institutionalize what Raymond Schwab dubs the 'Oriental Renaissance': when English and French philologists discovered Sanskrit, Arabic, and Persian classical texts as crucial to Europe's cultural revivification as were the Greek and Latin classics discovered by their Italian predecessors three centuries prior. This second rebirth sparked European enthusiasm for an India dominated by the British, as expressed by Friedrich Schlegel in 1800. His often-quoted dictum that 'we must seek the supreme romanticism in the Orient' led M. H. Abrams to conclude, before Schwab did, that orientalist philology had incubated a Romantic lyric consciousness (qtd in Schwab 13).[2] Orientalism, then, disciplined the sovereign Western subject in indirect ways. The rights-bearing, bourgeois (male) individual who presumes to possess a mind independent from society and nature gave rise to a political liberty predicated on the myth of psychological depth that others lack, even when orientalist tropes are absent (Makdisi 605). By contrast, the panorama's Orient demands a bodily shift in geographic orientation that inspires viewers to identify with and as strangers.

Applying Sarah Ahmed's queer phenomenology, I treat the orientalism operative in spatial and cartographic markings as a homing device by which raced, sexed, and gendered bodies are spatialized unevenly. Making subjects cohere around a given point in space facilitates an epistemic dominance vulnerable to cognitive dissonance, which compels them to find their home in racially queer geographies (14, 160). Accordingly, queerness refers to mediated desires that reorient social consciousness toward an alien environment in which sexual and gender norms are kept in abeyance. To track such a disorientation, the first half of this chapter maps out the wartime mediations that warped Barker's patriotic representation of warless conquest: spectators who pretend to be Ottoman subjects eager to submit to a foreign British authority, even as the discord between form and ideology can sometimes lead them astray. In the second half of this chapter, I argue that Abu Talib's poetry takes this detour to find Islamic hospitality among Ottoman strangers, a vision that complements British foreign policy in the Levant but without reproducing an orientalist world view. His poetic tribute to Barker's art dis(re)orients Englishness in three respects: the negation of Europe's Greco-Roman patrimony, the queering of the heteronormative distinction between a masculine West and an effeminate East, and the irrepresentability of intercultural relations in a peacetime haunted by war. Whereas, for Daniel O'Quinn, these connected crises of empire find their history in Antoine-Ignace Melling's topographical prints of Constantinople and in Lord Byron's Turkish Tales, for me these crises come to roost in a metropolitan social media not yet Western enough to subject its own strangers to a homogenous nationality (364–412). The panoramic view from nowhere integrates London virtually into an Ottoman cityscape that normalizes what the British consider an aberrant imperial–sexual subject position.

Europe in Asia

Henry Aston assisted his father, Robert Barker, who, on May 25, 1793, opened the Leicester Square panorama for exhibiting a vast circular painting that immerses viewers in a virtual reality, instantly transporting them from the familiar metropolis to an exotic city or a remote battlefield. According to Robert's 1787 patent, this invention was first called *la nature à coup d'oeil*, or 'nature at a glance,' as seen inside a circular enclosure, with indirect lighting from the top and accessible through a darkened corridor leading to two raised platforms: an upper circle 30 feet in diameter and a lower circle 50 feet in diameter ('Specification' 165). By turning 360 degrees, viewers cross-examine the two views from 'whatever situation he [they] may wish they should imagine themselves, feel[ing] as if really on the very spot' (167). The sensation of being in two places at once has led scholars to locate in this aesthetic an outlet for resisting totalizing ideologies. Yet this critical agency is taken to be a tool of governmentality, panoramic bodies that internalize a one-sided nationalism under the state's 'absolute dominance' (Comment 19).[3] Government by consent is the fantasy through which viewers 'would confer power on themselves as British subjects,' writes Denise Blake Oleksijczuk, so the more they compared Barker's two paintings of Constantinople, 'the more they were subjected to the views' political claims' (94). A closer look at these views alongside their accompanying printed keys and map presents a different picture: a desire for total world possession mapped onto, and potentially disrupted by, a hospitable Islamic imperium. Such a cosmopolitan reckoning induces the 'sense of always looking at one's self through the eyes of others' that, for W. E. B. Du Bois, characterizes Black subjects' abjection and redemption in white-dominated society (8). Double consciousness, I argue, is precisely what Henry Aston Barker's panorama exhibit inculcates in viewers to provincialize England vis-à-vis the Ottoman empire's gendered topography.

Wartime conditions Barker's perilous artistic quest. On August, 26 1799, he left Portsmouth and crossed a Mediterranean recently retaken by the British navy, disembarking at Palermo. He sought out the British ambassador at the court of Naples, Sir William Hamilton, in the hope of securing permission for future painting expeditions to Italy, only to meet his wife, Lady Hamilton. She introduced him to Admiral Horatio Nelson, who praised Barker's panorama on the 1798 Battle of the Nile as a great patriotic service to Britain's war with France. These contacts paved the way for the gracious reception the painter received in Constantinople on January 4, 1800. His plan to paint the city was approved by the chief commander of the Ottoman army, Ghezzar Pasha, after the British ambassador for the Sublime Porte, Lord Elgin, had intervened. Elgin had hired several London artists to draw ancient Greek ruins and sculptures in Ottoman lands, and between 1801 and 1812 had the marble frieze from the Parthenon in Athens shipped to London with the approval of Sultan Selim III, who ruled over Greece and had switched alliance from France to Britain. Elgin hosted Barker in Galata's French palace as the latter began work atop the Tower of Galata and afterwards the Tower of Leander on the Bosphorus's opposite bank under the watchful eyes of the Sultan's personal guard (Oleksijczuk 104–7). His sketch of the serene city was made possible by the intercultural sociability that Melling also experienced during his residency in the Ottoman court between 1784 and 1802.

Indeed, his *Voyage pittoresque de Constantinople et des rives du Bosphore* informs Barker's perspectival focus on nautical social life. Published in France in 1819, this large two-volume folio contains forty-eight black-and-white, wide-angle views of Constantinople and its environs, with twenty engravings of the city itself. These engravings vividly depict buildings and boats from a bird's-eye perspective that resonates with Barker's eight-part aquatints and the original painting they refer to, except that the horizontal line is unbroken in the panorama's circular rotation whereas Melling's separate prints favor discontinuous viewing. In the former, viewers physically turn on a vertical axis as if they were looking out from the tower in real time. They can look straight at the horizon across the crescent-shaped harbor called the Golden Horn or tilt their heads down toward the dense foreground of tiled rooftops, treetops, narrow streets, and pedestrians in Turkish and European dress, located in suburban Galata and Pera. In other words, they can switch sights at will between the domain where the Sultan rules over his subjects and the quarters where European merchants and diplomats reside as his guests. Notwithstanding differences in medium, the aquatints' first plate adheres to the division between foreground and background in Melling's *View of a Part of the City of Constantinople with Seraglio Point Taken from the Suburbs of Pera* (Figure 15.1 and online figures). Drawn from the Swedish Palace, the latter collapses the middle ground

Figure 15.1 Antoine-Ignace Melling, *View of a Part of the City of Constantinople with Seraglio Point taken from the Suburbs of Pera*, 1819. Engraving, 25.6 × 38.2 cm. Getty Research Institute, Los Angeles (93-B15373)

into the bustling waterway with ships sailing to and behind the Tower of Galata (pictured on the right) that is part of Pera's old Genoese fortifications, diagonally opposite the Hagia Sophia Mosque on the central horizon. Barker reproduces a similar vista symbolically oriented toward the sultan's palace at Seraglio Point, where Anatolia terminates in the harbor separating Asia from Europe. The unsettled middle ground in Melling's prints signifies 'a future for Franco-Ottoman cooperation against rising British power in the post-Napoleonic world,' which Barker repurposes to claim the future for the present Anglo-Ottoman alliance instead (O'Quinn 385). Yet this nationalist message is at odds with the directive that panorama-goers adopt the precarious viewing position of the artist, dependent on the Ottoman military for his safety.[4]

This disjunction in visual messaging is mitigated by the textual materials that direct viewers toward select spots on the giant canvas. The original panorama painting of the first view can be inferred from the eight aquatints, each overloaded with visual information that is packaged into a coherent cultural–political narrative in the 1801 descriptive key (Figure 15.2) and reference guide, both distributed at the Leicester panorama as souvenirs and memory aids. Seraglio Point's Topkapi Palace marks the 'Divan, where the Grand Signior gives Audience,' as the graphic cue for where a peaceful revolution begins and ends: the gaze is led circuitously to the 'green Kiosk,' where the Sultan parts with 'Captain Pasha,' who will sail back to him to perform a grand ceremony (as specified in the reference guide[5]); eleven indexed mosques, including those of Hagia Sophia and of Sultan Suleiman I; the Sublime Porte, where the Grand Vizier lives; the burnt column built under the Roman Emperor Constantine; three caravansaries for merchant travelers; the Eski Serai or old palace; the palace of the Janissary Aga; the Fortress of the Seven Towers (Yedikule), where state prisoners are held; the Captain Pasha's harem; the Swedish and English palaces; a school for preparing youth to serve the Sultan; the Tower of Leander; Prince's Islands; and 'Lord Elgin's Embassy by Water.' Intermixed military and religious sites gravitate around an auspicious event: Lord Elgin's ship, the *Phaeton*, is on course to block from view the Sultan's palace while Captain Pasha's ship, the *Selim of 120 Guns*, lags behind (Oleksijczuk 90).

The revolutionary turn anticipated in this scene becomes apparent in the second view from the Tower of Leander, which can be reconstructed from the diagram (Figure 15.3). Most prominent is 'a Division of the Turkish Fleet, returning into Port and saluting the Seraglio' with cannon fire, pictured in smoke, as it approaches the same spot in the peninsula, with indexes for the six mosques in the vicinity. This naval procession heading toward Seraglio Point subjects panorama viewers to Ottoman

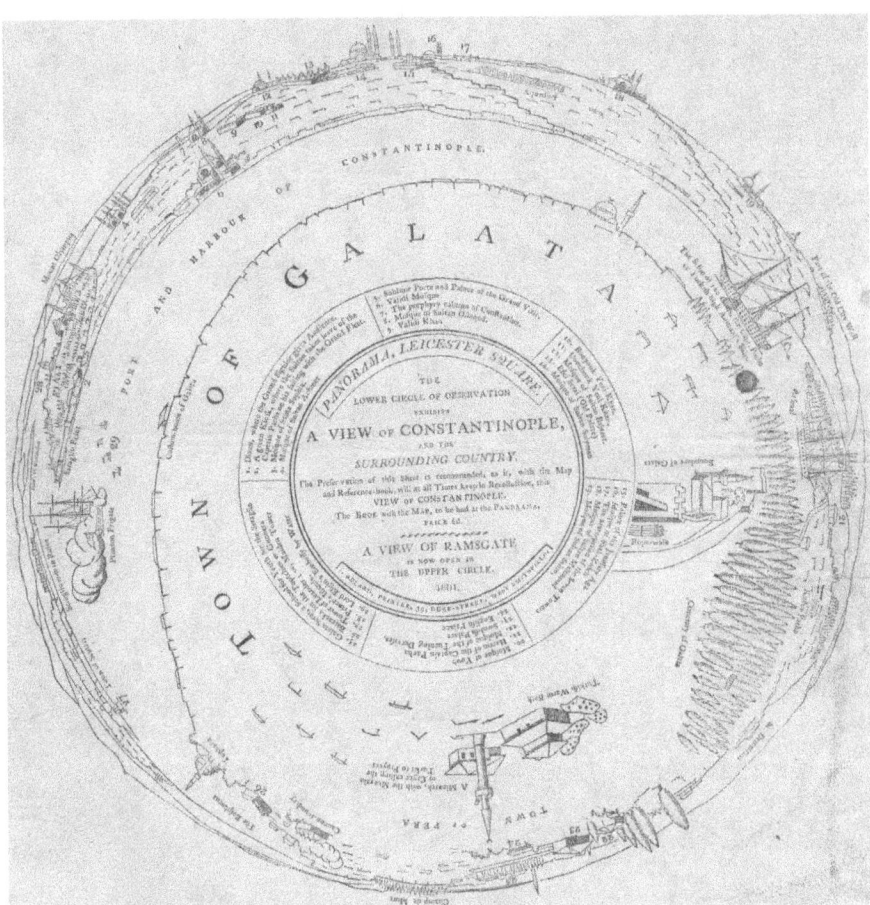

Figure 15.2 Henry Aston Barker, *View of Constantinople from the Tower of Galata*, 1801. Engraved key, 15.2 × 12.5 inches. John Johnson Collection Entertainments Folder 6 (4). Bodleian Library, University of Oxford.

imperial stagecraft. The Sultan departs from this point for his summer home by the Bosphorus, the 'Palace of Dolma Baktché,' joined by his attendants in seven boats as he is shown returning in a different barge, as 'customary,' alongside the chief Black eunuch in another ship, to culminate in a homecoming celebration. On the key's opposite ends are the 'Turkish Fleet' and 'A Turkish 74' sailing ceremoniously in the Sultan's direction. These ships occupy the respective positions of the *Phaeton* and *Selim of 120 Guns* in the first key, as if Lord Elgin had taken over the Ottoman navy. Because 'both [paintings] are intended as explanatory of each other,' as written on the diagram, this visual parallel has ideological resonance. Presumably, the British alone are destined to protect peacetime sociability on this international waterway

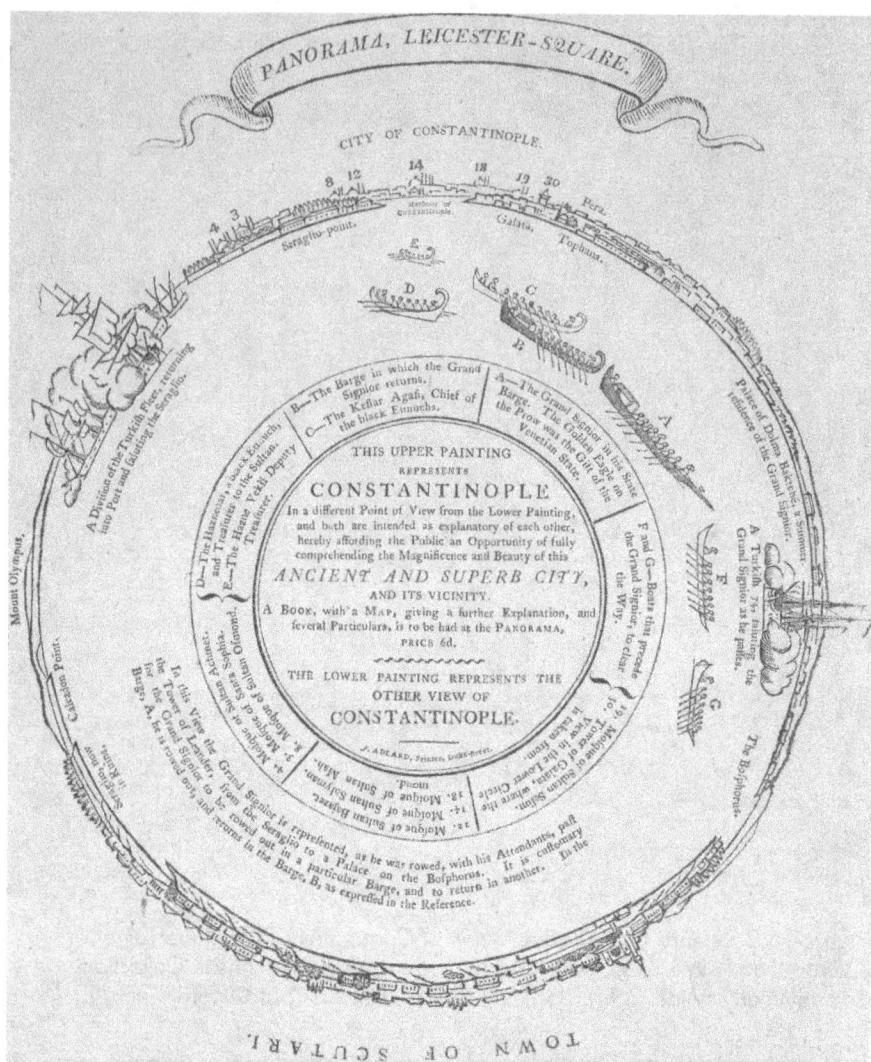

Figure 15.3 Henry Aston Barker, *View of Constantinople from the Tower of Leander*, 1801. Engraved key, 15.2 × 12.5 inches cut to 9.5 × 8 inches. © Victoria and Albert Museum, London.

non-violently by upholding Ottoman ceremonial protocols. In this circular displacement of power, the smoke billowing from *Phaeton*'s fired cannons, as graphically depicted in the key, initiates the welcoming ceremony for the Sultan before the *Selim of 120 Guns* does so on its return voyage. Viewers participate in Lord Elgin's conquest without war.

That the Sultan travels with 'Keslar Agafi, Chief of the black Eunuchs' is another important detail that the pamphlet guide, *A Concise Account of the Views of Constantinople*, symbolically links to Britain's geopolitical supremacy. The text considers what lies inside the buildings shown in the painting while withholding details, unlike the textual voyeurism deployed in Melling's *Voyage pittoresque* to entertain a peep into the Sultan's harem (O'Quinn 382). The final paragraph dwells on these impenetrable erotic interiors:

> The word Seraglio means a Palace, and that of the Grand Signior is divided by an intermediate apartment, which separates the Harem from what is properly the Seraglio; and though the whole is in general called the Seraglio, that part which is called the Harem, strictly signifies the apartments of the women, and the inclosures [sic] appropriated to their use. The other part signifies those buildings occupied by the Grand Signior, and his household. Foreign ambassadors have each a Seraglio, but no Harem; and every Turk may have a Harem; but the Vizer [sic] himself has no Seraglio. The Grand Signior has both. (Barker, *A Concise* 8–9)

The male–female spatial divide that only the Grand Signior can traverse recalls orientalist fantasies about the harem, where his many wives remain secluded under his eunuchs' supervision. In European political thought, this fantastical space for illicit sex constitutes a decadent despotism peculiar to the effeminate East, functioning as a negative foil for rational heteronormative governments in the manly West (Grosrichard). The digression as to which imperial subjects possess either a palace or a harem, while seemingly irrelevant to the painting, is crucial to its disciplinary regime. Visitors who consult the guidebook are assured that the Sultan's sexual politics will not corrupt Lord Elgin on his journey to supersede the Captain Pasha at Seraglio Point because 'foreign ambassadors' stay in a palace without a harem whereas the reverse pertains to the Turkish high admiral. One might surmise that his ship's diminishment in stature is occasioned not so much by British naval ingenuity but by his harem's proximity to the royal arsenal from where he sets sail (Figure 15.2; number 21 in the key).

Geographic boundary-making in gendered and sexualized spaces is what reorients metropolitan desire in Barker's exhibition. As described by Oleksijczuk, between November 23, 1801 and May 15, 1802 'the first view the European side' was shown in the larger, lower circle alongside the second 'view from the Asiatic side' in the smaller, upper circle (94). Each view affords a geographical–temporal distinction – Europe associated with the past, Asia with the present – that corresponds to a male–female binary (112–15). On the one hand, the Tower of Galata presents the city from a masculine perspective fixated on strongman politics – the Lord Elgin and Captain Pasha race to the seraglio. On the other, the Tower of Leander presents the city from a feminine perspective, as symbolized in its name – the Greek myth about a young man, Leander, who swam nightly from the eastern shore to unite with his lover, Hero, a priestess of Aphrodite who lit the way for him to meet her in the tower on the other side. One night, when a storm extinguished the light, he drowned midway. *A Concise Account* forestalls the philhellenic nostalgia conveyed in this legend by preferring the name 'Maiden Tower,' which refers to the Turkish story about 'a Greek princess [who] was confined in it' (14). Spectators shuffling back and forth between the two circles engage in a self-reflective circularity: the first painting pictures the Tower of Leander that they would virtually inhabit in the second painting, which pictures the Tower of Galata that refers to their initial viewpoint. They imagine themselves looking back like strangers in a bifurcated mirror (Oleksijczuk 120). Their selves split into European-male and Asian-female. This double consciousness is rationalized by the commentary on the seraglio/harem or, in the 'Cemetery of Galata,' on the gravestones with marbled turbans signifying interred males and those without turbans signifying females (Barker, *A Concise* 15). In other words, spectators' imaginary mobility across divisions in gendered sociality makes them as privileged and perverse as the Sultan himself, seeing the city queerly through his eyes.

While the guide's references to 'Arsenal with Men of War,' 'Mosque of the Turning Dervises,' 'Cemetery of Galata,' 'Turkish Warm Bath,' and 'a Minareh, with the Muezzin or Cryer calling the Turks to Prayer' invoke orientalist clichés, some descriptors emphasize cultural similitude. For example, 'at a distance ... appears Mount Olympus, ever covered with snow, with various scenery of classical ground,' the backdrop to ancient Greek myths. It 'rises on the Plain of Troy' near 'the City of Brusa, built by Hannibal, and formerly the capital of the Turks' (5–6, 15). Similarly, Constantine's 'Porphyry or Burnt Column ... had on the top a statue of Apollo, which was blown down and demolished' (11). The city, 'called now by the Turks Stambol' (6), incorporates Greco-Roman antiquity insofar as the House of Osman, which hails from Islamic and Turkic Anatolia, considered itself the heir of *Rum*, comprising the former Roman and Byzantine territories (Ergul). By privileging this Ottoman identity, the guide erases the aesthetic gains made by European antiquarians who, since the 1760s, had de-Ottomanized the Ionian peninsula to reconceive it as the birthplace of Western civilization (O'Quinn 213–66).

The city's architecture is traced to 'Pausanias, the Lacedemonian king,' Roman 'emperor Severus,' and Constantine when he rebuilt the city, later conquered by 'the Grecian Emperor Constantinus,' followed by 'the Turks, under Mahomet the Great, with an army of 300,000 men' (Barker, *A Concise* 6–7). Accordingly, Stambol (Istanbul) is a trans-imperial palimpsest. 'The Seraglio' that Elgin's ship triumphantly approaches in the key is not an exotic destination but a familiar 'space which formerly contained the City of Bizantium [sic]' (8). He is in effect claiming Europe's long-lost second home for the British empire. To convey this lesson, *A Concise Account* quotes Richard Knolles's *Generall Historie of the Turkes* and François Baron de Tott's memoir, two authoritative sources on the Ottoman empire. Their polemic against Muslim despotism and the Turkish menace to Christendom is nonetheless muted in the guide, as the Ottomans were no longer the formidable military adversary they once were. From Knolles's work readers learn that this 'noble city' is 'most fitly seated for the empire of the world' and from de Tott's that it was 'the most favourable for establishing a capital of the world' to one day become 'the center for the most useful productions and the most flourishing commerce' (8). Barker assimilates Britain's imperial aspirations into a Byzantine imaginative geography – adopted by the Ottomans – that casts this cosmopolitan city as the 'eye of the *oikoumenē*': the Greek phrase for a centrally located world civilization (Angelov 54–5).

To determine global positioning, viewers could consult the guide's map insert depicting the city from a southwest orientation (Figure 15.4). In locating the city and the surrounding area on the top facing south, 'Europe' on the bottom facing north, and 'Asia Minor' on the left facing east, the map decenters British cartography as the basis for universal

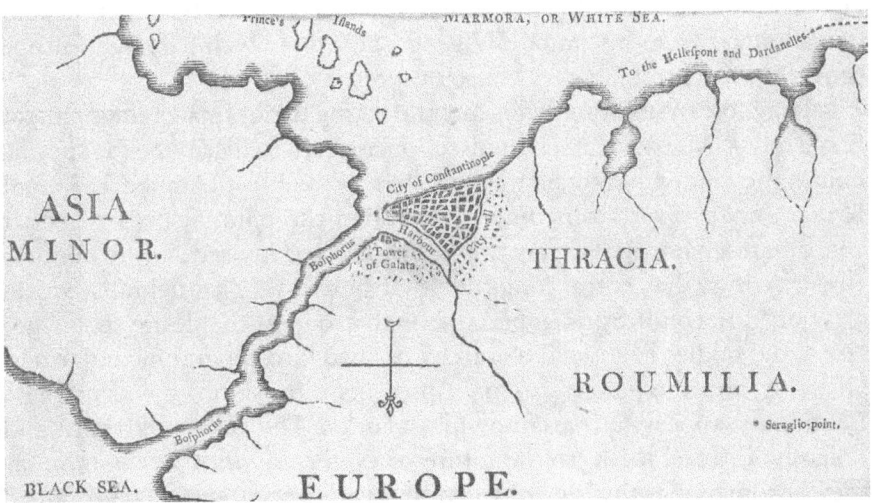

Figure 15.4 Henry Aston Barker, 'Map of Constantinople,' *A Concise Account of the Views of Constantinople ... at the Panorama, Leicester Square*. London: J. Adlard, 1801. © The British Library Board, shelfmark T.163(9.).

knowledge. At first glance, Europe appears near Asia, making it difficult to establish a singular vantage point for assessing the paintings. To the west, viewers would lose their bearings altogether. 'Thracia' is the ancient Greek name for the Balkan peninsula north of the Aegean – Thrace in northeastern Greece – paired with 'Roumillia' or Rumelia, whose etymology is the 'land of the Romans' covering Thrace, Macedonia, and Albania. The name pairing designates on the map an Ottoman territorial and administrative unit populated by *Rum*'s descendants. Where Western Europe should be located, according to modern European maps, is the phantasmagoric space where the Ottoman empire's Greco-Roman patrimony resides. Londoners looking for direction in this map would have had their imperial compass thrown off course. Their visual field would be reoriented toward an Islamic–Ottoman cartographical tradition that centers Stambol as the new Rome, emblematized in the directional cross capped with a crescent pointing to the 'Tower of Galata' (the masculine European side) in large type and aligned with Seraglio Point. The Tower of Leander is conspicuously absent. Again, a Eurocentric philhellenism is kept in abeyance. Instead, the map adapts a Muslim geographical schema akin to how the sixteenth-century Ottoman admiral and geographer Piri Reis had mapped out the capital in a southwestern aerial angle taken from the Tower of Galata.[6] This drastic reorientation foregoes the Greenwich prime meridian that by this time had made the British empire the planet's epistemic epicenter, which marginalized ancient Greek, Indian, Chinese, Persian, and Turkish cartographic knowledges and techniques (Sudan 156). Viewers' sense of national belonging would be dislodged from an immobile geography for which a fictive Europe provides access to planetary consciousness.

Feeling lost or confounded is integral to the panorama's remapping of Englishness. Maps normalize a direction as given to discipline the specific bodies they index – right as the East, left as the West (Ahmed 113). But Barker's map inverts this binary, disabling the paintings' race–gender coordinates. Metropolitan awareness is directed inward, not to confirm Greenwich as the central longitude that buttresses an orientalist world view but to orbit a trans-imperial axis that queers the desire to categorize sexed bodies in a racial hierarchy ossified into geographic polarities. Glancing into the Sultan's domain presents a topsy-turvy world where Londoners appear as harem-owning Turks. The map politically and sexually 'orients' them 'to the future or even *to a future occupation*' as they become what they behold: Ottoman subjects about to be subdued by the British foreigners whom they resemble (115).

In this imaginary doubling, who is the occupier and who is the occupied? Who is the guest and who is the host? These distinctions collapse into a societal togetherness that defies representation after Ottoman expansion was curtailed by the 1699 Treaty of Karlowitz, what O'Quinn calls the 'void place' for staging intercultural peace (50). How to capture this void in art is what dogged Barker on the ground. Although his diary abounds with racist remarks about the city's Greek and Turkish residents, he relied on them to pursue his artistic mission. As Melling had done when sketching the city, Barker participated in two-sided cultural exchanges as European empires vied for the sultanate's future, the key to controlling east–west trade routes after Napoleon's failed campaign to invade British India via Egypt and Syria created a power vacuum. Ottoman–European sociability entailed reciprocal borrowings in pictorial styles, genres, and practices, including cartographic knowledge production since the fifteenth century (Fraser; Curry; Andrea). The intimacy between strangers renders spatiality and temporality deeply problematic in Barker's gendering of peacetime. Cooperation before and after war indexes a social tension evident in his diary entry: 'Smoked a pipe, and drank coffee with a Turkish Gent'n,' despite 'the many instances of Turkish barbarity' (qtd in Oleksijczuk 109).

Nowhere are the panorama's disorientations more apparent than in those who felt at home among tolerant strangers. Consider the following observer riveted by Barker's art insofar as it transcends national and religious parochialisms: 'Constantinople, with its bearded and turbanned multitudes, quietly pitched beside a Christian thoroughfare, and offering neither persecution nor proselytism' (Hardcastle 152). Homing in on the scenery of plates five and six (see online figures), this person is more captivated by the amiable pedestrian interaction in the foreground than by the naval bravado in the middle ground. Peace affords the opportunity for living with an Islamic toleration preferable to an intolerant Anglican polity (Garcia, *Islam*). Double consciousness familiarizes the stranger as a friend, a relational term that Julie A. Carlson in this volume attributes to self-affirming justice in white society. The friend-in-difference confounds a stranger in the Leicester Square panorama, only to find himself at ease inside the abode of Islam; a realistic illusion that teleports Abu Talib Khan into the eye of the *oikoumenē*.

Hosting the Ottoman Romans

World peace was a mirage when the Indo-Persian Shi'i scholar, poet, and administrator had reached London via Cork and Dublin in January 1800. Desperate to evade court intrigues in the Indian state of Awadh, which drove him into poverty and despair as the British consolidated power in the region, the forlorn Abu Talib found solace among metropolitan strangers. They kindly took him to entertainment hubs that enveloped social life in a wartime mediascape, enabling him to befriend elite patrons and politicians while the British were at war with French, Irish, and Indian enemies. Elsewhere I have discussed his horror and dismay upon beholding simulated battles in London and Dublin, and his impression that Henry Barker's panorama of Nelson routing the French at Abu Qir in July 1798 presages Judgement Day (*England* 160–8). The sense of apocalyptic rapture that exhilarated Romantic poets was uppermost in Abu Talib's thoughts as he left London on June 7, 1802 to complete a pilgrimage. The Peace of Amiens, an insecure one-year truce between Britain and France, gave him enough time to scurry home via Paris, Genoa, Malta, and Constantinople in transit to Baghdad, where he worshipped at the shrines of Shi'i Imams in Kazmain, Najaf, and Karbala before sailing for Bombay. The entire journey is recorded in his *Masir-i Talibi fi Bilad i Afranji* (Travels of Talib in the Lands of the Franks), completed in 1803 and translated from Persian to English in 1810. It is a *rihla*, a travelogue that instills spiritual wisdom in South Asian readers. For this Persianate audience he also wrote, partly while in London, *Diwan-i Talib*, a poetry collection that has never been entirely translated into English.[7] In it are a few verses glorifying panoramic Constantinople. Mixed with English and French words, his hybrid poetics grapples with the profound disorientation he felt on seeing in Leicester Square the Islamic capital he would visit in person. His poetry rips the space–time continuum to create a virtual loophole wherein an untranslatable co-existence with strangers becomes spiritually redemptive, relocating Britain from the edge to the core of the Islamic homeland.

Diwan-i Talib is a *masnavi* (rhyming couplets) cataloging the markets, theaters, parks, and other popular amusements that make London a paradise on earth. Persianate writers in Central and South Asia had written similar poetry to praise the topographical features of major urban centers in the Safavid, Mughal, and Ottoman empires, focusing on the excellence or virtue of city dwellers and their architectural wonders (Sharma 6, 11, 90–5, 109). In Abu Talib's repurposing of this genre, Constantinople appears as London's heavenly counterpart:

> When you go there, all of a sudden,
> The first thing you find displayed is an excellent city
> Its entire design and all of its modes are
>   Exactly how they were during its real time
> When people appear there from the door
>   From the first look they praise everywhere
> Everyone recognizes their own house and place

>   Which increases their happiness
> When I was in a Constantinople home
>   One of the Romans appeared
> And was kind with me
>   And showed me each street and neighborhood
> There is also the picture of the renowned Hagia Sophia
>   That very famous mosque
> After that in their circular/traveling city
>   They showed me twenty-five mosques of the world
> The tongue cannot describe its wonders
>   The ambition of every soul should be to see it (qtd in Garcia, *England* 327–8)[8]

These verses appear in a section subtitled 'A description of modern/daytime showplaces,' without naming the Leicester Square panorama. However, the poet must have been there to see one or both of Barker's paintings sometime between April 21, 1801 and May 15, 1802. He mentions 'an excellent city' that looks historically accurate ('Exactly how they were during its real time'), onlookers who find 'their own house and place' in this display, a 'Constantinople home,' the Roman guide, 'the picture of the renowned Hagia Sophia,' and the 'circular/traveling city' revealing the 'twenty-five mosques of the world.' Obliterated from consciousness are the seraglio, the ships, the towers, the Sultan, Lord Elgin, palaces and harems, or any details that point to contemporary geopolitics. These are discernible only by consulting the textual supplements that Abu Talib would not have been proficient enough to read in English.

Instead, his poetry concentrates on the visuals to envision himself in *Dar al-Islam*, literally the sovereign territory or house of the true believers who surrender in peace to Allah. His focal points are the splendid mosques of Hagia Sophia, Sultan Achmet, Sultan Suleiman I, and Sultan Selim III, among others, located near the horizon line as shown in the plates (online figures). Most of the mosques glisten in sunlight, distracting the eye away from shady Galata and Pera in the foreground. *Dar al-Harb* – the domain of war, irreligion, and anarchy – is peripheral to a peacetime simulation assimilated into an Islamic intellectual and aesthetic vision. The idea that Londoners are overjoyed in seeing such an 'excellent city' and that 'everyone recognizes their own house and place' in the painting is a powerful homing device for the Muslim traveler. Welcoming strangers into one's home and offering them shelter and respite is how divine mindfulness shines forth in Islamic societies: a cardinal virtue that demands living with others and drawing them near, regardless of differences in religion and ethnicity (Siddiqui 10–11, 33–5). Muslim thinkers since Abu Nasr al-Farabi (c. 870–950) have taught that

Islamic hospitality is most optimal in urban habitats (Olsson 504). Such moral perfection enthralls Abu Talib inside a London rotunda while looking at Istanbul in a reverie of the Hagia Sophia: a Greek orthodox cathedral ordered to be built by the Byzantine Emperor Justinian I in 532–7 and converted to a mosque by the self-proclaimed Roman Caesar, Mehmed the Conqueror, in 1453. Beyond the violent imperial rivalries of the modern age lies an illusory no-place imbued with a timeless Islamic universality, for 'the ambition of every soul should be to see' the panorama's 'wonders.' Constantinople's historic grandeur is accessible only by looking through Londoners' eyes.

A mediational dynamic unlike the one in the panorama's guide and keys is at work in Abu Talib's poetic exuberance. Nothing in the quoted verses implies that he was lulled into thinking that 'British supremacy is masqueraded as objectivity,' nor had he lost his cultural bearings (Oleksijczuk 93). For that matter, he does not experience the double consciousness reserved for patriotic Britons in the audience. Nonetheless, he momentarily forgets his location in London when speaking as if he were in Constantinople, imagining the future as the present: 'When I was in a Constantinople home / One of the Romans appeared.' Feeling disoriented in space and time activates an abrupt switch in direction lacking sequential order, even as this lapse in cognition does not register as loss. Such a spatial–temporal dislocation reveals what Ahmed describes oxymoronically as a present absence, 'an object, thick with presence' (158).

The overwhelming nowness conjured by the panorama figures forth gender- and genre-bending in Abu Talib's poetry. Most likely written after he crossed the Mediterranean, the verses concerning the anonymous 'Roman' who 'showed me each street and neighborhood' transitions proleptically to the prose description of Constantinople in *Masir-i Talibi*, which documents the traveler's twenty-eight-day layover in the city. He stayed in the elegant house of Lord Elgin and his wife in Galata, moving in the same diplomatic circles that Barker had in the hope that the ambassador would secure for him travel accommodations from the British consulates in Basra and Baghdad, which he did. Abu Talib was 'received in the most gracious and friendly manner' by the ambassador, who 'possesses an amiable and liberal disposition' and put him in contact with officials in '*Istanbole*,' the city center 'where the Emperor, the nobles, and all the opulent Mussulmans reside' (*The Travels* 278–9). The gentlemanly demeanor that Elgin and Barker exhibited before their Ottoman hosts extends to the Indo-Persian visitor, and this shared gender orientation is made queer by a 'Roman' who is unmarked as male or female, elite or commoner, native or foreigner, in the interruptive leap from poetry to prose.

Hence, a future sociable event in the Islamic capital colors his poetic description of Barker's virtual art in the past, and vice versa: the Islamic city that he describes in prose is a panoramic spectacle. For example, upon entering the Golden Horn by ship he sees from afar 'a regular and magnificent city' that is 'the grandest place I had ever seen,' even though the street-level view 'disappointed' him (279). And he identifies most of the mosques featured in Barker's paintings. Unlike what he sees as the dilapidated and flea-infested wooden houses of the present Turkish inhabitants, these mosques 'are built in a handsome style, and highly ornamented; but the great Mosque of *Sufyeh* (Sophia) excels, in grandeur and elegance, any building I have ever seen,' superior to St Paul's Cathedral and 'the superb domes of Paris and Genoa.' The 'twenty-five public mosques' attracts his eyes more than the architecturally inferior 'private mosques,' and his poetry extols the 'twenty-five mosques of the world' as visualized in the panorama (285–6). A detail from plates two and six sticks out to him (online figures): 'the minars, on which the Mauzins stand to call the people to prayer' (286).[9] These perceptual matrices blend the authentic with the counterfeit, as if the city he visits for a social and religious purpose were shown on a canvas similar to the one he had seen in London. The hospitality shown to him in that city mirrors the kindness shown to him by a 'Roman' host inside a 'Constantinople home.' In other words, his writings are mediated by the panorama's self-reflexivity. The metacognition that panorama-goers exhibit as they observe observation itself stays with them after returning to a first-order reality, allowing the traveler to ponder indefinitely where the actual ends and the artificial begins (Otto paras 12–14, 17). Disrupting the unidirectional flow of space and time, in poetry and prose, this mediation injects uncanniness in all host–guest relations, diffusely so across figural economies that posit a home away from home.

His dreaming with open eyes raises consciousness about the constructed spaces of the social in ways that correspond to Barker's gendered experiences. Muslim women were offended by his sketching 'the Minarets [to the mosque] of Sultan Achement' and 'one of them cryed [*sic*] bitterly at seeing a Christian committing such an act of Sacrilege,' forcing the painter to leave with an 'imperfect View' (qtd in Oleksijczuk 108). Sunni Islam's objection to figurative art could explain what Barker considers a barbaric reaction, yet socio-political considerations factor heavily. Europeans had outworn their welcome due to rising tensions in Pera after Napoleon invaded Egypt (Zarinebaf 273–90). The peace transpiring between war was a source of gender conflict for Barker, whose artistic mission was authorized by powerful Ottoman men in the government yet impinged upon by Muslim female commoners on the streets. Consequently, his work became a resource for a London-bound Muslim gentleman who found tranquility in the painted mosques. In both cases, panoramic peacetime is like a Möbius strip in which one end, hospitality, circles to the other end, hostility: a feedback loop that, for Jacques Derrida, structures the stranger's right to visitation as a prelude to xenophobic violence (53–5).

Masir-i Talibi completes this circuit in likewise condemning Constantinople's Turks: they live in 'disgusting' quarters, their inns are 'horrid places' to stay, their horse stables are poorly kept yet overpriced, their cookery is terrible, and their multiple coffeehouses are loud, boisterous, dirty and impolite (Khan, *The Travels* 280–4). He stereotypes these people as coffee and tobacco addicts prone to sloth, lust, indolence, and idle storytelling, as they lack *adab*: an Arabic–Persian term for those who act nobly, speak and write elegantly, and welcome strangers (Steiner 669–71). In other words, the Turks are deficient in gentlemanly civic virtue. What made him contemptible to the predominantly Sunni Turks was his dressing 'in the '*ajamī* fashion,' as worn by men in Mughal courts, affiliating him with Persian speakers (not necessarily Shi'a) and the former Safavid empire in Iran (Kia 160). Yet this identity made him commendable among the Persian-speaking Ottoman male elite, such as 'the Prime Minister, Yusuf Pasha,' who 'received me with much politeness' (*The Travels* 290–1). 'The well-educated Turks are the admirers of the Persian language,' Abu Talib writes (291). Although he believes that the empire is corrupt and its army effeminate, he was charmed by Sultan Selim III. Exemplifying *adab*, the ruler granted him a *mehmandar* (a court conductor), honorary robes, an imperial order permitting travel to Mosul and Karbala, and treasury funds to finance his pilgrimage. In return, Abu Talib gifted him his Persian translation of al-Firuzabadi's *al-Qamus al-Muhit*, a large and widely used Arabic dictionary completed in 1410. The guest requested that this precious book be printed with his name in the preface and that it be distributed to the population for their education, to which the Sultan agreed (291, 295). Ottoman patronage of Persian *belles lettres* made the city endearing to Abu Talib, albeit from a distance. Because cultural exchanges between Ottoman courtiers and Iranian envoys were as common under Selim III's reign as the European artists who worked for him, the verses on the panorama could have been influenced by the turn-of-the-century vogue for Ottoman court poetry that lavished praise on Istanbul's architectural layout (Hamadeh 153, 232).

Still, Abu Talib's masculinist posturing among the Ottomans begs the question: who is the kind 'Roman' who took him on a sightseeing tour? The *Diwan-i Talib* often employs the term *Rum* to describe the Italian opera divas and actresses whose performances on the London stage ravished him (Garcia, *England* 322–3, 327). An Italian was most likely assigned to him by Ahmed Effendi, 'the Vizier for the Home Department,' who 'ordered one of his servants to attend me to the Mosque of St. Sophia, and to shew [*sic*] me all the sacred places, and other public buildings of Constantinople' (*The Travels* 291). This servant could also have been a Persian, Indian, Afghan, or Armenian, all of whom he 'had a very extensive society' with in the city, given his aversion to inhospitable Turks (292). Attuned to *Rum*'s semantic suppleness, Abu Talib uses this term inconsistently in ways that muddle gender, ethnic, and regional identities.

Taking Barker's map into consideration, *Rum* could refer to eastern Rome or Byzantium, the region incorporated into the Ottoman heartland in Anatolia. This multivalent term also applies to the Ottoman upper classes, who 'carried the privileged position of the people close to the sultan, or *kayser-i Rum*. Hence, the expression of *Rum* mainly related to the geography around Istanbul' (Ergul 634). In his geographical work titled *Lubbu-s Siyar wa Jahannuma* (The Essence of Biographies, and the World-Reflecting Mirror), composed between 1793 and 1796, Abu Talib indeed calls 'Constantinople' the 'capital' of 'the lands of Ottoman Rum from [the] European part,' located in a temperate climatic zone conducive to civilization and continuous with the white people living in Italy, France, Spain, Portugal, and the islands 'on the other side of [the] western ocean [the Americas]' (ff. 402).[10] On the empire's southeastern border and along the Anatolian coast lie 'Greek cities,' even though he recognizes the English as the translators and transmitters of ancient Greek histories. Yet it is Ottoman *Rum* that unites a Europe and an Asia divided by the Marmara Sea (Kia 91–2). By normalizing Turkish geographical knowledge, the panorama not only confirms Abu Talib's belief that Constantinople is the civilized world's imperial meridian, but also insinuates that British gentlemen's classicism is partial and, by extension, aberrant in prioritizing as their model the old Rome over the new Rome.

Hence, the ambiguous Roman/*Rum* registers the aporia that vexes Barker's art: that the place for intercultural cooperation is too evanescent, permeable, and indeterminate to sustain itself, dialectically inseparable from its constitutive opposites – war, xenophobia, and violence. Such hermeneutical indirection is not a problem to be solved but an invitation for endless self-regeneration. The 'Roman' communicates an untranslatable strangeness, the interpretive strategy that Emily Apter considers crucial for disrupting the 'cultural equivalence and substitutability' posited by English translations (2). This strategy forestalls the urge to make ethnic identities legible under a World Literature that masks neoliberal capitalist hegemony as benign globalization. The panorama disorientates such translative appropriations, more so in the city's inscrutable queer interiors, as made palpable in Abu Talib's gender non-descript 'Roman.' This sexless host without an ethnicity (a symbolic eunuch?) takes him inside the local mosques and homes where panorama viewers are barred from access. The *Diwan-i Talib* is radically open to an absolute other free from any moral obligation or need to self-identify, for the guest poet hosts the host in verse without codifying this relationship in law. 'Unconditional hospitality' obviates coding Ottoman Rome as European or Asian, masculine or feminine, and thus suspends the binary logic of philhellenic and orientalist discourses (Derrida 25). The poet's love of strangers knows no bounds in that gender signifiers do not translate into territorial–ethnic differences as the boundary between poetry and prose dissolves. The colonial gaze is turned back on itself to de-universalize Europe and return it to its Islamic homeland, minus the pro-British propaganda.

But this reorientation in art, religion, and politics does not terminate in an anti-imperialist critique or a solipsistic utopianism. Rather, it reaffirms Abu Talib's earnest belief that 'the common people' in England 'enjoy more freedom and equality than in any other well-regulated government in the world' (*The Travels* 174). For him, the British are indispensable to restoring law and order on the global stage during the Napoleonic Wars. They are militarily capacitated to administer justice in Mughal India's multiethnic Islamic imperium, a vision amenable to the cosmopolitan detour built into an artistic illusion about universal sovereignty. While Barker's panorama encouraged 'absorption into and mastery over exoticized landscapes,' it was neither bound to a nationalist script nor governed by a state-centered ideology (Zitzer 21). The optical technology that Abu Talib designates the 'circular/ traveling city' has the potential to transport a heterogenous audience into that which feels irreducibly strange and untranslatable, the affect that dispossesses them as they struggle to find a common ground from which to possess foreign lands as agents free to imagine alternative lifeworlds. Most crucially, this technology expands consciousness in an enchanted third space between empires in which the European episteme is non-hegemonic. Therein lies the power to reimagine the self otherwise, against the heteronormative desire to divide the earth's surface into gendered and ethnic territories.

In this respect, O'Quinn's conclusion about Melling's *Voyage pittoresque* and Byron's *The Giaour* (1813) pertains as well to Abu Talib's poetry: the 'demand that the reader remain fully engaged with relationality rather than fixed identity, for it is with the latter fixing that intersubjective and geopolitical violence unfolds' (412). Indeed, these three travelers negate Europe's monopoly over Greco-Roman antiquity, along with the heteronormalizing of sexed and gendered bodies that holds the past hostage to European fantasies about a future Eastern empire. They dismantle Eurocentric car(di)nal directions to make room for fluid subjectivities receptive to queer amalgamations of communal belonging that are reparative, culminating in Ottoman theaters of war and inspiring liminal self-fashioning. Unlike O'Quinn, however, I have shown that these multimedia vexations can transform a Muslim into a peace mediator, unwilling to serve as a passive literary foil for Europeans to masquerade as other.

Overall, I have argued that Romantic self-estrangement is endemic to a broader, interconnected media ecology than the contributors of *Romanticism and Consciousness* could fathom. Harold Bloom's paradigmatic 'quest-romance' for 'finding paradises within a renovated man ... in the arena of self-consciousness' encompasses social networks that embed subjects virtually in non-European environments (6). My hope is that the foregoing analysis has dislodged what Andrea K. Henderson calls the 'depth' model of consciousness in Romantic literary studies: the autonomous rational mind that gave expression to a Eurocentric selfhood. Abu Talib, too, is a poet 'of surfaces, of context, and of varying forms,' as drawn to 'insubstantial and spectral' selves as the British Romantics were (5). But only inside Barker's panorama is he redirected to his natal faith in feeling at home among those who share his strangeness. The moment when he surrenders (in Islam) without the pressure to assimilate to the host society happens in a virtual space–time warp where 'understanding and affinity founder,' in spite and because of the interimperial warfare that brought strangers together in peace.

Notes

1. Circa 1800, strangers were a pervasive cultural and literary phenomenon due to revolutionary politics, rapid urbanization, industrialization, increased social mobility, and the diversification of English vernaculars (Simpson, Melville, Sorensen, and Vernon).
2. M. H. Abrams considers Sir William Jones's translations of Persian, Arabic, and Sanskrit poetry a forebear of the non-imitative expressive aesthetics adopted by Romantic poets (87–8).
3. Scholars have proposed two divergent explanations for the early panorama's virtual effects: its illusion of totality either suspended critical reflection (Grau and Comment) or made perception itself perceptible to cast doubt on external social reality (Otto). The evidence presented in this chapter

supports the latter.
4. Newspaper advertisements would have informed panorama viewers that Elgin had facilitated Barker's permission to sketch the city and that a janissary had attended him the entire time (see, for example, 'Panorama, Leicester-square').
5. See Barker, *A Concise Account* 10n2.
6. A late seventeenth-century copy of Piri Reis's *Kitab-i Bahriye* (Book of Sea Lore) contains a realistic map of Istanbul and its surrounding topography. Though most likely embellished by a later copyist, this map strives for representational accuracy, with Topkapi Palace identified in the leftmost triangle that encompasses the city's boundaries and corresponds to Seraglio Point in Barker's map (Soucek 132–6; Goodrich 123).
7. Abu Talib's pupil, George Swinton, partially translated this work into English as *Poems of Mirza Abu Talib Khan* and published in 1807. It excludes the verses on the panorama.
8. These translated verses from *Diwan-i Talib* are based on the manuscript copy housed in the Bodleian Library, MS. Pers.e.9, pages 106–7.
9. The guide glosses this detail as 'a Minareh (which always accompanies a Mosque), on which is represented the Muzzin, or Crier, calling the devout Mussulmans to prayers' (Barker, *A Concise* 16).
10. He locates Istanbul in the fifth climate zone, which includes most of the urban centers in the northern European peninsula. According to Islamic geographical ethnologies of the seven latitudinal climes, this zone is temperate enough for humans to flourish psychologically and physiologically (Olsson 492).

References

Abrams, M. H. *The Mirror and the Lamp: Romantic Theory and the Critical Tradition*. Oxford: Oxford University Press, 1953.

Ahmed, Sarah. *Queer Phenomenology: Orientations, Objects, Others*. Durham, NC: Duke University Press, 2006.

Andrea, Bernadette. 'Columbus in Istanbul: Ottoman Mappings of the "New World."' *Genre: Forms of Discourse and Culture* 30 (1997): 135–65.

Angelov, Dimiter. '"Asia and Europe Commonly Called East and West": Constantinople and Geographical Imagination in Byzantium.' *Imperial Geographies in Byzantine and Ottoman Space*. Ed. Sahar Bazzaz, Yota Batsaki, and Dimiter Angelov. Cambridge, MA: Harvard University Press, 2013. 43–68.

Apter, Emily. *Against World Literature: On the Politics of Untranslatability*. London: Verso, 2013.

Barker, Henry Aston. *A Concise Account of the Views of Constantinople ... at the Panorama, Leicester Square*. London: J. Adlard, 1801.

—. *A Series of Eight Views, Forming a Panorama of the Celebrated City of Constantinople and Its Environs, Taken from the Town of Galata, by Henry Aston Barker, and Exhibited in His Great Rotunda, Leicester Square.* Engraved by Charles Tomkins, Frederick Christian Lewis, and George Robert

Lewis. London: Thomas Palser, 1813.
Bloom, Harold. 'The Internalization of Quest-Romance.' *Romanticism and Consciousness: Essays in Criticism*. Ed. Harold Bloom. New York: W. W. Norton, 1970. 3–24.
Comment, Bernard. *The Panorama*. London: Reaktion Books, 1999.
Curry, John J. 'An Ottoman Geographer Engages the Early Modern World: Katip Çelebi's Vision of East Asia and the Pacific in the *Cihânnümâ*.' *Journal of Ottoman Studies* 40 (2012): 221–57.
Derrida, Jacques. *Of Hospitality*. Trans. Rachel Bowlby. Stanford: Stanford University Press, 2000.
Du Bois, W. E. B. *The Souls of Black Folk*. Ed. Brent Hayes Edwards. Oxford: Oxford University Press, 2007.
Ergul, F. Asli. 'The Ottoman Identity: Turkish, Muslim or *Rum*?' *Middle Eastern Studies* 48.4 (2012): 629–45.
Fraser, Elisabeth A. *Mediterranean Encounters: Artists Between Europe and the Ottoman Empire, 1774–1839*. Philadelphia: University of Pennsylvania Press, 2017.
Garcia, Humberto. *England Re-Oriented: How Central and South Asian Travelers Imagined the West, 1750–1857*. Cambridge: Cambridge University Press, 2020.
—. *Islam and the English Enlightenment, 1660–1840*. Baltimore: Johns Hopkins University Press, 2012.
Goodrich, Tom. 'Supplemental Maps of the *Kitab-i Bahriye* of Piri Reis.' *Archivum Ottomanicum* 13 (1993–4): 117–41.
Grau, Oliver. *Virtual Art: From Illusion to Immersion*. Trans. Gloria Custance. Cambridge, MA: MIT Press, 2003.
Grosrichard, Alain. *The Sultan's Court: European Fantasies of the East*. Trans. Liz Heron. London: Verso, 1998.
Hamadeh, Shirine. *The City's Pleasures: Istanbul in the Eighteenth Century*. Seattle: University of Washington Press, 2008.
Hardcastle, Ephraim [Pyne, William Henry]. *Somerset House Gazette, and Literary Museum: or, Weekly Miscellany of the Fine Arts, Antiquities, and Literary Chit Chat*. London: W. Wetton, 1824.
Henderson, Andrea K. *Romantic Identities: Varieties of Subjectivity, 1774–1830*. Cambridge: Cambridge University Press, 1996.
Khan, Mirza Abu Talib. *Lubbu-s Siyar wa Jahannuma*. c.1793–6. Bodleian Library, Oxford, shelfmark Ms. Elliott 181.
—. *The Travels of Mirza Abu Taleb Khan*. Trans. Charles Stewart. Ed. Daniel O'Quinn. Peterborough, ON: Broadview, 2009.
Kia, Mana. *Persianate Selves: Memories of Place and Origin Before Nationalism*. Stanford: Stanford University Press, 2020.
Kristeva, Julia. *Strangers to Ourselves*. Trans. Leon S. Roudiez. New York: Columbia University Press, 1991.
Makdisi, Saree. 'Romantic Cultural Imperialism.' *The Cambridge History of English Romantic Literature*. Ed. James Chandler. Cambridge: Cambridge University Press, 2009. 601–20.
Melville, Peter. *Romantic Hospitality and the Resistance to Accommodation*. Waterloo, ON: Wilfrid Laurier University Press, 2007.
Oleksijczuk, Denise Blake. *The First Panoramas: Visions of British Imperialism*.

Minneapolis: University of Minnesota Press, 2011.
Olsson, J. T. 'The World in Arab Eyes: A Reassessment of the Climes in Medieval Islamic Scholarship.' *Bulletin of the School of Oriental and African Studies* 77.3 (2014): 487–508.
O'Quinn, Daniel. *Engaging the Ottoman Empire: Vexed Mediations, 1690–1815*. Philadelphia: University of Pennsylvania Press, 2019.
Otto, Peter. 'Between the Virtual and the Actual: Robert Barker's Panorama of London and the Multiplication of the Real in Late Eighteenth-Century London.' *Romanticism on the Net* 46 (2007): paragraphs 1–56. https://doi.org/10.7202/016130ar (last accessed September 24, 2020).
'Panorama, Leicester-square.' *The Morning Chronicle* April 21, 1801: 1.
Said, Edward W. *Orientalism*. New York: Vintage Books, 1994.
Schwab, Raymond. *The Oriental Renaissance: Europe's Rediscovery of India and the East, 1680–1880*. New York: Columbia University Press, 1984.
Sharma, Sunil. *Mughal Arcadia: Persian Literature in an Indian Court*. Cambridge, MA: Harvard University Press, 2017.
Siddiqui, Mona. *Hospitality and Islam: Welcoming in God's Name*. New Haven, CT: Yale University Press, 2015.
Simpson, David. *Romanticism and the Question of the Stranger*. Chicago: University of Chicago Press, 2013.
Sorensen, Janet. *Strange Vernaculars: How Eighteenth-Century Slang, Cant, Provincial Languages, and Nautical Jargon Became English*. Princeton: Princeton University Press, 2017.
Soucek, Svat. *Piri Reis and Turkish Mapmaking after Columbus: The Khalili Portolan Atlas*. London: Oxford University Press, 1996.
'Specification of the Patent Granted to Mr. Robert Barker.' *Repertory of Arts and Manufactures* 4 (1796): 165–7.
Steiner, Enit Karafili. '"Not to Abandon the Whole": Cosmopolitanism and Management in *The Travels of Mirza Abu Taleb Khan* (1810).' *European Romantic Review* 29.5 (2018): 657–80.
Sudan, Rajani. *The Alchemy of Empire: Abject Materials and the Technologies of Colonialism*. New York: Fordham University Press, 2016.
Vernon, James. *Distant Strangers: How Britain Became Modern*. Berkeley: University of California Press, 2014.
Zarinebaf, Fariba. *Mediterranean Encounters: Trade and Pluralism in Early Modern Galata*. Oakland: University of California Press, 2018.
Zitzer, Edward. 'Orientalist Panoramas and Disciplinary Society.' *The Wordsworth Circle* 32.1 (2001): 21–4.

Chapter 16

Doubling Down: On White Consciousness, Friends, and *The Friend*

Julie A. Carlson

This chapter doubles down on the relation of the friend to consciousness as part of two broader propositions. The first is that the extensions of mind that undergird Romantic-era concepts and promotions of friends are crucial to Romantic depictions of consciousness and hopes for facilitating firmer trust between people. My basic contention is that the linkage among friendship, literary creativity, and social justice posited and enacted by Romantic-era writers is the radical promise and under-recognized legacy of the 1790s. The second proposition is that championing the friend, whether in British Romanticism or current 'social justice activism,' has validity only if said friend is credible to doubly conscious minds: that is, to persons whose consciousness lets them know that consciousness is informed by structural asymmetries embedded in racism (Banerjea et al.).[1] Thus a doubly conscious self-dividing friend recognizes the privileges accorded to whiteness and opposes the good/s undergirding classical–romantic philosophical concepts of friends. This means that any path toward social justice envisioned as undertaken via the friend begins from conceptual and societal starting points that differ for white and for non-white aspirants.

To elucidate these propositions, I focus on Coleridge's *The Friend*, issued first in periodical format (1809–10) and ultimately codified into a book (1818). As the title suggests, *The Friend* is the most explicit and sustained reflection on the friend in British Romanticism, a reflection that is avowedly self-divided and textually overdetermined and indeterminate. It epitomizes several of the reasons why I propose 'the method of the friend' as the legacy of white radical Romanticism. First, friendship for these writers is the relational model best inclined toward justice because it is least tied to hetero-biological imperatives and because the bonds established between friends are extra-legal and non-institutionalized, and thus sustained largely by inclination. Espoused by new philosophical writers in the early 1790s who were intimate friends, their friend is a pivotal concept (self as friend and friend of humanity) and an enactable method of moving out from the given toward a diverse collectivity. They envision and characterize themselves as 'United helpers forward of a day / Of firmer trust' by virtue of being writer–friend–activists (Wordsworth, *The Prelude* 13.438–9 [1805]). A second reason is that their friend as concept and out-reaching project founders, sometimes colossally so. Scholars often read the humanitarian failure in tandem with the interpersonal failures, both instantiations of friend indicating these writers' naïvety regarding human nature, insufficient grasp on reality, and willed blindness to the destructivity in creativity (Thompson). This reading is why the centrality of friendship to the period's revolutionary and creative energies remains under-appreciated. But the assessment effaces the political significance of their writing in the wake of disheartenment over attempts to attain either end-point of friend, and it perpetuates idealistic conceptions of friends, which they are in the process of shedding as they confront the impossibility of mutuality between persons and peoples. A third reason is their conscious attribution of 'friend' to texts, by which they affirm the porosity between lives and texts and the depth of human attachments to literature.

Coleridge's *The Friend* exemplifies all three rationales in such extremes that the danger of losing consciousness of the friend or faith in friends through reading it is real. The danger exists without factoring in the overt xenophobia that makes objections to the whiteness of its consciousness such low-hanging fruit. Nonetheless, I mean to show how *The Friend* educes a 'method of the friend' that is conducive to reducing racism and building trust between different kinds of person. The textual transformation from periodical (1809–10) to book (1818) and, within the periodical, from espousing principles (numbers 1 to 11) to producing a miscellany (numbers 12 to 27) demonstrates some of what is lost to writer-friends in the solidification of improvisational mentation. Building from this, I elaborate what *The Friend* partially delineates as an 'friend-in-difference'[2] – partially because the claim is at best enacted, not overt, and partially because its type of in-difference does nothing to dislodge the supremacy of whiteness and its thirst for sameness. The second section of my chapter then posits interracial friendship as an anti-racist methodology that departs in both senses from *The Friend*. Conceptually, the friend-in-difference requires differentiating operations of split consciousness from those of double consciousness and assigning each to different networks and entanglements of mind/brain/environ interaction. As practice, it necessitates that changes in and to the consciousness of white aspirants must be evident to non-white potential partners before any possibility of developing a friendship will occur. This means that structural changes to cognitive and societal operations are preconditions, not end-points, of trustworthy relations between persons of different races. It also means that determining who can embark on this endeavor is one of the few instances in which categorically subordinate persons have the upper hand.

Self-divided as Friend

Issued (more or less) weekly during a period extending from June 1, 1809 to March 15, 1810, *The Friend: A Literary, Moral, and Political Weekly Paper, excluding Personal and Party Politics, and the Events of the Day* is written to revitalize the minds of a generation of youth who have lost hope in thinking owing to the failed revolutionary experiment in France.[3] The advertised 'chief purpose and general business' of *The Friend* is 'to examine, to evince and ... to remedy or alleviate' the 'unsteadiness, or falsehood or abasement of *the Principles*, which are taught and received by the existing generation' by helping readers regain fixed principles on the basis of which they would be able to discern whether any particular manifestation in the spheres of 'Literature, the Fine Arts, Morals, Legislation, and Religion' is to be trusted and adopted (30, 13). *Contra* 'our hurrying Enlighteners and revolutionary Amputators,' this recourse 'to Principles in all things' involves the 'referring of the Mind to its' [*sic*] own Consciousness for Truths indispensable to its' [*sic*] own Happiness,' an urgently needed safeguard against 'the thunder and earthquakes and deluge of the political world' (45, 13, 73, 30). Since this referral entails 'severe thinking, and thinking is neither an easy nor an amusing employment,' it involves removing the 'Evils and Impediments' that prevent receptivity to 'Knowledge,' including 'our aversion to all the toils of reflection' (48, 70, 86).

A guide, then, for solidifying autonomy of reflection and (white) personhood by distinguishing and recoordinating cognitive and moral imperatives, this process of principle recovery cannot occur without the friend. The connection is not simply titular. On the basic level, the primary friend in *The Friend* is Coleridge's mind, which is on display as a model of error and recovery chiefly in regard to the mistaken political consequences of affirming a 'friends of man' philosophy, acquaintance with which trajectory grants readers the knowledge and incentive to examine their own mistaken thoughts or flagging powers of thinking. Rejecting the role of 'Legislator of the opinions of other men' for that of 'Biographer of my own Sentiments,' *The Friend* humanizes and seeks to convey the 'entertainingness' of 'severe thinking' as a means of 'winning' rather than 'forcing my way' (9, 12, 17). The periodical format assists by building in temporal intervals between the issuing and uptake of one principle and the next, so that 'the Shock of the first Day might be so far lessened by Reflections of the succeeding Days, as to procure for my next Week's Essay a less hostile Reception' (17). In general, and especially in a climate of widespread disillusionment, *The Friend* acknowledges that mind does not enjoy thinking, much less struggling, on its own. Minds want model company to lessen the strain, a recognition enacted through the second basic manifestation of friend in *The Friend*: repeated reference to 'my honoured Friend William Wordsworth' and frequent citation of his published and unpublished works, endorsements of which are 'an act of mere justice both to myself and to the Readers of THE FRIEND' (108).

The structural tension, of galvanizing independence of mind through befriending minds in the process of thinking, barely grazes the surface of the multiplications and disseminative forces characterizing this exemplum of mind. It is next to impossible to discern who is speaking in or as *The Friend* and which mind/brain at any point is being remodeled and disseminated. The famous 'obscurity' of the first number starts at sentence two in massive pronoun confusion over how to refer to itself (Rooke lix–xii). Affirming that every writer confronts difficulty over how to begin a major work, 'THE FRIEND may be allowed to feel the difficulties and anxiety of a first introduction in a more than ordinary degree. *He* is embarrassed by the very circumstances, that discriminate the plan and purposes of *the present weekly paper* from those of *its* periodical brethren,' which, had it 'been *my* ambition to have copied,' 'I should have exposed *my* Essays to a greater hazard of unkind comparison' (5; emphasis added). This triune voice of *The Friend*, usually an I (assumed to be Coleridge) and sometimes identified as 'S. T. C.,' sometimes a persona (THE FRIEND), sometimes the weekly paper, is nowhere clarified or explained later in the text. Moreover, after 'I' confesses in number 11 to feeling 'depressed' over the 'frequency with which you hear The Friend complained of for its abstruseness and obscurity,' the text comes to rely heavily on the insertion of letters as well as on anecdotes of or passages written by other writers (150). The first number also introduces the obscurity attendant on its metaphysics by presenting self-division as the key phenomenal witness to the integrity and unity of (white) personhood. Waiving pleasantries by claiming the 'privileges of a friend before I have earned them,' it 'proceeds at once' to a 'subject, trite indeed and familiar as the first lessons of childhood': 'the sense of a self-contradicting principle in our nature, or a disharmony in the different impulses that constitute it.' This principle 'essentially distinguishes' humans from 'all other animals' and separates empirical persons 'from the idea of [their] own nature, or conception of the original man' (6, 7). In sum, the 'great definition of humanity' is 'that we have a conscience,' whose function is to coordinate the recognition of *what we are* (later, 'the worthless "thing we are"' [218]) with the concept of *what we are born to become; and thus from the End of our Being to deduce its proper Objects*' (17).

A world of indignity ensues from this conviction regarding the grounds of 'our humanity.' The hallmark of Christian exceptionalism, the conviction posits the subhumanity of non-Western minds, races, cultures, and spiritual traditions (Wynter, 'Unsettling'). Self-applied, it threatens Coleridge with worthlessness on almost every level except race and nationality. Anguished adjudications of self-worth as moral being, poet, man, friend of liberty, and friend of particular men and women suffuse Coleridge's writings. It is much of what 'Coleridgean' means. But that Coleridge, the 'damaged archangel' Coleridge, is much less apparent in the 1809–10 *The Friend* than in other quasi-autobiographical writings or later editions of *The Friend* (Fruman). My claim is that this degree of relative security is owing to the friend's place in consciousness and to 'honoured' friend Wordsworth's place in the writerly consciousness of the periodical *The Friend*. Perception of anchorage does not last even through to the in/completion of *The Friend*. But the model exists for those so inclined to adopt.

Up until number 12, the consciousness on display aiding those reluctant to resume thinking owns its self-division but not as grounds for lamentation or despair.[4] Especially in the early numbers, the voice of *The Friend* is surprisingly upbeat – even casting compositional and moral failings as reasons to subscribe to *The Friend*. As the Prospectus announces, 'the Number of my unrealized Schemes, and the Mass of my miscellaneous Fragments, have often furnished my Friends with a Subject of Raillery, and sometimes of Regret and Reproof.' Yet 'this Want of Perseverance has been produced' by an 'Over-activity of thought, modified by a constitutional Indolence, which made it more pleasant to me to continue acquiring, than to reduce what I had acquired to a regular Form' (16). The assurance in tone is bolstered by the methodological orientation of *The Friend*: retrospection, and hence knowledge that error has led to recovery, and focus on conscious, rather than on unconscious or aberrational, thought. While various numbers discuss anomalous processes, these accounts of 'ghosts and apparitions,' the 'progress of madness,' and 'guilt as the madness of the heart' are literary-clinical, not confessional, and are affixed to historical (Luther), actual (Maria Eleonora Schoning) or fictional figures (the widow in *The*

Three Graves), who are not obvious Coleridgean stand-ins.[5] At the same time, consciousness in *The Friend* is known and shown to be constituted through engagement with other minds for not only the development of content but also initiative to explore external objects – initiative in *The Friend* understood as equally a cognitive ('leading thought') and affective feature of mentation. Each number is initiated by an epigraph that jump-starts the argument that then is fleshed out through additional citations from other authors. It is as if mind in *The Friend* does not know itself or sense the worth of its existence when isolated from other texts or friends. Moreover, the need to feel shored up by textual and/or live friends intensifies as readers' voiced dissatisfaction with *The Friend* mounts, starting at number 11.

The shoring up is staged primarily through letters inserted into the text and to which it responds, sometimes as THE FRIEND, sometimes as Coleridge, and once by Wordsworth, who is invited to respond to a lengthy letter from 'Mathetes.' Moreover, *The Friend* is seemingly indifferent to whether the letter writer is actual (R. L., Mathetes), an actual friend (Wordsworth, Southey), or an authorial persona (Satyrane), so long as mind finds itself in conversation with something. Growing estrangement from readers prompts a show of authorial connectivity, whose aim is reassurance on both cognitive and relational planes. Whether actual or fictional, received letters of 'encouragement' relieve 'anxious thoughts and gloomy anticipations' of ongoing critique and are thanked for facilitating recovery of authorial confidence and fluency (247; cf. 283). They literally recompose his/its mind. Acquired emotional composure aids progress of thought by externalizing incoherent elements, differentiating one faculty from another, and re-presenting these splits as bearable, coherent, sometimes entertaining.[6] Making up one's correspondent works even better; writing as recipient to percipient, letters voice anticipated objections, the better to defang them.

Proleptic stalling of reproof later becomes inseparable from Coleridgean imagination and the self-defenses on display in *Biographia Literaria*. But at this stage, the chief aim in printing letters-from-a-friend to a self in the guise of THE FRIEND is keeping alive *The Friend* and the friendship with Wordsworth, both at a tipping point. The overdetermined relation of *The Friend* to Coleridge's 'honoured friend' has been explored largely in terms of the psychodynamic implications of the periodical's compositional triangulated context. Every number is composed and issued while Coleridge is living in the Wordsworth household and, starting at number 4, is dictated to muse and amanuensis Sara Hutchinson, long upholding Coleridge's dejection and puncturing each man's confidence in the other's integrity (Coleman 21–40, Parker

159–74). Hutchinson's abrupt departure to family in Wales owing to the strain of these tensions occurs after number 26 and leads to other ruptures. Less than two weeks after she leaves, *The Friend* leaves off at number 27 with '(To be concluded in the next Number).' Seven months after this, Wordsworth declares all hope is lost for Coleridge, and the two men never again cohabit or collaborate.

The rupture is never fully repaired and remains a painful illustration of the psychic pressures apt to emerge in close friends, especially co-creating writer-friends. My point here is that *The Friend* provides a different account of their friendship and, by extension, the nature and longevity of Coleridgean friendship that is worth taking seriously. The felt reality of friendship with Wordsworth buoys the authorial voice from the start. As confidence falters and ensuing numbers shift from 'abstruseness' to a 'miscellany,' the voice increasingly enfolds itself in Wordsworth's, by quoting various of his poems and prose writings and by intoning his name. This poet-friend's presence also is evident in the stance adopted by *The Friend* as 'Biographer of my own Sentiments' and cartographer of their windings toward recovery. The analysis given in numbers 10 and 11 of what was wrong-headed about youthful enthusiasm over the French revolutionary experiment not only echoes Wordsworth's account in Book Ten of *The Prelude* ('golden shield,' blameworthy conduct of 'experienced men'). It also cites passages from the yet-unpublished poem that function simultaneously to inform, validate, and clinch his own account, at the same time as it promotes his friend's poem and status as the 'greatest living Poet' by being the first to print selections from it, including what has become its most famous passage recalling the 'bliss' of 'we who were strong in love' at that 'dawn' (147). The extent to which *The Friend* befriends *The Prelude* and the growth of its writer's mind is a compelling example of how writer-friends fortify their minds to proceed independently together. In this regard, the consciousness rediscovered in number 10 as grounded in principle both is and is not hard won. When 'strong in love,' erring is less unbearable. Consciousness is on its own neither in making the error – 'young Men of loftiest minds' were together in this – nor in avowing it because an 'honoured' friend and the 'greatest living Poet' already has done so (just not in print). Knowing this helps to defuse whatever self-doubt is occasioned by envisioning less charitable readers. He (and we) need only resort to *The Friend* for confirmation that his and Wordsworth's words are in accord and mutually supportive.

The concept of 'cognitive scaffolding' does not capture the full complexity or idiosyncrasy of *The Friend*, but it approximates what 'the friend' at this stage accomplishes in Coleridge's literary biography. The friend is a precondition and an aid to self-reflection in his own writing and is what his writings offer readers in their process of portraying thought as a biographical record also of sentiment. John Savarese's argument that *Aids to Reflection* (1825) 'models' extended cognition and exemplifies Coleridge's 'conviction that thinking is not the inner business of enclosed individual minds, but a networked process that t[akes] place between an embodied mind and various linguistic and technological aids' is germane to the method and purpose of the 1809–10 *The Friend* (Savarese 141). So is his account of how *Aids* registers a mind losing control over its initial object of annotating selections of Bishop Leighton's sermons in order to encourage 'young readers' in their spiritual development. 'What begins as a set of scaffolded mental exercises to promote autonomy gradually comes to appear more dispersed, an increasingly intricate series of texts about texts' (144).

Enactive accounts similarly draw on Coleridge's later philosophical writings in reformulating a secular 'theory of life,' both the unfinished essay of that title (1816) and subsequent Coleridgean attempts to elaborate it. In Lisa Ann Robertson's rendering, Coleridge's essay posits life less as an 'organic' than an 'autopoietic' unfolding that differentiates, without polarizing, subject and object from the eternal, thereby producing a cognitive theory that is 'stripped of its theological baggage' (Robertson 119, 124). Robert Mitchell's reading is even more apposite to 'the friend' and *The Friend*. Beyond shared registration of 'abandoned experiment[s],' Mitchell's proposition that Coleridge's philosophizing is more in the genre of 'life-manual' than metaphysical disquisition is both enacted in and anticipated by the generic recoding in the 1809–10 *The Friend* of Coleridgean dejection. Textually, *The Friend* is a secondary revision of this affective state: elaborated in prose, not in a 'verse-letter' or ode, that shifts midstream from confident to frustrated and from abstruseness to a miscellany of genres (poems, letters, anecdotes, biographical elegy) and affects (151). Also, as a periodical, *The Friend* is not a book but is en route to becoming one that, when such, takes its place in a series devoted, largely, to political philosophical theology – *The Stateman's Manual* (1816), *Lay Sermons* (1817), *Biographia Literaria* (1817), *The Friend* (1818), *Aids to Reflection* (1825), *On the Constitution of Church and State* (1830). In other words, the periodical *The Friend* is a work of neither philosophy nor literature nor biography nor literary auto/biography, though it is an amalgam of all of them; instead, it is a companion to self-reflection where the 'self' ostensibly being reflected cannot perceive itself apart from the 'friend.'

The usefulness of applying Mitchell's notion of 'life-manual' to *The Friend* is heightened if we consider the chief difference in content between the periodical and book version. *The Friend* of 1818 contains the 'Essays on Method,' one of Coleridge's most prized philosophical contributions. They substitute for the numbers devoted in 1809–10 to 'Satyrane's Letters' (14, all of 16, most of 18, and a small part of 19) that, in the interval, have been inserted into the second volume of *Biographia Literaria*, primarily as filler. This is such a waste to consciousness of the friend as key to creativity. In *The Friend*, the lengthy wind-up that precedes the printing of actual letters sent in 1799 to wife Sarah and friend Thomas Poole during Coleridge's sojourn in Germany (with and apart from the Wordsworths) attributes the capacity to recall friends to mind as the incentive to writing. The first explanation describes a work that he claims to have begun as a student at Cambridge, modeled on 'the well known MISERIES OF HUMAN LIFE' and to which he had affixed an Appendix listing 'the Sights, Incidents, and Employments, that leave us better men than they found us; or, to use my original phrase, *of the Things that do a Man's Heart good*.' After an intervening 'eighteen years' of 'experience and reflection,' he now would 'rank foremost' 'a long winter evening devoted to the re-perusal of the Letters of far distant, or deceased Friends' (185). A second explanation, which conflates two separate walking tours with William Wordsworth, Dorothy Wordsworth, John Chester, and himself, recalls their plan to launch a 'joint Work to be entitled, "TRAVELLING CONVERSATIONS",' an idea that has since often 'recurred' to 'me' as possessing the 'merit of harmonizing an indefinite variety of matter by that unity of interest, which would arise from the Characters remaining the same throughout, while the Tour itself would supply the means of introducing the most different topics by the most natural connections.' Travelling conversations is how readers at this point are invited to envision *The Friend*, though the idea is never mentioned again (185, 186).

The two psychological portrayals given of Satyrane, presented in *The Friend* as an actual friend to the four traveling companions rather than as synonymous/pseudonymous with S. T. C. in the *Biographia*, further accentuate the friend's centrality to balancing a mind. The poem that introduces this section portrays Satyrane's mind as a harmonious blend of poetic and philosophical proclivities (184).[7] The concluding prose paragraph (186–7) ascribes Satyrane's increasingly 'pensive and almost gloomy' state of mind to his eventually discovering that people were more flawed, and thus disappointing, than he originally had conceived, a recognition that pains him, 'for to love and sympathize with mankind was a necessity of his nature.' All of a sudden, an 'I' intervenes into a formerly third-person (self-)description. 'When I first knew him, and for many years after, this was all otherwise. The sun never shone on a more joyous being!' 'That I may introduce him to my Readers in his native and original character, I now place before them his first Letter, written on his arrival at Hamburg' (187).

Such flights of self-division as other-division and self-fictionalization are dizzying. They put any reasonable reader on guard against the 'Truth' indispensable to 'Happiness' proffered as the reward of self-reflection in *The Friend*. Yet they have prompted generations of both worshipful and resistant readers of Romanticism to try to get closer or to stay close to such a mind. Why is hard to say. But the difficulty of answering the question is crucial to identifying the value of humanistic inquiry and training. Partial insight is gained by considering the many who continued to befriend a live Coleridge, like James Gillman, with whom Coleridge co-authors the fragmentary 'Theory of Life' (1816) and to whom he dedicates the 1818 *The Friend* in acknowledgement of Gillman's 'kindly' 'partiality' that has 'its strongest foundations in hope' to which, along with his 'medical skill,' 'I owe in great measure the power of having written at all.' Or the many pilgrims to Highgate seeking primarily to listen to the sage man. The pathology that limns the depth of Coleridgean co-dependence obscures the truth his literary life exposes of what writers owe to friends for the ability and incentive to write at all. Put the other way, Coleridge's growing preference for 'far distant, or deceased Friends' as a chief source of writerly self-protection soon 'infects the whole' of a literary life that is turning philosophical and increasing in rigidity and subterfuge in the process. The tipping points instanced in the periodical are toppled by the book version: the possibility of balancing poetic and philosophical approaches is excised with loss of Satyrane; re-cognizing miscellany as a compositional principle is dwarfed by Method; envisioning hope in days of firmer trust is transferred to medicine. Even the title demotes the literary: *The Friend: A Series of Essays in Three Volumes To Aid in the Formation of Fixed Principles in Politics, Morals, and Religion with Literary Amusements Interspersed*, as does substituting 'Principles of Method' for the high jinks and traveling conversations of Satyrane's Letters. This *Friend* and consciousness I now leave to fend for itself. I am back to tracking what the lived reality of the pivotal pivoting friend in the periodical *The Friend* augurs.

Whatever else one wants to say about Coleridge and friends, his friendships are mind-epochal and dramatize their new-world-bringing features. Making a new friend in his case can initiate a whole new intellectual enthusiasm, living arrangement, and opportunity to shed old habits in favor of more propitious living conditions. The tenets propelling the Pantisocracy scheme change massively over his life but the impulse to reshape domestic and political conditions through prioritizing intercourse with friends remains. This affective–cognitive–societal re-engineering and circuitry is what the method of the friend enjoins and keeps entwined, practices of living in which changes in thought move in tandem with changes in societal and institutional arrangements and where both kinds of transformation mandate and educe changes in the structuring of desire. As a model of friend Coleridge fails on countless scores that are clinical, critical, and quotidian: addict, plagiarist, depressive, mooch, prevaricator, fantasist – tendencies, to say the least, that weaken the likelihood of intersubjective exchange. But as a methodological model in the periodical *The Friend*, several features are worth entertaining: that minds function best when they perceive their thought to be companionate; that patterns of thinking and feeling are disrupted and extended through making friends; that the friend as a relational category pivots between self and collectivity, psychology and sociology; that the bonds that link friends are at once easiest and impossible to dissolve. The question is whether this conception appears credible or desirable to minds whose perceptual framework is double consciousness and consequently not predisposed to welcome overtures emerging from white mindsets. But if the doublings of consciousness prized in friend consciously affirm and unconsciously manifest the capacities inherent in Du Boisian double consciousness, then friends-in-difference have a fighting chance.

Doubling Down

This section ponders two questions: (1) Can the friend-in-difference shed the mono-conscious history that has informed 'friend' as concept-practice, or does it remain white-self-serving? (2) How is trust garnered between parties long socialized to be enemies? One compelling reason for skepticism is that Black persons typically do not use 'friend' to designate Black non-familial intimates or associates, preferring terms like 'brother,' 'mother,' 'cousin' and reserving 'friend' primarily for white familiars. How deep do the reservations that this terminology bespeaks lie? It is one thing to consider the advantages of interracial friendships if one's history of friendship has been mind-expanding both conceptually and at least occasionally in lived reality. It is quite another if that history has been both genocidal and epistemocidal (de Sousa Santos 9).

Consciousness of this asymmetry positions white and non-white aspirants at radically different starting points on each question. To start with the first, while few contemporary white theorists of mind deny the non-sovereignty and deeply entangled nature of mind/brain/environ operations, few of their elaborations of false consciousness, split consciousness, the dynamic unconscious, or four-E cognition approach such phenomena from a racially double-conscious perspective. Put a different way, solving the 'hard problem' of consciousness (Chalmers) – that is, how subjective experience arises out of neurobiological mechanisms – rarely proceeds from study of mind/brains that are not 'WEIRD,' as Joseph Henrich puts it, meaning Western, educated, industrialized, rich, and democratic [Henrich et al.]). WEIRDness also characterizes the field's gatekeepers. Steven O. Robert's recent analysis of more than 26,000 empirical articles published between 1974 and 2018 in cognitive, developmental, and social psychology found that of the sixty editors-in-chief of these journals, 83 percent were white, 5 percent were Black, Indigenous, and People of Color (BIPOC), 12 percent were unidentifiable, and no editors of the journals studied that were devoted to cognitive psychology were BIPOC. Of the publications with research that highlighted race, 87 percent were edited by whites; when editors were BIPOC, the journals were three times more likely to publish articles related to race. Moreover, those studies demonstrated that cognitive processes such as 'auditory processing, categorization and memorization, do indeed vary as a function of racialized experiences.' 'To not acknowledge this, or to only study human thinking with white participants, is a disservice to science' (Roberts).

This mono-focus not only disregards epistemological alternatives that exist within avowedly WEIRD nations like the US that are less individualist and enamored of competition. As Sylvia Wynter argues, it also skews how researchers address the 'hard problem' by ignoring 'what it is like to be black' and why this existential reality confounds a strictly first-person or third-person perspective (Wynter, 'Sociogenic' 31). Drawing on Frantz Fanon's concept of 'sociogeny' in *Black Skins, White Masks*, which depicts the origin and development of identity as a consequence of social factors, Wynter exposes 'sociogenic' laws that, although inseparable from physical and neurobiological processes, are non-reducible to these processes but also are not ontogenetic. As Fanon's account of 'the Caribbean Negro going to France demonstrates,' there are subjectively experienced processes whose functioning 'cannot be explained in the terms of *only* the natural sciences, of only physical laws' but are also 'culturally and thereby socio-situationally determined, with these determinations in turn, serving to activate their physicalistic [and biochemical] correlates.' Consequently, 'if the mind is what the brain *does*, *what* the brain *does* is itself culturally determined through the mediation of the socialized *sense of self*, as well as of the "social" situation in which this *self* is placed' (Wynter 36–7; also 41–2). This means that the concept 'human' functions neither to designate nor to cultivate a species. It is an invention coincident with European colonialism and elaborated in two forms and phases (civic humanism during the Renaissance and liberal–economic humanism at the end of the eighteenth and during the nineteenth centuries); in other words, 'human' is an ethno-class construct that ensures self-preservation of the dominant group.

This history of consciousness informs and impedes mutual understanding not only between, but also of, white and non-white persons and peoples. No wonder it occasions white flight on the score of consciousness in both parties. Insufficient internalization of this history is also evident in efforts to reduce racism by mapping its neurocognitive and psychic coordinates, efforts that actually weaken the trust that their conclusions regarding interracial contact are intended to bolster. A 2018 meta-analysis of twenty-seven intergroup contact studies modifies influential results from a 2006 study claiming to demonstrate 'that intergroup contact can contribute meaningfully to reductions in prejudice across a broad range of groups and contexts' (Paluck et al.). The 2018 analysis found far less evidence of reduction in prejudice when the contact measured pertained to racial and ethnic groups rather than to 'individuals with disabilities' or to 'lesbians and gays' (Paluck et al. 152). Also, its governing idea of 'contact' sidelined a prior researcher's prediction that 'the more contact the more trouble' (Allport 263) *unless* casual contact proceeds to 'deeper engagement' (Paluck et al. 153). Taking a different approach, neuroimaging studies of the 'race network,' by localizing perceptual, affective, and cognitive regions involved in race perception, are able to disentangle cognitive from affective and behavioral responses to race (Amodio). For example, Brittany Cassidy and Anne Krendl connect neural activity in a 'simple race perception task' (viewing Black and white faces) to two separable aspects: 'evaluative racial trust disparity (i.e., perceiving less trust in Black versus White faces) and racial differentiation disparity (i.e., differentiating Black less than White faces).' They draw the conclusion that increased activity in 'executive' areas of the brain underlies later attenuation of race disparities in differentiating faces that are relatively independent from bias. Because people have stronger empathic responses to those who look trustworthy, increased contact with races other than one's own 'may potentially alter neural response to race in a way that decreases racial trust disparity and also reduces race disparity in empathy' (Sessa et al., Cassidy and Krendl).

Such race-inflected accounts of social cognition confirm on the neural level not only that perception is guided by salience but also that quality of perception (speed, accuracy) influences quality of reaction toward the 'object' perceived. It thus confirms by inverting the directional logic underlying implicit bias training: that once having been made conscious of disavowed racial biases, well-meaning white liberals will recognize their responsibility consciously to undo them. Here the argument is that more contact with other races improves perceptual capabilities to see 'others' as individuated and thus to perceive them as 'worthy' of trust on that basis. But these inversions still privilege white consciousness in at least two respects. One is the ongoing faith in consciousness implied in summations to studies that have just detailed the neural entrenchments that make cognitive evaluation so efficient and thus biased. 'The understanding gained from these findings can be leveraged by future work to reduce the pernicious societal consequences of race disparities in social cognition' (Cassidy and Krendl). Worse is the implied faith in societal institutions (housing, education, policing, public health, law) that limit and foreclose opportunities for interracial relations, arenas ensconced in the 'codependence of Black exclusion and white ascension' (Johnson 43). A second symptom of white-privileging is assumptions that non-whites view interracial contact as a desirable starting point or white people's lack of trust in them as the chief impediment. Such conclusions drawn from maps of brain processing remain racial wishful thinking to the extent that they skip over the need for reparative work on their structural conditions.

A conceptual bridge exists in current neurocognitive accounts of improvisation as an example of autopoiesis.[8] This bridge positions enactivists (predominantly white) in the company of Black theoretical-activists who have long championed improvisation as a cornerstone of 'blues epistemology' and as the 'aesthetic' of the Black radical tradition (Woods 16–21, Moten *In the Break*). Both anti-conceptual 'schools' prize interactive, unscripted, and unpremeditated practices of co-creation, and each perceives acute self-consciousness as threatening successful performance. The difference is that while both approaches recognize the influence of local environments on cognitive–somatic processing, only blues epistemology is sociogenic in identifying race as a structural feature of natural–cultural environments and acknowledging the salience of racism in the cultivation of improvisational skill. Blues-epistemological improvisation takes flight from dominant terms of order and embodies a rich heritage of interlinking aesthetic and social practices and rearrangements; it acknowledges combos as the precondition to solo performance and temporary individuation (Monson). This is why training institutes, like the International Institute for Critical Studies of Improvisation in Guelph, affirm this interconnection as a vital part of their curriculum and ethos. They offer techniques of 'Community' and 'Social Practice' that are honed through jazz: skills in deep listening, attunement to surprise, trust in process rather than outcome (Fischlin et al. 189–230).[9] One could say that such institutes critique systems that claim to be 'self-regulating' because of the false neutrality and false equality assumed by such modeled interactions.

As a conceptual bridge between white and Black enactments of autopoiesis, improvisation is a method of extended minds and anti-individualist musicianship that hones techniques of non/mastery: leaderless, contextual, spontaneous, surprising, dissonance-attuned. Most importantly, by modeling the process through which conscious practice develops procedural memory that allows extraordinary creativity to steam up and take shape, improvisation both demonstrates and perpetuates the cyclical feedback of motivation, manifestation, and desire: willed surrender to processes whose outcome cannot be known in advance; positive experiences of the before-unapprehended emergence that increases trust in a process to which one more readily surrenders. This training and hedonic experiencing are important preconditions of anti-racist thought and action. Again, they are asymmetric. For BIPOC, structural racism prompts skill at and delight in improvising, whereas white improvisers generally disregard the critique of white supremacy implied in it.

Internalizing the anti-racist logic and history in improvisation is the im/methodical promise of the friend-in-difference - the conceptual practice of which friend desires difference, not self-sameness, as the ground of interpersonal interracial relations. Making any new friend brings new interests, points of view, familial and social traditions, but defamiliarization is greatly intensified when a new friend also unsettles one's cultural foundations and ethno-class working assumptions. At the same time, even being in position to venture this kind of friendship means that significant structural transformation already has occurred in the mind, body, and environs of each potential partner. It is dumbfounding how racially and class-segregated most US neighborhoods, places of worship, consumer goods, health services, and educational systems remain, and how rarely white people enter – let alone choose to enter – predominantly non-white spaces or stay long enough to be affected by the experience. Thus espousing a 'color-blind' perspective is a friend-in-difference non-starter because it effaces what each partner initially confronts in and via the face of the other - and must confront if anything deeper, less categorical, and more mutually differentially sustainable is to develop (Blake et al.). White people, especially middle- and upper-class, have little experience of being reduced to a category and little patience over being deemed a suspect category. This gives BIPOC partners the edge, practiced as they are in strategic runs-around and having the goodness of their intentions denied. This edge disrupts a second circularity, at once defeatist and white-privileging: since making friends is a small-scale solution to a huge structural problem, why bother? Yes; improvising has to start somewhere. Also, it shifts the discourse, especially on race discourse. If unearthing societal and cognitive entrenchment is a precondition to making friends-in-difference, then the desire that is augmented through expanding one's growing circle is the best engine and impulse of societal change.

Landing Place

My brief for the friend-in-difference of *The Friend* touches on current discussions regarding 'whiteness and the humanities' and the efficacy of curricular revision in countering institutional racism and the hegemony of Western thought. The contortions of my argument illustrate the challenge of enlisting writers to overturn a history of white supremacy that their writings construct and perpetuate. In a recent salvo, Simon During characterizes the effort as at an 'impasse' because 'race talk' and humanistic discourse have 'different logical structures' and therefore the impasse cannot be broken from 'inside the university.' '[W]hat is needed' instead is 'a genuine reckoning with the continuing history of white power and racism, especially in the U.S.' 'In the meantime,' the '*official* role' of anti-racist-inclined humanists is 'limited to that which honors the protocols, interests, and methods of our disciplines' – that is, 'commitment to inventiveness, interpretation, dialogue, persuasion, problematization, historicization, and so on' – a role that 'does not include dividing the world into friends and enemies, banning texts and words, or racially labelling archives and whole disciplines' (12, 9, 12).

The binary logic underlying this mapping of where impasse or resolution resides contradicts characterization of the humanities as dialogic and problematizing, though it is inventive. My interest, however, is in suggesting how 'the method of the friend' breaks the impasse as characterized and, in so doing, points the way to less supremacist humanities and societies. It is reductive to refuse to read works because an author happens to be a straight white male, but it is equally reductive to disarticulate the ambiguity and polyvocality of literary discourse from support of white supremacy or academic training from societal transformation. As *The Friend* makes clear, acts of reading, interpreting, educing do not occur in a vacuum; nor do minds work well or even wish to start if they have little hope of being encouraged by what they encounter. Literary texts are not determined or contained by the structures that inform them but neither are they external to them. This is what systemic racism means, and it will remain an informing condition unless conscious steps are taken to alter people's conscious and unconscious thought and desire. Reshaping unconscious desires is the special province of literature. If we wish to endorse literature's anti-disciplining approach to bodies and minds, we need to dismantle protocols that have disciplined and disappeared non-white ones.

The emphasis in *The Friend* on the friend's pivoting function between individual and collective, text and person, deadness and aliveness, suggests why it is unwise to underestimate the impact of the humanities on society. How else can structural change happen unless the cognitive, affective, and societal structures that undergird white consciousness are not only undone but also recoordinated? We shortchange the potential of the humanities to actually befriend humanity if we minimize either the damage it has done or its diffusive reach into social conditions. Oddly, the composition history of *The Friend* stages the importance of the literary through its titular and methodological demotion of it. Recall that the 1809–10 *The Friend* is 'a Literary, Moral, and Political Weekly Paper,' whereas the 1818 *The Friend* is 'a Series of Essays in Three Volumes to Aid in the Formation of Fixed Principles in Politics, Morals, and Religion with Literary Amusements Interspersed.' Part of my argument is that the 'literary' is not accommodatable to formulating 'fixed principles' for the reasons that During cites and that the career of Coleridge exemplifies, riven as it is over the conflicting appeals of poetry and abstruse research. That is what the 1818 *The Friend* brings to readers' consciousness: literature functions as a 'landing place,' an 'interlude' and temporary repose from strenuous thinking. It grants minds space to integrate and synthesize – to gather and personalize – what otherwise stays foreign, abstruse, and external. Providing landing places is the affective logic, and method, of *The Friend*, where 'love of knowledge' requires interposing essays for 'amusement, retrospect, and preparation,' and where 'delight' 'rewards the march of Truth' (I, xciii, 15–16). Though not in so many words, *The Friend* demonstrates its own aversion to the fixity of principles, at once craving relief from their punitiveness and accessing through literature trust in the benevolence of knowledge.

Most of this chapter has focused on the preconditions to making friends whose minds/brains/bodies are extended through co-mingling different histories of consciousness, struggle, sociality, and correlation between effort and reward. Focus on preconditions is required because of the cognitive and societal impediments to forging such friends, removal of which impediments is the outcome of conscious commitment and activity. Focus on preconditions is necessary also because, as in any intimate relationship, the particulars are co-created, and thus before-unapprehendable, as well as without guarantee of amounting to much. But unlike other forms, including intraracial friendship, this type intensifies opportunities for incomprehension because so many grounding assumptions are not shared – including whether friendship is more open-hearted or other-directed than blood ties, a point of debate between white and BIPOC radical thought. The asymmetry in priorities is often painful, to the white partner desiring partnering alternatives through friendship, to the non-white partner whose selfhood and kinship are threatened by affiliating with whiteness (Moraga 6–15). Relatively uncharted as well is how to navigate the dissolution of categories that occur once a deep connection is made, whereby the histories that deform interracial relations no longer are uppermost in either partner's mind.

Fortunately, there are landing places for the unsettledness within both the friendships and the texts that stimulate the process. Regarding the latter, the enlivening presence of textual models companionates minds in the process of destructuration and provides deepening acquaintance with other minds and the otherness of any mind. Also, it relieves BIPOC of the repeated demand to instruct anti-racist aspirants in how to behave like one. Having recourse to texts written from non-white or non-Western perspectives deepens both partners' interest in getting to know the other. White partners gain the cognitive benefit of double consciousness in acquiring more than one world view; BIPOC partners gain confidence that knowledge acquisition does not come at the expense of their minds or kin. Each begins to see what each has been missing, both cognitively and relationally, by being constructed as, or constructing others as, other. This is why curricula in the humanities should be evaluated on how well their texts and training inspire socio-cultural transformation through affective–cognitive transformation. Internalizing an array of non-white perspectives affects the nature and quality of the society that college students envision themselves as remaking. Enacting the internalization is visible in their 'choice' of friends.

The radical unpredictability of this project, the necessarily uncharted nature of its improvisational method and performance, leaves both parties deeply vulnerable, though again differently so. This situation makes perceiving diverse texts and friends as landing places so vital to the process. Each type of temporary landing offers relief, companionship, welcome distraction from the stresses and strains of socio-cognitive anti-racist exertion. Even better, each type is capable of functioning separately and in tandem. The advantage of separateness is that each is available to spell the other when the moving forward with one feels too strenuous, demanding, or no longer worth the effort. Reading texts that theorize and/or fictionalize racial identity help to keep friends-in-difference on track through their secondary processing of raw experience. They provide terms, delineations, guidance on what otherwise threatens to overwhelm by virtue of being 'self'-annihilating. Alternately, being with close friends revives the ease and joy of the not-knowing intensified in difference-oriented attraction. Availed of in tandem, the landing place provided by cross-racial friends as texts and multiracial texts as friends involves no longer having to explain oneself to the other or justify a life process of cultivating friends-in-difference to oneself as well as others. It is a space of un-self-soothing where the association of improvisation with friendship is part of procedural memory. Extending this way of becoming-with is the working method of the friend. It involves periodically doubling down on the depth of my attachment to *The Friend*.

Notes

1. A recent spate of books accommodate racial and sexual difference in their conceptualizations of friendship. Among others, Alexander Nehamas, *On Friendship*; P. E. Digeser, *Friendship Reconsidered: What It Means and How It Matters to Politics*; Niharika Banerjea, Debanuj Dasgupta, Rohit K. Dasgupta, and Jaime M. Grant, eds, *Friendship as Social Justice Activism: Critical Solidarities in a Global Perspective*; and Tim Delaney, ed., *The Friendship Issue* in *Philosophy Now* (June/July 2018).
2. Here I adapt Avery Gordon's concept of 'being-in-difference' to 'friend,' a 'being' characterized as a 'political consciousness and a sensuous knowledge' that offers 'a standpoint and a mindset for living on better terms than what we're offered' (v; cf. 48, 193). See also 75–112 where Gordon ties this mode of consciousness to the 'work' of friendship in an exchange with Céline Condorelli.
3. 'So grievously deceived by the showy mock theories of confident mock Thinkers, there seems a tendency in the public mind to shun all Thought, and to expect help from any quarter rather than from Seriousness and Reflection: As if some invisible Power would think for us, when we gave up the pretence of thinking for ourselves' (85).
4. A striking early passage presents suffering – whether it result from 'sickness, or grief, or remorse, or the deep yearnings of love' – as the incentive to reading because it renders one 'docile to the concurrent testimony of our fellow-men in all ages and in all nations.' By the way, '(there have been children of affliction, for whom all these have met and made up one complex suffering)' (7).
5. The account of Luther is arguably Coleridgean in ascribing the 'common effect of deranged Digestion in men of sedentary habits, who are at the same time intense thinkers,' a nervous 'irritability' fostered by 'the theological

Systems of his Manhood' that is 'sufficient to explain all his Apparitions and all his nightly combats with evil Spirits' (116). Still, his tone is unalarmed and analytical, and the focus serves as prelude to 'future Numbers [devoted] to the Subject of Dreams, Visions, Ghosts, Witchcraft, &c., in which I shall first give, and then endeavor to explain the most interesting and best attested fact of each, which has come within my knowledge, either from Books or from personal Testimony' (117). For Schoning, see 177–82, and the widow 89–96, 172. On the valuation of poems as psychological curiosities in the era, see Faflak.
6. 'You will grin at my *modest* account of Satyrane,' Coleridge writes Southey (*The Friend* II: 185n).
7. The poem portrays Satyrane's mind as 'strong' 'in joy' to 'follow the delightful Muse' to 'the fount of Hippocrene,' having often 'trac'd it upward to its source' and thereby grown familiar with every 'rill.' It then portrays that joyful stream as leading him into the 'long-neglected holy cave' of 'old Philosophy,' whose 'starry walls' he 'alone' with 'lifted torch' makes 'sparkle' as once they did to ancient 'Saint and Sage' (ll. 19–20, 24–5, 29–33). This is because, in name and disposition, 'studious poet' co-habits with 'Philosopher,' a combination that renders his disposition 'docile, childlike, full of light and love.'
8. For neurocognitive accounts of improvisation, see Berkowitz, Beaty, López-González, and Landau and Limb; for autopoietic and enactive accounts, see Luhman, Schiavio and van der Schyff, and Torrence and Schuman. For the deepest elaboration of jazz improvisation and blues epistemology, see Moten, *In the Break* and *Black and Blur*.
9. See especially Research Projects and Research Library on the IICSI website.

References

Allport, Gordon. *The Nature of Prejudice*. New York: Basic Books, 1954.
Amodio, David M. 'The Neuroscience of Prejudice and Stereotyping.' *Nature Reviews Neuroscience* 15 (2014): 670–82.
Banerjea, Niharika, Debanuj Dasgupta, Rohit K. Dasgupta, and Jaime M. Grant, eds. *Friendship as Social Justice Activism: Critical Solidarities in a Global Perspective*. London, New York, and Calcutta: Seagull Books, 2018.
Beaty, R. E. 'The Neuroscience of Musical Improvisation.' *Neuroscience and Biobehavioral Reviews* 51 (2015): 108–17.
Berkowitz, Aaron. *The Improvising Mind: Cognition and Creativity in the Musical Moment*. Oxford: Oxford University Press, 2010.
Blake, Felice, Paula Ioanides, and Alison Reed, eds. *Anti-Racism Inc: Why the Way We Talk about Racial Justice Matters*. Punctum Books, 2019. https://punctumbooks.com/titles/antiracism-inc-why-the-way-we-talk-about-racial-justice-matters/ (last accessed December 8, 2021).
Carlson, Julie A. 'On Literary Fractures.' *The Wordsworth Circle* 42.2 (2011): 129–38.
Cassidy, Brittany S. and Anne C. Krendl. 'Dynamic Neural Mechanisms Underlie Racial Disparities in Social Cognition.' *NeuroImage* 132 (2016):

238–46. https://www.sciencedirect.com/science/article/abs/pii/S105381191600152X#ab0010 (last accessed December 15, 2021).

Chalmers, David. 'Facing Up to the Problem of Consciousness.' *Journal of Consciousness Studies* 2.3 (1995): 200–19.

Coleman, Deidre. *Coleridge and* The Friend *(1809–1810)*. Oxford: Clarendon Press, 1988.

Coleridge, Samuel Taylor. *The Friend*. Ed. Barbara E. Rooke. 2 vols. Vol. 4 of *The Collected Works of Samuel Taylor Coleridge*. Gen. ed. Kathleen Coburn. Princeton: Princeton University Press, 1969.

Delaney, Tim, ed. *The Friendship Issue*. *Philosophy Now* 126 (June/July 2018). https://philosophynow.org/issues#126 (last accessed December 8, 2021).

Digeser, P. E. *Friendship Reconsidered: What It Means and How It Matters to Politics*. New York: Columbia University Press, 2016.

Du Bois, W. E. B. *The Souls of Black Folk*. 1903. New York: Penguin, 1996.

During, Simon. 'Whiteness and the Humanities.' *The Chronicle of Higher Education*. September 2, 2021.

Faflak, Joel. 'Psychology.' *A Handbook of Romanticism Studies*. Ed. Joel Faflak and Julia Wright. Malden, MA: Wiley-Blackwell, 2012. 391–408.

Fanon, Frantz. *Black Skin, White Masks*. 1952. Trans. Charles Lam Markmann. New York: Grove Press, 1967.

Fischlin, Daniel, Ajay Heble, and George Lipsitz. *The Fierce Urgency of Now: Improvisation, Rights and the Ethics of Co-Creation*. Durham, NC: Duke University Press, 2013.

Fruman, Norman. *Coleridge the Damaged Archangel*. New York: George Braziller, 1971.

Gordon, Avery. *The Hawthorn Archive: Letters from the Utopian Margins*. New York: Fordham University Press, 2017.

Henrich, Joseph. *The WEIRDest People in the World: How the West Became Psychologically Peculiar and Particularly Prosperous*. New York: Farrar, Straus, and Giroux, 2020.

—, Steven J. Heine, and Ara Norenzayan. 'The Weirdest People in the World?' *Behavioral and Brain Sciences* 33.2–3 (2010): 61–83.

Johnson, Walter. 'What Do We Mean When We Say "Systemic Racism"?: A Walk Down Florissant Avenue, Ferguson, Missouri.' *Kalfou* 3.1 (2016): 36–62.

Landau, Andrew T. and Charles J. Limb. 'The Neuroscience of Improvisation.' *Music Educators Journal* 103.3 (2017): 27–33.

Lipsitz, George. *How Racism Takes Place*. Philadelphia: Temple University Press, 2011.

López-González, Mónica and Charles Limb. 'Musical Creativity and the Brain.' *Cerebrum* 2012: 2. https://www.ncbi.nlm.nih.gov/pmc/articles/PMC3574774/ (last accessed March 10, 2021).

Luhman, Niklas. 'Self-organization and Autopoiesis.' *Emergence and Embodiment: New Essays on Second-order Systems Theory*. Ed. Bruce Clarke and Mark B. N. Hansen. Durham, NC: Duke University Press, 2009. 143–56.

Mitchell, Robert. *Experimental Life: Vitalism in Romantic Science and Literature*. Baltimore: Johns Hopkins University Press, 2013.

Monson, Ingrid. 'Improvisation as Conversation.' *The Improvisation Studies Reader: Spontaneous Acts.* Ed. Ajay Heble and Rebecca Caines. New York: Routledge, 2015. 35–51.

Moraga, Cherríe. *A Xicana Codex of Changing Consciousness: Writings 2000–2010.* Durham, NC: Duke University Press, 2011.

Moten, Fred. *Black and Blur.* Durham, NC: Duke University Press, 2017.

—. *In the Break: The Aesthetics of the Black Radical Tradition.* Minneapolis: University of Minnesota Press, 2003.

Nehamas, Alexander. *On Friendship.* New York: Basic Books, 2016.

Paluck, Elizabeth Levy, Seth Green, and Donald P. Green. 'The Contact Hypothesis Re-evaluated.' *Behavioural Public Policy* 3.2 (2019): 129–58.

Parker, Reeve. *Romantic Tragedies: The Dark Employments of Wordsworth, Coleridge, and Shelley.* Cambridge: Cambridge University Press, 2011.

Roberts, Steven O., Carmelle Bareket-Shavit, Forrest A. Dollins, Peter D. Goldie, and Elizabeth Mortenson. 'Racial Inequality in Psychological Research: Trends of the Past and Recommendations for the Future.' *Association for Psychological Science* (2020): 1–15.

Robertson, Lisa Ann. 'Enacting the Absolute: S. T. Coleridge's Theory of Knowledge.' *Distributed Cognition in Enlightenment and Romantic Culture.* Ed. Miranda Anderson, George Rousseau, and Michael Wheeler. Edinburgh: Edinburgh University Press, 2019. 118–38.

Rooke, Barbara E. 'Editor's Introduction.' *The Friend.* 2 vols. Vol. 4 of *The Collected Works of Samuel Taylor Coleridge.* Gen. ed. Kathleen Coburn. Princeton: Princeton University Press, 1969. xxxv–cv.

Savarese, John. 'Cognitive Scaffolding, Aids to Reflection.' *Distributed Cognition in Enlightenment and Romantic Culture.* 139–55.

Schiavio, Andrea and Dylan van der Schyff. '4E Music Pedagogy and the Principles of Self-organization.' *Behavioral Science* 8 (2018). https://www.cbi.nlm.nih.gov/pmc/articles/PMC6115738 (last accessed March 10, 2021).

Sessa, P., F. Meconi, L. Castelli, and R. Dall'Acqua. 'Taking One's Time in Feeling Other-race Pain: An Event-Related Potential Investigation in the Time-course of Cross-racial Empathy.' *Social Cognitive Affective Neuroscience* 9.4 (2014): 454–63.

de Sousa Santos, Boaventura. *The End of the Cognitive Empire: The Coming of Age of Epistemologies of the South.* Durham, NC: Duke University Press, 2018.

Thompson, E. P. 'Disenchantment or Default? A Lay Sermon.' *Power and Consciousness.* Ed. Conor Cruise O'Brien and William Dean Vanech. New York: New York University Press, 1969. 149–81.

Torrence, Steve and Frank Schuman. 'The Spur of the Moment: What Jazz Improvisation Tells Cognitive Science.' *AI and Society* 34 (2019): 251–68.

Woods, Clyde A. *Development Arrested: The Blues and Plantation Power in the Mississippi Delta.* New York: Verso, 2017.

Wordsworth, William. *The Prelude, 1799, 1805, 1850.* Ed. Jonathan Wordsworth, M. H. Abrams, and Stephen Gill. New York: W. W. Norton, 1979.

Wynter, Sylvia. 'Towards the Sociogenic Principle: Fanon, Identity, the Puzzle of Conscious Experience and What it is Like to be "Black".' *National Identities and Socio-political Changes in Latin America*. Ed. Antonio Gomez-Moriana and Mercedes Duran-Cogan. New York: Routledge, 2001. 30–66.

—. 'Unsettling the Coloniality of Being/Power/Truth/Freedom: Towards the Human, After Man, Its Over-Representation – An Argument.' *CR: The New Centennial Review* 3.3 (2003): 257–337.

Index

Page references to illustrations are in *italic* type.

Abrams, M. H., 2–3, 4, 6, 19n, 76, 196, 285, 340, 359n2
abstraction, 13, 16, 96, 97, 105–7, 110, 113n10
accentual meter, 270, 275, 276, 278–9
Adam, Nicolas, 294
Adams, Frederick, 262n11
Addison, Joseph, 268–71, 273, 276, 281
Adorno, Theodor W., 49, 177, 204
affect
  'after-affects,' 17, 146, 154–5, 157, 162
  and art, conjunctions of, 150–2
  and body budgets, 10–11, 21n19, 112n4
  and emotion, 123
  'impersonal,' 317–18, 321
  post-Romantic, 146–50
  primary, 131–7, 138–41
  rethinking of, by Wollstonecraft and Eliot, 152–5
  Wordsworth's 'simple affections,' 155–7
affect theory, 123, 153, 163n2–3, 164n11
affective narratology, lyrical balladry as, 121–41
affordances, 8, 10, 13, 14, 20n13, 96, 98, 112n7
African diasporic culture, 313
Agamben, Giorgio, 113n12, 169, 190n1
Ahmed, Sarah, 340, 350, 354
Aikin, John, 213, 271–2, 273, 275, 281
Aikin, Lucy, 275
Aizawa, Kenneth, 262n11

Alaimo, Stacy, 312, 314, 317
Alison, Archibald, 42
Allewaert, Monique, 329
Althusser, Louis, 75, 77, 84
analytic panpsychism, 52–5
Anderson, Amanda, 113n9
Anderson, Miranda, 273
animal rights, 62
animism, 49–51, 54, 56–8, 60
Anthropocene, 55, 60
anthropomorphism, 50, 51, 55, 57–8, 63, 69n11
anxiety, 35, 79, 99, 144
apostrophe, 50, 56–7, 58, 63, 300, 318
Apter, Emily, 357
Arendt, Hannah, 298
Arnold, Matthew, 311
art and affect, conjunctions of, 150–2
artificial intelligence, 88
Asia: in Barker's panoramic paintings, 339, 344, 347, 349–50, 357
Austen, Jane, 32, 41, 42–3
automatism, 34–5, 278
autopoiesis, 95, 103, 203, 370, 376, 377
Averill, James, 134, 139

Baars, Bernard, 8
Baillie, Joanna, 14, 41
ballad antiquarianism, 270, 273, 281, 282n3
ballad meter, 18, 126–8, 136, 274–5
balladry, 18, 121–41, 268–82
Barad, Karen, 312, 319, 326, 334n14
Barbauld, Anna Letitia, 213, 270, 271, 273–6, 281

Barker, Henry Aston, 339–59
  map of Constantinople, 349, 349–50, 357
  View of Constantinople from the Tower of Galata, 18, 339, 344, 345
  View of Constantinople from the Tower of Leander, 339, 346
Barker, Robert, 341
Barrett, Lisa Feldman, 10, 14, 21n19, 112n4, 113n10
Baucom, Ian, 168–9, 191n2
Beardsley, Monroe, 121, 123, 141n1
beauty, Kantian, 111n1, 179, 298, 305n10
belief: and faith, 84–5
Bell, Charles, 40–1
Belsey, Catherine, 31
Benjamin, Ruha, 102, 329
Bennett, Jane, 57, 58, 61, 69n13, 312, 317, 321
Bernard of Clairvaux, Saint, *158*, 158–62, *161*, 164n13
Bersani, Leo, 174, 181, 191n19
Black, Indigenous, and People of Color (BIPOC), 374, 377–8, 380
Black feminist theory, 325–6, 329, 334n13
Black studies, 312–13
Blake, William, 3, 7, 11, 17, 94–111
  annotations, 4, 5, 100, 173
  'The Chimney Sweeper,' 100
  'The Clod and the Pebble,' 109
  'The Divine Image,' 108
  'Holy Thursday,' 100, 108
  Illustrations from the Book of Job, 171–6, *172*, 191n12
  imagination, 98, 99, 105, 107, 108–9
  'Infant Sorrow,' 107
  innatism and idealism, 105–9
  and Kant, 99, 102, 107, 108
  'The Lamb,' 111
  'The Little Black Boy,' 103–4, 107
  'The Little Vagabond,' 104–5
  'London,' 259
  The Marriage of Heaven and Hell, 98, 101, 109, 175
  and meaning of 'experience,' 94, 98–9, 101, 104
  meter, use of, 279
  Milton, 175
  'On Another's Sorrow,' 100
  panpsychism, 61, 62, 67, 94, 109–11
  'The Shepherd,' 106
  Songs of Innocence and of Experience, 94, 98–111
  view of nature, 101, 109
  and Wordsworth, 4, 5
Bloom, Harold, 1–6
  Deconstruction and Criticism, 20n10
  essay on Percy Shelley, 249
  and Freud, 2, 73, 199
  'quest-romance,' 2, 29, 74, 359
  see also Romanticism and Consciousness: Essays in Criticism
Bloom, Paul, 14
'blues epistemology,' 376, 382n8
Bode, Christoph, 214–15
Bohrn, Isabel C., 137
Bolter, Jay David, 201, 202
Borromean knot, 87
brain, human
  body budgets, 10, 21n19, 112n4
  emotion-processing systems, 134–5
  frontal cortex, 9, 21n17
  mind–brain interaction, 52, 113n11
  models of cognition, 292–3, 295
  neuroimaging studies, 7–8, 20n12, 21n17, 137, 375
  orbitofrontal cortex, 135–8
  plasticity, 8, 111, 191n7, 293–4
  reading paradox, 293–4
brain mapping, 9, 20n12
brain–mind–consciousness debates, 311–12; *see also* mind–body problem
brain science, 34, 250
Brennan, Teresa, 318, 321
Brooke-Smith, James, 201
Brown, Marshall, 111n1
Brown, Richard, 114n17
Browning, Robert, 87–8
Bruhn, Mark J., 19, 251
'bundles of perceptions,' 12, 114n23, 252–3, 312, 316
Bürger, Gottfried August
  'The Lass of Fair Wone,' 138–9
  'Lenora,' 270, 275–9
Burke, Edmund, 18, 152, 153, 286–90, 297, 301, 304
Burkett, Andrew, 201
Butler, Judith, 102, 103, 114n20
Byron, George Gordon, 30, 36, 44, 340, 358

Cabanis, P. J. G, 38, 40, 41
Carlson, Julie A., 18, 264n32, 334n15

Carter, Benjamin, 31
Cartesian dualism, 13, 15, 88, 97, 104, 114n19, 204, 311
Cartesian theater, 115n27
Caruth, Cathy, 185
Cassidy, Brittany, 375, 376
Castellano, Katey, 301
Cavell, Stanley, 50–1, 57–8, 61, 64, 75–7
Cavendish, Margaret, 53
Chalmers, David, 7, 11, 76, 113n8, 261, 311
   argument for panpsychism, 11, 98
   'extended mind' theory, 251–5, 261, 263n25, 269, 295–6
   'hard problem' of consciousness, 68n3, 75, 84, 97–8, 374
Chandler, James, 103, 106, 191n2, 290, 301
Changeux, Jean-Pierre, 16, 21n6
characters, fictional, mental states of, 228, 241–2
Cheeke, Stephen, 250, 258
Chen, Mel Y., 318
Chester, John, 371
childhood, Romantic idealization of, 238–40
children
   brain plasticity, 293
   imagination, 18, 227–8, 232, 238–40, 244, 245n9, 246n15
   infants, 40, 41, 106–7, 115n26
   metacognitive abilities, 231–4, 237–43, 245n8
   reverie and 'vegetation,' states of, 42, 254
   skepticism, 228, 232–3
Christ, 100, 103, 225, 227, 229–31, 233, 245n1
Christensen, Jerome, 134, 167
Cisek, Paul, 8
citation analysis, 128–32, 133, 139, 141, 142n5
Clare, John, 58–60, 62, 63, 67
Clark, Andy, 7, 8, 13
   embodied cognition, 17, 21n18, 109–10, 114n19
   enaction, 110, 113n8
   'extended mind' theory, 251–5, 261, 263n25, 269, 295–6
Clark, David L., 170, 191n6
Clark, T. J., 173, 191n16
Clune, Michael, 114n15, 114n19, 115n31

coexistence thinking, 228–31, 234, 236, 237, 243
cognition
   distributed, 2, 13, 18, 69n15, 272–4, 281
   embedded, 101, 113n10, 273, 281, 282, 295
   enactive, 2, 95, 110, 111n2, 113n8, 272, 370
   'entangled' view of, 13–15, 21n23
   extended, 13, 252, 253, 262n11, 273, 296, 370
   see also embodied cognition
cognitive linguistics, 88
cognitive literary studies, 121, 122, 200, 241–4
cognitive neuroscience, 36, 293
cognitive psychology, 44, 227–8, 234, 238, 244, 374
cognitive 'scaffolding,' concept of, 257, 263n25, 270–5, 369–70
cognitive science, 2, 131, 286, 290–7, 311
   and consciousness, 31, 52, 88
   and literary criticism, 228, 240, 243
Cohen, Jeffrey, 318
Colebrook, Claire, 190, 211
Coleridge, Samuel Taylor
   Aids to Reflection, 370
   and automatism, 34
   Biographia Literaria, 54, 74, 368, 369–71
   'Christabel,' 31, 35–6, 171, 179, 268, 270, 278–80
   On the Constitution of Church and State, 32, 370
   'Dejection: An Ode,' 11, 213
   'The Eolian Harp,' 65
   and fairy tales, 239
   The Friend, 363–82
   friendships, 367, 368–9, 370–3
   'Frost at Midnight,' 171, 174, 196
   on instinctive behaviors, 40
   interest in mesmerism, 36
   and Kant, 212
   'Kubla Khan,' 36, 38, 42, 171
   lexical innovation, 32–3
   Lyrical Ballads, 33, 124, 141
   metrical experimentation, 268, 270, 278, 279, 280
   on poetic faith, 74, 84–5
   'Rime of the Ancient Mariner,' 11, 33, 35, 36, 44, 167
   sublime suspension, 5

'Theory of Life,' 370, 372
  and Wordsworth, 124, 136, 141, 367, 368–9
Coleridge, Sarah, 371
collective epistemology, 253
Collings, David, 12, 126, 134
common meter, 270, 274–5, 276, 277, 280–1
communications technologies, 203
computer learning, 291–2
Constantinople, 339–59
  map, 349, 349–50, 357
  panoramic paintings, 18, 339–59, 345, 346
corporate consciousness, 313, 318, 320, 322, 327
'correlationism,' 78, 211, 212
cosmopsychism, 51, 64–7
Crisafi, Anthony, 296–7
critical imagination, 238–41
Csikszentmihalyi, Mihaly, 5
Culler, Jonathan, 300
Curran, Stuart, 263n19, 315
cybernetics, 291

Dacre, Charlotte: *Zofloya*, 34, 37, 38
Damasio, Antonio, 2, 5, 9, 14–15, 20n9, 21n24, 123
Darwin, Charles, 80, 286, 290–2, 294, 305n5
Darwin, Erasmus, 38, 39, 40, 42, 65, 80, 203
Davy, Humphry, 213
de Bolla, Peter, 186, 188, 192n25
de Luca, Vincent, 176
de Man, Paul, 6, 56, 58, 68n9, 73, 76, 84, 95, 187, 285, 318
De Preester, Helena, 9
De Quincey, Thomas, 6, 31, 32, 41, 88
Deacon, Terrence, 132
deconstruction, 1, 57, 58, 73, 285, 286, 299, 333n1
Dehaene, Stanislas
  fMRI studies, 7–8, 21n17
  global workspace theory, 8–10, 21n17, 21n23
  innatism and abstraction, 106, 107, 115n26
  on learning, 106, 107, 293–4, 305n7
Deleuze, Gilles, 163n1, 164n10, 169, 176, 203
Dennett, Daniel, 20n, 115n, 316, 321
Descartes, René, 52, 53, 113n12

Diderot, Denis, 37, 53
disenchantment, 54, 55
disorientation, 18, 167–8, 171, 175, 188, 339–59
distributed cognition, 2, 13, 18, 69n15, 272–4, 281
divinity, 107, 108–9
double consciousness
  and Barker's panoramas, 341, 348, 351, 354
  in *The Friend*, 364, 373–4, 380
  in 'Ode to Autumn,' 319–20
  in Prince's narrative, 329, 331
Dove, Guy, 8
dreams and dreaming, 31, 36–8, 44, 83, 181–2
Du Bois, W. E. B., 341, 373
dualism, 13, 52–7, 65, 97, 98, 200, 202, 204, 212, 263n20; *see also* Cartesian dualism
Dürer, Albrecht, 225, 245n3
  George Slaying the Dragon, 226
During, Simon, 378, 379
Düttmann, Alexander García, 177–8

ecologies
  gothic ecologies of mind, 268–82
  media ecology, 18, 196–216, 218n11, 359
'ecology' (term), coining of, 55
efficiency, 6, 8–9, 11, 21n18, 111
ego psychology, 6, 73, 199
Elfenbein, Andrew, 241, 243
Elgin, Lord, 342, 344–9, 353, 354, 360n4
eliminative materialism, 52
Eliot, George, 146, 149–54, 157–63, 163n4, 164n11
  Middlemarch, 146–50, 154–5, 157, 162, 163n6
  'Notes on Form in Art,' 150–1
  Romola, 157–62, 164n13
Eliot, T. S., 3, 19n4
Ellenberger, Henri, 30, 285
embedded cognition, 101, 113n10, 273, 281, 282, 295
embodied cognition, 8, 9, 13–18, 95–7, 101, 107–11, 112n2, 295
  ballad studies, relevance to, 268, 269, 272–3
  and Cartesian dualism, 13, 104, 114n19, 200
  and 'efficiency,' 11, 21n18
  grades of embodiment, 114n19

embodied cognition (*cont.*)
  and Romantic writers, 14, 16, 34, 269, 370
embodied mind, 14, 31, 95–7, 101, 200, 269, 370
emotion: and affect, 123
emotion, 'quartet theory' of, 135, 142n7
emotional thinking, forms of, 144–63
empathy, studies of, 14
empiricism
  and Blakean experience, 98–9, 100, 109, 113n14
  eighteenth-century, 85, 272
  false beliefs, 112n6
  of Locke and Hume, 98
  'qualia empiricism,' 19n8
  Wordsworth's, 113n14
enaction, 96, 97, 101, 110, 112n5, 113n8, 114n22
enactivism, 2, 15, 95–8, 102, 110–11, 112n2, 113n8, 272, 296, 370
Enlightenment, 3, 36, 198, 288, 313, 324, 332, 333n1
'entangled' view of cognition, 13–15, 21n23
epistemology, 98–9, 199, 204, 210, 211, 212, 216
  'blues,' 376, 382n8
  collective, 253
  Kantian, 20n13, 211
Europe: in Barker's panoramic paintings, 339, 344, 347, 349–50, 357
everyday, aesthetics of the, 124, 146, 150, 163
evolution, biological, 11, 12, 106, 290–1, 293
experience
  Blakean, 17, 94–111
  in Smith's *Beachy Head*, 208–9, 215, 216
extended cognition, 13, 252, 253, 262n11, 273, 296, 370
extended mind, 249–61, 281, 286, 294–7, 301, 303, 377

Faflak, Joel, 6, 17, 31, 191n14
fairy tales, 239, 240, 246n15, 246n17
faith, the Real of, 73–93
Fanon, Frantz, 329, 374
fantasy genre, 228, 240–1
fantasy structures, 82, 83, 84, 85, 86
Felman, Shoshana, 76

feminism, 1, 2, 89n4, 210, 311, 334n12; *see also* Black feminist theory
Fenwick, Isabella, 124, 141n3
Ferguson, Adam, 271, 278
Feuerbach, Ludwig, 159, 164n13
Flanagan, Owen, 20n9, 108, 112n5, 115n27
Fodor, Jerry, 20n13, 52, 164n10
Foglia, Lucia, 295
Foucault, Michel, 7, 69n10, 169, 216n4, 304
François, Anne-Lise, 12
'free spirit,' 278–9
free thinking, 65
freedom
  concept of, 107
  from consciousness, 43
  poetic, 281
  of 'studio states,' 176–9
French Revolution, 63, 66, 152, 206, 287, 302–3, 369
Freud, Sigmund, 75, 83–4, 89, 199, 285
  assessment of legacy, 73–4
  and Bloom, 2, 73, 199
  concept of the unconscious, 31, 285
  and Lacan, 6, 73, 83–4, 89n3, 89n4
  psychoanalysis, 29, 31, 84
  theory of the human mind, 6, 199
'friend' (term): use of, 373
friend-in-difference, 373, 377, 378
friendship, 18, 351, 363–81
Frye, Northrop, 2, 3, 5, 11, 102, 114n25
Fuller, Matthew, 202–3, 218n11
functional magnetic resonance imaging (fMRI), 7–8, 20n12, 21n17, 137
Fuseli, Henry, 323
Fussell, Paul, 278

Gall, F. J., 40, 41
Gallagher, Shaun, 13, 96, 98, 102, 112n7, 296–7
Galperin, William, 69n18
Garcia, Humberto, 18, 76
Garofalo, Daniela, 77
gender, 2, 18, 187, 210, 313, 324–7, 340, 350, 354–8
gendered identities, 189, 197, 198, 202
geology, 197, 204, 211, 212, 213, 216, 219n15
George, Saint, 225, 226
Ghossainy, Maliki E., 231–2, 245n5–6
Gillman, James, 372

Gitelman, Lisa, 218n9
global workspace theory, 8–10, 9–10, 21n15–17
Goddard, Michael, 203
Godwin, William
   Caleb Williams, 37, 264n30
   Enquiry Concerning Political Justice, 288
   on institutions, 18, 286, 288, 289, 290, 297
   and Percy Shelley, 263n15, 264n30, 290, 305n3
   Thoughts on Man, 41, 42
   on Wollstonecraft, 323
Goff, Phillip, 11, 62, 69n20, 113n11, 115n30
Goldsmith, Steven, 99, 102–3
Goodman, Kevis, 184, 204, 278
Gordon, Avery, 381n2
gothic ballad revival, 268–82
gothic novels
   parasomnia motif, 36–7
   representations of unconscious mental acts, 34
Gottlieb, Evan, 319
Goya, Francisco, 170, 191n6
Gravil, Richard, 125–6, 140
Gray, Thomas, 125, 209
Green, André, 182
group-mind theory, 253
Grusin, Richard, 201, 202
Guattari, Félix, 169, 203
Guillory, John, 217n8
Gumbs, Alexis Pauline, 325, 326, 334n13
Guyer, Sara, 318

Haeckel, Ernst, 55
Haekel, Ralf, 18
Hamilton, Paul, 250
Hamilton, Sir William, 342
Hansen, Mark B. N., 212
happiness, 65–7, 208–9
Haraway, Donna, 318
'hard problem' of consciousness, 52–3, 68n3, 75–6, 84, 94–8, 113n11, 374
   responses to, 52, 98, 112n4, 311
harems, 347
Harman, Graham, 57, 58, 68n2, 312, 319, 333n1
Harney, Stefano, 316
Hartman, Geoffrey H., 5, 19n2, 44, 68n2, 74, 76, 285
   'Beyond Formalism,' 29
   'Romanticism and "Anti-Self-Consciousness"', 3–4, 30, 73, 95, 111, 311
   Wordsworth's Poetry, 301
Hartman, Saidiya V., 334n11
Havelock, Eric, 218n10
Hayles, N. Katherine, 15, 35
Hays, Mary, 208
Hazlitt, William, 3, 38, 39, 290
Hebb, Donald O., 305n7
Hegel, G. W. F., 12, 29, 163n6, 218n9, 285, 286, 289, 294–7
Heidegger, Martin, 180, 218n10, 285, 322
Heise, Ursula, 203
Hemans, Felicia, 33–4
Henderson, Andrea K., 12, 263n20, 359
Henrich, Joseph, 374
Herder, Johann Gottfried, 35, 271, 278
Hertz, Neil, 76
Hobson, J. Allan, 31
Hoffmann, E. T. A., 18, 225–44
   aesthetics, 246n20
   Dürer and, 225, 245n3
   fairy tales and children's fantasy, 241, 246n17
   The Nutcracker and the Mouse King, 225–44, 245n1, 245n4
   The Serapion Brothers, 246n20
Hogan, Patrick Colm, 134–6, 243–4
Hogg, James, 6
Hogg, Thomas Jefferson, 65
Hogle, Jerrold, 261n6
Hollander, John, 277, 278–9, 280
Holmes, Richard, 2
Holzer, Jenny, 83
Hume, David, 12, 84–5, 114n23, 153, 164n10, 252–3, 312, 316
Hurley, Susan, 7
Hutchinson, Sara, 368–9
Huxley, Thomas, 52, 216n3
hypermediacy, 201–2

idealism
   and Blake, 105, 107
   and embodied cognition, 13, 96, 110
   and enactivism, 96, 97, 110, 113n8
   Hegel's, 285, 296
   Kant's, 78, 212
   and panpsychism, 51, 68n4, 69n12, 70n24
   Romantic period, 68n4, 285

ideas, standard: Kant on, 297–9
ideology
   and consciousness, 94, 101–2, 108, 111
   Romantic, 3, 19n7, 73
   and utopia: in Blake, 99
Imaginary, the, 77, 79, 87
imagination
   and Blake, 98, 99, 105, 107, 108–9
   of children, 18, 227–8, 232, 238–40, 244, 245n9, 246n15
   mythopoeic, 3
   and nature, 51, 94, 95, 311, 333n1
   and self-estrangement, 339
   Wordsworth's definition of, 126
Imlay, Gilbert, 323
improvisation, musical, 376–7, 382n8
inactive theories of consciousness, 19n8
incest: in Shelley's *The Cenci*, 256, 257, 258, 261, 263n18
Industrial Revolution, 205
infanticide, 138
infants, 40, 41, 106–7, 115n26
innatism, 94, 105–9
innocence
   Blakean, 99, 105–6, 107, 108, 114n25
   in Smith's *Beachy Head*, 208–9, 215, 216
'innocence,' etymology of, 107
instinct, 34, 40–1, 153
institutions
   and 'extended mind,' 18, 286, 294–7
   gothic, 269, 270, 271
   and interracial relations, 376
   Romantic era, 287–90
   Wordsworthian, 299–304
integrated information theory, 15, 22n25, 110
intentionality, 55, 61, 96, 102, 177–8
'interoception,' 21n19, 38–9, 112n4
interpellation, 77, 81, 88
interracial friendships, 364, 373, 377, 380–1
intuitions, 16, 34, 41, 52, 53, 99, 106, 212
irony, 97, 110

Jackson, Noel, 12, 280
Jackson, Zakiyyah Iman, 313, 324, 326, 329
Jacobus, Mary, 6–7
Jager, Colin, 11, 17, 113n11

Jagoda, Patrick, 16, 22n27
James, William, 53, 69n12
Jameson, Anna, 158
Jameson, Fredric, 11, 17, 75, 204
Jarvis, Simon, 185, 188, 272
Jay, Martin, 97, 98, 113n12, 114n24
Jesus, 100, 103, 225, 227, 229–31, 233, 245n1
Johnson, Barbara, 56–7, 58, 69n10, 318
Johnson, Mark, 3, 264n29
Jones, Sir William, 359n2
Jordan, Neil, 330
Juengel, Scott J., 168
Jung, Carl, 7, 84
Juno Ludovisi, 188–90

Kames, Lord, 42
Kant, Immanuel, 297–9
   aesthetics, 111n1, 179, 298, 305n10
   and Blake, 99, 102, 107, 108
   'common human understanding,' 298, 299
   'correlationism,' 78, 211, 212
   critical philosophy, 199, 212
   Critique of Judgment, 168, 286, 298
   Critique of Pure Reason, 211
   'dark room' vignette, 167–8, 190
   epistemology, 20n13, 211, 212
   on human freedom, 107
   idea of enlightenment, 168, 169
   and the imagination, 99, 114n22
   and perception, 74–5, 95, 114n22, 298
   on populations, 286, 297–9
   purposiveness, notion of, 20n13, 179, 334n17
   on race, 298, 305n10
   and Romantic concept of consciousness, 199
   'standard ideas,' 298, 299
   thing-in-itself, 10, 50, 78, 111n1, 211, 212
   transcendental idealism, 212
   truce with skepticism, 50
Keats, John
   class consciousness, 324
   Endymion, 40, 44
   The Eve of St. Agnes, 37–8, 39–40
   'La Belle Dame Sans Merci: A Ballad,' 15
   letters, 41, 74, 301

'living hand,' 167
'Mansion of Many Apartments,' 179
medical training, 34, 41
'Ode on a Grecian Urn,' 78
'Ode to Autumn,' 319–21
'Ode to Psyche,' 34
and Percy Shelley's *Adonais*, 81–4, 85, 90n12
Khalip, Jacques, 12, 17, 262n10
Khan, Mirza Abu Talib, 339, 340, 351–9, 360n7
King, Tiffany Lethabo, 327, 329
Kittler, Friedrich, 217n7
Klein, Melanie, 6, 29
knowledge: in Smith's *Beachy Head*, 196–216
Koch, Christof, 11, 15, 96, 110
Koestenbaum, Wayne, 167, 176
Köppe, Tilmann, 200
Kramnick, Jonathan, 7, 8, 10, 20n13, 69n13, 96, 272, 322
Krendl, Anne, 375, 376
Kristeva, Julia, 76, 86, 89n4, 339

Labbe, Jacqueline, 196, 198, 205
Lacan, Jacques, 6, 29, 73, 75, 77–89
 and Freud, 6, 73, 83–4, 89n3, 89n4
 psychoanalysis, 6, 29, 73, 83–4, 86, 89n3, 90n10
 and the unconscious, 75, 86, 90n8
Lakoff, George, 3, 264n29
Langan, Celeste, 201, 202
language, Romantic, 55–9
Latour, Bruno, 333n1
LaVie, Peretz, 31
Laycock, Thomas, 31
learning, 42, 105–9, 287, 289, 291–4, 305n6–7
Leclercq, Jean, 160
LeDoux, Joseph, 114n17
Lee, Debbie, 11
Legare, Christine, 229, 230
Leibniz, Gottfried Wilhelm, 53, 170
Levinson, Marjorie, 95, 302–4
Lewis, C. S., 19n4
Lewis, Matthew, 34, 268, 276, 280, 282n1
lexical innovation, 32–3
Leys, Ruth, 163n2, 164n11
Libet, Benjamin, 19n8
Lindgren, Astrid, 240
linguistic fictions, 63
linguistic scaffolding, 263n25
Lippi, Filippino: *Apparition of the Virgin to Saint Bernard*, 157–62, 158
literary criticism, 51, 121–2, 228, 238–42
literature, knowledge in: connection to consciousness, 198, 199–203
Liu, Alan, 16, 174
Llinás, Rodolfo, 112n4
Locke, John, 12, 75, 98, 99, 102, 105, 106, 183–5, 188
locodescriptive poetry, 272
London, England
 in Mary Robinson's poem, 314–17, 318
 panorama exhibit (1801–1802), 339–59
Louverture, Toussaint, 170
Lovejoy, Arthur O., 2, 3, 19n3, 282n12
Lucretianism, 51
Lukacher, Ned, 84, 90n15
Lupton, Christina, 218n9

machine consciousness, 88, 110
machine learning, 107, 291–2
McCarthy, Anne C., 5
McCarthy, John, 293
McDonald, Peter, 134
McGann, Jerome, 1, 3, 73
McGinn, Colin, 112n5
McLuhan, Marshall, 202
Malabou, Catherine, 8, 9, 18, 21n6, 111, 171, 191n7, 294
Malthus, Thomas, 18, 286–91, 294, 297, 299–301, 305n5
Manzotti, Riccardo, 112n6
Marcone, Jorge, 58
Marder, Michael, 318
Massumi, Brian, 123, 313, 318, 321
materialism, 3, 57, 65, 69n12, 167
 eliminative, 52
 new, 35, 311, 312–14, 317, 324, 333n1
 philosophical, 52, 68n4
Mathews, Freya, 54–5
Matlak, Richard, 39
media ecology, 18, 196–216, 218n11, 359
media technologies, 201–2, 217n7, 217n8
media theory, 198–203, 212, 217n7, 218n10
medieval poetics, 279
Meillassoux, Quentin, 78, 211–12

Melling, Antoine-Ignace, 342, 351
  View of a Part of the City of Constantinople with Seraglio Point Taken from the Suburbs of Pera, 342, 343, 344
  Voyage pittoresque de Constantinople et des rives du Bosphore, 342, 347, 358–9
mental extension *see* extended mind
'mental theater,' 30, 325
Mercier, Hugo, 228, 234, 237, 241, 244
Merleau-Ponty, Maurice, 322
mesmerism, 36
metacognition, 228, 231–4, 237, 238–44, 245n7–8, 355
metaphysics: and politics, relation between, 59, 64
meter, 4, 13, 18, 126–31, 140, 155, 268–70, 274–82
Miles, Josephine, 19n2
Miles, Robert, 79, 89n1
Miller, Jonathan, 31
Milton, John: *Paradise Lost*, 209
mind–body problem, 52, 88, 97, 104, 200, 204, 216n3; *see also* Cartesian dualism
miracles, 84–5
mirror stage, 89
Mitchell, Robert, 12, 18, 370
Mitchell, W. J. T., 99
monads, 53, 170
monism, 55, 64, 69n21, 70n24, 322
Montag, Warren, 180
moral change, primary affect as agent of, 138–41
moral psychology, 99, 150
moral sentimentalism, 152–3
Moretti, Franco, 77
Moten, Fred, 104, 316, 331
'multiple drafts' theory, 20n9, 115n27
Münchow, Michael, 76
musical improvisation, 376–7, 382n8
mutual consciousness, 313, 314–21
mythopoeic imagination, 3

Nagel, Thomas, 311
Nancy, Jean-Luc, 76, 89n4, 173
Napoleonic Wars, 208, 340, 351, 355, 358
narcissism, 15, 96, 113n8, 282n12
natural history, 197, 204, 213, 215, 219n15

nature
  Blake's view of, 101, 109
  and consciousness, 5, 51, 78, 94, 95, 199, 311
  and imagination, 51, 94, 95, 311, 333n1
  panpsychism, 57–8, 62–3, 65
  'return to,' 311, 313, 333n1
  rights of, 62–3
  and Romanticism, 4–6
  separation from, 51, 78, 94, 311, 332
  in Smith's *Beachy Head*, 196, 209–14
  treatment of, 6, 54
  and Wordsworth, 76, 122, 151, 156, 210, 301, 304, 311, 332
necropolitics, 314, 333n3
Nelson, Horatio, 342, 352
neogothicism, 268, 269, 275–6, 279, 281
neurobiology, 88, 121, 374
neuronal populations, concept of, 18, 286, 290–4, 297, 299, 301
neuroscientific studies, 7–8, 14, 20n12, 21n17, 106, 137, 243
New Criticism, 1, 3, 19n6, 29, 164n12
new materialism, 35, 312–14, 317, 324, 333n1
Newton, Isaac, 53
Noë, Alva, 7, 13, 96, 110, 272
nonce meters, 268, 269, 280, 281
nostalgia, 56, 95, 96, 97, 348

object-oriented ontology, 311, 312, 319, 333n1
O'Doherty, Brian, 177
O'Donnell, Brennan, 127
Oleksijczuk, Denise Blake, 341, 347
O'Quinn, Daniel, 105, 340, 344, 347, 348, 351, 358–9
ordinary, the, 61, 69n13, 150, 152, 154, 157, 163
O'Regan, J. Kevin, 112n4, 114n22
Orient, the, 339, 340
orientation
  Kant's 'dark room,' 167–8, 190
  see also disorientation
O'Sullivan, Emer, 240, 241
Ottoman empire, 341, 349, 350, 352, 356, 357

Pandemonium architecture, 291–3, 305n6–7

panoramas, 18, 339–59, *345*, *346*
panpsychism, 49–67, 98, 109–11, 311–13, 319, 322
　analytic, 52–5
　in Blake, 61, 62, 67, 94, 109–11
　'combination problem,' 59–63, 64, 67, 69n18
　cosmopsychism, 51, 64–7
　and idealism, 51, 68n4, 69n12, 70n24
　revival of, 11, 51, 53, 60, 109
　and skepticism, 17, 52, 57
　smallism, 59–64, 66, 67, 69n14, 70n24
　as solution to 'hard problem', 52, 98, 311–12
　Victorian period, 69n12, 70n24, 333n2
　in Wollstonecraft, 51, 60, 65–7
parasomnias, 36–8, 44
Parikka, Jussi, 203
Parrish, Stephen Maxfield, 122–3, 141n1
Pascal, Blaise, 167
passions, 14, 40, 122, 123, 144–7, 156, 272, 333n8
pattern recognition, 291–3
Peirce, C. S., 53
Penrose, Roger, 15, 22n26
Percy, Thomas, 271, 276
Pfau, Thomas, 169
philistinism, 231, 240, 244
Phillips, Adam, 73–4, 76, 77, 262n11
philosophical materialism, 52, 68n4
philosophy of mind, 31
physicalism, 52, 53, 115n27, 164n10
Pinch, Adela, 69n12, 70n24, 333n2
plasticity, mental, 8, 111, 191n7, 293–4
pluralism, metaphysical, 69n14, 70n24
poetic cognition, 272, 282
poetic faith: Coleridge on, 74, 84–5
poetic histories: and the scaffolded mind, 270–5
poetic language, 89n4, 150, 271–2, 285, 302
poetic principles, 210
Polidori, John, 36–7, 38
politics and metaphysics, relationship between, 59–60, 64
Pollan, Michael, 88
Poole, Thomas, 371
populations, 8, 18, 286–94, 297–301, 305n6

porousness, 5, 7, 17, 94, 96–7, 101–2, 114n20
posthuman consciousness, 18, 88, 312–32
Postman, Neil, 202
poststructuralism, 1, 16, 29, 73, 89n4, 203, 285
primal scene, 84, 90n15
primary affect
　as agent of moral change, 138–41
　measuring, 131–7
Prince, Mary, 9, 18, 328–32, 334n18, 335n19
Pringle, Thomas, 328
Prinz, Jesse, 5, 8, 9, 15, 19n8, 20n9, 21n17
priority monism, 64
'prone mind,' metaphor of, 18, 249–51, 257, 260, 261n5
prosody, 272, 276, 277–8, 281
prosopopoeia, 313–14, 318–21, 324, 327
proverbs, 137
psyche, 7, 34, 199, 215, 269
psychedelics, 88
psychoanalysis
　emergence of, in Romanticism, 83–4, 89n3
　Freud's, 29, 31, 84
　Lacan's, 6, 29, 73, 83–4, 86, 89n3, 90n10
　and the Real of Romanticism, 75–84
　Romantic consciousness and, 6–7, 12, 73–5
　transference in, 100
psycholinguistics, 121
psychology, 6, 7, 12, 20n13, 31, 73, 99, 113n9, 373
　and 'cognitive revolution,' 121–2
　developmental, 231–2, 374
　of fictional characters, 228, 231–2, 241
　journal editors, 374
　see also cognitive psychology; ego psychology; moral psychology
Purdon, James, 218n10

'qualia empiricism,' theory of, 19n8
quantum physics, 14, 334n14
'quartet theory' of emotion, 135, 142n7
queer phenomenology, 340
quest romance, 2, 29, 74, 359
Quinney, Laura, 105, 113n14

racial consciousness, 324, 328, 331, 374
racial disparities: social cognition, 375–6
racism, 102, 103, 107, 363, 364, 375–9
Radcliffe, Ann, 37
Rancière, Jacques, 22n27, 189
rapid eye movement (REM) states, 36
reading paradox, 293–4
Real, the, 75, 83, 87
  of faith, 73–93
reason, social functions of, 227, 228, 234–8
Redfield, Marc, 185
reductionism, 98
Reinfandt, Christoph, 198, 201, 206
religion, 50, 74, 78–81, 84–9, 288, 306n12, 353, 358
remediation, 199–203, 210, 217n8
reverie, states of, 42, 44, 254
Richardson, Alan, 12, 17, 239, 250, 256, 262n7, 281, 325
Roberts, Steven O., 374
Robertson, Lisa Ann, 13, 370
Robinson, Daniel, 268–9, 276
Robinson, Mary, 5–6, 18, 314–18, 324
robotics, 295, 297
Romanticism and Consciousness: Essays in Criticism (1970), 1–7, 29–30, 44–5, 73, 76, 78, 121, 199, 285
  Bloom's essays, 2, 29, 74, 249, 359
  consciousness and nature in, 5, 15, 51, 94, 199, 269
  contributors, list of, 19n2
  de Man's essay, 6, 56, 68n9, 73, 75, 76, 95, 285
  Hartman's essays, 3–4, 30, 44, 73, 76, 95, 111, 285, 311
  Hollander's essay, 277, 278–9
  impact of, 1, 29, 73, 285
  model of consciousness, 2, 17, 94–5, 97, 101
  and psychoanalysis, 6, 7, 73
  Romantic ideology, 1, 3, 19n7, 73
  Romantic self-estrangement, 339, 359
  self-consciousness, 2, 4, 30, 68n2, 199
  title, 19n7, 29
Rosch, Eleanor, 95, 96
ruin: in *Frankenstein*, 181–3
Rupert, Robert, 253

Russett, Margaret, 278
Ruston, Sharon, 250–1

Said, Edward, 340
Savarese, John, 13, 18, 370
Sayers, Frank, 275
'scaffolding,' mental, 257, 263n25, 270–5, 369–70
Schelling, F. W. J., 285
Schiller, Friedrich, 4, 188–9
Schlegel, Friedrich, 246n20, 340
Schopenhauer, Arthur, 74–5
Schwab, Raymond, 340
Schwitters, Kurt, 218n11
Scott, Walter, 275–6
Seager, William, 69n12
Sedgwick, Eve Kosofsky, 76, 187, 242
self-consciousness, 2, 4–5, 30, 68n2, 156, 199, 311, 339, 359, 376
Selfridge, Oliver G., 291–3, 305n6–7
Selim III, Sultan, 342, 344–8, 353, 356
Sellars, Roy, 132
sentimentalism, 106–7, 153
sexsomnia, 37
sexuality, 97, 289, 313, 327, 335n19
Sha, Richard C., 12, 17, 259, 321, 333n1
shamanism, 58
Shamdasani, Sonu, 76
shapeshifting, 311–32
Shaviro, Steven, 61, 312, 313, 319, 333n9
Sheats, Paul, 127, 130–1, 140
Shelley, Mary
  Frankenstein, 15, 35, 178–83, 187, 192n21, 290
  and Percy Shelley, 87, 290
Shelley, Percy, 73–93, 249–64, 325–8
  Adonais, 11, 69n21, 81–9, 90n12
  Alastor, 15, 43–4
  brain science, influence of, 250–1
  Browning on, 87–8
  The Cenci, 18, 249–61, 261n6, 262n10, 263n20, 264n26–31
  and consciousness, 88, 334n13
  cosmopsychist thoughts, 65, 69n21
  A Defence of Poetry, 34, 41, 77, 87–8, 262n10
  Epipsychidion, 87
  and faith, 17, 73–93
  and Godwin, 263n15, 264n30, 290, 305n3
  Laon and Cythna, 254
  and Mary Shelley, 87, 290

and mental extension, 251, 261
'Mont Blanc,' 6
'Ode to the West Wind,' 56
'On Life,' 253–4, 260, 262n10
'On Love,' 254
Prometheus Unbound, 254, 261n5, 325–8, 334n13
'prone mind' metaphor, 18, 249–51, 257, 260, 261n5
Queen Mab, 38, 80, 87, 305n3
and race, 18, 326, 328, 334n13
similes, 264n32, 334n15
skepticism, 80, 82, 262n10, 333n1
The Triumph of Life, 9, 83–9, 325
Sigler, David, 6, 77
Singer, Kate, 12, 18
Siskin, Clifford, 11, 198, 201
situated cognition, 272, 281
skepticism, naïve, 231–4
Skrbina, David, 53
Sky, Jeanette, 239
slavery, 9, 103, 107, 324, 329–32
sleep, 36–8, 51, 184
Sliwinski, Sharon, 181
Sloterdijk, Peter, 6, 12
smallism, 59–64, 66, 67, 69n14, 70n24
Smith, Charlotte
  Beachy Head, 5, 18, 196–216, 219n15
  Elegiac Sonnets, 209, 216
  and feminism, 210
  History of England, 208–9
  knowledge of natural history, 197, 209–10, 213, 219n15
Snow, C. P., 216n3
social cognition, 18, 339, 375–6
socially extended cognition, 253, 261
'sociogeny,' concept of, 374
solipsism, 96, 339
Solomon, Robert, 164n11
Solomonescu, Yasmin, 18
Somerset, Fiona, 163n2
somniloquy, 36, 37
soul, the, 37, 52, 65–6, 105, 183–4, 197, 218n10, 250, 263n15
speculative realism, 2, 78, 211, 312, 314
Speitz, Michele, 329
Sperber, Dan, 228, 234, 237, 241, 244
Spinoza, Baruch, 53, 98
Sprevak, Mark, 273
Stewart, Dugald, 275–6
Strauss, David, 159

Strawson, Galen, 53–4, 57, 59–62, 64, 68n6
stream of consciousness, 102, 105, 108, 115n27, 197
Strickland, Susanna, 328
'studio states,' 167–90
subatomic particles, 49, 51, 61, 64
subconscious, 32, 44, 269
Sunni Islam, 355
supernatural thinking, 229–33, 245n4
supernaturalism, 61, 74
Swann, Karen, 334n16
Swedenborg, Emanuel, 173
Sylvester, David, 176
Symbolic, the, 77, 80, 81, 82, 85, 87, 88, 89n4
sympathy, 97, 100, 153, 262n10

Taylor, Charles, 74, 81, 262n15
Taylor, Thomas, 62
Taylor, William, 138–9, 270, 275–80
Te Awa Tupua (Whanganui River, New Zealand), 63
Terada, Rei, 176
Thelwall, John, 39
thing-in-itself *(Ding an sich)*, 78, 211, 212
Thompson, Evan, 95, 96
Thomson, James, 272
Tiffany, Daniel, 170, 180
Tononi, Giulio, 110
'trans-corporeality,' concept of, 312, 314, 317
transcendence, 80–1, 82, 113n14, 159, 160
transcendental idealism, 212
Twombly, Cy, 176–8, 181, 186
Tylor, E. B., 49

unconscious, the, 7, 15, 30–3, 38, 73, 75, 87, 90n8, 285
universe: consciousness of, in cosmopsychism, 51, 64–7
unsought thoughts, 183–90
utopia, 99, 170

vacancy, mental, 17, 43–4
vampire tales, 36–7
Varela, Francisco, 95, 96
vegetative states, 42, 101
Vermeule, Blakey, 244
Victorian period: panpsychism, 69n12, 70n24, 333n2

Vidal, Fernando, 12
Vikings, 207–8, 216
Virgin Mary, 157, 158, *158*, *161*, 164
vitalism, 51
Vivieros de Castro, Eduardo, 58
Vogl, Joseph, 200, 216n4

Wang, Orrin N. C., 333n1
Warren, Calvin L., 329
Wasserman, Earl R., 82, 90n12, 254
Weber, Max, 54
WEIRDness, 374
Weiskott, Eric, 279
Wellmann, Janina, 323
Wheeler, Michael, 273
white consciousness, 313, 332, 363–81
white supremacy, 18, 325, 326, 377, 378
Whyte, Edward, 276
Wiener, Norbert, 291
Williams, Nicholas, 99
Williams, Raymond, 304, 306n12
Wilson, John, 138, 140
Wilson, Robert A., 295
Wimsatt, William K., Jr., 121, 123, 141n1
Wollstonecraft, Mary, 65–7, 152–5, 322–3
    moral sensibility, 153, 164n11
    panpsychism, 51, 60, 65–7
    women's rights, 62; *see also* feminism
Woolley, Jacqueline D., 231–2
Wordsworth, Dorothy, 43, 60–1, 64, 67, 302, 371
Wordsworth, Mary, 32
Wordsworth, William, 4, 5, 123–41, 144–63, 299–304
    aesthetics of the everyday, 146, 150, 157, 163
    and Blake, 4, 5
    and Coleridge, 124, 136, 141, 367, 368–9
    and fairy tales, 239
    forms of 'emotional thinking,' 144–5, 146, 150, 151–2, 154, 155–7, 163
    French Revolution, 63, 66, 152, 302–3, 369
    'Guilt and Sorrow,' 43
    'The Idiot Boy,' 128, 138, 140, 300
    'Intimations' Ode, 62, 63
    lexical innovation, 32, 33
    Lyrical Ballads, 123–41, 131, 286, 300–1
    'The Mad Mother,' 156, 300
    meter, use of, 4, 126–31, 136, 140, 155
    and nature, 76, 122, 151, 156, 210, 301, 304, 311, 332
    'Preface' to *Lyrical Ballads*, 126, 144–5, 150–2, 155–7, 163n7, 186, 290, 300
    The Prelude, 11, 31, 32, 39, 44, 124–5, 141, 215, 369
    The Recluse, 4, 76
    self-consciousness, 156, 311
    'A slumber did my spirit seal,' 184–9
    and states of reverie and mental vacancy, 42, 43
    'The Thorn,' 56, 122–41, 142n5, 300
    'Tintern Abbey,' 3, 33, 39, 96, 196, 202, 209–10, 213, 301–4
    'We are Seven,' 156, 300
Wynter, Sylvia, 326, 329, 367, 374–5

Young, Edward, 152
Yousef, Nancy, 12, 17

Zajonc, Robert, 112n2
Zerilli, Linda, 298–9, 305n10
Zipes, Jack, 246n17
Žižek, Slavoj, 77–9, 83, 85–6
Zunshine, Lisa, 18, 200

EU representative:
Easy Access System Europe
Mustamäe tee 50, 10621 Tallinn, Estonia
Gpsr.requests@easproject.com